DATE DUE

RECEIVED	SEP 2 2 1998	
DEC 0 1 2001		
SEP 0 3 2002		

DEMCO NO. 38-298

NTC's
Dictionary
of
Korea's
Business and Cultural
Code Words

Boyé Lafayette De Mente

NTC Publishing Group

Library of Congress Cataloging-in-Publication Data

De Mente, Boyé.
    NTC's dictionary of Korea's business & cultural code words / Boyé
Lafayette De Mente.
        p.   cm. — (NTC's dictionaries of cultural code words)
        Includes bibliographical references.
        ISBN 0-8442-8362-2
        1. Korea—Social life and customs—Terminology.   2. Korean
language—Terms and phrases. I. Title. II. Title: NTC's
dictionary of Korea's business and cultural code words.   III. Title:
Dictionary of Korea's business & cultural code words.   IV. Title:
Korea's business & cultural code words.   V. Series.
DS904.D43   1998
306'.09519'03—dc21   97-49357
                                              CIP

Other books by Boyé Lafayette De Mente

Behind the Japanese Bow—Understanding & Predicting Japanese Behavior
Chinese Etiquette & Ethics in Business
Chinese in Plain English
Discovering Cultural Japan
How to Do Business with the Japanese
Japan Encyclopedia
Japan Made Easy—All You Need to Know to Enjoy Japan
Japanese Etiquette & Ethics in Business
Japanese for the Travel Industry
Japanese in Plain English
Korean Etiquette & Ethics in Business
Korean in Plain English
Mexican Etiquette & Ethics—Anticipating and Understanding Mexican Business &
    Social Behavior
NTC's Dictionary of China's Cultural Code Words
NTC's Dictionary of Japan's Business Code Words
NTC's Dictionary of Japan's Cultural Code Words
NTC's Dictionary of Mexico's Cultural Code Words
Subway Exit Guide to Tokyo
The Japanese Have a Word for It

Published by NTC Publishing Group
A division of NTC/Contemporary Publishing Group, Inc.
4255 West Touhy Avenue, Lincolnwood (Chicago), Illinois 60646-1975 U.S.A.
Copyright © 1998 by Boyé Lafayette De Mente
Printed in the United States of America
International Standard Book Number: 0-8442-8362-2
18   17   16   15   14   13   12   11   10   9   8   7   6   5   4   3   2   1

*This book is dedicated to my wife,
Margaret Warren De Mente,
who made it all possible.*

Contents

Guide to Key Cultural Themes   *xi*
Acknowledgments   *xiii*
Understanding and Interacting with Koreans   *xv*

 1   *Aboji* / The "Father" Culture   *1*
 2   *Achom* / Massaging Male Egos   *3*
 3   *Adul* / The "Son" Culture   *5*
 4   *Aeyok* / Eroticism in Korean Life   *7*
 5   *Amhuk Ki* / The Dark Period   *8*
 6   *Anae* / Wives: The Inside People   *11*
 7   *Anshim* / Peace of Mind   *13*
 8   *Anun Saram* / Someone You Know   *14*
 9   *Arirang* / The Korean Soul Song   *16*
10   *Chaebol* / The Industrial Colossi   *17*
11   *Chaegim* / Dealing with Responsibility   *20*
12   *Chae-myun* / Saving Everybody's Face   *22*
13   *Chagun* / Compassion and Mercy   *23*
14   *Chakupjachok* / The Self-Sufficiency Syndrome   *24*
15   *Chamulsong* / You Gotta Have Patience!   *26*
16   *Changpi* / The Shame Culture   *27*
17   *Chang Sung* / Staying in Touch with the Spirits   *28*
18   *Chayu* / The Power of Freedom   *30*
19   *Chebol* / Collective Punishment   *31*
20   *Chib* / Getting Family Approval   *33*
21   *Chimsul* / Needling Cosmic Power   *34*
22   *Chingu* / Cultivating Friends   *35*
23   *Chinshim* / Sincerity Comes First   *37*
24   *Chiwi* / Paying Attention to Rank   *38*
25   *Chiyok Kaldeungui* / The Scourge of Regionalism   *41*
26   *Chodae* / The Home-Meal Invitation   *42*
27   *Choe* / Sin in a Godless Society   *43*
28   *Cho Guk* / The Mother Country   *45*
29   *Chok* / The Korean Clan System   *47*
30   *Chol* / The Versatile Bow   *49*
31   *Chomjangi* / The Fortune-Tellers   *51*
32   *Chon Do Kyo* / The Heavenly Way Religions   *53*
33   *Chong* / Ties That Bind   *55*

34 *Chongbu* / Big Brother 57
35 *Chonggyo* / Faces of Korean Religions 58
36 *Chongmal* / The Color of Truth 61
37 *Chongshik* / Doing Things by the Book 63
38 *Chongui* / Justice Korean Style 64
39 *Chongyong* / Paying Proper Respect 66
40 *Chonjung* / Deferential Honor 67
41 *Chontu* / *Ssa-um* / Fighting at the Drop of a Hat 69
42 *Chorhakcha* / The Perennial Philosophers 70
43 *Chosang Sungbae* / Ancestor Worship 72
44 *Choson* / Land of Morning Calm 73
45 *Chung* / Groupism as Morality 76
46 *Chung* / Loyalty in a Korean Setting 78
47 *Chungjaein* / The Go-Betweens 79
48 *Chung Mae* / Arranged Marriages 80
49 *Chuso* / Finding the Right Place 83
50 *Dong Ari* / Hobby Groups 85
51 *Enuri* / Bargaining as a Social Skill 86
52 *Haengbok* / The Pursuit of Happiness 87
53 *Hakgajok* / Two-Generation Families 88
54 *Haksaeng* / The World of Korean Students 90
55 *Han* / The "Force" Is with Them 92
56 *Hanbok* / People in White 94
57 *Hanguk* / The Korean Nation 97
58 *Hanguksaram* / The Korean People 99
59 *Hanguk Yoksa* / Korea: A Historical Saga 102
60 *Hangul/Hantcha* / Korea's Writing Systems 117
61 *Han-Jong Shik* / A Korean Meal 121
62 *Hankuk Mal* / The Korean Language 124
63 *Han Yak* / The Herbal Way to Health 128
64 *Him* / A Passion for Power 130
65 *Hoesa* / The Korean Company 131
66 *Hopae* / Identifying the People 134
67 *Hwa* / Striving for Harmony 135
68 *Hwandae* / Surviving Korean Hospitality 137
69 *Hwangap/Jingap* / Celebrating Sixty/Seventy Years 138
70 *Hwarang* / The Knights of Korea 139
71 *Hyo* / The Power of Filial Piety 142
72 *Ilbonsaram* / The Japanese Factor 144
73 *In* / The Benevolent Society 146
74 *In'gan Kwan'gye* / Interpersonal Relations 148

75   *Injong* / Affection and Compassion   *150*
76   *Innae* / A Culture of Enduring   *151*
77   *Insa* / Rounds of Greetings   *152*
78   *Insam* / The "Man-Root"   *154*
79   *Irum* / What's in a Name?   *156*
80   *Isangajok* / The Divided Families   *160*
81   *Jeol* / Showing Respect to Elders   *161*
82   *Jolbu* / The Suddenly Rich   *162*
83   *Juche* / Searching for Self-Reliance   *164*
84   *Kaeinjuui* / In Search of Self   *166*
85   *Kajong* / The Korean Family   *168*
86   *Kamdong* / When Emotions Were Taboo   *170*
87   *Kanan* / Taking Comfort in Poverty   *172*
88   *Katun Sosuy Pap* / Eating from the Same Rice Bowl   *173*
89   *Ki* / The Cosmic Force   *174*
90   *Kibun* / Feelings Come First   *176*
91   *Kiddokyo* / Christianity in Korea   *178*
92   *Kimchi* / The Spice of Life   *180*
93   *Kisaeng* / The Pleasure Girls   *182*
94   *Kolpum* / Twin Pillars of Shilla   *186*
95   *Koman* / The Perils of Arrogance   *188*
96   *Komdo* / The Way of the Sword   *190*
97   *Komun* / Getting Good Advice   *191*
98   *Kongja / Yugyo* / The Master of Masters   *193*
99   *Kongpyong* / Korean Fairness   *197*
100   *Kongson* / Courtesy vs. Morality   *199*
101   *Kosa* / The Good Spirits   *200*
102   *Kukche Kyolhon* / International Marriages   *202*
103   *Kukkajuui* / Korean Nationalism   *204*
104   *Kunsa Munhwa* / The Military Culture   *208*
105   *Kwago* / Selecting the Brightest   *212*
106   *Kwalli* / Management Korean Style   *214*
107   *Kwallyojui* / Bureaucratic Authoritarianism   *220*
108   *Kye* / The Group Approach   *221*
109   *Kyeyak* / Contracts in Korea   *223*
110   *Kyojesul* / Business Drinking   *226*
111   *Kyolhon* / Marriage Customs   *227*
112   *Kyong* / Controlling the Mind   *232*
113   *Kyongjaeng* / Competition Korean Style   *233*
114   *Kyosop* / Korean Negotiating   *235*
115   *Kyoyuk* / Education and Power   *237*

116 *Mangshin* / Avoiding Shame 243

117 *Matbulibubu* / Two-Income Families 244

118 *Mi* / Worshiping Beauty 246

119 *Mishijok* / The Swinging Wives 247

120 *Mudang* / The Spirit Mediums 249

121 *Munhak* / Literature and Culture 250

122 *Munhwa* / Culture Then and Now 254

123 *Musokchi* / The Cultural Umbilical Cord 257

124 *Myongham* / Playing Your Name Cards 261

125 *Myongye* / The Need for Honor 263

126 *Namja /Nampyon* / The Outside Person 264

127 *Ne-Anio* / Yes and No 266

128 *Nolda* / Work Never Ceases 267

129 *Nolli* / Beware of Being Logical 268

130 *Noemul* / Bribery vs. Gift Giving 270

131 *Nongbu* / The "Good" People 273

132 *Norae* / Singing Your Way to Success 274

133 *Norae Bang* / The Singing Salons 277

134 *Noye* / The Pre-modern Slave Culture 278

135 *Nunchi* / Korea's Cultural Telepathy 280

136 *Oegugin* / Encounters with Foreigners 282

137 *Oegugin Songyosa* / Foreign Missionaries and Korea 285

138 *Ogi* / The Stubborn Streak 290

139 *Omoni* / Mothers as Saints 291

140 *Omsal* / Gaining Sympathy 293

141 *Ondol* / Hot Times on the Floor 294

142 *Orange Jok* / Playboys and Playgirls 295

143 *Origwan-Unsok* / Selfless Love and Indulgence 297

144 *P'a* / The Faction Syndrome 298

145 *Paduk* / A Learning Game 299

146 *Paik Il* / The Hundredth Day Party 301

147 *Pipyong* / The Pitfalls of Criticism 302

148 *Pohojuui* / Protectionism Korean Style 304

149 *Pojungkum* / Paying "Key Money" 305

150 *Pok/O-Bok* / Blessings from the Spirits 306

151 *Poksu* / The Need for Revenge 308

152 *Pongnyok* / The Violent Side 310

153 *Pop* / The Less Law the Better 313

154 *Pop Ko Chum* / The Law Drum Dance 315

155 *Pujong* / Keeping Women Down 317

156 *Pulda* / Eliminating Office Stress 318

157 *Pulgyo* / The Buddhist Wave *320*
158 *Pumjil* / Quality as a Cultural Thing *324*
159 *Pungnyu* / Going with Nature's Flow *325*
160 *Pungsu* / Keeping in Cosmic Harmony *327*
161 *Puseo Jang Hoe* / The Weekly Scoldings *329*
162 *Room Salon* / Sex in a Glass *331*
163 *Sagwa* / The Role of the Apology *333*
164 *Sajokuro/Yonjul* / Personalism and Connectionism *335*
165 *San* / Korea's Sacred Mountains *337*
166 *Sashil* / Forget the Facts! *339*
167 *Sayang* / Keeping a Low Profile *340*
168 *Segyehwa* / Korean-Style Globalization *342*
169 *Seon* / Spouse Hunts *344*
170 *Shi* / The Poetic Culture *345*
171 *Shigan* / On Fast Time *348*
172 *Shilpae* / Avoiding Failure *349*
173 *Shin* / Life Without God *351*
174 *Shinyong* / Operating on Trust *352*
175 *Shipijikan* / Living by the Numbers *354*
176 *Shiropka* / Businesspeople Redeemed *355*
177 *Shisaem* / The Jealousy Taboo *360*
178 *Sil Hak* / The Coming of Practical Learning *362*
179 *Sodo* / Writing as a Cultural Discipline *364*
180 *Sogae* / Limiting Introductions *365*
181 *Sogaejang* / Letters of Introduction *367*
182 *Soktam* / Wisdom in Proverbs *368*
183 *Sonbae/Hubae* / Seniors and Juniors *369*
184 *Sonbi* / The Ideal Human *371*
185 *Song* / Integrity vs. Law *373*
186 *Song* / Sexual Mores *374*
187 *Songnihak* / Cosmic Thinking *378*
188 *Songshilhan* / The Importance of Loyalty *379*
189 *Sonmul* / Gift Giving as "Social Oil" *380*
190 *Sonnim* / Honorable Guests *382*
191 *Ssirum* / Korean Wrestling *383*
192 *Sujupngun* / The Shyness Syndrome *385*
193 *Sulpum* / Sadness in Korean Culture *386*
194 *Suyong* / Cleansing Body and Spirit *387*
195 *Tabang* / Coffee Shops and Cafés *388*
196 *Taedo* / Manners as Morality *390*
197 *Taejop* / Let the Good Times Roll *391*

198   *Taekshi* / Riding Korean Taxis   *393*
199   *Tae Kwon Do* / Hand-and-Foot Combat   *395*
200   *Tangol* / Creating Special Customers   *397*
201   *Todok* / Circumstantial Morality   *398*
202   *Tojang* / Sealed with a Chop   *401*
203   *Tomanghada* / Escaping from Obligations   *402*
204   *Tongchang Hoe* / Alumni Groupism   *404*
205   *Tong Hak* / The Eastern Learning War   *405*
206   *Tong Il* / The Great Reunification Dream   *407*
207   *Tongnip* / Independence vs. Tradition   *408*
208   *Uimu* / Duty and Morality   *409*
209   *Uiri* / The Burden of Obligations   *411*
210   *Uishik* / Contents of the Korean Mind   *412*
211   *Ujong* / Friendships in Korean Life   *413*
212   *Umju* / The Great Equalizer   *415*
213   *Um-Yang* / Duality of the Korean Mind   *418*
214   *Unhye* / Social Indebtedness   *420*
215   *Unmyong* / The Demise of Fate   *421*
216   *Uri Nara Saram* / Our Country's People   *423*
217   *Wiom* / Dignity Comes First   *424*
218   *Wonmang* / The Grudge Syndrome   *426*
219   *Yangban* / The Mandarins of Korea   *427*
220   *Yatpoda* / Underestimating Koreans   *432*
221   *Yeon/Yeonjul* / Relationships and Connections   *434*
222   *Yeui Pomjol* / Etiquette as Morality   *436*
223   *Yobo/Yoboseyo* / Hey There, Darling, Hello!   *437*
224   *Yoja* / Korean Women   *438*
225   *Yolshimhi Hapsida* / Let's Do Our Best!   *446*
226   *Yoltunguishik* / The Fading Inferiority Complex   *447*
227   *Yonae* / Courting and Mating   *449*
228   *Yongmu* / Business as Religion   *451*
229   *Yongo* / The Language Burden   *454*
230   *Yonse* / Venerating Age   *455*
231   *Yopjon Sasang* / Looking Down on History   *457*

Selected Bibliography   *459*

Guide to Key Cultural Themes

Business Morality and Practices
10, 26, 51, 65, 84, 106, 109, 114, 155, 157, 159, 164, 168, 171, 172, 176, 181, 183, 189, 200, 202, 203, 204, 220, 228, 229

Communication and Consensus Building
7, 15, 16, 33, 36, 37, 40, 47, 52, 55, 67, 73, 74, 75, 86, 90, 95, 99, 112, 113, 118, 129, 135, 147, 161, 221

Culture and Customs
1, 3, 9, 11, 17, 19, 21, 22, 26, 27, 31, 32, 35, 42, 45, 48, 50, 56, 62, 63, 68, 69, 77, 79, 87, 88, 89, 92, 93, 96, 101, 102, 111, 120, 122, 140, 141, 145, 146, 149, 150, 154, 160, 170, 180, 191, 193, 194, 198, 199, 230

Education, Ethics, and Morality
54, 57, 61, 105, 115, 121, 127, 174, 177, 178, 179, 188, 201, 205, 208, 209, 214, 218

Etiquette and Role-Playing
2, 30, 39, 81, 100, 130, 143, 144, 163, 166, 167, 192, 196, 217, 222

Family, Society, Men, and Women
4, 6, 8, 20, 29, 45, 53, 71, 82, 85, 108, 117, 119, 124, 126, 131, 139, 142, 169, 186, 211, 223, 224, 227

Foreign Elements
91, 98, 120, 123, 136, 137, 158

History, Myths, Militarism
28, 44, 58, 59, 60, 70, 72, 94, 104, 134, 165, 219

Hospitality, Eating, and Drinking
68, 110, 132, 133, 162, 190, 195, 197, 212

Philosophical Beliefs and Practices
12, 46, 116, 125, 128, 138, 173, 175, 182, 184, 187, 210, 213, 215

Politics, Power, Law, and Nationalism
5, 13, 25, 34, 38, 41, 64, 66, 80, 97, 103, 107, 148, 151, 152, 153, 185, 206, 207, 216, 226, 231

Acknowledgments

I am deeply grateful to Dr. Martin H. Sours, an authority on Korea and professor of international studies at the American Graduate School of International Management (popularly known as Thunderbird) in Glendale, Arizona, for editing the final draft of this book, in the process of which he significantly improved the content of many of the entries and added to the clarity of others. I am also indebted to the following persons for reading the manuscript when it was in first draft and generously sharing their experiences and knowledge of Korea.

John H. Koo, Ph.D.
Professor of Korean, Center for Asian Studies
Arizona State University

Heon Jin Chang
President, Semco International, Seoul

Ernest Gerald Beck
Taekwondo Master, Orlando, Florida

Don Hackney
Korean Trade Specialist, Seoul

Hawk Sohn
Business Consultant, Seoul

Sokbom Han, Ph.D.
Arizona State University

Hosoon Ku, Ph.D.
Arizona State University

Understanding and Interacting
with Koreans

Koreans share many cultural characteristics with the Chinese and Japanese because of their geographic proximity, long history of contact, and the mutual influence of animism, shamanism, Buddhism, Confucianism, and Taoism. China was, in fact, the primary wellspring of Korean civilization from around 108 B.C. until modern times. But the Korean people have retained a unique character and personality that sets them apart from the Chinese and Japanese as well as other Asians—a difference that derives from their deepest spiritual and philosophical beliefs and from an image of themselves that has been shaped by both internal and external factors over the centuries.

A significant part of the Korean character was obviously forged by the rugged mountainous terrain of the country and by a climate that runs to the extremes of hot and cold. Another part of the character of Koreans was wrought in the bloody crucible of ongoing battles with raiders and invaders from the north and from the sea. Whatever the individual factors that went into the makeup of the Korean character and personality—and there were many others—the end result was a formidable people who have yet to achieve the full promise of their potential and from whom the world will hear a great deal more.

Contemporary Korean scholars and observers, including Dr. Jae Un Kim,* a developmental psychologist and the author of several books on the Korean mind-set and behavior, have noted a variety of surface changes in the attitudes and behavior of Koreans since the end of the nineteenth century, but they say that the national character of Koreans has remained essentially the same.

As is the case with all ancient cultures created within highly refined and meticulously structured social systems over thousands of years, one of the keys to understanding traditional Korean attitudes and behavior is the language of the people—or, more precisely, key words in the language. These key words provide access to the Korean mind—to core concepts and emotions, the attitudes and feelings that make up the Korean psyche. These key terms reveal both the heart and soul of Koreans and provide bridges for communicating and interacting with Koreans on the most fundamental level.

I have selected more than two hundred of the most culture-laden words in the Korean language and attempted to explain their special role in history and in Korean life today in a way that is both meaningful and useful.

Boyé Lafayette De Mente
Seoul, Korea

*Note on Korean Names

Approximately half of all Koreans share only five family names, and distinguishing among them is a genuine challenge. The roman letters used to represent Korean sounds may also vary with the geographic region and with individuals, resulting in the same names often being spelled differently. Brothers and sisters in a family also usually share a second given name that distinguishes their generation and is known as their "generational" name.

Generational names usually come after the personal or "first" name—and therefore appear like "middle names" to Westerners—but some people may put them first, further complicating matters. Some names are written with the first name and the generational names separate and with the initial letters capitalized. Others connect the two names with a hyphen, sometimes with the initial letter of the generational name capitalized and other times with it in lower case. Some people run the two names together as if they were one. The same editions of English-language newspapers and magazines published in Korea and abroad often present Korean names in two or three different ways.

Not surprisingly, foreigners who are not familiar with Korean family names, with the last-name-first custom, and with the use of shared generational names often have difficulty recognizing which is which.

For this book I have chosen to present all Korean names in the Western style—first name, the generational name as the individual concerned writes it, and family name—because Westerners are used to this system and it reduces the possibility of confusing the names. The most famous example of Koreans who combined their first and generational names was probably Syngman Rhee (1875–1965), the controversial patriot and statesman who was president of the Republic of Korea from 1948 until 1960. His original name was Sung Man Yi.

For more very important details about Korean names, see "*Irum* / What's in a Name?"

NTC's
Dictionary
of
Korea's
Business and Cultural
Code Words

아버지

Aboji

(Ah-boh-jee)

"The 'Father' Culture"

When asked to list the most important word in the Korean language, most older Koreans are likely to respond with *aboji* (ah-boh-jee), the common term for "father." A formal and honorific term is *abonim* (ah-boh-neem). In fact, Korea's traditional culture might be described as a father culture because of the central role that fathers played in the social structure and in day-to-day living for more than five centuries.

The reason for the development of a father-based social system in Korea is bound up in the Neo-Confucianism adopted in 1392 by the newly established Choson (or Yi) dynasty as the official government ideology. From around 1200 the preceding Koryo dynasty had become dominated by an elite class of officials and Buddhist priests who became increasingly corrupt and inefficient. Korean scholars of that era blamed the situation on the royal court's continuing obsession with supporting Buddhism at the expense of the welfare of the country.

These scholars began to advocate political reform based on a more detailed and stronger version of Confucianism, known as *Neo-Confucianism*, or "New Confucianism," that had been developing in China for several generations. This new form of the ancient sage's teachings emphasized filial piety and ancestor worship as the best possible foundation for the family and society as a whole. In 1386 the newly established Ming dynasty of China invaded Korea in an attempt to reassert hegemony over the peninsula. This precipitated the fall of the Koryo dynasty in Korea and the formation of a new dynasty in 1392 by a young charismatic Korean general named Song Gye Yi.

General Yi and those who succeeded him purged all Buddhist influence from the government and adopted Neo-Confucianism as the paramount ideology of the new regime, making it the law of the land socially as well as politically. Under this much more detailed and stricter form of Confucianism, Korean family members were precisely ranked by sex and age, with *aboji* or "fathers" having absolute authority over all other members. By law and by custom fathers were to be obeyed without question in all things.

There was a special relationship between husbands and wives, but first sons ranked second in the family hierarchy because they automatically inherited the mantle of the father's power, along with most of his property, and were responsible for performing the all-important rituals pertaining to ancestor worship. In this social and political context Korean fathers reigned as masters of their households in every traditional sense of the word. Love and affection played no formal role in this family system because attitudes and behavior based on such emotions would have been disruptive and were therefore taboo.

General Yi's successors (he took the name Taejo when he assumed the throne as king) continued his policy of promoting Neo-Confucianism as the state and social ideology, and by the middle of the next century they had won out over those continuing to favor Buddhism.

Over the following several generations Neo-Confucianism was turned into a ritualistic cult that controlled almost every aspect of Korean behavior, particularly the etiquette of interpersonal relationships and the role of the father. Under this Confucian concept of government and society, the king was regarded as the symbolic father of the people, who were expected to obey him as children obey their fathers. By extension, people were also expected to obey all government authorities because they were official representatives of the father-king.

A generally unspoken corollary of the king-as-father concept was that people were not expected to respect or obey an unethical king and were justified in rebelling against him. But that was something that normally occurred only after generations of abuse, during which the strength and will of the ruling faction gradually degenerated and the government could no longer stifle the dissent. The Confucian-oriented dynasty founded by General Yi was to last for more than half a millennium and fundamentally influence the attitudes and behavior of all Koreans.

All activity in Korean families was based on the dominant role prescribed for the male sex in general and on *aboji* and sons in particular. Fathers were the foundation of the family system, and sons were the pillars of each household. Until around the 1960s, Korean parents "babied" their young children, especially sons, longer than most Western parents. Mothers nursed their children longer and would often carry them on their backs until they were three or four years old.

Fathers generally had close, warm relationships with both their male and female children until they were three or four years old, tolerating behavior that would sometimes shock Westerners. But as soon as the process of preparing the children for adulthood began, the father's relationship with sons changed dramatically. Fathers became very strict and very formal, resulting in the relationship between fathers and sons gradually becoming more distant, ultimately reaching the point that interaction between them was virtually limited to formal occasions.

The whole thrust of the fathers' attitude and behavior was to condition their sons to obey them, to be dependent on them, to pay them a highly formalized style of respect in both language and behavior, and to carry on the Confucian traditions of the family, including the chauvinist treatment of females.

One of the more irrational aspects of this system was that it generally created an unbridgeable emotional gap between fathers and sons. It is recorded voluminously that the system resulted in a great many sons hating their fathers, and there are equally numerous references in social literature to the relief that sons felt when their fathers died, freeing them at last. From the outside, it often seems that most of the effort of Korean fathers while they were alive was to become *chosang* (choh-sahng), or "ancestors," whose descendants would remember and honor them.

Despite the strict Confucian image of the traditional Korean family it was rare that fathers exercised absolute dictatorial power over their wives and children. No matter how restricted wives were in their public behavior, within the walls of their homes they could and often did influence their husbands and sons.

It is also amply recorded that sons did not always obey their fathers and that among the ways they resisted paternal control was by physically avoiding their fathers—staying out of their sight. Another way was to listen to their fathers' orders, not object to them, then do as they pleased and apologize later—an approach that is common in the behavior of Confucian-oriented people.

Anthropologist Roger L. Janelli notes in *Making Capitalism—The Social and Cultural Construction of a South Korean Conglomerate* that young Korean men often used "avoidance, deception and reinterpretation" to thwart the wishes and commands of their elders.

There have, of course, been dramatic changes in Korean society and the role of fathers since the introduction of democratic principles in the mid-1900s and the economic transformation of the country. Among other things, many contemporary Korean fathers in urban areas work such long hours and are away from home so much that they play very little role in the upbringing of their children. Some, especially those who choose to play golf and network on Saturdays, see their younger children only on Sundays and holidays. In more affluent families many sons and daughters from provincial villages, towns, and cities spend their college years in Seoul on their own.

Sons who migrate to Seoul after graduating from provincial schools, as well as those who attend university in Seoul and remain in the capital after graduation, generally thereafter see their parents only a few times a year, further loosening the Confucian ties and altering traditional behavioral patterns. Even with these changes, however, fatherhood in Korea brings with it a special status and special responsibilities to families that incorporate many of the best facets of Confucianism—respect for seniors and the elderly, a powerful compulsion to achieve the highest possible education, close-knit families, mutual responsibility for the welfare of the family and relatives, and a deep commitment to social order.

2

아첨

Achom
(Ah-choam)

"Massaging Male Egos"

People in Korea, including foreigners, who have some special skill but no specific title, particularly if it involves intellectual efforts, are frequently addressed as *sonsaeng* (sohn-sang), which is the Korean equivalent of "teacher" but has a somewhat higher status connotation than the English word. *Sonsaeng* is commonly made even more honorific by adding *nim* (neem) to it: *sonsaeng nim*. *Nim* is one of the Korean equivalents of "Mr.," "Mrs.," and "Miss."

The use of *sonsaeng* outside the educational field is symptomatic of the Korean custom of linguistically elevating the rank of people to make them feel good—and often to get something out of them. But it is only a small part of the social protocol that Koreans have traditionally used to maintain friendly, positive relationships within their families, among their relatives, friends, and co-workers.

Demands put on Koreans by their etiquette resulted in the use of *achom* (ah-choam), "flattery" or "compliments," becoming an integral part of the culture to the point that it took on a life of its own. *Achom* was a normal and required part of interpersonal relationships. Failure to use it at the appropriate times and in the appropriate manner was a serious transgression.

Newly arrived foreigners who are subjected to the effusive use of *achom* by their Korean contacts tend to be disarmed by the experience, all too often lower their standards and expectations, and become much more susceptible to manipulation by their Korean hosts. While newcomers need not become cynical about this traditional kind of behavior, they do need to be aware of its role in Korean society and not read more into it than is actually meant.

Another related word that can cause problems for the unwary is *chansa* (chahn-sah), which means "compliment" or "compliments." Korean men are constantly complimenting each other and their male associates and friends, and Korean women regularly compliment each other. But it was traditionally rare if not unthinkable for Korean men to compliment their wives, daughters, or other females on their appearance or their accomplishments. And it was certainly not the custom for women to compliment men.

This old cultural tradition is changing among the younger generations, but older men still tend to believe that it is improper to compliment women in the presence of others and especially for foreign men to compliment Korean women in the presence of Korean men. At the same time, there is a significant exception to this taboo. Korean men are especially pleased when foreign men compliment them on the beauty and desirability of Korean women. In fact, they often have an exaggerated opinion of both the virtues and beauty of Korean women because in the past the women were in such demand by upper-class Koreans as well as the imperial court of China and invaders as concubines and slaves.

Another general exception to the taboo about complimenting women on their appearance and sensuality is when men are out at night drinking and enjoying themselves with *kisaeng* (kee-sang), Korea's geisha, or hostesses in nightclubs and cabarets. In this setting, virtually anything goes.

Foreign males in Korea are especially well advised to refrain from making comments about Korean women, whether flattering or derogatory, to Korean men with whom they do not have a long and deep relationship.

아들
Adul
(Ah-duhl)

"The 'Son' Culture"

During Korea's last—and longest—dynasty (which began in 1592 and did not officially end until 1910), the structure and ethics of society came to revolve around ancestor worship. It also became a matter of law that the primary rituals of ancestor worship had to be performed by the oldest male in each family, making it essential that each family have at least one *adul* (ah-duhl) or "son" to carry out these vital ceremonies.

The rituals of ancestor worship and the importance of having sons became the central theme in the lives of all husbands and wives, resulting in the appearance of attitudes and practices that were to have a profound effect on the culture, with women being held responsible for producing male children—it not being known at that time that it is the sperm that determines the sex of offspring.

In addition to virtually compelling men to take secondary wives when their primary wives failed to have sons, this cultlike custom resulted in females in general being treated as instruments of utility. Among other things, the process of selecting wives for sons took on a pseudoscientific air, with mothers judging the potential capacity for would-be brides to bear sons on the basis of a long list of physical attributes.

Eventually these attributes were codified into thirteen "physical requirements" that prospective mothers-in-law and other marriage go-betweens used to measure the potential for young girls to bear sons:

1. Eyebrows that were straight (a masculine characteristic) and slanted downward, along with flat, smooth foreheads
2. Large, wide buttocks and correspondingly large, wide stomachs
3. A voice that was even toned and a well-developed chest that indicated good breathing capacity
4. Smooth, silky skin that was translucent, "like water"
5. Hands that were shapely and tapered (instead of square and stubby)
6. An angular face that had the profile of a goose or flea
7. Rounded shoulders and a thick back that denoted physical balance and strength
8. Well-developed breasts, with dark, firm nipples
9. A nose with a high ridge and slanted eyes
10. A stomach muscle that was thick and well developed, and a deep-seated navel

11. Wide eyes with "long, slender" corners that were dry
12. Skin that was shiny and fragrant
13. Rosy palms

These qualifications took precedence over beauty and other feminine features typically associated with women. In contrast, there were twenty-nine physical attributes that were believed to indicate that a woman was unlikely to bear sons. These features included a fragile body, a small squeaky voice, small breasts with pale nipples, a flattened nose bridge, ears turned inside out, a small mouth with a broad face, yellow or red hair, thin eyebrows, thin lips that were pale, a small shallow navel, protruding lips, and unruly coarse hair.

In addition to attempting to follow these physical qualifications in selecting brides, parents provided their sons and daughters with written instructions on how to perform sexual intercourse so as to enhance the possibility of conceiving sons instead of daughters. These guidelines were based on the belief that the uterus had two openings, one that resulted in the conception of a male fetus and one that produced a female child. It was believed that if the male sperm entered the left opening a son would be conceived; if it entered the opening on the right side, a female child would be conceived. This resulted in wives lying on their left side and remaining very still after intercourse in the hope that the male sperm would enter the left opening.

It was also believed that intercourse on the first, third, and fifth days after the menstrual period was most likely to produce male children, while intercourse on the second, fourth, and sixth days would result in female children. In their obsessive desire to have sons, most couples avoided having intercourse on these latter days. There was a variety of other beliefs and rules pertaining to conceiving sons, including the best time of the day or night and the best positions for intercourse, all of which were depicted graphically on colorful charts provided to newlyweds by their parents.

Special prayers and a number of ceremonial rituals were performed by mothers-in-law, brides, and their husbands in an effort to ensure the conception of sons. One of these practices was to place a mixture of blue salts, musk powder, and ground-up mugwort in the sonless wife's navel and set it afire. Records show that this cauterization process was sometimes carried out as many as two hundred times by husbands anxious to have sons—and that the custom was still widely practiced until the mid-1900s. Also until modern times, women could not serve as midwives unless they themselves had given birth to several sons, and the more sons a woman had the more highly she was esteemed as a midwife.

Families celebrated the birth of sons with special fanfare. One of the customs was to attach red peppers, symbolic of penises, to ropes and leave them hanging outside their homes for several days for all the neighbors to see. It was common for adults to ask small boys to show them their "pepper" (penis) as public proof of their maleness. In the case of girls, pieces of charcoal were tied to the ropes.

Most of the superstitions and practices involving efforts to have male children have gone by the wayside in modern-day Korea, but sons are still particularly important because males continue to play a dominant role in Korean society.

4

애욕

Aeyok

(Aye-yohk)

"Eroticism in Korean Life"

Prior to the ascendancy of Neo-Confucianism in Korean society in the early 1400s, historical records indicate that Koreans in general enjoyed a relatively robust erotic life, not only in keeping with their belief that large families were vital to the existence of the family and family clan but also because there were no religious, social, or political sanctions against extramarital sex as a pleasurable activity—at least for men.

Furthermore, Korean males had adopted many of the traditional erotic pastimes of China soon after large-scale contact between China and Korea began in 108 B.C. These early Koreans did not, however, let the Chinese male fetish with small feet persuade them to begin binding the feet of young girls, as it did in China. Historical records show that prior to the massive introduction of Confucianism into Korea from around A.D. 600, upper-class Korean women as well as men had considerable freedom of choice in establishing intimate liaisons with lovers and engaging in *aeyok* (aye-yohk), or "eroticism." But for women this freedom dwindled in direct proportion to the growing strength of Confucianism.

With the founding of the Choson dynasty in 1392, and its adoption of Neo-Confucianism as the ideology of Korean society, women in all classes became totally subject to the will of men. Sexual activity outside conjugal relations undertaken by husbands and wives for procreation became the exclusive preserve of men, who were allowed to have concubines (second wives) and patronize the famous *kisaeng* (kee-sang), or "entertainment girls" (if they could afford them). It was also common for upper-class men to make use of maids and other female servants in their households—another custom widely practiced in China.

Outside of professional female entertainers and those who caught the eye of well-to-do men, the women of Korea were forced to repress their sexual desires, a system that resulted in emotionally and psychically induced illnesses becoming endemic among them. With rare exceptions (see *Kisaeng*) only virgins were acceptable as legal primary wives.

From the first generations of the Choson dynasty in 1392 until the beginning of the twentieth century, Korean women in urban areas lived as virtual prisoners in their homes. They could leave their homes and go shopping or visiting only at night during a special *sodung* (soh-duung), or "curfew," period when men were required to remain indoors. This system did, however, provide an opportunity for braver women (almost always the wives of well-to-do officials) to establish sexual liaisons with men, usually young Buddhist monks whom they ostensibly visited for spiritual solace. Among the freest women in Korea during the long centuries of the Choson era were spinsters, widows, and women who had been cast out by their husbands for not bearing sons or for breaking one of the "wives'" commandments (see *Yoja*) and had taken up prostitution to earn a living.

Korean women have long been known—and prized by invaders—for their beauty and other attributes, but it was not until the introduction of democratic principles into Korean society following the end of World War II in 1945 that they began to have a choice in their sexual behavior. By the 1960s it was common to hear from international businessmen and travelers that the sensual attributes of Korean women were one of the best-kept secrets of Asia.

There is still a significant degree of public puritanism in Korea, but as in most countries that have different sexual standards for men and women, eroticism in all of its usual forms exists behind the public facade.

5

암흑기

Amhuk Ki

(Ahm-huuk Kee)

"The Dark Period"

In the 1870s, Japan began to take actions that would cast Korea into an *amhuk ki* (ahm-huuk kee), or "dark period," the likes of which it had never before experienced. Within less than twenty years after its own self-imposed isolation from the West had been ended by American gunboat diplomacy, Japan began using the same approach against the weak and squabbling Choson court in Seoul.

The Japanese government, with its warrior mentality and a rapidly modernized army and navy at its disposal, began a systematic campaign to replace the traditional suzerainty of China over Korea. In 1876 the Choson court was forced to sign a treaty with Japan, opening the country up for trade and other ties that quickly became financial, military, and political.

In 1894 a rebellion by Korean dissidents against the weak Choson court prompted both China and Japan to rush troops to Seoul supposedly to protect the king. The Japanese got there first, seized the royal palace, killed the queen (Queen Min), deposed the king, and appointed a puppet regent in his place. This led to all-out war between China and Japan, with the Japanese victorious on land as well as at sea. Under the terms of the peace treaty, signed in 1895 and approved by most of the leading Western nations, Korea became a protectorate of Japan. Japan immediately began strengthening its presence in Korea, both overtly and covertly treating the country like a colony.

Nine years later Japan went to war again, this time against Russia, successfully eliminating it as a rival in East Asia. With a free hand in Korea, the Japanese continued their program of converting Korea into a Japanese appendage. Responding to this threat, Korean patriots formed underground resistance groups and guerrilla bands to combat the Japanese. Finally in 1910 Japan gave up all pretense of "protecting" Korea, annexed the country, and began an all-out political, military, and cultural campaign to condition Koreans to accept their fate.

Japanese administrators in Korea repressed all political activity and cultural life. Spies were dispatched into every corner of the country to report on the activities of intellectuals, religious leaders, and former politicians, beginning an era that Koreans were later to call *Amhuk Ki* (Ahm-huuk Kee), or "The Dark Period."

Japan dispatched a large number of its notorious *kempeitai* (kem-pay-e-tie), or "thought police," to Korea, charging them with ferreting out and punishing anyone who spoke ill of the Japanese or Japan. They also created a large corps of *koto keisatsu* (koh-toh kay-e-saht-sue), literally "high police"—approximately half of whom were Koreans who had agreed to work for the Japanese. These police were charged with the responsibility of overseeing political activity, education, health, morality, tax collection, public welfare—in fact every facet of life in Korea—and they had virtually unlimited powers to search, arrest, pass sentences, imprison, or execute anyone accused of breaking their laws.

One of the extremes to which the Japanese went to enforce their laws and impress on Koreans their power and the importance of obeying them without question was a provision that required government officials and teachers to wear swords as a means of intimidating people. Koreans who refused to act as spies and informers themselves became subject to arrest and punishment as enemies of the Japanese regime. The slightest suspicions were grounds for arrest, torture, and imprisonment or death. Punishment was typically collective, with hundreds punished for the crime or rebellious conduct of a single person or a small group.

The psychic damage caused by this kind of control by force and fear was magnified beyond all reason because so many Koreans themselves were intimidated into participating in the brutalities inflicted on the population, making it impossible for people to trust anyone except their own families.

Despite these draconian measures, the Japanese annexation and continued occupation of Korea did not go smoothly. More and more Korean patriots took to the hills as guerrillas and began a campaign of attacking Japanese troops and their facilities. Urban residents staged street demonstrations, resulting in thousands of them being killed. In retaliation Japan began a campaign to totally eradicate Korean culture. Schools were required to teach only in Japanese. All Koreans were ordered to take Japanese names, speak only Japanese when dealing with the Japanese, and behave in the Japanese manner. Leading artists and craftsmen were killed or imprisoned to prevent them from passing Korean culture on to the next generation. Hundreds of ancient palaces and temples were destroyed.

Dozens of thousands of Korean men were inducted into the Japanese army. Thousands of Korean women were forced to serve as prostitutes for the Japanese military. Other thousands of men and women were shipped to Japan as slave laborers to work in factories and mines. Rather than submit to Japanese rule and enslavement, thousands of Koreans fled their homeland, some making their way to Manchuria and China and others to the United States. Many of the refugees who fled to nearby China and Manchuria formed clandestine guerrilla groups that carried out commando raids against Japanese facilities.

Other exiles formed assassination teams that targeted Japanese government officials and military officers. One member of a group in China that organized an *Aeguk Tan* (Λγc-guuk Tahn), or "Patriotic Society," succeeded in killing several high-ranking Japanese military officers with a bomb, greatly encouraging all Koreans as well as the beleaguered Chinese.

The great *Amhuk Ki* ended on August 15, 1945, when Japan was defeated by the United States and its allies and Korea quickly reclaimed its sovereignty. But one kind of dark period ended only to have another one start just five years later. The United States agreed that Russian troops could occupy the northern half of Korea and disarm the Japanese troops there, while the U.S. forces would do the same thing in the southern half of the country. Both sides were to withdraw their forces from Korea as soon as the Japanese troops had been disarmed and shipped home. The United States fulfilled its commitment, but the Russians refused to withdraw from the northern half of Korea and quickly set up a Communist government under the leadership of Il Sung Kim, a dedicated Korean Communist. The Soviets then shipped most of the Japanese troops in North Korea to Siberia to be used as slave laborers rather than sending them home. (By the time these ex-Japanese soldiers who survived enslavement in Siberia were finally allowed to return to Japan in the 1950s, they had been so thoroughly brainwashed in communism that they immediately began staging strikes and sit-ins against the Japanese government and the American military forces in Japan, becoming an international embarrassment to Japan.)

Il Sung Kim, with massive Soviet aid, immediately began building up a large army of North Koreans and fortifying the line along the thirty-eighth parallel that had been selected as the boundary between the Soviet and American zones. But all was not calm in South Korea either. As soon as the U.S. withdrew its forces from the southern half of the peninsula, political factions began fighting over which group was going to run the government.

Finally, in September 1947, the United Nations called for elections in both the northern and southern portions of the country. The Soviet Union refused to allow North Korea to participate in the process, so elections were held only in the South. On August 15, 1948, three years to the day after the end of World War II, the UN presided over the establishment of the Republic of Korea, with veteran politician-patriot Syngman Rhee as its first president. Three weeks later the Soviet-backed Il Sung Kim proclaimed the establishment of the Democratic Republic of Korea, with himself as president.

On June 25, 1950, North Korea launched a full-scale invasion of South Korea, capturing Seoul within a matter of hours and pushing the ill-prepared South Korean forces into a tiny pocket at the end of the peninsula. The United States, with UN approval and help from fifteen other UN member nations, quickly rallied a counterattack under the command of General Douglas MacArthur, who had commanded American forces in the successful war against Japan and was then commander of the Allied forces occupying Japan.

The Allied counterattack succeeded in pushing the North Koreans out of South Korea, but when the Allied forces continued to pursue the North Koreans beyond the thirty-eighth parallel, China entered the war on the side of North Korea. Allied forces suffered enormous losses, and once again Seoul fell to combined Chinese and North Korean forces. General MacArthur proposed to attack China's staging areas north of the Yalu River in Chinese territory and was fired by U.S. president Harry Truman because Truman and his advisers were afraid that would result in all-out war with China.

With Allied forces bowing to political pressure to stop at the thirty-eighth parallel, the fighting finally ended in a stalemate on July 27, 1953. Peace talks were begun in a special complex built hastily in a three-mile-wide demilitarized zone straddling the boundary between North and South Korea.

The war devastated both North and South Korea. In addition to some 1.5 million people killed on both sides, hundreds of thousands of families were torn apart by the division of the peninsula into two parts separated by a barrier that was one of the most heavily guarded strips of land in the world.

The second *Amhuk Ki* of the twentieth century was over for South Korea, but by that time communism had an even firmer grip on the northern portion of the peninsula and was imposing a different kind of darkness on the hapless people there.

6

아내

Anae
(Ah-negh)

"Wives: The Inside People"

Few societies have limited, or twisted, the lives of women as much as Korea's Choson dynasty, which began in 1392 and formally ended in 1910. Under the influence of a Confucian ideology that restricted the role of urban women to childbearing and housework and farm women to childbearing, housework, and farmwork, the Choson court created a society in which the two sexes were segregated into different worlds.

Women were not allowed to meet, talk to, or associate in any way with any males outside their own families. When passing men—on the rare occasions that they did—they were required to avert their eyes. But the tradition of segregating males and females goes back much further in Korean history. The word for wife, *anae* (ah-negh), basically means "inside person" and reflects the image of wives that had existed in Korea since ancient times.

From the beginning of Korea's recorded history, which more or less dates from the peninsula's falling under the hegemony of China in 108 B.C., until modern times lower-class women were treated very much like property. To survive in this environment, women had to develop extraordinary resilience and willpower, characteristics that were regularly put to the test by internal strife as well as invasions from the outside.

In all social classes marriages were arranged to benefit the families. Wives could not initiate divorce or prevent husbands from divorcing them. Young women were regularly sold into slavery. Groups of young women, selected especially for their beauty, were also regularly sent as tribute to the harems of the imperial capital of China.

Korean women began to fare somewhat better in the last decades of the nineteenth century, by which time the Choson court had become virtually impotent and the country was being threatened by Japan as well as Western powers. But the few changes that did occur then mostly benefited a small number of unmarried girls from noble and well-to-do merchant families who were allowed to venture outside their walled homes, attend school, and participate in limited social activities. These first breaks with Confucian-oriented society generally did not extend to wives.

Korean wives were to remain virtually locked in the Middle Ages until the 1960s, by which time Korea had embarked on a remarkable economic as well as social transformation that was to sever many of its Confucian roots and greatly loosen the remainder of its ties with the past. This time the revolution was to benefit married as well as single women. By the 1980s Korean wives had caught up with their Japanese counterparts and in many respects had begun turning the tables on their work-harried husbands.

Like their Japanese neighbors, present-day Korean housewives are in day-to-day charge of their childrens' education and generally act as the family bankers. Among the blue- and white-collar working classes, husbands generally turn their salaries over to their wives, keeping only a weekly or monthly allowance. Wives play equal or leading roles in deciding on major expenditures. Wives also initiate and manage most noncompany social events in which their families participate. About the only area that is still regarded as a strictly male obligation is the leading role in rituals honoring ancestors, but this too is gradually weakening.

One of the most important cultural changes in the lives of Korean *anae* was the almost mandatory rule that they give birth to sons or be divorced. Sons are still highly valued in Korean society, but without the force of law requiring strict obedience to the rites of ancestor worship and enforcing patrimony, male children are no longer absolutely necessary for Korean wives to maintain their roles and status.

Korean wives are no longer denied the right to enjoy *aejong* (aye-johng), or "love and affection." *Aein* (aye-een), "lover" or "sweetheart," is no longer a taboo word in the vocabulary of the young, and like their counterparts in other countries, more and more unmarried girls, formally addressed as *Agassi* (ah-gahs-she), which is the equivalent of "Miss," take it for granted that it is morally permissible for them to have *aein* before they marry, and they are willing to confront society at large on the issue.

At the same time, *kyurhon* (kure-hoan), or "marriage," is no longer viewed as a trap that condemns them to a life of servitude and loneliness from which there is virtually no escape. The possibility of *ihon* (ee-hohn), or "divorce," is only one part of the changing scene for Korean wives.

A generic term for "housewife" or "mistress of the house" is *chubu* (chuu-buu). The male equivalent is *chuin* (chuu-een), which is variously translated as "host," "employer," or "master of the house."

7

안심
Anshim
(Ahn-sheem)

"Peace of Mind"

Another key element in traditional Korean culture that was to have a fundamental influence on the character of the people was an abhorrence of disorder, of chaos of any kind, physical or mental, something that no doubt derived from their indoctrination in Buddhism and Confucianism. Buddhism taught nonviolence in the strictest form, including respecting and preserving all life forms. Confucianism imbued the people with an equally strong sense of order and form, to the point that the *way* they did things generally took precedence over feelings and other personal considerations.

However, these two influences neither protected Koreans from their more aggressive and rapacious neighbors nor guaranteed domestic peace and tranquillity at all times. But they did establish a philosophical and spiritual foundation in Korea for a state of mind referred to as *anshim* (ahn-sheem), which literally means "peaceful heart," and made this the ideal mental and spiritual state for which all were expected to strive.

Korean history, particularly since the end of the nineteenth century, may seem at variance with the *anshim* element in Korean culture, but most of the violence that has been endemic in Korea since that time has been the result of invasions by both foreign forces and foreign ideologies, against which Koreans had no suitable defense.

Contemporary culture in Korea still holds *anshim* up as the ideal, and much of the Korean language, etiquette, and ethics is designed to create and sustain an environment of *anshim* in personal relations, in business, and in any other public activity. The fact that these efforts fail almost as often as they succeed is generally not for lack of trying but because the whole society is undergoing revolutionary changes.

Much of the ongoing Korean behavior that outsiders perceive as irrational and disruptive in some way is a manifestation of their efforts to maintain *anshim* despite new circumstances over which they have little or no control. The employee who keeps quiet about a mistake, the employee who does not complain about an injustice, and the businessperson who misrepresents a situation are all trying to avoid upsetting their own *anshim* as well as that of others.

Rather than express themselves directly in many situations that are routine to Westerners, Koreans keep quiet and expect other people to pick up on their desires or intentions via subliminal signals that are referred to as *nunchi* (nuun-chee), a kind of cultural intuition. It is fair to say that in Korea one cannot maintain an acceptable level of *anshim* in a work group (or in a family) without being skilled in *nunchi*—something that may put newly arrived and uninitiated foreigners at a very serious disadvantage.

One way for foreign businesspeople newly assigned to Korea to avoid some of the more dire consequences of disrupting the *anshim* of their Korean co-workers and failing to pick up on their silent messages through *nunchi* is to confess up front that although they are familiar with the terms and understand they refer to behavior that is crucial to maintaining good morale and productivity, they do not yet have the cultural skills to react to them or use them effectively. This kind of confession generally results in the Koreans concerned helping the foreign novice bridge the cultural gap. In any event, such a confession lays the foundation for the newcomer to ask questions when in doubt about anything.

Just letting a Korean friend or business associate know that you will do everything possible to protect his or her *anshim* can significantly enhance the relationship for the better.

8

아는사람

Anun Saram
(Ah-nuun Sah-rahm)

"Someone You Know"

Describing a person as *anun saram* (ah-nuun sah-rahm) or "someone I know" does not sound like a significant statement in its Western context. In the course of a busy lifetime, Westerners have traditionally made dozens to hundreds of acquaintances with whom they would engage in social activities or conduct business if an occasion arose.

Such was not the case in pre-modern Korea, however. There the collective and exclusive nature of each core family and its extended family made it impossible for individuals to develop relationships and obligations freely with more than half a dozen or so "outside" people during their lifetimes.

Generally, individuals were not free to make private or public commitments to nonfamily members on their own because one way or another such commitments impacted the whole family or even the whole clan. This situation resulted in Koreans generally viewing nonfamily members and people with whom they had no personal connection as strangers to be wary of and avoid, or simply to ignore as if they did not exist.

The Korean custom of avoiding casual outside relationships was driven in part by the fact that additional relationships would make it necessary to behave in a carefully calculated way toward the outsider to prevent either side from losing face and to avoid the possibility of creating enemies. Outside relationships could also create obligations that conflicted with existing ones. New relationships that were not specifically sought for some special advantage were therefore considered both socially burdensome and potentially dangerous. In effect, nonfamily members were culturally conditioned to repel each other.

Until recent times, ordinary Koreans had absolutely no say in government policy or practices, a circumstance that worked against their developing any concept of public responsibility. This situation was another key factor in Koreans' generally limiting their contacts and relationships to family, kin, and a few close friends who usually dated back to their childhood and school days.

In present-day Korea the tendency for people to limit their involvements to *anun saram*, or people with whom they have established personal relationships as a result of school or work, is still a significant factor in both private and public affairs. The exceptions to this are generally age and experience related. The younger the people, the more likely they are to be more casual in developing acquaintances. The more individual Koreans have been exposed to Western influence, through education or work experience, the less likely they are to limit their contacts to *anun saram* and the more likely they are to feel comfortable about establishing new relationships for personal or business reasons.

However, present-day social critics continuously deplore the low level of civic and public interest in Korea and the tendency for people in public to ignore or be discourteous to strangers—in most cases, other Koreans rather than foreign residents or visitors. Koreans normally put non-Asian foreigners in an "honored guest" category and most of the time treat them with special courtesy. Often their assistance to lost and otherwise helpless foreigners can go so far beyond normal expectations that it becomes embarrassing.

One conspicuous occasion when Koreans typically treat foreign residents or visitors the same way as other Koreans, however, is when they are all competing for taxis during rush hour and on rainy days.

Foreign businesspeople who visit and spend time in Korea have a significant advantage in establishing relationships with Koreans since in this respect Koreans regard foreigners as "culture free." Thus natives do not have to be concerned about upsetting social harmony or incurring unwanted obligations by establishing relations with foreigners.

아리랑

Arirang
(Ah-ree-rahng)

"The Korean Soul Song"

Few people have visited Korea for any length of time without hearing the song that vies with the country's national anthem in popularity and, in fact, serves more or less as the unofficial theme song of Koreans. The title of the song is "*Arirang*" (Ah-ree-rahng), which is usually translated by Korean-English dictionaries as "folk song" because it apparently is a coined word that has no literal meaning. According to bicultural business executive H. J. Chang, "it expresses the inner soul of Koreans."

In 1926, in spite of the presence of Japanese occupation forces, Korean actor-director Un Gyu Na somehow managed to produce a movie entitled *Arirang* that was a powerful protest against Japan's colonial oppression of Korea. The title of the movie was taken from a famous folk song by that name that is said to have originated in Chongson gun (Chongson County) in Kangwon Province.

According to local folklore, a young girl from the village of Yoryang fell in love with a young man who lived in the nearby village of Auraji, which was separated from Yoryang by a river. On the pretense of picking camellia flowers that grew on the other side of the river, the girl would cross the river on the daily ferry and secretly meet her sweetheart. A fall flood caused ferry service to be suspended for several days. The girl composed a beautiful, sad song to express her longing. The song eventually came to be known as "Chongson Arirang."

The movie was a huge hit with Korean audiences and has since become a classic, but it was the song, "*Arirang*," which reminded Koreans of their suffering under Japanese rule and their longing for freedom, that was to have the most lasting influence. In 1995, Korean writer Jung Rae Cho rekindled interest in the popular folk song and its connection with the colonial period by publishing a twelve-volume novel called *Arirang*, which recounts in painful detail the crimes of the Japanese colonial administrators as well as those of Koreans who collaborated with the Japanese. The book sold more than one million copies during the first year following its publication. Cho said the book was built on the anger and hatred that the Japanese colonial rulers left in their wake and that his purpose for writing it was to correct historical distortions and help relieve the feelings of disgrace suffered by so many Koreans.

Foreigners who would like to ensure themselves of a permanent place of honor among older Koreans need only to learn how to sing "*Arirang*" with all of the passion and soul that is so dear to Korean hearts. Unfortunately, since the 1990s the role of this poignant song has waned significantly among Korea's younger generations. They are more attracted to popular foreign songs.

10

재벌

Chaebol

(Chay-buhl)

"The Industrial Colossi"

One of the most powerful forces contributing to Korea's astounding economic transformation between 1953 and the 1980s was the emergence of a number of corporate conglomerates patterned after Japan's pre–World War II *zaibatsu* (zigh-baht-sue). Japan's *zaibatsu*, epitomized by Mitsui, Mitsubishi, and Sumitomo, were owned by individual families and together dominated Japan's economy. All of them were used as instruments of the Japanese government in carrying out its expansionist political policies from the 1880s on, including the annexation of Korea in 1910 and its administration as a colony until 1945.

Korea's post–World War II *zaibatsu*like enterprise groups are called *chaebol* (chay-buhl), which is the Korean pronunciation of the same Chinese ideograms that are pronounced *zaibatsu* in Japanese—meaning "financial clique" or "group." (A group of affiliated companies as well as financial groups are collectively known as a *jaebul* / jay-buhl.) More than one hundred Korean enterprise groups are labeled as *chaebol* by the government, with the largest and best known being Daewoo, Hanjin, Hyundai, Kia, LG Group (formerly Lucky Goldstar), Samsung, Ssangyong, and Sunkyong. Like their Japanese counterparts, Korea's *chaebol* had government support in their early years, but unlike the Japanese firms the support they received from the government was generally unofficial—and, according to their critics, often illegal.

Another significant difference between Korean *chaebol* and Japan's pre–World War II *zaibatsu* is that the Japanese groups had their own banks to arrange financing for them, while the Korean *chaebol* did not. This made the Korean groups more dependent on the government and therefore more susceptible to pressure from the various agencies and ministries controlling finance, manufacturing, importing, and exporting. One of the results of this difference is that the larger and more successful the Korean companies became, the more independent their decisions and actions.

Like their Japanese *zaibatsu* role models, however, Korea's *chaebol* were motivated by an urge to diversify and to control every aspect of their operations, from the sourcing of raw materials and manufacturing to marketing finished products. Most of the groups also entered totally unrelated businesses, taking advantage of their financial resources and government contacts. In many cases they were able to monopolize the categories they entered by emphasizing market share rather than profits. This compulsion to diversify included becoming major stockholders in other companies.

By the 1970s the *chaebol* were often referred to as *muno* (muu-noh), or "octopuses," because they had their "tentacles" in many things. Part of this negative image arose from the general public opinion that the combines profited unfairly from their close ties with government officials and agencies. There were numerous accusations of *pujong chuk chae* (puu-johng chewk chay), or "illicit wealth accumulation," that not only involved illegal activity but went against the Confucian concept of morality and virtue that went with political power.

The Vietnam War was a boon to the growing Korean *chaebol*, especially Hyundai and Hanjin. With the backing of the U.S. Army, Hanjin became virtually the sole operator of the key Vietnamese port of Qui Nhon and provided both marine and land transportation for the American forces in Vietnam. In support of this effort, Hanjin established an air and sea transport company in Korea to ferry supplies and workers to Vietnam. Using the enormous profits generated by this activity—and paid for by the American military forces in Vietnam—Hanjin bought the then ailing Korean Air (KAL) from the Korean government and subsequently turned it into one of the world's premier airline companies.

Hyundai and the hurriedly established construction divisions of other *chaebol* were given major construction contracts in Korea by the U.S. Army, providing them with a fund of experience as well as huge profits, which made it possible for them to bid on and win numerous construction contracts in the Middle East and elsewhere when the Vietnam War ended. Records show that in just four years in the latter part of the 1970s Korea's top ten *chaebol* made $22 billion on construction projects in the Middle East.

Each of Korea's conglomerates has its own corporate culture that began as a manifestation of the background and beliefs of its founder. Samsung, for example, was founded by the youngest son of an old *yangban* (yahng-bahn) gentry family. Its employees regard the company and themselves as the best and the brightest. It emphasizes high-tech industries. Hyundai, on the other hand, was founded by the son of a farmer, is known for its conservatism, and emphasizes heavy industries. The first generation of post–World War II *chaebol* employees, tempered by the experience as a colony of Japan (1910–45) and the horrors of wars that had devastated their homeland, were educated, hardworking, totally diligent, and fiercely loyal.

Korean-American anthropologist Choong Soon Kim, in his book *The Culture of Korean Industry*, described the first generation of *chaebol* managers as authoritarian, inclusive, and worried about the continuity of their enterprises. This led them to staff their executive positions with sons, sons-in-law, and other close relatives. In the early days of the *chaebol* there were few stockholders. The founder and his family usually owned controlling interest. Stockholder meetings were programmed to last for only half an hour or so, with outside stockholders given no chance to speak up about anything.

Not surprisingly, the founders or chairmen of the largest conglomerates were generally referred to by the press and others as *chongsu* (chohng-suu), a military term meaning "commander in chief." The personal income of some of the founders became enormous, amounting to several hundred million dollars a year, adding to criticism by those who saw the giant combines as immoral parasites.

Much of the unsavory reputation of the *chaebol* in the 1970s and 1980s was apparently well deserved. Their founders and senior executives (along with other companies and individuals who owned substantial real property assets) were accused of using *kamyong* (kah-myohng), or "pseudonyms," and the names of relatives to disguise the true ownership of stocks, land, bank accounts, and so on. This practice, which goes back to ancient times in Korea, eventually became a national scandal, and in the early 1990s a law was passed forbidding the practice. But the law apparently succeeded only in reducing the use of the subterfuge, not eliminating it.

In some *chaebol* and other large firms the workday began with the playing of the national anthem over the public address system. During the playing, employees stood at attention. At 5:00 P.M. the national anthem was again played to signal the official end of the workday, but unlike some of their Western counterparts, employees made no mad dash for the door. Women usually continued working for another hour or so, while the majority of the male employees worked for two or three more hours. The few people who left the office at "quitting time" invariably had a special reason for leaving and did so only after clearing it with their superiors.

The reputation of the *chaebol* reached a low point in the 1970s and 1980s, particularly among their own employees. Union agitation and strikes increased. A number of the conglomerates created special strike forces called *kusadae* (kuu-sah-day), or "save the company corps," made up of tough young men the companies used to physically break up strikes and other union activities.

Still, university graduates were so anxious to obtain employment with one of the *chaebol* that they would take the entrance exams of several firms in the hope of being accepted by at least one of them. This resulted in the government's ordering the conglomerates to hold their *ipsa sihom* (eep-sah she-hohm), or "entrance examinations," on the same day so that graduates from the most prestigious and best schools could not monopolize the available jobs. Smaller companies held their entrance exams on a later date. Candidates who passed the entrance exams then had to pass rigorous personal interviews that were designed to weed out prospects who did not meet the character and personality standards of the companies concerned.

By the early 1990s the *chaebol* had matured and reformed their managerial practices to the point that their labor problems had disappeared. They had also grown to the point that it was difficult to buy any domestically manufactured or imported item that had not been touched by one of the combines. The names of the leading groups had also become well known around the world. But in 1995 the close ties between the conglomerates and the government suddenly came to a head. President Young Sam Kim ordered the arrest of his two immediate predecessors, Doo Hwan Chun and Tae Woo Roh, on bribery charges, and implicated twenty-four of the country's top *chaebol* in payoffs to the former presidents. Government officials were quick to point out, however, that they had no intention of dismantling the conglomerates because that would cripple the economy. They said their purpose in calling in and interrogating the leaders of the twenty-four *chaebol* was to impress on them the importance of their voluntarily reducing their role and power in the economy—something that, in keeping with their dedication to the well-being of the nation, most of them agreed to do.

In *chaebol* jargon, the founder company is often referred to as *moche* (moach-eh), or "the mother company," while subsidiaries are often called *chamae hoesa* (chah-my hoh-eh-sah), or "sister companies."

There was to be an even more serious downside to the rapid growth the *chaebol* had relentlessly pursued for more than three decades. In 1997 their overextended financial obligations caught up with them, and several of them went bankrupt—something that had been virtually inconceivable to Koreans up to that time.

11

책임

Chaegim
(Chay-geem)

"Dealing with Responsibility"

Korea's traditional culture precluded the development of individualism and a sense of self. The Confucian system of filial piety and familism required that the self and the individual be merged into the family collective. Centuries of conditioning in the concept and practice of collective identity as opposed to individual identity resulted in Koreans' failing to develop a clear sense of personal *chaegim* (chay-geem), or "responsibility."

Chaegim was seen as a family or collective thing, not as a personal or individual matter. The father and family as a whole were responsible for the attitudes and conduct of each individual member, particularly when the conduct was regarded as immoral or disruptive. When a member of a family committed a crime or transgression against someone else or against government authorities, the whole family was considered guilty and was subject to punishment.

The demands on the "collective character" of individuals eventually became so strong that the personal pronoun *I* was seldom used. Koreans typically thought and spoke in terms of *we*, not *I*. In this environment, people generally did not think in terms of personal responsibility.

Present-day Koreans are still being culturally programmed in the concept of family-centered collective responsibility, but not nearly as much as in the past. At the same time, they are also being taught to develop individual *chaegim*, particularly in high-tech, highly competitive businesses, where the ideas and efforts of individuals acting on their own can make the difference between success and failure. This does not mean, however, that foreigners dealing with Koreans in business or in politics can automatically expect individual Koreans either to act on their own or to take personal responsibility for projects—or even their own actions.

Chaegim in Korean enterprises and institutions continues to be far more collective than it is in their Western counterparts. The Western practice of identifying and dealing with the "man in charge" often does not work in Korea. Typically there is no single individual company member who is directly and exclusively in charge of a particular matter. It is a section or group responsibility. There is usually a person in sections and divisions who has been designated as the "window" to the outside world. But he or she is generally an extension of the group and cannot act alone.

However, there are very conspicuous exceptions to the rule of divided responsibility in Korean companies that are still being run by their founders as well as in family-owned and operated companies. In fact there is a specific *shijo* (she-joe), or "company founder," syndrome in Korea that played a significant role in South Korea's rapid development into an economic powerhouse. Most Koreans who founded companies between 1945 and around 1970 were totally traditional (Confucian) in their attitudes and behavior, meaning that they looked on their employees as family members who were expected to show them the utmost respect and obey them absolutely.

These company founders typically worked seventy to eighty hours a week and expected the same of their employees. They ran their companies like feudal kingdoms, delegating very little authority to their subordinates. But anytime a company failed, all of the employees got a share of the blame—a factor that scholar-essayist Kyu Tae Yi explains in *The Shape of Korean Life*. He notes that when things are going well, Koreans who are involved in any way characteristically claim as much of the credit as possible, but when things go wrong they typically blame others.

In present-day Korea, managers of departments and divisions in larger companies typically give an impression of authority and power because they are almost always surrounded by a retinue of aides who respond to their orders like well-drilled military teams. But this impression is usually deceiving. For the most part these managers can act only after arriving at a consensus with a number of other managers. Adds H. J. Chang, president of SEMCO International, a leading consulting firm in Seoul, "There is, however, a slow but nevertheless discernible shift toward the Western way of decision-making by individuals."

Although Koreans are assuming more and more personal responsibility for their actions in family as well as business affairs, there is little likelihood that collectivism will disappear entirely from the culture in the foreseeable future. Sharing responsibility is deeply embedded in the Korean character. They are acutely conscious of the fact that if a society is to survive and prosper in a harmonious environment, individualism must inevitably give way to group responsibility. They are not likely to discard that hard-earned wisdom.

체면
Chae-myun
(Chay-me'yuun)

"Saving Everybody's Face"

At the beginning of Korea's Choson dynasty in 1392 the new government strengthened the divisions between the already segregated social classes by making a much sterner version of Confucianism the national political ideology as well as the state religion. The government made the system work by imbuing its religious aspects with a cultlike status that conditioned people mentally and physically to behave according to a precise etiquette and by severely punishing any dissent.

Since this system made a carefully prescribed etiquette the essence of morality while also providing the social factors that gave people identity based on their sex, age, social class, and official position, it created in people a permanent obsession with making sure that others treated them with an exaggerated level of formal courtesy and respect.

People became extremely sensitive to the behavior of others and to their own behavior because everything that was done or said impacted their highly honed sense of propriety, self-respect, and honor. Protecting and nurturing one's "face" and the "face" of one's family thus became an overriding challenge in Korean life and had a fundamental influence in the subsequent molding of the Korean language and culture in general. *Chae-myun* (chay-me'yuun), or "face saving," often took precedence over rationality, practicality, and truth.

In this face-sensitive society, speaking clearly and candidly became taboo. Speech became indirect and vague. Direct criticism, especially of superiors, was prohibited, and there were serious sanctions for breaking the ban. When something disruptive happened between individuals or groups, one of the institutionalized ways of "repairing" the damage was for a mutual agreement to *opton kosuro haja* (ohp-tohn koh-suu-roh hah-jah), which means "pretend it never happened."

During the long Choson dynasty (1392–1910), the practice of *chae-myun* contributed significantly to cultural, social, and economic stagnation because it did not permit open, free, and critical discussion of matters at hand. It was not only safer to say nothing and do nothing to change things, it was the spiritually and morally correct thing to do.

Face is still of vital importance to Koreans. People continue to be extremely circumspect in their speech and behavior. The goal is to guarantee that everyone is in a constant state of *anshim* (ahn-sheem), which means "peace of mind" or "at perfect ease." The first priority is to avoid any kind of direct confrontation by using only polite terms and refraining from saying or doing anything that would upset anyone. In business situations this may include not telling the truth about something, withholding bad news, and not bringing up mistakes that have been made. Naturally this kind of behavior can be very confusing and can mislead people who are not capable of reading between the lines. Foreigners dealing with Koreans may be especially disadvantaged.

Well before the formal end of the Choson dynasty in 1910, however, public institutions and the government had lost their Confucian immunity to criticism. By the 1950s criticism and direct action designed to bring about change were not only common in Korea but also were engaged in with a special vehemence. Physical violence and bloodshed were often included in the overreaction to the centuries during which such behavior occurred only when people were oppressed beyond the limits of their endurance.

Despite evolutionary changes in Korean culture since the end of the Choson dynasty, however, Koreans continuously engage in *chae-myun* in all of their personal and business relationships. Foreigners in Korea must do the same. Face saving, in fact, remains Korea's "cultural lubricant," without which things cannot and will not run smoothly.

13

자선

Chagun
(Chah-guun)

"Compassion and Mercy"

Westerners tend to be both fascinated and repulsed by the contradictions in Asian attitudes and behavior. The stylized etiquette and tranquil harmony that reflects one face of the Chinese, Japanese, Koreans, and other Asians simply does not fit with their other face of rage and savage brutality. These inconsistencies in character apparently arose from centuries of emotional, intellectual, and physical programming that compelled Asians to repress their natural instincts and desires and conform to an artificial kind of behavior that created contradictory impulses.

As long as the pressure on Asians to conform to this contradictory lifestyle was strong enough and steady enough to maintain a balance of the conflicting impulses, there was peace and tranquillity. But when this pressure weakened or became more than people could endure, their suppressed rage was unleashed, and the only way open to them to express this rage was through violence.

Korea's pre-modern history is a series of long cycles of peace and tranquillity ending in periods of great violence. The Koreans survived both forms of these cycles because they were tough, resilient, and determined and also because of a cultural element expressed in the word *chagun* (chah-guun), which can be translated as "compassion and mercy."

In keeping with the humanistic side of Korea's multiple philosophies (shamanism, Buddhism, and Confucianism), the harshness of life in Korea has traditionally been tempered by *chagun* most of the time. Except in rare cases of truly evil men, the officials who administered the authoritarian regimes down to modern times were generally compassionate men who, during times of peace, interpreted and enforced the laws from a humane rather than legalistic viewpoint. During periods of turmoil, however, the dark side of the Asian character inevitably came to the fore, and *chagun* was frequently replaced by absolute ruthlessness.

Broadly speaking, the cycle of violence and change that began in Korea in the 1870s has not yet ended. But this time there is a good chance the violence will end not because of the imposition of a new authoritarian political regime but because the national will of the people will succeed in bringing about the formation of a truly democratic government.

In the meantime, foreign residents of Korea may benefit from the *chagun* factor *if* they are aware of it and learn how to use it. On occasions when people run afoul of the law, whether the situation is minor or major, it is normal for them to get a special measure of leniency—a kind of justice that is applied to Koreans and foreigners alike—if they invoke the *chagun* element by apologizing and expressing regret.

There is another side to the dispensation of *chagun* if the situation involves a business matter in which Koreans are pitted against foreigners. In such situations it typically takes on a nationalistic flavor and can be expected to come down on the Korean side. To help prevent this from happening, or at least to mitigate the results, the foreign side is well advised to present its case with as much emotion and "humanism" as possible. Koreans are invariably more receptive to humanistic approaches than they are to hard facts and logic.

The Korean custom of giving precedence to human factors over facts and logic is usually upsetting to most Western businesspeople when they first encounter it—and may continue to upset them for months, years, or forever, depending on their own character and attitudes. Those who are perceptive enough to combine the Korean way with the Western way, using a combination of logic, humanism, and personalism, are usually the ones who succeed in Korea.

14

자급자족

Chakupjachok
(Chah-kuup-jah-choke)

"The Self-Sufficiency Syndrome"

In the early 1990s, Korean business and political leaders began talking about the importance of internationalizing or globalizing the Korean economy in keeping with the worldwide trend among leading industrial powers—something that is such an extreme departure from traditional Korean thinking that it suggests changes in the Korean mind-set that, in fact, have not occurred. Those who are expressing this viewpoint are few in number and are not speaking for the overwhelming majority of Koreans.

A number of Korean companies have become multinational to the point that they appear to have been internationalized, but that too is misleading because behind the foreign facade of Samsung, the LG Group, and other Korean conglomerates, both the heart and soul are still Korean. True and complete internationalization and globalization are so directly opposed to the traditional Korean mind-set that the whole culture would have to be transformed before either could happen—a circumstance that is, of course, common in some degree to all nationalities.

For all practical purposes Koreans were isolated from the world community until 1965, when diplomatic relations were reestablished with Japan, and although they have since made remarkable progress in catching up with the rest of the world in a material sense, they (like the Chinese and Japanese) are still generations behind most Westerners in viewing themselves as members of the world family—racially as well as culturally.

In addition to their geographic and cultural isolation until recent times, Koreans have traditionally been programmed in the concept of *chakupjachok* (chah-kuup-jah-choke), or "self-sufficiency." While this cultural conditioning naturally began as a matter of survival, it was eventually institutionalized in the Korean political, economic, and social systems. Until the first decades of the twentieth century the vast majority of all Koreans were, in fact, virtually self-sufficient, raising their own food and making their own clothing. While there was some exporting and importing in pre-twentieth-century Korea, the volume was so minuscule and limited to such a few items that foreign trade had no impact at all on most people.

Thus the concept of *chakupjachok* has permeated Korean thinking since ancient times and still is a significant part of the policies and practices of the government and business in general. The larger a Korean enterprise, the more it tries to control all of the factors involved in its operation, from sourcing raw materials to selling and servicing finished goods. Korean companies also have a phobia about coming under the control of foreign firms. On a national scale the Korean government is determined to prevent the country from ever again coming under the political and economic hegemony of any foreign power.

Foreign businesspeople and diplomats dealing with Korea invariably encounter the *chakupjachok* syndrome at one time or another, and generally it plays some kind of role in all of their relations with Korea. It will no doubt be a full generation or more before most Koreans are sufficiently internationalized to participate willingly in the globalization of their economy.

참을성
Chamulsong
(Chah-muhl-song)
"You Gotta Have Patience!"

One of the sights that early foreign visitors to Korea were most impressed with, and invariably described—almost to the point that it appears to have been required of them—was that of elderly Korean men and women seated in calm repose outside their homes, in parks, or along rural walkways. These elderly people, dressed in the national male and female costumes, were generally assumed to be the embodiment of the revered grandmother, grandfather, or wise old Confucian scholar and the famed Korean trait of *chamulsong* (chah-muhl-song), or "patience"—all of which represented the best of Korean culture in the popular mind.

Contemporary Korean philosophers, psychologists, and other social scientists proclaim that *chamulsong*, or "patience," is one of the primary national characteristics of the Korean people. They do not add, however, that this characteristic developed because the people of pre-modern Korea had no choice but to passively endure the abuses of authoritarian and backward-looking governments with as much dignity and patience as possible for century after century.

In old Korea any outward sign of impatience at the behavior of government officials and others in authority was traditionally taken as disrespectful and met with some kind of reaction that made things worse. In present-day Korea, *chamulsong* remains a prerequisite for survival and achievement. The government is not nearly as oppressive as it was in the past, but bureaucratic red tape, the personal nature of business transactions, limited facilities, and competition for virtually everything make patience essential if one is to avoid an emotional breakdown. Westerners in Korea generally have to undergo substantial cultural transformation before they can emotionally adjust to the slower pace of officialdom.

Probably the most conspicuous changes in the famed patience of Koreans is on the political front. Younger generations who have never known the hardships or the oppression that were the lot of their forebears are becoming more and more impatient in demanding political and economic rights that have long been taken for granted in the United States and other countries. Like other Asian societies that are attempting to accommodate principles of democracy and individualism within the context of their enduring Confucian cultures, present-day Koreans who live in larger cities and have college educations essentially have two personalities—a traditional Korean personality and what might be called a Western-oriented personality.

Generally speaking, these "two-sided" Koreans are able to assume whatever personality best fits the situations they are in. Problems arise, however, when the situations are not clear-cut and when they try to switch back and forth between the two modes or attempt to fuse them in an effort to please everyone.

Koreans who work with other Koreans in companies managed by expatriate foreign managers are especially challenged because they must be sensitive to a wide range of contradictory emotional needs and expectations from both their foreign managers and Korean co-workers. On an individual basis, Koreans can be as impatient as anyone else. But in any normal situation the larger the number of people involved the more likely the group is to assume a *chamulsong* mode and behave in the traditional fashion.

Generally speaking, as the famed English poet Rudyard Kipling did, trying to hurry things up in an Eastern culture like Korea usually makes them worse.

Another common term for patience—and endurance—is *innae* (een-nigh).

16

창피

Changpi
(Chahng-pee)

"The Shame Culture"

Many people are familiar with the concept of a "shame culture" as a result of Ruth Benedict's classic book *The Chrysanthemum and the Sword*, published in the 1940s, in which she delved into the cultural characteristics of the Japanese. As it happens, Korea also has a "shame culture" and for the same reasons—the influence of Confucianism, which makes saving face one of the most important elements in proper, moral behavior. In fact Korea was a "shame culture" before Japan, because Confucianism became entrenched in Korea well before it arrived in Japan.

In its Confucian context shame is regarded as the root of morality, and in shame cultures morality is driven externally. People in shame cultures try to avoid causing emotional pain to others and being subjected to such pain themselves—pain that is caused by being looked down on by others, by being embarrassed, by being disgraced in the eyes of others. Shame-centered people do not try to "be good" so as to avoid committing a sin that endangers their soul; they try to behave as is required by their social status and station to avoid losing their reputation.

Historically, the greatest sources of *changpi* (chahng-pee), or "shame," in Korea were failing to live up to the expectations of the father, the family, the kin, and one's circle of friends and associates and not being treated as one's status demanded. In the case of the latter, Koreans were honor bound to wipe out the shame by somehow, at some time, taking revenge against the person or persons who shamed them.

In contrast to both Korea and Japan, the United States and other Christianized countries have "guilt cultures." The primary sanction of the Christian religion is guilt feelings, and the more influence Christianity has on people the more guilty they feel about what they do—or think. Because these guilt feelings are internalized, people who have "sinned" can suffer on their own and in silence to the point that they go crazy—something that is rare in *changpi* cultures.

While Christianity peddles guilt and Confucianism purveys shame, there is a fundamental difference in the effects of the two sanctions. Shame-centered people can get by with all kinds of "immoral" conduct and not suffer any pangs of shame as long as it doesn't become known to others. In shame cultures it is not doing that is shameful so much as getting caught. Among the many things that people in *changpi* cultures can "morally" do that are considered immoral in Christianized guilt cultures is treat people as inferiors, take financial advantage of people, conceal the truth, use devious tactics, and—for men anyway—engage in premarital and extramarital sex.

It should be noted that some 20 to 25 percent of all present-day Koreans are classified as Christians, which could imply that this large number of Koreans today are more influenced by *maume kengginun* (mou-may keng-ghee-nuun), or "guilt feelings," than by shame and are therefore easier for Christianized foreigners to deal with. There is some truth in this belief, but not a lot. Koreans who regard themselves as Christians but were born and raised in Korea are generally Koreans first and Christians second—meaning that they continue to be more influenced by the traditional shame culture than by the Christian guilt culture. Their Christianity is more of an intellectual addition to their beliefs than spiritual or emotional guidelines for behavior.

In male-female relations, in family matters, and in other personal and professional matters that really count, traditional Korean beliefs and behavior generally take precedence over Christian dogma and customs. *Changpi*, as it applies to Korean culture, is, in fact, far more powerful as a social conscience than spiritual guilt because it is precisely detailed and is much more visible to the eye. Guilt can be disguised and denied. Shame often stands out for everyone to see.

The one transgression that Koreans cannot accept is being shamed.

17

장성
Chang Sung
(Chahng Suung)

"Staying in Touch with the Spirits"

Concern with the supernatural and with superstitions has historically been a primary trait in Korean character—an attitude that was part of the shamanistic beliefs that made up the spiritual cosmos of Koreans since the earliest times. As in all societies, including the latest and most modern, the Koreans used a variety of rituals and symbols to communicate with and appease the unseen gods and spirits they believed ruled over human affairs.

Today, despite its modern, high-tech veneer, Korea has not lost contact with the spiritual side of life. One of the most interesting signs of this ongoing connection is the *chang sung* (chahng suung), or "spirit posts," that historically have served as village guardians. These large totems, made of wood or stone, with grotesque humanlike faces painted on them, are still seen along rural roads and on the outskirts of villages. The spirit posts have huge, bulging eyes, big noses, and wide mouths that are designed to embody a wide range of human emotions, from anguish to ecstasy. To some the expressions of the spirit post faces are comical; others see them as frightening.

There are generally two spirit posts in each setting, one male and the other female. One of the posts will usually be inscribed with the Chinese ideograms that read *Chon Ha Dae Jang Gun* (Great General Under the Sky), and the other, *Chi Ha Dae Jang Gun* (Great General Under the Earth).

In earlier times, the *chang sung* were an integral part of village rites designed to ensure peace and prosperity and to ward off diseases and other calamities. The posts were cleaned and repaired regularly and replaced periodically so as not to offend their spirits. The materials and shapes of the *chang sung* varied with the location. In central Korea, pine, chestnut, and alder trees were used commonly. In southern Korea, where they were more susceptible to damage by weathering and decay, they were often made of stone.

In addition to village gods, all Korean homes traditionally had "ancestor gods," "house master gods," "fire gods," and "house site gods."

Among the more personal of the various religious symbols in Korea are the *pujok* (puu-johk), or "spiritual talismans," found in Korean homes, places of worship, and other public places. *Pujok* consist of slips of paper, usually white or yellow mulberry paper, with special Chinese characters and other symbols painted on them in red ink. (In Korean thought, red possesses the power to ward off evil and is the reason why the color is so common in the culture.) The *pujok* are placed on gates, on ceiling beams, over doors and other such places to ward off evil spirits.

Pujok come in a variety of types, ranging from single Chinese ideographs to religious symbols, geometric patterns, star charts, and the like. In addition to being used as barriers against evil, and unpleasant, disastrous events, they also are used to invite unlimited good fortune, from a long and healthy life to all of the other things that normally bring bliss to people.

While fewer and fewer Koreans take *pujok* seriously, they are still commonly seen throughout the country, especially at the beginning of the new year and at the beginning of spring. Many foreign residents in Korea adopt the *pujok* custom as a simple and pleasant way of demonstrating their appreciation of Korean culture—and to make sure they don't miss any bets in avoiding misfortune.

18

자유

Chayu
(Chah-yuu)

"The Power of Freedom"

The official date for the "creation" of the Korean people is 2333 B.C.—a time that probably marks the appearance of the first combined clan-state. Koreans thus claim a history of more than four thousand years. From that long-ago time until the 1970s, Koreans lived under authoritarian governments that were dominated by a tiny, elite class that denied common people the right of freedom of choice in almost every aspect of their lives.

In fact the concept of *chayu* (chah-yuu), or "freedom," in its present-day sense was totally alien to Korean culture until recent times. The political and social ideologies that prevailed during the long span of Korean history simply did not include the concept of personal freedom or personal choice. Personal freedom of any kind was regarded as an evil and corrupting ideology that had no place in Korean society because it contradicted virtually every facet of traditional shamanistic morality as well as the later Buddhist and Confucianist ideologies.

The historical lack of *chayu* in Korea not only warped the minds and spirits of Koreans but also kept the social, political, and economic state of Korea frozen in time. During all but the last decades of the 518-year-long Choson dynasty (1392–1910) the whole ideological weight of the Confucian-oriented government was focused on preventing change; on keeping the elite *yangban* (yahng-bahn) class in power and the common people in their place.

Despite more than four thousand years of conditioning in antifreedom ideologies within a hierarchical, authoritarian society, Koreans did not lose their desire for *chayu* because it is inherent in the human psyche; it was something their spirits yearned for. But the first serious movements toward democracy and change in Korea in the latter part of the 1800s were subverted by Japan, which began colonizing the country in 1895 and took over completely in 1910.

Koreans had fewer freedoms under the thirty-six-year Japanese colonial regime (1910–1945) than during the Choson dynasty and were to continue to suffer under strict authoritarian governments for another thirty years after regaining their sovereignty in 1945. But even the modest amount of freedom Koreans gained following the expulsion of Japan in 1945 was to have a dramatic social and economic effect on the country.

Free to make many economic choices and exercise their own initiative and energy for the first time in the history of the country, Koreans began working at a frenzied pace. By the early 1960s, economic growth had begun to change the country visibly. The more *chayu* Koreans won, the faster the economy grew. The larger and more powerful the economy, the more the people pressured the government for still more freedom.

Beginning in the 1960s and continuing over a period of several years, the Korean government gradually lifted the restrictions on ordinary Koreans traveling abroad. First only businessmen with special permission could travel overseas. Then the privilege was extended to people over the age of fifty who wanted to go abroad as tourists. Finally, in 1989, all restrictions on overseas travel were removed. The right to travel freely outside the country, perhaps more than any other change in Korea, spoke volumes about the progress that had been made in democratizing the government. The fact that hundreds of thousands of Koreans could *afford* to travel abroad was equally significant.

Legally, present-day Koreans are as free as the citizens of Australia, Canada, the United States, and other democratic societies. But there are numerous traditional social customs and cultural taboos that reduce their options and obligate them in many ways that prevent them from being as free as people in other democratic countries. These customs and taboos range from their manner of speech and behavior in general to what is acceptable as wearing apparel. Another factor that limits the freedom of Koreans has to do with the law itself. In Korea the accused person is considered guilty until proven innocent. Furthermore, the hand of the law is much harsher in Korea than it is in countries with long traditions of human rights.

19

체벌

Chebol
(Cheh-bohl)

"Collective Punishment"

Historically in China, Korea, and Japan the Confucian principle of collective guilt and *chebol* (cheh-bohl), or "collective punishment," were practiced with determined zeal in an effort to maintain absolute *anjong* (ahn-johng), or "stability," in society. In Japan whole families were sometimes executed for the crimes of single members (and to eliminate potential political rivals). In China collective punishment as well as political elimination were often even more draconian, covering extended families out to second cousins—a practice that was used regularly by Chinese Communists between 1930 and 1976 as a means of both eliminating enemies and suspects and intimidating other people through terror.

In early Korea, which historically was generally regarded as the most Confucian country in the Confucian sphere of Asia, entire families, and sometimes whole communities or villages, were held responsible for the behavior of each member. This provided an extraordinary incentive for individuals to behave and for families and group members to severely police their own members, resulting in the ultimate in Big Brotherism.

This collective coercion began in each individual family unit, the smallest political unit in the society. The father was responsible for the behavior of the family. The same concept of collective responsibility was extended to neighborhood communities and villages.

Today the Korean concept of morality is still based loosely on collective guilt, even though the law is not. Generally speaking, Korean society holds a family responsible for the misdeeds of any of its members, and by the same reasoning individuals cannot exonerate their families simply by declaring that their families are not responsible for their behavior. This is not to suggest that Koreans traditionally approved of *chebol* unconditionally. Quite the contrary. When applied arbitrarily by public authorities, it was regarded as one of the primary evils of the ruling powers. But it persisted in virtually full force in schools, in the military, and in various social organizations until the early 1970s.

Collective responsibility works especially well as a social sanction against misbehavior because Korean culture is a "shame culture." (See *Changpi* on page 27.) There is extreme pressure on all Koreans to avoid shaming themselves and their families. Foreigners living and working in Korea invariably encounter the shame factor in Korean culture, but generally they are not exposed directly to collective punishment.

(Although the concept of collective guilt and punishment may be anathema to most individualistic Westerners, if it is not carried to extremes it is the ideal social mechanism for ensuring maximal harmony in society. There is, in fact, constant dialogue in the United States in particular about a return to this ancient practice—holding parents responsible for the misconduct of their children.)

In present-day Korea *chebol* continues to be an important aspect of society, but it is generally enforced by private social response rather than official or government action. Individual Koreans are traditionally well behaved because they know their families will suffer if they misbehave.

As in other societies, however, violence is sanctioned in certain situations by Korean society, and those who refrain from such action are the ones criticized. The most common and conspicuous of these circumstances involve the need to focus attention on government abuses. Deliberately disobeying government edicts and attacking government officials and facilities are extremes historically deemed necessary because there was no other way of influencing the government.

In present-day Korea most such incidents are not aimed at actually killing anyone or destroying government property but are more symbolic in nature.

20

집
Chib
(Cheeb)
"Getting Family Approval"

One of the legacies of Confucianism that still impacts life in Korea is the concept and practice of filial piety, which has always gone far beyond honoring and obeying one's parents. One might say that filial piety has been the mortar of Korean society for more than seven hundred years. Until the last decades of the twentieth century, the instruction of Korean children in filial piety, in respecting and obeying their parents without question and taking care of them in their old age, was in effect the foundation on which Korean society rested.

Children who were conditioned in the home to honor and obey their superiors (their parents and other seniors in age and status) and to fulfill their social and economic obligations to their families could also be expected to be obedient, diligent, and loyal employees and citizens. The practice of Korean-style filial piety required individual members of families to suppress their own individuality and give the family or the group precedence in all things. Rather than identify themselves as individuals, people identified themselves with their families or work units in a totally collective sense.

In the Western view, individual Koreans hardly existed. They were first and last members of a *chib* (cheeb), or "household," or some other group, depending on the circumstances. Individual members of *chib* (or *chip* / cheep, depending on the usage), particularly younger members and females, could not make decisions or act on their own. Korean children in particular were required to think and behave in terms of their *chib* to avoid bringing dishonor on the family and disrupting its hierarchical standing. Parents constantly admonished their children to behave "like a family," not as individuals.

In the Confucian concept, *chib* were the building blocks of Korean society, and it was in the family that the foundation was laid for hierarchical social and political order based on the absolute submission of inferiors to superiors.

While the overall importance of the Korean *chib* has diminished considerably in modern times, there are many instances when it still takes precedence over the desires of individual family members and determines the opportunities that are available to them. When Koreans evaluate others, as possible marriage mates, as employees, and in other capacities, they look at the family as well as the individual, and the more important the matter at hand, the more weight the status and overall character of the *chib* has in their judgment.

One of the obvious results of this Confucian-oriented custom is that it contributes enormously to social harmony, a mutually cooperative spirit, and national cohesiveness—all qualities that are just as dramatically missing from many non-Confucian societies. Koreans commonly use the term *chip an* (cheep ahn), which literally means "inside the household" or "inside the family," in the sense of "my home," "my family," and "my company" (employer), as an indication of the commonality of themselves and the units they belong to. In other words, Koreans generally regard their places of employment as families, with all the attendant family-type responsibilities.

Among the biggest challenges facing Koreans today is how to maintain the positive aspects of the character and role of the *chib* while taking advantage of many of the Western attitudes and customs that do, in fact, contribute to the quality and ambience of life—particularly the freedom to develop one's own talents and lifestyle. If Koreans can successfully resolve this problem, by fusing ancient wisdom and modern knowledge, they could have one of the best of all social systems.

21

침실

Chimsul
(Cheem-suhl)

"Needling Cosmic Power"

Chimsul (cheem-suhl), or "acupuncture" (also sometimes spelled *shimsul* in roman letters), is another of the many concepts brought to Korea from China some two thousand years ago that has survived into modern times and now exists side by side with Western ideas. The principle of acupuncture is based on the belief that the "life force" that animates the body and energizes the various organs flows through the body in precise channels. When this energy is weakened or disrupted for any reason, the particular organ that is affected and the body as a whole cannot function normally.

As long as three thousand years ago, Chinese doctors identified and mapped the body's network of energy channels, then located more than 650 "points" where needles could be inserted into these channels to achieve some desired result. Acupuncturists say that inserting tiny needles into these energy channels has a variety of effects, ranging from stimulating and increasing the energy flow to blocking the flow, depending on where in the channels the needles are inserted.

Surprisingly enough, the channels and insertion points relating to particular body organs are often nowhere near the organs themselves. The insertion point for a problem involving the head or upper portion of the body may be located on the feet. (Western doctors agree that the bottoms of the feet are a mass of nerve endings, but they do not agree that the nerves "connect" with any of the other parts of the body.)

Practitioners of acupuncture say that it is not an instant cure for the variety of more serious ailments that develop over a long period of time. In such cases, they say, the treatment must continue for months to years if it is to have any chance of reversing the condition.

There is no question that acupuncture works in reducing or eliminating a number of ailments. It has been in use for more than three thousand years and has proven itself over and over again. One of its most dramatic uses is as an anesthetic in serious surgical operations on the brain. However, neither the Koreans nor the Chinese, who discovered and developed acupuncture, can explain in acceptable scientific terms exactly how and why it works. But in the 1980s Chinese medical authorities began a research program, with modern-day scientific guidelines, in a determined effort to resolve the mystery.

Acupuncture clinics are common throughout Korea, attesting to the continuing popularity of the treatment. In the past, practitioners routinely rotated the inserted needles by hand to increase their efficacy. Many have "modernized" the system by attaching wires to the inserted needles and sending weak electrical pulses through them. Some of the *chim* clinics in Korea cater specifically to foreign residents and visitors.

Western medical authorities are gradually accepting the premise that there is much more to therapy than drugs and surgery, and growing numbers are adding acupuncture to their medical repertoire. An interesting historical note: During the early decades of the Choson dynasty (1392–1910) a special group of women were taught how to treat upper-class female patients with *chim* because it was forbidden for men, including doctors, to touch women who were not their wives.

22

친구

Chingu
(Cheen-guu)

"Cultivating Friends"

Chingu (cheen-guu), or "friends," have traditionally occupied a special place in Korean society, but not just for the reasons that Westerners regard as obvious. Until well up into the twentieth century, Koreans were severely limited in the number and kind of personal relationships they could develop outside their families and kin. Each family was virtually an exclusive unit. The obligations that individual members had to each other, both individually and as a unit, precluded them from establishing close relationships with all but a select few outsiders. Females were especially limited in their outside relationships. With few exceptions, girls and women were not allowed to associate on intimate terms with anyone other than family members and close same-sex relatives.

During most of the long Choson dynasty (1392–1910) the majority of Korean women who lived in urban areas spent their entire lives without speaking to any men other than those in their immediate families and close kin. Their contact with females outside their families was limited by law to a few hours in the evening after dark, during which men were required to stay indoors.

When the Choson dynasty began to break up near the end of the nineteenth century, the segregation of males and females also began to end, as did the isolation of females in their homes. But it was not until the mid-1950s—after almost forty-five years of occupation by Japan and the havoc caused by war between North and South Korea—that Koreans began, slowly, establishing the kind of casual and intimate male-female friendships that are common in the West.

Korean men had always had more freedom to develop relationships outside their families—with other men as well as women (the latter in the *kisaeng* houses, tea houses, and bars making up Korea's exclusively male-oriented entertainment industry)—but it would not be until the last decades of the Choson dynasty, when the feudal class system was abolished and Western-type companies were introduced into the country, that men began to associate freely with relatively large numbers of other men. For the first time in the history of the country men were politically as well as socially free to expand their circle of friends.

These legal changes did not end the Confucian-oriented family system or the class differences, and both of these continued to limit the circle of intimate friends that men had. What was new and dramatic was that, because of the personalized nature of all relationships in Korea, large numbers of businessmen were compelled to meet and develop personal relationships with people in other companies and in a variety of government offices as part of their job.

In Korea today most businesspeople and all politicians count the number of friends and contacts they have in high places as among their most important professional assets. *Ujong* (uh-johng), or "friendship," remains one of the primary foundations for most business and professional dealings.

Fortunately, there are almost no cultural restraints on Koreans' meeting and establishing close relationships with foreigners, and many go out of their way to initiate such contacts for their own personal reasons. This is common enough that newly arrived foreigners are often advised by old-timers to be cautious about adding just anyone they meet to their circle of friends. There always seems to be a collection of unsavory characters in each city who are notorious for taking advantage of such relationships.

진심
Chinshim
(Cheen-sheem)

"Sincerity Comes First"

Koreans and other Asians regularly accuse Westerners of being shallow-minded, of giving priority to things that are secondary, and of often ignoring altogether matters that are most important. This contrast in attitudes and behavior, which often does exist, results from a fundamental difference in Asian and Western cultures. Westerners characteristically opt for short-term goals—immediate advantages, quick profits, instant satisfaction, and so on. Asians, on the other hand, have been conditioned culturally for centuries to take a long-term view, to approach things slowly, often by circuitous routes, and to be satisfied with making progress in small incremental steps.

While the typical Western approach calls for fast decisions based on whatever information is available at the time, combined with fast, concentrated action and force designed to overwhelm any obstacles, Asians have traditionally preferred to accumulate every shred of information possible, study it thoroughly over a relatively long period of time, and then devise strategies that take all possible contingencies into account.

Of course there are now numerous exceptions to this traditional form of Asian behavior, but many of the attitudes associated with this mind-set remain vital factors in everyday life in Asia and are especially conspicuous in personnel management and other areas of business. In Korea, for example, one of the most important attributes that employers look for in job applicants is expressed in the term *chinshim* (cheen-sheem), which literally means "true heart" and is the Korean word for "sincerity."

As is the usual case, however, *chinshim* is far more culturally laden than the English word *sincerity* and is used and understood in a different way. In its typical Western context *sincerity* is used in a rather casual manner. In contrast, *chinshim* in its Korean context refers to the philosophical beliefs, including spirituality, general attitude, and overall character, of an individual. People with a "true heart" are those who can be trusted to behave according to the highest social and ethical standards, which includes being unselfish, scrupulously honest, loyal to their superiors, hardworking, and willing to make extraordinary sacrifices to achieve more than what they are asked and expected to do.

Despite the importance of education—and experience—in Korean industry today, employers continue to give *chinshim* high priority on their list of qualifications when interviewing candidates for employment. Their view is that in the long run character and spirit are more important than anything else in determining the potential of job applicants.

Koreans automatically measure the *chinshim* of every person they meet—subconsciously when the meetings are casual and are not expected to lead to any kind of relationship, but consciously and very deliberately on other occasions. Their "sincerity radar" automatically switches to its most sensitive setting when they first meet foreign businesspeople, especially Westerners, with whom they might become involved. It is far more difficult for them to read the character of foreigners, and therefore whatever reading they get is all the more critical.

Westerners seeking to establish long-term positive relationships with Koreans can speed up the process by using the word *chinshim* in their dialogue because it sends a very clear message to their Korean counterparts that they are aware of the importance of "sincerity" in Korean culture and that they too desire a relationship based on *chinshim*.

24

지위

Chiwi
(Chee-wee)

"Paying Attention to Rank"

For nearly two thousand years Koreans were carefully conditioned to conduct themselves according to a minutely defined social status based on gender, age, class, education, and official position. This behavioral programming made all Koreans extraordinarily sensitive to *chiwi* (chee-wee), or "rank," and all of its symbols.

Koreans became so habituated to titles of respect that these titles were practically indistinguishable from their names. The most common such title for ordinary people is *ssi* (ssee), which is a generic term (like the Japanese *san*) used when addressing both males and females. Another generic title heard fairly often is *sobang* (soh-bahng), which basically means the same thing as *ssi* but is considerably lower than *ssi* on the respect scale. It is generally used only by superiors to some inferiors—and sometimes by people who are arbitrarily assuming a superior social status to put someone down.

In addition to these generic personal titles there is the usual array of bureaucratic titles for government officials and functionaries, as well as titles associated with occupations and managerial positions in companies and professional organizations, all of which are vital facets of the cultural protocol governing interpersonal relationships in Korea.

Of course none of this is unique to Korea (the Western world has its own traditions of ecclesiastical, military, political, professional, and social titles), but in Korea, as in China, Japan, and other Confucian-oriented Asian societies, the formal use of titles permeates society and is essential to maintaining friendly, even casual, relationships with people.

Social and professional ranking in Korea is acknowledged and demon-strated spatially as well as by title. Every space, from offices and meeting rooms to cars and elevators, has a "head" and a "foot." The "head" space belongs to the highest-ranking person or people involved, with lower-ranking people posi-tioned in the order of their rank down to the "foot" space. The head space of a room or hall is normally the most distant from the entrance. Therefore, one can assume upon entering a large "community" office in Korea that the people whose desks are nearest the entrance are the lowest-ranking people in the office.

In large-scale companies especially, managers can also be quickly identified by the size and quality of their desks and chairs. As a rule, the larger the desk and the more drawers it has, the higher the rank of the individual who sits there. Top-ranking executives with private offices have filing cabinets as well as many-drawered desks. Chairs without armrests mean ordinary staff members. Chairs with armrests indicate section chiefs. Chairs with armrests plus a high back denote department heads. The desks of ordinary employees are usually arranged classroom style, with the manager's desk in the front, facing them.

In a car driven by a chauffeur the ranking space is the right rear seat. The second rank is the left rear seat. If there is a third-ranking person, he or she will normally sit in the middle in the backseat or in the right front seat next to the driver. In a car driven by its owner, the ranking seat in the car is the right front seat.

From around 1960 until the early 1990s it became fairly common for peo-ple involved in international business to address people with the English titles *Mister*, *Mrs.*, and *Miss*, not only because of the international flavor but because these terms were rank neutral and could be used without fear of slighting any-one's social sensitivities. People who were not involved in international business in any way also picked up on the custom, and it became vogue among some internationally minded young people. But the almost miraculous growth of the Korean economy during those decades was also accompanied by a resurgence of pride in Korean culture and the feeling that using foreign gender and social titles was demeaning, resulting in many people discarding the practice.

There are now signs that the pendulum is once again swinging toward the mixing of foreign and Korean forms of address as people become more secure in their identity. The use of *Mr.*, *Mrs.*, and *Miss* by foreigners is perfectly accept-able to Koreans in all classes. However, when people have professional titles, it is important that they be used. Foreigners wanting to develop and maintain good relations with Koreans should learn and use both generic social and pro-fessional titles so as to be socially correct. Learning and using professional titles is also vital in helping to distinguish among the large number of people who have the same last name. Here are some of the common social titles:

Yobo (yoh-boh), apparently an early Korean equivalent of "hey you," was originally used by superiors to inferiors, but eventually men began using the term when calling their wives, resulting in foreigners' translating it as "wife." In more modern times the word took on a personal, intimate nuance and is com-monly used by older husbands and wives when calling each other, in the sense of "dear" or "darling." Younger Koreans, on the other hand, regard the term as sexist, and among them it is out of fashion.

Paksa (pahk-sah) is the title used for anyone who has a Ph.D. and is used routinely when addressing professors and other professionals. Whether used to address people with doctorates or others, the term has a strong nuance of both respect and flattery. Not using the term to people who have a doctorate degree is likely to be perceived as arrogance and taken as an insult.

Sonsaeng (sohn-sang) means "teacher" and is also used in the sense of "senior" or "someone who is older than me." It is commonly attached to the names of craftsmen and other specialists as a polite and somewhat flattering form of address. Koreans also often use it in a flattering sense to address foreigners who have some special skill or knowledge, particularly when the Koreans are nurturing a personal relationship with them for whatever purpose. It is not used by itself.

Kun (kuun) is a word used by teachers when addressing male students and also by some Korean managers when addressing younger male staff members in their sections or departments. It is always used in combination with the last name and is the equivalent of the old English use of the word *master* when addressing young boys.

Titles denoting family relationships are among the most important words in the Korean language. There are several different terms for each relationship, depending on the circumstances. Here are the various terms applying only to grandfathers (although only the first two terms are used commonly today):

Haraboji (hah-rah-boh-jee)—a familiar term for one's own grandfather
Chobu (choh-buu)—a formal term used when speaking to or about one's own grandfather
Wangbu (wahng-buu)—used when speaking to others about one's own grandfather
Songjogo (sohng-joh-go)—used when referring to one's own deceased grandfather
Chobujang (choh-buu-jahng)—used when speaking about someone else's grandfather
Wangdaein (wahng-die-een)—same as above but formal
Wangbujang (wahng-buu-jahng)—same as *Chobujang* but formal
Wangjonjang (wahng-john-jahng)—same as *Chobujang* but formal
Sonjobujang (sohn-joh-buu-jahng)—used when speaking about someone else's deceased grandfather
Sonwangdaein (sohn-wahng-die-een)—same as *Sonjobujang*
Sonwanggojang (sohn-wahng-goh-jahng)—same as *Sonjobujang*

There are six different words for "grandmother," fifteen for "father," seven for "mother," twenty-three for "elder brother," seventeen for "uncle," nine for "aunt," seven for "husband," sixteen for "wife," ten for "son," eleven for "sister"—with the use of each one determined by the blood relationship between the individuals involved.

지역갈등기
Chiyok Kaldeungui
(Chee-yohk Kahl-dung-we)
"The Scourge of Regionalism"

Birthplace and home village or hometown continue to be vitally important factors in life in Korea, significantly affecting the lives of people socially, economically, and politically. This widespread influence has its roots in the clan system that has prevailed in Korean society since ancient times and in the political, social, and economic divisions that have also existed since early times.

In present-day Korea this carryover from the past is generally expressed in terms of *chiyok kaldeungui* (chee-yohk kahl-dung-we), or "regionalism." It has to be taken into account to understand Korea as a nation and deal effectively with people individually as well as in groups. Economist Eui-Young Yu notes that people from Honam, for example, have routinely been discriminated against on a local, regional, and national basis for more than a thousand years. Yu says that the people of Honam are distinguished from other Koreans only by a slight accent, but the discrimination continues because it has been built into the culture.

Yu traces the origins of regionalism in Korea to the so-called Three Kingdoms period, which began in the first century B.C. and lasted until the seventh century A.D. During that long period the kingdom of Kokuryo held sway in what is now North Korea, the kingdom of Paekche was located in what is now the southwestern portion of the peninsula (the Honam and Chungchong regions), and the kingdom of Shilla was made up of the southeastern side of the peninsula—now designated as the Youngnam region.

Following the emergence of Shilla as the dominant power on the peninsula in the seventh century, people from the Youngnam region have dominated the government ever since. Discrimination against Honam people became the official policy of the government. In the tenth century legislation was passed prohibiting the hiring of Honam people for any government post. As time went by this government ban was transformed by geomancers into a folk belief that the topographical features of the Honam region were so negative that they fundamentally affected the mentality of the people, making them unfit for government service and untrustworthy in any endeavor. Yu notes that "this ridiculous myth" persists today and that regional antagonisms resulting from this factor remain a major influence in the political and economic life of both North and South Korea.

Since 1948 the government in North Korea has been dominated by people from North Hamkyong Province, where the late Il Sung Kim, founder of the North Korean regime, was active as a guerrilla leader during World War II. Since that time people from the North Korean provinces of Hwanghae and Kangwon, which are the closest to South Korea, have been virtually banned from high government offices because they are considered untrustworthy and unfit. In South Korea the government has been controlled mostly by natives from North Kyongsang Province in the Youngnam (formerly Shilla) region.

In South Korea the preference for people from Youngnam can be discerned in the professions and in business as well as in government. According to data compiled by Yu, being from the Honam region was more of a handicap in getting a highly desirable job in Seoul than gender. He found that the majority of both Honam men and women in the capital worked in blue-collar jobs and in lower-end clerical positions. Ongoing competition and conflicts between people from Cholla and Kyongsang Provinces are said to be serious enough that they have significant negative impact on national politics, the economy, and life in general.

Foreign employers in Korea routinely encounter situations involving friction and outright conflicts between managers and workers who are from different regions of the country. Much of this friction results when the foreigners inadvertently put Honam people in managerial positions over employees from Youngnam or other regions whose natives consider themselves superior to Honam residents. The best solution to this problem is to confront the situation from the beginning and make it clearly understood that employees will be treated equally and fairly on the basis of their qualifications and experience—not where they were born. Younger Koreans generally prefer this approach and accept it readily if it is made company policy, and is impartially enforced. Where older employees are concerned, however, foreign managers may have to make a special effort to see that they do not continue using this regional superiority syndrome to lord it over fellow employees.

26

초대

Chodae

(Choh-day)

"The Home-Meal Invitation"

Among the many things that have traditionally distinguished Koreans from most other Asians (in particular the Japanese, who are their closest racial and cultural relatives) is their custom of not only allowing but welcoming newly made foreign friends as well as casual acquaintances into the inner circle of their lives. Unlike the Japanese, who were traditionally conditioned to distrust and dislike foreigners and to keep them at a distance, Koreans are characteristically much more open in their relationships with foreigners.

In Japan the tradition was for people to entertain friends and guests outside the home, in restaurants, inns, bars, cabarets, and the like. In Korea, on the other hand, it was common for men of means to invite their friends and guests into their homes and to shower them with hospitality. Homes of the upper class generally had a special room in the front where the male members of the family spent most of their free time and entertained their guests.

With the introduction of democratic principles and equal rights for women in Korea, this tradition of entertaining guests in one's home was extended to women as well. Like Americans and other nationalities outside Asia, Koreans today take both pleasure and pride in extending *chodae* (choh-day) or "invitations" to friends and associates to come to their homes for meals that are marked by the variety and volume of food served. Part of this tradition no doubt comes from the old Korean custom for affluent families to invite their less fortunate relatives to their homes often for large meals.

The custom has since become one of the defining traits of Koreans. In fact Koreans who have become bilingual and bicultural typically list *chodae* as one of the key words in Korean culture and one of the terms (and customs) that foreigners must learn to fully understand and appreciate the Korean lifestyle.

Chodae is one of the reasons foreigners are able to establish closer, more intimate relationships with Koreans than are generally possible with other Asians. The custom makes many foreigners feel much more at home among Koreans than among other Asians. Foreign families wanting to create and nurture close relationships with Koreans should take advantage of the highly regarded *chodae* custom.

27

최

Choe
Choh-eh

"Sin in a Godless Society"

I have long believed that the fascination the Orient has traditionally held for Western men was originally based on the beauty and perceived availability of Asian women and on the fact that a great many of the things that were regarded as sinful in the Western world were looked on as perfectly normal in the East. I don't think that Marco Polo would have stayed in China so long or that the Portuguese, Dutch, English, and later the Americans would have persevered in their pursuit of trade and conquest if it had not been for Oriental women and the very different concept of sin that existed in Asia.

My own personal experience and observations in Asia in the last half century indicate very clearly that at least a significant part of the attraction that the

Orient has for Western men has not changed since the time of Marco Polo. Both the reality and the promise of "sin" are for many still a major attraction. Of course, Koreans have traditionally had a very clear concept of *choe* (cho-eh), which is usually translated as "sin," but *choe* is primarily a Confucian concept, and sin is a Christian thing. *Choe* is concerned mostly with outward appearances and Christian sin with internal thoughts as well as external behavior.

Choe in the eyes of Neo-Confucianism, which was adopted as the state ideology and national religion of Korea by the Choson dynasty (1392–1910), was concerned primarily with the failure of inferiors to behave in a respectful manner toward superiors and to obey them without question; the failure of children and especially sons to honor and obey their parents, especially their father; the failure of family members, particularly eldest sons, to revere their ancestors; and the failure to protect the "face" or reputation of the family.

A secondary level of *choe* in Korea involved breaking any of the rules of etiquette involving "proper" behavior between the sexes, husbands and wives, the young and the old. This included not using the prescribed form of speech, not bowing at the right time in the right way, not responding properly to the prescribed behavior of others, and so on.

In other words, sin in the traditional Korean context was any kind of behavior that upset the carefully balanced hierarchical relationship between people that was designed to maintain absolute social harmony in a minutely structured system of etiquette. Morality in this context was more of a physical thing than an intellectual standard of behavior based on a universal concept of right and wrong. In Korean society morality and sin were circumstantial things. What was perfectly moral for some people was a capital sin for others.

When Westerners began arriving in Korea in the late 1800s, they found the Korean concept of sin deplorable or delightful, depending on their own moral viewpoints and habits. Foreign missionaries were shocked by much of the traditional behavior of Koreans. But most foreign sailors, traders, and fortune hunters generally found the inferior position of women, uninhibited drinking by men, unrestrained pursuit of sexual pleasures by those of means, authoritarian rule by officials, and might-makes-right mentality of those in power very much to their liking.

When this latter category of foreigners in Korea ran afoul of the law, it was generally because they did not understand the circumstantial nature of Korean etiquette and ethics and assumed that they could get by with virtually anything at any time.

There have been significant changes in the Korean concept of sin since the nineteenth century. Large numbers of people have accepted the Christian concept of morality and Western democratic ideals, particularly as they relate to government in general and to the treatment of women in particular. Other Western influences, from films and love marriages to traveling and studying abroad, have greatly diminished the more inhuman facets of Confucian-oriented morality.

But generally *choe* in Korea continues to be Confucian *and* Buddhist first, and often last as well. The Korean criteria for sin are not based as much on universal absolutes as on the effect actions have on individuals, on the family, on co-workers and friends, and on society at large. Sin is not tied to what may happen to the spirit or soul after death. In fact, Koreans have never really been frightened by the prospect of going to a Christian-type hell.

One of the many advantages that Korea's *choe*-based morality has over a sin-based ethic is that it gives people far more leeway in what they can do and how they do it. Generally speaking neither businesspeople nor politicians judge their actions on the basis of any universal principles of right or wrong. They judge them on the basis of the risk involved and how beneficial they will be if they succeed.

28

조 국

Cho Guk
(Choh Guuk)

"The Mother Country"

From the 1950s through the 1970s hundreds of thousands of South Koreans fled their country in search of a safer and better life elsewhere. During the 1980s thousands of others went abroad to study and ended up staying in their host countries. By that time, however, political and economic conditions in South Korea had changed to the point that many expatriate Koreans began to return home, responding not only to unique opportunities to take advantage of the burgeoning economy but also to a deep-seated attachment to their *cho guk* (choh guuk), or "mother country." (This term may also be translated as "native country" and "fatherland.")

Unlike the Japanese, who have traditionally had powerful prejudices against other Japanese who went abroad and returned, regarding them as no longer Japanese at best and dangerous traitors at worst, Korea's major enterprises not only welcomed their countrymen back but offered them special incentives as well.

The most notable among these Korean returnees included many who had become successful technicians, engineers, and scientists and were subsequently given high-level positions in Korea's leading multinational firms. This factor alone played an enormous role in the rapid progress Korean companies made in the electronic and computer industries—progress that stunned the Japanese and others who did not believe that Koreans were capable of using, much less creating, high technology.

There is another curious difference between Koreans and Japanese that appears to be a part of their respective national consciousness. When the Japanese go abroad, they tend rapidly to lose their Japaneseness unless they spend most of their time in overseas Japanese enclaves with other Japanese. Koreans, on the other hand, seem to be much more adept at absorbing foreign cultures while retaining their own.

No doubt the key to this difference is that traditionally the Japanese were conditioned to believe that they were unique; that their language and their culture were so exclusive that no non-Japanese could ever learn them; and that any exposure to other cultures was like some disease for which there was no cure. The Japanese believed these things largely because their country had never been invaded successfully and they had never been forcefully exposed to other cultures (until the country was occupied by American and Allied troops at the end of World War II in 1945).

Koreans, on the other hand, had been subjected to repeated invasions from the dawn of their history. Forced to play a subordinate role to the Chinese (as well as the Mongols and Manchus) throughout most of their history, they learned very early to survive and prosper by accommodating foreign cultures while preserving their own identity. The call of the *cho guk* remains especially strong among Koreans because of their long history of survival against such fearsome odds. Their economic success since the 1950s is in considerable part due to the extraordinary pride that they have in being Koreans.

Munhwa undong (moon-whah uhn-dohng), or "cultural nationalism," is another important factor in the "mother country" pride that imbues Koreans with extraordinary energy and ambition. *Munhwa undong* is said to have originated in the 1920s as a movement to thwart the plans of the Japanese occupation forces to obliterate Korean culture and transform Koreans into Japanese. Korean scholars began to teach, surreptitiously as well as publicly, that the survival of the nation depended on preserving the culture.

When Japan was defeated and Korea regained its sovereignty in 1945, a number of Korean patriots who had absorbed the teachings of the scholars and survived the annexation by Japan became leaders in the new Republic of Korea. They unobtrusively made the concept of cultural nationalism part of their official platform, integrating it with their economic policies.

But it was not until the 1980s, by which time Korea had begun to flex its economic as well as its cultural muscles, that "cultural nationalism" became a primary theme in the country's domestic and international policies. Much of this phenomenon was precipitated by the United States government and American companies beginning to bring political pressure against Korea to open more doors to American-made imports.

None of these efforts were more controversial among Koreans or did more harm to the Korean image of America as a sympathetic "big brother" than the campaign to force Korea to allow the importation of American-made cigarettes. This campaign resulted in Korean intellectuals and industrialists creating a counter-campaign that appealed to the patriotism and nationalism of all Koreans. Signs disparaging American cigarettes and the American efforts appeared all over Korea.

It was during this campaign that the Korean phrase *Uri Hanguk saram* (Uhree Hahn-guuk sah-rahm), meaning "We Koreans," took on new meaning that was pregnant with emotional connotations. In its new emotionalized context the expression was meant to distinguish Koreans racially, culturally, socially, geographically, economically, and politically from all other people. It meant "we Koreans are a unique people," with the additional connotation that their cultural values should not be trampled on by foreign companies or governments interested only in financial profits.

Munhwa undong continues to buttress the "mother country" feelings of Koreans and to play a leading role in the planning and design of new public facilities as well as construction in the private area. The feelings that Koreans have for their country are often expressed in the term *aeguk* (aye-guuk), which literally means "love of country."

29

족

Chok
(Choak)

"The Korean Clan System"

Korea began as a collection of clans that gradually coalesced into tribal states and finally a unified kingdom. But the ancient *chok* (choak), or "clans," did not disappear, and today Koreans still commonly identify themselves and others by their ancestral clan roots. Contemporary terms for "clan" include *ssijok* (sshejoak) and *tangpa* (tahng-pah).

Korea's clan system survived into modern times because of shamanism, Buddhism, Confucianism, and the political ideology that evolved from these beliefs. Shamanism, Korea's indigenous spiritual philosophy, taught that the spirits or souls of individuals survived death, continued to influence the welfare of the living, and therefore had to be treated with reverence to avoid making them angry.

Chok leadership eventually became hereditary, with the families of the leaders becoming the royal houses and therefore vitally concerned about their genealogy. At the same time the roles of court officials, military officers, and other ranking members of the various tribal kingdoms also became hereditary, making it imperative that people in these families keep track of their bloodlines.

Buddhism, the state religion in Korea from around the seventh century A.D. until the end of the Koryo dynasty in 1392, also fostered the belief that the spirit survived death and was reincarnated time and again in an attempt to achieve total enlightenment, be liberated from the cycle of birth and death, and thereafter remain in paradise. Gaining merit by memorializing and revering one's ancestors was an important part of the teachings of Buddhism. This religious requirement added to the importance of keeping track of one's family tree.

Confucianism, which became increasingly influential in Korea from the twelfth century and was decreed the state religion in 1392, made ancestor worship the law of the land. Social classes, based primarily on ancestry, were minutely prescribed and hereditary. Local government offices kept detailed records of all families. From that time until the end of the nineteenth century, keeping track of one's genealogy was not just a religious and social commitment but a legal requirement as well.

Another factor in the perpetuation of the *chok* system in Korea was the requirement that all families be listed in a national registry for tax, corvée labor, military service, and other administrative purposes, a procedure that provided a permanent record of the bloodlines of families from one generation to the next.

Probably the most important element in the perpetuation of the *chok* system, however, was the fact that the ruling elite in each of the earliest clans tended to make their positions hereditary, resulting in both power and wealth accruing to their individual families. Over the generations a few hundred of these families grew into large clans. By the beginning of the so-called Three Kingdoms period in the first century B.C., in any particular generation a handful of these clans were able to maintain a virtual monopoly on government power, often with the king and most of the higher court officials from the same clan.

Each of Korea's three great unified dynasties, Shilla (669–935), Koryo (935–1392), and Choson (1391–1910), was dominated by the clans of their founders and their allied clans.

Korea's largest and most famous clans cannot be separated from the country's hereditary gentry class, the so-called *yangban* (yahng-bahn), a title first used in the early Shilla kingdom, prior to the unification of the country in 669, to describe scholars who served as both civil service officials and military officers.

Clan lineage in the *yangban* class became of overriding importance during the early centuries of the Choson dynasty (1392–1910) because each family's social status was determined primarily by its clan and by its relationship to the patrilineal founder of the clan. This made it extremely important for people to maintain detailed records of their ancestry, and as a result the study and publication of *chok po* (choak poh), or "clan genealogy," became a major industry in the early 1600s.

Among the clans that were prominent and powerful in Korea during the Three Kingdoms period (100 B.C.–A.D. 668), the ones that stand out were Kim, Pak (now often written as Park), Yi (usually romanized as Lee), Sol, Suk, Sin, Kang, Yo, Ro, Om, Chu, and Myong.

There are said to be thirty-nine "root clans" throughout the country, each with a number of branches. The largest and most prominent of these "root clans" is the Kim family, which has thirty-two branch clans and accounts for some 24 percent of the population of the country. The Yi (or Lee) family has five branches. (The literal meaning of Kim is "gold.")

Some Korean families can trace their clan ancestry back twenty-five hundred years. The main clan heir is known as *chongson* (chohng-sohn), which refers to "the oldest offspring." The place where a clan originated is known as *pongwan* (pohn-gwahn), or "original place."

30

절

Chol
(Choll)

"The Versatile Bow"

While all ancient people apparently bowed down to superiors and to symbols of power as a sign of inferiority, humility, and respect (behavior that seems to have been inherent in the human species), the Chinese ritualized and institutionalized the bow and made it a formal, official part of all greetings, farewells, apologies, petitions, religious rituals, acknowledgments of orders, and so on. When the Chinese invaded Korea in 109 B.C. and established a four-hundred-year-long political hegemony over the small kingdoms on the peninsula, one of the customs they introduced into Korea was their highly stylized form of bowing.

Over the next thirteen centuries the *chol* (choll), or "bow," gradually became embedded in Korean behavior. But it was the founding of the Choson or Yi dynasty in 1392 by General Song Gye Yi that was to make the bow into a vital part of the lives of all Koreans. General Yi adopted a much more structured and strict form of Confucianism, referred to as Neo-Confucianism, as the foundation for Korean society and implemented this new social order with military precision and discipline.

A key part of the relationship between individuals in the newly organized Choson dynasty was a precise form of etiquette that included respect language, a demeanor that was appropriate to the social rank of the people involved, and the *chol*.

General Yi's successors continued the policies and practices that he had instituted until the very end of the Choson dynasty in 1910. When the Japanese annexed and colonized Korea in 1910, they brought their own highly institutionalized and stylized bow with them and required that all Koreans adopt it. The result of all this intensive conditioning is that the bow is still an important part of Korean etiquette.

The deeper the bow, the more humility, respect, sorrow, gratitude, etc., it indicates. In earlier times it was common for people to kneel down (if they were not already sitting) and touch their foreheads to the floor or ground when bowing to rulers and other high-ranking dignitaries and on special occasions such as funerals. This was the infamous *k'ou t'ou* (kowtow) long associated with China. *K'ou* means "head," and *t'ou* means "bump" or "knock"—in other words, to knock one's head against the floor or ground to demonstrate servile deference.

European traders and others who began visiting Asia in the 1700s and 1800s were shocked when they observed people performing the kowtow. They regarded it as dehumanizing and insulting. One historically famous "bowing" incident involved the leader of a British delegation who was scheduled to be presented to the empress of China. When he was informed that he would have to perform the kowtow before the empress, he became outraged and announced that he would rather go to war than submit to such a barbaric custom. (Finally the matter was settled when the Chinese agreed that he could remain standing and just bow from the waist.)

If one is accustomed to sitting on the floor or ground—as the Chinese and other Asians were—bowing until the head touches the floor is not such a big deal—a perspective that was, of course, totally alien to Europeans.

In Korea, as in Japan and most other Asian nations, bowing remains the formal method of acknowledging, greeting, and paying respect to people, to religious symbols, and so on, although where casual meetings and farewells are concerned internationalized Koreans and other Asians routinely combine the bow—and sometimes replace it altogether—with the Western custom of handshaking.

The *chol* is, in fact, a very effective means of nonverbal communication and for Koreans is far more culture-laden than verbal greetings and handshaking. The message given by a *chol* is determined by its depth and its duration. The deeper the bow and the longer its duration, the stronger the message.

There are bows for a variety of occasions and the people involved. The lower-status person generally bows first, unless the superior is formally apologizing for some serious transgression. Differences in the social standing of the parties, as well as the circumstances, determine the type of bow that is appropriate. People of conspicuously senior status may barely nod in response to bows from those who are young and very junior to them (professors/students; parents/children; corporate presidents/ordinary employees). By the same token, the more emotional content the bower wants to express, the deeper and longer the bow.

As someone who has been bowing for more than fifty years, I can personally attest to the efficacy of the *chol* as a means of relating emotionally, spiritually, and intellectually to others. When expressing sorrow, humility, or gratitude, for example, a deep, prolonged bow can be far more powerful than a handshake or a comment. (In greeting and saying farewell to people, however, it is not nearly as expressive as a hug!)

Bowing properly is not as simple as it may seem. It requires a great deal of intuitive understanding of the situation and practice in the physical technology involved, both of which are generally learned only through long experience in the culture. Training programs conducted for new employees by larger Korean companies usually include lessons in bowing.

For those who want to learn and use the *chol* properly, it is normally accompanied by expressions that are appropriate for the occasion. When meeting someone for the first time in a day, the standard expression is *Annyong haseyo!* (Ahn-n'yohng hah-say-yoh!), which is the Korean equivalent of "Good morning," "Good afternoon," and "Good evening." When parting or seeing someone off, the bow is accompanied by *Annyonghi gaseyo!* (Ahn-n'yohng-hee gah-say-yoh!), which literally means "Go in peace." The person leaving generally responds with *Annyonghi gyeseyo!* (Ahn-n'yohng-hee gay-say-yoh!), or "Stay in peace."

Korean children traditionally began learning when and how to bow as toddlers. One of the more important bowing occasions in Korea was early on New Year's Day. On this day members of families performed deep bows, called *sae bae* (sigh bay), before photographs of deceased ancestors and to the older members of their families.

Many Korean families have continued all or part of this old Confucian ritual, and it is especially popular among some older children and teenagers because their grandparents customarily give them money, called *sae bae ton*, or "*sae bae* money," to mark the occasion. However, younger Korean generations are rapidly becoming Westernized in virtually all of their casual behavior when only their peers are involved. In casual leave-takings among this group one is more apt to hear "good-bye" or "bye-bye" than any of the traditional Korean greetings.

Westerners who spend more than a few weeks in Korea generally find themselves becoming acculturated to the bow without realizing or working at it. The best solution for cross-cultural encounters, practiced by more and more internationalized Koreans, is to use both the bow and the handshake, often at the same time.

31

점장이
Chomjangi
(Choam-jahng-ee)

"The Fortune-Tellers"

Historically Koreans were conditioned to believe that their lives were in the hands of spirits and only direct intervention by the spirits could change their fortunes for the better. This was especially true of common people, whose lives were predetermined primarily by their ancestry, social class, and gender. They were not free to change occupations, to move their place of residence, or to alter the way things were done.

Because of these political restrictions and social conventions, common Koreans generally could not improve their fortunes through their own efforts. Members of the elite class as well, particularly women, were also severely limited in their options. Therefore people on all social levels naturally turned to the supernatural for solace, guidance, and blessings.

Since communicating with the supernatural requires special knowledge and powers, the profession of the *chomjangi* (choam-jahng-ee), or "fortune-teller," became an important aspect of Korean society from the earliest times. Virtually everybody, from the king on down, consulted with *chomjangi* about important decisions and actions.

Fortune-telling is still a thriving industry in Korea. Young men and women consult *chomjangi* about their marriage prospects. Mothers ask fortune-tellers to evaluate potential sons- and daughters-in-law. Parents of newborn babies get help from fortune-tellers to select the most favorable names for their offspring. More than a few businesspeople regularly consult *chomjangi* prior to making important decisions. Shamans, who abound in Korea, are also believed to be able to predict the future and are commonly consulted on all kinds of matters by many people.

The Korean belief in the supernatural and its relationship to their fortune hinges on astrological factors surrounding the year, month, day, and hour of their birth—the familiar zodiac, with its twelve animal symbols. When all of the astrological factors are combined, they are known as *saju* (sah-juu).

Despite the fact that many intellectuals and other Western-oriented sophisticates in Korea tend to look down on *chomjangi*, it is generally accepted that they provide an important service—on the order of psychiatrists in the West—and there is no stigma attached to patronizing their services.

The most popular forms of divination in Seoul are said to be reading horoscopes, consulting with spirits, reading faces and figures (physiognomy), casting lots, and numerology. Horoscopic divination is based on the idea that the time of birth fixes one's personality and fortune. Divination through spirits involves diviners going into trances and consulting with various spirits. Some people in Seoul specialize in reading faces as a means of discerning character, personality, sexuality, and potential for future success. There are also diviners who include face and hand reading in their practice. Casting lots consists of tossing eight sticks of bamboo, metal rods, or three coins a set number of times and "reading the patterns" they form. Numerology is one of the tools used by spiritual diviners.

On New Year's Day and for the following two weeks many Koreans engage in the popular custom of consulting fortune-tellers to find out what their fortunes are going to be for the next twelve months. The most popular method of fortune-telling during this period is by use of the *Tojong-Pigyol* (Toh-johng-Pee-gyohl), a book that purports to reveal the secrets of one's fortune based on the yin-yang principle of negative and positive forces and the five cosmic elements, metal, wood, water, fire, and earth. (The book was written by a man named Ji Ham Lee, an authority on the principle of yin-yang, whose pen name was Tojong.)

Those wanting their fortunes told provide the *saju* (sah-juu), or year of their birth, according to the lunar calendar, along with the month, date, and hour of their birth. One day is divided into twelve hours instead of twenty-four hours, and each of the twelve segments of time has its own name or label (Ja, Chuk, Im, Myo, Jim, Sa, Oh, Mi, Sim, Yu, Sul, and Hae).

천도교
Chon Do Kyo
(Choan Doh K'yoh)
"The Heavenly Way Religions"

The influence of *Chon Do Kyo* (Choan Doh K'yoh), or "Heavenly Way Religions," on Koreans—beginning with shamanism and continuing with Buddhism, Confucianism, and Christianity—has been both profound and contradictory. Shamanism was their original link with their ancestors and all the gods and spirits in the universe. It taught them that all things in nature had spirits that had to be kept benign and friendly by prayer, offerings, and other rituals.

Buddhism, introduced into Korea from China in the fourth century A.D., brought with it virtually all of the arts, crafts, values, and beliefs, including reincarnation, of the already ancient and sophisticated civilization of China. Life in Korea became an amalgam of Korean and Chinese cultures and civilizations—often Chinese on the surface but stubbornly Korean on the inside.

From around A.D. 700 until the last decade of the fourteenth century, Buddhism was generally treated as the official state religion, while shamanism was practiced as more of an unofficial folk belief. But Buddhism was much too tolerant, too unfocused, and too susceptible to manipulation and corruption to provide either the ideology or the political structure necessary for the survival of a society. Ultimately neither shamanism nor Buddhism could compete with the aggressive and politically potent Confucianism, which was first introduced into Korea as a political and social ideology soon after China invaded the country in 109 B.C. and turned the existing kingdoms into vassal states.

By the thirteenth century, reform-minded Chinese scholars were advocating a much more focused form of Confucianism that was based on absolute filial piety and ancestor worship, which would give the government much more control over society. It was this form of Confucianism that was made the state religion by Korea's Choson dynasty in 1392.

During the 518-year reign of the Choson dynasty, Koreans were so thoroughly programmed in the concepts of Neo-Confucianism from infancy on that both Buddhism and shamanism became little more than private folk beliefs involved with the spiritual welfare of the people, while Confucianism controlled their practical everyday values, attitudes, and interpersonal relationships.

Christianity, introduced to the common people of Korea in the late 1800s, near the end of the Choson era, was to have a dramatic effect on the thinking and behavior of Koreans within a very short period of time. The Christian ideas of universal brotherhood and social equality were new and exciting concepts to Koreans and caused a great deal of ferment among the small literate class, completely overshadowing Buddhism and causing the validity of Confucianism to be questioned.

In fact, some Korean scholars like Tong Shik Yu say that Buddhism had virtually nothing to do with forming the modern-day Korean mind, despite its long history in the country. Yu says that traditional Korean mentality is a mixture of Confucianism, shamanism, and Christianity. Yu adds that shamanism satisfies the Koreans' need for spiritual solace, Confucianism provides answers for social and political challenges, and the concepts of universal equality and brotherhood taught by Christianity appeal to their intellect.

Yu's description of the Confucian contribution to Korean culture is essentially negative. He lists these negatives (paraphrased) as dependency on others because of a lack of a strong sense of self, conservatism and fear of change that grows out of lack of personal control over their lives, pragmatism that is self-centered because of the first two elements, a powerful tendency to form factions that are bound together with religious fervor, submission to bureaucratic control by authoritarian politicians and corporate bosses, and a hedonistic obsession with enjoying the good life now because the future is so uncertain.

Yu goes on to identify the shamanist elements in the traditional Korean character as a strong belief that the fate of individuals, good or bad, is determined by supernatural spirits; a deep-seated resistance to changes in attitudes and values; a strong concern for present-day, here-and-now needs; and a "pleasure orientation" manifested by copious singing and dancing.

Korean historian Sang Yun Hyon offers an additional list of the effects of Confucianism on the Korean mind—all of them negative. He says Confucianism kept Korea dependent on China and thereby discouraged the growth of an independent and self-reliant spirit, resulted in the creation of a family- and faction-centered society that tended to ignore all public responsibility, brought about severe discrimination against people based solely on their social class, justified an authoritarian government and an all-powerful bureaucracy that controlled and limited the lives of the people, prevented economic development by regarding profit making as immoral, encouraged people to resort to bribery and other unscrupulous means to raise their social status, and kept people focused on the past, thereby further discouraging progressive changes.

Hyon does say there is a plus side to the effects of Confucianism, however. He notes that Confucianism made Koreans famous for their stylized etiquette (Chinese officials originally referred to Korea as "The Eastern Country of Correct Manners and Propriety"), promoted the concept of mass education and the importance of learning, provided an ethical foundation for Korea's feudal society, promoted the idea of human relatedness and mutual responsibility, and encouraged people to be content with "honest" poverty and develop their character rather than attempt to accumulate material wealth.

Not all Korean historians are totally critical of Buddhism. Buddhist scholar Ki Yong Yi holds that Buddhism is a far more humane religion than Confucianism; that Buddhism promoted good, discouraged evil, called for evildoers to be punished, promoted mercy and charity, advocated the development of endurance to withstand the daily challenges of life, and endorsed individuals' sacrificing themselves for others and for their ideals.

A recent semigovernment study that focused on the influence of Christianity in Korean society, in comparison with shamanism, Buddhism, and Confucianism, came up with some intriguing conclusions. The study concluded that Korean shamanism had become much more practical, Buddhism had become nationalistic, and Confucianism was giving way to Christian thought because the latter is human and personally oriented rather than bureaucratic-authoritarian-harmony oriented.

The study also reported that Buddhist and Christian thought and behavior were publicly very conspicuous in everyday life in Korea, while the influence of shamanism and Confucianism was generally "below the surface" and more subtle. Ultimately an amalgam of Korea's four great "Heavenly Ways" may prove to be their most important legacy.

33

정
Chong
(Chohng)
"Ties That Bind"

Historically Koreans have had especially strong bonds with their families, kin, schoolmates, teachers, work colleagues, and other people from their birthplace—bonds that come under the label of *chong* (chohng), or "feelings." These bonds were of special importance because the people could not depend on laws, government agencies, or outsiders to assist them in times of need. Generally their only recourse was to call on people with whom they had personal *chong* bonds derived from a common relationship, preferably *chinchok* (cheen-choak), or "blood kinship."

Despite the dramatic changes that have taken place in Korea since the mid-1900s, *chong* continue to be one of the most important factors in Korean society. Koreans still think in terms of their *chong* links in private matters as well as in business and politics. Businesspeople prefer to hire family members, relatives, fellow alumni, and people from their home village or home town, usually in that order. When people find it necessary to contact a government or business office for any purpose, they first try to find out if they have any *chong*-bound links in the office or in any related office.

Korean social scientists say that *chong* was also the basis for the *hwa* (whah), or "harmony," that was long associated with their culture. It was this emotional element, they add, that made it possible for groupism to take precedence over individual interests, even overriding the concept of personal identity. Not surprisingly, the official end of the feudalistic family system in Korea in the mid-1900s and the demise of the authoritarian state power that was used to enforce the Confucian philosophy of *hwa* have since resulted in dramatic changes in Korean attitudes and behavior.

Koreans are still primarily family and group oriented, and a great deal of their behavior that confounds and frustrates foreigners derives from the lingering influence of generations of programming in avoiding confrontation, but Confucian-style harmony is rapidly becoming a thing of the past.

The personal feelings of young Koreans are no longer totally smothered in family or group bonds. They generally conform to high standards of etiquette in interacting with seniors and superiors with whom they have social relationships, particularly in school and the workplace, but in other situations they do not hesitate to express their *chong* as individuals.

Still today, Koreans are inclined to overreact both vocally and physically when expressing their feelings in public as well as private settings—a symptom that is no doubt exaggerated because such behavior was totally forbidden in the past. To some Western eyes Korean women, for example, are masters at using emotion to achieve their goals. In the words of one longtime foreign resident in Seoul, "they will rant and rave and carry on like banshees until they get what they want." Traditionally, Korean behavior was characterized by extreme swings from stone-faced passivity to loud and sometimes violent outbursts.

All Koreans are apt to resort to institutionalized outpourings of emotion, some angry and aggressive and others designed to express humility, sorrow, anguish, and the like, in situations that in the West would more likely be resolved by calm, rational consideration. This conspicuous use of *chong* no doubt derives from the fact that historically matters were never settled by rational consideration or debate in Korea. The Korean language itself was not designed for clear, objective reasoning. All relationships, personal as well as public, were based on predetermined factors that included gender, age, social class, and position and were officially immutable but could be influenced by emotional factors.

Broadly speaking, since Koreans were traditionally prohibited from basing their personal relationships on *chong*, or changing their relationships because of ill feelings, their only recourse was to use feelings to influence these set relationships and to try to manipulate the system through *chong*.

In present-day Korea, feelings still often take precedence over all other considerations, a factor that just as often becomes a major roadblock for rational-minded, fact-oriented Western businesspeople and diplomats. Usually the best way through this cultural quicksand is to address the personal, emotional factors along with the hard facts of the situation at the same setting, intertwining them so that they buttress each other. In some cases, however, the most effective approach may be to lead with the facts and then bring in *chong*, or vice versa.

34

정부

Chongbu
(Chohng-buu)

"Big Brother"

Centuries ago the Koreans, like their Chinese and Japanese neighbors, perfected the "Big Brother" kind of government made famous by George Orwell in his novel *1984*. Until the 1980s *chongbu* (chohng-buu), or "government," in Korea was controlled by a tiny elite class of scholar-bureaucrats, or by military authoritarians, who in turn controlled virtually every aspect of life in the country. Common people had no voice in the government. There was no such concept as human rights and only the vaguest concept of civil rights. (The literal meaning of *chongbu*, a Chinese word, is "big brother," or "oldest brother." The native Korean word for the same concept is *mat-hyung*/maht-hyuung.)

Until the end of the nineteenth century the government of Korea not only prescribed the official religious beliefs and rituals but also prescribed and enforced the etiquette for all personal and public relationships. Only "right thinking" was permitted. People who criticized the government or did not follow the prescribed protocol were either ostracized, exiled, or executed, depending on the nature of their offense.

It was not until the 1970s that demands by the Korean people finally began to result in the powers of the government being curbed and some of the worst government abuses being prohibited by law. It was another two decades, however, before additional reforms by a new generation of leaders actually brought about significant changes in the attitudes and behavior of government officials.

Still today, government bureaucrats and appointees on every level tend to view themselves as Korea's first line of defense against unwanted intrusions by outsiders and as "big brothers" to the rest of the population. These attitudes are subsumed in a number of key words that have long been associated with the government and continue to play a significant role in business as well as in the private lives of the people. Some of the most important of these words:

Chido (chee-doh), or "guidance": This term is probably best known for its use in reference to the influence that the Korean government exercises over business. An elaboration on this word is *haengjung chido* (hang-juung chee-doh), meaning "administrative guidance," a specific reference to how the government influences business through the power that is inherent in its control of licenses, import and export quotas, taxes, government financing, etc. In addition to the various laws pertaining to these functions, there are numerous *nae kyu* (nay k'yuu), or "unwritten laws," that the ministries and agencies of the government utilize in their efforts to control the economy.

One of the "unwritten rules" commonly invoked by government bureaucrats involves a practice known as *gara mungeida* (gah-rah muun-gay-dah), or "crushing with one's rear end." In other words, killing applications or proposals by sitting on them—something that bureaucrats are noted for in almost every country. Government bureaucrats are also noted for subjecting people to a runaround known as *jajungga bakwi dolligi* (jah-juung-gah bahk-wee dohl-lee-ghee), or "pedaling a stationary bike."

Government control of *mok* (moke), or "quotas," on some categories of imports and exports has traditionally played a key role in the Korean economy. In some product categories annual quotas are based on the previous year's performance, virtually guaranteeing that certain companies are able to monopolize these import and export categories.

Another method used by the government to influence business in general is the official sponsorship of a large number of *hyopoe* (h'yahp-poh-eh), or "associations." There is an association for almost every profession and industry in Korea, all of which are required to operate within guidelines set down by the government. Those pertaining to business are invariably designed to achieve goals that the government approves of or goals that the government itself has set.

Hyopoe that are sponsored directly by the government and designed to promote the export industry (like the Korean Traders' Association) can be very helpful to foreign businesses wanting to import from Korea. These associations maintain extensive data banks of information on virtually every manufacturing category in the country and provide free staff help in identifying suppliers and setting up appointments with them. Associations sponsored by Korean manufacturers, wholesalers, and retailers, on the other hand, have as one of their primary goals controlling foreign access to the Korean market.

Another factor that has long been an integral part of doing business in Korea is putting up with the age-old practice of bringing social, economic, or political leverage against companies to force them to make *kibu* (kee-buu), or "donations"—a custom that has traditionally involved people in all walks of life but is especially associated with top-level politicians, particularly presidents, because the sums going to them amounted to millions of dollars.

35

종교

Chonggyo
(Chohng-g'yoh)

"Faces of Korean Religions"

Traditional Korean beliefs and day-to-day behavior were an amalgam of four schools of spiritual and philosophical thought, or "religions" if you will—shamanism, Buddhism, Confucianism, and, to a lesser degree, Taoism. Early foreign Christian missionaries in Korea (in the last decades of the 1800s) noted that Koreans were Confucian in their social life, Buddhist and Taoist in their philosophical attitudes, and shamanist in their attempts to ward off and deal with life's calamities—all without apparent conflict.

Korean educator and developmental psychologist Jae Un Kim has surmised that the "success" of so many *chonggyo* (chohng-g'yoh), or "religions," in Korea was a direct outgrowth of the people's need for spiritual comfort in an authoritarian society that oppressed and abused them. Kim also says that Koreans showed little interest in the theological foundations of religions because they were more interested in relieving the hardships of their daily lives than in contemplating abstract notions of a better life in the hereafter.

Kim explains that several religions could coexist in pre-modern Korea because none of them had theological underpinnings that demanded absolute exclusivity. None of the early religions of Korea—shamanism, Buddhism, or Confucianism—has a "jealous" God in the Christian sense. And strictly speaking, they also do not have a Christian-type hell designed to frighten them into worshiping a single deity.

The only conflict between Buddhism and Confucianism in early Korea was over government and royal patronage and political power—not in the religious or philosophical sphere. Confucianism provided the social, political, and educational ideology that determined how Koreans thought and acted in regard to these matters, while Buddhism (along with shamanism) influenced their spiritual beliefs and behavior.

Generally speaking, Korea's Confucian scholar-philosophers paid no heed to practical social and economic matters until around the fourteenth century, and even then it was only a small group of powerless "outside" scholars who began advocating "practical learning." When Christianity, a religion that *is* based on an exact theological premise, was introduced into Korea, Kim adds, most Koreans ignored its theological teachings and saw only its political and social implications.

Korea's oldest religion, originally called *Ko Shin Do* (Koh Sheen Doh), or "The Way of the Gods," is now officially called *Tae Jong Gyo* (Tay Johng G'yoh), which translates as "old religion." *Tae Jong Gyo* incorporates Korea's creation myth, which says that *Tangun*, the legendary founder of the Korean race, became a great teacher and lawgiver who reigned over the people of Korea until he ascended into heaven.

Early Koreans offered prayers to the *sajik* (sah-jeek), or "gods," of the land and harvests before *sajiktan* (sah-jeek-tahn), or "god altars." This eventually resulted in the so-called "Founder's Altar," a system under which new tribal chieftains and later incoming kings offered their prayers. These altars eventually evolved into shrines where shamanist rituals were conducted.

Buddhism was "officially" introduced into Korea in A.D. 372. By the time the Shilla kingdom had unified the Korean peninsula under its rule in A.D. 668, Buddhism was already generally accepted as the national religion. During the following Koryo dynasty (918–1392) Buddhist monks became politicians, courtiers, and warriors, usurping much of the power of the court and causing a steady decline in private as well as public morality. The more wealth and power Buddhist monks achieved, the more corrupt they became.

Ultimately those who opposed the corrupt government and eventually ended the Koryo dynasty associated Buddhism with its evils, resulting in Buddhism's being replaced by Confucianism as the new state ideology when the Koryo dynasty fell in 1392.

Confucianism was brought into Korea much earlier, presumably by Chinese government officials and others who flocked to the peninsula after it was conquered by the armies of Emperor Wu-Ti in 108 B.C. But it was more of a social ethic than a religion and did not impinge on the spiritual beliefs or customs of the people. By the beginning of the Choson dynasty in 1392, however, Confucianism had been developed into an all-encompassing political, social, and philosophical ideology with cult status. Over the next five hundred years it was to become the core of Korean culture.

Taoism was "formally" introduced into Korea sometime in the seventh century A.D. Over the next several generations many Buddhist temples were converted into Taoist temples as part of the general decline of the influence of Buddhism. While Taoism did not develop into an independent cult, it was to have a significant influence on Korean thinking, particularly its emphasis on long life (*su*) and happiness (*pok*), whose symbols are still used widely today.

The basic philosophy of Taoism was that people should live simple, spontaneous, meditative lives; that they should ignore social conventions and worldly affairs and stay in harmony with nature. (This impractical approach to life was no doubt the primary reason that Taoism never became a widely practiced philosophy.)

In an effort to discover ways to transcend life, Taoist devotees experimented with elixirs and potions and with transforming metals. During one period Taoists advocated engaging in copious sexual activity as the best way to achieve enlightenment—a policy that resulted in a significant increase in the philosophy's followers.

In number of adherents, the third-largest religion in Korea today is *Chon Do Gyo* (Chone Doh G'yoh), or "Religion of the Heavenly Way," which originated in the *Tong Hak* (Tong Hahk) or "Eastern Learning" movement that developed in the latter part of the nineteenth century in response to pressure on Korea from Russia, Japan, and European powers and the weaknesses of the Choson court. *Chon Do Gyo* is described by Korea's religious authorities as a nationalistic mixture of Buddhism and Confucianism.

Islam is one of the officially registered religions in Korea but is of recent origin. Koreans who were moved to Manchuria between 1895 and 1928 by the Japanese and were subsequently converted to Islam brought their new religious faith with them when they were finally returned to their homeland. The first inaugural service of Korean Islam was held in 1955, following which a Korean Imam was elected. The Korean Islamic Society was established in 1966, and the Ministry of Culture gave the organization official status in 1976.

Many Koreans still do not think very much about any religion. Surveys indicate that younger people do not believe that religion should be a part of the education of their children. At the same time, they say the moral teachings of religion are necessary for a wholesome outlook on life.

This apparently contradictory view results from the fact that throughout Korean history religious beliefs and rituals were an inseparable part of the lifestyle, not something seen or regarded as distinct and separate from everyday living. Koreans simply did not associate the concept of religion with the way they lived. They did not think in terms of "this is a Buddhist ritual" or "that is a shamanistic practice."

It was not until the widespread introduction of Christianity into Korea from the late 1800s on that ordinary Koreans began to consciously recognize religion as a distinctive field of thought, and there is still a tendency for Koreans to see Christianity and other new religions as "religions" but not to label Buddhism, Confucianism, and shamanism as such.

There are some 240 so-called "new religions" in Korea, all of which are combinations of Buddhism, Confucianism, and Taoism. The largest of these new religions are *Ilshin Gyo, Taejing Gyo, Chondo Gyo, Murong Chondo, Pong Nam, Todokhoe, Chongilhoe*, and the Unification Church. *Chondo Gyo* began in the nineteenth century as *Tong Hak* (Tohng Hahk), or "Eastern Learning," a political movement against inroads being made into the country by foreign colonial powers and Catholicism.

Internationally the best known of Korea's new religions is the Unification Church, founded in the 1950s by the Rev. Sun Myung Moon. Notorious for its cultlike practices in attracting and keeping converts and in fundraising, the Unification Church has branches worldwide. In the United States, members of the church are popularly known as "Moonies," a less than flattering term probably coined by a journalist. In 1982 the founder, Rev. Moon, was convicted by a U.S. court for income tax evasion and spent nearly a year in a federal prison.

The public platform of the Unification Church is "the Global Family" and "Love Will Save the Earth"—themes that it uses to stage mass gatherings that attract high-profile celebrity speakers. However, the most unusual of the church's huge gatherings are mass weddings, the largest of which (at the time of this writing) involved more than seven hundred thousand couples around the world.

According to government statistics, some 25 percent of the population of South Korea is listed as members of the various Christian denominations that have flourished in the country.

36

종말
Chongmal
(Chohng-mahl)

"The Color of Truth"

When the first Westerners took up residence in Korea in the sixteenth century—unwillingly as the result of a shipwreck on Cheju Island—they were almost immediately presented with a kind of behavior that confused and frustrated them. They quickly learned that virtually everything of substance that they were told by their Korean captor/hosts turned out to be untrue. It seemed to them that it was the official policy of the authorities to lie rather than tell the truth.

What these early visitors to Korea encountered was a version of *chongmal* (chohng-mahl), or "truth," that was based on the reality of Korean life rather than abstract principles. In Korea's authoritarian feudal society "truth" was an arbitrary factor that was determined by circumstances, not by hard, objective facts. In effect *chongmal* was what the government said it was and what the people had to accept to survive in that cultural environment.

In other terms people were not free to determine or express objective truth in their personal relationships or any of their affairs. The "truth" in all matters was an artificially constructed political and social paradigm that had been designed to preserve the harmony of a hierarchically arranged authoritarian society that denied personal individuality and human rights. All personal feelings and concerns were secondary to the interests of the state, which based its policies on a corrupted form of Confucianism that the government used to justify itself.

In this environment, *chongmal* was an artifice that people were forced to use to maintain the inferior-superior relationships that were prescribed precisely for family members and between friends, co-workers, and the authorities on every level of government. A "truthful" response was whatever would sustain and enhance the harmonious actions and reactions of people within this minutely controlled culture. Thus "real truth" was sacrificed to the system. People were forced to "lie" as an essential part of the role playing demanded by the etiquette they were forced to follow.

When Westerners were first confronted with this form of reality, they took it to mean that Koreans had no principles and no honor and that they knowingly lied for malicious purposes rather than as a part of their normal behavior.

In the latter decades of the nineteenth century a few Westerners—mostly missionaries and their families—became longtime residents of Korea, learned the language, and became familiar enough with Korean culture to understand the difference between Western reality and Korean reality. They also learned that when Koreans were interacting with foreigners in a relatively culture-free, nonthreatening atmosphere they not only understood the concept of objective reality and truth but were perfectly capable of telling the truth and behaving in a rational manner.

Although the political, economic, and social systems of Korea have been transformed since the mid-1900s, and the people have undergone dramatic intellectual changes as well, enough of the traditional mind-set remains that it continues to play an easily discernible and significant role in society. In purely Korean settings people are still under immense pressure to tailor the truth in their responses to others and for the same reasons—to save face for themselves and others and to keep everything harmonious on the surface.

But there are now powerful forces at work within Korean society, fueled by increasing economic and political involvement with the West, by a critical mass media and the internationalization of education, that are gradually eroding the use and the need for circumstantial truth. It is unlikely that this erosion process will totally eliminate subjective truth from Korean society in the foreseeable future, but it has already gone far enough in Korea's "international community" that it is no longer a major barrier to communication, understanding, and cooperation. As a general rule, however, it is still important for foreigners doing business in Korea to maintain a "truth alert" in their relationships with employees and others and to regularly confirm the information they receive.

37

정식

Chongshik

(Chohng-sheek)

"Doing Things by the Book"

Life in ancient Korea was structured around the tenets of shamanism, with precise rituals governing all religious ceremonies, including planting, harvesting, and various other activities that were believed to be influenced directly by spirits and sundry gods. The ritualization of these functions consisted primarily of creating and following precise ceremonial actions designed to honor and placate the various spirits, from making food and drink offerings to performing dances, chanting prayers, and singing.

The introduction of Buddhism and Confucianism into Korea from China between A.D. 300 and 600 brought a variety of new rituals, both religious and social, that were to have a profound effect on the overall attitudes and behavior of Koreans down to the present time. For century after century Koreans were physically, emotionally, and intellectually programmed in all of the *chongshik* (chohng-sheek), "processes" or "procedures," making up the Korean lifestyle—from worshiping, bowing, sitting, eating, performing household chores, and working, to the way they used their language.

This behavioral conditioning was so pervasive that it eventually became an integral part of Korean culture, something that was automatically taught to each child, directly as well as indirectly, and thus became a part of his or her character and personality.

A deep attachment to *chongshik*, which is also the Korean word for "formality," remains a key element in Korean culture. Although most present-day Koreans, particularly those in younger generations, are significantly less formal in their behavior than what was characteristic until the last decades of the twentieth century, the legacy of millennia of conditioning in *chongshik* continues to distinguish Koreans from most Westerners, particularly Americans.

Some of the formalities that remain characteristic of Korean behavior include their treatment of guests in both their homes and places of work, their use of respect language, their dress, their conduct of meetings and ceremonies, and so on.

While this ceremonial behavior may be time consuming, it nevertheless adds a certain nuance to life in Korea that most foreign visitors and residents—especially those from countries where the niceties of social etiquette have become so diluted that they are hardly noticeable—find reassuring and often pleasant if not charming.

There is another facet of *chongshik*, however, that generally elicits a negative reaction from foreigners as well as a growing number of Koreans. This is the ongoing penchant for people in both business and the government to formalize their activities to the point that initiative, spontaneity, and innovation become difficult or impossible. Even the most mundane activities must be done "according to the book" in the ultimate bureaucratic mode, almost inevitably complicating and delaying things.

In recent years the Korean government as well as private organizations, including commercial enterprises, have inaugurated policies and programs to eliminate some of the *chongshik* from their operations, but it persists to varying degrees, especially in many government offices, because it continues to be part of the traditional culture. The challenge now is to find the degree of formality that continues to add decorum to personal relationships but does not detract from getting things done.

38

정의

Chongui
(Chohng-we)

"Justice Korean Style"

During Korea's long feudal era, which actually did not begin to end until the mid-1900s, whole families were held responsible for the behavior of individual members, with the primary responsibility falling on the male heads of families. This Confucian-based system provided extraordinary incentive for Korean patriarchs to rule their families with an iron hand and was at the heart of the order and harmony that existed in pre-modern Korea.

In ruling their families, Korean patriarchs were prosecutor, jury, and judge. Their rules and their decisions were based primarily on Confucian ethics instead of man-made laws, and to that extent there was uniformity in the standards society required of people. But Confucianism was not so cut-and-dried that it required the same kind or degree of punishment generally demanded by man-made laws. Confucian "law" was more situational and was generally applied according to personal rather than objective circumstances.

In the Korean concept of things, *chongui* (chohng-we), or "justice," within families was what served the best interests of the family, which is quite different from a universal concept of punishing an individual for misdeeds. Legal justice applied by the official judicial system of pre-modern Korea also had a personal element that made it different from Western justice.

In both family and official justice in feudal Korea the first consideration of importance was whether or not the accused admitted guilt, expressed remorse, and asked for forgiveness or maintained his or her innocence. If the accused confessed and begged to be forgiven, crying and carrying on in the process, the punishment was invariably less. (Or, in the case of people accused and convicted by authorities of capital crimes, the death sentence could be carried out in a more humane manner.)

Ordinary Koreans are extraordinarily sensitive about the concept of *chongui* because throughout the history of the country common people were treated by the government and the elite ruling class as second-class or third-class citizens, with few inherent human rights and no legal rights except those granted to them by the ruling powers. They therefore looked on those in power as arrogant and unjust and on themselves as eternal victims whose only recourse was to pretend to obey the laws and to get by with as much as they could without getting caught.

In the minds of most ordinary Koreans today the government is still more authoritarian than democratic, still denies them rights that they should have, and tramples on those that have been enacted into law. It often seems that the greatest—and sometimes only—champions of justice in Korea today are university students. Knowing that government officials would pay little if any attention to them if they presented their criticisms and demands in petitions—the traditional practice of scholars and others—the students take to the streets.

The Confucian-oriented concept of proper behavior, collective responsibility, and personalized justice still prevails in Korea. While punishment is no longer officially collective, most Koreans still believe that misbehavior by one member of a family dishonors the whole family, and there is extraordinary pressure on family members to obey both customs and laws. (Korean students who are active enough in street demonstrations to attract personal attention to themselves endanger their chances of getting jobs with prestigious companies after their graduation. Some companies have a policy of not hiring former student agitators.)

There is one other important factor in the Korean concept of *chongui* that is not totally unique to Korea but is much more developed there than in most cultures. When someone confesses to misconduct or a crime, expresses remorse, and asks for forgiveness but is subjected to the full measure of punishment anyway, the person typically takes it as an injustice, resents it deeply, never forgets or forgives, and, if possible, exacts some kind of revenge in the future.

Justice in Korea also has a nationalistic element that favors the Korean side in any situation involving foreigners. Some of this bias is to be expected. Consciously and unconsciously, most people favor their own kind. But in business and political disputes with foreigners, the tilt toward the Korean side is generally open and aggressive.

There is also often an easily discernible clan, regional, and relational aspect to local justice in Korean courts. The local judicial system can be expected to favor people who are members of the same family lineage or the same community. Part of this bias is a holdover from earlier times when local people regarded the central government as an adversary rather than an ally and generally resisted what they regarded as unfair treatment by bending laws or ignoring them altogether to benefit the local community.

Still today, the concept of Korean justice is generally based on what is best for society rather than on what is best for the individual. Because of this concept, individualistic foreigners who become involved with Korean courts are likely to be disappointed with the decisions handed down.

39

존경

Chongyong
(Chohn-gyohng)

"Paying Proper Respect"

One of the key Confucian principles of Korea's traditional lifestyle was maintaining absolutely harmonious relationships among all people at all levels of society. The basis for this interpersonal harmony was the suppression of individual interests and desires coupled with unquestioning obedience to all superiors and the authorities, along with unselfish service to the family, the local community, and the nation.

This abrogation of virtually all "human" and personal rights by the Confucian-oriented government was cloaked in the guise of *chongyong* (chohn-gyohng), or "paying proper respect"—to one's parents, siblings, elders, the authorities, and so on.

While the Confucian concept of *chongyong* was emminently admirable when presented in principle, translating it into practical day-to-day rules that governed all human behavior turned out to be primarily a political maneuver that stifled the lives and spirits of the Korean people. Common Koreans had almost no personal choice in their lives. They were required to submit to the will of their parents, particularly their fathers, who in turn were subject to the will and authority of the government. With only a few exceptions during the long pre-modern dynasties, this system kept Korea locked in a social, political, and economic time warp.

Particularly between 1392, the beginning of the Choson dynasty, and the latter decades of the 1800s, changes in Korea were few and far between because the emphasis was on a kind of harmony with the status quo and the past that made change immoral. But modern times were to bring to Korea in just one century as many changes as most European countries went through in five hundred years.

One of the facets of traditional Korean culture that has survived these changes, however—albeit in significantly altered form—is *chongyong*. For the first time in more than five hundred years, paying respect in Korea is more a matter of personal choice than of government edict. Koreans today continue to show exceptional respect toward their parents, teachers, and superiors who have legitimate authority over them. But they draw the line at respecting people they consider undeserving, especially government officials.

The most important facet of *chongyong* in Korea today is the respect that individuals expect and demand for their own feelings and face. People are extremely sensitive about any comment or demeanor that appears to be disrespectful in any way. The respect that bosses expect from their employees, for example, includes bowing to them at all appropriate times, addressing them by their titles and using other respect language, not leaving the office or workplace before they do, and doing—or trying their utmost to do—anything asked of them.

There is also a strongly nationalistic facet to the respect that Koreans expect. They are fiercely proud of their country and their culture and react very emotionally to any comments or actions that disparage either one. Foreigners dealing with Koreans must therefore be equally sensitive about their feelings, keeping in mind that their reactions are likely to be emotional rather than logical and that once they have taken a position they will typically defend it well beyond all reason.

To maintain effective working relations with Koreans, foreigners must continually demonstrate Korean-style sincerity, loyalty, and respect for all of the things that Koreans hold dear.

40

존중
Chonjung
(Chohn-juung)
"Deferential Honor"

Until the latter decades of the 1900s the Korean lifestyle denied people on all levels of society the right to exercise personal prerogatives, to demonstrate any significant degree of individuality or self-interest. In fact, there was virtually no time and no situation in which Koreans could think or do exactly as they pleased. Their lives were programmed to conform to a very precise and strictly enforced vertical system based on gender, social class, age, order of birth, education, and occupation.

Every individual had a specific place in this hierarchically arranged society that generally was fixed at birth. In most of the fundamental things in life—such as education, occupation, place of residence, marriage, and so on—people usually had little or no personal choice. These were things that were prescribed by custom and by law. Life was further controlled by a system of stylized etiquette that was designed to maintain harmonious relationships among all the ranks and categories of people.

In such a society self-esteem derived mainly from following all of the rules prescribed for one's class and category rather than from individual efforts, skills, or accomplishments. With but few exceptions, personal ambition, initiative, innovation, and anything else that might disturb or change the status quo was taboo.

One of the most important cultural factors in the existence and survival of this system was the role of *chonjung* (chohn-juung), or "paying deferential honor to superiors." Koreans were literally programmed from childhood to treat those above them with extraordinary deference at all times. Deferential respect for parents, especially fathers, for the male sex in general, for senior members of the family, for elders in general, for government authorities, and for spirits and the gods was a prime directive in the culture and resulted in *chonjung*'s becoming a key element in the foundation of the social system.

The repeal of Korea's feudal family laws following the end of World War II in 1945 and the gradual introduction of democratic principles into Korean government over the next several decades removed almost all of the legal coercion and much of the social pressure that had artificially supported the respect syndrome in Korean culture since ancient times. But by that time *chonjung* was so deeply embedded in the culture that, although greatly diminished in many respects, it has continued to be a significant factor in Korean life.

Koreans are still distinguished by their respect for their parents and family, for their seniors and elders, for scholars, for discipline, for form and formalities, for education, and so on, but they no longer passively accept or automatically respect government authority or its elected or appointed officials. For the first time in the history of the country the people of Korea not only have a legal right to criticize and oppose government authorities but also are protected by laws that guarantee this right. And even though these laws are not always enforced fully or fairly, Koreans now have a voice in their government, and they are as verbal—and sometimes as violent—in asserting this voice as other people with much longer democratic histories.

Present-day Koreans have made great progress in personalizing *chonjung*— that is, *they* decide who and what they are going to respect according to their own criteria, not according to traditional customs or authoritarian government regimes. In this new environment, self-respect takes precedence over all other people and institutions. Individual Koreans are, in fact, extraordinarily sensitive about being respected—in itself this is nothing new, but in the past the respect they demanded was based on external factors such as their age, gender, rank, position, and so on. Now it is based primarily on their image of themselves as individuals with personal rights and only secondarily on other circumstances. Koreans also have great respect for themselves as a national group, with virtually unbounded confidence in their combined abilities.

Chonjung is therefore an especially important word in the Korean vocabulary and one that foreigners dealing with Korea should learn in all of its nuances.

전투 씨움
Chontu / Ssa-um
(Chohn-tuu / Ssah-uum)
"Fighting at the Drop of a Hat"

The ancient view of Koreans as paragons of good behavior and of Korea itself as "The Land of Morning Calm" stands out in stark contrast to another aspect of Korean life—the inherently volatile character of Koreans and their willingness to fight whenever verbally insulted or physically confronted. Korean social scientists invariably rank a "peaceful" nature high on any list of Korean traits. But this one-dimensional reading of the character of Koreans is based on the fact that historically Koreans were not aggressive toward their neighbors (the Chinese, the Khitans, the Japanese) and did not go out looking for trouble.

The home front was a different matter altogether. The code of Confucian etiquette and ethics that Koreans lived under from the fourteenth century until modern times was so all-encompassing and so strict that it required Koreans to suppress virtually all of their emotions and confine themselves to a highly stylized form of behavior that was contrary to practically everything that is normal and natural for human beings.

This behavioral conditioning made Koreans extremely sensitive to any deviation from the prescribed Confucian manners, particularly any behavior they regarded as disrespectful toward them or their family, and primed them to take quick action on such occasions. It could be said that Korean men in particular were something like water in covered pots that was normally just below the boiling point but hot enough for considerable pressure to build up inside the pot. When the "heat" on Korean men was turned up by anything that was upsetting, the pressure inside them increased rapidly, often resulting in their "blowing their lids."

The propensity for Korean men to engage in *chontu* (chohn-tuu), or "fights," especially public brawls, became such a disruption that one of the early kings of the Choson dynasty issued an edict requiring adult men to wear heavy ceramic hats in place of the lightweight horsehair hats that were traditional at that time. (*Chontu* is a Chinese term. The Korean equivalent, also commonly used, is *ssa-um*/ssah-uum.)

The edict went on to say that any man who became embroiled in a fight and lost his *chungsan mo* (chuung-sahn moh), or "pot hat," would be punished severely. It is said that this decree was successful enough that it significantly diminished the amount of public violence in Korea. (What has not been mentioned, however, is how acrobatically skilled many Korean men became in balancing their heavy hats while still defending their honor.) The story goes that the "pot edict" was soon repealed because it interfered too much with the normal routine of men.

Korean men still do not go out looking for *chontu*, and by other social standards they are exceptionally well behaved even when drinking, but when they are called on to fight in a socially and politically approved situation they are fierce fighters who are inclined to give no quarter. During the Korean War men as well as women, on both sides of the conflict, routinely performed incredible feats that required extraordinary bravery.

In the late 1960s and early 1970s close to 250,000 Korean soldiers were sent to fight in the Vietnam War (under a financial arrangement with the United States), where they again proved their fighting spirit and skills and were especially feared by the Viet Cong. Since the 1970s most of the fighting spirit of Koreans has gone into transforming the country into an economic powerhouse—a challenge they met with the kind of ferocity once directed toward enemies on the battlefield.

42

철학자

Chorhakcha
(Chorr-hahk-chah)

"The Perennial Philosophers"

Early Korea, like China, had its great *chorhakcha* (chorr-hahk-chah), or "philosophers," who were generally the most esteemed men in the country. As also in China, Korea's philosophers typically expressed their beliefs in poetry as well as prose, further ensuring that their names and beliefs would become known to the masses. (Many *chorhakcha* were as famous for the artistic quality of their calligraphy as for their philosophical concepts. The ability to write calligraphy in a highly refined style was, in fact, a yardstick for measuring the cultural achievement of all men in Korea's gentry class and was regarded as the mark of a gentleman.)

Korea's most outstanding philosophers included Ik Chae Yi (1287–1367), Kun Kwon (1352–1409), Hwang Yi (1501–70), I Yi (1536–84), and Hae Wol Choe (1829–98).

Ik Chae Yi's main theme was that all education should focus on realism, that metaphysical subjects, which abounded in his time, were just empty talk. Kun Kwon emphasized *shilli* (sheel-lee), or "realistic reasoning," and *shilshim* (sheel-sheem), or "realistic mind," in his teachings. Hwang Yi (known as Toegye) was also a proponent of practical learning, which was counter to the Confucian-oriented system of education that had prevailed in the country for the previous thousand years.

I Yi (known as Yulgok) taught that reverence for sincerity in attitudes and behavior would prevent the victory of evil over good—that only the sincere man could know the "realism of heaven." I Yi believed that government should be conducted on the basis of national consensus and that a loyal opposition was essential to keep those in power honest. He said that if demagoguery was not kept under control it would eventually destroy the state; that no man who depended upon demagoguery could survive no matter how high his position; that no amount of eloquence or courage could save a country once its leaders were caught up in the quagmire of demagoguery.

I Yi added that the more incompetent and corrupt the leadership, the more public resentment there would be; that morality would crumble and the penal system would become ineffective. He said that as long as corrupt officials escaped punishment, injustice could not be eliminated.

Hae Wol Choe (who was probably influenced by European and American philosophers) held that all men were created equal and that there should be no distinction as to origin or class—both concepts that were diametrically opposed to the political and social ideology of the ruling *yangban* (yahng-bahn) class.

While all of Korea's early philosophers were themselves members of the *yangban* class, those who held beliefs that were contrary to the philosophy prevailing at the royal court were invariably "outsiders" with little or no political power. Thus for generation after generation, their wisdom came to naught.

Korea's dissident philosophers played a background role in the disintegration of the country's backward-looking Choson court in the last half of the nineteenth century, but their warnings and counsel were too little too late. The government was so outdated, weak, and inept that it was simply overwhelmed by the tidal wave of Western influence that began sweeping the country in the 1870s, culminating in a period of colonization and destructive wars that lasted until 1953.

The philosophical conditioning of Koreans in coping with authoritarian governments throughout their early history was a major factor in their survival during the turbulent period when they were ruled by the Japanese and subjected to the brutality and havoc of modern warfare. But it was not until they had regained their sovereignty and accomplished a virtual economic miracle that they had the luxury of applying philosophy in its higher moral, spiritual, and social sense to their daily lives. This did not come easily.

The harsh military occupation of Korea by Japan for some five decades (essentially from 1895 to 1945), followed by the communization of the northern portion of the peninsula and a devastating civil war, resulted in the resurgence of a degree of militant authoritarianism that had not been experienced in the country since the founding of the Choson dynasty in 1392. And it was mostly Korean students, the heirs of the still-unused higher philosophical wisdom that had been accumulating for centuries, who defied one militaristic government after the other, eventually making it possible for more democratic leaders to achieve political power and, for the first time in the history of the country, begin heeding the philosophers.

Koreans on all levels of society are now engaged in a fundamental philosophical transformation, trying to fuse ancient beliefs and traditions with independence, individualism, democracy, and a totally new technology-driven lifestyle. How well they succeed will have international repercussions for the foreseeable future.

43

조상숭배

Chosang Sungbae
(Choh-sahng Suung-bye)

"Ancestor Worship"

It is generally assumed that the ancient Korean practice of *chosang sungbae* (choh-sahng suung-bye), or "ancestor worship," was imported from China, but that is not entirely the case. There was a substantial element of ancestor worship in shamanism, Korea's indigenous religion. Shamanism taught that the spirits of people who died survived death and continued to play an important role in the lives of those still alive and that those still living had to make sure their deceased ancestors were comfortable and content to keep them from causing trouble. (It was long believed that the spirits of people who died childless, called *yongsan*/yohng-sahn, were the most likely to be violent and cause problems.)

But of all the cultural values and customs introduced into Korea from China, none was more insidious or influential than the version of *chosang sungbae* originated by Buddhists and later elaborated on and espoused by Neo-Confucianists as a political and social ideology.

Neo-Confucianism itself was a product of reform-minded Confucian idealists in China during the thirteenth and fourteenth centuries. In their efforts to rid China of its hated Mongol overlords, they began advocating a form of Confucianism that they believed would revitalize Chinese society and at the same time strengthen government control. This new form of Confucianism, based on absolute filial piety and ancestor worship, was adopted as Korea's state creed in 1392 by General Song-Gye Yi, founder of Korea's last and longest dynasty (Choson).

Building on the Buddhist teachings of the survival of the spirit after death and the importance of revering the spirits of ancestors, Neo-Confucianists created a minutely structured hierarchical society in which males were inherently superior to females, the family unit was a patriarchy, and the father or oldest male in the family had absolute authority over all the other members. Individualism was taboo. Responsibility was collective.

The bond that held this system together, intellectually, spiritually, and emotionally, was the cult of *chosang sungbae*—which was not only adopted as the national philosophy but also made the national political ideology as well as the state religion. This meant that it was mandatory; people had no choice in the matter. The eldest son in each family was charged with the responsibility of performing the various rituals concerned with ancestor worship, a requirement that made it absolutely essential for each family to have at least one male offspring to perform the rituals as well as to carry on the family line.

The general rule was that ancestors back to the fourth generation were to be honored by their direct descendants several times a year, including their death days, *ki-il* (kee-eel), at their home *sang chong* (sahng chohng), or "mourning shrine," where the memorial tablets (wooden slats bearing the deceased ones' names) were kept. Ancestors from the fifth generation and back were to be commemorated only once a year during the Harvest Festival visits to grave sites. Some people who were the descendants of illustrious forebears going back several more generations chose to honor them as well.

Chosang sungbae was the central theme in Korean culture for more than five hundred years, impacting virtually every aspect of society. The cult contributed to the custom of arranged marriages and was directly responsible for the obsession with having male children. It also contributed to the practice of men taking "second wives" or concubines when their first wives failed to have sons, displeased them, or weren't sufficiently attractive to hold their interest.

Early Korean critics of the cult of ancestor worship blamed it for the relative lack of social and economic progress in the country until the advent of modern times. They said that the cult forced first sons to spend so much time involved in the process of maintaining the family system, and themselves preparing to become ancestors, that it made their lives as well as the lives of their families an aberration.

Today more traditional Korean families hold memorial services in their homes for grandparents going back four generations on the anniversaries of their deaths. For ancestors from the fifth generation and beyond, combined memorial services are held at the family tomb once a year during *Chusok* (Chuusoak), the Harvest Moon Festival (the Korean equivalent of America's Thanksgiving Day), held on the fifteenth day of the eighth month on the lunar calendar (which ranges from late August to early October). Less traditional Koreans pay respect to their ancestors just once a year during *Chusok*. Ancestor worship rites are known as *chesa* (cheh-sah) or *jesa* (jeh-sah).

44

조선

Choson
(Choh-suun)

"Land of Morning Calm"

Some three thousand years ago, when the Chinese first began to pay serious attention to what is now the Korean peninsula, they found it occupied by a people who were racially akin to them but had their own distinctive language and culture. It appears that one of these early Chinese visitors, no doubt some kind of official, was so impressed with the peaceful atmosphere of the Korean countryside that in his report he used the Chinese characters *cho son* (choh suun), meaning "morning calm," in reference to the region.

According to one Chinese myth, China itself founded the first Korean nation (now referred to as "Old Choson") in 1122 B.C. In any event, by 109 B.C. (when China's emperor Wu-Ti led an invasion army that conquered the Korean peninsula) the Chinese were officially referring to Korea as *Choson*. Later *Choson* came to be translated into English as "Land of Morning Calm" and became a phrase associated not only with the Korean landscape and unpretentious lifestyle but also the spirit and character of the people. (*Choson* is also commonly written as *Chosun*, which is closer to the phonetically correct pronunciation.)

Unfortunately, it seems that the peaceful character of the early Koreans was more of a bane than a blessing. Throughout its long history the Korean peninsula was invaded repeatedly by the Chinese and others, including Khitan tribesmen from the north, Mongols from the west, and, in later centuries, Japanese pirates and armies of the Japanese warlord Hideyoshi Toyotomi from the east. In 1386 still another invasion by Chinese forces precipitated the founding of a new dynasty in Korea in 1392 that was officially named *Choson*, no doubt in the hope that it would live up to that old description.

General Song Gye Yi, the founder of the new dynasty, took the title of King Taejo. To reward his supporters, he seized control of all the land in the country, thereafter parceling out much of it to them on the basis of their rank. Peasants were guaranteed the right to till the land, but they were required to pay half of their annual crops to the state as rent on the lands they tilled. Taejo reigned from 1392 until 1398, when he was ousted by the powerful literati who dominated the Privy Council. His youngest son and designated heir was assassinated on the orders of his fifth son, who also disposed of the fourth son and became King Taejong (1400–18).

King Sejong, who ruled Korea from 1418 to 1450, is generally considered the greatest of the Choson kings. In addition to a number of inventions and innovations he is said to have created himself, he instituted many reforms and established the *Chip Hyonjon* (Cheep H'yohn-joan), or "Hall of Worthies" (sometimes spelled *Jip Hyonjon*/Jeep H'yohn-joan and translated as "Symposium of Wise Men"), made up of a select group of scholars and scientists. In 1443, King Sejong ordered this group to create a native writing system for the Korean language, which was subsequently made available to the public in 1446. These scholar-scientists also researched various other subjects, wrote books and manuals, and acted as advisers to the king.

The next Choson king (Sejo) was neither as scholarly nor as benevolent as King Sejong. Sejo and his supporters exterminated virtually everyone who opposed him, including the country's leading scholars, ministers, and his own younger brother, then devised a national code that was to bring the full force of Neo-Confucianism to Korea for the next five-hundred-plus years.

Under this new code the Choson court sought to control every aspect of society, including the size of dwellings (which had to be appropriate for the status of the individual family concerned), the number and placement of gates in the walls around homes, the apparel that people wore (including the materials they were made of), the accessories people wore, and their personal behavior in virtually every situation. Political purges and killings continued during most of the 1500s, but by the end of the century most organized resistance to Neo-Confucianism had ended.

Because the Neo-Confucian-based regulations were enforced strictly by the Choson court, a great calm did, in fact, descend on the countryside (a world far removed from the squabbling *yangban*, or "scholar-officials," who continued to dominate the higher echelons of the government and the bureaucracy) and lasted for nearly a century.

In 1592 Japan, then ruled by warlord Hideyoshi Toyotomi, launched the first of two massive invasions against Korea, according to some historians to punish the Koreans for having aided the Mongols in the thirteenth-century invasions of Japan and for refusing to help Japan invade China at this time. These Japanese armies sent to Korea were made up mostly of *samurai* (sah-muu-rye), Japan's professional warrior class, who marched to and fro in Korea, looting and then destroying virtually everything in their paths.

Despite the destruction wrought by the Japanese on land, the Koreans, under General Sun Shin Yi (usually referred to as Admiral Sun Shin Yi), eventually won the first encounter by using the world's first ironclad warships to devastate the Japanese naval fleet. Japan's second invasion of Korea, launched in 1597, was called off the following year by the Japanese when Toyotomi died and the fief lords in his kingdom began fighting among themselves.

Just three decades later the Manchus launched the first of another two invasions of Korea, the first in 1627 and the second in 1636, to establish their own hegemony over Korea. Unable to defend itself against the Manchu hordes, the Choson court once again agreed to accept the status of a vassal state under the new rulers of China. But the Choson court went further than that. It closed the country's borders to all outsiders except the Chinese, eventually becoming known to the outside world as "The Hermit Kingdom."

External enemies were not the only thing that frequently disturbed the calm of Korea. Other Choson rulers ranged from mediocre to tyrants who squandered huge amounts of tax money and carried out purges and reigns of terror resulting in the execution of hundreds of scholars and officials.

During the last two hundred years of the Choson dynasty the system gradually broke down, in part because growing numbers of *yangban* lost their elite status when no one in their families could pass the civil service exams. Commoners could legally sit for the civil service examinations during the *Choson* period, but appointments to all public offices were monopolized by the leading *yangban*, who formed factions and fought continuously, overtly and covertly, for power.

As more time passed, people from the middle and "technical" classes began rising in the bureaucracy. The number of slaves began to drop dramatically. In the 1700s a number of young *yangban*, along with members of the *chugin* (chuu-gheen), "middle class," and the lower class were converted to Christianity and its principles of equality and democracy.

When Western missionaries began flocking to Korea after the country was forced to reopen its doors to the outside world in 1876, they reported enthusiastically on the peace and calm that reigned in the countryside as well as the towns and cities. One missionary wrote in a 1908 letter that Korea was a nation of silence, that there was very little recreation for common people, and that among the most common sights were farmers working in their fields and middle-aged and older men sitting around outside, smoking tobacco in quiet contemplation.

But the Korea that emerged in the 1880s from its long hermit period was soon to become anything but a "Land of Morning Calm." Japan began dominating the peninsula in the 1890s and in 1910 annexed the country, making it into a province in the Japanese empire. The normally peaceful Koreans did not accept Japanese domination casually. Prior to and after the annexation Korean patriots engaged in violent street protests, local rebellions, and guerrilla activities in the mountains.

The Japanese period ended with Japan's defeat in World War II in 1945, but within seven years after regaining its sovereignty Korea was torn apart by the Korean War (1950–53).

Choson still has meaning for Koreans, evoking nostalgic images of golden ages of the past. In addition to the internationally known Chosun Hotel in Seoul, the name is also widely used in company names. *Chosun Ilbo* (Choh-suun Eel-boh), or "The Daily Chosun," is one of Korea's most important newspapers.

45

충

Chung
(Chuung)

"Groupism as Morality"

Koreans have survived for five millennia or more as a society and as a distinctive people because they are bound together and influenced by common beliefs, aspirations, and dangers. But there is more to the coherence of Korean society and the national character of Koreans than what normally results from these shared influences. One additional element was the emotional and intellectual homogenization of Koreans to the point that *chung* (chuung), or "group consciousness," virtually replaced individual awareness. (*Chung* is also the Korean word for "loyalty." See the next entry.)

In areas where the emotional and intellectual fusion of Koreans was incomplete, powerful sanctions were brought into play to force people to behave in the same way even if they did not think in exactly the same way. *Chung* was the goal, no matter what it took to achieve. To make group consciousness totally acceptable to people, Korea's elite ruling class deliberately introduced the most powerful psychological factor of all. They equated *chung* with morality, making conformity in both thought and action the ultimate standard for moral behavior.

From the beginning of the Chosun dynasty in 1392 until modern times, the moral value used to support *chung* was a new brand of Confucianism that made filial piety and ancestor worship the primary foundation of society. While total *chung* was never achieved at any time in Korean history, it came close during the middle centuries of the long Choson era—close enough that most Koreans seemed to have been cast from the same cultural mold, as fraternal if not identical cultural twins.

Between 1400 and 1900 the concept of group consciousness became so deeply embedded in the psyche of the people that its influence is still readily visible today, even though Koreans are no longer compelled to think and act alike for political or moral reasons. In many areas of life opinions and behavior vary greatly, but in such things as courtesy, dignity, respect, pride, and ambition, *chung* continues to prevail.

Foreign diplomats and businesspeople involved with Korea must deal with *chung* in almost every encounter, which often means repressing their tendency to concentrate on and depend on the individuality of their contacts. In most cases Koreans are still not free to act as individuals because the effects of centuries of conditioning to think and behave in terms of group interests continue to permeate their culture. Acting on their own is tantamount to disowning their group and virtually assuring that they will be severely criticized if not ostracized.

When self-centered Westerners are first exposed to the degree of *chung*-based morality that exists in Korea, they generally regard it as both irrational and inhuman. But the fact is, of course, that a substantial degree of *chung* is absolutely essential for the smooth functioning of any society and represents an advanced state of social maturity that is sorely and conspicuously absent in the United States and many other Western countries.

Individualistic Western businesspeople often find themselves seriously handicapped by the groupist morality of Koreans. But rather than viewing *chung* as a negative and as something that Koreans should give up, these self-directed Westerners should try to meet their Korean counterparts halfway and develop some *chung* of their own.

Educated Koreans with cross-cultural experience are well aware that their group-based morality often conflicts with the interests, intentions, and actions of Westerners. Many are under constant pressure to give up their traditional way of thinking and doing things and adopt the Western way. A few Koreans are making the switch to accommodate their foreign business associates. But most Koreans feel very strongly that their traditional way is superior to the Western way and are not inclined to change.

46

충

Chung
(Chuung)
"Loyalty in a Korean Setting"

Koreans traditionally emphasized *chung* (chuung), or "loyalty," in their literature, teaching, and behavior. But loyalty in the traditional culture of Korea was not a universal concept or practice that applied to people in a general sense. It was a carefully defined and prescribed kind of behavior that was based on Confucian concepts of male superiority, authoritarianism, a hierarchical society, ancestor worship, regionalism, and other circumstantial factors. In its Korean context, loyalty came under the heading of what is now called *situation ethics*.

In general terms the first obligation of individual Koreans has traditionally been absolute loyalty to their immediate families. The second priority was loyalty to kin, followed by loyalty to friends, community, and the nation at large. Most of these loyalty obligations were fixed at birth and in essence were immutable regardless of the feelings involved. The closed nature of Korean families, communities, and society in general severely limited the number of personal relationships individuals could develop and therefore kept obligations for loyal behavior narrowly focused.

Chung in its Confucian context was, of course, a social principle linked to virtue. On an individual basis, virtue was demonstrated by acts of loyalty. The other side of the *chung* principle was that those to whom loyalty was extended were expected to be virtuous and therefore deserving of the loyalty, implying that people were not required to be loyal to the undeserving. In actual practice, however, lack of virtue in the case of fathers, other family members of superior status, and local or national authorities did not automatically release people from obligations of loyalty. Those in power could and usually did demand loyalty regardless of their own character and punished those whom they considered disloyal.

The Confucian concept of loyalty still prevails in Korea, but it has become less focused and less one-sided in response to the growth of individualism, personal choice, and personal responsibility. Young people no longer blindly obey abusive or unfair fathers; wives no longer remain loyal to abusive or distant husbands, opting for divorce instead; workers who feel they are not being paid or treated properly regularly change jobs without suffering any pangs of Confucian shame.

Probably the most conspicuous example of *chung* in Korea today is toward the nation as a whole. Koreans are especially proud of their country. Their pride and loyalty results in their willingly making sacrifices to benefit all of Korea.

Foreign managers in Korea should keep in mind that Koreans still relate the loyalty they extend to foreign relationships, particularly foreign employers, with their perception of the degree of virtue, including *chung*, exhibited by the foreigners involved. Any sign, real or imagined, that the foreign side is disloyal (looking out primarily for itself at their expense) releases them from their *chung* obligations.

Maintaining mutual loyalty in Korea requires extraordinary sensitivity to a variety of cultural expectations and both the willingness and ability to fulfill those expectations. Acquiring this level of awareness and experience usually takes several years of dedicated effort. Until foreigners achieve that level of expertise, they should make a point of establishing a close personal relationship with one or more older, experienced Korean men and women willing to be their mentors.

47

중재인
Chungjaein
(Chuung-jay-een)

"The Go-Betweens"

One might say that prior to modern times Korea was not a land of laws but a land of religious beliefs and customs. Until 1910, when the last of Korea's royal dynasties officially ended, behavior was controlled primarily by Confucian ethics, which detailed all interpersonal relationships, including those between citizens and government authorities. A number of laws and codes had been established over the centuries by various kings and their ministers, but the ruling Confucianists believed that the fewer laws the better.

One of the reasons for this Confucian attitude toward laws was that if there were no precise laws, the government was free to interpret any action or idea to its best advantage. Another rationale was that if there were no precise laws covering a situation, people would be more circumspect in their behavior because of uncertainty over what might get them into serious trouble.

Confucius himself taught that the more laws a society has, the less people will obey them and that societies that depend on laws to control the behavior of their citizens will eventually self-destruct. His philosophy was that people will conduct themselves in a peaceful, cooperative manner only if they are taught by their parents and teachers to respect, obey, and support their seniors and superiors.

Throughout Korea's history parents and government scholar-officials were the judges of good behavior and were responsible for keeping order. Since there was no great body of law on which to base decisions, most disputes were settled by officials or others acting as *chungjaein* (chuung-jay-een), or "mediators."

Generally speaking, people preferred to make use of the services of private *chungjaein* rather than go to government officials, because the latter tended to be much harsher in their judgments and because it was always dangerous to bring oneself to the attention of the authorities. Over the centuries this extreme reluctance to get involved with government officials on any level became deeply embedded in the psychology of the common people, giving the role of *chungjaein* special importance in Korean society.

This attitude remains very strong in present-day Korean society, and mediators continue to play an important role in private as well as business affairs. Korean businesspeople especially prefer to use mediation to settle disputes that arise in their international relations and are upset when foreigners bring in lawyers, or threaten to bring them in, and resort to court action.

The best way for foreign companies to protect their own interests in Korea is to have ready access to the services of a Korean *chungjaein* who is senior enough in age to be genuinely respected by the other side; who has had a distinguished career in business, in diplomacy, or as a high-ranking government official; who was educated abroad and/or had extensive experience in acting as a go-between in international situations; and who is known to be objective and fair-minded.

Generally there is no lack of such individuals in Korea. Korean culture influences people to become philosophical as they age, and for most this means becoming logical, objective, and fair in their judgments—all things that were often denied to them during their youth and younger years.

Naturally, the better educated, the more experienced, and the more successful Koreans are in their primary careers, the more likely they are to mature into sages who think and see beyond the confines of their own culture and become true internationalists.

48

중매

Chung Mae
(Chuung May)

"Arranged Marriages"

Until Korea's feudal family system was abolished in 1945 following World War II, virtually all marriages were arranged and were subject to a number of government regulations and social customs, some of which extended back to the first appearance of Koreans as a distinctive group of people.

By the unified Shilla period (669–935), marriages between people with the same family name, between blood relatives, and between different classes were prohibited. During the Koryo period (935–1392) young men and women could not marry if either any of their parents or grandparents were serving prison terms or if it was during the official period of mourning for a deceased parent or spouse. Also in earlier times, there was a form of serial monogamy in which the two parties getting married were already related to each other through marriage that was known by the interesting name of *tae bagu* (tay bah-guu), which is translated colloquially as "substitute sex partner" and figuratively refers to a surrogate husband.

During the latter years of the Koryo dynasty (918–1392) the gradual encroachment of Confucian influence in the government resulted in measures being taken to prevent widows who had married a second time from marrying a third time. Anyone who married a third time was blacklisted in an official book called *chanyoan* (chah-n'yoh-ahn), which was tantamount to being labeled a prostitute. In 1485 the Choson government totally banned widows from remarrying in an edict called *Kyong Guk Taejon* (K'yohng Guuk Tay-joan), which means "Great Book of Honorable Nation." To add force to this edict, the sons and grandsons of upper-class women who disobeyed the law and remarried anyway were permanently prohibited from taking the civil service exams that were a prelude to government positions. The only males that this law did not apply to were sons-in-law of kings.

The *Kyong Guk Taejon* edict resulted in the development of so-called "kidnap marriages" among commoners and those below them. Men arranged with their male friends to steal widows from their homes. Once they had slept with the stolen brides, the marriage was recognized by society and the law as legitimate. In many cases, widows, usually with the help of friends, arranged for their own kidnapping since that was the only way they could remarry.

During the Choson dynasty (1392–1910) there was a ban on marriages among the upper class when the court was looking for brides or husbands for royal princes and princesses. Most upper-class families did not want their children to marry into the royal family because they became virtual prisoners in the court, were in special danger during factional uprisings, and could end the family line if their sons or daughters who were wed to royal spouses died childless.

In addition to being kept isolated in their court quarters, the women of the court, including the queen and princesses, were required to do various kinds of work. All, including the queen, had to tend silkworms because this particular activity was considered to be training in moral thought and virtuous conduct. Another reason why most women did not like being selected to serve in court as ladies-in-waiting was that after they were released they were officially prohibited from getting married.

Early in the Choson period all marriages were prohibited during mourning for the death of members of the royal family. It was eventually made law that all betrothed couples had to wait for two years if a death occurred in either of the two families concerned prior to a planned marriage. Punishment for violating this law was a hundred lashes with a bamboo staff, which was usually disfiguring and could be fatal.

The legal age for marriage during the Choson era was fourteen for girls and fifteen for boys, but it was common for girls to be married earlier, especially when a parent was ill with an incurable disease or was over the age of fifty.

Upper-class Choson men could have as many secondary wives (concubines) as they wanted and could afford to support. Secondary wives from the commoner class were called *yang chop* (yahng chope). Those from the "lowly class" (butchers, entertainers, slaves) were called *chon chop* (chohn chope). When a man took a commoner as a second wife, there was a simplified ceremony. No ceremony was required when the woman was from the lowly class. Secondary wives had no legal position, and their children were regarded as illegitimate. Their sons were prohibited from taking the exams for government service, the highest form of employment in the society.

Until recent times in rural areas, immediately following a wedding the bride was presented to her new in-laws and other members of her husband's family in a ceremony that was called *pyebaek* (peh-bahk). Another old practice that has fallen by the wayside was the custom for members of the wedding party to escort the new bride and groom to the room where they were to spend their first night together. There their relatives, mostly drunk by that time, would poke peep-holes in the paper doors to watch the couple. But once the couple had started ceremoniously removing their wedding robes, the groom extinguished the candle lighting the room (by squeezing the flame between sticks rather than blowing it out so as not to breathe out good luck), thereby preventing the peepers from seeing anything.

The *chung mae* (chuung may), or "arranged marriages," that occur in Korea today are more likely to be among the upper class, whose members are more concerned about social and economic standing, and among common people in rural areas, where the old traditions persist. Arranged marriages that do occur generally follow centuries-old customs. The first of these customs is careful scrutiny of the so-called "four pillars" of the prospective couple, which refers to an astrological study of the year, month, day, and hour of their birth.

Predictions based on the "four pillars" concern the health, life span, and material success of the two individuals—not the relationship itself. Whether or not the couple can be expected to live together in harmony is revealed by their *kung hap* (kuung hahp), or "harmony quotient," which is usually determined by a fortune-teller. The results of the *kung hap* generally take precedence over the "four pillars." If the harmony quotient of the couple is low, the proceedings are usually called off, and the search for potential partners begins anew.

If both the *kung hap* and "four pillars" are positive, the next step is an engagement ceremony at the girl's home, at a restaurant, or at a hotel. At the meeting the young couple exchange gifts, and the young man's parents ceremoniously present the girl's parents with a piece of handmade white paper on which his "four pillars" have been written. The two families then decide on the wedding date. The first private meeting between prospects for an arranged marriage is called the *matson* (maht-sohn).

From this point on, the customs for *yon-ae* (yohn-aae), or "love marriages," and *chung mae* marriages are similar. A day or so before the wedding is scheduled to take place, the young man's family sends a large wooden box of gifts to the bride-to-be. The box is called a *ham* (hahm), which literally means "box" but refers specifically to a box used to convey wedding gifts. The gifts, normally jewelry and several yards of red and blue cloth used in making a traditional dress, are known as *yemul* (yehm-uul), or "courtesy gifts." (On the day of the wedding acquaintances and work associates generally bring money, in special white envelopes, as gifts. Close friends often give the bride and groom personal items.)

Friends of the young man, usually in a merry mood from drinking and cutting up, carry the box of gifts to the girl's home. My alumnus-brother Don Hackney, who was married in Korea, notes that the groom's friends who take the *ham* to the bride's home are divided up into a leader, a "horse" (the man actually carrying the box), and two "knights" guarding the "horse." The "horse," who may be wearing a dried squid mask, cannot make a move without being told to do so by the leader. As the group approaches the door of the bride's home, the leader repeatedly orders the "horse" to stop and allows it to proceed little by little as the bride's family and her friends hand over sums of money to the leader. The money is later used to take the whole group out for more drinks, food, and fun.

Most present-day weddings in Korea are held at wedding halls, in hotel banquet rooms, or in Christian churches. More likely than not, the bride and groom wear Western-style dress. The wedding ceremony itself is very much like the typical Western wedding. The father of the bride escorts her to the groom's side. The bride and groom face the wedding officiant and exchange vows. The officiant then makes a long speech about the obligations of the couple and how they must strive to make a successful marriage.

When the speech finally ends, the couple turn to the guests and bow. This concludes the formal ceremony, following which photographs are taken. An elaborate buffet-style meal in an adjoining or nearby room follows (some guests leave the ceremony early or skip it altogether and head straight for the buffet). Couples who get married in Western-style dress invariably do a quick change into traditional Korean attire after the ceremony for the picture-taking session.

When the bride and groom are Christians, which is often the case since some 25 percent of Koreans are officially registered as Christian, the wedding may be completely Western, cake and all.

주소

Chuso
(Chuu-soh)

"Finding the Right Place"

Finding *chuso* (chuu-soh), or "addresses," in Korean cities approximates finding the proverbial needle in a haystack. In fact there is no better illustration of the difference in Korean and Western thinking than the naming of streets and the numbering of buildings for addressing purposes, for here the contradictions between the logic and rationality of the West and the "illogic and irrationality" of the East are plainly visible for all to see and experience on a daily basis.

Historically in Korea (as in Japan) most streets were not named, numbered, or otherwise identified in any way, making it impossible for people to orient themselves or locate buildings or homes by referring to the lanes or streets that they were on or near. Furthermore, houses and buildings were not numbered in sequence according to their locations on or near streets. Instead they were numbered on an area basis in the order in which they were built. In other words, there was no such thing as "street addresses"; instead there were "area addresses." Individual addresses had nothing to do with their street locations.

To further complicate the problem of finding places in Seoul and other cities, there was little or no order in the relationship of many lanes and streets, resulting in mazes that were virtually impenetrable by outsiders. This fuzzy system resulted in Koreans' (as well as foreign residents') navigating in the cities primarily by means of well-known landmarks. After arriving in the vicinity of a desired location, it was then a matter of "needle-in-a-haystack" searching.

Still today, many streets and most lanes in Korean cities are not named. Generally, the only streets that are named are major thoroughfares (and in some cases they were first given names by foreign residents). The house and building numbering system has been rationalized in some new districts, but in most urban areas it remains a maze with no obvious relation to streets—a system that is just as inconvenient for Koreans as it is for foreigners.

Korean cities are divided into wards (*gu* or *ku*), districts (*dong*), and sections or blocks (*ka*). There are several *dong* in each *gu*. (Seoul has 24 *gu*, and over 500 *dong*.) Houses and buildings are numbered, but for the most part the numbers are not attached to the buildings or displayed where they can be seen readily. Addresses begin with the appropriate ward (*gu*), followed by the district (*dong*), the section or block (*ka*), then the house or building number, and finally the name of the householder or the building name.

A typical address (in the Korean language), for example, is "Seoul, Choong Gu, Sokong Dong, 87, name of the building or householder." (The Korean postal system accepts—and delivers—international mail addressed in the Western manner: addressee, building or house number, district, ward, city, country.) In rural areas, counties (*gun*) and villages (*ri*) take the place of cities and wards in the addressing system.

The best approach for non-Korean-language foreigners who want to go to private homes or less than well-known office buildings by taxi is to have a Korean call the location concerned, get precise instructions on how to get there, and then draw a map of the location, with the names of the ward, district, and section written in *Hangul* (Hahn-guhl), along with markers indicating nearby landmarks, to give to the taxi driver.

Almost all hotels in Korea keep a ready supply of their own "address cards," in both English and Korean, at their check-in and information counters for the convenience of their guests. The cards are designed to be shown to taxi drivers and others to make sure that guests can get back to their hotels.

동아리
Dong Ari
(Dohng Ah-ree)

"Hobby Groups"

From early in Korea's history until the 1960s and 1970s, the hierarchical structure of the society, the separation of the sexes, the exclusivity of the family, community, and clan groups, and the lifestyle in general severely limited friendships outside these groups and any activity not directly related to making a living and engaging in the various religious rituals and celebrations. Recreational activities in the modern sense were virtually nonexistent for most people.

There were games that children played, some festivals featured athletic events (including rock battles), and adult men were privileged to frequent a variety of tea and wine houses, but for the most part life in Korea did not permit individuals to pursue their own personal or professional interests for any purpose.

All this was to change with the abolition of the feudalistic family system and the coming of affluence in the last half of the twentieth century. For the first time in the history of the country people were not only politically and socially free to pursue personal interests but had the financial means to do so. Large numbers of people began to indulge themselves in the kinds of *ch'wimi* (chee-we-me), or "hobbies," that had long been popular in affluent Western nations.

One of the more interesting of these new developments in Korean society was the emergence on college campuses of *dong ari* (dohng ah-ree), which might be translated as "hobby groups" and gradually spread into the general population. The "hobbies" pursued by these early college groups came to be known as "circle activities" and encompassed such things as singing, general discussion groups, book readings, *soyangjanggi* (soh-yahng-jahng-ghee) or "Oriental chess" (the Koreanization of the English word *chess* is also used—*ch'essu/*cheh-ssuu), and various volunteer activities.

In Korea today there are *dong ari* for virtually every recreational activity one can image, from poetry readings and travel groups to computer users who have formed electronic networks for personal and professional purposes. Most of the *dong ari* have female as well as male members, and, depending on their activities, age is no barrier. There is a nominal fee for membership in the groups.

Like the Japanese, Taiwanese, and other Asians who got their first real taste of freedom following the end of World War II and the introduction of democratic principles into their lives, Koreans take their *dong ari* seriously, devoting a great deal of time and money to them. They represent a degree and kind of freedom never before experienced in Korea, even among the elite *yangban* class and members of the royal court, and are symbolic of the extraordinary progress Korea has made since the 1960s.

In addition to their importance in the social emancipation of Koreans, the rapid growth of *dong ari* made a significant contribution to the emergence of Korea's mass market by increasing the demand for recreational supplies, accessories, and equipment of all kinds, from books to hiking boots.

Foreign residents in Korea who want to expand their personal and professional networks of friends and colleagues should look into joining one or more appropriate *dong ari*.

51

에누리

Enuri
(Eh-nuu-ree)

"Bargaining as a Social Skill"

In most old societies bargaining was a natural part of economic exchange because there were no universally recognized principles for establishing set prices for goods or labor. Everything was a matter of personal choice. Korea is one of the many societies around the world in which *enuri* (eh-nuu-ree), or "bargaining," has survived as an important economic and cultural activity, especially in public markets and among smaller, family-operated businesses.

Since *enuri* has long been part of the regular social intercourse of Koreans they are generally good enough at it that they do not feel they are at a disadvantage when dealing with established merchants. Where sidewalk vendors are concerned, however, they are cautious but take pride in being able to hold their own.

Visitors in Korea who have not had any experience in bargaining tend to feel very uncomfortable when faced with a choice of haggling or paying an inflated price—especially when there is a language problem. The first experience that foreign travelers have with bargaining in Korea is often at one of Seoul's two huge public markets, the famous *Tongdaemun* (Tohng-day-muun), "Great East Gate," or *Nandaemun* (Nahn-day-muun), "Great South Gate," or in *Itaewon* (E-tay-wahn), Seoul's most famous tourist shopping and entertainment district, where hundreds of shops and sidewalk vendors compete for buyers.

Supermarket chains, department stores, and other first-line retailers in Korea have fixed prices on their products, and customers are not expected to bargain. (But I have received discounts of 10 percent in name department stores in Seoul simply by asking for them—a special service they may extend to foreign customers who buy several relatively expensive items.)

Veteran foreign bargainers in Korea advise that shoppers in places where bargaining is the accepted practice carefully scrutinize any item they are interested in, especially internationally known brand items, because it may turn out to be an unlicensed copy. Another thing to look for is any kind of flaw. In either case, it is usually best to start out with a casual offer that ranges from 60 to 70 percent of the asking price. Of course, shoppers have to be willing to walk away if vendors refuse to accept their offers. But in the larger shopping districts the same items are usually sold by several vendors, so there are a number of opportunities.

Koreans have traditionally been skilled bargainers, whether in public markets or business offices, because the nature of their class- and rank-based society made it imperative that they develop substantial verbal skills and learn how to deal with people on an emotional basis. Present-day Korean society is much less hierarchical and hidebound than it was during the country's long pre-modern period, but enough of the traditional culture remains that the same kind of skills are still essential in both private and public matters.

Bargaining sessions involving groups are often noisy affairs at which many people may talk at the same time, often in loud voices, in a traditional process that is known as *chugoni-batkoni* (chuu-goh-nee baht-koh-nee), which means "give-and-take," something at which most Koreans are masters. Another well-used old term referring to several people haggling over something is *oksinkaksin* (ohk-sheen-kahk-sheen), which might be translated as "pushing back and forth."

Western business and political negotiators who have been conditioned to depend on facts and logic rather than emotion and verbal skills often find themselves seriously disadvantaged in dealing with their Korean counterparts. There is a major element of stagecraft in Korean bargaining techniques that simply floors people who are not skilled in using theatrics to achieve their goals.

52

행복

Haengbok
(Hang-bohk)

"The Pursuit of Happiness"

The founders of the United States of America believed that human beings have the *right* to be happy and that they should have the freedom to strive for happiness—something that neither religions nor social contracts anywhere in the world had formally recognized up to that time.

In Korea, as elsewhere, the concept of *haengbok* (hang-bohk), or "happiness," as a birthright was totally alien—first because the lives of most people were routinely hard and often cruel and second because they had virtually no control over the quality of their lives. In this environment, *haengbok* was a rare and incidental thing. People came to believe that happiness was something dispensed by the gods in heaven—not something that they could or should strive for on their own. Happiness was therefore something that came to people who were favored by the gods and was more a matter of luck than a reward for hard work or righteous living.

According to Korean essayist Kyu Tae Yi, people who claimed to be or appeared to be happy in pre-modern Korea were often viewed by the majority with suspicion because they themselves were unable to experience happiness. It was not until the political freedom and economic progress of the 1960s and 1970s that ordinary Koreans for the first time in the history of the country were able to achieve a level of affluence and security that allowed them to experience *haengbok* over relatively long periods of time.

Surveys today indicate that Koreans in general are "fairly happy." For the first time their more important material and sensual needs are being met and they acknowledge regularly enjoying themselves by eating and drinking with family and friends, traveling, and attending or participating in cultural events. In fact, many in the upper middle class and upper class now indulge themselves in a surfeit of material and sensual pleasures in a pendulum reaction to the hardships of earlier times. While they may not describe themselves as "happy," their level of *manjok* (mahn-joak), or "satisfaction," is the highest it has ever been.

Koreans say that the biggest obstacle to happiness in the country today is the authoritarianism and elitism that still pervades the political and economic systems, despite progress that has been made in democratizing the presidency and society in general. These complaints are primarily about the bureaucratic nature of the government and the militaristic approach to both government and business management that continues to prevail in Korea.

Having tasted intellectual and spiritual freedom for the first time in their history, Koreans yearn for freedom from other restraints as well. But they are also beset by a dilemma, by the question of whether or not giving up more and more of their traditional ways will, in fact, lead to more happiness or to the kind of social ills that now plague the United States and other Western countries.

This dilemma represents one of the greatest social challenges the Koreans have ever faced. But of all the people in the Confucian sphere of Asia, they are much more likely to be successful in retaining the best parts of their traditional culture while pursuing the *haengbok* that is possible only in a society that guarantees the right as well as the means for achieving happiness.

53

핵가족

Hakgajok
(Hahk-gah-joak)

"Two-Generation Families"

Until the 1970s the characteristic Korean household consisted of three to four generations. From earliest times it had been customary for the oldest sons to replace their fathers in the same households. After younger sons got married, families that could afford the expense helped them establish their own households. They then repeated the process, becoming three- and four-generation families sharing the same abode.

This custom caused an endless array of problems in Korean families because it made friction inevitable, but it also ensured that no member of any family would be left completely helpless. One of the primary obligations of oldest sons was to look after their aged parents—a responsibility that they invariably laid on their wives. As a result of this custom most aged parents were able to live out their lives in relative comfort, without worry about having a place to live, food to eat, and someone to take care of their other personal needs.

Korea's transformation into a highly industrialized, affluent society during the 1960s and 1970s changed this ancient custom dramatically by introducing a totally new element into the society—the *hakgajok* (hahk-gah-joak), or "two-generation family." By the early 1990s the preponderance of *hakgajok* had fundamentally changed not only the social structure of the country but much of the economy as well. The change from three- and four-generation households to two-generation households resulted in a striking increase in the demand for housing, furniture, kitchen appliances and utensils, household accessories, and so on, giving an extraordinary boost to the development of a mass market in Korea.

There are still many multigenerational families in Korea, particularly in rural areas, but they are becoming the exception rather than the rule. The move away from multigenerational families was not caused solely by the desires of newly married young people to be independent from their parents. Parents themselves, newly affluent and used to far more independence than their own parents had experienced, often preferred to live alone rather than be relegated to the position of housekeepers, cooks, and baby-sitters for their married offspring.

Because the phenomenon and various influences of *hakgajok* families were totally new to Korea, by the mid-1990s the term itself had become a catchall for many of the changes taking place in the social infrastructure as well as the psyche of the people. *Hakgajok* now represent a growing majority among Korean households, impacting on every area of the social, economic, and political life of the country.

Among the numerous cultural changes that are being encouraged by *hakgajok* are a significant decrease in the role of ancestor worship as well as in the age-old custom of respecting and honoring parents in general, a decrease in the use of respect language, and a general loosening of the family bonds that have been so crucial to survival and success in Korea.

While *hakgajok* played a positive role in the creation of a mass-market economy in Korea and helped fuel a dramatic rise in the standard of living, their overall cultural impact may prove to be negative.

학생
Haksaeng
(Hahk-sang)

"The World of Korean Students"

Until the 1880s higher education in Korea was generally reserved for the sons of the elite scholar-official *yangban* (yahng-bahn) class, who went on to monopolize virtually all local and national government posts in the country. Becoming a student at an institute of higher learning was therefore an impossible dream for the majority of young Koreans. When this monopoly on education ended, hundreds of thousands of ordinary Koreans flocked to newly opened high schools and colleges, joining the ranks of the formerly exclusive, privileged class of *haksaeng* (hahk-sang), or "students."

Unlike most of the sons of the hereditary elite, this new breed of Korean *haksaeng* was not dedicated to maintaining the social and economic status quo that had kept the *yangban* in power and generally wealthy for more than a thousand years. They wanted, and demanded, change. And it was this new class of educated Koreans who were at the forefront of resisting the colonization of Korea by Japan from 1910 to 1945 and again took up the struggle against their own militaristic leaders after Korea regained its independence.

From the 1950s through the 1980s, Westerners in Korea were often surprised and sometimes shocked at the propensity for Korean *haksaeng* to engage in antigovernment protests. But these students were not setting precedents or imitating politically active students in the West. They were following an Asian tradition that goes back to ancient times.

Throughout the Confucian sphere of Asia, intellectuals had traditionally regarded it as their right and their responsibility to monitor the behavior of government leaders and to demand that they step down if they misbehaved. Thus in earlier centuries the only Korean voices raised against authoritarian and corrupt governments were those of a few scholars who had the courage to put their lives on the line for their beliefs—and more often than not they made the ultimate sacrifice by doing so.

When the *yangban* monopoly on education ended in the late 1800s and schools were opened for hundreds and then thousands of ordinary Koreans, many of them went on to become both the conscience and the voice of the people, and unlike their scholarly predecessors they advocated direct action. When Japan began the process of invading and annexing Korea in the early 1900s, this new class of students was in the vanguard of those who took up arms to defend the country.

But it was the latter part of the 1950s, after thirty-six years of occupation by Japan and a devastating civil war that followed the division of Korea into north and south camps, before the students of South Korea had a major impact on the political system and subsequently the lifestyle of all Koreans. Always more courageous and aggressive than their teachers and elders, students once again took the lead in uprisings against inept, corrupt, and militaristic leaders. They helped bring down administrations and influence political reforms that were subsequently enacted by succeeding governments.

By the 1970s student uprisings of one kind or another had become so common in Korea that there were special police units to deal with them. Most of these demonstrations were on a limited scale and were controlled by determined police action without serious damage to either side. However, larger uprisings were invariably crushed by the police and the army, occasionally with great loss of life. The resolve with which Korean students undertook protests against dictatorial governments was indicated by the term *hyolso* (h'yohl-soh), one of the words that bound them together. The literal meaning of *hyolso* is "written in blood," and it referred to a "blood-brother" kind of bond between those who chose to defy the government openly and physically.

The sacrifices by Korean students were not in vain, however. By the early 1990s the authoritarian rule by a long line of ex-generals and their military aides had been replaced by a democratically elected civilian leadership, and the militarism that had marked the South Korean government since 1948 had begun receding into the background. This success, combined with continued economic progress, resulted in most students' going back to their books and to an easy life on campus before they joined Korea's fast-paced corporate world.

In 1995 thousands of Korean students once again took to the streets in a massive effort to force the democratically elected government of President Young Sam Kim to punish his predecessors, Doo Hwan Chun and Tae Woo Roh, who were accused of accepting several hundred million dollars in bribes from Korean and American firms. The protests, backed by strong media support, succeeded. Both Chun and Roh were arrested and sentenced to long prison terms. Thirty-six leaders of the country's giant *chaebol* (chay-buhl) conglomerates were also called in for questioning about the "donations" they had given to Roh. But the general consensus was that such political corruption was so widespread and deep that it would not be pursued beyond token punishment of the two ex-presidents.

Present-day Korean students are politically aware and continue to make their influence felt in the country, but student violence in the streets is no longer common. The biggest challenge facing Korean students today is to get on the "escalator to success"—the schools, beginning with elementary schools, that are most successful in sending their graduates on to successively higher institutions whose graduates end up with the plum jobs in industry and government.

This "success escalator" is narrow and crowded, and the competition to stay on it grows more fierce as it goes up. Students must pass highly competitive entrance examinations for each higher level of school—a system that makes junior, middle, and senior high school a "living hell" for the more ambitious students. High school students are pressured by their parents—especially their mothers—to study hard in school and then continue their studies at home for up to six more hours each weekday evening. Many mothers arrange their lives and manage their households in support of the study efforts of their children, especially their sons. Because of this unrelenting pressure, many students are burned out by the time they enter college and literally coast through their university years.

In the early 1990s the ministry of education took a number of steps to alleviate the pressure on Korean students competing to get into the most prestigious high schools and universities by adopting a universal quota system separate from entrance examination scores. According to Dr. Martin H. Sours, Professor of International Asian Studies at the American Graduate School of International Management and an authority on Korea, some students are now admitted to schools "on qualifications other than test scores."

55

한

Han
(Hahn)

"The 'Force' Is with Them"

There is always something in the cultures of nations that defines the character and personality of the people—something that is responsible for the essence that we label American, Chinese, Japanese, or Korean. The nature of this essence is influenced by geography, climate, the flora and fauna of the region, religions, political systems, the proximity to other cultures, and so on. At the same time, there is an inherent spiritual quality in most people that encourages them to endure under the most trying of circumstances and, when the opportunity arises, to improve the quality of their lives dramatically.

There is, perhaps, no better example of all this than the Koreans, a people who have not only survived the hardships of nature and the depravities of their own fellow men but were so tempered by the experience that, once freed from the more onerous restraints and oppressions of the past, they astounded the world with their rapid intellectual and material progress.

Among the forces that were responsible for the character, personality, and aspirations of the Korean people, none were more fateful, for good and bad, than the feudalistic form of government imposed on them from the dawn of their history until the last decades of the twentieth century. It was within this crucible that the essence of the Korean people was forged.

There is a single word in Korean that encompasses and explains to a remarkable degree the spirit, the aspirations, the strength, and the fierce will of the Korean people. This word is *han* (hahn). *Han* is an abbreviation of the phrase *han tan* (hahn tahn), which is defined by Korean sociologists as "unrequited resentments." But its meaning is far stronger than this definition implies. It refers to a degree of anger and bitterness that wells up from the very depths of the soul and has been passed on from one generation to the next. It is a word that, like primordial matter compressed into a tiny ball, contains unbounded energy and a universe of references and meanings.

Korean social and medical authorities identify many different kinds of *han*, all of them spawned by the spiritual, emotional, intellectual, and physical oppression under which the Koreans lived for so many centuries. There is the *han* of political abuse, the *han* of status immobility, the *han* of sexual discrimination, the *han* of poverty, the *han* of wartime suffering, the *han* of stifled ambitions—all of the institutionalized limitations on human freedom and all of the hardships the people of Korea were forced to endure over the ages.

Expressed in another way, *han* refers to the buildup of unrequited yearnings that were created by oppressive religious and political systems; by life in a society in which most of the normal human drives were subverted or totally denied; by a state of constant fear; and by intense and permanent feelings of frustration, repressed anger, regret, remorse, grief, deprivation, and helplessness.

For centuries, political leaders kept the people of Korea inside a sealed cage that prevented them from developing even a fraction of their potential. They became like steel springs pressed nearly flat, with no way to release their energy, curiosity, or creativity. In an article on the values of the Korean people, essayist In Hoe Kim noted that the feelings of *han* had a kind of magical power that could cause disaster, because it could easily turn into hatred that became a curse.

Submerged in the psyche of every Korean is the heart and soul of a fierce warrior. When pushed just a little too far, the warrior returns with a rush that shocks the uninitiated foreigner. (This can be particularly disconcerting to foreign men who unintentionally unleash the warrior in Korean women.)

Korean poetry abounds with expressions of *han*—deep feelings of sadness, frustration, and resentment. The submissiveness of Koreans throughout their feudal history was related directly to the degree of power holding them down. Any lessening of that power resulted in an equal increase in their aggressiveness. If the pressure went beyond a certain point, however, they exploded in violence.

Psychologist Tae Rim Yun attributes this dual nature of Koreans to contradictions between their cultural programming in humility, harmony, and the inherent goodness of man and the harsh reality they actually faced. In his book *The Koreans: The Structure of Their Minds*, Yun says that although Koreans were forced to be submissive and obedient no matter what the provocations, the "knife of resistance" was turning in their hearts and souls.

All of this repressed energy, all of the repressed needs and aspirations of the Koreans over a period of some five thousand years, is what makes up the *han*, or the psychic force, that motivates and energizes those Koreans who are now free for the first time in their history. It is this released energy of *han* that drives Koreans to get an education; to work with a kind of frenzy; to be adaptable, disciplined, and tenacious; to sacrifice themselves for the betterment of their families and their country.

The political, economic, and social successes of South Korea since the mid-1950s demonstrate that no matter how heavy, how old, or how widespread the burdens of *han*, once the yoke of political oppression has been removed, people can and will help themselves to rise to the level of their abilities.

Nothing produced more *han* for Koreans than the annexation of the country by Japan in 1910 and the mental and physical pain inflicted on them by the Japanese over the next thirty-five years. Many Koreans say openly that this *han* is the driving force behind their efforts to outdo the Japanese economically and become a member in good standing of the international community. Certainly the old as well as the new *han* that continues to influence the attitudes and behavior of Koreans provides much of the *himssuda* (heem-ssuu-dah), or propensity for Koreans to be "diligent, industrious" and "exert" themselves beyond the norm, notes Korean cultural authority Dr. Martin H. Sours, Professor of International Asian Studies at the American Graduate School of International Management.

56

한복
Hanbok
(Hahn-boak)
"People in White"

The traditional national costume of Korean men and women is known as *hanbok* (hahn-boak), which literally means "Korean dress." One of the more intriguing things about *hanbok* is that it is so different from the traditional costumes of China and Japan that one might question the cultural relationship among the three countries.

Perhaps because of the influence of Buddhism and Taoism, which promoted a sedate manner and prolonged periods of inactivity, the primary characteristic of the formal traditional costumes of China and Japan is that they were extremely confining. Consisting of full-length "robes" that wrapped around the body more or less like straitjackets, they forced the wearers to take short, mincing steps and limited all other physical actions. Chinese history reveals that many of China's battles with less civilized tribes of the North and West were lost because the ground-length robes worn by Chinese troops made it impossible for them to move freely and quickly.

In Japan, the whole way of fighting by that country's famed samurai warrior class was fundamentally influenced by the kimono. (When industrialization began in Japan, the Japanese kimono proved totally incompatible with getting onto streetcars, buses, and trains, working in factories, etc.)

After following Chinese styles for several centuries, the Koreans adopted a new national dress in the thirteenth century that was an adaptation of the attire worn by Mongols, who invaded and exercised suzerainty over the Korean peninsula for more than one hundred years (1231–1366). During the Mongol occupa-

tion, the costume worn by Korean men evolved into short jackets (*chogori*/
chohh-goe-ree) tied at the chest, baggy trousers (*paji*/pah-jee) tied at the ankles,
and boat-shaped shoes. Men, particularly those in the aristocratic *yangban* class,
also adopted the stiff, broad-brimmed Mongol hat (*kat*) made of horsehair to
complete their ensembles.*

During this period the national dress for women became a short, tight jacket
(also called *chogori*), a long voluminous skirt (*chima*/chee-mah), a slip that was
a shortened version of the men's pajamalike trousers, and sandal-like shoes that
curled up at the toes. The ankle-length skirt was worn high, tightly wrapped
around the chest so that it covered the bust. The skirt was fastened at the chest
with a large bow or brooch. In one version, the skirt came only to the waist, leaving the breasts exposed for nursing. Except for being fastened snugly around the
chest, it was designed to allow free movement and to be cool in summer and
warm in winter.

From the fourteenth century on, when the cultivation of cotton was introduced into Korea from China, the *hanbok* were made from this popular fabric.
(The production of cotton cloth quickly became the main household industry in
many peasant homes. In addition to producing cotton cloth for their own use,
each household was required to produce a specified amount of fabric every
year as a "tribute tax" that went to landlords and the government—the latter for
the manufacture of military uniforms and for export.) The fact that Koreans
chose to pattern their national dress after the costumes worn by horse-riding
Mongols would seem to be an early indication that they were more practical
than either the Chinese or Japanese. But the *hanbok* has also come in for its
share of criticism in more recent times—not only because of its design but also
because white was long regarded as the "national color." The Korean affinity for
white clothing resulted in the phrase *Paek-i Min Jok* (Pake-ee Meen Joak), or
"Country of White-Clothed People," becoming a synonym for Korea.

Since white was traditionally associated with the national costume of Korea
it is somewhat surprising to discover that contemporary Korean writer-scholar
Hyon Bae Choe says that white symbolizes poverty, inactivity, senility, sorrow,
and femininity and is therefore symbolic of all that has traditionally been irrational, inefficient, and negative in Korean society. In actuality, white clothing was
the prescribed, official attire only for commoners, who were permitted, however, to don brightly colored *hanbok* when participating in special events such
as festivals and weddings. Members of the royal court and the elite upper class

---

*As recounted in the *Chontu* entry, one of the more interesting stories (unverified) about
the propensity of early Koreans to fight among themselves involves hats. As a result of the
influence of the Mongols, who captured and dominated the peninsula during the thirteenth and fourteenth centuries, Korean men began wearing high stovepipe hats made of
tightly woven hair taken from the manes and tails of horses. Sometime during the early
decades of the Yi or Choson dynasty, which began in 1392, the ruling king became so upset
by public drunkenness and fighting that he decreed men had to wear heavy ceramic hats
instead of the lightweight horsehair hats, and if they got into a fight and the hats fell off
of their heads they would be punished severely. I have always presumed that this was the
origin of the old saying about "fighting at the drop of a hat," although I have no idea how
it might have gotten from Korea to the West.

were permitted to wear colored versions of the national costume, made of silk, as their daily attire. Choe, a severe critic of traditional Korean culture, says that the Korean style of clothing was awkward to wear, got soiled easily, forced women to spend an inordinate amount of time doing laundry, and was therefore one of the primary weaknesses of the traditional Korean way of life. The design of Korea's traditional clothing, Choe observed, restrained the movements of both women and men and contributed to both a disdain for manual labor and effeminate attitudes and behavior by men in the upper class.

Among a series of reforms enacted in 1894 was one that abolished the law designating wearing apparel for the upper class and commoners and made it legal for Koreans to wear Western-style apparel. It is still common to see elderly retired men in rural areas wearing the traditional *hanbok*, but since the 1960s the Western business suit has been the new "uniform" of Korean men in the white-collar class. Korean girls and women wear the traditional female costume on special occasions such as weddings and festivals. Now it comes in a variety of colors. Unmarried girls often wear yellow jackets and red-and-blue skirts to indicate their single status. Brides may wear yellow jackets and pink skirts as a sign of their new status.

Both Korean men and women are especially concerned about their appearance, no doubt because historically wearing apparel was a conspicuous sign of one's social class and occupation. The government not only designated the wearing apparel for each class but also designated the dates on which winter attire would be changed for summer wear and did not take into account any changes in the weather. Wearing winter clothing after the date set for changing to summer attire was not only illegal but eventually became unthinkable. (After Korea opened its doors to Westerners in the 1870s, Koreans would often express amazement when they saw Westerners wear winter-type clothing during cold spells in June. To them, one simply did not wear winter clothing in summer, no matter how cold it might be.)

Present-day Koreans regard dressing up as raising one's class in the eyes of others. Formal attire is so common among white-collar male workers in Korea that there has long been a saying that baby boys are born already dressed in three-piece suits. Young Korean women are especially concerned about *yuhaeng* (yuu-hang), "fashion," and go to considerable expense and trouble to keep up with the latest trends. When it comes to the quality and style of clothing, virtually all Koreans have exceptional *mot* (moht), or "good taste." This special sensitivity to wearing apparel, a legacy of the past, has provided extraordinary impetus for Korea's fashion apparel industry.

In many larger corporations and other organizations the programming of Korean life extends beyond behavior to include grooming and dress codes. The historical government practice of setting precise dates for seasonal attire has been continued by some of Korea's leading firms, with the dates for these changes posted on company bulletin boards.

Foreigners visiting Korea for business or other purposes should be aware that they will be judged by their wearing apparel and grooming. Western attire is known as *yangbok* (yahng-boak) in Korea.

한국

Hanguk
(Hahn-guuk)

"The Korean Nation"

"Let us love, come grief, come gladness,
this, our beloved land!"

There is probably no better way to describe the feelings that Koreans have about their *cho guk* (choh guuk), or "homeland," than the last line in the Korean national anthem.* Few people have suffered more for the sake of their homeland than Koreans, not because of *who* they are but because of *where* they are. *Hanguk* (Hahn-guuk), or Korea (the literal meaning of which is "Cold Country"), is located on a peninsula that extends southward from the eastern seaboard of Asia, with the Yellow Sea on the west and the East (or Japan) Sea on the east. The peninsula, directly opposite central and southwestern Japan, is approximately 1,000 kilometers (600 miles) long and 216 kilometers (135 miles) wide at its narrowest point. It is 190 kilometers from the west coast of the Korean peninsula to China's Shantung Peninsula and 180 kilometers from the Korean city of Pusan on the southeast coast to Japan's main island of Honshu.

Northern Korea shares a 1,025-kilometer (636-mile) boundary with China, marked in the northwest by the Amnok Gang or Amnok River (better known by its Chinese name, Yalu River) and in the northeast by the Tuman (Tuu-mahn)

---

*The Korean national anthem in its entirety:

Dong Hae Mul Gwa Paek Tu San I, Ma Ru Go Dal To Rok
Ha Nu Nim I Bo U—Ha Sa, U Ri Na Ra Man Se
Mu—Gung Hwa Sam—Ch'ol Li Hwaryo Gan San
Dae Han Sa Ram Dae Han—U Ro, Ki Ri Bo Chon Ha Se!

Until the East Sea waves are dry, (and) Mt. Paektusan worn away
God watch o'er our land forever! Long live our Korea!
Rose of Sharon, thousand miles of range and river land!
Guarded by her people, ever may Korea stand!
Like that Mt. Namsan armored pine, standing on duty still,
Wind or frost, unchanging ever, be our resolute will.
In autumn's arching evening sky, crystal and cloudless blue,
Be the radiant moon our spirit, steadfast, single, and true.
With such a will (and) such a spirit, loyalty, heart and hand,
Let us love, come grief, come gladness, this, our beloved land!

—*Translation by John T. Underwood*

Gang—Tumen in Chinese. The last 16 kilometers of the Tuman River form the boundary between North Korea and Russian Siberia.

The Amnok River (790 kilometers in length) flows southwest into the Yellow Sea. The Tuman River (521 kilometers/313 miles) flows northeast and then southeast into the East (or Japan) Sea. Large rivers in the interior of Korea include the Han (514 kilometers/308 miles), which flows through Seoul, the Kum (401 kilometers/241 miles), and the Naktong (525 kilometers/315 miles).

Total land area of the Korean peninsula is approximately 221,370 square kilometers, which makes it about the same size as New Zealand or England. The peninsula has a range of spectacular mountains, made mostly of granite and limestone, running down its northeast coast. The western and southern regions of the peninsula consist of hills, valleys, and plains that slope down to the coastlines. Hills and mountains account for some 70 percent of the total land area of Korea. Until recent times the chains of mountains running down the peninsula were major barriers between the east and west sides of the country, influencing the culture and the history of the two areas.

The geology and climate of the peninsula has resulted in numerous caves, deep canyons (many with vertical walls of solid granite), and waterfalls, some of them spectacular. The largest and most famous cave in Korea is the Tongnyong Gul, near the city of Yongbyon in North Korea. It is 5 kilometers long and has several chambers that are some 150 meters wide and 50 meters high.

There are no active volcanoes in Korea (although it is only a short distance from the Japanese archipelago, which is one of the most active volcanic regions on earth), but there is ample evidence of major eruptions in the past. There is also no history of strong earthquakes in Korea. Of the two-hundred-plus quakes recorded since 1905, only 48 of them caused measurable damage.

More than three thousand four hundred offshore islands add to the ambience of Korean life and the picturesque beauty of the land and seascape.* The largest and most famous of these islands is Cheju Island, a semitropical volcanic uprising that is eighty-five kilometers from the southern tip of the Korean peninsula in the South Sea. Cheju (Cheh-juu) has the political status of a province.

Korea has a so-called temperate climate, in this case meaning that it has four distinct seasons, gets hot and humid in the summer (except in the mountains), and gets cold in the winter. The farther north on the peninsula, the longer and colder the winters. In winter the southeast coast is warmer than the west coast because of the warm Kuroshio Current that comes up from the Philippines. The northern portion of the East Coast is influenced by a cold *Puk Han* (Pook Hahn), or "North Korea" current that comes down from the Okhotsk Sea. In central and northern Korea, rivers freeze during the winter, some for three to four months. (The hot summer period is referred to as *tae so*/tay soh, or "big heat." The coldest winter period is known as *tae han*/tay-hahn, "big cold.")

Korea is in the East Asia monsoon zone and gets some 70 percent of its rain in the summer months (June through September). There are light to heavy rains from March through June, with heavy rains in July. October is marked by warm-

---

*Koreans have long recognized and treasured the natural beauty of their homeland. In South Korea alone (which occupies 45 percent of the peninsula) there are twenty large national parks and nineteen provincial parks.

to-cool days with clear skies and low humidity, making it the most comfortable period of the year. Cyclones that originate in the Yangtze Valley of China regularly cross the Yellow Sea and hit Korea during March and April, bringing heavy rains. Annual typhoons are also common during July and August and account for much of the rain that falls in the southern part of the peninsula during that period.

In addition to its scenic mountains and coastlines, Korea's geography and weather support a wide variety of flowers, trees, and other flora that add to its seasonal beauty. In earlier times, large numbers of tigers, leopards, bears, and wild boars roamed its hills and mountains.

The history of Korea is inseparable from that of China, Manchuria, and Japan. Viewed from a political perspective, it is a saga of tribal nations, kingdoms, and dynasties marked by long periods of order and peace that were then shattered by short periods of violence as factions seized power, ruled for a time, grew corrupt and weak, and then were replaced by the rebels who brought them down. As in China, each new Korean regime justified its authority to rule by invoking *li* (lee), or the "mandate from heaven," an ancient Chinese concept.

Between 1876 and 1910, the weak and divided Choson court was first victimized by China and then by Japan, which gradually took over the administration of the country, finally annexing it into the Japanese empire in 1910. In 1945 the United States and its allies defeated Japan and restored sovereignty to Korea. However, just days before this momentous event, armies of the Soviet Union invaded north Korea and set up a Korean Communist, Il Sung Kim, as head of a Communist-controlled regime in Pyongyang, the largest city in the northern portion of the peninsula. In Korean, South Korea is *Nam Han* (Nahn Hahn); North Korea is *Puk Han* (Puuk Hahn).

58

한국사람

Hanguksaram

(Hahn-guuk-sah-rahm)

"The Korean People"

America's Nobel Prize–winning writer Pearl S. Buck, who was born in China in 1892 and was a frequent visitor to Korea during the first half of the twentieth century, expressed her feelings about the country and its people in an essay that began, "Korea is a gem of a country inhabited by a noble people." The beauty of the Korean peninsula is indisputable. But the character of the people has long been clouded by man-made calamities that did not begin to subside until the last decades of the twentieth century.

Paleontological evidence indicates that there were human beings living on the Korean peninsula as long as five hundred thousand years ago. Other than what is suggested by these fossilized remains, however, nothing is known of these ancient people. Some thirty thousand years ago small tribes of people began moving eastward from the Altaic mountain regions of central Russia into what is now Siberia, Manchuria, and Mongolia—apparently also the original homelands of the Japanese, Finns, Turks, and Mongols, with whom they shared some racial characteristics and language similarities.

About five thousand years ago some of these Altaic people began moving onto and down the Korean peninsula. There they encountered a race of people now referred to as paleo-Asians and gradually drove them off the peninsula. The descendants of these paleo-Asians are said to be the Ainu of Japan, the natives of Sakhalin, and the Eskimos of eastern Siberia and Alaska.

The creation myth of present-day *Hanguksaram* (Hahn-guuk-sah-rahm), or "Korean People," precisely dates their formal appearance as a distinctive people and nation in 2333 B.C. This auspicious event is said to have taken place somewhere on the slopes of Mt. Paekdu, Korea's highest mountain (2,744 meters), which sprawls across the border separating North Korea and China and has since been regarded as the holiest place in Korea.

According to Korea's creation myth, the divine creator sent his son, Hwanung, from the heavens to rule over the earth. One version of the myth from this point on is that Hwanung heard a female bear praying to become human. He gave the bear twenty cloves of garlic and some sacred mugwort and told it to spend a certain number of days (twenty-one or one hundred, depending on the source) in a cave. At the end of this period, the bear had been transformed into a beautiful woman. A modernized version of this myth is that the woman concerned was a member of a tribe whose totem symbol was the bear, and the divine son was a tribal leader (king) named Hwanung who had three thousand "spirit companions" with him when the tribe settled on the slopes of Mt. Paekdu—a fairly obvious reference to the number of people making up the first large group of Koreans on the peninsula.

To go on with the story, the woman prayed for a son, was impregnated by Hwanung, and in due course gave birth to a boy who was named *Tangun* (Tahn-guun), which literally means "Birch Lord"—apparently a reference to the prominence of birch trees in the region where he was born, but it could be translated figuratively as "generalissimo" or "First Supreme Leader." (Other sources say that the beautiful woman was Hwanung's granddaughter and do not mention the father of Tangun. These sources also say that the capital of the dynasty Tangun founded was the walled city of Pyongyang in the northern half of Korea.)

In any event, Tangun became the founder of the first Korean dynasty, which lasted until 1122 B.C. At that time, according to legend, a Chinese army under the command of China's King Kija showed up in Korea, heralding the formation of a new dynasty in Korea and a vassal-like relationship with China that was to continue off and on for more than three thousand years.

One interpretation of Korea's creation myth is that it was such a beautiful country that even the gods wanted to live there—emphasizing the point that the divine beings who founded the Korean race were not exiles from heaven but volunteers who were enthralled by the beauty of the peninsula. Early Chinese visitors to the peninsula were equally impressed with its beauty and wrote about it voluminously. One famous verse went: "I would rather live in Korea and see the Diamond Mountains [Mt. Kumgang]." These early Chinese visitors also noted that the Koreans were so courteous they would walk on the side of the road to avoid inconveniencing others.

The people of the legendary first dynasty of Korea, called Old Choson in Chinese records, were described by the Chinese as *Tung-i* (Tuung-ee). The term can be translated either as "Eastern bowmen" or "Eastern barbarians" (*i* has more than fifty meanings in Chinese), but when used by the Chinese it meant "Eastern barbarian." Later Chinese visitors referred to Korea as *Tongbang Yeui Chi Kuk* (Tohng-bahng Yay-wee Chee Kuuk), or "The Country of Eastern Decorum," in reference to the diligence with which Koreans of that day followed a strict protocol in their interpersonal relationships.

Whatever their origins, the people of Korea are more racially homogeneous than most, indicating that their gene stock has been relatively pure for a long time. Interestingly, however, only some 80 percent of Koreans have the epicanthic eyefold that is associated with the Mongolian race, and they generally have high, prominent cheekbones that distinguish them from most Chinese, Japanese, and Southeast Asians of Mongolian descent. They also have the distinctive blue "Mongolian spot" birthmark on their lower backs that is characteristic of Mongolians. As a rule, Koreans were taller and more muscular than the Japanese and Chinese—no doubt because their diet traditionally included more meat and nonrice grains.

Another apparent reason why *Hangugin* (Koreans) were generally taller than the Japanese in particular was the conspicuous difference in their lifestyles. Until the 1970s, most Japanese had legs that were unusually short in comparison to their body trunks—the result, apparently, of eating a rice-heavy diet, swaddling infants, and spending a lot of time sitting on their legs. (A dramatic change in the diet of the younger generations of Japanese, beginning in the 1960s, resulted in an equally dramatic change in the length of their legs.)

Koreans, on the other hand, especially upper-class urban Korean women, have traditionally been known for their attractive figures and overall beauty—so much so, in fact, that for centuries they were prized as loot by Chinese, Japanese, and other invaders and were among the tribute Korea was required to pay to China as a vassal state. Many young Korean women exude a kind of sensual charm, expressed in the term *maeryok* (mayer-yohk), that is so powerful it virtually entrances most men. The term *minyo* (meen-yoh), meaning "beautiful woman" (or "beautiful women"), has traditionally had a special significance in Korean history.

The most traumatic event in the history of the Korean people occurred in 1910, when the country was invaded and annexed by Japan. The annexation lasted until 1945, when Japan was defeated in World War II. During that thirty-six-year period, the emotional, spiritual, and intellectual suffering inflicted on Koreans reached new heights of cruelty. In the last decade of the occupation, the Japanese government did everything it could to crush the spirit of Koreans and destroy their identity as Koreans. The use of the Korean language was prohibited and all Koreans were ordered to take Japanese names and to follow Japanese etiquette.

Because the Japanese occupation of Korea lasted only thirty-six years and became more brutal with each passing year, their efforts to destroy Korean culture and Korean identity backfired. The Koreans who survived the occupation and the brutalities inflicted on them became even more determined to preserve their culture and developed an intense hatred for the Japanese that still colors the view that Koreans have of Japan.

Some Koreans claim that the organized violence and brutality regularly inflicted on them by foreign invaders since the beginning of their history resulted in their developing a "blood taboo"—a taboo against spilling blood, against killing. But this taboo did not prevent them from vigorously defending themselves when they believed they had a chance of success.

Western residents of Korea during the late 1800s often described Koreans as being "the Irish of the Orient"—a reference to their poetic nature, outgoing spirit, temper, fondness for strong drinks, and willingness to fight when wronged. Present-day *Hangugin* are often described by people who know them well as less ethnocentric than the Japanese, less devious than the Chinese, more direct than either the Chinese or Japanese, and more fun to be with.

Despite political and geographic divisions of Korea that go back to ancient times, the homogeneity of Koreans is expressed in many ways, including the use of the words *Han minjok* (Hahn meen-joak) to mean either "Korean nation" or "Korean people," depending on the context.

Also, despite the personal passivity that was forced on Koreans for generations by the strict demands of their Confucian-oriented social system, there was always just below their calm surface an unquenchable individualistic spirit that raged to be free. This only partially freed spirit was the source of the aggressive entrepreneurship that transformed Korea into a modern industrial nation in just one generation and continues to drive Koreans to achieve even more.

Despite the extraordinary changes that have occurred in the character and behavior of Koreans since the days of Pearl Buck, the quality of *kosang* (koh-sahng), or "nobility," that so impressed her is still discernible in the national character of the people. This *kosang* includes elements of refinement and high-mindedness that continue to be a significant part of Korean culture. Koreans also pride themselves on their *chilgida* (cheel-ghee-dah)—their "toughness, durability, and tenacity"—and their *chinshim* (cheen-sheem), or "sincerity."

59

한국 역사
Hanguk Yoksa
(Hahn-guuk Yoke-sah)

"Korea: A Historical Saga"

The first historical mention of Koreans occurs in Chinese records written in 1122 B.C., apparently as the result of an expedition of some sort to the Korean peninsula. These early Chinese visitors to Korea were so impressed with the behavior of the people that they referred to the country as *Dongbang Ye Yiji Kuk* (Dohng-bahng Yeh Yee-jee Kook), or "Eastern Nation of Decency and Manners."

During Korea's Bronze Age (900 B.C.–400 B.C.) several relatively large clan societies developed as walled city-states, including Chinbon, Imdun, Old Choson, Puyo, and Yemaek. Old Choson emerged as the largest of these states and was ruled by a priest-king, called Tangun Waggom, who was said to have descended from a sun god. By the fourth century B.C. the power of Old Choson had declined to the point that a rebel leader broke away from the Chinese-dominated court and formed a new kingdom called Wiman Choson.

In 109 B.C. the famous Han Chinese emperor Wu-Ti (known as the "Martial Emperor") invaded and captured Wiman Choson, bringing the whole peninsula under China's military and administrative hegemony—a period that was to last for some four hundred years. Under Chinese rule the several small kingdoms on the peninsula were consolidated into three larger kingdoms. These three kingdoms were Koguryo (37 B.C.–A.D. 668), Paekche (18 B.C.–A.D. 660), and Shilla (57 B.C.–A.D. 935).

After the conquest of Korea by China, large numbers of Chinese administrators, artists, craftsmen, and scholars took up residence in Nangnang, near present-day Pyongyang, turning the city into a thriving center of Chinese culture. The three consolidated kingdoms adopted the Chinese style of government, which was based primarily on Confucian principles, and eventually the Buddhist religion as well.

Most of the cultural institutions introduced into Korea from China were "Koreanized," then passed on to Japan, where they played a key role in unifying and civilizing that country. There is, in fact, evidence that the first imperial court in Japan was established by Korean horsemen—something Japanese history books dispute. Korean records indicate that in A.D. 815, some one-third of Japan's noble families were of Korean descent.*

As the Han dynasty in China weakened, the Korean kingdoms became more and more independent. During the seventh century, China's Tang dynasty, which

---

*The Paekche kingdom, first located in the vicinity of present-day Seoul and then on the southeastern side of the peninsula, where Pusan is now located, introduced Buddhism, silk culture, the forging of iron, and a wide variety of arts and crafts into Japan. Another facet of Korea's early influence on Japan that most present-day Japanese are not aware of is that the official name of Japan—*Nippon* (Neep-pone)—originated in Korea, not Japan. In the seventh century, Korean scholars of the Shilla dynasty changed the name of Japan from *Wa* (the original Chinese name for Japan, meaning "dwarf") to *Nippon* in all of their references. A short time later (in 670) Japan's imperial court officially adopted the new name—although the old name, *Wa*, also pronounced *Yamato* (Yah-mah-toe), continued to be used unofficially for several generations. *Nippon* literally means "Sun Source" or "Source of the Sun"—the East, as seen from Korea. *Wa* is the Japanese pronunciation of the Chinese ideogram *Wo* (Woh), which is what the Chinese first called the Japanese when they became aware of their existence sometime before the first century B.C. In its Chinese connotation *Wo* (or *Wa*) could mean "dwarf" or "barbarian." The Japanese later altered the meaning to "peace" or "harmony" and adopted a different Chinese ideogram to write it.

In the eighth century, Japan's imperial court ordered scholars to "correct" and complete the history of Japan up to that time. In the process of doing so, according to Korean and Western scholars, they "changed" history to enhance the status of the imperial family and court, stretching the history of the imperial family back to 666 B.C. and removing virtually all references to Korea and Koreans.

had replaced the Han, invaded Korea several times in an attempt to reestablish Chinese hegemony but each time was repulsed by the Koreans. While fighting to keep from being swallowed up by China, the three Korean kingdoms also competed for supremacy among themselves. In the early centuries, Koguryo was the largest and most powerful of these kingdoms, controlling some two-thirds of the peninsula and southeastern Manchuria.

The peasant population of these three Korean kingdoms was ruled by an elite that lived in walled towns. For the first several generations, religious and political leadership were the same, but as the societies grew and became more sophisticated, the duties of the leaders were gradually separated into political and religious spheres.

As the centuries passed, Shilla grew in wealth and power. In A.D. 668 Shilla defeated its two rivals and established its hegemony over the entire peninsula. This resulted in Tang China's dispatching an expeditionary force to reassert its power over the peninsula. But Shilla's armed forces succeeded in repulsing the Tang China advance, forcing the Chinese government to withdraw its "Protectorate-General for Pacifying the East" from Korea. Shilla then negotiated a treaty with China that resulted in a lively exchange of goods between the two countries. The volume of Korea's "cultural borrowing" from China also increased dramatically.

The social ranking system in Shilla was so precise and all-encompassing that it designated the kind of houses that different-ranked people could live in, their wearing apparel, the kind of personal transportation they could use, even their kitchen utensils. Shilla's elite ruling class became known as *chin gol* (cheen gohl), literally "sacred bones," a reference to their blue-blood ancestry.

Between 668 and 932 the Shilla kingdom carried on a brisk foreign trade with both China and Japan. In 788 the Shilla government instituted the Chinese system of holding annual civil service examinations to qualify candidates for all government positions—*munban* (muun-bahn), or "civil service officials," and *muban* (muu-bahn), "military officers." Those who passed the tests became "scholar-officials," eventually known as *yangban* (yahng-bahn), which literally means something like "double duty." Kyongju, the capital of Shilla, prospered. Its main streets were more than ten kilometers long. Shilla scholars specialized in such things as medicine, mathematics, astronomy, diplomatic correspondence, personnel management, and government service.

The seventh and eighth centuries of the Shilla dynasty were a golden age, but then decline set in. "Secondary capitals" were established by the royal court in an attempt to get some of the elite families to move out of the dynastic capital of Kyongju. Most of the *yangban* refused to move but were given grants of "tax villages" in perpetuity, allowing them to siphon off much of what the peasant class produced and making them wealthy. As the estates and wealth of the provincial gentry grew, they began building fortified compounds and maintaining their own private guards and armies. Some of the estates grew into provinces or fiefs, with the clan head serving as both governor and military commander. Eventually these clan chiefs came to be known as "castle lords."

This system resulted in numerous peasant rebellions in the latter centuries of the Shilla dynasty and in factional strife between contending court officials and provincial clan lords. Thousands of peasants fled their villages to escape their untenable existence, offering their services to local castle lords or taking to the hills and becoming bandits.

As time passed and the size of the royal family as well as the families of the elite class grew, there were not enough court or government posts to provide for them. The larger the class of *chin gol*, or "sacred bones," grew, the more its members became lazy, self-indulgent, and corrupt. Intraclan conflicts led by more ambitious *chin gol* who were out of power resulted in numerous coup attempts. Historians say that during the first decades of the ninth century, the Shilla dynasty was "torn apart" by rebel *chin gol* leaders and their private armies.

In the meantime, during the eighth century, a former Koguryo general gained control of the northern portion of the peninsula and much of what is now Manchuria and established a kingdom known as Parhae, which declared itself the successor to Koguryo. This new state was sometimes called Koryo—from which comes the name Korea.* In 926, Parhae was conquered by the Khitans from Manchuria, causing most of its ruling class to flee southward and join the Koryo group that was contesting for power with the weakened Shilla court. In 918 one of these rebels, Kon Wang, declared the founding of the Koryo dynasty, but it was 936 before he gained full control of the peninsula. The last Shilla stronghold fell in A.D. 935 and was formally replaced by the Koryo dynasty.

Koryo's founders changed the social status system, eliminating the *chin gol* system and creating a number of "orders" that included court officials, ministry officials, military officers, clerics, artisans, and soldiers and made the categories hereditary. The peasant and slave classes remained hereditary.

The new Koryo court established a system of appointing all officials down to the county level, thereby creating a national bureaucracy that gave it virtually absolute control over the whole country. The court also appointed officials from many different clans in a move to broaden its political power base. But as the generations passed, the more influential families continued to amass power through intermarriages, with the result that by the twelfth century a few hereditary aristocratic families controlled the government.

Taxes on public land were set at 25 percent of whatever was produced on it; on privately owned land the taxes were set at 50 percent—all to be paid in produce and woven cloth. All commoner males between the ages of sixteen and sixty were subject to conscription for corvée labor. The law specified that no individual be required to work for more than a total of six days each year, but this provision was ignored regularly by local and regional authorities. One of the largest public works programs of this era was the completion between 1033 and 1044 of the Great Wall along the northern boundary of Koryo to help keep invaders out.

The early centuries of the Koryo dynasty were another brilliant age. The leaders were renowned for their scholarship, statecraft, and literary accomplishments. Their primary forms of recreation included holding poetry contests,

---

*Marco Polo called Korea *Cauly* from the Chinese word *Kaoli*, which in turn came from the Korean word *Koryo*. Polo's spelling resulted in Korea's being variously spelled *Coree* and *Corea* by Westerners.

in which the participants were required to create poems extemporaneously, and staging large banquets. Ranking Buddhist monks were given the status of nobility. Hundreds of great temple complexes were built throughout the country. During this period there were six classes of people: the royal family clans; the *yangban* civil and military officials; the *nanban* higher-ranked palace bureaucrats; the *hyangni* clerks and other lower-ranking palace bureaucrats; the *sang min* (sahng-meen), which translates as "good people" but meant peasants and fishermen; and, at the bottom, *paekchong* (pake-chohng), or "outcasts." These *paekchong* included slaves and people in occupations considered unclean (butchers, hide tanners, etc.) as well as everyone whose work required travel (entertainers, hunters, peddlers, seamen).

Domestic and international trade flourished during the Koryo period. So many foreign traders visited Korea during that time that a network of inns was built in port cities and up and down the coasts to accommodate them during their visits and travels within the country. The first monetary coins were minted in Koryo in 995. A national mint was established in 1097, and great efforts were made to encourage the use of coins instead of cloth and grain as mediums of exchange. (Paper currency was first issued in Korea in 1401.)

But growing corruption among the ruling class and powerful Buddhist monasteries led to creeping decadence in the Koryo court. In 1170 the Koryo military seized power, massacred many officials, and purged others. A series of coups, peasant rebellions, and slave uprisings followed. Some slaves who burned their family records went on to become generals and high-ranking government officials.

When the military took over Koryo, the former literati (*sadaebu*) scholar-officials became bureaucrats. (They were to make a comeback under the banner of General Song Gye Yi, the scion of a famous military family who founded the Choson dynasty in 1392.) Although all administrative power in Koryo was in the hands of a military junta after the coup in 1170, the military leaders chose to maintain the Koryo king and his court as symbolic leaders of the country.

In 1223 Japanese pirates (known as *Wako*/Wah-koe in Japanese and *Waegu*/Wie-guu in Korean) began raiding Korea's coastal shipping and thriving seaports. The raids stopped in 1231 when the Mongol armies of Genghis Khan invaded Korea, beginning a long, drawn-out war that was to end with the Mongols devastating the peninsula, killing more than a hundred thousand Koreans, including all of the artists and craftsmen responsible for Korea's famed celadon industry, totally wiping it out. The war ended when the Koryo court agreed to become a tributary state to Khan's new Yuan dynasty in China.

As part of Koryo's status as a vassal state, Khan required all Korean crown princes to be educated in Beijing, marry Mongol princesses, and remain in Beijing until the ruling Koryo king died, thereby exercising virtually complete control of the country. Koryo was also required to pay annual tribute to China (gold, silver, ginseng, and women). The Mongol court required so many Korean women for its harems that two offices were set up in Korea to locate, screen, and ship women to Beijing.

Another of the more notable events in the thirteenth century was the invention of movable type by a Korean printer in 1234 (two hundred years before the same feat was accomplished by Gutenberg in Europe), resulting in a booming publishing industry.

In the early 1270s the Mongols began amassing a huge naval fleet and army in Korea to attack Japan, which they did in 1274 and again in 1281. In both cases the invasions ended in disaster when the combined Mongol and Korean fleets were destroyed by typhoons (giving birth to Japan's "divine winds" belief).

In 1350 the Japanese *Waegu* pirates again began raiding Korea, with some of the raids involving as many as five hundred ships. These pirate fleets not only raided the coastal areas for loot and captives but sent large bodies of brigands marching overland to raid royal granaries, libraries, and museums. Records show there were some five hundred such raids between 1350 and 1388. Chinese rebels known as Red Turbans also invaded Korea twice in the 1360s, adding to the woes caused by the Japanese pirates. (The Mongol domination of Korea lasted until 1368, when the Yuan dynasty founded in China by Khan was overthrown by the Chinese.)

In 1380 the Koreans finally started getting the better of the *Waegu* by arming a flotilla of ships with cannons—a first in the world. In one battle in the estuary of the Kum River, the small Korean flotilla completely destroyed a pirate fleet of some four hundred vessels. Following this Korean victory and the emergence of Korea as a formidable naval power, Japan's *Daimyo* (Die-m'yoe) warlords in the fiefs facing Korea agreed to suppress the *Waegu* and to begin formal trade relations with Korea.

In the late 1380s the new Ming dynasty in China once again attacked Korea in an attempt to reestablish hegemony over the kingdom. The Korean general sent to repel the Chinese, General Song Gye Yi, quickly realized that his forces were no match for the Chinese, turned back, deposed the ruling Koryo king, and in 1389 put one of his own supporters on the throne. In 1392 Yi completed the coup against the Koryo throne, established what was to be Korea's last and longest dynasty, and became its first king. Yi chose to call the country *Choson*, the ancient name, which can be translated as "Morning Fresh," "Fresh Morning," or "Morning Serenity." (There would to be a total of 27 *Choson* kings by the time the dynasty ended in 1910.)

General Yi, who took the title King Taejo, adopted a newly reformed version of Confucianism as the official state ideology, relegating Buddhism and Taoism to the ignoble status of heretical folk beliefs. In 1394 he established his capital in Hanyang (present-day Seoul), which had been the Paekche seat of government some fifteen hundred years earlier. A great ten-mile-long wall, with numerous gates, was built around the city. Huge palace and garden complexes were also built, making the city one of the most spectacular metropolitan areas in the world. The Choson dynasty was to become the period during which the national character of the Koreans that is known today was forged in a crucible of Neo-Confucianism.

General Yi kept China at bay by signing an accord that guaranteed Korea its independence in exchange for once again becoming an official tributary state of China and paying annual tribute to the Chinese government (this time the tribute included women, ginseng, eunuchs, gold, silver, horses, artisans, and hawks). The Choson court sent four regular diplomatic, trade, and tributary missions to

China each year—at the beginning of the new year, the emperor's birthday, the birthday of the crown prince, and the winter solstice. Later the Choson court solved the problem of feeding and clothing its army of conscripts by requiring that every conscripted soldier be supported by a "paired provisioner" from his own village—an obligation that doubled the already heavy burden on the peasant class.

With the Mongol armies gone from Korea, Japanese pirates once again began attacking Korean merchant vessels and raiding coastal ports and villages. In 1419, King Sejong, who had succeeded his father, King Taejong, the second Choson king, launched a military expedition against the Tsushima-based pirates in an effort to eliminate them. Following this successful effort, he then agreed to open three Korean ports to legitimate trade with Japan under strict Korean supervision. But Japanese merchants began importing so much from Korea there was fear that the stores of rice and cotton cloth would be depleted. The Choson court negotiated a new agreement in 1443 limiting the Japanese to sending fifty trading ships a year to Korean ports.

In 1444, King Sejong, the third and most illustrious Choson king, reduced the tax on farmers from one-tenth of their harvest to one-twentieth. Among the cultural highlights of this remarkable period in Korean history was the development of *Hangul* (Hahn-guhl), the Korean alphabet, in 1446. Other inventions included the rain gauge (in 1442, two hundred years before it was invented in Europe), water clocks, and sundials. A new class of people rose up between commoners and the *yangban* gentry that was given the label *chung-in* (chuung-een), which literally means "middle people." This class was made up primarily of technicians, doctors, lower-ranking military officers, translators, and the like. Common people were officially called *sang-min* (sahng-meen), which means "good people," as well as *yangin* (yahng-een). Outcasts were still known as *paek-chong* (pake-chohng), which literally means "butcher" (a dealer in meat products) and grew out of the Buddhist condemnation of slaughtering animals and eating meat.

In the century following the foundation of the new dynasty, scholar-bureaucrats who had been steeped in Neo-Confucianism gradually took over the government, instituting a stern political and moral code that was to control and color Korean society until the end of the nineteenth century.

In 1519 the new Choson dynasty gave Korean farmers a degree of self-government under a contract called *hyang yak* (h'yahng yahk), or "village contract." The social contract called for mutual encouragement of morality, mutual supervision of wrongdoing, mutual decorum in social relationships, and mutual aid in times of disaster.

The Choson dynasty engaged in brisk foreign trade and cultural exchanges with China and Japan. Much of the trade with Japan was handled through the Japanese-held island of Tsushima, only thirty-five kilometers (twenty miles) from Korea in the straits that separate Korea from Japan. (The northwestern tip of Kyushu, one of Japan's main islands, is 200 kilometers [120 miles] from Korea.) Because of its proximity to Korea, Tsushima became the "Hong Kong" of the day for trade between Korea and Japan. The island had long been used as a base for Japanese pirates.

But the restrictions on the number of Japanese trading ships that could call at Korean ports resulted in Japanese traders stationed in the ports staging a protest rebellion in 1512, following which the Korean government reduced the number of ships permitted each year to twenty-five to make it easier to control the Japanese traders.

In 1592, Japan's paramount military leader, Hideyoshi Toyotomi, decided to conquer China and sought Korea's cooperation and help. The Koreans refused. Toyotomi then ordered the lords of several fiefs in the south and southwestern parts of the country to field armies and launched a massive attack against Korea. These armies, acting separately and in competition with each other, marched northward from the southern end of the Korean peninsula, overrunning the country in less than a month, destroying just about everything in their path, and collecting both booty and captives to be sent back to Japan.

These Japanese invaders were harassed by Korean guerrilla forces known as *ui hyong* (we he-yohng), or "righteous armies," that were led mostly by local literati. Buddhist monks also formed guerrilla bands to harass the Japanese. China sent an army of fifty thousand men to help Korea fight the Japanese invaders. (Korea's righteous armies went back to seventh-century peasant rebellions against the ruling elite.)

However, what stalled Toyotomi's plan to conquer Korea and use it as a staging ground to invade China was not the combined Korean-Chinese forces, arrayed against his forces, but the introduction of the world's first ironclad warships into the battle by Korea's admiral Sun-Shin Yi. Admiral Yi had large studded iron plates cast like modern-day siding, then attached them to the hulls of wooden ships, making the ships virtually invulnerable to enemy cannonballs. These ships were quickly dubbed *kobuk son* (koh-buuk sohn), or "turtle ships," because of their iron shells.

In their first encounter with the Japanese fleet, Admiral Yi's small flotilla sank some 250 ships. (There is a statue of Admiral Sun-Shin Yi [1545–98], who is one of the two or three most admired men in Korea's history, in downtown Seoul.) After this inglorious defeat, Toyotomi agreed to peace talks with Korea, but the demands he made were so onerous that the Korean government refused to accept them. Toyotomi ordered a second attack on Korea in 1597. In the meantime, Admiral Yi had been relieved of duty because of court intrigues against him, and this time most of the Korean fleet was destroyed before Yi was recalled. He once again sank most of the Japanese invasion fleet, but in the last battle he was killed by a stray bullet.

Fortunately for Korea, Toyotomi died in 1598. His leading generals in Korea hastily withdrew their troops from the peninsula and rushed back to Japan in an effort to keep the Toyotomi family in power. However, the two back-to-back invasions had a devastating effect on Korea. In addition to the physical destruction and the loss of thousands of Korean artists and craftsmen taken back to Japan as captives, the invasions caused a famine and epidemics of diseases that resulted in a dramatic drop in the population.

In addition to destroying almost every building in their path, the Japanese deliberately destroyed census and tax records as well as family histories—all of which were of vital importance to both the Korean government and the people in general. What cultural artifacts the Japanese could not transport back to Japan they destroyed.*

In 1627 Korea was again invaded, this time by the Manchus when they began their campaign to conquer China. The Manchus captured Pyongyang and Seoul in 1636 and once again made Korea a vassal state. Nine years later the Koreans rebelled against the Manchus, but this time they were completely crushed by the vengeful Manchu armies. The Manchus went on to conquer all of China in 1644, establishing the famous Ching dynasty in Beijing.

By this time, continuing invasions and stories of the activities of foreign missionaries and traders in Japan and elsewhere in Asia resulted in the Choson court's closing Korea's doors to all of the outside world except China (and later Japan) and becoming what was known in the West as the "Hermit Kingdom." Korea was to remain isolated from the Western world from 1637 until 1876. Historian Sik Lee Chong described the Korea of that period as "a proud, dogmatic, closed society."

Korea was also to remain a tributary of the Ching-dominated China until 1894–95, when Japan attacked China—the Sino-Japan War—and forced the Chinese to give up their interests in Korea.

Despite Korea's closed doors from 1637 until 1876, new ideas continued to seep in, primarily via China, fueling growing criticism of the authoritarian Confucian-oriented government and society. By the early 1800s there were increasing demands from intellectuals that the system be reformed and the country opened up to the outside world. Peasant rebellions in 1812 helped to bring about a number of welfare programs and other reforms, but they were no more than Band-Aid measures. Rebellions flared up again in the 1860s.

At this time, Seoul had hardly changed in some five hundred years. The gates of the great wall surrounding the city were closed at sunset, so anyone wanting to enter or leave the city after that hour had to climb the wall. As darkness came on, large fires were lit on the tops of the four hills surrounding the city as signals that all was well in the capital. An hour after sunset all men were required to remain indoors, leaving the streets strictly to women, who were confined to their homes during the day.

From 1832 on, foreign naval and merchant ships began appearing off Korea's coasts. Attempts by Japan, Russia, European powers, and the United States to open Korea began in 1866, with Russia leading the way. All these powers subsequently sent naval forces into Korean waters. In the 1860s and early 1870s Japan's noted nationalist Saigo Takamori, who had helped bring the downfall of the Tokugawa Shogunate and restore the emperor to power, was a powerful advocate of a policy known as *Seikan* (Say-e-khan), which was short for "Conquer Korea Agitation."

French warships bombarded Korea's West Coast ports in 1866 following the execution of a number of French Catholic priests who had smuggled them-

---

*The Tokugawa Shogunate, which replaced the administration of Hideyoshi Toyotomi in Japan in 1603, reopened diplomatic relations with Korea and negotiated a trade agreement between the two countries that was to become one of only three "windows" that Japan itself had to the outside world from the 1630s until the 1850s. The other two windows were with the Chinese and the Dutch.

selves into Korea. In 1871 an American flotilla attacked Kanghwa, an island compound just off the coast west of Seoul that was favored by the royal family, but gave up in the face of determined Korean resistance. The attack was intended to punish Korea for the destruction of the American ship *General Sherman* and the slaughter of its crew.

As told by F. A. McKenzie, a correspondent for the *Daily Mail* in London, in his book *The Tragedy of Korea* (Yonsei University Press), the American ship (only the captain, a man named Preston, and three of the crewmen were Americans) left Tientsin, China, intending to plunder the royal tombs at Pingyang. The ship sailed up the Tai Tong River to Pingyang, causing an uproar. The ruling regent ordered the local garrison to prevent the ship from docking and force it to leave Korean waters. If the captain refused to sail away, the ship was to be destroyed and the crew killed. The captain refused to leave. A company of Korean soldiers and enraged civilians tried to storm the ship. Dozens were killed and wounded by the ship's guns. The captain tried to move the ship out of the range of fire from the shore but got stuck in shallow water. The siege continued for four days. The Koreans then floated scows loaded with burning firewood down the river, finally managing to set fire to the ship. The sulfur and saltpeter on the ship ignited. The crew tried to escape by jumping into the water and climbing ashore, some of them carrying white flags in surrender. All were cut into small pieces, with some parts of their bodies kept for use in medicines and the remainder burned.

These attacks prompted a movement to strengthen Korea's tiny armed forces and gave rise to such slogans as *Cha-Gang* (Chah-Gahng), or "Self-Strengthening," and *Pu Guk Kang-Byong* (Puu Guuk Kahng-B'yohng), translated as "Enrich the Nation and Strengthen the Military." This was followed by *Kae Wha* (Kigh Whah), or "Enlightenment and Progress."

Between 1876 and 1894 a number of "memorials" were submitted to the Choson court by conservative Confucianists who opposed any modernization of Choson's political, social, and economic systems. During the same time frame more than a hundred memorials advocating reform were submitted to the court.

This resulted in both China and Japan sending large expeditionary forces in Korea to protect what they claimed were their interests. In 1876 the Japanese government sent a fleet of warships to Korea in a show of force to compel the weak and divisive Yi court to open the country up to foreigners (in an exact replay of the gunboat diplomacy that the United States had used on Japan in the 1850s).

After Korea signed a treaty with Japan in 1876, the Japanese took charge of training Korean military forces, exacerbating an ongoing struggle with China to control Korea politically as well as economically. Bowing to the realities of the situation, the Choson court later that year sent a group of young aristocrat-scholars to Japan to study how Japan was transforming itself from a medieval kingdom to a modern power. In 1881 another group of young Korean students went to China.

The first treaty that Korea signed with a Western nation was with the United States, in 1883, following which the Choson court sent a goodwill mission to Washington, D.C. Other treaties quickly followed, opening several Korean ports to foreign ships and allowing foreigners to enter the country for business and other purposes. In preemptive moves against Japan and the Western powers, the Chinese began aggressively pushing their own interests in Korea, taking over many of the functions of the court. The rivalry between China and Japan escalated, with the United States, Russia, France, and England playing their hands more cautiously.

In 1884 a progressive group of scholar-officials staged a coup attempt against the court, expecting support from Japan. The Japanese failed to come through. This resulted in an attack on the Japanese legation by an angry mob of Koreans. Chinese army units in the city took command. They arrested the leaders of the attack and executed them, then promised Japan that Korea would pay a heavy indemnity, provide the Japanese government with a new legation, and guarantee them additional trade and travel rights in Korea. All but eight of the Korean conspirators were caught and executed by the Chinese. The eight escaped to Japan.

The Korean court was in complete disarray and was no match for either the Chinese or the Japanese. There were more than four thousand people attached to the palace, including large numbers of eunuchs, sorcerers, and soothsayers. The sorcerers, made up of a powerful guild of the blind, had long been especially feared by the public because of their arbitrary use of power.

In what was presented to the world as an attempt to settle the matter, both China and Japan formally agreed to withdraw their troops from Korea, but Japan reneged on the commitment. In 1894 the Japanese army created an incident it used to justify an attack on China (the Sino-Japanese War, 1884–5) in a deliberate move to end Chinese influence on the Korean peninsula. Korea's Queen Min was an influential voice against inroads being made by Japan. When Japan began its attack against Chinese forces in Seoul, Japanese soldiers chased the queen down in the corridors of the royal apartments, killed her with swords, forced her attendants to confirm her identity, killed them, then dragged her body out into the garden and burned it. Ten years later, the Japanese went to war against Russia (the Russo-Japanese War, 1904–5) to eliminate Russia as a competitor in the region.

In 1905 U.S. president Theodore Roosevelt rejected the advice of the American minister in Seoul to oppose Japanese demands following their victory over Russia and made a secret agreement with the Japanese that if they would not object to the United States' takeover of the Philippines the United States would not object to Japan's taking whatever measures were necessary for it to "guide, control, and protect" Korea. Historians further point out that until the Russo-Japanese war in 1904–5, most Western nations, including the United States, were on Japan's side, believing that Japan would help end the chaos in Korea and keep the Russians at bay.

With this assurance from the United States, the Japanese gradually took control of Korean business, financial, and foreign affairs, but not without a costly struggle. The Japanese had disbanded the small Korean army, but armies of Korean peasants, eventually totaling some seventy thousand men, began attacking Japanese garrison troops and facilities, mounting some 1,451 such engagements in 1907 alone.

The Japanese struck back with overwhelming arms, burning hundreds of

Korean villages and killing more than eighteen thousand insurgents. To intimidate the people of Korea, the Japanese instituted a policy of massacring large numbers of civilians, including women and children, when demonstrations occurred. Japanese secret police swarmed out across the country, reporting on the slightest infraction of Japanese rules.

British foreign correspondent Frederick Arthur McKenzie, who was in Korea in 1904 and again in 1906, wrote that "coolies" from Japan swarmed into Korea by the dozens of thousands and went through the country "like a plague," brutalizing the people and seizing their homes and land at will. He records visits to villages that had been totally destroyed and others that had been abandoned by their frightened inhabitants who had fled into the mountains to escape the marauding Japanese. None of the Japanese, he adds, were ever punished for these outrages.

To further weaken the Choson court, the Japanese seized much of the land from which the court received taxes and turned the land over to Japanese interests. Finally, in 1910, Japan annexed Korea, turning it into a colony. In addition to more soldiers, Japanese businessmen as well as farmers poured into Korea, with the latter taking over much of the best land in the country. During the first years of the colonization, the ownership of much of the land and timber stands in Korea was transferred to Japanese interests.

The largest uprising against the Japanese occupation forces occurred on March 1, 1919, and became known as the *Samil Undong* (Sahm-eel Uhn-dohng), or "March First Movement." Spearheaded by all the various religious groups in Korea, the mass revolt was crushed quickly by the Japanese army. Korean records indicate that more than 7,500 people were killed, some 15,000 were seriously injured, and over the next several months more than 45,000 were arrested and imprisoned.

In the 1930s Japan began a draconian campaign to totally eradicate the cultural identity of Koreans. All education was in the Japanese language. All official records had to be kept in Japanese. All Koreans were required to take Japanese names. The educational system was designed to indoctrinate Korean children in Japanese manners and ethics and in Japanese history. The history taught in Korean schools was distorted and falsified to show Japan in a favorable light.

The Japanese came up with the slogan *Nai Sen Ittai* (Nie Sen Eet-tie), "Japan and Korea as One Body!" As the Pacific War turned against Japan, the colonial administration in Korea imposed a *kong chul* (kohng chuul), or "quota delivery," system on Korean farmers as a means of forcing them to produce more for the Japanese war effort. In 1944 this quota system was expanded to include manufacturers as well. A few Koreans managed to establish companies during the annexation period, but they were forced to coordinate them with Japan's interests. Some of these Korean businessmen nonetheless showed extraordinary entrepreneurial ability, foreshadowing what was to come in the 1960s and beyond.

Japanese records show that some 365,000 Korean men were drafted into the Japanese army during World War II, and another 725,000 were conscripted to work on military installations in Korea and Manchuria, which Japan had seized from China. More than 150,000 Korean men were killed during the war or disappeared without any trace. Conditions became so bad in Korea that in between harvests people were reduced to eating the roots of wild plants because the Japanese commandeered most of the crops to feed their armies.

Japan's onerous colonization of Korea came to an end in August 1945 when the Japanese empire was defeated by the United States and the Allied powers. But the end of Japanese rule in Korea did not bring peace to the peninsula. It was immediately caught up in the struggle between the West and communism. Communist roots in Korea went back to 1920. That year a small group of Korean scholars and patriots who viewed the Soviet Union as a friend to the poor and disenfranchised and believed that *kongsangjuui* (kohng-sahng-juu-wee), or "communism," would be the savior of common people all over the world established the Korean Communist Party (*Koryo Kongsan Dang* / Koh-re-oh Kohng-sahn Dahng).

The Korean Communists acted in concert with Korean exiles in Japan, Shanghai, and Siberia who had come under the influence of the leftist thought then being exported by the Soviet Union. The party promised relief for workers and students, the two most militant groups in Korea. The Communist movement resulted in Korean nationalists dividing into quarreling factions, greatly weakening their efforts and their image in the international community. The Japanese cracked down on the nascent Korean Communist movement with extraordinary vehemence.

At the end of World War II and the ousting of Japan from Korea (at which time more than 750,000 Japanese civilians were living in Korea, along with several hundred thousand Japanese troops stationed around the country), the Communists came back out in the open. They proved to be better organized and had clearer goals than the divided nationalists and were to play leading roles in the political division of the peninsula into North and South Korea. Among the best-organized Korean Communist-oriented guerrilla groups was one in Manchuria that was headed by Il Sung Kim, who had forged close ties with the Soviets. When the war ended with Japan's defeat, all of these exiled political groups rushed back to Korea and began battling to take over the country. The peninsula was divided into Soviet-dominated North Korea and United States-dominated South Korea. Il Sung Kim and his former guerrilla forces, backed by the Soviet Union, seized control in North Korea. In 1948 the division became permanent when the Republic of South Korea was proclaimed in Seoul, and a short time later the People's Republic of North Korea was inaugurated in Pyongyang.

The division of Korea into north and south parts was a shock to Koreans, not so much because of political considerations but because of personal factors. It separated hundreds of thousands of families, which was far more important to ordinary people than politics. The fact of the matter was that historically North and South Korea had been divided by ideological and social gaps often so wide that they behaved very much like separate countries. The long Choson dynasty (1392–1910) was dominated by southerners who, through their high government posts, also dominated the North. For some five hundred years few high government posts went to northerners, even though they held the highest degrees awarded in the *kwa go* (kwah go) state civil service examinations. Politically speaking, there had been bad blood between the North and South for centuries.

Two years after the founding of North and South Korea the peninsula once again became a bloody battlefield, this time with North Korea and its Chinese ally pitted against South Korea and the United States—a war that ended in a stalemate.

The founder of the North Korean People's Republic, Il Sung Kim, was to rule that hapless half of the peninsula as a Communist despot until his death in 1994, leaving the people of North Korea impregnated with Communist ideology. The southern half of the peninsula was to go through years of struggle between authoritarian and democratic factions but remained solidly committed to capitalism and the West.

Over and above the emotional trauma caused by the North Korean attack on South Korea, the physical destruction was incredible. In Seoul over half of all private dwellings, three-fourths of all business offices, and over 80 percent of all public buildings, utilities, and transportation systems were destroyed. Ultimately, however, Koreans turned this vast destruction into an advantage because when they rebuilt their factories, office buildings, and homes they had no choice but to bring in more modern equipment and use new materials.

In May 1961 Chung Hee Park (Pak Chong Hui), a ranking South Korean general, took over the government in a bloodless coup. Park turned out to be a master administrator. He later resigned from the military, was elected president, and ruled the country with an iron hand until October 1979, when he was assassinated.

In 1972 Park declared martial law, dissolved the government, and forced a new constitution on the country that he referred to as the *yusin* (yuu-sheen) constitution. *Yusin* means something like "revitalization," or "restoration." The new constitution promised a number of reforms but in effect made Park an absolute dictator. Park used his dictatorial powers to complete the transformation of Korea into an economic powerhouse by promoting exports and keeping the country closed to imports, in a series of five-year plans that were carried out with ruthless efficiency. Park and his hand-picked ministers in effect acted as general managers of the economy, forcing ostensibly private enterprises to follow the government's plans regardless of their own agendas.

Under the authority of the National Security Law and and the Anticommunist Law, the Park government used arbitrary arrests, torture, imprisonment, and execution to throttle anyone who dared to oppose the so-called *yusin* constitution and the government's policies and actions. But eventually the opposition, led by students, intellectuals, unions, and Christian groups, became a nationwide movement against the government. Historians of the period say that students and young writers, musicians, and artists created an entire subculture of rebellion against the Park regime, using art, poetry, songs, plays, and other means to indict the government. The government retaliated by arresting, torturing, and imprisoning thousands of people. All during this time, the Park regime had the full backing of the United States.

It was Park's policies that made it possible for the rapid rise of the now famous *chaebol* (chay-buhl), or "conglomerates," which still today are responsible for over half of the country's total gross national product. Finally, on October 26, 1979, Jae Kyu Kim, head of the Korean Central Intelligence Agency, shot and killed Park (and his chief bodyguard) at a private dinner in the KCIA compound near the palace. Park's death did not bring a quick end to the abuses of the *yusin* constitution. Some steps were taken by the new government to eliminate the worst abuses, but it would be the latter part of the 1980s before any real semblance of democracy would appear in Korea, with the interim period marked by more military coups, assassinations, arbitrary arrests, torture, and widespread bloodshed in the streets.

It was not until June 29, 1987, that genuine political reforms were announced by the government—many say primarily because the government had committed itself to staging the 1988 Summer Olympic Games in Seoul as Korea's international "coming out" celebration and did not want the event to be spoiled by violence in the streets. By this time, the United States was also pressuring the government to avoid again using the army to quell student and union demonstrations.

The Park years were an era of unprecedented economic progress in South Korea. Adopting the same industrial and mercantile policies that had revived and transformed Japan, Korea rapidly became an export-oriented economy led by the huge *chaebol* industrial combines that were patterned after Japan's notorious prewar *zaibatsu* (zigh-baht-sue) and postwar *keiretsu* (kay-e-rate-sue), or "aligned companies." The economic success of Park's policies left Koreans with ambivalent feelings about him.

Korea, like Japan, benefited enormously from the Vietnam War. Some 300,000 Korean troops, all paid for by the United States, served in Vietnam between 1965 and 1973. In addition, Korean construction companies were awarded many of the major building projects the United States funded in Vietnam. By the 1990s South Korea had joined the ranks of the world's top eleven industrial economies, while Communist-dominated North Korea appeared on the verge of economic collapse but continued to resist all efforts to reunite the two halves of the country.

In the mid-1990s the government of South Korea officially adopted a policy of globalizing its economy in keeping with the worldwide trend among the leading economic powers. But it set no precise timetable for achieving that goal. (See *Segyehwa*.) The most extraordinary events of the mid-1990s, however, were new student demonstrations that were followed by the arrest and indictment of former president Tae Woo Roh on bribery charges, followed a few weeks later by the arrest of his predecessor, Doo Hwan Chun, with both Roh and Chun charged with complicity in the killing of several hundred students and union members during the May 1980 antigovernment demonstration in Kwangju. (See *Nomul, Sonmul*.) The leaders of several of Korea's largest business conglomerates were also questioned about paying bribes to the former presidents, then indicted and bound over for trial. Both ex-presidents were convicted and sent to prison.

By the 1980s the Korean national flag, or *taegu ki* (tay-guu kee), had become recognized around the world. The *taegu ki* depicts the yin and yang forces of the cosmos and the elements that are in constant movement within the sphere of infinity. The yin-yang figure in the flag represents balance and harmony. The four trigrams in the flag represent the elements originally believed to make up the universe: heaven, earth, fire, and water. The flag is a powerful metaphysical symbol to Koreans.

Historian Donald Stone Macdonald notes in his book *The Koreans—Contemporary Politics and Society* that since the invasion in 109 B.C. by Emperor Wu-Ti of China, the Korean peninsula has been invaded approximately nine hundred times. One of the few things now shared equally by all Koreans, North and South, is a powerful resolve never again to be invaded by outside forces.

Visitors wanting to have a brief organized glimpse of the lifestyle of Old Korea may do so at Folk Village near Suwon, 41 kilometers (26 miles) south of Seoul. The village, built in 1973, is an authentic duplication of the culture of the early Choson period in Korean history (1392–1910). Among the buildings are the home of a *yangban* (aristocrat official), a number of other homes, a farmhouse, and several craft shops. The village is staffed by people going about their work and social life as it existed for hundreds of years. There are regularly scheduled events in the village square, ranging from weddings and funeral processions to kite flying, tightrope walking, and dancing.

Koreans celebrate Foundation Day, or *Kae Chon Jol* (Kay Chohn Johl), literally "Sky Opening Day," on October 3. On this day, the historical museum within the grounds of the Kyongbok Palace in downtown Seoul is open to the public.

60

한글 한자
Hangul/Hantcha
(Hahn-guul/Hahn-jah)

"Korea's Writing Systems"

In 109 B.C., when China invaded the small kingdoms on the Korean peninsula and established suzerainty over them, the Koreans had no writing system. But well before the end of the following four hundred years of Chinese domination, scholars in the Korean kingdom of Shilla had created a makeshift system, called *Idu* (Ee-duu), of writing their own language using *Hantcha* (Hahn-jah), or "Chinese ideograms." (*Hantcha* is also sometimes written in roman letters as *Hanja*.)

Although Korean words were written with Chinese characters, they were pronounced in Korean as long as that word originally existed in Korean. Whenever possible, the Chinese ideograms were selected to match the meanings of the Korean words they represented. In many cases, however, there was no relationship between the meaning of the ideograms and the Korean words.

Korean scholars resolved part of this disparity by using many Chinese ideograms as phonetic symbols, simply ignoring their original meanings. This hybrid writing system did not please all Korean scholars, but they had no choice since learning how to read the ideograms was the only route to scholarship. For nearly two thousand years the Chinese ideograms remained Korea's official writing system, requiring years of study to learn the thirty thousand or so complicated characters necessary to become literate.

Generally only male members of the elite *yangban* class were allowed to learn how to read and write. (The only official exception to this was the small, select group of young women chosen to be professional entertainers and extramarital companions for men in the ruling class. See *Kisaeng*.) All government records and communications, as well as all literary works produced during this long period, were written in Chinese characters, meaning that the vast majority of Koreans were illiterate.

In 1443, the reigning king of the Choson (Yi) dynasty, King Sejong, himself a scholar of high repute, put together a team of scholars in a large hall called *Chip Hyonjon* (Cheep H'yohn-joan), variously translated as "Hall of Worthies" and "Hall of Talented Scholars," on the grounds of his palace and charged them with creating a simplified, purely Korean writing system. The goal was to make it easier for Koreans to become literate so literature would be accessible to more than just the well-to-do.

After laboring for three years—apparently with King Sejong often participating in the process—the king's scholars presented him with the results of their work, which later became known as *Hangul* (Hahn-guul), literally "Korean writing" or "Korean script." The king was overjoyed and enthused that thereafter anyone could learn how to read and write in a matter of days or weeks at most. Soon after the writing system was completed, King Sejong established a publishing agency to produce and distribute *Hangul* translations of Buddhist texts. Agricultural manuals and military manuals were also published in *Hangul*, the latter to help keep them confidential from foreigners.

Use of *Hangul* spread quickly among women in the upper class, including the royal family, upper-class women attached to the palace as ladies-in-waiting, and the wives and daughters of senior officials who used it for writing letters, poetry, and diaries. One of the first books King Sejong ordered printed in the new script was *Yongbi Ochon Ka* (Yong-bee Oh-choan Kah), or "Songs of the Flying Dragons," which praised his ancestors.

The government officially designated the new script as *Hangul* much later. At first it was called *Hunmin Chongum* (Hune-meen Chohng-umm), "Proper Sounds for Instructing the People." Also translated by some authorities as "Script for the People," it consisted of twenty-eight characters, or "letters," used to construct syllables made up of ten vowels, fourteen consonants, and eleven "vowel blends."

The best way of understanding what is meant by a "character" in this sense is to visualize each of the characters in the Korean "alphabet" as representing one of the familiar ABCs or a combination of these letters, as in *ch*, *kg*, and *ya*. In other words there is a Korean character for *a, b, ch, ya, yo, yu*, etc.

Just as in English, it usually takes two or more *Hangul* characters (letters) to form syllables and one or more syllables to form words. When the *Hangul* characters are assembled into a syllable, they look quite a bit like simplified Chinese ideograms, which was obviously the purpose of their creators. The big difference between Korean characters and Chinese characters is that the Korean characters by themselves have no meaning. They are merely phonetic symbols like the English alphabet, whereas Chinese characters are literally pictures of concepts and things—highly stylized but still drawings of things.

Not surprisingly, a majority of Korea's educated upper-class men, particularly its professional scholars, greatly resented the creation of *Hangul*, which anyone could easily learn, and some of them predicted that it would bring the wrath of China down on Korea because allowing common people to become literate would lower the exalted Chinese system to the level of barbarian scripts. They were able to keep *Hanja* as Korea's official writing system until the 1890s, some 450 years later, though many common people used *Hangul*.

The first real inroads on the monopoly that Korea's scholars had on knowledge were not made until the 1880s, when Western missionaries began arriving in Korea in large numbers and chose to translate their Bibles and religious tracts into *Hangul* instead of Chinese characters to reach the common people. A number of these missionaries created their own phonetic system of writing the Korean language in roman letters, resulting in all kinds of confusion in spelling. The Korean government also devised its own system.

These spelling difficulties arose from the fact that the pronunciation of many Korean syllables and words is very subtle and subject to different interpretations by different people. In addition, a number of roman letters are used interchangeably—*ch* and *j*, *b* and *p*, *d* and *t*, *s* and *sh*. It was not until 1939 that two Americans, George M. McCune and Edwin O. Reischauer, both scholars with long family missionary experience in Korea and Japan, devised a system that has since become the standard method for romanizing Korean.

One of the most distinctive features of the McCune-Reischauer romanization system is its use of apostrophes to indicate aspirated consonants and to differentiate between *n* and *ng*—as in *Han'gul* (Korean writing). Actually, *Han'gul* is two words: *Han* (Korea) and *gul* (writing), and it seems to me that simply separating them as they are in English would be a much better solution.

Still today there are numerous variations in the spelling of family names (that are the same in Korean), as well as in the spellings of towns, cities, and so on. Two conspicuous examples: Yi, Lee, and Rhee are all the same family name; Pak and Park are also the same in Korean.

The romanization of Korean follows a pattern that will be familiar to those who have had experience with the Japanese system. Consonants are pronounced very much as in English. Vowels are pronounced much as in Spanish: *a* = *ah*, *i* = *ee*, *u* = *uu*, *e* = *eh*, and *o* = *oh*. Grasping the essentials of Korean pronunciation is fairly easy (certainly it is much easier than tonal Chinese), but it does require some study and practice.

Two decades after Japan annexed Korea in 1910 the Japanese government mandated that all Koreans learn to read, write, and speak the Japanese language, and that eventually the Korean language no longer be used. Fortunately, the Japanese regime in Korea ended in 1945 with Japan's defeat in World War II, and both the Korean language and *Hangul* survived.

In 1959 the Korean Ministry of Education came up with yet another system for romanizing Korean, but it created so much confusion that it was revised in 1984 and is now practically the same as the McCune-Reischauer system. (Another idiosyncrasy brought on by the romanization of Korean is the use of numerous pleonasms, particularly in the names of islands, mountains, rivers, and monasteries. For example, the *do* in *Cheju Do*, usually written as *Chejudo*, means "island," but it is invariably rendered in roman letters as *Chejudo Island*—which is "Cheju Island Island.")

In 1970, some hundred years after the American missionaries had chosen *Hangul* over *Hanja* to bring their message of Christianity to the Koreans, the government of the Republic of South Korea finally took the dramatic step of inaugurating a "use *Hangul* only" campaign. In a move motivated by nationalism and "modernization," President Chung Hee Park ordered that all Chinese *Hanja* be eliminated from elementary and high school textbooks.

But Park's well-intentioned campaign caused so much confusion and met with so much resistance that in 1975 the government agreed to allow *Hanja* to be placed in parentheses after Korean words in high school textbooks (but not elementary-level books). This new approach called for all students to learn eighteen hundred *Hanja* characters over a six-year period. But the ideograms were taught in class only once a week and were only a small portion of the examination credits. The overall result was that very few Korean students became fluent in reading and writing the ideograms.

In the early 1980s, In Sung Kwak, headmaster of Shinsa Elementary School in western Seoul, chose to publicly defy the ban and began teaching his pupils the imported Chinese characters. He claimed that besides being able to read Korean publications using a combination of *Hangul* and *Hanja*, his students had shown remarkable improvement in their overall academic standing. To prevent their students from being seriously disadvantaged, other elementary schools unofficially resumed teaching the Chinese characters as a basic part of their curriculum.

Most older people in Korea opposed President Park's *Hangul*-only edict because virtually all of the country's collection of ancient books were written exclusively in *Hanja* or, after 1446, in a combination of *Hangul* and *Hanja*. Their point was that young people who could not read the Chinese characters would be cut off from most of their cultural heritage. In addition to the writing itself, approximately 70 percent of the Korean language is made up of words that originated in China. But these words have become so completely fused into Korean and the Korean culture that Koreans generally use them without being conscious of their origin.

By the end of the 1980s, changing political and economic factors had dramatically altered the context of the advocacy for the reintroduction of *Hanja* into Korea's education system from one based on maintaining links with its past to taking advantage of the fact that *Hanja* was the writing system for nearly one-fourth of the world's population. The Korean business community as well as educators and a growing number of government officials pointed out that not only the Chinese and Japanese used *Hanja* but also the overseas Chinese who dominate business in Indonesia, Malaysia, the Philippines, and Singapore.

Dae Kun Lee, professor of economics at Sung Kyun Kwan University, stated the case succinctly: "We have every reason to learn Chinese characters in pursuit of an economic alliance among Asian nations." Headmaster Kwak added: "To prepare our students for an increasingly competitive global society *Hanja* should be given the same weight as computers and English."

North Korea's paramount leader Il Sung Kim was the first to prohibit the teaching of Chinese characters, a step he took shortly after he gained power in 1945. He was also the first to reverse the policy—in 1964—as a result of increasing trade with China, Japan, and Southeast Asia.

When the Communists took power in China in 1948, they began a program to reduce the number of characters in regular use from around 5,000 to 2,238 and to simplify the way they were written. This caused communication problems not only in China but also in other countries that continued using the traditional way of writing the ideograms and using larger numbers of them. Some Chinese publications eventually ended up publishing two editions—one using the reduced number of simplified characters and the other using the old style.

In 1990, linguists from China, Japan, and Korea began holding regular meetings to discuss ways of integrating the writing styles as well as the meanings of the *Hanja* used in the three countries to facilitate communication. As predicted, the common usage of Chinese characters throughout East and Southeast Asia now plays a significant role in political, economic, cultural, and social relationships between Korea and its Asian neighbors.* Now virtually all Korean students are required to study the basic eighteen hundred *Hanja* characters, and many go on to study the Chinese and Japanese languages.

61

Han-Jong Shik
(Hahn-Joong Sheek)

"A Korean Meal"

One of my earliest and strongest memories of Korea is the sight of men and women, often in their fifties and sixties if not older, carrying loads on their backs—a custom known as *optta* (ohp-tah)—that would daunt people half their age and twice their size. The feats of physical strength routinely exhibited by

---

*Koreans, like the Chinese and Japanese, do not normally insert spaces between written words and combine many phrases as if they were single words. The martial art *tae kwon do* ("the way of the feet and hands") is written as *taekwondo*. This makes learning, reading, and understanding Korean more difficult than it should be.

Texts written in Korean also do not include conspicuous spaces between words, as English does, further complicating the learning and reading process for those studying Korean. Another factor that hinders communication between Koreans and foreigners is that Koreans are not required to study the McCune-Reischauer romanizing system, which is favored by English-speaking foreigners, as part of their formal education, and when they have occasion to write their names or other words in roman letters they often use some other system or make up one of their own.

these people were simply astounding. My unscientific explanation for the unusual strength of these men and women was the food they ate. Unlike traditional Japanese food, which emphasizes the natural taste of individual ingredients and is therefore relatively bland, most Korean food is highly spiced with red pepper, garlic, and scallions. Soy sauce and sesame oil are also used regularly in Korean cooking.

In any event a *han-jong shik* (hahn-joong sheek), or "full-course Korean meal," is a culinary experience of the first order. Basically a *han-jong shik* consists of servings of rice, soup, barbecued beef, steamed short ribs, grilled fish, *kimchi* (pickled cabbage), and up to eight other side dishes. It is customary in Korea for all of the main dishes making up a meal to be served at once. Usually the only exception is fresh fruit, served after the meal as dessert.

While Korean cuisine is not nearly as extensive, as elaborate, or as imbued with metaphysical properties as Chinese cuisine (I have been in some Chinese restaurants that had more than four hundred dishes on their menus and have been prompted endlessly on the importance of eating food in a certain order), food nevertheless occupies a similar position in Korean culture, not only from the nutritional aspect but also in the social role it plays in Korean life.

In Korea as in China and elsewhere eating together has traditionally been an important part of the bonding process, with the difference in pre-modern Korea being that men did not bond with women because the sexes were socially segregated. Until the middle decades of the twentieth century it was customary for males in Korean families to be served separately from the females, either in separate areas of the home or with the menfolk eating first.

Special foods also played key roles in shamanistic ceremonies and the rituals of ancestor worship that were at the core of family religious practices until well up into the twentieth century. The abolition of the feudal family system after Korea regained its sovereignty in the 1940s officially ended the segregation of the sexes at meals. Sanctified foods continue to play a leading role in shamanistic rituals, but in most urban families ancestor worship has been relegated to the status of an annual event.

Since the end of the feudal family system in the 1950s males and females have been eating together in private as well as in public, and meals, particularly large, formal banquets, are an integral part of the process of nurturing friendships and business relationships, and honoring guests. In fact, a great deal of the wealth of Korea is spent each year on *yonhoe* (yoan-hoe-eh), or "banquets," to the extent that there are frequent calls for the government to prohibit such expenditures.

Traditionally Koreans did not distinguish among breakfast, lunch, and dinner foods. Each meal consisted of one or more main courses and four, five, or more *pan chan* (pahn chahn), or "side dishes." Like most hosts everywhere, Koreans make a point of encouraging their guests to eat heartily.

Generally speaking, there are two types of table settings in Korea: daily dining and ceremonial dining—the latter referring to such things as weddings, the hundredth-day celebration for babies, memorial services for ancestors, and banquets for VIPs. Regardless of what Korean dishes are served at a meal, or the occasion for the meal, the *sang-cha rim* (sahng-chah reem), or table-setting etiquette, remains the same and is observed strictly.

Steamed ribs or strips of beef on a chafing dish are placed in the center of the table. Other dishes of broiled fish, raw fish, greens, and so on are placed around the large chafing dish in an order that is pleasing to the eye. Soup and steamed rice or noodles are placed in front of each diner. Hot dishes and meat dishes are placed to the right of the diner. Cold dishes and vegetable dishes are placed to the left of the diner. *Kimchi*, which is made of cabbage, is placed to the right of diners, apparently in recognition that it is spicy hot.

The custom in Korea is to eat soup and rice with a spoon and use *chotkkarak* (choat-kah-rahk), "chopsticks," for eating other dishes. Unlike in Japan and China, Koreans consider it bad manners to pick your rice bowl up and hold it in your hand while eating the rice—although this old taboo is now ignored by many in the younger generations.

Unlike Chinese meals, at which loud conversation and laughter have traditionally been an important part of the ritual of eating, until recent times Koreans tended to be much more reserved and quieter. Sipping soups and slurping noodles was common, however. While some people say making such noises is a sign that one is enjoying the food, the original reason was probably to cool the food, since it has long been customary to eat soup and noodles while they are hot.

Korea's traditional eating etiquette remains a lesson in the country's unique culture, however. If there are elders present, proper etiquette calls for all diners in the group to wait until the elders have picked up their soup or rice spoons. In earlier times younger people could not leave the table until their elders had finished eating, and talking was considered bad manners. Both of these customs have long since gone by the wayside, and Korean meals are now lively affairs.

In early April, usually the fifth or the sixth, many Koreans observe a grave-tending day known as *Han Shik* (Hahn Sheek), which literally means "Cold Food." Originally associated with ancestor worship when people were required to perform rituals in memory of their deceased ancestors, the custom now has more of the spirit of a picnic at which people generally eat cold food after cleaning family graves.

Korean dishes that are typically the most popular among foreigners include *pulgogi* (puhl-go-ghee), or marinated beef; *kalbi* (kahl-bee), or broiled ribs; *kimbap* (keem-bahp), rice and vegetables rolled in seaweed; *naeng myon* (nang m'yohn), cold noodles in soup; and *pibimbap* (pee-beem-bahp), a vegetable-rice dish. Western food in Korean is *Yang Shik* (Yahng Sheek).

In addition to an amazing proliferation of full-scale restaurants and other places that serve food items, Korea is noted for its *pojang macha* (poh-jahng mah-chah), or "tent stall street restaurants," that spring up in the early evening along sidewalks, in parking lots, and in other open areas. Larger collections of *pojang macha* have a carnival atmosphere that attracts large nightly crowds, making them ideal places for getting a taste of the culture of contemporary Korea. While some visitors shy away from eating at the "tent stalls" for sanitary reasons, they should know that Koreans are fanatical about cleanliness, and the foods are well cooked. For many, however, actually eating at *pojang macha* is secondary to whiling away an evening at the outdoor stalls sipping beer or rice wine and engaging in animated conversations with friends. In any event, strolling these outdoor nighttime food "malls" is a rewarding social experience that is highly recommended.

Other things to keep in mind when in Korea: people invited out for a meal sometimes bring an unannounced friend, a custom that is perfectly acceptable; ordinary restaurants generally do not have individual menus for their patrons—they post them on the walls on large signboards; when there is no defined host in a restaurant outing involving two or more men of different ages, a younger member of the group will often pay the bill as a way of catering to and showing respect for the older men; rice is *ssal* (ssahl) when uncooked and *pap* (pahp) or *chinji* (cheen-jee), which is more honorific, when cooked.

Don Hackney, a veteran expatriate American businessman stationed in Seoul and an avid student of Korean culture, notes that originally *Han Shik* was one of the twenty-four seasonal divisions based on the ancient Korean agricultural calendar. "Koreans used the calendar to mark the seasons for planting, watering, harvesting, etc.," he said. Hackney added that the Korean "thanksgiving," *Chusok* (chuu-soak), was another one of these seasonal divisions and is called *cholgi* (chohl-ghee).

62

한국말

Hankuk Mal
(Hahn-kuuk Mahl)

"The Korean Language"

The origins of the native Korean language or *Hankuk mal* (Hahn-kuuk mahl) are lost in the mists of time. But it is classified as an Altaic language because it is believed to have originated in the Altaic region of what is now Russian territory. It is also said to be related distantly to Finnish, Japanese, and Turkish, which are identified with the same region. The relationship between Korean and Japanese is quickly obvious. Their grammatical structure is exactly the same—subject, object, verb—and many Korean and Japanese words vary only slightly in pronunciation.

There is no direct linguistic relationship between Chinese and *Hankuk mal*, but in fact the language is more "Chinese" than Korean. Some 70 percent of the entire Korean vocabulary is Chinese in origin. (This does not mean, however, that Chinese can understand 70 percent of the spoken language of Korea. The pronunciation of the Chinese terms has been Koreanized, and they may or may not sound like Chinese.)

Korea's massive importation of vocabulary from China occurred because the civilization of China was already highly advanced when the first Korean kingdoms appeared. Korean culture was primitive, and the language had a limited vocabulary. Thousands of new words came with the new products and ideas that flowed into the country from China.

Another key reason why Koreans adopted so many Chinese words was that they did not have a way of writing their language and adopted the Chinese system. Many of the Chinese words came with the ideograms used to write them. Among other things, such abstract words as *truth, evil, goodness,* and *courage* did not originally exist in the Korean language. The words now used to denote these meanings were adopted from the Chinese language. The concept of *if* is also of Chinese origin.

Koreans also adopted the Chinese system of counting because the original Korean system only goes up to ninety-nine. As time went by, it became customary to use the old Korean system of numbers to count minutes, hours, days, and distance up to 99 kilometers, while the Chinese system was used for counting money. Native numerals were used to express the hour, while Chinese numerals were used to express minutes. Now the Korean system is used for counting things and the Chinese system for counting money as well as things.

As in all cultures, the Korean pattern of thinking and the national character of Koreans are related directly to the nature of the language. In Korean there is generally no distinction between the singular and plural. Until recent times, the word *I* was uncommon in Korean speech, and it is still much less used than in most other societies. *I* and *we* are often used interchangeably, and there is no relative pronoun in the language.

This phenomenon is explained by Korean ethnologists Chang Don Yu and Il Chol Shin as resulting from the traditional custom of Koreans to think in terms of the family, the kinship group, or factional groups rather than individuals. The social scientists add that this custom is one of the ways that Koreans have traditionally used to distance themselves from personal responsibility, diffuse it among whatever group is concerned, or simply broadcast it into empty space.

More often than not, the sociologists continue, people take advantage of this custom to escape responsibility rather than to unselfishly put the interests of their family or faction above their own—a practice that they refer to as escaping into a "collective identity."

Subtlety in personal relationships in Korea resulted in the creation and use of several words that mean "you." There is a *you* that is used between equals (*nuh*), to inferiors (*ja-ne*), to superiors (*dang-shin*), and so on. But the word *you* is usually left out of Korean speech, because it is understood. Titles are also commonly used in place of *you*, especially when people do not know the names of those being addressed. People who are senior in age and status or who have some special skill are frequently addressed as *sonsaengnim* (son-sang-neen), or "teacher." It is also common for older men who appear to have some status to be addressed as *sajang* (sah-jahng), or "president," which means "company president." Older men with no particular standing are usually addressed as *ajossi* (ah-joh-shee), or "uncle," older women as *ajumoni* (ah-juu-moh-nee), or "aunt," and young females as *akassi* (ah-kah-sshe), or "young lady."

Use of the right *you* as well as many other courtesy and honor words remains a vital part of Korean etiquette. If the correct term is not used, determined by the relative social status of the individuals as well as the content and purpose of the dialogue, the flub can result in serious offense with all kinds of unpleasant repercussions.

Korean language experts Yu and Shin say that *Hankuk mal* is designed to reveal and maintain the social status of speakers. In any conversation, who is the superior and who is the inferior quickly become obvious. They add that because Koreans have become so sensitized to language it is extremely important for people to use humble and modest expressions to avoid offending each other. They add that Koreans are "slaves" to the demands of language etiquette.

Shin says that it is difficult to speak logically in Korean because the language is designed to be vague and lacks sufficient abstract terms. He adds that a great deal of the communication between Koreans is based on intuition and "hunch," combined with physical cues, rather than precise verbalization. (See *Nunchi*.)

Shin and Yu suggest that until modern times the nature and use of the Korean language acted as a specific barrier to scientific thought and investigation. Shin further notes that pure *Hankuk mal* does not lend itself to logical thought because there are no relative pronouns in the language, the predicate is usually missing, the distinction between singular and plural is vague, and sentences often have no subject. Shin adds that these linguistic "weaknesses" are the reason why logical and philosophical reasoning did not develop to any significant degree in Korea despite its long history. (The many Korean scholars who became famed as philosophers transcribed their thoughts in Chinese.)

Tae Rim Yun, in his book *The Koreans: Their Thought Patterns*, agrees that inadequacies in the Korean language are one of the primary reasons why Koreans are prone to rely more on intuition and what he calls "approximation by hunch" than on systematic reasoning to make their points. Still today social positions in Korea are so finely graded and people are so sensitive about them that using the wrong vocabulary can be a serious transgression—and is one of the reasons it is difficult for foreigners to learn the Korean language well enough as adults to always be culturally correct.

Korean speech continues to be characterized by the use of many honorific expressions that denote class and hierarchical differences, some designed to humble the speaker and others aimed at exalting the hearer. One of the unique characteristics of Korean is that it has two honorific suffixes—*shi* and *supnida*—that are attached to words in keeping with the linguistic etiquette system. *Shi* honors the subject of the sentence; *supnida* indicates the speaker's respect for the hearer.

Another idiosyncrasy that makes Korean unusually difficult for foreigners to learn is that the pronunciation of some words is based on their context. One commonly used example, the word *kaps*, which means "price," may also be pronounced as *kap* or *kam*, although it is "spelled" the same in *Hangul* (Hahn-guul), the native Korean writing system. Fortunately, Koreans do not automatically expect foreigners to use the Korean language "correctly" and are tolerant of their misuse of honorifics and the like.

There are presently six recognized Korean dialects, usually designated as Central, Northwest, Northeast, Southeast, Southwest, and Cheju Island. The five mainland dialects are similar enough that everyone who speaks them can understand each other.

When Japan forcibly colonized Korea in 1910, one of the aims of the Japanese government was to incorporate Korea into the Japanese empire culturally as well as politically and economically. The Japanese understood the importance of language in the survival and success of a people and in the 1930s began a program to eliminate the Korean language and force all Koreans to learn and speak Japanese.

In 1936, after the Japanese government had begun its program to eliminate the Korean language, a small group of Korean scholars designated the Seoul dialect as the standard language of Korea as part of their efforts to preserve the language. The Japanese retaliated by quickly arresting and imprisoning all of the leading linguists in the country.

In 1943, when the "Great Asian War" (as Japanese historians often call World War II) began going against Japan, Japan's colonial administrator in Korea ordered that only the Japanese language be used for official purposes in Korea. To help enforce this new decree, the Japanese government charged a Korean branch of its notorious *Kempei Tai* (Kem-pay-e Tie), or "Thought Police," which had its own private strike force, with seeking out and eliminating all Koreans who resisted its attempts to Japanize Koreans.

Japan's defeat by the United States and its allies in 1945 ended the Japanese occupation of Korea and their efforts to eliminate the Korean language. Since that time Korea's emergence as a world-class economic power and a leading member of the international community has resulted in the teaching of the Korean language in many universities and business schools around the world.

Because there are several levels of the Korean language, created by different vocabulary and word endings that are used to reflect the social status of the speakers, it is especially difficult for foreigners to become "culturally fluent" in the language. Learning to speak Korean correctly goes well beyond vocabulary and grammar. It must also include intimate knowledge of what words and what word endings are appropriate for each social setting—or, as Paul Shields Crane says in his insightful book *Korean Patterns*, you must know the rules of social intercourse.

While Koreans are very tolerant, and appreciative, of attempts by foreigners to learn and speak Korean, the safest approach for new students of the language is to use only the polite form until they have also mastered the very precise and very sensitive social etiquette that is normally communicated through the language.

There is a special term, *mal porus(i) opta* (mahl poh-ruus-(*i*) ohp-tah), meaning "crude language," which is commonly used in reference to language that does not meet the courtesy standards in Korean society and to people who use such language. Marketing consultant and old Korean hand Don Hackney adds: "Another important term in the Korean vocabulary is *chondae mal* (chohn-day mahl), which means 'polite speech' or 'honorific speech,' and refers to the especially polite or honorific speech that is used to elders and seniors."

한약
Han Yak
(Hahn Yahk)

"The Herbal Way to Health"

Like all ancient peoples, Koreans have a long history of treating physical and mental ailments with herbal medicines—a tradition that probably evolved along with humanity (it being well known that many animals seek out certain plants and roots to eat when they are sick). In any event, the shamans of ancient Korea were doctors of both the body and the mind and made use of a wide variety of herbs in their rituals and treatments. Until the sixth century A.D., the practice of herbal medicine in Korea had changed very little for uncounted generations. In 561 Chinese visitors to the court of Koguryo presented the king with a number of treatises on herbal medicine, some of them dating back to 3000 B.C.

This new knowledge gradually spread to the other kingdoms on the Korean peninsula, merging with the traditional shamanist practices and coming to be known simply as *Han yak* (Hahn yahk), or "Korean medicine." *Yak* by itself means "natural medicine." Up to that time one of the most important herbs in the shamans' medical kits had been the root of the ginseng plant (*insam*). In fact ginseng had been one of the most important tribute products shipped to China each year for half a millennium. In both countries ginseng was used to make potions for a wide variety of illnesses, from general weakness and fatigue to nervous disorders.

The second most prized herb in the shaman's bag was a mushroom called *yongji posot* (yohng-jee poh-sot), which translates as "spiritual mushroom." Other herbs included anise, cinnamon, chrysanthemum petals, ginger, and dried fruit skins. Powdered deer antlers and other animal products were also used.

During the Koryo dynasty (918–1392) and especially during the first centuries of the following Choson or Yi dynasty (1392–1910), *Han yak* flourished in an age of extraordinary scholarship. In the latter period, a whole publishing industry grew up around *Han yak*, reaching its zenith in 1610 with the publication of a twenty-five-volume medical encyclopedia called *Tong I Po Gam* (Tohng Ee Poh Gahm), or "Treasures of Eastern Medicine."

This compendium, written by court physician Jun Ho over a period of sixteen years, is still in print today and is used by herbalists throughout Asia. Koreans of that time had a holistic approach to health that just began to gain credibility in the United States and other Western countries in the last half of the twentieth century. Hundreds of years ago many well-to-do Korean families retained doctors to visit them regularly and advise them on diets and other habits that would keep them healthy, with the aim being to prevent illnesses in the first place.

When a Korean became ill despite the advice of the family doctor, payment to the doctor ceased and he was held responsible for curing the illness without further charges. If the patient died, the doctor was discharged as incompetent.

Both shamanism and herbal medicine have survived into modern times, the latter successfully competing with Western medicine and, in fact, growing in popularity among some because its effect on the body is presumed to be more natural. And, in keeping with old traditions, Korean medicine still emphasizes prevention, particularly from the yin-yang viewpoint of living a balanced and harmonious life. Koreans are especially sensitive about the effects of diet on health, and visitors who are hosted by Korean friends are invariably advised on which dishes are noted for their health-giving properties.

There is a historical anecdote about medical care in Korea that starkly reveals the nature of the sex segregation policy enforced by the government during the Choson dynasty (1392–1910). During this long period, when men and women lived in separate worlds and it was literally taboo for a man to touch a woman not his wife or lover and for a woman to touch a man not her husband, the medical practice took on some facets that were beyond all common sense. Because a male doctor could not physically touch a female patient—a taboo that was especially strong in the royal family and elite ruling class—physicians could take the pulse of upper-class female patients only by touching the end of a silk thread that had been wrapped around the wrist of the patient by a female servant or assistant. In some cases involving members of the royal family doctors had to conduct their entire examination of patients from behind a screen or outside the room, with the silk thread extended through a crack in the door.

The problem created by this sexual segregation was partially resolved by the Choson court's ordering that some of the young girls being trained to become *kisaeng* (kee-sang) or female entertainers also be trained in medicine so that when female members of the court became ill they could be treated by women. (This caused another problem because male members of the court and aristocracy were invariably attracted to the "physician *kisaeng*" because they were originally chosen for their beauty and then trained in singing, dancing, writing poetry, and conversing—educational skills denied to all other women.)

Kongang (kohn-gahng), or "health," remains a major concern of Koreans and is constantly on their minds and in their speech. Western doctors have noted that there are some unusual differences in the health of older Koreans and their Western counterparts. Apparently because of their diet and lifestyle, Koreans are significantly less likely to suffer from arteriosclerosis, senility, and varicose veins. But strokes and stomach cancer, particularly among men, are common.

64

힘

Him
(Heem)

"A Passion for Power"

Until the introduction of some democratic principles into Korea following the end of World War II in 1945, all political power in the country was traditionally in the hands of the government and bureaucratic administrators drawn from the elite *yangban* class. Common people had no voice in choosing their rulers or in influencing their behavior by any systematic, peaceful means.

Citizens who had been wronged or were seeking help of some kind were traditionally allowed to petition the authorities on a local level. But there were no guarantees that their petitions would be accepted, and if local officials were embarrassed or angered by the requests, petitioners were liable to be punished. Since local officials in pre-modern Korea had considerable personal leeway in their reaction to petitions, the system led to rampant corruption, with petitioners attempting to influence officials to make favorable judgments by presenting them with "bribes" in money and in kind.

Because all political power in Korea was reserved exclusively for government officials, and because virtually all government officials were able to use their power to make themselves and their families well-to-do, the dream of ordinary Koreans was to become an official and live the good life. At the same time, the Confucian family system relegated all social power to the senior male in the family, leaving wives totally subservient to their husbands and children subordinate to their fathers and grandfathers. Eldest sons inherited the power of their fathers.

In this political and social environment, the overwhelming majority of all Koreans remained virtually powerless all their lives. And because of this system, all Koreans became extremely sensitive to *him* (heem), or "power," and *kwollyok* (kwohll-yohk), or "authority." Authoritative power so impregnated Korean culture that it was the first and last thing that had to be considered in any social, economic, or political action.

Him, rather than knowledge, reason, ability, or hard work, thus became the holy grail to Koreans, because it was only thing that could improve their lifestyle and guarantee any degree of safety from those with power.

In present-day Korea *him* is still vitally important. But now almost anyone can achieve some degree of power through education and work. In fact Korean social scientists say the real reason Koreans are so determined to get the best possible education is their obsession with *him*. They know from their history that education can be translated into power.

The ability to earn money by working and by engaging in business has also emancipated most Koreans to a considerable degree, giving them the power to make choices of their own and have some say over their lives for the first time in the history of the country. The power provided by money is another of the reasons present-day Koreans work so hard and with such diligence. (It also accounts for the fact that many Koreans list *don*/dohn, or "money," among the most important words in the Korean vocabulary.)

Business management in Korea is generally based on the exercise of executive power, despite the importance historically relegated to consensus building. Most consensus building in Korea is, in fact, a facade—role playing that those in power allow to take place to give the impression of mutual agreement. Koreans at all levels of government and business are virtually obsessed with the exercise of the power they have. They may share it symbolically, but when it comes down to the final word they prefer to be the voice of God.

This Korean reaction to *him* is not likely to change very much in the foreseeable future. Korean culture has been a "power culture" for some four thousand years, particularly since the adoption of Neo-Confucianism as the state ideology by the Choson dynasty in 1392. The whole fabric of the culture will have to change, gradually over generations, before it can become a genuine consensus culture.

65

회사

Hoesa

(Hoh-eh-sah)

"The Korean Company"

The Korean word for company or firm, *hoesa* (hoh-eh-sah), literally means "social organization," and any understanding of the role that Korean companies play in society in general and in the lives of their employees in particular must begin with this meaning. In broad terms smaller Korean companies operate very much like close-knit individual families; larger companies operate more like military organizations.

Hoesa are hierarchical in structure and generally paternalistic in function. Larger companies are "societies" within themselves, and each tries to be as self-sufficient as possible. All of Korea's great industrial conglomerates, called *chaebol* (chay-buhl) in Korean, were founded by individuals who patterned them after the traditional Korean family, with all of its Confucian trappings, from emphasis on obedience and loyalty to the importance of family, school, and regional ties.

Korean employees are not just outsiders who come in and work and then leave. They are members of the company family at all times, and the larger and more important the company, the more obligations they have as "family." What they do outside the company reflects directly on the image of the company and their standing in the company. Where larger companies are concerned, company orientation has become as important as, and sometimes more important than, the traditional family orientation—a factor that is gradually replacing family-centered morality with corporate-centered morality.

Practically all large Korean corporations attempt to express their social philosophy and morality in their *sahun* (sah-hoon), which is generally translated as "company instructions" but is more in the nature of a motto or statement of the company's values and goals. Among the elements generally found in *sahun* are expressions of *chango* (chahng-goh), which is a combination of entrepreneurial spirit and creativity, and *inhwa* (inn-whah), or "harmony." Other common *sahun* elements are unity, sincerity, diligence, and credibility.

Sahun are printed, framed, and hung in offices, hallways, and meeting rooms. They are included in annual reports, on company brochures and manuals. The motto of Poongsan Corporation, Korea's largest manufacturer of copper and copper-related products, is *Changui, Silchon, Hwakin* (Chahng-we, Seel-chohn, Hwah-keen), which means "Creativity, Performance and Execution, Verification and Confirmation."

Another aspect of the personalized familylike environment of Korean companies, particularly larger firms, is the traditional practice of the *chohoe* (choh-hoh-eh), or "morning meeting," which is staged ritualistically just before the workday begins. In some companies the *chohoe* is little more than formal greetings at which the staff stands and bows to the manager, who may or may not make some pronouncement. In other companies "morning meetings" may last for several minutes, with announcements or comments by a number of people. In some companies the national anthem is played over the PA system as part of each morning's ceremony.

Virtually all Korean companies have *jimmu kyuchik* (jeem-muu k'yuu-cheek), or written "company rules." In larger firms these rules are detailed and comprehensive, and all new employees are required to sign them. It is especially important for foreign companies in Korea to have *jimmu kyuchik* to avoid the kind of problems that often arise in joint venture and cross-cultural situations. It is also vital that foreign firms get competent help from labor and legal consultants in preparing their *jimmu kyuchik*.

There are a number of key words involved with hiring practices in Korea. *Junggi chaeyong* (juung-ghee chay-yohng) means "periodic hiring" and refers to the traditional custom for Korean companies to hire high school and university graduates in groups when the school year ends each spring. *Kioe chaeyong* (kee-way chay-yohng) means "hiring out of season" and refers to hiring new employees at times other than the annual spring hiring period. Another interesting term that one might hear in connection with firing employees in Korea is *mogaji* (moe-gah-jee), which literally means to cut off one's head.

Mogaji may be the fate of an employee who becomes known as a *nat dung-jang* (naht duung-jahng), or "day lamp"—a derogatory term used in reference to employees—often managers and executives—who never seem to do anything and make no contribution to the company, like lights left on during the day.

When valued employees of a Korean company decide to quit and go with some other firm—something that began to occur fairly often in the 1980s—they are expected to write a formal letter of resignation called *sapyo* (sah-p'yoe) explaining their reasons for leaving. If they are key employees with special talents, their seniors in the companies usually mount intensive campaigns to convince them to change their minds, including talking to their wives.

Many midsized and larger Korean companies are "aligned" with one of the huge conglomerates (Daewoo, Samsung, LG Group, etc.), and are referred to as *keiyul hoesa* (kay-e-yuhl hoh-ch-sah), or "affiliated companies." Which conglomerate a particular company is affiliated with can have an important influence on its operation, from its ability to raise capital to the kind of distribution it has. It is therefore important for foreign companies looking for tie-ups in Korea to determine in advance if prospective partners are affiliated with one of the conglomerates and the nature of the affiliation.

One word that foreign managers newly arrived in Korea learn quickly is *ponosu* (poe-no-suu), which is the Korean pronunciation of "bonus." Companies in Korea are expected to pay *ponosu* twice a year—in midsummer and just before the end of the year. They are considered an integral part of employee income, not something special, even when the companies concerned are not operating profitably.

Despite ongoing parallels between Korean *hoesa* and the traditional Korean family and clan, relationships between workers and employers changed dramatically during the 1970s and 1980s as employees went to extremes in seeking better treatment, higher wages, and more security. They complained bitterly that since they were not really "family" and had no proprietary interest in the companies they worked for, it was patently unjust and unacceptable for employers to treat them like "children" who could be overworked and paid starvation wages because they were "family."

In addition to staging strikes and engaging in other disruptive activities that broke all the conventions of the traditional family, many employees began doing something that was unthinkable in the family concept—they began quitting the companies that hired them upon their graduation from high school or college and going with other firms that offered them better deals.

Despite the stigma that still attaches to people who change jobs of their own accord, the number is growing. People who frequently move from one company to another looking for more pay and better working conditions are sometimes referred to as *chamsae jok* (chahm-say johk), or "a flock of sparrows."

호 패

Hopae
(Hoh-pay)

"Identifying the People"

In 1413 the Choson court issued an edict requiring all Koreans to carry or wear *hopae* (hoh-pay), or "identification tags," at all times. The edict specified that ranking members of the elite *yangban* class would carry ID tags made of ivory. Middle-ranked *yangban* officials were ordered to wear tags made of deer horn. Lower-ranking officials were to identify themselves with tags made of yellow poplar wood. Commoners were required to wear small tags made of ordinary wood. Outcasts (slaves, people who worked with meat and hides, and people who had no fixed abode because their profession kept them on the road—peddlers, entertainers, sailors, etc.) had to wear large wooden tags.

The ID tags had to bear the name, birthdate, social class, and address of the wearer. The tags served several purposes. They immediately identified the social class of the wearer, making it possible for other people to react to them with the appropriate language and etiquette, which differed dramatically between the upper and lower classes. The ID system also played a major role in the collection of taxes, conscripting corvée labor, and rounding up recruits for military service—programs that applied to all except the upper class.

Since farmers and slaves were not permitted to change their occupation or their home of their own accord, the *hopae* made it much easier to keep track of them. In times of economic hardship the *hopae* system was a major deterrent to peasants abandoning the land they worked and escaping into the mountains or trying to move their residence.

In the fifteenth century, following a series of regional rebellions by dissident rural gentry and peasants, the *hopae* system was strengthened. Again in the seventeenth century the system, which had become lax over the decades, was reconfirmed and strengthened.

The *hopae* system was especially essential to the national corvée labor program that required all males between the age of sixteen and sixty to donate labor to government and civic projects. According to the corvée labor law in effect at that time, individuals could not be required to work more than six days a year at prescribed times, but in reality people were conscripted for such labor anytime they were needed and often for longer periods of time.

Individuals were permitted to pay someone else to take their place in fulfilling their corvée labor obligations, but the cost set by the government for such replacements was so high few peasants could afford to buy their way out.

In present-day Korea everyone over the age of eighteen is required to have and carry a "citizen's ID card" at all times—a regulation that was especially important during the early decades of the division of North and South Korea into separate political entities, when North Korea carried out a regular campaign of dispatching secret agents into South Korea.

67

화

Hwa
(Whah)

"Striving for Harmony"

The first historical references to Korea appear in Chinese records and literature dating back some four thousand years. These writings include comments about the decorum with which the Koreans went about their daily lives, attesting to the importance of *hwa* (whah)—also written *chohwa* (choh-whah)—or "harmony," in Korea's indigenous shamanistic culture.

From around 108 B.C., when the Korean peninsula came under the direct military and cultural hegemony of China, Korean leaders began adopting Confucianism as a new political and social structure for their own age-old shamanistic philosophy of harmony. In the Confucian system of government, *hwa* was achieved through the repression of individualism and the supremacy of collectivism or groupism. Society was divided vertically into inferiors and superiors, with very precise rules of etiquette for each social layer. The administration of family as well as government affairs, on all levels, was authoritarian. Absolute obedience was the only acceptable norm.

In this environment, the lower people were in the social stratum, the more limited their choices and the more detailed their obligations. Friction of any kind was forbidden. Public harmony reigned most of the time. One of the natural results of demanding absolute conformity to strict rules of behavior was that within each social layer people tended to think and behave alike. Any unprescribed behavior stood out like the proverbial sore thumb and brought quick retribution.

As the generations passed, this tightly controlled system produced a composite ideal image of men, women, and children for each of the two primary social classes—the *yangban* gentry and *chon min* (chohn meen) common people. This ideal became the defining model for all Koreans in their particular class. The lifestyles of each of these groups, from wearing apparel and work to housing, was determined by this common image. The whole of society functioned as groups, not as individuals. Primary responsibility for keeping harmony was on each family.

This system of communal living for generation after generation conditioned Koreans to living and working within specific groups (families, collectives, associations, etc.) to the point that it became second nature. People were literally programmed to think and act alike to avoid friction and confrontation.

Foreign scholars and writers have emphasized the presence and role of

Confucian-oriented harmony in traditional Korean society. But in reality this harmony existed only on the surface and was broken regularly by outbursts of disharmony that ranged from verbal battles to armed conflicts.

Despite its aura of public harmony, behind the scenes Korean society has always been very competitive on every level and in virtually every facet of life and work. Overt competition and violence were endemic in Korea from the late 1800s, when the Choson dynasty began breaking up, until the end of the 1980s. Violent street demonstrations staged by students, union members, and opposition political parties were regular occurrences from the late 1950s until the latter part of the 1980s.

The authoritarian rule that was essential for the maintenance of surface *hwa* in South Korea did not begin to end until well into the 1970s. The same forces that encouraged a more democratic government also motivated ordinary Koreans to demand and arbitrarily assume more rights of choice and behavior. Parental and governmental authority declined in tandem. Koreans began learning how to think and act like individuals. Not surprisingly, *hwa* was one of the first things to weaken in this new atmosphere.

However, present-day Koreans still pride themselves on the existence of *hwa* in their culture, attributing a great deal of their emergence as an economic powerhouse to its influence. Conditioning in group behavior and passive obedience to authority was historically such a large part of the lives of Koreans that a great deal of it lingers on in the average Korean mind-set. Only Big Brother has changed. Today much of the authoritarian power that was formerly wielded by Korea's fathers and government officials is exercised by corporate executives and managers.

Expatriate businesspeople in Korea need to be acutely aware of the relationship between harmony and authoritarianism in the workplace and how to use it in a positive manner. Probably the most important point for foreign businesspersons to keep in mind is that the more authoritarian their management in Korea, the more they are expected to treat their employees with paternalistic care.

In the past, foreign businesspeople in Korea who attempted to introduce democratic principles into their management generally failed because their employees did not know how to conduct themselves as equals and still maintain *hwa*. Inevitably the Korean employees ended up with their own Korean-style management infrastructure that was almost invisible to the foreign bosses.

There is a growing community of internationally educated and experienced Koreans who have learned how to work harmoniously in a democratic environment. But the natural environment of typical Koreans remains a hierarchical relationship in which their attitudes and behavior are determined by their place on the vertical ladder of sex, age, authority, and seniority.

68

환대

Hwandae

(Hwahn-day)

"Surviving Korean Hospitality"

One of the truly humane and enjoyable tenets of Korea's traditional culture is an emphasis on *hwandae* (hwahn-day), or "hospitality," in the form of food and drink. Koreans typically roll out the red carpet for friends and visitors alike—often to the point that it becomes embarrassing to those who are not familiar with such largesse.

The fundamental reason for the extraordinary *hwandae* of Koreans derives from the Confucian concept that materialism is immoral, that piling up material goods beyond one's own needs is sinful, that virtue is gained by sharing whatever one has with others—a philosophy that was also practiced by a number of Native American tribes who lived along the northwest coast in what is now Oregon, Washington, and Alaska.

Koreans did not go as far as these Native Americans (who would regularly hold parties at which they made sure that all of their extra goods were distributed among their guests), not so much because they didn't have the impulse to go that far but because the average Korean families of old had little if anything extra in their households. However, even the poorest Korean family felt deeply obligated to treat guests with special hospitality, even when it meant that they would later have to do without.

The tradition of *hwandae* remains strong in Korea, and the degree to which individuals and families go in extending hospitality has grown with their affluence—so much so that they are often accused of being *mumohan* (muu-moe-hahn), or "extravagant," a term that continues to have negative Buddhist and Confucianist overtones.

Korean hospitality extends into the workplace. When clients or guests visit offices, they are invariably served some kind of refreshment, usually without being asked. Some offices automatically serve coffee (often with cream and sugar already in it), while others maintain a supply of fruit juice or other soft drinks. (I have been offered beer before noon in some factory offices.)

Corporate hospitality is such an institutionalized custom in Korea that when Koreans visit the offices of foreign companies and are not served anything it is very conspicuous and reflects negatively on the character and cultural level of the management. Korean businesspeople invariably host dinner and drinking parties for visiting customers and suppliers, generally making a point of taking them to places that are well known for the quality of their food and entertainment. One veteran expatriate businessman in Seoul commented that it often seems as if Koreans prefer pleasure before business, instead of the other way around.

Another aspect of this inbred *hwandae* syndrome is that Koreans have been culturally conditioned to pay restaurant and bar bills even when they are not the host. When two or more Koreans are out for lunch or the evening, especially the latter when drinking is involved, they will fight over the bill. Part of this syndrome no doubt derives from the age-old Korean custom of genuine hospitality. Another part is a response to feelings of Korean pride and sense of face. One gains face by playing the role of the generous host.

By the same token, the Western concept of "going Dutch" is naturally alien to the traditional Korean way of thinking and behaving, and except among students it is still unusual.

Westerners visiting Korea for the first time should be wary of allowing their Korean friends or business counterparts to gain face at their expense unless they know for sure that they will have an opportunity to reciprocate. Koreans who insist on paying bills that are not rightfully theirs often attempt to get their way by saying that since the visitor is in their country it is their responsibility to act as the host and that the visitor's turn will come when they come to his or her country.

69

환갑 신갑

Hwangap/Jingap
(Hwahn-gahp/Jeen-gahp)

"Celebrating Sixty/Seventy Years"

Life in pre-modern Korea was hard—and short—for most people. Infant mortality was high, and fatal illnesses among children and adults were common. Reaching the age of sixty was an extraordinary achievement that was marked with a special celebration known as the *hwangap* (hwahn-gahp), which literally means "returning age" and figuratively "starting one's life over." The custom, Chinese in origin, was based on the lunar calendar concept of recording time in cycles of sixty years and regarding sixty years as a full lifetime, with the cycle of time, and life, starting over on the sixtieth year.

People who were fortunate enough to live to sixty were generally privileged to give up all responsibility—to behave like children again if they wanted to—and spend the rest of their lives as respected seniors, taking their ease, enjoying their grandchildren, traveling, and so on. In earlier times age was more or less equated with wisdom, and the older a person was, the wiser he or she was presumed to be. In a certain sense this was generally true, because most of the wisdom involved in the challenges of daily living in early Korea was based on practical experience and accumulated folk knowledge, not academic or scholarly learning.

Although men who retired after reaching the age of sixty (or earlier) generally gave up direct responsibility for supporting their families and running their businesses, their authority usually remained intact throughout their lifetimes. It was especially common for elderly people to upbraid and sometimes spank misbehaving children—something that still occasionally happens today. (Unlike in the West, Korean parents and teachers customarily paddle children on the bared calves of their legs, not on their buttocks or back.)

The sixtieth birthday of a parent or grandparent is still an occasion for a major celebration and is often the biggest event in the lives of many families. Sons and grandsons participate in sending out invitations. If the number of guests expected is too large for the home to accommodate, a hall or a banquet room in a restaurant is usually rented. If the celebration takes place in a rural village, straw mats and canopies may be erected outside the homes, and the parties may last for several days.

At these important birthday celebrations honorees and their spouses are seated at a main banquet table at the head of the room or hall. They dress in their finest traditional clothing, like newlyweds. Piles of fruits and cakes are spread on low tables before them. Sons and daughters, in the order of their age, take turns bowing before their parents, pouring wine for them, and wishing them many more happy years. After the members of the immediate families have completed their obeisances, younger brothers of the fathers and then their sons take their turns. Then the parents' friends pay their respects in the same manner.

Music, usually provided by professionals playing traditional drums and flutes, is a major part of *hwangap* ceremonies. Members of the family and guests sing, dance, and act like children to make the old couple feel young again. "Another part of the custom is for those celebrating their sixtieth birthday to reflect on their life up to that point and give serious thought to their 'second' or new life as an elder"—Ernest G. Beck, American taekwondo master and student of Korean history and culture.

Now that people are living longer, some skip the traditional sixtieth birthday festivities in favor of their seventieth birthday, *jingap* (jeen-gahp). This celebration is sometimes referred to by an old name, *kohi* (koh-hee), which means "old and rare."

70

화랑

Hwarang
(Whah-rahng)

"The Knights of Korea"

In the sixth century, when King Chinhung and the chief ministers of Korea's Shilla kingdom were faced with the problem of recruiting the best-qualified candidates for upper-level civil service officials, they came up with the idea of establishing a kind of quasi-military training school, or corps, and inviting the sons of nobles to compete for entry into the elite group. The corps was given the name *Hwarang To* (Whah-rahng Toh), or, poetically, "Circle of the Knights of the Flower." The first member of the corps is said to have been a warrior named Sorwon.

The concept of the *hwarang* (also referred to as "flower princes") grew out of a Buddhist cult that featured godlike beings of superior virtue and talents. Young men selected to become members of this elite order of knights were destined to be warriors as well as civil administrators. According to King Chinhung, the young men were to be schooled in filial piety, brotherly love, loyalty, sincerity, and the other qualities most desirable in future ministers, governors, and military leaders. The young knights were to be bound by a code called *Hwarang Do*, figuratively "The Way of the Warrior,"* which incorporated the famous Five Injunctions proclaimed in the early 600s by a noted Buddhism monk, Wongwang.

These injunctions were:

1. To serve the king with absolute loyalty
2. To serve one's parents with filial piety
3. Never to retreat in battle
4. To be faithful in friendships
5. To refrain from wanton killing

Records show that the training of the *hwarang* candidates was also referred to as "the five constant ways" (goodness, righteousness, decorum, wisdom, and fidelity) and the "six arts" (etiquette, music, archery, horsemanship, calligraphy, and mathematics).

Hwarang warriors practiced *Taegwon Do* (Tay-gwahn Doh), or "The Way of the Sword," and the use of other weapons. They were also trained in singing, dancing, and other entertainment skills and were required to stage performances before the court. Finally, the young knights were steeped in the Taoist ethics of simplicity, harmony, patience, and contentment.

All of the training of *hwarang* knights was designed to integrate their minds and bodies to the point that they could combine psychic power and physical power to achieve perfection in their actions. In this concept the ultimate goal was to be able to match their actions with their words. "Flower warriors" were also charged with the responsibility of keeping the spirit world on the side of the kingdom by performing ceremonial singing and dancing, praying, and participating in pilgrimages to sacred mountain and river sites.

New members for this elite corps of warrior-scholars were recruited only from the sons of the ruling class, further buttressing the hold that this class had on the government and on the affairs of the country in general.

---

*Korea's *Hwarang To* or "Knights of the Flower Circle" predated Japan's better-known samurai and their code of Bushido by more than five hundred years.

In 576, King Chinhung decided that the ranks of the *hwarang* should be opened to female candidates, and some three hundred of the most beautiful and talented girls in the upper class were inducted into the corps and given the name *wonhwa* (wohn-whah), or "female leaders." But in no time there was so much intrigue, jealousy, and illicit sexual activity that the coed policy was dropped. It is said, however, that thereafter the theme of feminine beauty was continued by requiring the young male members of the corps to wear makeup and fashionable clothing to enhance their appearance, resulting in their being especially popular among male members of the court who favored the charms of young men.

Historians say that later generations of the "Knights of the Flower Circle" played a leading role in Shilla's success in defeating the two rival kingdoms of the seventh century, Paekche and Koguryo, and unifying the peninsula for the first time in the history of the Korean people.

The importance of the *hwarang* in Korean society grew with the passing generations, not always for the good. As members of the elite *yangban* class that monopolized government offices, the *hwarang* generally belonged to one faction or another and were regularly caught up in the political intrigues and infighting that historically characterized the upper class.

The Shilla dynasty lasted for approximately two hundred years after it achieved supremacy on the peninsula, and in part it was a degeneration in the training and code of the *hwarang* that brought its downfall. But after the winners of the rebellion against the Shilla had established their own regime, the Koryo dynasty (918–1392), they continued the tradition of the *hwarang*, breathing new life into the training of their own corps of warriors.

For the first several generations of the Koryo dynasty the "flower knights" once again played a key role in the survival and success of the new dynasty, only to succumb again to factionalism and corruption and contribute to the downfall of the Koryo court. The history of the *hwarang* was to be repeated again in the succeeding dynasty, the Choson, which was founded by a dissident general in 1392.

As time passed and peace endured for generation after generation, particularly after 1650, the military training of the knights waned and they became more scholars than warriors. By the mid-1800s the martial traditions of the *hwarang* had been virtually forgotten, and they were little more than aristocrat dilettantes. Thus when Japan, Russia, the United States, and Europe's colonial powers began threatening Korea, the Korean armed forces were too weak and ill led to resist, resulting in Korea's becoming a victim of Japan's aggressive colonial policies in 1910.

It was not until the end of World War II, when Korea regained its sovereignty, that its military forces were rebuilt in the martial spirit of the ancient knights, but without the traditional emphasis on training in the various arts.

71

효

Hyo
(H'yoh)

"The Power of Filial Piety"

Any understanding of Koreans must take into account the lingering heritage of *hyo* (h'yoh), or "filial piety," which refers to a cultlike devotion and reverence of children for their parents and grandparents that was instilled socially and politically into Koreans from the fourteenth century until the last decades of the twentieth century. Filial piety may have existed in Korea prior to the introduction of Confucianism sometime around 108 B.C. (if not before), but it was the Confucian concept of ancestor worship that forged *hyo* into the core of the traditional Korean social system.

According to Korean psychologists, the traditional concept of *hyo* regarded children as extensions of their parents, not as separate individuals. This meant that the two could not be separated and that sons and daughters could not become fully functional individuals by themselves. They remained linked to their parents by a spiritual, emotional, and intellectual umbilical cord that could not be severed.

On the surface of this system children owed their parents and ancestors *chongjung* (chohng-juung), or "respect," and unlimited devotion in return for the care they received from their parents and grandparents. First sons were also charged with the obligation of carrying on the family line. While this system virtually guaranteed that parents would be cared for throughout their lifetimes, it also had many negative facets. Among the negative factors of this kind of *hyo* was that it tended to make people very conservative, static, splintered into exclusive family groups, and unable to communicate and cooperate readily with people in other groups.

There were more demands on older sons because they were the primary family heirs, responsible not only for the survival of the family name but also for honoring the family's deceased parents and grandparents.

In this system individuals had many obligations but very few rights. They were conditioned to put their parents and their families first, to avoid actions or innovations that would upset or endanger the equilibrium of the group, and to submit to the authoritarian rule of the family patriarch, to public officials, and to the government in general. *Hyo* was undergirded by strict ancestor worship, which meant that filial piety crossed the boundary of death, binding the generations together in an unbreakable bond.

Korean psychologist Kun Hi Yi has analyzed the nature and role of *hyo* in traditional Korean society in terms of the Oedipus complex, which refers to the sexual attraction between children and their opposite-sex parents. Whether or not this is a valid method of analyzing *hyo* is beyond me, but it nevertheless makes for some interesting views of Korean mentality.

Yi states that *hyo* represents the ultimate in the relationship between mature offspring and their parents. He goes on to say, however, that in actual practice in Korean society it resulted in neurotic symptoms of dependency and masochism between fathers and sons and pathological behavior between sons and mothers. He adds that the Oedipus complex was used as a control mechanism to help sons sublimate conflicts with their fathers and eventually to transfer power smoothly from the aged father to the mature son.

A fourth point Yi makes is that the rampant hedonism in present-day Korea is a reflection of an unconscious urge to return to times when things were simple and peaceful.

The Confucian code of filial piety required that all sons, but older sons in particular, "do what was best" for their parents. This provided sons with significant leeway because what was best for their parents was often an arbitrary judgment that they assumed the right to make. If there were complaints from their parents or other relatives, they could defend their actions by claiming that they were benefiting their parents even if their parents didn't recognize or accept the actions as beneficial.

A report on present-day Korean mentality by the Korean Institute for Policy Studies notes the continuing legacy of *hyo* and attributes its power to the fact that filial piety was the core of the kinship community for centuries and that independence and autonomy of the individual were simply not recognized, that children were seen as physical and mental extensions of their parents in a concrete sense.

The final link in filial piety in Korean society was that it transcended generations. The living remained connected physically and mentally to their ancestors. The overriding obligations each person owed to his or her family and community made it impossible for individuals to establish similar obligations with outsiders. The most that the individual could do was to have relationships with a small number of same-sex peers.

This extreme degree of cultural programming in filial piety began to diminish prior to the downfall of the Choson dynasty in 1910, but it was to remain a major part of the upbringing of Korean children until the last half of the twentieth century. Not surprisingly, the old idea that a woman's failure to produce a male child in itself constituted a lack of filial piety was one of the first of the traditional *hyo* beliefs to be discarded following the introduction of Western knowledge and human rights into Korea (mostly by American missionaries) in the 1880s and 1890s.

Despite other changes in Korean culture since the end of the Choson dynasty, and particularly since the introduction of social equality and democratic principles into Korea from the late 1940s on, filial piety continues to be an important aspect of Korean society. Generally speaking, the family comes before the individual.

일본사람
Ilbonsaram
(Ehl-bohn-sah-rahm)

"The Japanese Factor"

One of the great ironies of Korea is the relationship it has had with Japan since around the fourth century. With the western end of the main Japanese islands of Kyushu and Honshu only 180 kilometers (288 miles) from the southern tip of Korea, and the small Japanese island of Tsushima midway between these points, Korea was the primary source of immigrants to Japan as well as the bearer of virtually all of the Chinese arts, crafts, philosophies, and religions that were to make up most of Japan's civilization and culture.

There is, in fact, considerable hard evidence indicating that it was Korean immigrants who first unified Japan and founded the imperial family. In any event, Koreans and Japanese have been related racially and culturally since ancient times. But these ties did not guarantee a peaceful and cooperative relationship between the two countries. According to Korean records, there was some raiding of Japan's coastal areas by Korean pirates between the second and fourth centuries A.D., but they stopped and were never again repeated.

However, from around the sixth century until recent times it seems that different generations of Japanese were obsessed with the idea of inflicting as much suffering as possible on Koreans. In addition to large-scale pirate raids on Korea—raids that sometimes amounted to invasions—during the thirteenth century and again during the sixteenth century, Japan launched a major invasion of Korea in 1592, and over the next seven years virtually destroyed the country's infrastructure and decimated its population.

But it was the *Ilbonsaram* (Ehl-bohn-sah-rahm), or "Japanese" takeover of Korea between 1895 and 1910 and its annexation and colonization of the country between 1910 and 1945, that was to have the greatest psychological impact on Koreans. In addition to enslaving the Korean population, killing dozens of thousands, and imprisoning even more, the *Ilbonsaram* initiated a program of obliterating Korean culture and transforming Koreans into Japanese. The program would have succeeded had it not been for Japan's defeat by the United States and its allies in World War II.

Shortly after taking over Korea, the Japanese government established several women's organizations that were designed to influence Korean women to accept the colonial status of the country and cooperate with Japanese authorities. However, the growing number of Western-educated women opposed this blatantly obvious ploy by the Japanese government by forming associations and secret societies of their own, not only to further their goals of eliminating the traditional feminine roles but also to help male patriots liberate Korea from Japanese domination.

During the colonial period, large numbers of young Koreans were also sent to Japan for education and indoctrination purposes. Others went on their own because there were not enough opportunities for them to obtain a higher education in Korea. Thousands of Koreans were taken to Japan as laborers or migrated there to find better jobs. With each passing year Japan intensified its efforts to coordinate the Korean economy with Japan's growing needs. One of the slogans Japan promoted in an effort to reduce friction between the Japanese occupation forces and Koreans was *Ni-ssen Yuwa* (Nee-ssen Yuu-wah), or "Japan-Korean Harmony." As part of this program, the Japanese constantly harangued the Koreans on the benefits they were bringing to Korea and how lucky the Koreans were to be a part of the growing Japanese empire.

In late 1939 the Japanese government decreed that all Koreans would adopt Japanese names—a blow that surpassed virtually every injury the Japanese had inflicted on Koreans up to that time. To Koreans their names were their link with their families, their clans, their ancestors—their whole history as a people—and had a spiritual quality that made them almost sacred. The name-change decree, called the "Name Order," made it mandatory that all Koreans go to their local registry office and replace their Korean names with Japanese names.

But this did not mean that the "former" Koreans were then accepted as "Japanese." In all official use thereafter, Koreans were required to use both their old Korean names and their new Japanese names so the Japanese administration could keep track of who they really were. The outbreak of war on a massive scale and the enforced movement of huge numbers of Koreans to other parts of the peninsula, to Manchuria, and to Japan to work as slave laborers interrupted the process of reregistering all Koreans, however. When World War II ended in 1945, some 20 percent of the population had not yet changed their name registrations.

When World War II ended, there were more than three-quarters of a million Japanese civilians in Korea, occupying much of the best farmland in the country, working in factories, and administering the government and economy. There were also several hundred thousand Koreans in Japan, many of them born and raised there. All of the Japanese were quickly repatriated to Japan. But rather than go back to a war-ravaged Korea, most of the Japan-born Koreans decided to stay in Japan, the only home they knew, automatically becoming the largest contingent of foreigners in the country.

For the next twenty years or so, relations between Korea and Japan remained strained. Most Koreans looked on the Japanese with all the antipathy they could muster. That they would ever forgive the Japanese for all of the suffering inflicted on them seemed impossible. But Japan's rapid transformation into an economic superpower and Korea's own needs for technology and financing gradually brought about a grudging rapprochement between the Korean and Japanese business communities.

By the 1970s Japanese businessmen, flush with large amounts of money, were flocking to Korea seeking deals of one kind or another. Older Koreans who had been forced to learn the Japanese language as children found their fluency in the language a major advantage in dealing with the Japanese, a factor that helped relieve some of the anger they continued to feel toward Japan. As the number of Japanese investors in Korea continued to spiral upward, young Koreans began studying the Japanese language in school to get jobs in companies catering to the Japanese, particularly the new international hotels that began sprouting in Seoul and elsewhere in the country.

By the 1980s the Japanese travel industry had begun promoting Korea, especially the semitropical island of Cheju off the southern tip of the peninsula, as an attractive destination that was "foreign" but not so foreign that it would repel the ethnocentric Japanese. In no time hordes of young Japanese who had very little knowledge of the Japanese occupation of Korea or World War II were flocking to the island and to the port city of Pusan, only a short ferryboat ride from Japan. To them, simply making a trip out of Japan was a major event in their lives, even if it was only an hour away.

Today Koreans tolerate the Japanese and do business with them, but they do not view them as close relatives and are not fond of them, despite the racial and cultural similarities. Generally speaking they continue to regard the Japanese collectively as arrogant, overly aggressive, and opportunistic. The fact that the Japanese continue to treat Korean residents in Japan as outsiders constantly reminds Koreans of the superiority complex that has long been characteristic of the Japanese.

73

인

In

(Een)

"The Benevolent Society"

Like all people with a long history of authoritarian governments and state-sponsored religions, the national character of Koreans has traditionally been marked by an extraordinary number and variety of contradictions. Koreans were wont to swing back and forth between being sublimely peaceful and being extremely violent and from being excessively polite to being outrageously rude, depending on the circumstances. They could also be overbearingly solicitous on one occasion and callously indifferent on another.

While generally cheerful and fun-loving, Koreans were also subject to bouts of pessimism and sadness and readily engaged in crying binges. Women in particular have traditionally resorted to ritualistic wailing to get what they want because they were not allowed to engage in rational debates with their fathers, husbands, or mature sons. While these patterns of behavior are rapidly diminishing among the younger generations, they are still a significant part of Korean life.

The tolerance of Koreans to hardships of all kinds, and especially to ill treatment by those in power, is legendary. And yet they also have traditionally been quick to fight at the slightest provocation. But beneath all of these cultural characteristics there is a moral and ethical foundation that distinguishes Koreans and is one of the primary reasons many foreigners who have taken up residence in the country in the past have become deeply attached to the people.

Unlike many other Asians and many people in Africa, Europe, and the Americas, Koreans had no institutionalized traditions of barbaric savagery. In comparison with many other people around the world, Korean political and religious leaders (especially the latter) have not been especially cruel to their own people or to outsiders. This cultural foundation of Korean humanism is subsumed in the word *in* (een), which refers to the "humanity" or "benevolence" that, according to Korean scholars, makes up the core character of the Korean people. The word includes the concepts of wisdom, kindness, and meekness.

Korean scholars point out that it was this fundamental *in* aspect of their traditional culture that resulted in most people characteristically "turning the other cheek" when they were insulted or assaulted by anyone. They also point out that over the full range of their history they have never invaded another country, while Korea itself has been attacked and invaded hundreds of times over the centuries, particularly by the Chinese, Mongols, Manchus, and Japanese.

Koreans say they owe their *in* character and lack of interest in conquering and controlling other people to their native religion, which taught a peaceful coexistence with everything in nature as opposed to the aggression and domination taught by other religions and political ideologies. At the same time, Koreans are noted for their courage and their willingness to sacrifice for what they believe is right—a fact, they say, that is not incompatible with their basically peaceful and humble character.

While present-day Koreans have retained much of their traditional character, the lessening of political control over their attitudes and day-to-day behavior since the 1950s allows more of their traditionally repressed anger and dissatisfactions to emerge in the form of direct confrontations.

Following the declaration of democratic principles in the constitution of 1948, young Koreans, particularly high school and university students, quickly began to exhibit a tendency to use violence in attempting to redress political injustices. Violence by labor unions also became common in the 1960s and 1970s.

The *in* of present-day Koreans is more likely to hinge on a strong sense of justice fulfilled than on a meek acceptance of political or economic abuse. This factor impacts every facet of Korean life, from internal politics to international diplomatic and trade relations.

Foreigners dealing with Koreans must be equally sensitive to their feelings of *in* and develop considerable skill in harmonizing their relationships to succeed in any mutually cooperative enterprise.

인간관계
In'gan Kwan'gye
(Een-gahn Kwahn-gay)
"Interpersonal Relations"

There are few words in the Korean vocabulary that are more important than the phrase *in'gan kwan'gye* (een-gahn kwahn-gay), or "interpersonal relationships." The phrase is invariably used in all explanations of the structure of Korean society and how it functions, in private as well as public matters, including politics and business. It is frequently repeated that one cannot understand Korean attitudes and behavior without a solid grasp of the role of *in'gan kwan'gye*.

It is also said that Korean society is the most Confucian of all societies in the Confucian sphere of Asia, and since the hallmark of Confucian-oriented societies is harmonious relationships the outsider might assume that Korean society is peaceful and that the people are happy in their work.

Of course there are exceptions, but generally speaking there is an undercurrent of friction in Korean society that frequently results in verbal outbursts and physical explosions. The very same Confucian principles and etiquette that are designed to ensure a harmonious society also create an enormous amount of frustration and friction that is normally hidden below a facade of order, calm, and contentment.

While Koreans may be praised for their genuine commitment to peace and their generally peaceful behavior, they deserve even more praise for being able to survive for generations in a social system that was designed to suppress and subvert both their intellectual and emotional natures. It was not until recent times that the majority of Koreans became socially and politically free enough in their daily lives to truly enjoy personal relationships. Prior to the middle of the twentieth century their relations, private as well as public, were so prescribed and limiting that the vast majority led truncated lives.

Koreans are still in the process of emerging from the cocoon of Confucianism that for centuries kept them bound to each other by invisible webs and prevented them from developing their own identities and personalities. This metamorphosis is progressing very slowly because institutional Korea—its government ministries and agencies, its large commercial enterprises, its schools, and the like—are still bastions of Confucian thinking and rules and will no doubt remain so for a long time.

Virtually all Koreans who are employed outside their homes must strive constantly to abide by all of the intricate customs and rules controlling their interpersonal relationships to avoid upsetting co-workers and superiors and maintain surface harmony—a never-ending process that requires extraordinary *noryok* (nohr-yohk), or "effort." They are aided in this effort by a number of conventions designed to help them dissipate their anger and frustrations, with after-hours drinking and bitching sessions being one of the most common methods used.

In the meantime it is naturally younger Koreans who are becoming independent and individualistic enough that when they are outside the confines of these Confucian strongholds (and away from their superiors) they are able to express their own personalities, respond to their emotions, and exercise their own judgment.

On an individual basis Koreans regard themselves as equal to, if not better than, anyone else. But Korean society requires that every individual know his or her place on the hierarchical social ladder and strictly adhere to it. Another key factor in Korean society is that no matter how high one might be on the social totem pole proper etiquette requires that they maintain a humble attitude and allow others to elevate them to their proper position—by the use of honorific language, by directing them to the seat appropriate for their status, and so on.

In earlier times people who failed to rigorously follow these rules of etiquette were often described as *sangnom* (sahng-nohm), or "nonpersons," the same term that was generally used in reference to people in the lowest social classes—criminals, prostitutes, entertainers, butchers—and foreigners as well. The attitudes subsumed in the traditional meaning of *sangnom* continue to play a role in Korean society. People are still exceptionally sensitive to social class, and the higher one is in social status the more severe the etiquette requirements.

When Caucasian foreigners began showing up in Korea in the late 1800s, the attitudes and behavior of many of them, particularly sailors and other lower-class individuals, were so uncouth and barbarian by Korean standards that they were frequently referred to as *sangnom*. In the first place, the white skin, different-colored hair, and sometimes blue eyes of Caucasian Westerners was so alien to the Korean experience that the foreigners did not look like normal humans. When this was added to the xenophobia that was common among Koreans, it was no great leap for the average Korean to regard all foreigners as *sangnom*.

But Koreans did not, and still do not, discriminate only against foreigners and low-class people. Generally speaking, as far as Koreans are concerned, everyone in Korea, Koreans as well as foreigners, is more or less *sangnom* until a personal relationship exists. By lumping all strangers into the *sangnom* category, Koreans can ignore them, minding only their own business.

75

인정
Injong
(Een-johng)

"Affection and Compassion"

Social relationships in pre-modern Korea, including marriage, were not based on personal feelings. They were based on absolute imperatives demanded by the obligation to perpetuate households, perform the rituals of ancestor worship, and maintain order and harmony among inferiors, superiors, and the sexes.

Social relationships were defined and limited further by the stratification of people into precise classes and within these classes into exclusive family and kinship groups. The exclusivity of these groups was such that outsiders were generally treated more or less as enemies to be kept at a distance. Virtually all friendships were limited to members of one's own group—family, kin, school-mates, and, in the case of males, workmates.

In this environment *injong* (een-johng), or "personal affection and com-passion," were not universal characteristics that applied, or could apply, to peo-ple in general. They were limited to one's family and "in" group. Members of each of these groups were generally callous about the problems and suffering of others.

Broadly speaking, affection in pre-modern Korea was limited primarily to the relationships between parents and children—especially between mothers and male children. While there is ample evidence that men, and some women as well, in the elite class carried on extramarital relationships based on love, these were not socially sanctioned affairs.

Because affection and compassion—both of which are natural human attrib-utes—were so narrowly focused in the lives of Koreans, there was a tendency for people to go to extremes in expressing them, to the point that the emotions involved were overwhelming and burdensome. Westerners who have married into Korean families often remark that the affection showered on children, espe-cially male children, by their mothers and grandmothers is so strong that it tends to stifle their psychological development.

Generally speaking, strangers were treated with indifference and often with a degree of selfish callousness that was shocking to outsiders. The "good Samar-itan" syndrome, except for dedicated Christian converts since the 1890s, was never a part of the Korean experience.

Although there have been dramatic changes in social relationships in Korea since the 1950s, friendships are still naturally influenced by family background, education, degree of affluence, and so on. And compassion for others tends to be conspicuously selective. Yet Koreans have traditionally prided themselves on their *injong*, primarily because all of their personal relations were so carefully prescribed, so dependent on the character and goodwill of others, that there was an obsession with basing attitudes and behavior on compassion and affection to protect themselves from the absolute power of fathers, superiors, and government officials.

The fact that *injong* often failed to protect the people from those in power made it even more important that relationships within families and kinship groups be based on genuine compassion and affection. Foreigners who took up residence in Korea in the 1880s and 1890s often commented on the capacity of Koreans for *injong* toward people who posed no threat to them. As the authoritative nature of Korean society has diminished, particularly since the 1980s, feelings of universal *injong* have increased in direct proportion. The less threatened the people become, the freer they are to extend compassion and affection to those who are outside their circle of family and friends.

Having been subjected to extreme suffering so many times in their history and still having retained their capacity for compassion and affection, Koreans may end up as models for the rest of the world.

76

인내

Innae
(Een-nay)

"A Culture of Enduring"

Early visitors to Korea—first the Chinese and other Asians and much later Europeans—invariably commented on the peaceful nature of Koreans and the atmosphere of calm repose that enveloped the cities, towns, and countryside day and night. As these early travelers had it, there was no such thing as private "night life" in Korea for common people, and the only public entertainment as such were the country's religious-oriented festivals.

Although Korean history is pockmarked with peasant rebellions, clan wars, invasions by outside enemies, and sporadic coastal raids by Japanese pirates, until the last decades of the nineteenth century the country was peaceful most of the time.

Exactly why Korea was traditionally a nonaggressive country is open to debate. Some Korean historians claim it was because the country was small and surrounded by powerful warlike enemies. Others attribute their peaceful nature to shamanism and Buddhism (which seems doubtful because both Chinese and Japanese, who were also Buddhists and shamanists, have long been known for their warrior mentality).

Whatever contributions these factors might have made to the passive nature of earlier Koreans, their own political and social systems, in many ways onerous to the extreme, were primarily responsible for most of the traditional national character of Koreans, including their famed *innae* (een-nay), or "patience/endurance," without which they would not have been able to withstand the periodic invasions of their enemies, their own wars, and the hardships imposed on them by their own rulers.

Innae is still an important word in the Korean vocabulary and a vital factor in the day-to-day survival and success of Koreans. Even though the challenges Koreans face are no longer life-threatening or spirit-crushing, they must still deal with a degree of government bureaucracy and authoritarianism, and with a variety of social and cultural demands, that requires extraordinary patience and the ability to endure circumstances that would try the souls of people with less *innae*.

Few foreigners have ever become involved with Korean officialdom or larger Korean corporations without being advised repeatedly that they must have a virtually inexhaustible supply of *innae*, although there are now growing exceptions to this rule, particularly among companies involved in high-tech industries.

Koreans often explain that the ongoing need for *innae* results from the competitive factor in small, heavily populated Korea—among students striving to get into the best schools, among companies striving for more market share, among politicians and bureaucrats fighting to protect their turf and reap personal gain, and among people in general who want better jobs, better housing, and more social security.

In any event, the heritage from the past combined with the competitive nature of Korean life today makes it imperative that people learn and practice patience with extraordinary fortitude. And these imperatives are even more applicable to foreigners trying to do business, or doing business, in Korea because they generally do not have as many options or avenues as Koreans in bringing pressure to bear to speed things up or fundamentally influence their outcome.

Foreign businesspeople who have spent years in Korea frequently comment that those with a low tolerance level for bureaucratic obfuscation, situational ethics, and indirect communication might be better off avoiding the country altogether.

77

인사

Insa
(Een-sah)

"Rounds of Greetings"

The personal nature of all relationships in Korea, including business relationships, makes it imperative that Koreans have regular face-to-face meetings with their friends and business contacts. One category of these meetings has been institutionalized under the term of *insa* (een-sah), which literally means "greetings" in a formal sense that includes such connotations as salutation and recognition of the value of the other party to the relationship.

On both a private and a business level virtually all Koreans make a specific point of paying *insa* visits to friends and contacts several times during the year. This cultural ritual is especially important for businesspeople, politicians, and others whose welfare is affected directly by the relationships they have with people in other companies and government offices.

There are several varieties of *insa* meetings, all of which follow a precise protocol. These varieties include paying respects when someone suffers a death in the family, extending congratulations on the occasion of happy events, and nurturing business and political relationships.

Insa performed by businesspeople include bowing, expressing appreciation for past favors, help, business, and so on, along with requesting that the other parties continue to be helpful and cooperative in the future. Businesspeople traditionally make a round of *insa* visits from the middle of December until the end of the year to thank clients, suppliers, etc., for past business and follow this up after the holidays with *insa* visits to start off the new year. Some people take gifts to those they are visiting before the end of the year.

Among the most important of the annual *insa* occasions is the first day of business at the beginning of the new year, usually between January 3 and 5. It is de rigueur for businesspeople to make courtesy visits called *sebae* (say-bay) on the senior managers, directors, and presidents of the companies they do business with. The figurative meaning of *sebae* is "beginning of the year bow." Actually there is very little if any business done on this day because of a regular stream of visitors and because drinking toasts to each other is a key part of the ceremonial visits.

Another traditional custom followed by almost all Korean companies on the first business day of the new year is the *shimushik* (sheem-uu-sheek), or "starting business ceremony," which includes eating special foods, drinking, and hearing short speeches made by executives and managers in a very festive atmosphere.

Sebae (say-by), or "New Year's Greetings," expressed to everyone you meet are also an important part of Korean protocol. The traditional expression is *Saehae Pokmani Padushipshio* (Say-hay Pok-mahn-ee Pah-duu-sheep-shee-oh), or "Happy New Year!"

Another common ceremonial event in Korea, especially among larger international corporations, is *songbyul hoe* (sohng-buhl hoe-eh), or "farewell parties." When employees are being sent abroad on overseas assignments, their co-workers invariably stage *songbyul hoe* at which there are numerous speeches and even more numerous toasts. These events go beyond just providing employees with an opportunity to have a good time at the expense of the company. They are designed to reinforce ties among employees and their loyalty to the company.

Large Korean companies routinely rotate younger employees between departments and branches in early spring as part of their on-the-job training, a system that is known as *insa idong* (een-sah ee-dong), or "job rotation." *Insa idong* serves several purposes. It familiarizes employees with the operations of other departments and gives them a much better understanding and appreciation of how their companies operate as a whole, and just as important, it provides them with the opportunity to establish personal relationships with other staff members so they will have a basis for communicating with each other in the future.

While the *insa idong* system is obviously designed to integrate the cultural needs of Koreans with the business interests of their companies, it can be a serious handicap to foreigners doing business with those companies. The general consensus is that it takes three to four years for foreign managers or representatives in Korea to develop effective relationships with their contacts in Korean companies—a process that requires a significant investment in time and often money as well. Many of the relationships that are started, or developed, by foreign businesspeople are interrupted by these personnel transfers, forcing outsiders to start the relationship process over again and again.

The usual procedure is for the employees being transferred to introduce all of their contacts to their replacements and for as long as necessary to continue to serve as advisers and liaisons to both their replacements and their clients or suppliers. This is some help, but it slows things down because it takes weeks to months, or even years, for the individuals concerned to get up to par in their new assignments. Any problems that already exist or occur after the change are likely to be exacerbated.

When a business relationship between companies survives over a period of years, and the same managers or representatives of the foreign company remain in place, the *insa idong* system eventually becomes a significant advantage because the foreigners end up knowing individuals in several departments and can continue to use the relationships to help keep the business running smoothly.

78

인삼

Insam
(Inn-sahm)

"The 'Man-Root'"

It is impossible to spend more than a few days in Korea without encountering *insam* (inn-sahm), which literally means "man-root," in a variety of forms. *Insam*, in its more familiar English translation, is "ginseng"—which is an anglicized pronunciation of the Mandarin Chinese words *jen shen* (jun-shun), meaning "man limb" or "man root." (The resemblance of some ginseng roots to an anatomically correct man is so explicit that they are preserved and exhibited rather than being served up as tea or in some other form.)

Ginseng is any of several plants of the genus *Panax*, most of which have small greenish flowers and a forked root that suggests legs and tendrils extending out like arms. The two most important kinds of ginseng in Korea are red ginseng (*hong*) and white ginseng (*baek*). Red ginseng is said to be the most potent and is substantially more expensive than the white variety.

Insam is important in Korea because of its reputed medicinal properties. The ailments said to be reduced or cured by *insam* read like an encyclopedia of human complaints. The wondrous root was already well established as the centerpiece of Korea's folk medicine when recorded history began.

In 108 B.C., when troops under the command of Wu-Ti, emperor of the Han dynasty in China, invaded the Korean peninsula and turned the small kingdoms there into vassal states, one of the annual tributes he demanded was ginseng. The earliest Chinese medical manual, *Nei Ching* (Nay-e Cheeng), published around 1000 B.C., contained a large number of ginseng prescriptions. At that time, the ginseng used in China came from the mountains of Manchuria and the Korean peninsula.

Today ginseng is cultivated widely in the mountains as well as the lowlands of Korea, where the plants are grown in row after row of long plastic sheds visible from highways and train lines.

Ginseng was introduced into Europe in the 1800s and has since been subjected to exhaustive scrutiny by a number of scientists who found that it contains what appears to be the largest variety of minerals (some five hundred) of any other known plant. The cultivation of ginseng in the same fields year after year is said to be especially difficult because it absorbs so many nutrients from the soil that nothing else will grow there until the nutrients are replaced.

Insam is one of Korea's highest-profile and most profitable exports, and its cultivation and marketing are a tightly controlled government monopoly. The advertising and marketing of ginseng is as conspicuous in Korea as drug advertising is in Japan and the United States. One literally cannot escape the billboards or other advertising media hawking the miraculous plant.

But for those who want to have the total ginseng experience, the best bet is the small market town of Kumsan in the southwest corner of Chungchongdnam Province in west-central South Korea. Kumsan is the ginseng capital of the world, with over 80 percent of South Korea's annual *insam* crop sold in its markets.

The town's three largest *insam* markets are the Kumsan Ginseng International Market, Kumsan Undried Ginseng Center, and Kumsan Medicinal Herb Market. Each year from September 21 to 23, Kumsan hosts the Korean Ginseng Festival. Kumsan is about a thirty-minute car ride from Taejon, one of South Korea's largest cities.

The efficacy of ginseng as a medicinal product has been confirmed over and over again by Western doctors. It is said to be especially effective, when used regularly over a long period of time, in relieving digestive ailments, chronic fatigue, and a variety of nervous ailments. Devotees say that ginseng stimulates the nervous system, resulting in sharper mental responses and improving the overall functioning of the body. It has long been used in Korea as a hangover tonic.

Ginseng is marketed in Korea (and worldwide) in practically every form imaginable, from pills, capsules, and powder to chewing gum, tea, wine, candies, soap, and shampoo. However, most Koreans prefer to drink it as tea, in the traditional way, both at home and in the ubiquitous *insam cha jip* (inn-sahm chah jeep), or "ginseng tea houses."

Ginseng tea houses serve more than just tea made from ginseng roots (and other herbs). They offer a variety of potions that mix ginseng with pine nuts, ginger, jujubes (a kind of date), sugar, and other ingredients. (Just tell your Korean friends what ails you, and they will prescribe the most appropriate tea.)

Few foreign visitors ever leave Korea without at least one box of *insam* in their luggage.

79

이름

Irum
(Ee-ruum)

"What's in a Name?"

One of the most unusual facets of Korea's still-clannish society is the fact that the clan system, along with the hereditary upper-class system and a law that prevented common people from having surnames until the beginning of modern times, dramatically limited the number of *song* (sohng), or "family names," in the country. Still today there are only about three hundred surnames in all of Korea—a factor that plays a vital role in business as well as all other areas of life. (Male commoners were granted the right to adopt and use family names just before the end of the nineteenth century.* It was 1909 before the same right was granted to female commoners.)

Approximately half of all Koreans are named Choi, Kim, Lee, or Pak. Korean population statistics show that 21.7 percent of all Koreans are named Kim (there are 32 Kim clans), 14.8 percent are named Lee, and 8.5 percent are named Pak (also written in roman letters as Park). The seven other most common names are Choe (Chay), Chung, Kang, Cho, Yun, Chang (Jang), and Rim. Altogether, these ten names account for some 65 percent of the population.

This situation is said to derive from the fact that Korea was founded by a very few families whose names became imbued with a sacred aspect that was

---

*In Japan common people were not legally allowed to have family names until the end of the shogunate system of government in 1868, although most families had begun using surnames unofficially by the beginning of the nineteenth century.

maintained meticulously from one generation to the next. A significant part of this tradition no doubt came from Confucianism, which incorporated the concept of revering one's ancestors, encouraged the keeping of family names, and discouraged any inclination to adopt new surnames that would have no history and no honor.

Early in their history Koreans adopted the Chinese custom of using two *irum* (ee-ruum), or "given names"—a personal name and a generational name chosen by the parents, grandparents, or an onomancer (name-giver). Still today in most Korean families, all sons and daughters in that family are given the same generational name. As this family branches out over the generations, the generational names are continued in the male and female lines for five generations so that eventually people who are related very distantly may have a common generational name that goes back to a remote ancestor. After the fifth generation the cycle is started over with new linking names.

A great deal of thought goes into the selection of both personal and generational *irum*, and it is still common for parents to seek the help of onomancers. The object is to select a name that fits the child on the basis of the time of birth and the parents' expectations for the child. Among the more common given names are those that refer to things that are hard and virtually ageless, like stone and iron. The idea being, of course, that some of the qualities of these materials will be bestowed on the bearers of the names.

A rather strange aberration occurred during the Choson or Yi dynasty that resulted in female children sometimes being given odd names. The actual need for male children was so great that when female children were born fathers would often give them odd names reflecting their disappointment, regret, and sorrow. Some of the names given to female children under these circumstances were rather humorous. These included names that meant "The End" and "Hoping Against Odds."

Koreans, like the Chinese, traditionally put their family names first, followed by their two given names. (The Japanese also put their family names first, followed by their given name, but they did not adopt the Chinese custom of using generational names.)

The first Westerners to enter Korea after its "closed door" policy was ended in 1876 were confused and frustrated in their efforts to keep track of Koreans by their names. This frustration with names was one of the most compelling reasons why foreigners introduced the practice of writing Korean in roman letters, thereby eliminating the need for them to learn the Chinese ideograms with which their names were normally written. However, this did not end the problems that Westerners had with Korean names. Being unfamiliar with Korean-style names in the first place, they often confused the first given name with the last or family name. There was also an ongoing dilemma of how to spell many Korean names with roman letters because some of the sounds involved had no English equivalents.

Before long some Koreans began to connect the first name to their generational name with a hyphen (Kyong-Dong or Kyong-dong)—an artifice that was apparently intended to help foreigners avoid mistaking the first name for the family name. A few Koreans resolved the problem of distinguishing between their first name and generational name (writing their names in roman letters) by simply joining the two names. One of the best-known individuals to do this was Syngman Rhee, who became the first president of the Republic of Korea in 1948. (Note that he also chose to put his given names first and his family name last, in the Western fashion. This wasn't all that Rhee did. Earlier he had changed his name from Sung Man Yi to Syngman Rhee.)

Still today there is no universally accepted way of writing Korean names in roman letters. Some people and some publications connect the first name and generational name with a hyphen. Others do not. Some capitalize the first letter of generational names when they are connected to the first names. Others do not.

Because of the special, almost mystical, role that names play in Korean society, Koreans are very sensitive about their names, and there are numerous taboos about using them. Generally speaking, first names are used only by family members and close school friends. Traditionally, some older Koreans were so sensitive about their personal names that they did not like to hear other people say them aloud. Shortly after birth, female children were given personal names, but they were seldom used. Generally they were called by poetic or poignant nicknames until they married, after which they were known as Mrs. So-and-So, after their husbands' family names, and were entered in their husbands' family registers simply as *pae* (pay), or "spouse." As a result of this system, many women lived out their lives without ever hearing their personal names spoken, a practice that contributed enormously to their being treated impersonally and submerging their identity within their families.

Present-day Korean women do not change their names when they marry. They may be called by their maiden name or by the title *puin* (puu-een), which is used in reference to someone else's wife, or addressed as "the wife of Mr. Lee," etc. When men refer to their own wives (when talking to others), the commonly used term is *anae* (ah-negh). When older, more traditionally minded husbands call out to their wives (to attract their attention), they commonly use the word *yobo* (yoh-boh), which can be translated as an endearment ("Dear!") or as "Hey, you!" depending on the circumstances and the character of the husbands. Another old custom is for husbands to address their wives as "Mother of X" (the name of a daughter or son); e.g., *Hosoon ssi aemeoni*, or "Mother of Hosoon."

As is the case in so many other areas of Korean life, however, these old customs are gradually disappearing among the younger generations. Many younger couples have adopted the Western way of addressing each other and family members.

Close friends and married couples who are bilingual and bicultural because of their higher education abroad, who dated for relatively long periods before marrying, as well as others in the younger generations, commonly refer to each other by their first names. A new trend—that started in the 1970s and had become common by the 1990s—is the use of initials instead of foreign names and in place of first and generational names on name cards and in other written materials as well as when verbally addressing friends and regular business contacts. In some multinational Korean companies it is official policy that their employees will use the initials of their first and middle names in all of their foreign dealings.

To get around the fact that every other Korean they meet is either Kim, Lee, Pak, or Choi, Koreans use titles connected with their profession, place of work, and rank. In a large company where there are dozens to hundreds of Lees, Kims, Paks, and Chois who are all managers, they are distinguished by their titles (supervisor, manager, general manager, etc.) plus their section or division.

If there are two or more Manager Lees in one section, they may be referred to as Manager Lee of Production No. 1; Manager Lee of Production No. 2; and so on. For years the Public Relations Department of the Westin Chosun Hotel in Seoul had two Lees. One was called "Senior Lee" and the other one "Baby Lee." On the personal side, Koreans also use the areas where they live to identify each other: Lee of such-and-such an address or area, and so on.

A further problem for foreigners results from the fact that when romanized many of the most common names in Korea may be spelled two or three different ways. Some of the syllables of the Korean language are also pronounced differently by many people, making the names sound different even though they are the same. When spelled with roman letters, Yi, for example, may be spelled as Rhee, Lee, Ree, Rii, Le, or Ee. Pak often sounds like Park when it is pronounced, and some people with that name spell it that way when they write it out in roman letters.

This name situation creates special problems for foreigners who are new arrivals in Korea and try to telephone people they have met recently. Not being aware of the seriousness of the situation, they frequently fail to get or to remember the titles and sections or departments of the people concerned and are therefore unable to identify which person they are calling for.

It is very important for foreign travelers and businesspeople visiting Korea to carefully write down the full name, title (if any), and company section of all Koreans they might want to call or meet again. On a personal level, it is also wise to get their home addresses and often their position in the family (first or second son or daughter, etc.).

The surname problem is also one of the reasons name cards are so important in doing business in Korea. In addition to being used as general references, they are frequently presented as documents to help distinguish individuals from others with the same names.

Many Koreans with foreign business contacts and friends choose to use a foreign first name. But until recent times this was not always a matter of personal choice. In more traditional families, the decision by a member of a family to use a foreign name was a family matter. Some Koreans who adopted foreign names for use with their foreign contacts did not reveal them to their families because adoption of a foreign name is a very un-Korean thing to do. However, the problem of keeping all the Lees, Kims, and similarly named Koreans straight is mitigated by their traditions of goodwill, cooperativeness, and hospitality, especially to foreign visitors.

Koreans take great care in selecting the Chinese ideograms used for writing names. They believe that a person's name has a relationship to his or her character and fortune. Parents, often with the aid of close relatives or professional name-givers, select ideograms that express the kind of character and fortune they want for their children.

A growing number of Koreans today who have attended graduate and postgraduate schools abroad (and become bilingual and bicultural) combine their generational names with their first names the way Syngman Rhee did. A growing number of internationalized parents dispense with generational names altogether, giving their children single first names.

80

이산가족

Isangajok
(Ee-sahn-gah-joak)

"The Divided Families"

At the end of World War II in 1945 the Russian army occupied the northern half of Korea and the American army occupied the southern half of the country. In 1948 the two halves of the country were divided politically between a Korean Communist regime in the North and a Korean democratically oriented regime in the South—resulting in the appearance of two fiercely independent and antagonistic entities: North Korea and South Korea.

Well before the political division of the peninsula into two countries the situation between the rival groups was so serious and disruptive that dozens of thousands of Koreans in the northern half of the country, both people originally from the southern half of the country and many whose traditional homes were in the North, began a desperate attempt to escape from the Communist-controlled North and reach the South.

The North Korean Communists began a systematic campaign to prevent these people from leaving North Korea. Many were arrested and imprisoned. Others were shot and killed by North Korean soldiers guarding the border between the two halves of the country. When the division of the peninsula into North and South Korea was formalized, the North Korean government sealed off the border completely, trapping hundreds of thousands of South Koreans in the North and preventing both them and North Koreans from reaching the South.

In 1950, when the North Koreans unleashed a full-scale invasion of South Korea in an attempt to unify and communize the whole peninsula, dozens of thousands of Koreans in the North took advantage of the chaos of war to escape to the South. Untold thousands died in the attempt. When the fighting stopped in 1953, the border between North and South Korea was turned into one of the most heavily guarded borders in the world, permanently trapping hundreds of thousands of Koreans who were originally from the South.

This action created a huge group of Koreans who became known as *isangajok* (ee-sahn-gah-joak), or "divided families," in reference to South Korean families who had members trapped in North Korea. As the years passed and the Communist regime in the North refused to allow the South Koreans to return home, the term *isangajok* became one of the bitterest terms in the Korean vocabulary, conjuring up the anguish of the families involved and their anger at the North Korean government.

Several decades after the end of the Korean War in 1953, the North Koreans began a carefully calculated program of allowing small numbers of people from *isangajok* to meet briefly at Panmunjom on the border and in North Korea, always under strict, guarded conditions. While the people who were able to participate in these meetings were overjoyed to see members of their families once again, the meetings and the circumstances under which they were held also served to remind them of their anguish and the unconscionable behavior of the Communist rulers of North Korea.

At this writing North and South Korea are still divided, and the anguish of the *isangajok* continues.

81

절

Jeol
(Juhl)

"Showing Respect to Elders"

Confucius, the great Chinese sage (551–479 B.C.), taught that for societies to survive and prosper in a peaceful, cooperative atmosphere they had to be arranged in a hierarchical form, and that all people had to know where they belong in that vertical structure and fulfill all of the obligations that were inherent in their sex, age, social class, position, and circumstances.

The teachings of Confucius were introduced into Korea, along with the Chinese system of writing, around the beginning of the Christian era in Europe. By the fourth century there were a number of Confucian universities in the three kingdoms on the Korean peninsula, and from that period on, Confucianism gradually permeated Korean culture.

Unlike Christianity, Confucianism had no god and no single "authority" that was the source of morality for mankind. The only supernatural reference in Confucianism was to "heaven," by which Confucius meant a divine or cosmic order that was essential to all things in nature. He left it up to people to develop their own virtue through study, the observance of various rituals, and respect for their fellow men and for order in their lives.

One of the facets of order that Confucius taught was respect for parents, official authority, elders in general, teachers, and others with important skills. Already steeped in respect, ritualism, and order from their native shamanism, Koreans fused this new philosophy from China into their old beliefs, eventually becoming more Confucianist than the Chinese themselves.

The heritage of Confucianism lives on in present-day Korea and is the most conspicuous in the institutionalized form of respect paid to parents and other elders—a deeply entrenched custom known as *jeol* (juhl) in Korean. To most Koreans *jeol* is a national characteristic that distinguishes them from most Westerners and one of the facets of their culture that they point to with extraordinary pride. They add that *jeol* is one of the most important keys to understanding Korean culture.

There are several forms of *jeol* and a number of specific occasions when it is an essential part of Korean behavior. It is manifested in honorific forms of speech, in when and how one bows, and in a broad range of etiquette that determines how one behaves in the presence of elders, from seating arrangements to who gets on an elevator or in a car first to who begins to eat first. Juniors in schools and in places of work are expected to pay a specific kind of respect to students or fellow employees who are senior to them. This respect includes using special titles and generally deferring to seniors in matters of judgment and choice.

New Year's Day is an especially important occasion for performing respect rituals to parents, bowing to them, thanking them for their care and support, and serving them special food and drinks. On this occasion the ceremonial rites of *jeol* are known as *sebae* (say-bay), which is sometimes translated as "New Year's bow." One of my Korean friends says that *bae* refers to bowing and that *se* may refer to age because it is an occasion when one bows to those senior in age and a day when traditionally in Korea everyone became one year older (children born during the previous year were considered two years old on New Year's Day, which was calculated according to the lunar calendar).

Foreigners visiting or residing in Korea might be able to add a special dimension to their own lives by wholeheartedly adopting the custom of *jeol*.

82

졸부

Jolbu
(Johl-buu)

"The Suddenly Rich"

Between 1962 and 1980, Korea was transformed from a basically agricultural nation into a highly industrial society. Within this short time frame the appearance of the country changed dramatically. The once-denuded hills and mountains were reforested in cloaks of green trees and foliage. Fields in the valleys and on the small plains took on the look of well-kept gardens. New homes, many of them qualifying as mansions, appeared in both urban and rural areas. High-rise office complexes, shopping centers, and smart boutiques turned the country's previously drab cities into sophisticated urban areas on a par with those found in the most advanced countries of the world.

Seoul, the capital, and other cities like Taegu, Pusan, and Kwangju grew rapidly in population, spilling across their old boundaries into suburban areas and onto farmlands. Thousands of factories sprang up on the outskirts of cities and along the new freeways connecting the major cities. This unprecedented growth drove the price of land in these areas to unbelievable heights, turning thousands of ordinary people into instant millionaires. Thousands of new businesses that were started during these decades were also virtually overnight successes, creating a new class of people who became rich quickly. In the case of farmers who sold their lands, this transformation from poor to rich occurred without any effort whatsoever on their part.

The news media soon dubbed this new class of people *jolbu* (johl-buu), which literally means "sudden wealth," in a derisive comment on their having gained wealth without working for it and for generally not having the sophistication usually associated with the well-to-do. Descendants of the old aristocratic *yangban* class, which ruled Korea for nearly two thousand years, regard *jolbu* as undeserving upstarts and are often critical of their behavior.

There is also a tendency for people who are descendants of the old *yangban* class to look with some disdain on foreigners who unknowingly go into business with *jolbu*. While the newly rich should, of course, be judged on their own personal merits, there are considerations to take into account. Because of their social background, people who are publicly identified as *jolbu* cannot always make the same connections or get the same level of cooperation and help from government officials and others that members of the old upper-class can usually count on.

Social prejudices that the so-called *jolbu* are subjected to will no doubt dissipate with time, but in the meantime they are a highly visible group of people who represent something entirely new in the Korean experience and increase the strain and friction that results from the overall cultural revolution going on in the country.

Where foreigners are concerned, the existence of *jolbu* may be a plus or a minus, depending on the circumstances. Because of their upstart image and the fact that the old guard tends to look down on them, the newly rich are often more amenable to business deals with outsiders who have no social prejudices against them and are much less likely to discriminate against them in any way. They are also inclined to be more flexible and less mercantilistic than the old guard. The downside may be the fact they cannot always take advantage of the "old boy" networks that exist among the socially elite.

83

주체

Juche
(Juu-cheh)

"Searching for Self-Reliance"

Koreans traditionally had a strong sense of their national identity. But according to research conducted by the Korean Institute for Policy Studies, they lacked a sense of *juche* (juu-cheh), or "self-reliance," because they were conditioned by Confucianism to suppress their own personal identity and self-esteem in favor of the family and the group.

In the Confucian environment of traditional Korea, people were not permitted to develop their own ideas or to behave on their own. They were programmed from birth to accept without question the values, behavior, and standards prescribed by the government-sponsored Confucian social system. One of the facets of this system was the concept of *sadae* (sah-day), which means something like "serving the great" and referred to the Confucian idea that it was proper for junior or inferior people to obey and serve senior or superior people.

Probably the most conspicuous use of the term *sadae* was to describe the ideal relationship between subjects and the king. It was also used, often in a derogatory sense, to describe Korea's historical tributary relationship with China.

Given the fact that traditional Korean society virtually precluded the development of self-reliance in practically every sense possible, it seems contradictory that the word *juche*, "self-reliance," would have such a powerful meaning to Koreans. Korean sociologists say that the fundamental *juche* concept incorporates the idea that man is the master of all things and, with proper training and willpower, can achieve any goal—something that was deliberately denied to most Koreans until modern times.

This explanation suggests that in pre-modern Korea *juche* was a philosophical concept developed by *Son* (Sohn), or Zen Buddhists, who used meditation, concentration, and physical repetition to hone both mental and physical abilities to a very high level. (The extraordinary prowess of Japan's samurai warriors was based on Zen-inspired exercises that were imported from Korea and China and then refined in Japan.)

In modern-day Korea, *juche* is part of the force that motivates Koreans to get an education and succeed in business or one of the professions. Having been denied these opportunities in the past, and having suffered unbearably under foreign as well as domestic authoritarian rulers, Koreans as individuals and as a nation strive for self-reliance.

One of the most conspicuous facets of the Korean character that emanates in part from this compulsion to be self-reliant is that they automatically assume, or take the Zen position, that they can meet any design or production challenge if they work hard enough and long enough.

Another aspect of the force that drives Koreans is a virtual obsession to catch up with Japan, which historically was politically, culturally, and technologically behind Korea. Korean historical records indicate that it was Korean horsemen from the famous Puyo tribe who founded the imperial house of Japan in the fourth century A.D. and whose descendants made up the majority of Japanese nobles for many centuries. It is clearly recorded that most of the arts and crafts that became the foundation of Japanese civilization were introduced into Japan by Koreans, either as willing immigrants or as captives brought back from Korea by Japanese pirates and invaders.

Much of the *juche* that now energizes Koreans derives from their determination to disprove the Japanese attitude that Koreans are an inferior people, as well as to dispel the lingering legacy of inferiority resulting from Korea's traditional vassal relationship with China.

In 1972 the traditional Korean concept of *juche* was given an entirely new twist by North Korean president Il Sung Kim. He fused the concept with a strong dose of Marxist-Leninist doctrine and then had it incorporated into the country's constitution as the national ideology. Kim took the position that each country should have a *sur yung* (suhr yuung), or "supreme leader," in whom people have total confidence and to whom they give total support. While *juche* in its historical sense conveyed the idea that mankind's rightful role was to be the master of the world and to dominate and transform both society and nature by acting together in a collective sense, Kim was able to grasp all of this power in his own hands.

Kim used his revised form of *juche* to justify one-man rule and mass indoctrination of the population in his thinking—the same approach that had been taken earlier by the Soviet Union's Joseph Stalin and China's Mao Zedong. North Koreans were required to pay unconditional reverence to him, to literally memorize his sayings, and to obey his orders without question. He was subsequently deified as all-powerful and omnipresent.

Kim's philosophy of how to run North Korea was based on three absolute principles: *chaju* (chah-juu), or independence; *charip* (chah-reep), self-reliance or self-sufficiency; and *chawi* (chah-we), self-defense. While this form of *juche* imbued North Koreans with extraordinary national pride, it also made them xenophobic to an extreme. This contributed to North Korean leaders' often being completely irrational in their foreign relations policies.

개인주의
Kaeinjuui
(Keh-een-juu-wee)
"In Search of Self"

Until the twentieth century most ordinary Koreans had virtually no experience with thinking or behaving as individuals and therefore could not fully understand or appreciate the idea when it was first introduced into the country at the end of the nineteenth century. Prior to that time the Korean social system was so strongly family and group oriented that *kaeinjuui* (keh-een-juu-we), or "individualism," was regarded as immoral and was prohibited by both custom and law. Punishment for those who broke any of the taboos against personal attitudes and self-oriented behavior was severe.

In addition to personal independence being nonexistent in pre-modern Korea, there was no clear concept of individual property ownership. In a strictly Western sense, Koreans did not exist as individuals. In this environment, the words *mine* and *yours* played only a minor role in Korean life. *Kaeinjuui* and all that this word now implies was an alien concept.

Scholar-author Sun Mok Chong has taken the concept of lack of differentiation to what sounds like a supernatural extreme. He says that in traditional thinking the individual and his or her ancestors and future descendants all existed in that person at once. In this amorphous cosmos, Koreans were interwoven parts of a great mosaic that had no beginning and no end and did not distinguish between themselves and their families.

Other social scientists have more mundane explanations for the traditional Korean character and personalities of the people. Some say that the typical Korean house was also a major factor in molding the Korean character. Most houses have the huge beams, large columns, heavy roof tiles covered by a thick layer of earth, and an enclosing wall. The custom of "barricading" themselves in these fortresslike abodes, say certain sociologists, was another reason Koreans traditionally did not develop strong individualistic personalities and had a weak sense of community and public responsibility.

While this kind of construction was probably intended originally to withstand the heavy rains and strong winds that annually buffeted Korea and to ward off the numbing cold of winter, there is no doubt that Koreans saw them as private refuges and regarded anything or anybody outside the home as a potential threat.

While individualism now has taken root and is growing rapidly, a great deal of Korean behavior emanates from the lack of differentiation that still exists among individuals. They tend to view themselves as physically and spiritually connected to their families and to the places where they work. The influence that this view has on the attitudes and behavior of Koreans often confuses and frustrates foreigners who are used to thinking and behaving as individuals.

Koreans often say "we" when a Westerner would say "I," and until recent times it was common for a Korean man to say "our wife" when referring to his wife. The connotation of this usage was that men did not view themselves as separate from their families; that their wives were not exclusively theirs but belonged to the family.

Familism and groupism are still overriding factors in Korean society, in personal affairs as well as business and politics, but movement toward individualism by the younger generations is becoming more and more conspicuous. This movement naturally creates a certain amount of friction on every level and in every area of Korean society, first because it goes against everything Koreans have traditionally held as sacred, and second because many of those who are adopting this essentially alien philosophy do not get it completely right.

In its Western context, people who exercise their individuality and make personal choices are expected to take responsibility for their opinions and actions. But taking personal responsibility has traditionally been just as alien to Koreans as individualism. Despite significant changes in Korean society since the mid-1900s, generally speaking people are still not permitted to behave totally as individuals, even when matters concern what Westerners regard as their most private affairs.

Politics and business are two areas in Korean life where, with still rare exceptions, there are customs and rules that strictly prohibit individualistic behavior. Even though some company founders and more enlightened executives preach individual initiative and innovation to their employees, the traditional morality and conduct are so powerful that most of those who try to follow this new way are rebuffed. If they persist, they soon find themselves compromised and neutralized by their own co-workers.

Foreigners dealing with Koreans typically find themselves frustrated because they must deal with groups of people rather than individuals. This, foreigners point out, not only slows the process of decision making but also has a tendency to dilute agreements and diffuse responsibility—which, in its Korean context, is exactly what it is supposed to do.

Korean social scientists explain typical Korean behavior by saying that their people have a strong sense of "I," of themselves as individuals, but that they are forced to pursue their personal interests in the context of groups—their families, their co-workers, sports teams, and so on.

가정
Kajong
(Kah-johng)

"The Korean Family"

Korea's traditional Confucian social system was based on the family and on a combination of "virtues" made up of personal humility, respect for the elderly, and total subordination and obedience toward superiors. The *kajong* (kah-johng), or "family," was the pillar of the society. It was where the ethic of subordination and dominance, held together and enforced by collective responsibility and punishment, began. Each family was a precisely identified group in the society, its members arranged in an exact hierarchical order with the father as the paramount authority. Children owed absolute *poktchong* (poke-chohng), or "submission/obedience," to their parents. The family was therefore a microcosm of the whole nation.

In this traditional Korean family the father-and-first-son relationship took precedence over all other relationships because it was the first son who carried on the family line and was responsible for performing the rituals of ancestor worship. In principle and often in practice, the father's authority over the son, throughout the father's life, was absolute.

This concept became the central theme and the pillar of Korean family life, so deeply embedded in the culture that today it still influences the thinking and behavior of most Koreans, including those who have been educated abroad and adopted a layer of Western culture.

The typical Korean *kajong* continues to reflect the influence of Confucianism in many ways, although there has been a dramatic shift in the relationship between husbands and wives, sons and fathers, and other members of the family. In the past Korean husbands—unaware, of course, that it is the male that determines the sex of a child—routinely divorced wives who failed to produce sons, sometimes divorcing and remarrying two or three times in a valiant effort to produce male children. Others, especially well-to-do men in the *yangban* class, routinely took concubines in their efforts to produce sons.

In general terms married women were never really considered members of their husbands' families because their bloodlines were different. They were considered outsiders and were tolerated only if they produced male children and served the husbands' families, particularly their mothers-in-law, diligently and without complaining.

Surveys in the mid-1970s showed that the concept of filial piety was still an overriding factor in Korean families. Fathers used the concept to exercise authoritarian control over both sons and daughters. Children were not treated as individuals. The private ownership of property within families was not recognized. Couples generally did not express affection for each other. Kinship ties and hierarchical relationships were still emphasized.

In present-day Korea the *kajong* is still based on the male line. It is still regarded as a great tragedy for a family not to produce male heirs to carry on the name, so having sons remains of extreme importance. But it is no longer the overriding factor in many marriages. As a general rule Korean men no longer divorce wives who fail to have sons.

Most younger Koreans today, particularly urbanites, regard such things as the kinship organizations as old-fashioned and generally ignore them. They no longer feel a compulsive need to keep detailed genealogical records. They feel a strong commitment to their families and relatives but do not feel that they should sacrifice themselves to serving others.

It is no longer taboo—or "against the cultural nature"—for Koreans to develop and demonstrate affection and love for each other. Young Koreans are as romantic as their counterparts anywhere, and passionate relationships abound.

Still, old Korean values and customs exist side by side with Western values and customs. Rank and status in families are still signified by a large number of titles or words that designate the sex and position of the individuals. There are special words for older brothers and younger brothers, for older sisters and younger sisters, for paternal uncles and aunts, for maternal uncles and aunts, etc., that are used automatically but with everyone fully aware of their social implications. These built-in linguistic and behavioral habits are among the more obvious things that give Korean culture its special nuance, making it either fascinating or frustrating to foreigners, depending on their own character.

Position on the "family tree," expressed in the term *hangyol* (hahng-yohl), is a key factor in determining the rank of families and family members within kinship groups. The closer a family is to the "founding family," the higher its status. Koreans who share the same paternal ancestors are referred to as *tongjok* (tohng-joak), "paternal relatives." They frequently come together for ceremonial functions.

Another factor in Korean life that emanates from the central role played by the family, and differentiates Koreans from most Americans and other Westerners, is that the primary motivation to succeed is to enhance the prestige and security of the family—not to distinguish the individual. Generally speaking, Koreans "behave themselves" because of concern for the reputation of their families—not because of laws or any intangible morality. To be guilty of disgracing one's family is probably the worst thing that can happen to a Korean.

86

감동
Kamdong
(Kahm-dohng)

"When Emotions Were Taboo"

For centuries all Koreans, but especially women, were conditioned to suppress their *kamdong* (kahm-dohng), or "emotions," and avoid displaying their feelings openly. This conditioning had two effects that were especially conspicuous. It made Koreans irrationally sensitive to every nuance of social interaction and charged them with very short tempers that often erupted in extreme violence.

Yet, historically, according to Tae Rim Yun and Yong Man Cho in their book *The Charms of the Koreans*, not expressing one's emotions was considered a virtue and one of the special charms of the Korean people. Obviously, however, that was a very selective view of Koreans designed to justify the extreme measures necessary to force them to suppress all their emotions.

In the officially enforced social and political ideology of pre-modern Korea the direct, public expression of emotions was immoral, and there were severe sanctions against such behavior. The primary reason for this was the Confucian concept that emotions, including love, were disruptive to the harmony of society and should therefore be suppressed.

Since all relationships were based on personal factors rather than objective or rational reasoning, people were extraordinarily sensitive about slighting someone or being slighted. Within this environment Koreans had to conceal their emotions as a defensive measure to avoid exposing themselves to any kind of danger. This danger was present at all times because the hierarchical superior/inferior structure of the society demanded absolute conformity to a stern standard of etiquette between the different classes and the dozens of levels within classes. It was also simply impossible for the people to totally suppress their *inshim* (een-sheem), or "feelings."

The only practical way Koreans had of protecting themselves was to limit the number of people they had regular contact with, to keep their inner thoughts to themselves, to maintain a calm, neutral expression, and, when forced to speak, to speak only in vague terms. But despite all of the sanctions against disorder of any kind, and all of the overt and covert conditioning in maintaining a calm, peaceful demeanor, Koreans have traditionally been quick to anger and to fight. And when they do "lose their cool," their anger is something to behold.

Of course, the very same system that was responsible for the "charming" calm and harmony historically considered characteristic of Koreans was also responsible for their short temper and tendency to fight when crossed. Having to repress their emotions toward each other, especially toward the opposite sex and in particular toward spouses, resulted in the buildup of emotion that could be triggered by the slightest deviation from officially sanctioned behavior.

In earlier times, Koreans generally internalized their emotional frustrations or took them out on family members or people who were within their own circle of contacts because any other kind of behavior was life threatening. The constant presence of powerful government officials and police magistrates mandated to enforce peaceful coexistence resulted in Koreans' developing passive ways of defending themselves and openly competing only with those in their own circle.

One of these defensive techniques was to behave and speak in a humble way when confronted by superiors, both personal and official. This self-humbling behavior derived in part from centuries of conditioning in the concept of minimizing oneself and exalting others. It was also based on the goal of reducing the threat of anger and violence from authority figures (a kind of behavior that is, of course, fundamental in much of the animal kingdom).

As usual in societies that have long been dominated by authoritarian secular and religious regimes, there was another, contradictory side to the short temper and propensity for Koreans to fight. This was an extraordinarily well-developed sense of humor, including wry, biting jokes that they used to help them endure government shortcomings and abuse by government officials.

At the same time, Korean psychologist Jae Un Kim says that because Koreans are so emotional and rely so heavily on intuition, there is another side to their character that is anything but charming. He says that Koreans are also extraordinarily narrow-minded, opinionated, and uncompromising. He adds that there is a sadistic streak in government officials and what he calls "masochistic sheepishness" in the character of the people.

The importance of denying one's *kamdong* did not begin to change in Korea until the 1960s and 1970s, and the most public of these changes was the behavior between teenage boys and girls. Traditional Korean culture required that the two sexes be segregated from an early age. Young men and women simply did not socialize with each other in any sense, and marriages were arranged by their parents, relatives, or professional go-betweens. During the long Choson dynasty (1392–1910), females were programmed to repress all emotions such as envy, jealousy, love, anger, frustration, even happiness—with disastrous effects on their mental and physical health.

The appearance of limited political and social freedoms in Korea beginning in about 1960, combined with the influence of American movies, television, and the behavior of several hundred thousand American troops and civilian personnel stationed in Korea, spurred Korean teenagers to begin dating and publicly demonstrating affection for each other. The concept of *nim* (neem), or "romantic love," spread with amazing speed.

All relationships between Koreans today are more open and relaxed than ever before, but there are still severe restraints on how people behave in business and professional relationships. Korean society is still hierarchical and is still based on inferior-superior rankings. A very precise kind of protocol is still mandatory when inferiors address or respond to superiors. Care must still be taken at all times not to offend people by failing to follow the etiquette demanded by their status, whether inferior or superior.

Essayist Kyu Tae Yi says that Koreans still stress emotional ties rather than specific, concrete obligations (as the Japanese do), by which he apparently means to imply that Koreans are less predictable and more volatile than the Japanese.

In all normal situations, self-restraint—as a protective device rather than a sign of humility—is still a hallmark of Korean behavior—so much so that Western businesspeople in Korea are often frustrated because their Korean colleagues, employees, officials, and others are not more frank and forthcoming. One of the major concerns of foreigners dealing with Koreans is not to inadvertently and unknowingly trigger their tempers.

87

가난

Kanan
(Kah-nahn)

"Taking Comfort in Poverty"

Members of Korea's traditional ruling class, the *yangban* (yahng-bahn), like most ruling classes everywhere, typically used both religion and philosophy to justify their rule and their privileged existence. For centuries, state-sponsored religious and philosophical ideologies were used to imbue common people in Korea with the belief that there was virtue in *kanan* (kah-nahn), or "poverty." Each generation learned anew the expression (attributed to a member of the elite scholar-official class): "Be content with poverty and be pleased with the Way." (A contemporary term for *poverty* is *pingon*/peen-gohn.)

In this case "the Way" referred to the Buddhist and Taoist beliefs that materialism, over and above what one needs to survive in modest comfort, is one of the most insidious and destructive of all human instincts and must be exorcised or suppressed before one can achieve true happiness.

There was, of course, enough truth in this "happiness in poverty" philosophy that when the so-called *kanan* level was not below what is necessary to maintain health as well as life, it was not fundamentally cruel. But that did not allay the unrequited desires of ordinary Koreans to be able to indulge themselves in some of the attractions and pleasures routinely enjoyed by the upper class. Not surprisingly, this prompted Korea's upper class to attempt to blunt these ambitions by also preaching that envy was an evil that all moral and upright people should shun.

One of the results of this situation was that Korean proverbs and sayings, of which there are thousands, primarily emphasize the political and economic hardships suffered by the Koreans over the centuries. Psychologist To Hwan

Kim, who analyzed 7,300 proverbs, found that their most common subjects were concern with poverty, a desire for wealth, hostility toward government officials, disdain for the elite *yangban* class, contempt for people who did menial work, anxiety about social relationships, the acceptance of authoritarianism as the natural order of things, and expressions of both optimism and fatalism.*

By the 1980s about the only ancient proverbial sentiments that survived were an ongoing desire for wealth and hostility toward government officials. For the first time in their history ordinary Koreans had achieved a lifestyle that was conspicuously above the *kanan* level and made their lives so different from what had been traditional since their emergence as a people that it was, in fact, a different world.

In one short, intense generation Koreans virtually eliminated *kanan* and in the process of doing so exorcised a concept that had been promoted by the elite ruling class for more than two thousand years.

While no longer content with poverty, Koreans have not not become totally caught up in materialism. Both Taoism and Buddhism hold that materialism is one of the great evils that human beings must avoid—or overcome—if they are to achieve true happiness, and the legacy of this philosophy remains deeply embedded in the Korean psyche. The challenge facing Koreans now is to achieve a balance between materialism and asceticism that provides them with the best of both worlds.

88

같은솥밥
Katun Sosuy Pap
(Kaht-unn Soh-suut Pahp)
"Eating from the Same Rice Bowl"

Because food is essential for life, it is not surprising that it was apparently the first and most important religious offering in most if not all of humanity's religious cults. Food still has a semireligious aura in most countries today, particularly in countries like China, Japan, and Korea, where key elements of the culture have survived since prehistoric times.

Certain foods continue to have powerful religious connotations in all of these countries, and a variety of rituals involve food as offerings and as symbols of piety, commitment, togetherness, and so on. One of these ritualistic practices that has survived in Korea and plays a significant role in society, private as well as public, is known as *katun sosuy pap* (kaht-uun soh-suut pahp), which literally means "same pot rice/meal" and is used in the sense of "eating from the same

---

*To Hwan Kim. *A Psychological Analysis of Korean Proverbs* (Pusan; Haeyang Publishers, 1976).

pot." (The Japanese version of this saying is *onaji kama no meshi*/oh-nah-jee kah-mah no may-she, or "same pot food.")

Koreans have traditionally used eating together and sharing food from the same pots and platters as a means of consciously and deliberately bonding relationships, and the practice is even more common today because affluence has made it possible for more people to make use of the ritualized custom in their daily personal and business affairs.

Katun sosuy pap occasions range from large, elaborate banquets staged by politicians, bureaucrats, and businesspeople to one-on-one breakfasts, luncheons, and dinners that vary from informal to pretentious. With the exception of breakfast meetings, which are the most casual, "same pot meals" almost always include drinking alcoholic beverages, a custom that has its own set of ritualistic do's and don't's and plays an equally significant—if not more important—role in relationships in Korea.

Outsiders who become involved with Koreans for whatever purpose should be aware of the psychological and emotional role that sharing food and drink plays in Korean life and respond accordingly. This does not mean, however, that foreign guests should drink too much—something that is very common among newcomers in Korea because Korean hosts are typically very forceful in encouraging their guests to drink, and foreign guests are afraid it would be impolite and possibly damaging to the relationship to say no. There are ways of getting around this problem. See *Umju*.

An obvious aspect of the *katun sosuy pap* custom is when and how to reciprocate. The more of this kind of "hospitality" that one accepts without reciprocating, the greater the obligation that one has to the host and the more unequal the relationship becomes. Seniors customarily treat their juniors to food and drink as a key facet of their superior/inferior relationship. Both parties clearly understand the dynamics of the situation, and both are prepared to fulfill the obligations that are inherent in their relationship.

Foreigners should be cautious about allowing themselves to be put in an "inferior" position by keeping the "account" between themselves and their Korean contacts balanced or, better yet, in their favor.

89

ㄱ|

Ki
(Kee)

"The Cosmic Force"

Koreans, like all ancient people, first viewed the world as a spiritual phenomenon and saw themselves as linked inseparably with the earth and with everything in nature. Sometime after the Koreans established their first tribal states, the Chinese (whose civilization was already more than two thousand years old) introduced Koreans to a philosophical-scientific theory that the cosmos is animated by a "force" or "power" that provides the spark of life to all matter in the universe. This energy is called *qi* (chee) in Chinese and *ki* (kee) in Korean.

In this theory, *ki* energy is dualistic, meaning that it consists of a combination of positive and negative forces that must be in harmony for the "matter" or "life" concerned to function properly. The Chinese went on to explain further the nature and role of *ki* in their much better-known *yin-yang* theory, which divides *ki* energy and matter into *yin* and *yang* categories. These categories are made up of opposites: light-darkness, heat-cold, aggressive-passive, male-female, sweet-sour, health-sickness, explosion-implosion, and so on.

According to the Chinese theory of *ki*, which the Koreans integrated into their own cosmos, human life and all the forces that affect life are manifestations of *ki*, which can be controlled and manipulated. Like their Chinese tutors, the Koreans thereafter incorporated the principle of this universal power into their lifestyle. Houses and other buildings were positioned and constructed to attract the positive forces of *ki* and dispel negative forces. Graves were aligned to be in harmony with *ki*. The combination of foods eaten at meals was based on a harmonious balance between the dualistic forces of their *ki*.

In this theory of cosmic energy it was *ki* that determined a person's physical and mental health. Any imbalance in the energy resulted in some kind of ailment. In response to this belief, Chinese physicians some three thousand years ago identified "*ki* channels" in the human body and located some 650 "meridian points" where this energy could be stimulated or blocked by pressure, massage, or insertion of needles into the body. These discoveries led to the origin of the practice of acupuncture—*zhenjiu* (jen-juu) in Chinese, *harikyu* (hah-ree-que) in Japanese, and *chim* (cheem) in Korean.

Ki can be concentrated and enhanced through mental power—the power of thought—which sometimes occurs spontaneously, as during some kind of emergency when people lift objects they could not move under other circumstances. Ordinarily, however, it takes a great deal of mental and physical discipline over a period of time to tap into the power of *ki*. The best-known groups of people to deliberately seek to utilize the power of *ki* include Zen priests, Japan's famous samurai warriors, and martial arts practitioners, who in Korea are generally *taekwondo* students.

While the authenticated feats of some monks, warriors, martial arts experts, and acupuncturists are so remarkable that the power of *ki* seems self-evident, its nature—even its existence—is still widely disputed by Western scientists and others. However, modern-day technology appears to be rapidly proving that the Chinese and their Korean and Japanese protégés have been right all along. New electronic devices have shown that the human body, like all plants and other forms of life, has an aura emanating from an internal power source and that mind-power can dramatically affect the functions of the body.

It is quite possible, of course, that this internal power source, suddenly magnified, is responsible for incidents of spontaneous healing that Western scientists cannot explain. Koreans, along with the Chinese and Japanese, attribute many of their successes to their belief in *ki* and their conscious use of it in many of their endeavors.

An interesting side note: Don Hackney, an American businessman residing in Korea and student of all things Korean, notes that in the early years of the Japanese occupation of Korea (1910–45) the Japanese colonial administrators had large metal stakes driven into the summits of Korea's most sacred mountains to upset the *ki* of the country. It is believed that most of the stakes have been found and removed. Hackney adds that in 1995 there was a museum exhibit of the stakes that had been discovered.

90

기분

Kibun
(Key-boon)

"Feelings Come First"

The primary principle at work in social relationships in Korea has traditionally been Confucian-oriented harmony. In fact, most of the time in the past harmony took precedence over virtually everything else—over honesty, truth, accomplishment, and so on. Harmony is still a primary consideration of Koreans in almost all of their interpersonal relationships. It affects their attitudes and behavior directly and dramatically in every area of their lives.

Since harmony is an emotional state of mind, emotional factors rather than objective reasoning play an important role in how Koreans act and react in their daily lives. The key to interacting effectively with Koreans is therefore being able to divine and deal with their personal feelings and mood—in Korean terms, with their *kibun* (key-boon).

Kibun literally means "feelings," but its implications and importance go well beyond this English term. In its full cultural context *kibun* incorporates most of the values Koreans hold dear. It is the foundation of harmony. It sets the tone, style, and quality of all their relationships. Face, dignity, pride, respect, and more are bound up in the meaning and role of *kibun*. For Koreans to develop and maintain harmonious relationships they must be able to accurately "read" the *kibun* of others, adjust their own attitudes and behavior accordingly, and at the same time protect their own feelings. Richard Saccone says in his book *The Business of Korean Culture* the goal of *kibun* is for people to help each other stay "unthreatened, relaxed, comfortable and happy." This makes it imperative that people avoid or ignore many situations that are commonplace in business and everyday life, from minor mistakes and embarrassments to very serious matters.

Kibun can be be damaged—and cause a negative reaction—by a wide variety of things that usually involve failing to follow the very precise rules of Korean etiquette. Some of the more common of these transgressions are not bowing properly to a superior, not using the proper respect language, not using a person's official title, inadvertently treating a senior as a subordinate, giving an inappropriate gift, being the bearer of bad news, making critical remarks about someone or something that are contrary to the other party's views, and questioning the competency, veracity, or honesty of an individual. *Kibun* injuries invariably result in *wonmang* (wohn-mahng), "resentment" and "grudge," and the creation of a *chok* (choak), "enemy."

The ability to read a person's *kibun* is a cultural skill that is called *nunchi*, which literally means "eye measure." From early infancy on, Koreans are programmed in both the need for and the ability to be sensitive to and react properly to the *kibun* of others. In both personal and professional situations Koreans depend on the accurate measurement and understanding of *kibun* as much as if not more upon than on verbal communication. This is especially important in the workplace where people of different ages, backgrounds, and social status, and therefore different *kibun* requirements, must interact constantly in a cooperative and highly efficient manner.

The *kibun* factor in Korean culture puts most foreigners at a serious disadvantage in their dealings with Koreans because becoming attuned to it and developing the skills necessary to cope with it do not come quickly or easily. In fact many Westerners in Korea never get on the *kibun* wavelength, even though they may live and work in the country for years. Some don't bother to try. Others don't have the necessary cross-cultural or linguistic skills. About the only practical recourse newcomers and these people have is to develop a close confidant relationship with one or more older Koreans who will act as their counselors and sounding boards.

Given the hierarchical, authoritarian nature of Korean society, most *kibun* transgressions are committed by subordinates or inferiors upsetting people who are superior to them. A superior may criticize an inferior without damaging his or her *kibun* as long as the action is within the superior's area of responsibility. In other words, the *kibun* factor in Korean culture is designed primarily to ensure that inferiors cater to superiors, and avoid upsetting them, even when such behavior requires that they keep silent about vital information, tell lies, and otherwise obscure or misrepresent the true situation. The *kibun* of the superior normally takes precedence over all other considerations.

This is not to imply that people of lower social status do not have inner feelings that need protecting. All Koreans are impregnated with *kibun* and are extraordinarily sensitive about keeping it in harmony. The major difference is that the lower the social status of the individuals concerned, the more people there are above them that can push them around without worrying about upsetting them, and the more people whose *kibun* they have to protect.

Foreigners in Korea are in an especially sensitive position. Not being Korean and therefore not having the status that comes with being a member of Korea's hierarchical society, they do not have the privilege or prerogative of "looking down" on anyone or ignoring anyone's feelings.

Much of the friction that occurs between Westerners and Koreans results from the *kibun* of the Koreans being disturbed—often unintentionally by the foreign side because they are not aware of what the Koreans find disturbing. American military personnel and civilian employees of the U.S. government stationed in Korea from the end of World War II in 1945 until recent times created enormous ill will for Americans in general because of the superior attitude many of them exhibited toward Koreans of all classes.

The sensitivity of Koreans to their *kibun* is slowly decreasing as they become more individualistic and self-assured. The day-to-day use of the term itself is also diminishing. But the feelings subsumed in the word are so deeply ingrained in the Korean psyche that they will no doubt continue to play a vital role in Korean life for the foreseeable future.

91

기독교

Kiddokyo
(Keed-doh-k'yoh)

"Christianity in Korea"

Records indicate that the first Christian to enter Korea was a Catholic priest named Gregorio de Cespedes who accompanied a Japanese army that invaded Korea in 1597. One of the generals leading the invasion forces, Konishi Yukinaga, was a Christian convert, but there is no clear record of why he took the priest along. The Japanese invaders succeeded in killing dozens of thousands of Koreans (they cut off the ears of thousands of their victims, pickled them, and took them back to Japan to prove it), but there is no record of their having made any converts to Christianity.

The real introduction of *Kiddokyo* (Keed-doh-k'yoh), or "Christianity," into Korea was accomplished by a young Korean scholar named Sung Hun Yi, a member of the ruling family, who went to Beijing, China, in 1777 with his emissary father, was converted to Christianity by Jesuit priests, and on his return to Seoul founded a Christian church.

Religious historian Tong Shik Yu notes in his book *Korean Religions and Christianity* that shamanism, Korea's indigenous religion, did not impede the spread of Christianity in Korea because it was not an exclusive ideology and had many things in common with Christianity, from its prayer rituals to gain favor and ward off disaster to its emphasis on the supernatural and its conservatism.

Over the next twenty-three years scholar-turned-missionary Yi succeeded in converting some four thousand Koreans to Catholicism. But because many of the converts then refused to conduct the traditional ancestral rituals required by Confucianism, the state religion, they were severely persecuted, causing the movement to lose its momentum and go underground. Yi was executed in 1801, following which many of his followers were also put to death.

In the early 1800s the Vatican appointed an apostolic vicor for Korea, following which three French priests entered the country, established churches, and began making converts. After repeated requests by the newly converted Korean Catholics, Pope Gregory XVI ordered the consecration of the first Korean priest and the establishment of a Korean diocese in 1831—making the church in Korea independent from China.

In 1839 the Korean court, dominated by outside Confucian influences, ordered the three French priests and many of their Korean converts executed. Some years later the first Korean to be ordained as a priest, in China, returned and began preaching. He was executed in 1846. A few years later the court's anti-Catholic policy was relaxed, resulting in the arrival of several more French priests who began proselytizing and publishing books and tracts on Catholicism that had been translated into *Hangul* (Hahn-guhl), the simplified Korean writing system.

From about 1850 the influence of the Catholic church in Korea began to grow again, alarming the Yi Court, which saw the new religion as a threat to its Confucian ideology and to the state as well. In 1863 there were twelve Korean Catholic priests in the country and a like number of French Catholic priests residing in Seoul. Altogether there were some twenty-three thousand Korean converts to Catholicism.

In 1866 the Yi court ordered nine of the French Catholic priests living in Seoul executed (the execution, by beheading, was carried out on the banks of the Han River, which passes through Seoul) and unleashed a pogrom against Korean converts to Catholicism that resulted in the massacre of some eight thousand. (The French, in retaliation for the execution of the priests, sent a fleet of warships to bombard the west coast of Korea.)

The pressure against Korea to open its doors to foreign missionaries as well as foreign diplomats and traders was inexorable. In 1875 Japan claimed that some of its ships had been attacked by Korean coastal defense forces and used the ruse to occupy Seoul and force the Korean government to allow Japanese diplomatic and trade missions to set up permanent offices in Seoul.

This opened the gates for other foreigners to rush into Korea. In 1884, an American Protestant missionary-doctor named Horace Allen, who was serving as physician to the diplomatic corps in Seoul, was appointed physician to the ruling Yi family. Shortly afterward he founded the country's first Western-style hospital and thereafter used his political influence to bring in other Protestant missionaries and establish Protestant churches in the country.

Christianity appealed to many Koreans, especially women, because it advocated human rights, social equality, and other democratic principles. The occupation and annexation of Korea by Japan at the beginning of the twentieth century served as an extraordinary impetus for the spread of Christianity among dissident Koreans.

However, in a Christian sense many of these conversions were incomplete. Most Korean converts found it impossible to accept the Christian dogma that Christianity is the only religion that possesses and preaches "the truth." Today approximately 25 percent of the Korean population is listed as Christian, and

Korean Christians are prominent in government, business, and all of the professions.

As far as Koreans were concerned, the most impressive elements in Christianity were its teachings that all people are equal in the eyes of a Heavenly Being, that all men are brothers, and that universal love should be the foundation of all relationships. This was a startling concept in the experience of Koreans, because it contradicted the very foundations of their society and virtually every tenet of their culture. For centuries they had been taught that order and harmony based on a hierarchical ranking of all people and inferiors fulfilling their obligations to superiors were the foundation for all ethical and moral behavior.

A report published by the Korean Institute of Policy Studies on the influence of religions in Korea pointed out that Christian churches were the only place in all of Korea where men, women, the young and old, common people and rich people, and people who were not related to each other could sit together without any restrictions or protocol.

There are said to be more Christian churches in Korea than Buddhist temples—a testimony to the persistence of both foreign missionaries and their Korean converts.

Christianity, Buddhism, Confucianism, and shamanism coexist in Korea without any apparent turf conflicts. Each one basically overlays the other, with some elements from all of them fused together. The surface manifestations of Buddhism and Christianity in Korea make them more visible to the eye, but just beneath this surface layer one invariably finds a bedrock of Confucianism and shamanism in the Korean psyche.

Korean writer Chan-sup Chang calls Korean Christians "yin-yang Christians" because, he says, they have to balance their Christianity with their Koreanness. He says they are Christians when they are in church and "Korean Christians" when they are not in church.

92

김치

Kimchi
(Keem-chee)

"The Spice of Life"

Korean food is as distinctive as the character and traditional behavior of the people—robust and enduring. The Korean dish that most people regard as the "most Korean" of all is *kimchi* (keem-chee). Virtually everyone who has ever been involved with Koreans anywhere in the world, or spent more than a few days in Korea, is familiar with *kimchi*, a dish that is so potent some people have compared it to rocket fuel.

There are some two dozen varieties of *kimchi*, but probably the most common version consists of Chinese cabbage that has been pickled in a volatile mixture of red pepper, garlic, scallions, radishes, ginger, and salt. Although *kimchi* is often referred to as a side dish, it is, in fact, more like a main dish, and few Korean meals have ever been served without it. Cucumbers, radishes, and scallions are among the other vegetables that are routinely *kimchi*'d.

In the old days virtually every Korean family in the country made a fresh supply of *kimchi* daily during the summer months when the ingredients would ferment quickly in the heat. Preparing *kimchi* for the frigid winter months was a major fall event that was called *kimjang* (keem-jahng), which figuratively means "preparing winter *kimchi*." Whole families generally participated in the annual *kimjang* event. After the desired volume of ingredients had been prepared, they were placed in large pots that were then wrapped in straw and buried up to their necks in the ground. The last of the lot, eaten the following spring, would be ripe indeed.

Commercially made *kimchi* has been available in food stores and supermarkets in Korea since the 1960s, but many rural families continue to make their own and often supply their city relatives as well. Despite its popularity and positive symbolic relationship with Korean culture, the term *kimchi* is commonly used in a derogatory sense. Says Ernest G. Beck, an American *taekwondo* master and lifelong student of Korean culture, "In its negative sense *kimchi* is used to infer that something is of low quality—for example, 'Kimchi Cadillac' (Hyundai car); 'Kimchi GI' (Korean soldier)."

Another food item, or ingredient, in Korean cuisine that may go back even further than *kimchi* is *manul* (mahn-uhl), or "garlic." Early Western visitors to Korea quickly became aware that the breath of most Koreans smelled of a strong, unfamiliar odor, particularly powerful when they were confined with several people in a small, hot room. It didn't take these visitors long to discover that this unusual odor was garlic and that many Koreans ate so much of it that their bodies seemed to be literally saturated with the smell. It also wasn't long before many of the Westerners became immunized to the odor by doing as the Koreans did—eating copious amounts of *manul* in most of their meals.

Garlic has a long and glorious history in Korea as one of the most potent and important of the disease-fighting and health-giving herbs, first as a medicine prescribed by the country's shaman healers and then as a vital part of the people's daily diet. Early Koreans believed that *manul* had magical powers, so much so that it played a key role in their creation myth.

According to this myth, when *Hwanung*, the son of "God," was sent down to earth to create the Korean race, he encountered a female bear that was praying to become human. *Hwanung* gave the bear twenty pieces of garlic to eat (and some mugwort) and told it to spend one hundred days (some histories say twenty-one days) in a cave. During its stay in the cave the bear was transformed into a beautiful woman—the Korean Eve. (This first Korean woman subsequently became pregnant by "divine favor" and gave birth to a son, *Tangun*, who became the founder of the Korean race and established the first Korean dynasty, in 2333 B.C.)

Given this central role of garlic in the creation myth of the Korean race it is not surprising that it has continued to occupy a special place in Korean life—and is something that uninitiated visitors cannot avoid if they sample Korean cuisine. Many foreigners who spend any length of time in Korea develop a taste for *kimchi*, and it stays with them for life. (Canned *kimchi* is now exported to many countries of the world and is continuing to gain devotees among Westerners.)

93

기생

Kisaeng

(Kee-sang)

"The Pleasure Girls"

During the so-called Three Kingdoms period in Korea, roughly 57 B.C. to A.D. 669, it became the custom for a troupe of attractive young girls, especially trained in singing, dancing, and pleasing men, to be attached to the royal court for the pleasure of the king, senior ministers, and important visitors. These young women were called *yorak* (yoh-rahk), which might be translated as "entertainers."

By the advent of the unified Shilla kingdom in A.D. 669 the keeping of female entertainers at court had become an important part of the palace activities and had a far-reaching effect on society as a whole. These young women, who were eventually to become known as *kisaeng* (kee-sang), which means something like "art person" or "person skilled in various arts," were to play a major role in Korean history, socially, politically, culturally, and economically, down to present times.

In addition to singing and dancing at court, these early female "artists" entertained troops in distant outposts. It is also amply recorded that during the Koryo dynasty (935–1392) the *kisaeng* attracted the amorous attentions of kings and high-ranking court officials, particularly after power was seized in the twelfth century by military generals and during the suzerainty of the Mongol Yuan dynasty in China, when high Mongol representatives dominated the Korean court (1271–1368).

At different times the institution of the *kisaeng* became especially controversial because their dual role as mistresses and prostitutes resulted in numerous scandals, particularly involving young scholar-officials in Seoul, and there were demands that the institution be abolished. But the heyday of the *kisaeng* in Korea was to come during the Choson dynasty, which began in 1392.

The Choson court adopted as the state religion a new form of Confucianism that was to have a profound effect on the relations between the sexes. This new ideology, which was made the foundation of society, required that the sexes virtually live apart and that love play no role in marriage. In fact the expression of practically all emotions in interpersonal relationships between males and females was to be suppressed in favor of absolute surface harmony.

With the emotional element dramatically reduced in Korean life and almost eliminated from the husband-wife relationship, men in all classes begin to seek both emotional and sexual succor outside the home with professional prostitutes and mistresses who came in several categories, including widows and the relatively large number of women who had been kicked out by their husbands (for misbehavior or failure to bear sons) and were not permitted to remarry.

This extreme form of Confucianism greatly enhanced the role of the *kisaeng*—the Korean equivalent of the better-known *geisha* of Japan. In the late fifteenth and early sixteenth century the Choson dynasty's King Yonsan was especially notorious for partying with *kisaeng*. During his reign he increased the number of court *kisaeng* from one hundred to ten thousand. He referred to his chief *kisaeng* recruiter as his "red skirt envoy."

During this period the keeping of concubines by nobles and other upper-class men in Seoul became so widespread and involved so many women that teams of recruiters were kept busy searching the eight provinces for the prettiest girls. In many instances the girls and young women (some of whom were married) were simply kidnapped. The number of facilities and the volume of wearing apparel, food, and other supplies necessary to accommodate such a large number of young women was enormous and required a major organized effort. These supplies were commandeered from the provinces. The concubines themselves were classified into more than one hundred categories that delineated their origin, age, education, talents, and so on.

As time passed, the institution of the *kisaeng* became a large-scale commercial enterprise. *Kisaeng*, recruited from among the prettiest girls in the commoner class, were the only females in Korea who were legally allowed to become educated. To enhance their attraction to their upper-class patrons, novice *kisaeng* were trained carefully in reading, writing, composing poetry, and playing musical instruments, singing, and dancing. They were also instructed in a variety of topics that allowed them to engage their patrons in lively conversations—something that Korean men did not do with their wives or other women.

Kisaeng could wear cosmetics and gorgeous clothes, both of which were denied to ordinary women. They did not have to avert their eyes when passing men, and they could smile and talk whenever and as much as they pleased—all of which were also denied to other women. The law stated that girls had to be fifteen years old before they could officially become *kisaeng*, but their training began when they were eight or nine years old. Although only lower-class girls were eligible to become *kisaeng*, their skills and education made them very popular among upper-class men, who frequently took them as concubines and in some controversial instances married them as second wives, despite a law at that time prohibiting *kisaeng* from marrying.

The law also required that *kisaeng* retire upon reaching the age of thirty—a figure set to make sure that the women were at the peak of their physical charms during their careers.

In each generation there were *kisaeng* who became nationally famous for their exceptional beauty and skills. Many of the women in this category became well-to-do from monetary and other gifts received from their patrons. Those who were less fortunate often became nuns, mistresses, or prostitutes after reaching the age of thirty because no other employment was open to them and they were prevented from marrying.

The number of *kisaeng* grew rapidly during the first century of the Choson dynasty. The most attractive and brightest daughters of government slaves in Seoul and in the provinces of Chungchong, Kyongsang, and Cholla were trained in special *kisaeng* schools in the capital. After completing the training, the girls who had been recruited in Seoul and registered as official *kisaeng* were required to entertain the elite men of the day, including prime ministers, provincial governors, scholar-officials, poets, painters, calligraphers, and men from influential families. Girls brought in from outside provinces were generally returned to their home provinces to work in their own regions. Eventually a decree was issued permitting *kisaeng* to marry, following which their husbands acted as their managers.

The early Choson dynasty also saw the rise of two other categories of *kisaeng*: medical *kisaeng* and needlework *kisaeng*. The need for clothing by court women and the wives of nobles, ministers, and other upper-class men required a small army of women trained in needlework. Since the recruiting and training of large numbers of women for the entertainment industry was already well established, the court simply decided to create another category of *kisaeng*.

The impetus for the creation of a corps of medical *kisaeng* was much more extraordinary. Female members of the royal family, wives of nobles, ministers, and so on frequently died young from lack of medical care because it was culturally, politically, and socially taboo for them to expose their bodies to men or to be touched by any man other than their husbands. Since all doctors were men, many women who became ill refused to be seen by a doctor, subsequently received no treatment for their ailments, and often died.

When women were prevailed on to consult doctors, the doctors had to perform their examinations without touching the women and, in the case of members of the royal family, without seeing them. The female patients were kept hidden behind curtains, screens, or doors. It is recorded that princesses and other female members of the nobility who were ill would wind silk threads around their wrists and have the other end of the thread extended through a window or a slightly open door to an outside garden where a doctor would take hold of the thread and try to read the patient's pulse through it. The other means of diagnosing such unseen patients was listening to their voices and getting descriptions of their appearance and symptoms from their servants.

To remedy this situation, the court ordered that some of the young girls recruited to become *kisaeng* also be trained in diagnosing ailments and providing limited medical care to female patients. These so-called medical *kisaeng* were taught to treat patients by using *chim* (cheem), or "acupuncture," moxibustion (placing small amounts of shredded mugwort on key points on the body and setting them afire), and dispensing a variety of herbal medicines. Medical *kisaeng* students who got good grades and passed the final examinations received cash prizes and were assigned to duty in the capital or in their home province. Those who failed the examinations were punished by being made tea brewers.

The first *kisaeng* to be allowed to take ordinary men as husband-managers, called *kibu* (kee-buu), were those trained in medical treatment and needlework. This custom was implemented because it was decided that they would be more productive if they had someone taking care of their household affairs for them.

Near the end of the Choson dynasty, Prince Taewon became notorious for his policy of allowing upper-class men to have free access to the palace *kisaeng*. Between 1897 and 1906, a *kisaeng* union was formed and most of the *kisaeng* who practiced prostitution were rounded up and confined in a courtesan district called Sanghwashil in the southern part of Seoul. Also during the latter years of the Choson dynasty rich merchants and their sons often patronized *kisaeng* to the point that they bankrupted themselves and in some notorious cases were forced to become servants to the *kisaeng* they had previously supported. There were also numerous occasions when *kisaeng* who publicly "belonged" to an older patron had one or more secret lovers who were young men. Over the centuries, several of Korea's *kisaeng* became heroines in times of domestic turmoil and for their actions against invaders, particularly Japanese invaders.

Korea's *kisaeng* have survived into modern times. Every city has its *kisaeng* houses, but their professional training has been watered down, their social status has fallen, and they have competition from teahouse and cabaret hostesses. Nevertheless they continue to occupy a special niche in Korean society.

An old saying that love in a *kisaeng* house is as casual as a pinecone dropping from a tree is no longer valid. Patrons of present-day *kisaeng* houses have to throw a lot of money at the "trees" to get their "cones" down. In fact, the biggest complaint about Korea's *kisaeng* houses today is that they are too expensive for ordinary salaried men. They are patronized almost exclusively by politicians and company executives who are exceptionally affluent or have generous entertainment allowances.

Although present-day *kisaeng* generally have not undergone the specialized training that was required in earlier times, some of them can play traditional musical instruments, and all of them can sing popular Korean songs and perform folk dances with passable expertise. In houses that cater to foreign guests, *kisaeng* parties almost always begin with traditional Korean entertainment and then go Western or modern. Most if not all of the *kisaeng* know several songs in English and Japanese and are skilled at all of the popular Western styles of dancing. Typical *kisaeng* parties end with everybody soused and singing the popular Korean song "*Arirang*," which might be called the "Auld Lang Syne" of Korea. As in the past, some of the *kisaeng* are available for private after-hours parties with patrons who can afford their fees.

But the profession of the *kisaeng* may be on the verge of extinction. The number of *kisaeng* "houses"—actually inns, called *yojung* (yoh-juung), that have in-house *kisaeng* or call them in from the outside when guests request them— has decreased dramatically since the 1960s, when nightclubs and cabarets featuring hostesses proliferated in the country's major cities.

Historically one major difference between Korea's *kisaeng* and Japan's *geisha* was that the *kisaeng* were usually younger, invariably had better figures, and were prettier and more sensually attractive than their Japanese counterparts.* Some were so gorgeous that newly arrived foreign men who were not yet used to how beautiful Korean women can be found themselves stunned.

94

골품

Kolpum
(Kohl-poom)

"Twin Pillars of Shilla"

In the seventh century after the rise of the Tang dynasty in China, Shilla, one of the three kingdoms then existing on the Korean peninsula, allied itself with the Tang court. With Chinese assistance, Shilla was able to defeat the armies of the other two Korean kingdoms, Koguryo and Paekche. Then, in a move to prevent China from reestablishing total control over the peninsula, Shilla formed an alliance with the remaining Koguryo forces, drove the Chinese out, and in 668 unified the peninsula under a single banner for the first time in its history.

Shilla eventually had to reassume a vassal status to China and keep the Chinese at bay by paying an annual tribute, but the Shilla period (669–935) was to be Korea's first golden age and the term Shilla continues to have a special place in the historical memory of Koreans.

The Shilla court reorganized Korean society on the basis of *kolpum* (kohl-poom), a hierarchical ranking system based on ancestry, and a paramilitary organization known as *hwarang* (whah-rahng) for the education and training of the sons of the ruling class. The ranking system of the elite ruling class was based on "bone ranks," which Koreanologist Alan Carter Covell says apparently derived from a shamanistic concept that human bones were semimagical and related to the individual's social status. In this context they were the equivalent of bloodlines in tracing ancestry.

People in the highest class were categorized as *song gol* (sohng gohl), literally "sacred bones." Members of this class who made up the royal family and chief ministers were distinguished further by the term *chin gol* (cheen gohl), which means "true bones." The Shilla aristocracy practiced endogamy—marrying only within their own class. The *kolpum* system ensured that the class divisions in society would be permanent. The *hwarang* system limited all education and training in military and administrative matters to the sons of the elite, further ensuring that only members of the elite were prepared for leadership of any kind.

---

*Japanese *geisha* have never been subject to any mandatory retirement age, with the result that many continue in the profession until they are in their fifties, sixties, or even older. In earlier times the luckier ones continued to serve patrons they first met when they were teenagers. Such loyalty is rare in present-day Japan.

Setting up its capital at Kyongju in the south-central portion of the peninsula, the Shilla court began a program of sponsoring the arts and Buddhism that resulted in hundreds of Korean students being sent to China and India, and constructing large numbers of palaces, huge gardens, pagodas, temples, and tombs in the city and its environs. Shilla also expanded trade and cultural relations with Japan. Hundreds of Korean scholars, artists, and craftsmen took up residence in Japan, many on a permanent basis, greatly influencing that country's political, social, and economic development.

But the same rigid social organization and domination of all areas of life by warrior-aristocrats that made early Shilla powerful were also a cancer eating away at its core. As the generations passed, overindulgence and corruption in the Shilla court made it weak and inefficient. Rival warlords appeared in the outlying provinces. Its patron, the Tang dynasty in China, was also in trouble and unable to help.

Discontent among all of those who were excluded from power resulted in one rebellion after another. Finally, the ruling Shilla king handed his throne over to a resurgent Koguryo kingdom in the North. The capital was moved to Kaesong, north of Seoul, and a new dynasty took the name of Koryo. One of the first things the new dynasty did was abolish the *kolpum* system and revise the Chinese system of selecting all government officials by means of annual civil service exams that had been adopted by the Shilla dynasty shortly after its founding. Under the new Koryo regime, the right to hold office was less restrictive and was not limited to members of the elite ruling class. Anyone, including former soldiers recruited from the common class as well as slaves, could study and sit for the annual exams and, if they passed, win appointment to a government office.

The *kolpum* concept did not disappear, however, because it was so deeply embedded in Confucianism. But it was to be relatively dormant until the beginning of Korea's next—and last—dynasty, the Choson or Yi dynasty, which began in 1392.

General Song Gye Yi, the founder of the Choson dynasty, made Neo-Confucianism, based on absolute filial piety and ancestor worship, the state ideology and the state religion, which not only reinstated the philosophy of *kolpum* but also made it the foundation of Korean society. General Yi and his successors also chose to continue the *hwarang* paramilitary corps for the sons of the elite, again guaranteeing a steady supply of well-educated warrior-administrators to direct the affairs of the country.

The *kolpum* system remained virtually unchanged until the Choson dynasty began breaking down in the mid-1800s—a period of nearly five hundred years. It was finally ended altogether by the Japanese when they annexed the country in 1910. However, by the beginning of the twentieth century, the concept and practice of filial piety had become so much a part of the psyche of Koreans that it was the defining factor in their society, controlling almost every aspect of their lives, and it was to remain so until the 1970s.

Although *kolpum* no longer controls Korean society, it is still of vital importance in the lives of Koreans, influencing their interpersonal relationships, their education, and their work. But ancestor worship, the ultimate extension of filial piety, did not survive Korea's encounter with the outside world and is now little more than a curious reminder of the past. Koreans still show deep respect for their ancestors, however, and many of them continue to perform rituals on behalf of their departed forebears. But these rites are now more like folk customs than mandatory acts of worship.

The Choson dynasty's *hwarang* corps did not fare as well as the *kolpum* system, however. The corps of young warriors evolved with the times, gradually becoming less military oriented and more directed toward aesthetic and artistic pursuits, including the performance of folk songs and dances before the royal court—a factor that played a significant role in the gradual weakening of the military prowess and administrative ability of the elite class.

Thus, when Japan, Russia, the United States, and European powers began pressuring Korea to open its ports to foreign trade, political alliances, and religious missionaries in the last half of the nineteenth century, the effete and divided members of the Yi court and *yangban* ruling class were powerless to protect the country.

While the ancestor worship promoted by *kolpum* is no longer a significant cultural feature of Korean society, the martial spirit and mental toughness originally taught by the *hwarang* corps has been restored by a century of harsh military rule and conflict that gave birth to a fevered nationalism. Today virtually all Koreans are well educated, and all males who are physically able are required to undergo tough military training as part of an ongoing national defense effort.

95

거만

Koman
(Kuh-mahn)

"The Perils of Arrogance"

In the Confucian sphere of Asia there has long been a deep-seated abhorrence of public arrogance because of the teachings of Confucianism and Buddhism, both of which regarded such behavior, especially in leaders, as one of the greatest sins. In Korea, historically described as the most Confucian of all Asian nations, the entire culture from the beginning of the Choson dynasty in 1392 was based on an especially restrictive form of Confucianism that included taboos against *koman* (kuh-mahn), or "arrogance," in any form by anyone.

This does not mean, of course, that *koman* did not exist in Korea. Just as power breeds corruption, it also bred arrogance among a wide assortment of Korean rulers and officials who put power and privilege above the welfare of the people. But in general public *koman* was never as rampant in Korea as it was in other countries, and still few things rankle ordinary Koreans more than displays of *koman* by people in any position of authority.

Koreans have, in fact, traditionally been more tolerant of avarice and venality among their leaders and officials than of *koman*. But this tolerance changed dramatically in the 1970s and 1980s when a succession of presidents was found guilty of illegally amassing hundreds of millions of dollars from the country's largest corporations.

By that time Korea's underlying foundation of Buddhist and Confucian morality had been buttressed by an infusion of democratic principles that made the people far more sensitive to private as well as public misbehavior and more important made it possible for them to bring pressure against the leadership through unrestrained criticism, street demonstrations, and the ballot box.

Koman has not been exorcised from Korean society, however. To some extent the pendulum has swung the other way, and it is now more common than before. In the past the arrogance that did exist was generally limited to government officials and other members of the elite *yangban* ruling class because they were the only people who had any authority. Now it is commonly found among some academics as well as people in the business world as part of the plumage of their newly achieved power.

Korean sensitivity to arrogance plays an especially significant role in the foreign affairs of the country—in politics as well as in trade—because a great many of the attitudes and much of the behavior characteristic of Americans and other nationalities is regarded by Koreans as arrogant. This includes almost any public criticism of Korea and any demands that the Korean government, or any individual Korean company, abide by international laws and customs that Koreans regard as disadvantageous to them.

Many aspects of the Western way of doing business, especially practices that are the most closely associated with Americans, are viewed by Koreans as being arrogant. Korean employees of American and other Western firms in Korea often accuse their foreign bosses of *koman,* when the real problem is a difference in perception—not intent. Generally speaking the mere fact that foreign managers insist that things be done their way rather than the Korean way may be interpreted as an arrogant attempt to take advantage.

Obviously there is no quick, permanent solution to this cultural problem. The only practical, and best, approach to managing the problem is for foreign employers to maintain an ongoing dialogue with their Korean staff that is designed to keep both sides fully informed about their mutual expectations and feelings and to achieve a mutually agreeable consensus on how things are to be done. This is not something that can be accomplished with a monthly or even a weekly meeting. It must be based on a system of communication that is seamless and virtually constant. And, of course, the first challenge that the foreign side must meet and deal with is the Korean perception of *koman*.

96

검도

Komdo
(Kuum-doh)

"The Way of the Sword"

In the early years of Korea's Koryo period (918–1392) it was customary for young men in the upper *yangban* class to be taught a variety of martial arts, including archery, horsemanship, and fighting with the sword, as part of their normal education. Those who went on to become members of the armed forces, particularly the famed *hwarang,* or "flower warriors," were drilled in these arts until they were highly proficient. Some developed incredible skill that made them virtually unbeatable in fair combat.

Swordsmanship was one of the most important of these martial arts because the sword was a key weapon in both defense and offense. Over the following generations the Korean method of sword fighting and training in the art were systematized and institutionalized into what came to be known as *komdo* (kuum-doh), which literally means "the way of the sword" (and is the Korean equivalent of the better-known Japanese word *kendo*).

During the early years of Korea's next dynastic period, the Yi or Choson (1392–1910), Buddhist monks of the *Son* (Sohn) or Zen sect became more and more militant and began practicing *komdo* as part of their meditative exercises as well as to use in defending themselves and when attacking their enemies.

In the beginning, *komdo* was practiced with real swords and was known as *haedong komdo* (hay-dohng kuum-doh). But such practice involved considerable danger, and accidental injuries were common, eventually resulting in staffs made of bamboo being substituted for metal swords during all of the early stages of training. Practicing with a bamboo sword was known as *taehan komdo* (tay-hahn kuum-doh).

Unlike in Japan, however, Korea's ruling class did not develop *komdo* into an all-encompassing cult or make training in martial arts mandatory for all members of the upper class. During the latter centuries of the long and relatively peaceful Choson dynasty (1392–1910), *komdo* played a minor role in Korean life and was kept alive only by a small military force and a few Buddhist monks who continued to practice it as part of their training in self-control. When Japan took over and colonized Korea in the first decade of the twentieth century the Japanese colonial administration strictly controlled all training in martial arts to reduce the possibility of Koreans resorting to violence in their efforts to regain their freedom.

Taekwondo, which emphasizes use of the hands and feet as weapons, was the first of the Korean martial arts to gain international attention following the end of the Japanese occupation of Korea in 1945 and the end of the Korean War in 1953. It was not until the 1980s that Haeng Won Yi, a Buddhist monk who was a master of "Zen meditation swordsmanship," along with two of his disciples, Han Il Na and Yi Chol Shin, established a *haedong komdo* gymnasium and turned the ancient art of sword fighting into a martial sport. They then founded the Haedong Komdo Association and began promoting the art nationwide.

The execution of the movements of *haedong komdo* are very much like a precisely choreographed dance and are done in the three-beat rhythm that is common to Korean dance music. The movements, primarily circular and combined with smooth, curving lines, are designed for defense rather than offense. Master Na says that it is an art that is "designed to save, not to kill."

Like the famed *kungfu* of China, which was developed by Shaolin Temple monks, the movements of *haedong komdo* are patterned after the movements of animals, particularly the tiger, and plants, which sway with the wind, thereby dissipating their strength. Na says that the most important rule in the art is following the examples of nature, physically as well as mentally. In training, students of the art participate in one-on-one bouts as well as in group matches in which they must defend themselves against attacks by more than one person.

Na adds that training in *haedong komdo* is based on self-cultivation in the traditional ethics of Korea—filial piety, loyalty, diligence, honesty, and a highly refined etiquette—and that actual skill in swordsmanship is secondary to developing the character of the individual.

Within ten years after the founding of the first *haedong komdo* gymnasium in Korea the Haedong Komdo Association had branches throughout the country, as well as in Canada, Russia, and the United States. In the mid-1990s the association began training instructors destined to be dispatched to *haedong komdo* gyms abroad. The founders of the modernized art predict that it will soon become as well known and as popular as *taekwondo*.

97

고문

Komun
(Koh-muun)

"Getting Good Advice"

Because education in pre-modern Korea was generally limited to male members of the elite upper class, the only people in the country who were in a position to become experts at anything beyond manual skills were members of the gentry. All government officials in Korea were selected from the elite educated class. Many of the gentry who did not receive or solicit appointments to government positions became professional scholars and spent their lives studying, teaching, and dispensing advice. These men came to be venerated by the people, sometimes to the point of being regarded as saints.

This built-in admiration for scholarship and for *noryonga* (no-re-own-gah), or "experts," was carried over into industrial Korea but with a twist. In the early decades of Korea's rise to economic prominence there was very little understanding or appreciation for the concept of intellectual property or for the concept of paying outside *chonmunga* (chone-muun-gah), "experts" or "professionals," for advice. For years the common practice was to take every possible advantage of the expertise of outsiders—friends and even casual contacts—to get as much professional advice as possible from them without any thought of payment. Visiting foreigners, regardless of their field, were looked on as free sources of business information. Those with technical knowledge in particular were expected to reveal everything they knew, including what they regarded as proprietary information, to their Korean contacts.

By the 1980s, however, the executives of most larger Korean firms had made the quantum leap from a preindustrial mentality to a very modern approach to using foreign consultants, engineers, and scientists, retaining large numbers of them, and paying them well—something they learned and adapted to much more quickly than the Chinese and Japanese.

Foreign companies making their initial approach to Korea are strongly advised to qualify and retain a *komun* (koh-muun), or "consultant-adviser," to guide them through the cultural and political mazes. Broadly speaking, there are two kinds of *komun* in Korea. First is the professional consultant who bases his insights and advice on native cultural wisdom, research, and scholarship in general. Second is the formerly successful businessman or bureaucrat, turned consultant as a second career. These latter individuals may be referred to as *yuryukja* (yuu-ree-yuke-jah), or "a person with influence," meaning someone who has the clout to get things done.

In Korea retired government officials and high-level corporate executives do not automatically become nonpersons the moment they retire, as is usually the case in the United States and elsewhere in the West. Their successors, who are usually their handpicked followers, fulfill their Confucian-oriented obligations to them by continuing to take their advice and doing favors for them—knowing that when their turn comes to retire, their successors will continue the custom.

Generally speaking, the professional *komun* is the most valuable to start up companies, particularly in fashioning employment contracts, hiring, and employee training. *Yuryukja* render the most valuable service in helping companies resolve problems with the government and in initiating high-level relationships with other companies. *Yuryukja* with high, positive public profiles are often capable of accomplishing small miracles on behalf of their clients.

If younger foreign businesspeople make use of older Korean *komun*, it helps to treat them as respected *susung* (suu-suung), "teachers" or "mentors," something they will respond to in an exceptionally positive way. Asking advice from elders has long played a key role in Korean life, not only because of the genuine value of the counsel of older, more experienced people but also as a ploy to gain and keep their goodwill and help.

공자 유교

Kongja/Yugyo
(Kohng-jah/Yuu-g'yoe)
"The Master of Masters"

Confucius, *Kongja* (Kohng-jah) in Korean, was born in China in 551 B.C., lived until 479 B.C., and had more influence on more people than any other human being until modern times, particularly Koreans.* Korea has, in fact, long been reputed as the most Confucian of all the countries in the Confucian sphere of Asia. But generally speaking Koreans do not call themselves or consider themselves Confucianists. *Yugyo* (Yuu-g'yoe), or "Confucianism," has been so integrated into the culture for so many centuries that they are Confucianists (to varying degrees) without being conscious of it. (*Yugyo* also appears as *yukyo*.)

Yugyo became well known in Korea during the final centuries of the Three Kingdoms period between 37 B.C. and A.D. 668. It gained adherents as a political ideology during the last decades of the Shilla dynasty (669–935), by which time Shilla's Buddhist-dominated political system had become corrupt and inefficient, and Confucian scholars were to play a leading role in establishing the ideology of the following dynasty, Koryo.

But *Yukyo* continued to take a backseat to Buddhism until the latter part of the Koryo dynasty (918–1392), when a new form of the ancient doctrine that had been developing in China attracted the attention of reform-minded Koreans. The new orthodoxy was that success or failure in politics depended solely on Confucian education and precise following of Confucian doctrines, and it was this reasoning that resulted in the founders of the new Choson dynasty making Neo-Confucianism the foundation of both the new government and society in general.

Neo-Confucianists taught that *kongbu* (kohng-buu), or "hard study and the practice," of a series of spiritual exercises was essential for achieving enlightenment and following the right Confucian path. The first challenge in this pursuit was to cultivate oneself. Next was to instruct one's family, and last was to seek disciples on the outside.

General Song Gye Yi, founder of the Choson dynasty, blamed Buddhism for the corruption that had brought down the previous dynasty. He and his successors made this new version of Confucianism into the state religion in a draconian reform movement that was to shape Korean culture and society from then until modern times. (In the following generations the people became so deeply influenced by the Confucian concept that the king was inviolate that

---

*"Confucius" is an anglicized rendition of the sage's name in Chinese, *Kung Fu-Tzu*.

virtually all of the uprisings were aimed at the corruption and abuses of lower-ranking officials, not at the court or the king.)

The so-called Neo-Confucianism adopted by the Choson dynasty (*Songni-hak*, which translates as "School of Nature and Principle") emphasized a highly stylized form of etiquette, learning and wisdom, integrity, fidelity, a social system based on male supremacy in an age-related hierarchy, an authoritarian government, and ancestor worship. The system was designed to guarantee absolute social harmony. All emotions, including love between the sexes, were to be suppressed. All relationships were based on five principles: sons were required to obey their fathers absolutely; all subjects were required to be loyal to the ruler; husbands and wives had separate obligations in producing and raising children, with wives subject to the will of their husbands; the young were required to respect elders; and friends were to be bound by trust.

In an attempt to totally eliminate the traditional Buddhist and shamanistic rituals from Korean life and replace them with Confucian ceremonies, the new Choson government issued an edict requiring all families to build "domestic shrines," *kamyo* (kahm-yoh) or *sadang* (sah-dahng), in their homes, and make regular offerings to their ancestors. These "god-cabinets," usually enclosed behind twin swinging doors, contained the name tablets of deceased ancestors and various religious icons. Offerings of special foods were regularly placed on the shelflike *kamyo*, and family members bowed before the shrines to say their prayers.

The eldest son in each family was charged with the responsibility of performing formal ancestor-worship rituals before the shrines, but female members of each household were also required to pray before the *kamyo*.

Scholar-essayist Kyong Dong Kim says that the Confucian influence on the traditional education of Korean children was based on seven values as represented in the *Sohak* (Soh-hahk), or Confucian primer: authoritarianism, self-discipline, disregard for material comfort, an emphasis on teaching and learning, humanitarianism, morality, and ritualism. In more common terms this meant that Korean children were taught to be submissive, obedient, and self-sacrificing—to their fathers and mothers, to their superiors in any context, and to the state.

Confucianism provided the moralistic foundation for this kind of behavior by ritualizing the etiquette of interpersonal relationships and imbuing the rituals with both philosophical and religious sanctity. Authority was based on a preordained inferior-superior relationship, first between the ruling gentry and common people, second between family members, then between kinship groups. Power was concentrated in the hands of husbands, fathers, and government officials.

Families were bound together by filial piety and its ultimate extension, ancestor worship. Each family unit was required to think and act as a collective and was treated as a collective by the authorities. This meant that the whole family was held responsible for the behavior of its members. Because the collective nature of the family and kinship groups precluded individual thought and action, virtually all personal, economic, and political activities were based on connectionism—on using personal connections that had been developed and nurtured carefully for that purpose.

This new Confucianism continued to call for rulers to be moral, selfless, concerned only with the welfare of the people and the country. But this ideal was seldom if ever realized, as few kings lived up to the principles or standards espoused by the Confucianists, even in such simple areas as music. In his classic *Book of Filial Piety*, Confucius wrote: "For giving security to the ruler and order to the people there is nothing better than ceremonies, and for changing the mores and improving the customs [of the people] there is nothing better than music." Of course, the kind of music that Confucius was talking about was music that stills the beast in men and raises their humanity and conscience to a higher level. But over the centuries the kings of Korea maintained troupes of female musicians and singers whose duties went well beyond uplifting the mind.

As the decades of the new dynasty passed, the political-social ideology of Neo-Confucianism became codified in *O Yun* (Oh Yuun), or Five Ethical Standards, and *Sam Gang* (Sahm Gahng), Three Cardinal Principles. The five ethical standards were:

Ui (we)—Righteousness and justice between rulers and subjects
Chin (cheen)—Cordiality and closeness between parents and children (applying mostly to sons)
Pyol (p'yohl)—A clear distinction between the roles of husbands and wives
So (soh)—Order between elders and juniors
Shin (sheen)—Trust between friends

The three cardinal principles were:

Chung (chuung)—Loyalty to rulers
Hyo (h'yoh)—Filial piety toward parents
Yol (yohl)—Female chastity, obedience, and filial piety

Korean sociologists have identified seven key elements in the traditional Korean character that evolved from the Neo-Confucianism of the Choson dynasty. These elements include a deep commitment to hierarchical authoritarianism, collectivism, connectionism, personalism, and moralistic ritualism. Other characteristic traits developed during the Choson dynasty included a dual personality resulting from cultural contradictions and a wide gap between what was presented as real and what was actually real. Because the nature of all Korean relationships was based on personal factors rather than objective facts or principles, personalism, charged with heavy doses of emotionalism, became the overriding factor in all relationships.

The Choson social and political system produced a society that was highly controlled and controllable most of the time. But there were so many built-in contradictions in the system that it also created an intellectual dilemma that resulted in people with split personalities, who often behaved in a totally irrational manner and sometimes erupted in extraordinary violence. In an attempt to resolve this dilemma, basically by covering it up, Korea's gentry exaggerated the virtues of Confucianism and ignored its limitations, creating a constant disparity between the ideal and the real. As is virtually always the case, there was a penalty for ignoring the problem. It fueled discontent and encouraged corruption.

Neo-Confucianism stressed social inequalities based on sex, age, and position, the suppression of emotions and individual desires, the suppression of creativity and innovation, and absolute obedience to superiors, seniors, and government authorities. People were not viewed or treated as individuals but rather as members of families or collectives. The only relationship in the Choson Confucian system that was horizontal or equal was the one between friends, which generally meant that the two people concerned were of the same sex, approximately the same age, had the same or similar background, and usually had some long-term shared experience.

One of the most important and far-reaching tenets of Neo-Confucianism was the concept that ordinary people should regard poverty as the morally correct condition for them to be in and should be satisfied with it—a political ploy designed to keep common people "in their place" and preserve the status quo between the ruled and the rulers. Of course the policy of the Choson court to totally impregnate all Koreans with Neo-Confucianism was only partially successful among the illiterate lower classes, who were concerned primarily with survival rather than adhering to concepts that were designed to keep them poor and passive.

Critics of Confucianism say its overemphasis on formalism, bureaucratism, and theoretical debates discouraged industry to the point that there was very little economic development in Korea for more than two thousand years. Historian Sang Yun Hyon is more specific in his criticism of Neo-Confucianism. In his book *History of Korean Confucianism* (Seoul, Minuunsogwan) he says that the Neo-Confucianism of the Choson era was riddled with negative elements, some of which continue to impact Korea today. Hyon listed the negative elements of Choson-era Confucianism as a tendency toward flunkyism (first toward China and later toward the West), dependency, family-centered factionalism, class discrimination, exaltation of those in power, discouragement of industrial development, despising of the military, seeking of status and honor at virtually any cost, and an orientation toward the past rather than the future.

Despite the many obvious weaknesses and irrationalities of Choson Confucianism, much of the original wisdom of Confucius is still applicable today. For example, he preached that the way to peace and order in a society does not lie in passing and trying to enforce laws to control the behavior of people but in eliminating the sources of discontent and violence. Confucius also preached the efficacy of self-discipline, good manners, education, the almost miraculous influence of good music, goodwill, kindness, hospitality, and all the other attributes that are generally recognized as admirable.

Probably the most positive aspect of Confucianism was its emphasis on education. Koreans (and other Asians in the Confucian sphere) still give education the highest possible priority, and it shows. The scholastic achievements of present-day Koreans and other Asians are playing a seminal role in propelling Korea and other Asian countries into the front ranks of the industrial powers.

Confucianism is no longer the official social ideology in Korea, and younger generations no longer consciously condition their children to obey its tenets. But Confucian attitudes and behavior remain so much a part of the culture that it is naturally absorbed as part of the daily lifestyle.

Confucian attitudes and behavior are not a matter of conscious choice for most Koreans. Confucianism was the primary foundation of their culture for so many generations that it became the only behavior they knew and was automatic. Traditional values that interfere with individualism and freedom of choice are now criticized and often ignored to some extent by younger Koreans, but the effects of more than a thousand years of conditioning cannot be completely exorcised from the culture in just one or two generations.

All of Korea's Confucian-oriented culture was not derived directly from China. The country had its own great sages, eighteen of whom are enshrined in the National Confucian Temple in Seoul. The earliest of these sages, Chong Sol, lived during the seventh century. The latest, Se Chae Pak, lived from 1631 to 1695. These sages, as well as Confucius, are still honored annually with *sokchon* (sohk-chohn) ceremonies. *Sokchon* literally means "dispensing libations" and refers to the ceremonial offering of food and drink before icons of Confucius and the other Confucian sages.

On the first Sunday in May each year, descendants of General Yi and the noble Yi family, which ruled Korea from 1392 until 1910, gather at the Chongmyo Shrine in Seoul, where their ancestors are enshrined, to honor both their ancestors and Confucius, the master sage of Asia, by performing the *sokchon* ceremony.

There are several hundred *hyang gyo* (h'yahng g'yoh), or "private academies," in present-day Korea that teach young people traditional Confucian values and manners and how to relate them to modern society.

99

공평

Kongpyong
(Kohng-p'yong)

"Korean Fairness"

The Confucian ideology that prevailed in Korea from 1392 until modern times provided total justification for the existence of a hierarchical arrangement of society that was based on the permanent inequality of people. At the top of the Korean social pyramid was the king. Next came members of the royal family, court ministers, and so on down to the common people and the lowest of the low.

Within the context of this system the concept of *kongpyong* (kohng-p'yong), or "fairness," as either a moral or legal doctrine did not exist—or at least it did not exist in the Western sense. The Western concept of fairness, which is, of course, based on a fundamental principle of equality (*pyongdung*/p'yong-duung), is diametrically opposed to the Confucian concept of ideal social relationships. Korean gentry, the so-called *yangban* (yahng-bahn) who regarded themselves as inherently superior to lower-class people, no doubt considered their treatment of common people perfectly fair, since the relationship was preordained and sanctioned by heaven.

Industrialization and urbanization, particularly since the 1960s, have dramatically changed the social status of Korean bureaucrats and government officials. They are no longer seen as the exclusive representatives of heaven or even of the public at large. While the overwhelming majority of Koreans favor a government that is strong enough to maintain order and stability, their attitude toward individual members of the government, especially those on the highest levels, is cynical if not antagonistic. They are very much aware that politicians as well as bureaucrats have historically used their positions to enrich themselves and their families, and they naturally resent such avarice.

Fairness in its Western sense is growing in Korea but it is still not the norm. Generally it is still viewed—and practiced—from a hierarchical perspective in which social class, position, and power take precedence over the universal principle of equality. On a more personal basis, however, as in families and between husbands and wives, the younger the individuals and the better educated they are, the more likely that their relationships will be based on at least a partial sense of equality and fairness. The total dominance of wives by husbands is becoming a thing of the past. Koreans born after 1960 no longer accept the idea that they should follow the dictates of their parents without question, and most of them do not.

On the international front, Koreans generally think of *kongpyong* in its traditional Korean context, not in the Western sense of fairness. This means that all of Korea's international business, trade, and diplomatic relationships have to satisfy their cultural values and views of what is fair, which means they are often at odds with the Western concept of fairness.

Koreans do not believe it is fair or morally right for the United States and other larger, richer countries to demand equal trade rights with Korea because Korea is a small country with few natural resources and should not be expected to compete on an even basis. Executives of smaller Korean companies do not believe it is fair or right for large foreign corporations to demand that they sign contracts as equals, for the same reason. In its Korean context, fairness is a relative thing, not an absolute principle.

When considered from the Korean viewpoint, their concept of *kongpyong* is not only morally correct and therefore just but also democratic.

100

고사

Kongson
(Kohng-sohn)

"Courtesy vs. Morality"

Koreans, like the Japanese, have long been noted for their stylized etiquette and the effusive courtesy with which they treat friends and guests. But also like the Japanese, Koreans are selective in their use of *kongson* (kohng-sohn), or "courtesy." While few outsiders who are in Korea for even a few days have failed to be impressed by the extraordinary politeness of Koreans on the one hand, they are also just as likely to be shocked by equally extraordinary examples of rudeness on other occasions.

Probably the most common experience that newcomers have with what they regard as a blatant example of Korean rudeness is when they flag a taxi down in the street during rush hour and have one or more people—usually men—dart in front of them or physically push them out of the way and take the taxi.

This dichotomy in Korean behavior is, of course, a product of the traditional culture. While Westerners are generally conditioned to be courteous to everyone, especially to strangers, Koreans were traditionally conditioned to ignore strangers and be courteous only to friends and acquaintances. Koreans traditionally ignored strangers because to acknowledge them resulted in burdening themselves with a number of unwelcome obligations and was often dangerous as well. Acknowledging strangers meant treating them correctly according to their status, sometimes offering them food and drink, and later helping them if they got into trouble—all things that could make an already difficult life more onerous.

For a person of inferior status to become involved with someone of superior status when there was no specific obligation to do so was not only unthinkable under ordinary circumstances, it could be especially hazardous if it happened by coincidence or accident. If the person of rank happened to be arrogant and cruel, there could be serious repercussions.

Not only was the idea of a member of the upper class establishing a casual relationship with someone of inferior status unthinkable to upper-class Koreans, the minutely prescribed and strictly enforced superior-inferior social system within which Koreans lived acted as a virtually insurmountable barrier to their interacting freely with outsiders. They felt safe and secure only with their own families and in-groups.

Korean behavior toward strangers and the public at large is changing as the demands of the traditional etiquette weaken, but these changes are slow and depend on the educational level and background of the individuals involved. The better educated Koreans are—which invariably means the more Western or non-traditional influences they have experienced—the more likely they are to treat strangers with a reasonable degree of politeness.

It also seems that Koreans are more courteous to strangers—both other Koreans and foreigners—when they encounter them in first-class hotels, restaurants, office buildings, on trains and the like, perhaps because the location gives them something in common and is nonthreatening. The key point in the presence or absence of *kongson* depends on the relationship between the people involved. If there is no relationship, both other Koreans and foreigners alike may be treated as "nonpersons"—in other words, ignored.

Despite the traditional custom of ignoring strangers and being wary of foreigners, many Koreans feel an enormous amount of goodwill toward Westerners in general and are both polite and helpful toward those they encounter personally. Most of the automatic goodwill that Koreans extend to foreigners results from the fact that the foreigners concerned are *not* Korean and Koreans therefore do not have to worry about relative social rank, special etiquette, or undesirable obligations. Another aspect of Korean behavior toward foreigners is that foreigners automatically fall into the "guest category," which obliges Koreans to treat them with special courtesy. For foreigners, merely greeting Koreans politely is generally sufficient to establish a relationship that results in a friendly response.

But the American Graduate School of International Management's Professor Martin H. Sours notes that there is another situation where Korean courtesy and goodwill toward foreigners does not necessarily apply. Curiously, this involves foreign women driving cars. Some of the multinational firms with major operations in Korea have an official policy of not allowing the wives of their expatriate managers to drive cars in Korea. Their point is that the Korean concept of courtesy and justice in the case of accidents—in addition to most street signs being only in Korean—is different enough that it would put the wives in danger and could cause serious complications for the companies. These wives are required to use chauffeur-driven cars.

101

고사

Kosa
(Koh-sah)

"The Good Spirits"

When Korea entered the pages of history some four thousand years ago, *Musokchi* (Muu-soak-chee), or "shamanism," the belief that good and bad spirits inhabit the world and can be summoned and influenced by a variety of rituals, had long since been institutionalized as the prevailing religious and political ideology. But following the introduction of Buddhism and Confucianism into Korea between the fourth and sixth centuries A.D., the governments of the various kingdoms attempted to distance themselves from shamanism in favor of these new philosophies.

In 1392 the newly established Choson dynasty chose *Yukyo* (Yuu-k'yoe), or Confucianism, as the state ideology and turned it into a religionlike cult, leaving shamanism as an unofficial folk belief. But shamanism survived and still plays an important role in Korean life.

The most conspicuous demonstrations of the ongoing influence and importance of shamanism in Korean life is the custom of performing a *kosa* (koh-sah), or "shamanistic ceremony," at the beginning of new enterprises, particularly when starting the construction of new homes, new buildings, expressways, train lines, etc. The openings of new offices and other places of business are also generally marked by a *kosa* to seek the blessings of the appropriate spirits.

Kosa range from small affairs involving only a few people to large gatherings of hundreds. Some older, tradition-oriented housewives hold *kosa* at their homes once or twice a year to invoke the blessings of various household spirits. Corporations regularly stage large *kosa* events that are attended by employees, clients, and VIPS. Food and drink are mainstays of *kosa* ceremonies. A pig's head, symbolic of good fortune, is often the centerpiece of the main table. Larger *kosa* may also feature professional entertainers.

Probably the most common shamanistic ritual in Korea is the so-called "company *kosa*," which consists of the ceremonial offering of special foods to a variety of gods or spirits to prevent bad luck and ensure good luck and prosperity. Company *kosa* are held when new offices are opened, when new factories are opened, when new, elaborate equipment is installed, and so on. Some companies hold annual *kosa* as a routine custom just to stay on the safe side of the spirits.

At a typical company *kosa*, often managed by the wife of the president or chairman, large tables are laden with traditional foods like rice cakes, fruits, nuts, steamed pigs' heads, rice wine, and so on. Candles and incense are lit by the ranking attendee, who then bows twice to the other participants. They bow in turn. There are generally no public prayers or speeches of any kind, and after this short, silent ceremony the food is put into small boxes and given to the employees to take home.

Some Koreans take *kosa* ceremonies seriously, making a special effort to cleanse their spirits and bodies for several days or weeks prior to participating in the rituals. Others treat them as a pleasant break in their regular routine. A number of foreign companies involved with Korea have adopted the custom of staging *kosa* to mark special events, in some instances including those that occur in their home countries. The rationale of the foreign executives who initiate such ceremonies is that they won't hurt and they might help. All see them as valuable contributions to their Korean partnerships.

국제결혼
Kukche Kyolhon
(Kuuk-cheh K'yohl-hohn)
"International Marriages"

Korean culture, like other cultures in the Confucian sphere of Asia, has traditionally been racially and culturally exclusive to the point of obsession. In basic terms this meant that someone not born of the Korean race and raised in Korea simply could not become a Korean under any circumstances. In a broader sense this combined cultural and racial exclusivity meant that non-Koreans were always regarded as and treated as foreigners, as outsiders, even if they were born and raised in the country, spoke only Korean, and had never been outside of Korea.

A great deal of the cultural exclusivity that was traditionally characteristic of Koreans grew out of the Confucian-oriented family system in which relationships between parents and their children were fixed on the basis of a dictatorial inferior-superior hierarchical arrangement that was immutable. An equally important aspect of the Korean family system was that it required individuals to submerge their individuality in favor of the family unit. Wives and children were required to obey the senior male in the house without question.

Marriage was therefore an extremely important matter that involved the whole nuclear family as well as the closest kin. Marriages were arranged, and the lives of the new couple continued to be controlled by the parents of the groom. In other words, marriages were not the merging of two individuals into a new, separate social unit. They were additions to existing families, with profound social, political, and economic implications. Brides literally became servants to their mothers-in-law, and grooms remained the obedient sons of their fathers, subject to their will and their convenience.

The culture of the Korean family made it virtually unthinkable for a son or daughter to choose a mate. For parents to arrange or approve of a marriage between their offspring and a non-Korean was even more alien. This was the social environment in Korea at the end of World War II in 1945, which saw North Korea fall into the hands of Soviet-backed Communists. The economy had been devastated by the war. Hundreds of thousands of Korean men had been forcibly taken to Japan as slave laborers. Even larger numbers had been forced to serve in the Japanese army and had been killed in the fighting. This left several hundred thousand young Korean women without marriage prospects.

With the war's end, dozens of thousands of young American men, soldiers and civilians, began pouring into Korea to help repatriate the Japanese occupation forces and reestablish the country. Within weeks, many of these men had made friends with young Korean women. The first *kukche kyolhon* (kuuk-cheh k'yohl hohn), or "international marriages," took place the following year.

In 1950 North Korean forces invaded South Korea in an attempt to unify the country under Communist rule. This war, which ended in 1953 in a stalemate, was even more destructive to Korea and to Korean families and resulted in the number of young American and Allied troops and civilians in Korea being increased to several hundred thousand. Soon after the end of the Korean War, *kukche kyolhon* between foreign men and Korean women became commonplace, with most of the newly married couples moving to the husband's homelands within a matter of months or a few years.

In these international marriages it was invariably the wives who were required to adapt to a totally new lifestyle. Many of the marriages broke down because the cultural differences were simply too great. Others dissolved because once the foreign men were back in their homelands their commitment to their Korean wives—often more sexual than emotional—waned and they wanted out of the relationship. The more uneducated and unsophisticated the men, the more likely the marriages were to break up.

As the years passed, an increasing number of foreign-Korean couples remained in Korea for long periods or became permanent residents, where the foreign partners faced an entirely different kind of challenge. As the horrors and problems of war receded and order and a degree of affluence began returning to Korea, the traditional attitude toward *kukche kyolhon* reasserted itself. Mixed couples in public were often subject to derogatory comments and other slights. The children of foreign-Korean couples often suffered in a much more complex and damaging way. They were the butt of jokes and insults from Korean children and were often treated coldly by adult strangers as well—the kind of discrimination that has traditionally befallen mixed-bloods in societies throughout the world. Many of the children were also affected adversely by the obvious racial and cultural differences—and conflicts—in their own homes. Some of these children grew up speaking only Korean while their foreign fathers spoke only English.

Generally the only exceptions to these dysfunctional families were those in which both the husbands and wives were well educated, had strong unified values that they passed on to their children, and were affluent enough to live above much of the petty discrimination that is commonly inflicted on people who are different. (As late as 1997 a fight broke out on a Seoul subway as a result of derogatory comments directed toward a mixed-race couple.)

Over and above racial and cultural discrimination, mixed couples in Korea faced the problem of dealing with their Korean relatives. Some of the foreign husbands learned very quickly that they had acquired whole families as well as wives and were expected to behave, at least in part, like Korean sons-in-law. The closeness of Korean families and all of the obligations involved thus became a new, unexpected, and sometimes onerous burden to foreign husbands.

Western women who married Korean men generally fared better in their relationships with their husbands' families because the families expected less of them. An additional factor in most Western women–Korean men marriages was that the Korean men had usually been educated abroad, spoke their wives' language fluently, and had become accustomed to living Western style.

As Korea has become more modernized and more involved internationally, the number of *kukche kyolhon* has continued to increase, but generally speaking tolerance and acceptance of Korean-Western couples in Korea has not kept pace. Again, the exception to this rule is that the higher the social and financial level of the people involved, the less resistance they encounter when they first announce their intention to marry, and the less discrimination they face after marriage.

My Korean colleague H. J. Chang notes that international marriages are in fact becoming more and more common but that the majority of such marriages involve Western men and Korean women, with it still being rare for Western women to marry Korean men.

국가주의
Kukkajuui
(Kuuk-kah-juu-we)

"Korean Nationalism"

Uri Hanguksaram (Uh-ree Hahn-guuk-sah-rahm) means "We Koreans" and is a ringing pronouncement that is pregnant with cultural connotations. It is an expression that distinguishes Koreans racially, culturally, socially, geographically, economically, and politically from all other people. It figuratively means "We Koreans are a unique people"—often with the additional connotation that they cannot be compared to or mixed with other people and must therefore be treated differently.

Korea's recorded history officially began in 2333 B.C., which, according to the Korean creation myth, is the year that the son of "God" descended to the earth, turned a bear into a woman, and mated with her. She subsequently gave birth to a son, Tangun, who became the founder of both the Korean race and the first Korean nation. A more literal view of Korean history indicates that the first Korean "nation" was more likely a single tribe, made up of some three thousand people whose ancestors had migrated from the Altaic Mountains region of central Asia into Mongolia and Manchuria, moved from there onto the Korean peninsula, and eventually settled on the slopes of Paekdu Mountain, which straddles the border between what is now North Korea and northeastern China.

The myth goes on to say that the reign established by Tangun lasted for twelve hunded years (until 1122 B.C.), when it was replaced by a new dynasty, called *Chosun*, meaning "Morning Calm," that survived until 108 B.C.

In 109 B.C., China's Emperor Wu-Ti invaded Korea and after a year of pitched battles established suzerainty over the tribal kingdoms on the peninsula. During the first century of Chinese dominance, the several tribal states coalesced into three kingdoms—Koguryo, Paekche, and Shilla—all of which remained vassal states under China until A.D. 314, when the reigning dynasty in China fell.

For the next three-hundred-plus years Koguryo, Paekche, and Shilla survived as independent kingdoms. In the seventh century the Shilla kingdom, with the help of the Chinese, conquered Koguryo and Paekche, creating the first unified "Korean" state. From that time until 1945, the people of Korea were unified under a single state but with different ruling dynasties—the Shilla kingdom lasted until 918, the Koryo until 1392, and the Choson until 1910.

Fears that Korea was going to be carved up by China, Japan, and the colonial powers of the West resulted in the appearance of strongly nationalistic feelings among Koreans from the early 1870s. One of the results of these feelings (which were avidly promoted by American missionaries in Korea) was the formation in 1896 of a group known as *Tongnip Hyophoe* (Tohng-neep H'yoap-oh-eh), or "Independence Club," which was aimed at modernizing and strengthening the Korean government so Korea would be able to protect itself.

One of the most active members of the Independence Club was a young man named Sung Man Yi, who later was to become known internationally as Syngman Rhee. A member of the famous Yi clan that had founded the ruling Choson dynasty, Rhee was born in Seoul in 1875 and was graduated from an American missionary-run school (Paejae Boys School). The Independence Club became more and more nationalistic and began planning to replace the monarchy with a republic. The government ordered the club dissolved. When it refused to disband, many of the leaders, including Rhee, were arrested and imprisoned.

By the time Rhee was released from prison, the Japanese were running Korea. He went into exile in the United States and in 1909 in Hawaii formed the Korean National Association (*Taehan Kungmin Hoe*/Tie-hahn Kuung-meen Hoh-eh). The following year Japan annexed Korea and made it a part of the Japanese empire. For the next thirty-five years Rhee lobbied the U.S. government and other foreign powers in an effort to get Korean sovereignty restored.

Japan ruled Korea as a province until 1945. During that period the Japanese made an extreme effort to totally eradicate the national identity of Koreans by forcing them to adopt Japanese names, learn and speak only Japanese, consider themselves Japanese nationals, and be loyal to Japan. In a clandestine move to prevent this from happening, a number of Korean scholars began promoting *munhwa undong* (muun-whah uhn-dohng), or "cultural nationalism," which emphasized continued use of the Korean language and the traditional Korean way of life.

Oppressive rule by the Japanese also resulted in a number of Korean patriots and scholars calling on the business community to make economic self-sufficiency a national goal. Their idea was not only to encourage more Koreans to go into business but also to protect Koreans from being at the economic mercy of their Japanese overlords. A key part of the movement called for Koreans to buy and use only Korean-made products. There was also a spiritual element to this national economic self-sufficiency movement. Its leaders saw it as a way of helping Koreans endure the shame that had been inflicted on them by Japan.

The program, which became known as the "Korean Production Movement," enjoyed extraordinary success during the first year. Its promoters began publishing a monthly magazine and opened branch offices throughout the country. But the Japanese administrators of Korea did not approve of the movement and took a variety of steps aimed at hindering its progress and ultimately destroying it.

Korea regained its sovereignty in 1945 when Japan was defeated by the United States and its allies. American military forces occupied the southern half of Korea; Soviet forces took over the northern half of the peninsula. Virtually all of the Korean nationalists, including Korean Communists, who had exiled themselves during the Japan period rushed back to their homeland, intent on taking part in forming a new government.

With Korea divided between the United States and the Soviet Union at the thirty-eighth parallel (a line arbitrarily picked by two American military officers, Major Dean Rusk and Colonel Charles H. Bonesteel, who were in Washington, D.C., at the time and were given thirty minutes to make a decision on where to draw the line), the United States and the Soviets chose totally different methods of restoring order and reestablishing Korean administration of the two halves.

Il Sung Kim, a North Korean who had been converted to communism while exiled in the Soviet Union and fought the Japanese occupation forces as a guerrilla leader, was confirmed by the Soviets as head of a North Korean provisional government (he had kept his guerrilla army intact and was the most popular leader in the North). Kim quickly initiated a wide range of land and political reforms that were designed to totally eliminate the elite landlord and scholar-official class that had ruled for some two thousand years. Kim virtually exterminated the landholding upper class and replaced it with a Communist military dictatorship. He also nationalized key industries, established an eight-hour workday, created a social security system, outlawed concubinage, prostitution, and female infanticide, and decreed that women were to receive the same pay as men.

The United States, on the other hand, began by setting up an American military government—the U.S. Army Military Government in Korea (USAMGIK)—and chose to allow prewar and pre-Japan-period upper-class politicians and bureaucrats to resume power—a decision that was to have disastrous effects on South Korea because they continued the authoritarian, abusive style of government that had been traditional in Korea since early times, setting the stage for violent uprisings by students, union workers, and farmers over several decades.

The USAMGIK, with the approval of Washington, D.C., chose the old revolutionary Syngman Rhee (Sung Man Yi), already in his seventies, as head of the South Korean government. Rhee, who had spent most of his life in the United States and was a graduate of Harvard and Princeton, spoke fluent English and on the surface was thoroughly Americanized. But beneath that facade he was a throwback to the days of the Choson dynasty, an elitist authoritarian who proved to be as ruthless as any of his ancestors who had founded and ruled Korea's last and longest dynasty.

In addition to allowing most of the same officials and bureaucrats who had collaborated with the Japanese in running Korea to remain in office, the USAMGIK and Rhee reinstated thousands of Korean policemen who had been trained by the Japanese and worked alongside them during the brutal Japanese occupation. Rhee also passed a "National Security" law that made it possible for him to legally crush all criticism of and opposition to his regime.

Under Rhee's guidance, the concept of cultural nationalism created by Korean patriots during the Japan period was integrated into the political and economic platforms of the new Republic of Korea, established in South Korea in 1948. Shortly afterward, the Communist regime in North Korea established the People's Republic of North Korea and continued its intensive program to indoctrinate North Koreans in a rabid form of communistic nationalism.

In South Korea, Rhee used mass arrests, assassinations, and massacres to stay in power until 1960, when he was forced to step down by nationwide student uprisings and, finally, pressure from the United States. Il Sung Kim continued to rule as an absolute dictator in North Korea until his death in 1994. Today there are few names in modern Korean history that are more controversial and notorious than those of Sung Man Yi / Syngman Rhee and Il Sung Kim.

Despite this checkered political history, Koreans have always had a deep-seated sense of common racial and cultural identity that transcended artificial borders. And, in fact, this sense of common identity has been tempered and strengthened by repeated attacks by foreign enemies. Even the division of the peninsula into two "kingdoms" in 1945 was seen as just another imposition from the outside that could not shake the intangible bonds of race and culture.

From 1910 until 1945 the Japanese attempted to eradicate those bonds but succeeded only in reinforcing them. Subsequent attempts by the Communist regime in North Korea to remold North Koreans into Communist drones also failed—just as Chairman Mao Zedong failed in his attempt to remake the Chinese into Communist robots. The complete reintegration of North and South Korea politically and economically will no doubt take a long time, but with the artificial barriers eliminated the people will flow together like water.

In many ways, Korean *kukkajuui*, or "nationalism," is much stronger than the nationalism of Americans, Australians, Canadians, and most West Europeans. Their nationalism grows out of an absolute sense of racial and cultural uniqueness that goes beyond territory and borders. Anybody can become an American, an Australian, or a Canadian. No foreigner can become a Korean. Koreans are born, not made. The exclusivity that makes up the Korean mind-set is buttressed by nearly five thousand years of conditioning in survival that has given them an indomitable spirit. Like the Jews of Israel, they now have the will to achieve the power to protect themselves, to never again be victimized by others.

In the 1980s, by which time Koreans were beginning to accept the idea that they had become major economic players on the world scene and had begun to flex their economic as well as their cultural muscles, *munhwa undong* suddenly became a national issue. Much of the virtually sudden reappearance of "cultural nationalism" was precipitated by the U.S. government and American companies beginning to bring political pressure against Korea to open more doors to imports. None of these efforts were more controversial or did more harm to the American image as a sympathetic "big brother" than the campaign to force Korea to allow the importation of American-made cigarettes.

This American campaign resulted in Korean intellectuals and industrialists creating a counter-campaign that appealed to the patriotism and nationalism of all Koreans. Signs disparaging the American cigarettes and the American efforts appeared all over Korea. Since that time radical students opposing American support of the Korean government, which they regard as still authoritarian and corrupt, have routinely seized every opportunity to demonstrate against the American influence in Korea and to keep an exaggerated form of nationalism at a high pitch.

All foreigners dealing with Koreans today must take their heightened sense of *kukkajuui* into consideration.

104

군사문화

Kunsa Munhwa

(Kuun-sah Muun-whah)

"The Military Culture"

During Japan's annexation and occupation of Korea (1910–45) a Japanese scholar noted that Koreans were more interested in poetry and art than in militarism, implying that this was one of the reasons why Koreans were no match for the militaristic and aggressive Japanese. The Japanese scholar's judgment about the unmilitaristic nature of Koreans was obviously accurate at the time it was made. When Japan annexed Korea in 1910, there were fewer than five thousand men and officers in the Korean armed forces.

Korea's famed Three Kingdoms (Koguryo, Paekche, and Shilla), which flourished from around 37 B.C. until A.D. 668, were dominated by family clans that sustained their political power through military force. The Shilla kingdom, which succeeded in unifying the peninsula under its own banner in 668, created a hereditary corps of professional warriors to serve as both military leaders and government officials—the famed *hwarang* (whah-rahng), or "flower warriors"—which was to be continued by successive dynasties down to the end of the nineteenth century.

But unlike the early Chinese, Japanese, Mongols, and other North and East Asians, ordinary Koreans traditionally were not a warlike people. Even the famed *hwarang* warriors spent more time singing and dancing than they did practicing the martial arts and fighting. For the most part early Korean society was dominated by scholar-officials, not by military leaders. And while Korea's early kingdoms were often beset by small-scale internal strife, and over a period of several hundred years the kingdoms warred against each other for supremacy, these were battles fostered by small elite groups of people who were out of power or wanted to extend their control. They were not indicative of the nature of Koreans in general.

Although Koreans chose time and again to defend themselves against foreign invaders, they did not develop a philosophy of *kunsajuui* (kuhn-sah-juu-we), or militarism, and with the exception of occasional heroes who saved the nation from outside attackers soldiers were not highly respected. Historians say that Koreans developed a peaceful nature because the kingdoms and peninsula as a whole were small and surrounded by enemies that were much larger and stronger. They had no acceptable choice but to learn how to survive without depending on military power—a choice, however, that was to have a fundamental influence on their economy as well as their society in general.

Again with some notable exceptions at the end of the sixteenth century (when a Korean admiral built the world's first ironclad warship), Koreans did not actively pursue military technology and did not develop an industrial base to support large military organizations or invasions of their neighbors. Some contemporary Korean scholars say that since militarism has traditionally been a primary factor in economic development, the nonmilitant philosophy of Koreans deprived them of one of the most powerful economic forces in the history of nations and is one of the main reasons economic development in Korea did not occur much earlier.

During the last 250 years of the Choson dynasty (1392–1910) Korea depended on China to defend it from its other neighbors, resulting in the military forces of the country shrinking to little more than a token guard. (At no time during the feudal history of Korea were common people permitted to own and keep weapons privately.) The sons of the gentry, who had traditionally made up the elite officers' corps, enrolled in Confucian studies to take the civil service examinations and gain exemption from military service because the road to prestige, wealth, and power was through government service, not the military.

The great calm that settled over Korea during this era was deceptive, however. Koreans were peaceful and unaggressive only when they were not being threatened. When a perceived or genuine threat appeared, all of the anger, frustrations, and pent-up rage they had been suppressing over generations of political and social repression came to the surface and they would fight with incredible fierceness and tenacity.

It was the aggressive actions of the Japanese, along with the English, French, Russians, Chinese, and Americans, that precipitated a dramatic change in the attitudes and behavior of Koreans from the 1870s on. The primary catalyst in reintroducing militarism into Korean culture were the Japanese themselves. The Japanese colonial administration of the peninsula from the early 1900s to 1945 was conducted as a military operation, with all of the brutality and terror for which the Imperial Japanese Army was noted. Hundreds of thousands of Koreans were also inducted into the Japanese army and subjected to the kind of training that made its soldiers feared throughout Asia.

One of the results of this treatment by the Japanese was to instill a martial spirit in Koreans that had not existed for some three hundred years—in fact, not since the Japanese invaded Korea in 1592 and again in 1598 in an attempt to capture and colonize the peninsula. Another event that was to create what sociologists and others referred to as a *kunsa munhwa* (kuun-sah muun-whah), or "military culture," in Korea was the communization of North Korea following the end of World War II, and its subsequent invasion of South Korea in 1950.

Between 1945 and 1950 the Communist leaders of North Korea brainwashed the entire North Korean population in militarism. The constant threat posed by the North Korean Communist regime after the end of the Korean War in 1953 forced South Korean leaders to build a strong, dedicated military force as well. A law was passed requiring all young Korean men to serve on active duty in the military for a minimum of two and a half years and remain in the reserves and local militia for an additional twenty years.

The South Korean military leadership, virtually all of whom had been trained by the Japanese during the 1930s, adopted some of the rationale and methods previously perfected by the Imperial Army of Japan. This included creating a recruit training program that was so rigorous and dangerous that each year dozens of trainees were killed and thousands injured. One of the techniques used to discipline recruits was to force them to lick urinals clean with their tongues. Eventually the public outcry against this system became so severe that the training program was reformed. But it was to continue to have a fundamental influence on the attitudes and behavior of all draftees and officers that eventually permeated the entire society, giving it a conspicuously military flavor.

The training of new military recruits in Korea has traditionally been rough by any standards, contributing to a system of bribery that in some areas was known as *milpaeggi* (meel-pie-gghee), which refers to a traditional practice of people serving their parents and older relatives liquor and special foods a day or so before major celebrations. The custom was known colloquially as "giving medicine" to the people involved. Military recruits who wanted to make sure they got through the training without suffering too much "gave medicine" (in the form of cash in white envelopes) to their instructors. "Medicine" was also routinely prescribed for police officers and other officials by people seeking to avoid problems or to get out of trouble.

Koreans had already been indoctrinated for centuries in the Confucian concept of a hierarchical social structure made up of inferiors and superiors and a strict protocol controlling relationships between ranks, including unquestioning obedience of orders. So there was no great step from a Confucian culture back to a military culture. As the hundreds of thousands of young men returned to civilian life, they brought with them not only their Confucian heritage but also the effects of several years of harsh military training and service that made them ideal employees for the new industries that were springing up all over the country.

In the intervening decades the influence of Confucianistic conditioning in homes and schools, the strictness of the military training male Koreans undergo, and the management systems in Korean companies have become less rigid and formalistic, but there is still an easily recognizable militaristic flavor to the attitudes and behavior of Korean employees, especially in larger companies and government agencies.

The standing at attention when in the presence of superiors, the bowing, the singing of corporate songs, the ritualistic seating according to rank, and other formalistic behavior that is still characteristic of most Korean employees is right out of the marine manual. The self-discipline and diligence demonstrated by small groups of Korean workers, especially on the line and in the field, is also typical of highly trained military units whose safety and success depends on each member knowing and doing his job.

However, the reputation of ranking officers in the military suffered grievously between 1961 and the early 1990s. In 1961 General Chung Hee Park staged a coup, took over the government, and turned his administration into a military dictatorship. He was assassinated in 1979. In 1980 another general, Doo Hwan Chun, staged a second coup and ruled until 1988, when he maneuvered to have a fellow general, Tae Woo Roh, replace him as president of the country. Students, workers, and Buddhist monks throughout the country responded to this latest outrage with riots and strikes that brought the country to a standstill. With all-out civil war threatening, Chun approved of Roh giving in to the demands of the people, beginning the first real political reforms to be seen in the country since the 1880s and 1890s.

Most Koreans today readily admit that the militarism of General Chung Hee Park, president of the country from 1961 to 1979, in particular the military discipline and efficiency that he brought to the government, was a key factor in the rapid modernization of the country. In the view of many Korean historians, only the military could have wrested power from the entrenched elite class that had ruled the country for some two millennia.

As soon as Park took power, he purged most of the upper-level bureaucrats from the government and replaced them with military officers. After he resigned from the army and was elected president as a civilian, Park continued this policy, filling some 28 percent of all the key posts in the government with ex-army men—the first time since the founding of the Choson dynasty in 1392 that the government was basically run by soldiers.

Military men continued to dominate the Korean government and the life of the country until Young Sam Kim was inaugurated as president in February 1993, beginning the country's first genuine civilian administration in thirty-two years. Among the reforms initiated by Kim was a program to "cleanse" the military services of the legacy of harsh and sometimes brutal training left behind by the Imperial Japanese Army that had occupied the country from 1910 until 1945. However, given its historically vulnerable position and the instability of the present times, along with the regimentation and protocol that continue to characterize Korean behavior, chances are that a "militaristic culture" will prevail for the foreseeable future.

All Korean males who are physically and mentally able are required to spend 2-3 years in military service between the ages of twenty and twenty-five and thereafter to serve in the *hyangtoyebigun* (h'yahng-toh-yeh-bee-guun), or "reserve forces," from twenty-five to thirty-five and then in the *minpangwidae* (meen-pahng-wee-die), or local "people's militia," from the age of thirty-five to forty-five. Another category of military service called *pangwibyong* (pahng-wee-b'yohng) refers to companies of men between the ages of twenty and twenty-five who are allowed to fulfill their military obligations in their own hometown instead of in a regular military unit at a camp. These hometown units are administered by the local police department. Present-day Koreans tolerate their military forces as a necessary evil.

과거

Kwago
(Kwah-goh)
"Selecting the Brightest"

Early in its history Korea's Shilla dynasty (A.D. 669–935) adopted the already ancient Chinese practice of qualifying and selecting government officials by nationwide civil service examinations called *kwago* (kwah-goh), which means something like "learning test." The exams tested candidates on the Confucian classics and commentaries on the classics and required them to write poetry and essays on given subjects. Candidates were also evaluated on their skill in writing the Chinese characters in the stylized form known as *soye* (soh-yeh), or calligraphy.

Among the Chinese classics that made up the curriculum of aristocratic students were *The Classic of Filial Piety*, *The Book of Rites*, *The Analects*, *The Book of History*, *The Book of Poetry*, and *The Book of Changes*. Mastering these subjects was based on rote memorization and practice that required many years.

Despite good intentions, the *kwago* examination system was corrupted virtually from the start, as the hereditary nobility and members of the upper class were able to use their wealth and political power at court to get high-level appointments without taking the examinations. Relatives of the highest-ranking officials were also routinely appointed to high positions without taking the examinations. Not surprisingly, the *kwago* system was rife with other forms of corruption as well. Administrators, invariably underpaid for their services, were subject to bribes by the families of the candidates. Friction and strife caused by clan and factional competition to monopolize the exams and government offices were also constant.

At first the examinations were open to anyone except people in certain outcast occupations such as butchers, musicians, and actors. Doctors were also excluded from those who could take the exams. Among the offices that were filled routinely by graduates were magistrates (local police chiefs and judges combined in the same person), provincial governors, staff positions at the court, and army and navy officers.

Since passing the *kwago* was the only way most people could enter government service (which was the most prestigious of all occupations because only government officials were in a position to accumulate wealth and provide security for their families), the government examination office was deluged with candidates. To reduce this problem, the Shilla government established quotas for the different areas of the country. In a later, draconian move to keep government posts in the hands of the elite, the court issued an edict prohibiting anyone who had had an outcast ancestor during the previous eight generations from taking the civil service exams.

When the exams were first inaugurated, they were conducted every year. As the population and number of scholars expanded, the timing was changed to meet government needs. During one period they were held every three years. The age of the contestants ranged from sixteen to sixty, but the majority were in their late twenties and early thirties. At the highest level of the exams, only about one out of every thirty candidates received passing scores.

While the *kwago* set very high literacy standards for civil service, very little of what was learned could be translated into practical policies or programs. The majority of the most brilliant scholars, ensconced in their family estates, spent their lives involved in theoretical philosophizing on the nature of the universe and man's place in the cosmos rather than trying to help solve real problems.

Each succeeding dynasty continued the *kwago* system, with occasional revisions designed to meet certain needs or policies. But the policy of limiting the subject matter of the tests to Confucian classics and allowing only sons of the ruling class to take the examinations and become officials, was to undercut any virtue of the concept of qualifying civil service bureaucrats. Korean scholars now attribute much of the authoritarianism and stagnation that afflicted Korea throughout most of its pre-modern history to the *kwago* and their Confucian bias.

By the middle of the long Choson dynasty the *kwago* had become so corrupt that many Confucian scholars who lived in the countryside refused to take the exams. Revered as paragons of Confucian morality and integrity, these scholars became known as *sallim* (sahl-leem), which literally means "mountain and forest" but might be better described as "hermit scholars." Over the generations, especially when conditions were reaching a critical stage, it became common for the court to call on the most outstanding of these scholars to accept important government positions.

In a number of cases, however, unscrupulous leaders invited noted scholars to join their administrations just to quiet criticism and did not allow them to exercise any real authority. Because of this, later kings created a new government system that included a number of powerful posts that were reserved exclusively for *sallim*, thereby assuring that they would have executive powers.

The heyday of the *sallim* was from 1650 to 1720, when there were many outstanding individuals among their ranks. But because of resistance from official-scholars who had passed the *kwago* exams and were an entrenched part of the old system, the conditions surrounding the appointment and positions of the *sallim* became so bad that they refused to accept any more official appointments. From that time until the end of the Choson dynasty in 1910, most *sallim* scholars remained outsiders—and thus it came about that in the late 1800s, when Westerners began entering Korea, they often commented on this group, saying that although they did nothing but study and spend their time in idleness, they were still highly revered by all Koreans.

During this era the exams took place over a period of several days, beginning at dawn and continuing throughout the day. They were strictly supervised by government officials. Anyone caught trying to smuggle books or notes into the examination sites was arrested and banned from taking the exams for the next three years. Ayone inside the examination site found to have "crib notes" or any other aids was ejected and banned from taking the tests for six years. The exams covered civil administration, military strategies, and technical subjects and included oral as well as written tests. Recent research indicates that during the Choson era some commoners were allowed to take the exams.

Finally, in 1894, the *kwago* system was abolished by the Choson court, only sixteen years before the dynasty fell and was replaced by a Japanese colonial regime. In present-day Korea candidates for civil service employment and government employees seeking advancement are required to pass qualifying examinations.

106

관리
Kwalli
(Kwahl-lee)

"Management Korean Style"

Because Korea's traditional Buddhist philosophy regarded profit making as immoral, and Confucianism so tilted society in favor of an elite ruling class made up of scholar-officials, the spirit of individual entrepreneurship did not become a part of the Korean character in pre-modern times. Social status in early Korea was derived from one's educational level and political power, not from technical skills or business acumen.

It was not until the first century of the Choson dynasty (1392–1910) that the foundation for a genuine commercial class was inadvertently started. The Choson court licensed a fairly large number of merchants to act as wholesalers and agents on its behalf, allowing them to place contracts with growers and makers of a variety of products around the country. This system resulted in the chartered merchants creating a network of suppliers and gradually becoming a wealthy class separate from the semihereditary *yangban* gentry. But rather than invest their wealth in expanding the economy, these merchants chose the "morally correct" path of buying land and becoming landlords, changing nothing except their own standard of living.

But when the Choson dynasty began to fall apart in the last decades of the 1800s, there were many Korean merchant families ready to take advantage of their experience in business. However, most of them were to be frustrated by the inability of the Choson court to prevent the Japanese from taking over the country, and it was the Japanese who took the lead in industrializing Korea to serve its own needs.

It was not until Japan was defeated in 1945 that Korean businessmen became fully free to establish and run their own companies. All of the dozens of thousands of companies subsequently established in Korea between 1945 and 1973, including those that grew into huge industrial combines (*chaebol*/chay-buhl), were managed like family enterprises or private clanlike fiefs by their founders. And it was not until the 1970s that a genuine appreciation for professional management skills in the Western sense began to develop in Korea. Dozens of company founders sent their sons to business schools in the United States, creating a whole generation of Western-educated executives who began to take over many of the larger enterprises in Korea during the 1980s and 1990s.

Still, the *kwalli* (kwahl-lee), or "management," in typical Korean organizations remains Korean in style as well as in essence. One good way of explaining Korean *kwalli* in Western terms is to equate it with the military, particularly the Marine Corps. The typical Korean corporation is a vertical structure with a precise chain of command from the top "general" down to ordinary "troops." Anyone who dares to engage in *hakusang* (hah-kuu-sahng), "going over a superior's head," is asking for trouble and better be doubly sure of his or her position.

The strictness of management in Korean companies—a direct carryover from the traditional Confucian-oriented social system—is very intimidating and contributes to employees resorting to the age-old practice of *joja sei* (joe-jah say-e), or "lying low." Knowing very well that drawing attention to themselves can be dangerous, employees typically keep quiet about mistakes, mishaps, or other problems that management should be aware of. Upsetting the *kibun* (kee-buun), "feelings" or "mood," of a superior by being the bearer of bad news is something that most employees prefer to avoid. (When someone is demoted or transferred to a job that has less prestige, it is commonly referred to as *jwa chon*/jwah choan, which literally means "a change to the left," from the old custom of seating inferiors on the left side.)

Overall, corporate philosophy in Korea is characterized by extreme paternalism and strong emotional ties that are expressed openly. Decisions are a combination of a top-down and middle-management-up process subsumed in the words *kyul-jae* (k'yule-jay), which literally means "authorization" and refers to a formal procedure for submitting written proposals to senior executives. The word for the document system itself is *pummi* (pume-mee). This term is the equivalent of the Japanese *ringi seido* (reen-ghee say-e-doe), introduced in my book *Japanese Etiquette and Ethics in Business*, first published in 1959.

Unlike their Japanese counterparts, however, senior Korean executives do not routinely approve of written proposals simply because all or most lower managers have signed off on them. They use the procedure to maintain control. Further, the personalized nature of Korean management results in far fewer memos and other documents (*soryu*/soe-r'yuu) than what is common in the United States and elsewhere. Most disagreements or confrontations in Korean companies are resolved by authoritarian edicts from senior executives, not by discussions leading to compromise and consensus.

Training and discipline in Korean companies are as strict as they are in elite military organizations. Both attitudes and behavior are prescribed down to the smallest detail. Inferiors obey superiors. Etiquette between ranks is strictly enforced. Instead of the salute there is the bow. Everything proceeds according to the book. Employees are expected to wear the proper "uniform" and keep themselves neatly groomed.

There are, in fact, many areas of Korean management expectations that go beyond the Marine Corps. One of these areas is attitude. Except during emergency situations, the marines allow a certain amount of levity in both attitude and behavior. Joking and horseplay are common. Generally speaking, Korean *kwalli* makes absolutely no allowances for such behavior. Employees are expected to think and behave in a serious manner at all times, concentrating only on doing their jobs and on maintaining the proper relationships with their co-workers and superiors.

Most senior executives in larger Korean companies are the products of a "survival of the fittest" process that is known as *gong-chae* (gohng-chay), which refers to "open" competitive tests given to managerial candidates at the time of their hiring—candidates who have already qualified themselves through *gong-chae* entrance examinations. Managers who have been with Korean companies for many years and achieved a high level of influence are often referred to as *tobagi* (toh-bah-ghee), which means "native" or "aborigine," in recognition of their seniority and importance to the companies.

Another factor in Korean management is the relationship ties of managers and employees with the founders, owners, and top executives, that are expressed in the terms *hyul-yun* (h'yule-yoon), *hak-yun* (hahk-yoon), and *ji-yun* (jee-yoon). *Hyul-yun* means "blood ties," *hak-yun* refers to "school ties," and *ji-yun* means "regional ties." Individuals with these ties get preferential treatment in the hiring as well as in the promotion process and therefore represent an important element in the management of most Korean firms.

Given these personal factors in Korean management, it follows that many decisions top Korean executives make are value judgments rather than judgments based on empirical evidence or facts—something that often upsets fact-minded foreigners.

Most Korean managers work long hours—ten or more in the office and then several times a week two to six more hours interacting with associates in bars, clubs, and restaurants. Generally, junior managers will not leave their offices before their seniors do.

Managers in larger Korean companies go all out to promote *ilch egam* (eelch eh-gahm), or a "sense of oneness," by sponsoring employee recreational activities, celebrating special occasions, giving gifts, holding after hours drinking parties (usually for male employees only), directing mass singing of the company song, repeating the company motto, and making speeches emphasizing the oneness of the company and its efforts and the "we are all Koreans" theme.

Korean managers are constantly emphasizing the point that as far as effort and product or service quality is concerned only the best that is possible is acceptable. In speeches and in posters they exhort employees to purge themselves of the *choktangjuui* (choak-tahng-juu-wee), or "doing only a satisfactory job," mentality and strive for perfection.

Another concept that plays a significant role in Korean management is *songsil* (sohng-sheel), or "sincerity." But *songsil* means a lot more to Koreans than "sincerity" does to the average Westerner. To Korean managers and employees being *songsil* implies being totally dedicated to the company, which means being willing to sacrifice one's personal interests and obligations, including one's family, for the company.

The power and scope of *songsil* in Korean culture comes from its traditional role in the Confucian family system. It was a vital ingredient in making the inferior-superior male-dominated system work as smoothly as it did. Family members had to sacrifice most of their individuality to conform to the dictates of the system.

Songsil is still a major factor in all areas of Korean society, including business, but it is not nearly as strong or as limiting as it once was. The influence of democratic and other Western principles, along with new kinds of demands that are inherent in a fast-paced high-tech economy and totally new opportunities in both work and lifestyle, are gradually eroding the suffocating nature of *songsil*.

Among the attributes that Korean personnel managers look for in employee candidates is their knowledge of the etiquette pertaining to the traditional Confucian-oriented hierarchical system of inferior-superior relationships and their willingness to observe it.

Until recent times Korean companies generally did not fire anyone outright. Instead they conspired to make the situation so unpleasant for the individuals concerned that they would eventually leave on their own. This was done by assigning them to a desk that was not appropriate for their rank and therefore humiliating, not assigning them any work to do, transferring them to an undesirable location, and so on—all techniques previously perfected by the Japanese. Of course, employees being subjected to this treatment got the message quickly. Also like the Japanese, Koreans commonly use a euphemism such as *nagaya handa* (nah-gah-yah hahn-dah), literally "having to go out," when referring to being fired or quitting under pressure.

One type of employee-training conducted by many Korean companies, particularly larger firms, is called *kukki hullyon* (kuuk-kee huhl-yoyn), or "self-control training." This is a kind of training designed to break down the preconceived notions that recruits have of themselves and the world at large and reorient them into company men who can stand up under extreme pressure and not lose control of their emotions or their presence of mind. Another facet of this training is to condition them to think alike and behave alike, to become perfect organization men.

The self-control training programs, created by professional training companies, go well beyond self-control in the usual sense. They are designed to force the young employees to put the success of the group above their own interests; in other words, to suppress their "self" in favor of the group. Tests devised by the trainers include puzzles and tasks that can be accomplished only by close teamwork and include intellectual and emotional and well as physical challenges. Some of the tasks are impossible to accomplish and are designed to determine how the employees will react in such situations. The training programs are conducted with military precision and thoroughness, with the trainees required to demonstrate the kind of enthusiasm and response that first-year students must show in the strictest military academies. One important goal in the programs is to break down the traditional Korean reserve and etiquette where speech and physical behavior are concerned by forcing the trainees to do things they have never done before—such as accost strangers on the street and persuade them to do things that are out of the ordinary. Part of the program is to teach new employees how to endure hardships and persevere at difficult tasks, an experience called *kugi hulyon* (koog-ee huhl-yohn), which translates as "learning endurance." *Kukki hullyon* was pioneered and perfected by the *chaebol*, the large conglomerates headed by Samsung, Hyundai, Sunkyong, LG Group, Daewoo, and Ssangyong. The training includes a strong dose of Confucian-oriented morality, fighting spirit, nationalism, and pride. Employees are indoctrinated with the concept that they are civilian soldiers in a battle against great odds to continuously increase Korea's national product. To enhance the concept that the company's efforts correspond to and contribute to the goals of the nation, some companies have Korean flags on display at all times in all of their offices.

In its early years Samsung was famous for starting each workday with the broadcasting of the national anthem over its internal loudspeaker system. When the anthem was being played, employees faced their respective flags and stood at attention.

Company executives routinely emphasize the relationship between the success of their companies and the national welfare and in both subtle and conspicuous ways equate diligence and hard work with *aeguk chongsin* (aye-guuk chohng-sheen), or a "patriotic spirit." To be a good Korean is to be a hardworking Korean who willingly sacrifices for his company.

The larger the Korean company, the more likely it is to have a militaristic type of management and require its new employees to go through some kind of outside training program. Some of these programs are conducted by privately run Confucian-oriented academies that look very much like *Son* (Sohn), or Zen, temples. At the end of these programs there is a party at which the young employees are encouraged to drink as much as they can hold, to "forget etiquette" and say anything they want to about the program, the instructors, their new company, and so on. While this traditional custom is based on the idea that nothing that the candidates say will be held against them, it seems that most of them choose to keep any really critical thoughts they may have to themselves.

In stricter companies lower-ranking employees are required to behave with special respect toward managers. Some managers do not allow their subordinates to sit in a relaxed manner when in their presence. They must literally sit at attention. Crossing their legs and other types of casual behavior are strictly taboo. There are many occasions when employees of such companies are required to stand when senior executives enter their areas and to stand at attention when in their presence and responding to them.

Company events and the travels of senior executives are planned and executed with military thoroughness and precision. This often includes preparing
maps or sketches to show exactly where things are to occur and where specific
people are to be at exact times. A significant part of this regimentation mentality is a holdover from earlier years when there was an established process and
order for virtually everything in Korean life, from the manner of speaking, bowing, eating, and walking to working. The strict military service that almost all
male Koreans have been subjected to since 1950 also plays an important role in
orienting Korean employees toward militaristic behavior. As frustrating and as
humiliating as this kind of behavior can be to some people, there is no doubt that
it has been one of the factors contributing to the extraordinary progress made
by the Korean economy since 1960.

Foreign companies in Korea with relatively large numbers of white-collar
employees invariably have two levels or kinds of management—one foreign and
the other Korean. The Korean level of management is generally behind the
scenes and is operated by the Korean staff in keeping with their traditional values and social behavior. In some cases the foreign managers may be totally
oblivious to this "invisible management" within their own firms.

The more the foreign side ignores the factors that are meaningful to Koreans—their sex and age, their social class and clan, their birthplace, the schools
they attended—the more likely there will be both problems and a secondary
chain of command in the company. Whether or not this sub-rosa management
is positive or negative depends on how many and to what depth traditional
Korean values have been contravened, and the attitudes and agendas of the
ranking Korean staff members. They can use their influence to make things run
smoothly, or they can disrupt them—or somewhere in between.

It is therefore important for foreign executives setting up operations in
Korea first of all to be aware of these social factors and, second, to get outside
help in putting together a staff that is "socially correct" enough that the people
can work together without undue friction. Another thing to keep in mind is that
unwesternized Koreans do not like to involve *pyonhosa* (p'yone-hoe-sah), or
"attorneys," in business negotiations because legal terminology and the kind of
logic used by lawyers goes against their cultural grain.

Korea therefore does not have a large cadre of attorneys, and the government essentially regards them as quasi–civil servants who come under its jurisdiction, particularly when they are attempting to represent foreign clients, and
there are a variety of laws limiting their behavior.

관료주의
Kwallyojui
(Kwahll-yoh-juu-wee)
"Bureaucratic Authoritarianism"

For more than two thousand years Korea was ruled by a small class of scholar-officials who fostered the Confucian concept that their superior social status justified their right to rule and that common people should accept their inferior position and be both passive and obedient. As the centuries passed, this authoritarian system engendered a powerful sense of elitism among the ruling class that has continued to be characteristic of Korean politicians and officials down to the present time.

This form of government, which was perfected during the first centuries of the Choson dynasty (1392–1910), achieved an extraordinary degree of stability and harmony in Korean society over relatively long periods of time. But it had a serious downside. Throughout the Choson dynasty this systematic spiritual, social, and economic oppression of the common people alienated them from the ruling class and resulted in periodic protests and rebellions that were viciously put down by the authorities. The short-lived Japanese colonial period in Korea (1910–1945), added significantly to the conditioning of Koreans in bureaucratic authoritarianism because the Japanese civilian overseers and military occupation troops were even more domineering and strict in their administration of the country than the Korean ruling class had been.

The division of Korea into North and South Korea in 1945 under ruling regimes that distrusted and hated each other resulted in both halves of the peninsula being subjected to dictatorial military control that not only continued but strengthened the *kwallyojui* (kwahll-yoh-juu-wee), or "authoritarianism," that had marked Korean governments since ancient times. However, by the 1970s a modicum of democracy had been introduced into South Korea and this was to grow in the following decades, while the people of North Korea remained locked in an authoritarian and bureaucratic time warp that was typical of the most paranoid Communist regimes of the 1950s and 1960s.

Present-day Koreans, like most Asians in the Confucian sphere, are involved in an emotional and intellectual struggle between their traditional values and customs and the democratic, individualistic ways of the West. One facet of this struggle is the lingering influence of bureaucratic authoritarianism that continues to set the tone of government as well as business. Generally speaking, officials on all levels develop some degree of *koman* (kuh-mahn), "self-importance" or "arrogance," and see themselves as "fief lords" no matter how small or insignificant their bureaucratic fiefdoms might be. People having to deal with officials to obtain government approval or documentation of any kind must cater to their emotions and egos, which means being extraordinarily circumspect in their behavior and often showering them with some form of hospitality or favors.

Part of the authoritarianism complex that afflicts most Koreans when they achieve power, particularly in government, is that they invariably emphasize their authority and downplay, or ignore altogether, the responsibility that is supposed to go with the office. This situation makes official corruption inevitable and naturally impacts all areas of politics and business.

Generally speaking, Korean political leaders and officials continue to practice bureaucratic authoritarianism because they still believe it is the most efficient way to administer the country—besides being the only way they know how to conduct themselves. It is therefore rather unlikely that bureaucratic authoritarianism will disappear from Korea or even be diminished significantly in the next two or three generations. It is much too deeply entrenched in the Korean psyche and, like so many other traditional Korean beliefs and practices, will change only in concert with fundamental changes in the entire Korean culture.* Still, agitation for change in the Korean style of government is growing both vocally and physically, especially among high school and university students, who in the tradition of Korean scholars see themselves as responsible for defending the welfare of the people against immoral and unscrupulous government.

108

계

Kye
(Keh)

"The Group Approach"

Koreans have been conditioned for centuries to form cooperative groups made up of family members, friends, and fellow villagers to pursue a variety of goals. The key to the efficiency and importance of these groups was expressed in the word *kye* (keh), which means "agreement" or "bond" and is used in compounds that refer to a variety of social organizations formed to raise money for specific purposes. In this sense it means something like "money pool."

---

*There is a good side and a bad side to the autocratic behavior of Korea's government officials, which often depends on whose ox is being gored. Or maybe whose pig is being fed, as is demonstrated by an Environmental Ministry law that bans *issushigae* (ee-suu-she-guy), or "toothpicks," on restaurant tables so that pigs eating leftovers won't have to worry about chomping down on an upright toothpick. The fine for breaking this ban is several thousand dollars. Adds Don Hackney, an American businessman stationed in Seoul, "*Issushigae* may be available at the cash register desk, however."

One of the most common of these organizations today is the *wichin-gye* (weech-een-geh), which can be translated as "parents' organization." People who have aged parents organize *wichin-gye* to help them raise money and make arrangements for celebrating their parents' seventieth birthdays—an important occasion in Korean society that can be very expensive and require a great deal of advance preparations.

Another traditional type of rural *kye* are *sangjo-gye* (sahng-joh-geh), "funeral associations," which are organized to help families prepare and pay for a parent's funeral. Members of these groups donate money, serve as messengers, help dig the grave, carry the bier, and provide other services for the bereaved family. In a *sangppo kye* (sahng-ppoh keh), or "funeral *kye*," the people meet and work out the details of the group, beginning with a formal name, its location, and all of the provisions that the members must agree to follow, including the timing and manner of the monetary contributions and how they are to be distributed.

Kyorhon kye (k'yohr-hohn keh), or "wedding pools," are also popular because weddings are both a major undertaking and expensive. In addition to monetary donations and gifts such as bedding and household utensils, members of wedding *kye* also stage one or more receptions for the families and friends of the bride and groom.

There have also traditionally been village *kye* that were more or less standby organizations that went into action when there was some special need, such as repairing a home, building a new home, repairing and building community facilities, and providing emergency aid following typhoons, fires, or other disasters. At fixed times each family in the village contributes agreed-on sums of money to the village *kye* fund. Korean villages have also traditionally formed *pumasi* (puum-ah-she), "co-op labor groups," to help each other during the annual busy seasons.

"The most common type of *kye* not only in Korea but among overseas communities of Koreans is the 'wives *kye*,'" notes Martin Sours of the American Graduate School of International Management (AGSIM). "Each wife in the group contributes to the *kye* from her household budget. The accumulated funds are made available to the members on a rotation basis, each 'winning' in turn. If a member experiences some kind of emergency, she has access to the funds out-of-turn. The 'wives *kye*' are thus both an important form of savings and a source of financing among Korean families," Sours added.

In more recent times a new kind of *kye* has appeared among housewives in larger cities who want to broaden their social activities. These housewife *kye* raise funds that are used to finance parties at which the wives eat, drink, gossip, and generally have a good time.

Another form of cooperative in Korea is the *ture* (tuur-eh), which is work oriented. These groups are formed to provide the labor for planting, weeding, harvesting, digging or repairing wells, repairing bridges, and so on—a custom that originated during the Shilla dynasty (618–935). Each family in a village usually contributes one worker to a *ture*—usually men but sometimes women as well. When a *ture* group is working in a field or on a project the area is surrounded by banners identifying the group and their activity.

It has long been the custom for some of the work done by the *ture* to be accompanied by rhythmic music, with workers being accompanied to and from the fields by a *nong ak* (nohng ahk), or "farmers' band," made up of drummers, cymbalists, and ribbon twirlers. Workers are paid for their *ture* labors. Part of the money is contributed to the village welfare fund, and another part is used to pay for a party after the project is completed.

Another common form of cooperation and mutual help in Korea are the *kye*, or "money pools," established by a group of individuals who need extra money to finance business ventures or other kinds of investments and prefer to raise the money privately rather than go to banks. These private money-pool groups are limited to a small number of people who are carefully screened to make sure they are trustworthy.

Other types of *kye* include *chonchak kye* (chohn-chahck keh), a rotating syndicate for ceremonial food and liquor; *unsang kye* (unh-sahng keh), syndicates for raising money for a palanquin (*kama*/kah-mah) for carrying a coffin to a grave site; and *kap-kye* (kahp-keh), or "same-age associations," to raise money for sponsoring various programs. The chief or leader of a *kye* is called *kye jang* (keh jahng). A *kye* meeting is a *kye gori* (keh goh-ree).

109

계약

Kyeyak
(Keh-yahk)

"Contracts in Korea"

Western-style business *kyeyak* (keh-yahk), or contracts, are a relatively recent phenomenon in Korea and for the most part go against the traditional cultural grain. Prior to modern times (which basically did not start in Korea until the twentieth century), detailed written contracts were the exception. Most commitments made between individuals, between the government and its suppliers, and between manufacturers, merchants, and retailers were primarily verbal understandings. Also until modern times there was very little legal foundation for the conduct of professional and business affairs and in many areas no legal infrastructure at all.

The commitments that individuals and organizations made to each other were based on family and kinship ties and on personal contacts that often went back several generations. The system was held together by Confucian morality, which included a strict sense of obligation and responsibility based on "face," social class, and tradition. *Shinsa hyopchong* (sheen-sah h'yohp-chohng), or "gentlemen's agreements," were the rule.

An important part of this cultural scenario was that Koreans were not comfortable with making precise commitments of any kind. They preferred to keep things general so relationships could evolve as circumstances changed. Generally speaking, Koreans were more interested in the emotional and friendship aspects of relationships than in trying to tie down specific details. The Korean perspective was that as long as the parties to any relationship were sincere and gave precedence to personal and humane elements, they would be able to deal with the various circumstances that arose and the relationship would be solid and achieve its goals.

Because of this cultural attitude, verbal commitments were only as good and as binding as the relationship between the people involved. It was therefore often the case that as much or more effort went into sustaining friendly, cooperative relationships as in carrying out any duties or obligations involved.

The traditional Buddhistic view of the cosmos as cyclic helped program Koreans to think in broad terms and to be less concerned about precise details—something that now varies from being a serious handicap to being a significant advantage. Koreans often choose to ignore details of contracts and other matters in the interests of long-term goals. Westerners, who have been culturally conditioned to emphasize details and the here-and-now, often clash with their Korean counterparts in working out and following through on agreements.

The Korean attitude toward *kyeyak* has become more "Westernized" since the 1960s, when the country began transforming itself into an economic powerhouse. But there is still an easily recognizable element of traditionalism in both negotiating and servicing contracts, even among the most international of Korea's largest and most successful corporations. Koreans often use the term *kyeyak so* (keh-yahk soh), or "written contract," to imply that a contract may be no more permanent or important than the piece of paper it is written on.

Another interesting term often used in reference to contracts is *baek ji wiim* (bake jee weem), which means "trusting in white paper." The connotation is that someone who does business on the basis of written contracts rather than deep personal relationships is on very fragile ground. A contract may also be referred to as a *ko e kulmyun* (koe ee kull-m'yuun), which refers to something that can be used as either a "nose ring" or an "earring," implying that a contract or some other situation can be interpreted in two or more ways. It may also refer to a person who changes his attitude or position according to the circumstances.

One of my Korean colleagues says that when Koreans sign contracts they are merely engaging in a formality that is meant to indicate they have a relationship with someone. They do not mean to bind themselves to detailed, precise obligations and actions that are so dear to the heart of Western businesspeople. He added that Koreans look upon *kyeyak* as "symbols" of relationships rather than as something that defines and controls relationships. "We regard contracts as general guidelines that set perimeters around which we work," he said.

While Westerners interpret contracts from an exact legalistic viewpoint, Koreans generally interpret them in moralistic terms that are based on factors that Westerners regard as totally irrelevant. Koreans take into consideration the relative size and strength of the firms involved, the length of time the two parties have been involved with each other, any special difficulties involved in fulfilling the requirements of the contract, the relative advantages accruing to the two parties, unexpected changes in the market, and so on.

In its Korean context a *kyeyak* is more of a general statement of purpose and goals than a detailed document that binds the parties to absolute requirements. The fundamental aim of a Korean-style contract is to formally acknowledge that both parties to the agreement will do whatever is necessary, and within their capabilities, to ensure that neither side is disadvantaged or loses in any way. Korean *kyeyak* therefore have a substantial degree of built-in flexibility that makes it possible for the two parties to continuously adjust to the changing circumstances.

Koreans regularly point out that their *kyeyak*, as well as their whole approach to business, rests on a philosophical foundation of *injong* (een-johng), or "compassion for the plight of others"—which, they add, or imply, is typically missing from the Western way of doing business. Koreans regularly accuse Westerners of putting profits before relationships, thereby causing unnecessary friction between companies and instability in the marketplace.

This amorphous view of business and contracts does not necessarily apply to all Korean businesspeople. A few, especially among those who have had extensive educational and work experience abroad, are as detail-minded and as diligent about living up to contractual provisions as their Western counterparts. But fundamentally Koreans dispute the rationality of the all-too-typical Western-style contract that attempts to eliminate ongoing adjustments in the relationship. They point out that circumstances are continuously changing, and unless they are free to adjust their actions both parties will soon be at a serious disadvantage.

This presents a serious challenge to all businesspeople in or doing business with Korea, Koreans as well as foreigners. The traditional Korean solution to this problem is to establish strong personal ties with key individuals in all of their business relationships and then work to make as sure as possible that they can count on these personal ties to get fair treatment as circumstances change.

The Korean rationale is certainly valid, but what it does not state is that when they adjust their actions to account for changing circumstances their primary purpose is to protect their own interests. Only the rare Confucian paragons will give as much thought and concern to the interests of their business agents or partners as they do to their own.

The honesty, integrity, loyalty, and diligence of Koreans is intimately tied to their "face," to the degree of shame they would suffer if they failed to exhibit any of these qualities at the appropriate time. Foreign businesspeople seeking to qualify Korean partners and sign contracts with them should first try to measure their "face." The more face they have to lose the more likely they are to be trustworthy in every respect. And by the same token, if they have little face to lose, their ethics are likely to be loose and easily discarded.

Foreign companies wanting to establish long-term contractual relationships in Korea are well advised to get professional help in Koreanizing their contracts to the point that their Korean partners can sign them in good faith and will make a sincere effort to abide by them, while making very sure that their own interests are protected.

Foreigners who work out important, formal agreements with Koreans should be prepared to mark the occasion with a celebration that includes drinks and speeches. These events traditionally end with all the participants simultaneously raising their arms in the air and shouting *mansei!* (mahn-say-e!) three times. *Mansei* literally means "ten thousand years" and is the Korean equivalent of "Hip! Hip! Hooray!" and the Japanese word *banzai* (bahn-zie).

110

고제술
Kyojesul
(K'yoh-jeh-suul)
"Business Drinking"

The strict Confucian code by which Koreans lived for more than five hundred years called for a very precise kind of behavior that prevented the casual relationships and easy camaraderie so familiar to most Westerners and so important to the emotional and spiritual well-being of all people. Korea's strict code of manners prevented people from freely expressing themselves physically or verbally. There was a precise, stylized form of etiquette they were required to follow in all of their relationships, in speech as well as in bodily movements.

This system was even more of a mental and physical strain because the two sexes were required to live in virtually segregated spheres from an early age. The psychic stress that resulted from this custom was far more damaging to women than to men because they had far fewer outlets for relieving the stress.

Men, depending on their social station and means, had access to concubines, mistresses, professional prostitutes, professional female companions, and, most of all, to regularly drinking *sul* (suhl), "alcoholic beverages," "forgetting etiquette," and sometimes engaging in fighting.

As in most if not all cultures, drinking alcoholic beverages in Korea began as a religious ritual. The idea, apparently, was that it was possible to commune more directly with the spirits or gods when one was in a drunken or trancelike state. In earlier times Korean women were allowed to drink, but following the introduction of a new, strict form of Confucianism into Korea from China during the fourteenth and fifteenth centuries, the role of women in Korean society was changed dramatically. They became totally subservient to men. In addition to not being able to interact casually with males, even members of their own family, they were also prohibited from drinking.

Drinking thus became one of the many prerequisites reserved exclusively for men—and was something that they did during religious rituals, during festivals, and at "after-hours" dinners or parties with male friends. A key reason for the popularity and importance of drinking to male Koreans was that while drinking with co-workers and friends they could ignore much of the formal etiquette that normally applied to their behavior and act in a much more natural manner.

When industrialization finally came to Korea in the twentieth century, the custom of drinking was incorporated into the business world as a vital part of establishing and maintaining interpersonal relationships, not only within companies but with all outside contacts, including government officials. *Kyojesul* (k'yoh-jeh-suul), or "business drinking," thus became an integral part of Korea's business world.

Kyojesul thus has several dimensions. It first of all is essential in allowing participants to temporarily dispense with the strict etiquette that is the hallmark of Korean interpersonal relationships.This makes it possible for them to behave in an informal, casual manner, to the point of loudly disagreeing with each other and complaining about other people, including their own superiors. A second element in these drinking sessions is their role in making it possible for people to bond with each other—something that is difficult and limited at other times because normal etiquette does not allow either intimacy or openness. And finally, the ritualistic toasting of each other, business agreements, and other special events with alcoholic beverages imbues these ceremonial events with the same kind of sanctified religious authority that a priest brings to a christening or wedding.

Of course, alcoholic drinks have traditionally served exactly the same purpose in Western societies, but to a far lesser degree than in Korea. Foreigners interacting with Koreans should be aware of this very important difference in degree and take their *kyojesul* experiences in Korea seriously. Most Korean men also have well-established *sulchinku* (suhl-cheen-kuu), or "drinking partners," whom they commune with to relieve stress and aid in times of need—a custom that is highly recommended for expatriate businesspeople in Korea.

111

결혼

Kyolhon
(K'yohl-hohn)

"Marriage Customs"

In the age of the earliest Korean kingdoms (before 108 B.C.), *kyolhon*, or "marriage," was more of a communal and tribal affair than a personal matter. Marriages were arranged, and love played no role in the arrangements. In fact, love—even affection—was seen as an obstacle to a successful marriage because it introduced an element of emotion that would interfere with spouses meeting their responsibilities.

In some—if not all—of Korea's earliest tribal states husbands offered the sexual services of their wives to honored guests. When married men were killed or died early from other causes, their brothers were required to marry their widowed wives. Following the introduction of Confucianism into Korea during the Three Kingdoms period (57 B.C.–A.D. 669), marriage began to take on the forms that existed until modern times.

During the Shilla dynasty (669–935) and the following Koryo dynasty (936–1392) upper-class men were permitted to have several wives, who were considered equal. Newly married husbands in the commoner class customarily lived in their wives' homes (at least until the birth of their first child). Both of these customs were to change dramatically following the adoption of Confucianism as the state ideology by the new Choson dynasty in 1392. Under the Confucian-oriented social system devised by this regime the first wife was the primary or main wife. Other wives and concubines were relegated to a much lower status, causing innumerable inheritance problems and emotional conflicts.

In the fifteenth century the Choson court passed laws designed to prevent divorcees and widows from remarrying. These laws, aimed primarily at the upper class, made the sons and grandsons of women who married a second time ineligible for advancement in civil service positions, the most desirable of all occupations. Sons and grandsons of women who married a third time were banned from taking the civil service exams that led to government positions. Women in this latter category were more or less regarded as prostitutes.

Under the Confucianized social system instituted by the new Choson government, wives moved into their husbands' homes. After marriage men and women slept together for conjugal purposes, but there was a woman's world and a man's world that basically resulted in their living segregated lives. Brides and grooms often met each other for the first time on their wedding day or a short time before they were united in marriage. Parents, close relatives, professional matchmakers, and in some cases employers or masters acted as go-betweens in arranging marriages. Sociologist Sang Bok Han observed in his book *The Korean Patterns of Life and Way of Thinking* (The Academy of Korean Studies) that in keeping with the Confucian ideology of filial piety the primary relationship in a marriage was between fathers and sons, not between husbands and wives. Wives were vital to the production of progeny but other than serving as childbearers and domestic help they were incidental to the lives of men.

Also in old Korea it was the custom for parents to arrange early *kyolhon* for their sons and daughters. In many cases daughters were married off before they reached their teens. The rationale for this custom was very practical as far as parents were concerned. By marrying off a daughter they got a son-in-law who was beholden to them and had to serve them in many ways. By marrying off a son they got a daughter-in-law who was even more beneficial, because daughters-in-law essentially became servants in the parents' household.

During the latter centuries of the Choson dynasty (1392–1910) there were two approaches to arranging marriages. Young men could select several prospective brides from which their parents would then make the final decision. Or the parents, relatives, or a professional go-between would come up with prospects and the grooms would make the choice.

Also during this period, girls in better-to-do families were often married between the ages of twelve and sixteen and were generally one to two years older than their husbands. In peasant families, however, male children were usually not married off until they were in the later teens, to keep them as single workers. The more sons-in-law and daughters-in-law parents had, the greater their social status and the more people they had who were subject to their authority and who were required to serve them while they were alive and honor them after their death. Husbands whose wives failed to produce sons routinely took concubines, causing a whole new set of problems because the male offspring of concubines were generally regarded as illegitimate.

Korea's feudal family system was abolished in 1894. Early marriages were prohibited. The minimum age was set at sixteen for females and at twenty for males. Widows were allowed to remarry; sons of secondary wives could succeed their fathers. The following year the Western calendar was adopted and men were ordered to cut off their traditional topknots (for centuries men had worn their hair tied into knots on top of their heads). This latter edict was met with bitter resistance from large numbers of Korean men who considered it one of the most important things in identifying them as males and as Koreans.

Despite abolition of the feudal family system, male-female relations in Korea did not begin to change dramatically until the 1960s. Concubinage was made illegal by the Japanese colonial government in 1922, but the practice continued to be tolerated for several more decades. In 1951 the Seoul District Court ruled that if a husband took a concubine his wife was legally justified in seeking a divorce. Social discrimination against the offspring of concubines was still common in the 1990s.

Young people born after 1945 were raised in a far more democratic environment, educated, and exposed to foreign influences such as American movies and television. By the 1970s young Korean women could no longer be taken for granted by the male sex. Many young Korean women began picking their own husbands, and they had high standards, not only in physical size and appearance but also in education, earning potential, and character.

But still today, some 30 percent of all marriages in Korea, particularly in rural areas and among the rich, are more or less arranged. Present-day professional marriage matchmakers, like their predecessors, are usually elderly women who are skilled in astrological matters and can advise the couple and their parents when the match appears to be especially favorable for all concerned. Divining the qualities of a prospective bride is known as *napkil* (nahp-keel). The potential compatibility of spouses is called *kunghap* (kuung-hahp).

Parents provide matchmakers with all of the pertinent background information about their sons and daughters—family history, social status, education, and so on. They then go through their files and make new contacts in an effort to find suitable matches. Once the matchmaker has decided on a possible match, she invites both sets of parents and their respective offspring to a meeting at a teahouse or coffeehouse. In cities, name hotel coffee shops are a favorite location for such meetings—and such groups can be spotted easily virtually any day of the week in these places.

Matchmaker meetings are designed primarily for the parents to look each other over, sound each other out, and decide if they want to encourage the match. If both sides are favorable, the couple go out on dates to see if they are also compatible. There is often considerable pressure from one or both sets of parents for their sons or daughters to agree to the match, particularly if they are older than the average age or have some other "defect."

It has traditionally been customary for the oldest sons and daughters in families to marry first. If they are late in marrying, the pressure against them from both their parents and younger siblings can be intense. Some individuals marry just to escape this kind of pressure. But generally if either side does not want to go through with the wedding the whole process starts over.

Matchmakers are expected to have qualified both potential partners as far as social status and background are concerned, but many attempts at matchmaking fail because the woman is too independent-minded for the man's taste or the woman does not like the man's personality. After the matchmakers have made their recommendations, most mothers of would-be couples cover their bets by consulting fortune-tellers. If the fortune-teller finds that the astrological profiles of the young man and woman match, the mothers may be all the more forceful in encouraging the marriage. Generally in arranged marriages, social class, family background, and the economic status of the families take precedence over the appearance, personality, and ability of prospective brides and grooms.

When an unmarried son or daughter in a more traditional Korean family dies, it is customary to call in a shaman or a team of shamans and conduct a posthumous wedding ceremony for them, uniting them with the spirit of someone of the right age and sex who also recently died before being married. The purpose of this ritual is to provide the souls of the unmarried dead with "spirit mates" to keep them company in the afterlife. Such marriages were known as *sahon* (sah-hoan), "ghost marriages" or "spirit marriages."

One old Korean wedding tradition, now rapidly dying out, that is of special interest involves the so-called *ham* (hahm), which refers to a large wooden box that the groom's male friends use to carry wedding gifts to the bride's home, and the practices that surround this custom.

At a time that has been prearranged with the bride's family, the young men, who have usually been drinking, show up at the front gate (or, in the case of an apartment building, at the front door of the building) with the box. One of the men, acting as a "horse," carries the box on his back. Another member of the group leads the "horse," telling him when to stop and go. At the front gate (or at front door of the apartment building) the "horse" leader and the other young men announce loudly that the "horse" is so tired it can't move unless money is paid for each additional step it takes.

The bride's family and the leader noisily negotiate how much the group is going to be paid for each step the "horse" takes to reach the door—where the bride, her friends, and the groom are waiting. Once the amount is settled, the money is collected at each additional step, amid a great deal of noisy bantering. After the "horse" and other young men are inside the home or apartment and the *ham* has been handed over to the family, the group is served food and drinks. The men give half of the money they collected to the groom, then invite the bride's girlfriends to go out with them to spend the rest of the money on more drinks.*

Don Hackney, an American businessman stationed in Seoul, adds, "Since the early 1990s there has been growing controversy over a number of traditional wedding customs that some people consider incompatible with the times, particularly the *ham* ritual. The controversy became more heated after a bride jumped out of a hotel window to her death when her husband complained about the amount of money her family had given as *ham*. The custom is now rare, especially in urban areas."

"Love marriages" in Korean are *yonae kyolhon* (yoh-nigh k'yohl-hoan), which literally means "love marriage" with connotations of a sexual element. Arranged marriages tend to be more common among the new urban rich than among the middle class because they are especially interested in forming alliances with other families on their own level or higher. Farm families also tend to follow many of the old customs, including arranged marriages.

Until the 1980s descendants of the *yangban* class seldom if ever married outside of the class. Now it is becoming more and more common for them to marry into "common families" that have become wealthy through business and have formed a new elite class. As in most societies, the well-to-do and upper class in Korea tend to marry on their own social and economic levels. And as in Japan, families of professors at prestigious universities and high-ranking career military officers are considered upper class.

There is now a law in Korea stating that a husband cannot divorce his wife against her will if there is no one who will take her in or if she cannot support herself, if she has already participated in the traditional three-year mourning period for her husband's deceased parents, or if the husband has become well-to-do since their marriage. These very practical stipulations are obviously designed to prevent men from arbitrarily divorcing their wives—something they were historically privileged to do.

In 1995 the Korean government passed legislation making it legal for members of the huge Kim clan to marry as long as there were no direct traceable ties between the prospective brides and grooms. The clan accounts for some 24 percent of the entire population.

Korean women do not take their husbands' names upon marriage. They continue to be known by their own family names for all legal purposes. In social situations they are referred to as "the wife of so-and-so."

---

*The custom of having the *ham* box bearers repeatedly stop and refuse to go on until they have been given a sum of money has also traditionally applied to funerals. Pallbearers carrying the casket to the burial site stop several times and chant that they can't go on because it is so difficult. They refuse to go on until the chief mourner or other member of the deceased's family gives them money, which is turned over to mutual aid societies and the like, not kept or used by the pallbearers. Rather than being a somber custom as might be expected given the overall sad mood of funerals, this ritualistic practice is often done with an entertaining flair that lightens the mood of the mourners.

112

경

Kyong
(K'yohng)

"Controlling the Mind"

One of the great traditions of Oriental philosophy is the importance of gaining control of the mind and disciplining it to achieve specific goals in philosophy, religion, the fine arts, martial arts, architecture, garden design, and so on. In Korea an important aspect of this mental discipline was subsumed in the word *kyong* (k'yohng), which means something like "humble respect for mind control and the development of reason"—a concept that is both Confucian and Buddhist.

Because of the fundamental role of Confucianism in Korean society from the fourteenth century until modern times, it was essential that the government, in concert with the cultural establishment, promote mind control, including emotion control, to make the social system function smoothly. The detailed nature of the Confucian-based etiquette prescribed for all relationships in Korea made it mandatory that people learn, keep in mind, and meticulously perform the ritualistic forms of behavior appropriate for the inferior-superior status of individuals—an absolute obligation that required severe mental discipline.

Broadly speaking, there was no such thing as "free-form" behavior in pre-modern Korea. The form, order, and style of virtually every action was prescribed. This form was repeated so many times in childhood and the early years that by the time people became adults most of their physical actions and speech were automatic. Still, this prescribed behavior required extraordinary mental effort along with the *kyong* element because it impacted the emotions as much as the intellect, if not more so, and most people are far more influenced by their emotions than by their reasoning powers.

The other cultural foundation for *kyong* came from the teachings of Buddhism, particularly the *Son* (Sohn), or Zen, sect, which was based entirely on gaining control of the emotional as well as the intellectual facets of the mind to become attuned to the universal mind and the power that animates the cosmos.

Of course, it was the professional practitioners of *kyong*, Zen monks and Confucian scholars, who first articulated this philosophy, attempted to conduct their lives according to its principles, and set the example for others to follow. But it was the fact that the Choson court adopted its own version of *kyong* as a key part of its state ideology—a version designed to serve its own interest in order and conformity—that the philosophy became an integral part of the popular culture.

Although Koreans have traditionally been noted for their extraordinary physical strength and mental endurance—both of which were essential to their survival—they paid for these qualities in a number of ways, including an occasional phenomenon known as *momsal* (mohm-sahl), which refers to what amounts to a virtually complete shutdown of the mind and body.*

According to medical authorities, the phenomenon of *momsal* occurs when someone contracts some kind of relatively minor ailment, such as a cold or upset stomach. Instead of fighting the ailment, the person collapses mentally and physically and seemingly gives up—a state that lasts for anywhere from a few to several days and then ends as abruptly as it began.

Some observers say the *momsal* phenomenon is a reaction to the extraordinary stress brought on by the strict order and form of all behavior, including speech, required by the Korean social system. Traditionally, the only excuse for not following the proper protocol and fulfilling all obligations was to become physically and or mentally incapable of doing so.

In any event, the influence of *kyong* is still conspicuously discernible in the character and behavior of modern-day Koreans. It is manifested in their famed stubbornness, their dedication to achieving success in school and in work, and their overall "can do (anything)" attitude—which, in the 1980s, was officially proclaimed a national slogan by the government.

Predictions by the Korean government that the country will continue expanding its economy for the foreseeable future, and will become one of the world's top ten economic powers, are based in large part on the *kyong* element in Korean culture. Western nations would do well to incorporate more respect for *kyong* into their own child-raising and educational systems.

113

경쟁
Kyongjaeng
(K'yohng-jang)
"Competition Korean Style"

One of the most important aims of Korea's traditional Confucian-oriented culture was to control all *kyongjaeng* (k'yohng-jang), or "competition," depersonalize it, and channel it into precisely defined groups within social classes, ranks, professions, and political positions—an ideology that was designed to ensure social stability and to protect and preserve the state.

The key to this ideology was making competition immoral except when it was designed to advance the welfare of groups, beginning with the family unit and kin and progressing outward and upward to include the community, the

---

*Foreigners who spent time in Korea between 1945 and the 1960s were often astounded by the loads that both Korean men and women would carry on their backs on *chi-gye* (chee-geh), or "A-frames"—a word that in later years conjured up painful memories and often considerable pride for older generations of Koreans.

company, and society in general. Individuals were allowed to compete against each other but only to benefit their groups, not themselves.

The philosophy behind this ideology was admirable up to a point. It assumed that the needs of the many outweighed the needs of the individual and the few. But it did not allow for the inescapable reality that people are intrinsically different, have different needs, and inevitably resist any effort to limit their individuality. Maintaining this kind of social system required both the attitudes and behavior of people to be strictly controlled through social, religious, and political sanctions—a situation that was inherently inhuman because it forced people to suppress most of their emotions and natural instincts.

Despite the fact that this system eventually became an inseparable part of Korean culture, it did not kill the spirit or the individual aspirations of Koreans, and once they were freed of the feudalistic controls that bound them to the system, unleashing their competitive drive literally for the first time in their history, they quickly became one of the most competitive-minded people in the world.

Present-day Koreans, whether in school, sports, the workplace, or anyplace else doing anything, do not like to be outdone by anybody. They don't like being behind and don't want anyone to get ahead of them, and they will exert extraordinary energy to keep that from happening. This competitive drive, energized by centuries of accumulated deprivation, suffering, and frustration, was a key factor in the transformation of Korea from a devastated wasteland in the early 1950s to one of the world's top countries in terms of gross national product and living standards in one short generation and continues to play a major role in its ongoing progress.

Kyongjaeng in Korea continues to have its cultural as well as its political peculiarities, however, and foreigners must be aware of these idiosyncrasies and develop skill in dealing with them so as to compete in the Korean market and on an international basis. In general terms all Korean behavior, including competition, is still group oriented to a considerable extent. Business management in larger firms is minutely structured and conducted with military formality and precision. Success in business is seen as a matter of survival and is pursued with a dedication that borders on obsession.

There is a strong nationalistic flavor to large-scale business in Korea that transcends individual benefits and personal ambitions. Most Korean business moguls are not motivated by a desire to accumulate more and more personal wealth and polish their egos. They see themselves as patriots helping to raise the living standard of all Koreans and building a better nation.

Korean political leaders, in turn, see themselves not only as responsible for setting economic policies that favor business but also as partners—and often as senior partners at that—in the management of business. Government ministries are especially vigilant in protecting Korean companies from foreign competition with tariffs and other measures and otherwise keeping the playing field tilted in their favor.

Adds Martin Sours of the American Graduate School of International Management (AGSIM): "Business in Korea has traditionally been seen by the government as an extension of the family, which must be both protected and guided—a perfect example of the Confucian 'Big Brother' syndrome."

114

고섭
Kyosop
(K'yoh-sop)

"Korean Negotiating"

Kyosop (k'yoh-sop), or "negotiations," in Korea are a microcosm of the culture in action. Western businesspeople should be aware that negotiating with a major Korean corporation is very much like dealing with a sovereign nation—a dictatorship when the company is still run by a strong founder, and somewhat more like a democracy when it is in the hands of second- or third-generation sons and professional managers. In a typical Korean scenario, the heads or senior executives of two corporations meet and agree that the companies will do business with each other. Lower-ranking staff members are then charged with the responsibility of working out all the details of the relationship and getting them approved in advance. The top men then reenter the picture for a ceremonial signing of the agreement.

Koreans are skilled negotiators. While more open-minded and flexible than the Japanese or Chinese, they generally regard compromise as a form of weakness, and when bargaining they prefer to begin with a go-for-broke approach, drawing back only at the last moment if they meet insurmountable resistance. When they do meet resistance, Koreans typically alternate between confrontation and compromise, in an effort to achieve their goals in small increments.

Another facet of doing business in Korea that is surprisingly difficult for Westerners to accept and deal with is the Korean custom of not saying no clearly or directly. Among the expressions that are commonly used in place of "no" are "we will study it further," "we must consult with our top management," or the old standby, *keul se* (kay-uhl seh), which means "we'll see" or "we'll think about it." (Adds Semco International senior partner H. J. Chang: "True, but Korean businesspeople are generally more straightforward than their Japanese counterparts.") A similar expression: *kuroseyo* (kroh-say-oh).

All Koreans, from government and company executives down to individuals in the street, tend to be paranoid about becoming dependent on foreigners, and a great deal of their behavior that foreigners regard as unwise, irrational, frustrating, and so on derives from this fear. This trait is invariably a conspicuous part of negotiations involving joint ventures. There is no quick way around this factor. The only solution is to develop personal relationships to the point that Koreans can overcome their paranoia and respond with confidence.

Unlike American and other Western firms, larger Korean companies generally give more emphasis to market share than they do to quarterly or annual profits, giving Korean businessmen different priorities that may cause problems for their foreign partners.

One aspect of the negotiating behavior of Korean managers and executives that often confuses foreign businesspeople is their habit of suddenly switching their position 180 degrees without any warning or explanation—something that is common in all authoritarian, hierarchical societies. The rationale behind this kind of behavior seems to be that the people involved will maintain a certain position up to the point where the threat of its backfiring appears imminent and then reverse themselves as a protective measure.

Reversals of this kind may be prompted by the Koreans' recognizing that the opposing party is on the verge of breaking off the engagement or when a new element is introduced that somehow puts them in jeopardy. This kind of Korean behavior is difficult for outsiders to understand and accept because it often appears to be totally arbitrary and purposely disruptive. It is an arbitrary approach, but it is a serious one. The Korean negotiators are, in effect, gambling that the other party will fold and they will win.

When it is the Korean side that folds and reverses itself, it is a manifestation of the traditional "winner take all" attitude that is common in Japan and elsewhere in Asia. Losers subordinate themselves to the winners, usually without any psychic damage, and become wholehearted collaborators and supporters—a common survival technique among people whose morality has traditionally been based on circumstances rather than unbendable principles.

Another aspect of traditional Korean culture that continues to influence business behavior is the custom of revealing as little information as possible during negotiations. There is a strong tendency for Korean businesspeople to regard details about their operation as vital company secrets. They are especially cautious about revealing information to outsiders with whom they do not have an established relationship.

When negotiations (or a product) are not going well and Koreans decide to cut their losses and get out, they may resort to *danyomhada* (dahn-yohm-hah-dah), which literally means something like "cutting one's mind" but is used in the sense of "throwing in the towel." They are more likely, however, to spring a surprise move on their counterparts known as *sunsu chida* (suun-suu chee-dah), which means something like "first to draw" or "first to strike" and refers to a sudden maneuver designed to win a major point or put your opponents in a position where they have no more room to maneuver.

Foreigners are often surprised and chagrined by the degree of *kojip* (koh-jeep), "stubbornness," typically demonstrated by Koreans, particularly North Koreans, in negotiating sessions.

115

고육

Kyoyuk
(K'yoh-yuuk)

"Education and Power"

"One should not step even on the shadow of one's teacher," a saying that has long been a popular in Korea, is indicative of the role that education has played in Korean life since ancient times. *Kyoyuk* (k'yoh-yuuk), or "education," in the modern sense was introduced into Korea by Chinese officials and scholars more than two thousand years ago. China invaded Korea in 109 B.C. and by the following year had established suzerainty over the small tribal kingdoms existing on the peninsula at that time.

The Chinese military officers, administrators, and advisers who took up residence in Korea brought with them their writing system and collections of books and treatises on philosophy, religion, medicine, the arts of war, and other subjects and made them available to the leading members of these kingdoms. A small number of Koreans, mostly court ministers, officials, and religious leaders, began studying the Chinese language to communicate with their Chinese overseers and learn about Chinese culture and civilization.

For Koreans thereafter, becoming educated meant mastering the Chinese ideograms and a wide selection of Chinese literature, especially the *kyong* (k'yohng), or classics on Confucianism—a privilege that was theoretically open to anyone but in effect was limited to a very tiny segment of the population because only they could afford to invest years in the process. Even more important, Korea's ruling class also adopted the Chinese attitude that it was not desirable for common people to become educated.

In A.D. 372 the court of the Koguryo kingdom established a *Tae Hak* (Tay Hahk), or "Higher Learning [Confucian] Academy," the first such school in Korea. Soon after the king of Shilla succeeded in unifying all of the Korean peninsula under his rule in 669 he made the custom of restricting all education to the sons of the ruling class into official policy—a move that was to have a profound influence on Koreans until well into the twentieth century. In 682 the Shilla court established a *Kuk Hak* (Kook Hahk), or National Educational College.

The policy of primarily restricting *kyoyuk* to the sons of the elite was continued by the succeeding Koryo dynasty (918–1392), guaranteeing that some 90 percent of the Korean population would remain illiterate. The Koryo dynasty also institutionalized the *hwago* (hwah-goh), or civil service exam system, originally adopted from China by the preceding Shilla dynasty.

During the Koryo dynasty there were privately run schools for male children of the aristocracy. Buddhist temples also ran schools, but attendance there was also limited primarily to boys from the upper classes. In 992 a *Kuk Chagam* (Kook Chah-gahm), or National University, was established in Kaesong, the capital of the Koryo dynasty. The National University, founded by King Songjong, included several colleges that were open to the sons of lower-ranking officials as well as a few commoners—a first in Korea. These colleges taught accounting, law, and calligraphy. Later the king also sent scholars into rural areas to teach the sons of gentry.

The founders of the Choson dynasty (1392–1910) expanded the variety and range of educational facilities. Sons of the upper class began studying the Chinese classics at private elementary schools called *sodang* (soh-dahng) when they were three or four years old. At the age of seven (six or five in Western terms), these youths entered *hak tang* (hahk tahng), or secondary schools. Next came a higher-level school and a series of examinations whereby those who were successful were awarded increasingly higher degrees, with the highest being the equivalent of the modern Ph.D.

There were also schools that taught technical subjects such as astronomy, foreign languages, geomancy, medicine, and meteorology, which were open to people in the so-called *chungin* (chuung-een), or "middle people." A *Songkyun Gwan* (Song-kyuun Gwahn), or "National Confucian Academy," was founded during the first year of the Choson dynasty. (Foreign languages taught at these academies for the training of interpreters included Chinese, Japanese, Manchu, Mongolian, and Nuchen Tartar.)

In 1432 King Sejong, the fourth Choson ruler, ordered that manuals detailing guidelines for the behavior of women be written and distributed throughout the country. But the book was written in Chinese characters, which few women could read, and did not become influential until it was republished in 1481 in a combination of the new common script called *Hangul* (Hahn-guhl) and Chinese. To overcome this literacy problem, the government ordered local scholars to go from village to village, verbally instructing women in how to conduct themselves according to Confucian principles.

In 1443 King Sejong began a determined effort to break the monopoly that the ruling class had had on education since the Shilla kingdom and extend the privilege to the common people. He brought together a team of scholars and directed them in the creation of a purely Korean writing system based on phonetic symbols that anyone could learn in a matter of days or weeks at most. It was his intention that this new writing system make it possible for all Koreans to learn how to read, write, and become educated.

Unfortunately, the entrenched intelligentsia derided the new system, ignored it, and were able to maintain their monopoly on Chinese-oriented education until the Choson dynasty began breaking up in the latter half of the nineteenth century. As the decades passed, however, more and more women in the royal court and elite upper class took up the study of *Hangul* and prevented it from atrophying. (Many upper-class families unofficially retained tutors for their daughters to teach them writing as well as other subjects.)

In the sixteenth century Hwang Yi (1501–70), the most famous Confucian scholar of his day, established a private Confucian academy called *So Won* (Soh Wahn) in his own district after he became a magistrate. The ruling king endorsed the academy and gave it a royal charter. He also ordered that the state provide the academy with books, tax-free land, and slaves—the same status previously enjoyed by Buddhist monasteries.

This resulted in many other scholars establishing private Confucian academies throughout the country, all of them supported by the government. In line with the Confucian philosophy, the bonds between *so won* students and scholars became such that their impact had a major influence on both government and society thereafter. Students could not question the veracity or knowledge of their professors and in later years, after they became officials, could not refuse any requests of their former teachers.

This system not only stifled independent thought but also greatly increased the political, social, and economic influence of the Neo-Confucianists. The elite ruling class became more and more conservative and gradually lost its military ardor. As the generations went by, the Choson dynasty sank further and further into stagnancy.

Also in the sixteenth century a number of deadly purges waged against scholar-officials by opposition political factions in the *yangban* class resulted in large numbers of the literati giving up any thoughts of serving as government officials and thereafter devoting their lives to research and teaching. Thus a significant majority of the best-educated people in Korea spent their lives involved in studies and endeavors that were not connected with political or economic conditions. This period of time produced many great philosophers, but while they were contemplating the cosmos and the dualism in all things, the country marked time. As the generations passed, however, the *so won* gradually achieved a virtual monopoly on education and little by little gained considerable control over the government by providing officials for the court and consorts for the royal family.

In the latter part of the 1800s the waning Choson court began closing down the schools as hotbeds of political insurrection. Between 1864 and 1873 the ruling regent ordered all but forty-seven of the more than six hundred *so won* to close as a way of reducing the influence of the powerful families that ran them.

In 1882 the reigning Choson king (Kojong) issued a decree calling for the establishment of state-sponsored mass education based on Western knowledge instead of Confucianism. The first Western-style school, named Yugyong Kongwon, opened in 1886. Yugong Kongwon employed several Americans to teach English to its students. Other languages offered by the new school, and others that opened in the following years, included Chinese, French, German, Japanese, and Russian.

Despite the negative effects that Confucianism had had on Korean culture, in particular the low quality of life that it had forced on the majority of the people for so long, it left a positive legacy where education was concerned. Throughout Korean history all power had been in the hands of government officials. The only way to power was to become an official. The first step in the process of becoming an official was to pass the regional qualifying examinations and receive a degree as a *chinsa* (cheen-sah), or "licensed scholar." The next step was a second-stage examination held in Seoul.

Only well-educated upper-class people could become officials. Koreans therefore traditionally equated education with political power, and political power with wealth, security, and the good life.

Following the breakup of the upper-class monopoly on education in the latter decades of the nineteenth century, schooling in a relatively limited scale became available to common Koreans for the first time in the history of the people. At first hundreds and then thousands of Koreans enrolled in newly opened schools and began studying with obsessive energy and ambition, determined to improve their lifestyle and at last to share in some of the power of the elite ruling class.

But this effort was totally subverted in the first decade of the twentieth century. Beginning in 1875 Japan initiated a policy designed to bring Korea under its influence, a policy that resulted in the Sino-Japanese War in 1894–95 and the Russo-Japanese War in 1904–05, with Japan the victor in both wars. With China and Russia out of the way, Japan began turning Korea into a colony. Korean attempts to counter this Japanese move were met with massive military force and the outright annexation of Korea into the Japanese empire in 1910.

Japanese administrators, backed by a powerful police and military occupation force, took over all education in Korea and began a campaign to convert the Koreans into Japanese. They built hundreds of new schools but saw to it that the education for those Koreans who did attend school was focused primarily on vocational training that would serve Japan's political and economic interests. Fewer than 5 percent of all Korean students were allowed to go beyond the primary grades. It was decreed that the Japanese language was the national language, and all Koreans who were allowed to go to school were required to achieve basic literacy in Japanese. When the Japanese occupation of Korea ended in 1945, some 80 percent of all Koreans had had no formal schooling at all. But about 15 percent of the population could read, write, and speak Japanese fluently.

During this period only a few young people were allowed to attend college in Korea. Others who wanted a higher education were permitted to attend universities in Japan if they and their families had the "right attitude." Between 1905 and 1919 more than 2,250 private schools were founded throughout the country, but a major uprising against the Japanese occupation forces in 1919 resulted in the Japanese colonial administration closing most of the schools, which they accused of teaching patriotism and democratic ideals to their Korean students.

One of the most dramatic events in the history of education in Korea occurred in the spring of 1914, when the Ewha Women's University in Seoul graduated its first class. Described by Helen Kim (who was then a freshman student at Ewha) in her book *Grace Sufficient* (The Upper Room, Nashville, 1964), the ceremony was held in Chongdong Church, the leading Methodist Church in Seoul. When the ceremony began, the audience stood up and remained standing, most of them, including men, silently weeping.

Another graduate of Ewha, feminist author and lecturer Ducksoon (Diana) Yu-Tull, notes in her book *Winds of Change* that the school was founded in 1886 by an American missionary named Mary Scranton, who is credited with the first efforts to provide modern education for Korean women. Yu-Tull writes that Scranton bought a strip of land in what is now downtown Seoul that contained nineteen straw huts and christened the unlikely place *Ewah Haktang* (Eh-wah Hahk tahng), or "Pear Blossom Institute." But it was a year before she was able to enroll her first student—the concubine of a high official who was chosen to learn English so she could serve as the queen's interpreter. During the following two decades male resistance against educating females was so strong it was common for girls who tried to enter schools to be ridiculed and sometimes beaten. The tradition of keeping upper-class girls confined in their homes during the day was intensified by many fathers.

When World War II and the Japanese colonization of Korea ended in 1945, well over half of all Koreans were illiterate. Thus it was not until the middle of the twentieth century that all Koreans were actually free to pursue education of their own choosing. They did so with a vengeance, and as before they were motivated by an extraordinary ambition for the power that they knew came only with education. By 1965 Korea had one of the highest literacy rates in the world.

Present-day social scientists add that this Korean obsession with power is related to the concept and practice of filial piety, which was the basis for the traditional Korean family. The ultimate way that sons of the elite could serve and honor their parents and their families—demonstrate filial piety—was by achieving political power.

This compulsive need, say the sociologists, added an extraordinary dimension to the desire of upper-class Koreans to become educated and pass the government-sponsored tests that were the door to officialdom—a desire that was immediately adopted by lower-class Koreans when the elite *yangban* class's monopoly on education ended.

In the early post–World War II decades, entrance into high school and university was by competitive examination. The best jobs went to graduates of the most prestigious universities, so competition to get into these universities was extreme, resulting in the Korean version of Japan's notorious "Examination Hell." Korean parents became as notorious as Japanese parents for pressuring their children incessantly not just to do well but to do exceptionally well in school. The whole focus was to get on and stay on the "educational escalator" to highly prized jobs in government and private industry. Competition for these prized slots began on the elementary school level, with some schools having a much better record than others for getting a large percentage of graduates on the "escalator."

Today in Korea success is certainly not measured only in terms of civil service. Money, earned by commercial enterprise, is now on virtually equal footing with government office as a source of power. Generally, successful businesspeople have more status and prestige than all government bureaucrats except those at the very top—who usually have money as well as political power.

This does not mean that the importance of education has been downgraded, however. Access to the best commercial and government jobs in Korea is still through education. With rare exceptions the person who does not graduate from a university is forever relegated to menial work—which means he or she stays in or near the lower class.

Social psychologist Jae Un Kim refers to the obsession Koreans have with getting an education to elevate their social status as "diploma disease." He says a great deal of this obsession is a holdover from the Choson dynasty (1392–1910) days, during which the ruling class heaped humiliation and degradation on the lower class.

In 1969 the Korean government abolished middle-school entrance examinations and adopted a lottery system administered on a zone basis to eliminate the pressure on children as well as the distinctions between inferior and superior schools and put all schools and students on the same level. In 1974 the high school system was also revised. Examinations held by individual schools were replaced by state examinations, with successful applicants assigned to schools by a lottery system. In 1993 the college entrance system was revised to combine high-school test scores with nationwide state examination results to qualify applicants. High-school test scores must account for a minimum of 40 percent of the qualification requirements.

Many Korean mothers still go to shrines, temples, and churches to pray for the success of their children in their studies and particularly in school examinations. During periods leading up to examinations, virtually all of the activities in many Korean households are designed to enhance the efforts of the children to prepare themselves for the exams. This includes taking TV sets out of children's rooms and keeping households absolutely quiet.

Also as in Japan, once Korean high school graduates succeed in getting into university, the outside pressure for them to study practically disappears. Many, especially those who have been burned out by twelve years of classwork and homework, treat their college years as one long vacation. They spend their time involved with sports and social clubs or work part time.

The method of education in Korea is changing slowly. New methods of teaching have been introduced, and there is a growing realization that real-life experiences and the interest of the students should take precedence over old ideas and old ways. But education is still mostly a one-way experience, with professors and instructors lecturing and students learning by rote memorization. Students are indoctrinated in moral as well as academic subjects. However, social surveys indicate that the higher the level of education the less traditional Koreans are in their attitudes and behavior. Among the things that are the most dramatically affected are familism, the concept of male superiority, and the importance of a highly refined, stylized form of politeness. Recognizing the negative influence of this trend, the Korean government in the early 1990s began encouraging the development of private Confucian-type academies to offer instruction in ethics and etiquette to young Koreans.

In present-day South Korea, the three most prestigious schools in the country are Seoul National University, Korea University, and Yonsei University. And one of the most meaningful words in the vocabulary of students and their parents is *yuhak* (yuu-hahk), "studying abroad"—the golden grail of education for a growing number of Korea's university graduates. Much of the spectacular success that South Korea has experienced since the mid-1950s was fueled by a cadre of technicians, engineers, scientists, and marketers who took postgraduate courses abroad.

In the meantime, the Communist-dominated post–World War II educational system in North Korea was from its beginning in the 1940s designed to eliminate all individualistic tendencies in young North Koreans and turn them into socialists absolutely devoted to collectivism and totally loyal to the paramount Communist leader and the Communist Party. In this environment students were taught to be obedient, never to question the leader or the party, to discard all traditional attitudes and customs, to hate "class enemies," and to fight against all outsiders who threatened the system in any way. Students were also taught to "love" labor and to willingly sacrifice themselves for the state, to be a "group hero" and a warrior for socialism and against capitalism and imperialism. Students were required to engage constantly in self-criticism and mutual criticism as a means of destroying their individuality and fusing them into a great mass that thought and behaved as one.

A significant part of the education of North Korean students was memorizing the slogans and philosophy of the supreme leader, a program that eventually resulted in the first founder of the regime, Il Sung Kim, being worshiped as virtually divine. Deviations of any kind were not allowed. It was not until the death of Kim in the early 1990s and the onset of increasingly serious economic problems that North Korean leaders began to question the correctness of their educational system and to allow some individuality and independence. The impact over nearly fifty years of intensive brainwashing in the socialist doctrine and in antipathy toward outsiders will no doubt continue to plague North Koreans for many decades.

116

망신
Mangshin
(Mahng-sheen)

"Avoiding Shame"

Korea's traditional minutely prescribed etiquette, which incorporates both physical behavior and speech, makes it necessary for Koreans to spend a considerable amount of time and energy in maintaining friendly, cooperative relationships with family members, friends, co-workers, and others during the course of their daily activities. This kind of careful behavior is necessary because Koreans have been conditioned for generations to be especially sensitive about shaming anyone or themselves being shamed—something that can result from the wrong level of speech being used, from not using the "proper" form of address or title, from criticism, from weaknesses being revealed, and so on.

For Koreans, *mangshin* (mahng-sheen), or "shame," has traditionally been an unbearable burden that they would go to extremes to avoid and still greatly complicates their lives because it often precludes open, honest relationships and forces people to play roles that are more virtual than real.

The *mangshin* factor in Korean culture is a by-product of Confucianism, which teaches that the highest morality is a carefully prescribed form of conduct or etiquette that is based on hierarchical relationships between people. The Confucianism adopted by Korea's last and longest dynasty (the Choson dynasty that began in 1392 and lasted until 1910) divided Korean society according to hereditary social class, sex, age, and other factors and prescribed an etiquette based on male superiority, social class, seniority in age, official authority, and so on.

In addition to laws designed to enforce adherence to the prescribed etiquette where official authorities were concerned, the Confucian scholar-officials who administered the government propagated the concept of shame as the primary social sanction against any kind of undesirable behavior. In effect this system put everyone in jeopardy at all times. The slightest deviation from the prescribed etiquette was very conspicuous—as when an actor misses a cue or speaks the wrong lines. The system made morality visible as well as audible. Everyone was exposed to shaming someone or being shamed at every encounter.

Korean concern with shame is one of the cultural factors that often complicates their relationships with Westerners because Westerners generally are much less sensitive to things that Koreans find shameful—and there are many, including some that Westerners are familiar with, such as public criticism. Probably the two broad areas in which foreigners are most often guilty of shaming Koreans, usually unintentionally, is underestimating their ability (from the Korean viewpoint, of course) and being disrespectful toward them by manner or by word (again from their viewpoint).

Koreans are quick to identify another all-too-common breed of foreigner who, because of their own character failings, are openly arrogant and disdainful of most people and habitually belittle them in a variety of ways. There is another category of longtime resident foreigners who criticize Korea as a country and Koreans as a people, usually behind their backs, in the most bitter terms. But they continue living and working there year after year in a strange symbiotic relationship that they seemingly cannot end.

Westerners in Korea (or elsewhere in Confucian Asia) should keep in mind that in many ways shame cultures are more effective in promoting good manners, mutual responsibility, and group cooperation than their own guilt cultures, and make a special effort to avoid cultural confrontations.

117

맞벌이부부

Matbulibubu
(Maht-buu-lee-buu-buu)

"Two-Income Families"

Korea has long been regarded as the most Confucian of all Asian countries, especially in the traditional image that men had of women, how they treated them, and what they required of them. From around the twelfth century on, when Confucianism began to replace Buddhism as the favored social and political philosophy, the status of Korean women began to erode in direct proportion to the rise of Confucianism. Following the establishment of the Choson (Yi) dynasty in 1392 and the adoption of Confucianism as the state creed, the position of women degenerated to the point that they were little more than slaves to men.

The higher the social position of women, the more their prerogatives and activities were limited and carefully controlled by their fathers, husbands, oldest sons, in-laws, and the government in general. Women in rural areas worked in the fields and at various handicrafts and operated small family-type businesses, but they too were treated as inherently inferior to men and at the beck-and-call of male members of their households.

This virtual enslavement of women in Korea did not begin to end until the last decades of the nineteenth century, when the Choson court began to lose control in the face of new religious, economic, and political ideas coming in from the outside and encroachments being made on the sovereignty of Korea by China, Japan, Russia, the United States, and the colonial powers of Europe. But it was the middle of the twentieth century before Korean women were legally emancipated and the 1970s and 1980s before they had achieved a significant degree of social freedom.

One of the most far-reaching factors in the social emancipation of Korean women was the rapid growth of industry from 1962 on, a phenomenon that resulted in most Korean girls going to work outside their homes as soon as they finished high school or college. For the first several decades it was generally understood that these young women would work only until they got married, at which time they would quit work and become full-time housewives. By the 1980s, however, many young women had become independent enough that they insisted on keeping their jobs after they got married.

By the beginning of the 1990s there were enough wives working that they and their husbands had formed a new economic category known as *matbulibubu* (maht-buu-lee-buu-buu), or "two-income families"—something that, with rare exceptions, had previously been unthinkable in Korea. Now this term is bandied about by economists, politicians, and news media pundits as a significant and growing factor in the economy of the country.

The fact that more and more Korean women continue to work after marriage is indicative not only of the increasing cost of the new style of living that has been part of the industrialization process, but also of the extraordinary progress Korean women have made toward equality with men since 1962, when General Chung Hee Park took over the government in a coup and initiated the first of a series of five-year economic growth plans.

The impact of Korean females working in industry, first as young single women and then as wives, has already resulted in more changes in Korean culture than occurred in the previous six hundred years, and the changes are far from over. Given the hard work, resilience, courage, and talents that have traditionally been demanded of Korean women, there is every reason to believe that they will make the most of their freedom.

118

ㅁㅣ

Mi
(Me)

"Worshiping Beauty"

Institutionalized aesthetics have been an important aspect of Korean culture since the beginning of the country's recorded history. As is also the case in other Oriental cultures, Korea's aesthetic beliefs and practices first evolved from animism and then from Buddhism and Taoism, introduced into Korea from China between the fourth and sixth centuries A.D.

All of the beliefs and practices taught by these religious philosophies conditioned Koreans to minimize their physical and sensual desires in favor of spiritual and aesthetic goals—a philosophy that served the needs of the secular powers as much as it aided priests and helped provide ordinary Koreans with the fortitude that was necessary for them to survive at a subsistence level for generation after generation.

The institutionalization of aesthetics occurred during the golden years of the Shilla dynasty (669–935). Because the genesis of the movement to make beauty an integral part of the lives of all people was religious, it was originally expressed in chants and poetry, then in the construction of temples and the making of arts and crafts related to religious expressions. The goal of every architect, artist, and craftsman was to achieve the ultimate in beauty through harmonious symmetry and revealing the spiritual nature of the materials used— or, in the case of paintings, the subjects depicted. Both the creating and viewing of man-made as well as natural objects were regarded as a religious experience.

One of the crafts for which Shilla artisans became especially famous was the casting and embossing of temple bells, said by noted Korean art historian Dr. Jon Carter Covell to be superior to anything done in China or Japan.

Another important element in Korean aesthetics was their sensitivity to natural changes in the climate and the seasons. Because their lives and their comfort depended on clouds, rain, snow, sunshine, and wind, all of which were endowed with spiritual dimensions, Koreans became exceptionally aware of these forces and endeavored to see the beauty in them as part of their reverence of nature.

This nature reverence, taught by animism and buttressed by Buddhism, was especially important in making *mi* (me), or "beauty," a basic part of the everyday lives of Koreans. Animism taught that clay, metal, stones, and wood had spirits that were retained when these materials were used in making ceramics and other utensils. The making of such things, if done correctly, further enhanced their spirits and their beauty. Buddhism provided an element of refinement, style, and spiritualism that added to the aesthetics of accessories, furnishings, and buildings and gave virtually everything Koreans made a recognizable "Oriental" flavor.

Because the beauty that is inherent in the cultural artifacts of Korea goes well beyond physical harmony and utilitarian values, it touches and pleases the spirit of more sensitive viewers and plays a key role in the tranquillity and contentment that is inherent in the traditional Korean lifestyle. Contemporary scholar Hyon Bae Choe attributes the traditional importance of beauty in Korean life—as expressed in pottery, ceramics, and other handicrafts as well as paintings and drawings—to a belief that their purpose in life is to enhance the welfare of mankind by cultivating humanism and spirituality.

Korea's traditional dedication to *mi* has suffered grievously since the late 1800s, when inroads by colonial powers doomed the already weakened Choson dynasty. Japan's annexation of the country in 1910 and the havoc of the Korean War in 1950–52 made basic survival the paramount concern of the people.

But the economic prosperity that South Korea achieved between 1960 and 1980 was accompanied by a resurgence of interest in natural as well as man-made beauty, and since that time private as well as government-sponsored programs have restored much of the natural beauty to the peninsula. Denuded mountains were reforested. Parks and riverways were beautified. Urban landscaping around new homes of the well-to-do and professional buildings now reflect aesthetic principles that were perfected over a period of some two thousand years.

On the commercial front Koreans designed and made consumer products reflect the refinement that comes from generations of sophisticated cultural traditions. Korea's long history of revering beauty is once again making a major contribution to its culture.

119

미시족

Mishijok

(Me-she-joak)

"The Swinging Wives"

Of all the changes that have occurred in Korea since the end of that country's long period of isolation from most of the rest of the world in the 1870s, none have been more significant or more impressive than the strides made by Korean women to revolutionize their image and their role in the traditionally male-dominated society.

As late as 1960—nearly one hundred years after the female revolution began—the progress that Korean women had made could still be measured only in inches. For the most part they remained locked inside a Confucian-oriented culture that made them almost totally subservient to men, unable to express themselves beyond an excruciatingly narrow norm that had been established for them by chauvinist men during the Choson dynasty (1392–1910) and the following thirty-five-year domination of Korea by even more chauvinist Japanese military men.

For centuries the lives of Korean women, both single and married, had been so restricted, so limited, that as children they could not even play with boys after a certain age; as teenagers they could not associate in any way with boys their own age or men outside of their families; and as wives even talking to males other than their sons, husbands, or fathers was taboo for those in the upper class.

By 1970, however, the freedoms and opportunities extended to Korean women by the new constitution of 1948 and later legislation had made it possible for young Korean women to begin to metamorphose from human drones into colorful butterflies. On my visits to Korea during this period a day—or night—seldom passed that I was not literally stunned by the beauty, aggressiveness, and talents of young women—and finally understood why Korean women had been so prized by the emperors and ministers of China for so many centuries.

By the 1990s an entirely new category of Korean women had appeared that was in such marked contrast to the history of females in Korea that they were the subject of commentary by the news media, social scientists, and laymen alike. These are young married women who "dress and behave in public as if they are single," to use the words of a thirty-something Korean male.

These women, referred to as *mishijok* (me-she-joak), which might be translated figuratively as "modern women," are generally the wives of men who earn good money and are therefore able to indulge themselves by eating out, shopping, attending events of one kind or another, and generally enjoying themselves. The connotation of *mishijok* does not suggest outright that these wives engage in hanky-panky with other men. They have been singled out and labeled because their behavior is so different from the traditional behavior of Korean wives that it is remarkable. There is, however, a strong hint of illicit sexuality in this kind of behavior because it is at such variance with the traditional norm in Korea.

The reaction of older, more conservative men in particular—but some women as well—was reminiscent of the late 1800s when a small handful of very brave Korean women began appearing in public in Western-style attire, causing some people to equate their behavior with the outbreak of a dangerous plague and to predict that such behavior would contribute to the downfall of the nation. (Earlier, when the Choson court ordered Korean men to cut off their traditional topknot and adopt the Western hairstyle, riots broke out all over the country, resulting in numerous injuries and loss of property.)

Given the fact that Korea's newly emancipated young women are generally the trendsetters in both fashions and social customs, the example set by the *mishijok* will no doubt become the norm in a generation or so.

120

무당
Mudang
(Muu-dahng)
"The Spirit Mediums"

From the first appearance of Koreans in history until recent times, one of the few areas in Korean life where women played leading roles was in the practice of shamanism—the indigenous religious belief that there is a spiritual world inhabited by good and bad spirits who are able to influence the lives of the living and that all material things in nature have spirits which people must live in harmony with to enjoy good physical and mental health.

The involvement of women along with men in shamanism apparently came about because early in Korean history women were recognized as the mothers of humanity, as healers, and as the primary source of solace for those in pain. This led to their being accepted in the role of *mudang* (muu-dahng), or "shamanistic mediums," in early Korean society. (An honorific term for shaman mediums is *manshin*/mahn-sheen.)

Generally, women took up the role of *mudang* after going through some kind of psychotic experience such as falling into a trance and seeing a vision—a common phenomenon worldwide among so-called "faith-healers." As time passed, some daughters of *mudang* followed in their mothers' footsteps, and the profession gradually became hereditary. Thereafter the use of drums, cymbals, and dancing to achieve trances became an integral part of the profession.

Before the arrival of Buddhism, Taoism, and Confucianism in Korea between the fourth and sixth centuries A.D., *mudang* were figures of importance in their communities. As the priests of their day, they were respected and honored. But with the spread of these imported philosophies, shamanism gradually lost most of its official standing as the national religion.

When the founders of the Yi or Choson dynasty made Confucianism the state religion in 1392, the new government prohibited many of the ancient shamanistic practices in an attempt to further erode the official image of *mudang*. At least a part of this action was based on the Confucian principle that women were inferior to men and should not participate in important rituals of any kind.

But the tenets and practices of shamanism were too deeply embedded in the psyche of the people to be legislated away. Not only did the common people continue to engage *mudang* to perform the age-old shamanistic rituals, but members of the ruling class, including the royal family, also unofficially continued the custom. In fact during the long centuries of the Choson dynasty *mudang* were among the few women who were allowed to associate officially and publicly with men. (The others generally were professional female entertainers and high-class prostitutes.)

The profession of the *mudang* is still alive and well in present-day Korea—although their social status is akin to that of mediums in Western societies. Still, they are called in by people in all classes to perform rituals on a number of occasions, ranging from sickness and death to the dedication of new buildings.

However, present-day *mudang* can no longer get by with such common religious techniques as ringing bells, beating drums, and intoning incantations. Depending on the occasion, they must stage elaborate performances that include music, singing, dancing, comedy, and other vaudevillelike acts.

Shamanistic ceremonies are known as *kut* (koot) and *kosa* (koh-sah) in Korean. *Kut* refers to a *mudang* making contact with one or more spirits during a séance. Which spirit or spirits is determined by the occasions. Traditionally, *mudang* enter into trances by performing mind-altering dances to make contact with spirits. Expelling evil spirits is known as *narye* (nahr-yeh). A séance to "cleanse" a dead spirit of troubling matters is known as *ssitkimkut* (sheet-keem-koot).

Some families, villages, and towns retain *mudang* for annual as well as special *kut*. Some *kut* are open to the public and are advertised in newspapers like other spectator events. Public *kut* are usually held in scenic places alongside rivers or in mountains and are as much entertainment or recreation as they are religious. Foreigners may be invited to attend private *kut* and are welcome to attend public ceremonies without invitation. People who attend are expected to make small donations of money.

Mudang may also be invited to participate in the shamanistic ceremonies that are performed to dedicate new construction projects (homes, office buildings, ships) or the opening of new offices. These ceremonies are known as *kosa*, which literally means "prayer ritual."

Government records show there are some forty thousand *mudang* in South Korea alone, but media reports say the figure is probably closer to one hundred thousand because most *mudang* do not bother to register. There is a national association of *mudang* headquartered in Seoul.

121

문학

Munhak

(Muun-hahk)

"Literature and Culture"

Between 108 B.C. and the seventh century A.D. the small kingdoms on the Korean peninsula were in effect vassal states to China. During this long period *munhak* (muun-hahk), or "literature," in the form of Buddhist, Confucian, and Taoist treatises covering everything from arts, crafts, medicine, government, philosophy, and politics to poetry, was introduced to Korea's ruling class, first by Chinese scholars and later by Korean scholars as well.

From around the fourth century A.D. Confucianism was gradually adopted as the ideology of the Korean government, and Buddhism was adopted as the state religion. At the same time, Korean scholars developed a way of writing the Korean language using the already ancient Chinese ideograms. Legend has it that this system of writing, called *Idu* (Ee-duh), was developed by the love child of Wonhyo, a famous seventh-century monk, and a court princess. According to the legend, Wonhyo was motivated to create the new system of writing as a result of his efforts to unify the various Buddhist sects and popularize the religion among the masses. In the process he wrote many books in the *Idu* script.

Learning how to write the Chinese characters was a painstaking process that required years of study and practice, however, and was therefore something that only a few privileged people could accomplish. To restrict the spread of literacy further, the rulers of the Korean kingdoms also adopted the policy of limiting education to sons of the elite ruling class—a policy that was made official in the seventh century and was to be continued for most of the next twelve hundred years.

Thus, until modern times virtually all Korean literature was written in Chinese ideograms by professional scholars who had spent years learning how to read and write the complicated "characters," and, with the exception of professional female entertainers called *kisaeng* (kee-sang), the only people who had direct access to literature were male members of the *yangban* ruling class. Because of this government policy, the vast majority of Koreans were cut off from direct access to the Buddhist, Confucian, and Taoist literature that prescribed as well as defined their culture and was a reflection of all of the elements that went into the making of the traditional Korean character.

Historian Kuy Tae Yi says in his book *Rediscovery of the Koreans* that the main "elements" of Korean character revealed in classical Korean literature are a "this-worldly secularism," a longing for a hermitlike life of seclusion, a belief in miracles, deep resentment and remorse, and a lack of love caused by artificial barriers between people, especially between the sexes. Yi adds that early Korean literature also emphasized the importance of self-discipline and the suppression of truth as a means of ensuring absolute order and harmony throughout society. In some periods it was even taboo to emphasize beauty, to prevent jealousy and other emotional reactions.

The suppression of truth as a means of maintaining order and harmony is, of course, a common and well-known practice in authoritarian political regimes. But the suppression or, to be more exact, the disguising, of beauty is more complex and is typical only in the Confucian sphere of Asia.

Just as well-to-do Korean officials built homes with nondescript exteriors as a means of keeping their inner luxury from prying and envious eyes, it appears that there was an unwritten consensus among the *yangban* to play down the beauty of Korean arts and crafts as well as the beauty of Korean women to discourage envy among commoners and invasions by foreigners seeking loot.

But there was an ancient tradition of oral literature in Korea that helped to make up for the illiteracy of the common people. In the thirteenth and four-teenth centuries some of Korea's most celebrated scholars were those who wrote soul-stirring historical sagas for a new class of *paegwan* (paig-wahn), or "storytellers." Poetry, in particular, had long played a key role in Korean culture. All scholars were trained in writing and appreciating poetry, and many of them pursued the art as both a vocation and an avocation throughout their lives.

Reforms introduced by the founder of the Choson dynasty (1392–1910) and his early successors, including a simplified system of writing called *Hangul* (Hahn-guhl), resulted in the gradual appearance of a popular form of literature that expressed personal feelings, including such taboo emotions as love and discontent with the Confucian-oriented society. Most of the writers of these books were disaffected scholars who were still members of the elite *yangban* class but whose families had long since been out of power. Their writings planted the seeds of rebellion that were to contribute to the downfall of the dynasty at the end of the first decade of the twentieth century.

Other contributors to the literature of the Choson dynasty were female members of the royal court and the families of leading *yangban* scholars and officials who took advantage of the new, easy-to-learn system of writing. These rare women broke the ancient taboos against women becoming educated and speaking out by writing letters, poetry, travel accounts, diaries, and essays.

The most famous work produced by a female during this long era was a manual prescribing the attitudes and behavior expected of Korean wives and women in general. Entitled *Naehun* (Nie-huun), it was written by Queen Sohei and published in 1475. Reprinted numerous times and distributed nationally, this was the bible of Korean women until the Choson dynasty began breaking up at the end of the nineteenth century.

Generally speaking, there were three categories of Choson women who became educated enough to read and write, with some of them leaving impressive examples of their poetry and prose. These three groups of women were members of the royal and noble families, concubines of upper-class men, and *kisaeng*, women trained to be professional entertainers and companions for men of means. A fairly large collection of biographies, essays, letters, memoirs, and travelogues written by upper-class women and ladies-in-waiting are still extant.

One of the most quoted of all Korean *sijo* (she-joh) poems was written in the sixteenth century by a lady named Chin I Hwang.

> I cut in two
> A long November night, and
> Place half under the coverlet,
> Sweet-scented as a spring breeze.
> And when he comes, I shall take it out,
> Unroll it inch by inch, to stretch the night.

Another *sijo* verse, quoted below, was written by a *kisaeng* named Hong-nang in the sixteenth century. It was composed when she was saying farewell.

to her lover, a scholar-poet named Kyong Chang Choe, as he was about to leave on a government-sponsored tour. She gave him the poem as a parting gift.

> I chose a wild willow branch
> and plucked it to send to you.
> I want you to plant it
> by the window where you sleep.
> When new leaves open in the night rains,
> think that it is I that have come to you.*

The turmoil of the late 1800s created enormous interest in the history of the rest of the world and in literature of all kinds among younger upper-class Koreans. This interest spawned a new class of writers, including authors who wrote so-called *sin sosol* (sheen soh-sohl), or "new novels," which were written in the ordinary vernacular as opposed to a highly stylized literary language of the past and expounded on such themes as sexual equality, democracy, and other matters that had previously been alien in Korean thought.

One of the forms of literature that became prominent as a political tool was the use of wall posters (*pyok po*/p'yoke poh), and banners or streamers (*hyon sumak*/h'yohn suu-mahk), the latter usually hung in trees as well as on walls, that carried political messages aimed at the government and sometimes at individual figures. In the early 1800s the suffering of the peasants had reached the point that they began to voice their grievances through wall posters and banners inscribed with their complaints in the harshest possible language. A banner hung up in the city of Chongju resulted in the government punishing the city by reducing its administrative rank and changing its name.

But it was not until well into the twentieth century that mass education was made available to Koreans, making it possible for literature to became a direct influence in their lives.

The Japanese occupation and annexation of Korea in 1910 served as a powerful impetus for a new breed of educated Koreans to use literature to express their feelings of outrage and encourage people to resist the Japanese occupation forces. Koreans who took refuge in Manchuria, China, and the United States were leaders in this movement.

Literature, of all kinds, is now a major industry in Korea.

---

*Both verses are from *Women of Korea—A History from Ancient Times to 1945*, by the Committee for the Compilation of the *History of Korean Women*, edited and translated by Yung Chung Kim (Seoul: Ewha Women's University Press, 1983.)

문화

Munhwa

(Muun-whah)

"Culture Then and Now"

Traditional Korean culture had its origins in shamanism, the indigenous beliefs that gave shape to the spiritual world of the people and established the structure and rituals of their daily lives, socially, economically, and politically. Tribal leaders were both priests and chiefs at the same time, and the daily rhythm of life was determined by the need to keep the spirit world—and the priest-chiefs—placated.

Some time around 1000 B.C. or so the first Chinese influence began to impact this isolated, spirit-dominated world of the earliest Koreans. But Korean life was to remain much the same until 109 B.C. when the Chinese invaded the Korean peninsula and turned the various tribal kingdoms into vassal states.

From this period on, Chinese culture began flowing into Korea, first in small spurts that were limited primarily to the members of the ruling class. Over the next several centuries this flow grew into a large, continuous stream that was to add numerous dimensions to Korea's culture but neither destroy nor dilute the native shamanistic rituals.

Chinese culture entered Korea in the form of language combined with literature on Buddhism, Confucianism, and Taoism, all of which were to have dramatic effects on the attitudes and lifestyles of Koreans, from the form of their government to the food crops they depended on, the clothing they wore, the etiquette they followed, their arts and crafts, their entertainment, and their philosophical view of the world.

By the beginning of the Koryo dynasty in 935, Buddhism was entrenched as the state religion and, combined with shamanism and Confucianism, set the guidelines and standards for all Korean attitudes and behavior. The spread of Buddhism became the central policy of the Koryo government. The Koryo court as well as members of the elite class sponsored the building of hundreds of temples and pagodas (prayer stupas) and the transcribing and distribution of Buddhist literature.

Koryo kings and ministers became dedicated to collecting and preserving books. Numerous libraries were established, and thousands of scholars and woodblock printers were employed in the writing and printing of books. This impetus for accumulating knowledge led to the invention of movable metal type in 1234—a first in the world. Buddhism was replaced as the state religion by a new form of Confucianism in 1392, resulting in a new massive program of educating people in this new doctrine. Implementing this program required the services of thousands of Confucian priests, scholars, writers, and publishers, resulting in a new wave of Confucian-oriented culture that was to inundate Korea for the next five-hundred-plus years.

Today the *munhwa*, or "culture," of Korea is a sometimes curious and always fascinating amalgam of the East and West. In very broad terms it is often Western on the outside and Oriental on the inside. The most conspicuous facade of "Western" Korea are its streets and highways jammed with automobiles, high-rise buildings, nighttime neon signs, people dressed in the latest American and European fashions hurrying to and fro, and other such things that are found in any highly industrialized country.

But behind and beyond this facade of Western sights and sounds one still finds traditional Oriental Korea—the Korea of temples and palaces and the remnants of great walls; of teahouses and inns; of sitting on heated floors eating foods pungent with garlic, pepper, and spices; of a language that is so old nobody really knows where it came from; of a people who intellectually, emotionally, and spiritually are still primarily a fusion of ancient Korean and Chinese beliefs and customs.

At the same time, there is an ever-growing number of Koreans who have absorbed a patina of Westernism and are able to step out of their cultural skin when dealing with Westerners. But if they were born in Korea and lived there to maturity, this foreign coating is more like a cloak that they put on and take off as the situation demands.

In any event, it is traditional, Oriental Korea that provides the character and flavor of a unique culture that alternately repels and attracts outsiders. Among other things, one of the key facets of traditional Korean culture that lingers on is that it did not recognize or permit development of the self. It was designed to suppress the sense of self and force people to "lose" any sense of individualism they might have. Instead of being programmed to be self-centered, as most Westerners are, Koreans were conditioned to be group- or human-centered, to use a term favored by Korean sociologists.

In the 1930s, during the heyday of Japan's occupation of Korea, a Japanese observer noted that Korean culture was a culture of painters, writers, and scholars and was fundamentally defense oriented, while Japanese culture was a culture of warriors, swords, and political power and was aggression-centered.*

This was an astute and surprising observation, especially in regard to Japan. But where Koreans were concerned it applied only to Korea's traditional upper class, which, until modern times, had an almost total monopoly on education, literature, and the finer arts. A current and much more useful observation on Korean culture was made by social psychologist Dr. Jae Un Kim, who based his comments on a series of psychological profile studies he conducted on Koreans in all walks of life.

Dr. Kim said that in present-day Korea the level of education provides a remarkably precise measurement of the culture of individuals—how traditionally Korean they are and how Western they are in their attitudes and behavior. The higher their education, Dr. Kim reported, the "less Korean" people tended to be in their attitudes toward male-female relations, male superiority, the

---

*Yong Un Kim, *The Japanese and the Koreans* (Seoul: Purigipun Namu, 1981).

traditional etiquette, and so on. He said that Koreans with the most education tended to be more self-centered, less authoritarian, less humble, less polite, less emotional, less superstitious, less fatalistic, and less warm-hearted—as well as sloppier in the way they do things.

For this group there has indeed been a lessening of the traits associated with traditional Korean attitudes and behavior. But the traits are still there, easily discernible in every area and facet of their lives. And as for those who are less educated, and especially those who live in rural areas, the old intellectual and spiritual *munhwa* remains virtually unchanged. Rural Koreans use modern, high-tech conveniences, but shamanism still rules the spiritual lives of most of them. The social relationships of the older generations are still controlled by deep-seated Confucian concepts of filial piety.

Generally speaking, Koreans are selective about the old culture they give up and the new culture they adopt. In pre-modern times people who aggressively tried to improve their living standard were regarded as immoral and evil because such behavior was a threat to the status quo. Needless to say, this is one traditional concept that Koreans no longer accept. There is no resistance at all to adopting new material things because such things pose no threat to their mental cosmos. At the same time extraordinary success in the material world has given Koreans both the time and impetus to contemplate their traditional culture once again, this time with a far more objective frame of mind.

From the last decades of the dying Choson dynasty in the late 1800s until around the 1970s most Koreans felt that their traditional culture was a handicap that was responsible for most of the problems and suffering the common people had endured throughout most of the country's history. Western-oriented Koreans in particular looked on the old Confucian-based culture as an embarrassment and attempted to emulate the attitudes and ways of the West. But as Korea became more and more successful economically, this attitude began changing from disdain to respect and pride.

Korean scholars, writers, artists, businesspeople, and government leaders began promoting traditional values and customs of Korea as the main source of their national identity. One of the far-out but typical examples used by a Korean professor to illustrate the superior nature of Korean culture was to compare the *pojaegi* (poh-jie-ghee), a square wrapping cloth used to carry things, with Western-style briefcases, purses, and other small carrying bags.* The professor pointed out that the *pojaegi* is totally flexible and by its very nature conforms to the shape and size of anything that is to be carried, while the briefcase and other Western carrying devices are inflexible and limiting. He added that when a *pojaegi* is not being used it can be folded up and carried in a man's pants or coat pocket or a woman's purse, making it the ultimate in practicality and convenience.

---

*The same illustration has also been used by the Japanese as evidence of the superiority of some aspects of their traditional culture. In Japan the wrapping cloth is called a *furoshiki* (fuu-roh-she-kee). *Furo* means "bath," and *shiki* means "spread." It is said to have originated as a cloth that bathers took to the public bath to lay their clothes on or wrap them up in while bathing. Chances are the *pojaegi/furoshiki* traveled from China to Korea and then to Japan.

It is also common for Koreans to claim that *chotkarak* (choat-kah-rahk), or "chopsticks," which are commonly used in Korea for both cooking and eating, are superior to forks and spoons because those utensils are static in shape, size, and flexibility, while chopsticks are just the opposite. Some add that food tastes better when it is eaten with wooden chopsticks.

Despite this praise of Korea's traditional civilization, the use of *pojaegi* has virtually disappeared among urbanites as well as younger generations in rural areas. About the only people who continue to use them regularly are older women in the countryside. Chopsticks are still the primary eating utensil in Korea, however, and are not likely to be given up. (But it has long been customary in Korea to provide large ceramic spoons for eating soup.)

Still, pride in the traditional culture of Korea is synonymous with patriotism and is held up by *minjok* (meen-johk), or "nationalists," as the glory of Korea. Many Koreans truly believe that Korean culture is superior in many ways to Western cultures, particularly in its spiritual dimensions and its concern for human feelings. The struggle now is to protect and preserve those elements of the traditional culture that are seen as positive from inroads being made by Western influence.

Korean sociologist Yong Bok Koh has described the structure of Korean culture as "queer." He says that it consists of spiritual culture, behavioral culture, and physical culture and that spiritual culture takes precedence over the other two forms. He adds that the spiritual culture of Korea is far ahead of reality and that there is now a spiritual vacuum because spiritual culture has changed much more rapidly. This, Koh continues, has led to a reevaluation of traditional Korean culture, and the challenge facing Koreans today is to remerge and balance the three facets of Korean culture.

123

무속기

Musokchi
(Muu-soak-chee)

"The Cultural Umbilical Cord"

Linguistic authorities say that the word *shaman* (*musok*/muu-soak in Korean), originated in Siberia among Tungusic tribes and entered the English language via German. In any event *shamanism* is the English word used to describe the indigenous religious or spiritual beliefs of Koreans. During the early history of Korea shamans were called *mu* (muu), which meant "ritual specialists."

The essence of Korean *musokchi* (muu-soak-chee), or "shamanism," is that good and evil spirits pervade the world and can be summoned or communicated with through inspired mediums—a belief that appears to have been common among virtually all ancient humans and is still alive and well among many tribal societies around the world. Belief in the immortality of the soul was a major tenet of shamanism practiced during this early period. It was also believed that the living souls of ancestors were capable of influencing the well-being of their still-living descendants and that the souls therefore had to be treated with respect and care.

Shamanism was the only religious or spiritual philosophy in Korea until the introduction of Buddhism from China in A.D. 372. The cosmos presented by *musokchi* was a world in which existence was a human-centered, harmonious blend of the natural and supernatural, incorporating the good and the bad. To stay right with the world, people had to respect the spirits and pay obeisance to them. Shamanism taught Koreans that if they revered their departed ancestors and performed the various rituals prescribed to keep their spirits happy, the spirits would reward them with blessings. By the same token, if they did not "worship" their ancestors, their spirits would be angry and cause them to have bad luck.

Korea's shamanism was not replaced, and only slightly diluted, by the wholesale adoption of Buddhism in the fourth century A.D. Although Buddhism was a far more comprehensive and structured religion, it was not intolerant of other religions or aggressive (like Christianity and Islam). Buddhism not only tolerated shamanism's practices but incorporated some shamanistic rituals into its own practices. Most Buddhist temples in Korea have a *Sam-Song Gak* (Sahm-Song Gahk), or "Three-Spirit Hall," where shamanistic deities are enshrined. Buddhist priests also routinely pass out (or sell) good-luck charms, and some engage in fortune-telling—both of which are traditional shaman practices.

By the beginning of the unified Shilla period (A.D. 669) the majority of Korean shamans were female. They acted as priestess intermediaries between the people and the spirit world, including the gods of rain and agriculture and the spirits concerned with the well-being and blessing of the royal family. Their next most important role was in healing the sick and warding off disasters. In addition they were diviners, foretelling the future of individuals as well as the nation.

Female shamans were among the few women in ancient Korea who were permitted to practice a profession and participate in public life. (The other main category of women with this privilege were *kisaeng*/kee-sang, professional entertainers who generally doubled as prostitutes—and in later centuries as medical practitioners for treating female patients who would not allow male doctors to examine them directly.)

With the growing influence of Confucianism and the military from the middle of the Koryo dynasty (935–1392), shamans began to lose their privileged position and power—both because most of them were female and because Confucian scholar-officials resented their role in government and the national life. Government restrictions on the official role of shamans were gradually increased.

During the middle years of the Koryo dynasty (918–1392) shamanistic rituals became so common that the official court astrologer petitioned the king to expel all the "in-house" shamans retained by court ministers and other high officials. The petition was granted, but the shamans banded together and bribed leading ministers and officials to submit a counter-petition to the king. This petition pointed out that since spirits are formless there is no way to prove they are real or fake and that banning the shamans altogether could be disadvantageous. The king rescinded the ban.

Until the fourteenth century shamanism was also not especially threatened or diminished by the appearance of Confucianism in Korea because the teachings of the great Chinese sage were more of a political and social doctrine than a spiritual philosophy. However, with the adoption of a much stricter form of so-called Neo-Confucianism as the state ideology of Korea in 1392, the new Choson dynasty began a program to discredit shamanism. The ancient folk practice was forced into the background, but it persisted, even among members of the royal court. In fact contemporary Korean sociologists say that the depersonalizing and dehumanizing aspects of Confucianism contributed enormously to the continued survival and popularity of shamanism because shamanistic rituals provided direct, immediate relief to many of the intellectual and emotional problems caused by the strict Confucian code of conduct.

Furthermore, Korean society maintained most of its tribal characteristics until recent times, and shamanism played a leading role in the creation and survival of traditional Korean culture throughout the long Choson dynasty.

Korean educational writer In Hoe Kim said in an article entitled "The Values of Korean People," published in 1979 (Seoul, Munumsa), that the traditional shamanistic beliefs of Koreans had become identical with their most basic goals—a long life that was peaceful, mentally and physically comfortable, envied by others, and ensured continuation of the family line. But the very things that made shamanism an "easy" religion for people to accept and follow had a negative side that also fundamentally affected Korean attitudes and behavior.

Recent studies of shamanism conducted by the Korean Institute of Policy Studies (KIPS) say that shamanism promoted childish submission to the supernatural, precluded self-reflection, and discouraged any attempt to develop self-esteem, to improve one's own character or habits, or to be the master of one's fate and take pride in creative efforts of any kind. On the plus side, shamanism valued human life and human happiness and sought to maintain a harmonious relationship between people and the cosmos at large, from local nature spirits to the gods of the universe.

While the KIPS noted that the general influence of shamanism on people was that it made them passive and submissive, the flip side was that if their lives were disrupted by any outside force, regardless of its source, they were prone to blindly lash out with extraordinary violence.

In *Korean Religions and Christianity*, Tong Shik Yu says that it was primarily shamanism that satisfied the spiritual needs of the Koreans and that it in turn shaped their character. Yu lists the traditional "shamanistic character" of Koreans as dependency (supernatural spirits were responsible for everything in life), conservatism (there was no motive or incentive for changing things for the better), pragmatism (the only thing of importance was the here and now), and hedonism (singing, dancing, and drinking).

According to the KIPS, the only ethical element in shamanism was personal and circumstantial, not absolute or universal. Basically it was not concerned with the common good or with community spirit and mutual cooperation.

This said, Korea's shamanism is very practical. Rather than emphasize abstract theology, sacrifice, and otherworldliness, it is concerned with physical and mental well-being in this world, with an emphasis on material wealth and enjoying the here and now. There are no moral commandments, no threats of punishment in the hereafter in shamanism.

For these reasons as well, shamanism has remained a powerful influence in Korean life over the centuries because it is humanistic and because it serves perceived spiritual needs in a way that Buddhism, Christianity, and Confucianism do not. In a sense shamanism has traditionally been one of the umbilical cords that tied Koreans to their ancient past.

There are several types of shamanistic rituals. The most elaborate is the *kut* (kuut), where teams of male and female shamans perform various roles. Individuals or families wishing to have a *kut* performed because of a death in the family or some other catastrophe or serious problem retain a team of shamans, usually consisting of three or four people and sometimes made up of a husband, wife, and daughter team.

Shamanistic rituals that are designed to exorcise such harmful influences as stress, whether caused by some kind of tragic accident, an emotional conflict of some kind, or the demands made by Korean etiquette, are called *salpuri* (sahl-puu-ree), or "exorcising rituals."

These ceremonies have a showlike atmosphere, with cymbals and drums providing music for singing, dancing, and storytelling. The stories told vary from humorous to sad, since it is believed that the process of cleansing the soul requires both sadness and laughter. Participants for whom the ceremonies are being held sometimes perform dance rituals that put them into a trancelike state.

A key part of the *kut* ritual is communicating with the spirits of the recently dead, to let them know they are loved and to say good-bye to them. This part of the ceremony is always conducted by female shamans, called *mudang*, who act as mediums in making contact with the spirits. This kind of *kut* ceremony is generally attended by a fairly large number of people, sometimes an entire village. The ceremonies last for several hours, sometimes through the night. When the ceremony is over, all of the shamanistic images created for that particular ritual are piled up and burned.

Kut ceremonies for people who die of natural causes or are killed in accidents or disasters are generally attended by family members and friends, who gather to pay their respects and bid farewell to the deceased. Those closest to the deceased vent their feelings of remorse by sobbing loudly before their memorial photographs. When expressing this ritualistic grief the mourners repeatedly cry out, *"Edol! Edol!"* A similar ceremony that involves dancing and singing to music, also provided by drums and cymbals, was originally more of a private ritual and is known as a *kosa* (koh-sah). A third ritual, in which *mudang* simply rub their hands together while praying to the spirits, is known as *pison* (pee-sohn). *Kosa* rituals are now also used to invoke the blessings of the spirits on the beginning of new enterprises, the inauguration of new buildings, and the like. According to government records, there are some forty thousand registered shamans in South Korea. However, Korean anthropologists estimate that the actual number is closer to one hundred thousand. (They add that one of the reasons for the relative success of Christianity in Korea is the similarity between shamanistic rituals and Pentecostal Christian services.)

Shaman teams that specialize in the larger ceremonies travel about the country, the busier ones staging as many as fifteen rituals a month. A large *kut* ceremony can cost the equivalent of several months' pay.

124

명함
Myongham
(M'yohng-hahm)
"Playing Your Name Cards"

Family and given names are of special importance in Korean society, playing a much more specific and vital role than names do in most other countries. There are several reasons for this phenomenon. The first, or earliest, of these reasons is the fact that Koreans trace their ancestry as a people to a single tribe made up of a relatively small number of families. Tribal custom allowed only elite core families to have family names.

Over the ages, these elite families grew into clans and their names became more and more sanctified. Members of these families revered their ancestors and their names. (Early in Korean history given names were known as "taboo" names and were kept confidential from most people.) There was also an element of ancestor worship in *musokchi* (muu-soak-chee), or shamanism, Korea's indigenous religion, which contributed to the importance of keeping detailed records of names.

The introduction of Buddhism and Confucianism into Korea in the fourth century A.D., both of which also included reverence for ancestors as major tenets, brought more emphasis to family names and genealogies. In 1392 the new Choson dynasty proclaimed Neo-Confucianism, a much more detailed and stricter form of Confucian concepts, the state religion and the foundation of Korean society. The centerpiece of this new social system was filial piety and ancestor worship, making it mandatory that Korean families record the names and honor the memories of their ancestors.

The Choson dynasty formally lasted until 1910, but the custom of keeping track of and honoring family names had become so deeply embedded in Korean culture that it survives to this day. Still today there are only a few hundred surnames in all of Korea, each with its own historical pedigree and status. The "middle" or "generational" name is also a key to identifying individual Koreans within the context of their family tree and sometimes their birthplace as well.

More than half of all Koreans have only six family names—Kim, Lee (Li, Yi), Pak (Park), Cho (Choe), Jung (Chung), and Chang (Jang).

On a social level it is extremely important for Koreans who meet to get their respective names right and to quickly establish their relative status to know how to behave toward each other. Until the relative social position is clearly established, communication is severely limited. Both parties use a high standard of respect language to avoid the possibility of offending someone who may be higher on the social hierarchy.

On a business level getting names right is not only a social imperative but also essential to properly identifying individuals for any kind of future reference. *Myongham* (m'yohng-hahm), or "name cards," therefore play a vitally important role in Korean business and society in general. Name cards help overcome the serious problem of same and similar names by giving company affiliation, departments, sections, titles, phone numbers, and so on—all of which are usually necessary to distinguish among the hundreds of thousands of Kims, Lees, Choes, and Parks.

When a single large company has as many as two hundred, three hundred, or even more employees named Lee, Kim, and Pak, not having detailed information about a particular individual can make it impossible for telephone operators, receptionists, and others to identify and locate the right person.

Foreign businesspeople meeting Korean contacts for the first time must be especially diligent about getting their name cards and making sure that their cards provide enough information to distinguish them from other people in their company who have the same or similar names. Another aspect of the name problem is that there are several different ways of spelling the romanized versions of a number of Korea's most common family names. Name cards make it possible to use the spelling preferred by the individual concerned.

It is fairly common to receive a name card of an individual whose rank is given as *taewu* (tie-wuu), which means "high rank" or "senior rank," but does not give any additional information about the individual. These are generally people who do not have a specific position or title such as goes with being the head of a department or division manager, being a director, and so forth, but have been designated as *taewu* to indicate their status in the company. They are often former government bureaucrats who have joined the company but are not direct-line managers.

The term *taewu* is also used in reference to the kind of treatment that is given to VIPs and other special guests whom companies want to impress for one reason or another.

125

명예
Myongye
(M'yohng-eh)

"The Need for Honor"

Americans and other Westerners dealing with Koreans for the first time often find themselves encountering negative reactions that they did not anticipate, cannot understand, and are unable to overcome. There may be a variety of reasons for this common Korean reaction, but one that is of special importance has to do with *myongye* (m'yohng-eh), or "honor," and the distinctive role that it plays in Korean life. To Koreans, personal honor is not an abstract concept in the back of their minds. It is a living thing that is a constant force in their thoughts, influencing their behavior and their reaction to others.

Korean psychologists say that Koreans were traditionally obsessed with honor because of their deep-seated need to maintain face, which feeds on fame and honor. They add that still today it is virtually impossible to deal effectively with Koreans without protecting and stroking their sense of honor.

In earlier times the Korean obsession with honor was so overpowering that it often led to violence. Any action that was perceived as damaging to one's honor, whether something as mundane as a slur or a failure to use respectful language, called for evening the score by somehow punishing the guilty person. During the long Choson dynasty (1392–1910) this extreme sensitivity about personal honor caused so many street fights that it became a matter of national concern, resulting in a number of decrees designed to keep the level of violence down.

Contemporary essayist Kyu Tae Yi says that once a Korean loses face he or she feels like an outcast and that to keep face Koreans need regular recognition for their character and efforts. Yi adds that while Koreans are no longer totally obsessed with *myongye*, the desire for honor often leads them to sacrifice practical interests. Yi was specifically referring to South Koreans, not North Koreans, when he noted that Koreans are no longer obsessive about honor. The intransigence of North Korea's political and military leaders continues to be fueled by a compulsive preoccupation with face and honor that has not changed since the heyday of the Choson era.

Although the Korean need for honor continues to impact negatively in a number of ways, there is a positive side that more than mitigates the negatives. It is the ongoing concern with honor that motivates young Koreans to sacrifice much of their youth to study. It is the need for honor that compels virtually all adult Koreans to adhere to a strict form of etiquette, to dress well, to approach their obligations seriously, to work exceptionally hard, and to be concerned about the reputation of their country.

Much of the extraordinary spirit and strength that is characteristic of Koreans, and played a key role in their rapid rise to stardom as an economic superpower, was derived from their feelings of personal and national honor.

To succeed in Korea, both foreign businesspeople and diplomats must understand the nature and role of honor in Korean life and develop the ability to work cooperatively with Koreans, in the context of their need for *mongye*, without compromising their own principles. This requires a substantial degree of knowledge about Korean values, expectations, and behavior.

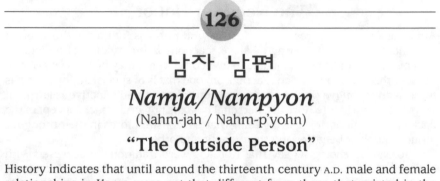

126

남자 남편

Namja/Nampyon
(Nahm-jah / Nahm-p'yohn)

"The Outside Person"

History indicates that until around the thirteenth century A.D. male and female relationships in Korea were not that different from those that existed in the more chauvinistic countries of the Western world. *Namja* (nahm-jah), or "the male sex," was dominant in society, and women, including those in the upper class, were often treated like property. Lower-class women were regularly given to the imperial Chinese court as tribute. Upper-class women were routinely married off in political alliances. Until the end of the nineteenth century Korean men were legally permitted to have concubines or secondary wives, while wives who gave any sign of being jealous were subject to severe punishment—in earlier times jealous behavior was punishable by death.

One of the primary reasons for the perceived superior status of men in early Korean society was spiritual or religious. It was believed that women were inherently "soiled" because of their menstrual period and therefore were not qualified to perform the various religious rituals that were a vital part of Korean society. This sexual stigma was extrapolated to deny female equality in virtually every area of life. Then there was the matter of disparity in male and female strength combined with men generally being more aggressive and more prone to violence than women.

From the thirteenth century on, the social gap between men and women became even greater as a much stricter form of Confucianism began to replace Buddhism as the national ideology. When this Neo-Confucianism was officially adopted as the state ideology in 1392, the superior status of men became a matter of strictly enforced government policy. The new Choson government passed laws that precisely detailed the most intimate details of the private lives of the people, from weddings and funerals to the process of ancestor worship, which was made mandatory. The role of women in Korean life was generally limited to managing the internal affairs of the household.

Houses were built so that the male and female members could spend most of their time in separate quarters. Affluent homes had a special room called *sarang bang* (sah-rahng bahng) that was the private sanctum of the male members of the family, used by them to meet and entertain male guests. Women in urban areas could leave their homes only during certain hours at night.

The Korean word for husband—*nampyon* (nahm-p'yohn)—may be translated as "outside person" and is indicative of the role husbands traditionally played in Korean society. Marriages were arranged. Husbands could discard wives and take new ones. But wives themselves were forbidden from leaving or divorcing their husbands. If they ran away, they could not return home (their parents wouldn't accept them), and generally they were prohibited from remarrying.

This social system persisted for the next five hundred years—until, in fact, the Choson dynasty began to disintegrate from its own internal weaknesses that emanated primarily from the backward-looking conservatism of its Confucian-oriented ministers. The gradual introduction of Christian and democratic concepts into Korea from the latter part of the 1800s began to slowly bring about significant changes in male-female relations in particular and between children and their parents in general.

But it was another half century of social turmoil and warfare before democracy began to break down the barriers separating the sexes in Korea. In the latter part of the 1940s and during the 1950s Korean women were legally emancipated for the first time in the history of the country. Women were guaranteed the right of choice in who they married, including when marriages were arranged, and the right to divorce their husbands. Wives born after 1960 generally regard themselves, and behave, as the equals of their husbands. But the heritage of more than five hundred years of total male superiority continues to influence the behavior of both Korean men and women.

Korea is still a man's world, and there is a universe of difference between the lives of *namja*, or "males," and *yoja* (yoh-jah), or "females." Generally speaking, male children are still preferred over female children, and some wives resort to aborting female fetuses. Boys are still given preference in education. Men have a virtual monopoly on political power and the best jobs.

Still, Korean men are no longer legally or morally the absolute masters of their homes and families. The Western concept of sexual equality and democratic ideals has, to a considerable extent, replaced the traditional Confucian system that put the male sex on a pedestal and controlled the lives of Koreans for dozens of generations.

네, 아니오

Ne-Anio

(Neh-Ah-n'yoh)

"Yes and No"

Like most Asians, Koreans were meticulously programmed for centuries to avoid confrontations, ultimatums, and commitments by speaking in circumlocutions and allusions or not responding at all—a form of communication that eventually became second nature. This linguistic development came about because in Korea's inferior-superior-ranked society giving a superior person a negative answer, an incorrect answer, or a disturbing answer could have very serious consequences. In this environment Koreans learned how to use cultural intuition or "cultural telepathy" to discern what was actually meant by speakers.

For example, there are simple, clear-cut words in Korean for "yes" and "no"—*ne* (neh) and *anio* (ah-n'yoh)—but they are seldom used by themselves. Saying "no" outright is still considered impolite by older generations—an attitude that can cause no end of problems to foreigners who are not tuned in to Korea's cultural communication channels.

In private as well as business matters, Koreans make what outsiders regard as promises only to fail to live up to them. In Korean reality what appears to be a promise is often no more than a way of saying *anio* that is designed to avoid discord and save the face of both parties.

One of the ways Koreans customarily turn down requests, petitions, applications, or whatever is to make the requirements so onerous that no one will pursue the matter. Koreans intuitively understand what is going on and back off. Foreigners are more likely to believe that the Koreans concerned are being hardheaded, uncooperative, dishonest, destructive, etc., and to persevere without realizing there is no chance of success. Foreign businesspeople in Korea can usually determine the difference between a promise and a put-off by requesting that the commitment be put in writing in an official document. If the document is not forthcoming, the answer is clear.

In private and personal situations, the challenge is more subtle. Foreigners who are aware of the Korean reluctance to say *anio* directly, and are diplomatic, can get by with breaking etiquette and asking for a clear *yes* or *no*.

There are three primary words for "yes" in Korean: *ye*, which is used when addressing superiors; *ne* (neh), which may also be used when addressing equals; and *kurae* (kuu-rye), which is used when addressing inferiors and has the connotation of the English word "right." But *ye* or *ne* does not always mean an unqualified "yes" in their Korean context. In many cases *ye* and *ne* do not mean agreement. Instead they mean "I hear you," or "I understand what you are saying (but)." If, for example, you ask if someone can do something by a certain hour or day and he says *ye/ne* (or *kurae*), it does not necessarily mean he *will* do it.

All too often, such responses are meant only to keep things on a pleasant, harmonious level, to avoid upsetting the other person's feelings.

About the only way to avoid this kind of cultural morass is to diplomatically pursue the matter by explaining how important it is that the time frame be established precisely and that if any problems are anticipated you want to know about them then and will understand if there are, in fact, problems.

Generally speaking, Koreans use the negative and positive of verbs, rather than plain *ye* or *anio*, when responding to direct questions such as "Are you going?"

128

놀다
Nolda
(Nohl-dah)

"Work Never Ceases"

During Korea's "Three Kingdoms period" (57 B.C.–A.D. 668) the adoption of the Chinese system of government by the rulers of the kingdoms was to have a profound effect on Korean society in a variety of ways. For one thing, it resulted in the appearance of a whole class of people—which eventually made up around 10 percent of the population—who regarded manual labor as beneath them.

According to a number of contemporary Korean sociologists, the Chinese system of government adopted in Korea eventually "feminized" the male members of the ruling class, making them conservative and fearful of any disorder or change and conditioning them to support an authoritarian government that could keep the lower classes in check. The sociologists add that by disdaining work and supporting the status quo, Korea's ruling class became the greatest obstacle to any kind of progress in the country.

In contrast to this attitude and behavior of upper-class Korean men, common Koreans believed that for a society to function smoothly in an ideal manner everybody except the young, the disabled, and the aged should work unceasingly. Koreans in this class traditionally looked on the absence of work as a vacuum that brought on misfortune and fear—a work ethic that is as formidable as anything ever created in the West.

Mrs. L. H. Underwood, an American missionary who lived in Korea during the 1880s and 1890s, wrote in *Fifteen Years Among the Top-Knots* that Koreans were among the hardest-working people she had ever encountered. She added that given the opportunity, Koreans were also as talented as the Chinese and Japanese, and that morally Koreans were as good as, "if not better" than, the Chinese and Japanese.

Mrs. Underwood also noted that most lower-class Korean wives were so ignorant, shy, filled with despair, and sorrowful from hard work, lack of love, and illnesses that they appeared to be in a daze most of the time. She then made the seemingly contradictory observation that Koreans in general were bright, had a wonderful sense of humor, were warm and kind and not given to revenge—as were the Chinese and Japanese.

The duality of these traditional Korean attitudes toward work is captured in the commonly used word *nolda* (nohl-dah), which refers both to play (not working) and to being unemployed (not having a job). Still today, the typical Korean is under tremendous psychological pressure to have a job and to work hard. Another interesting aspect of the work attitude of Koreans is that they have virtually unbounded confidence in their ability to do anything that others can do. As a rule Koreans believe they can accomplish anything if they work hard enough and long enough—something they learned from Zen Buddhism.

At the same time, however, modern-day Koreans are impatient for results, and if one method doesn't work quickly they tend to switch to some other approach—behavior that can be upsetting to Western managers in Korea who do not expect that kind of reaction from Asians and who may feel that such behavior reduces their ability to control the situation.

Unlike most of their Western counterparts, Korean workers, technicians, engineers, and designers are not eager to share their experience and expertise with anyone outside of their in-group. Americans, for example, often appear to be obsessed with sharing—or showing off—their knowledge to anybody who will listen. Most Koreans, however, are still in the grip of a strictly defined groupist philosophy and regard outsiders as competitors—or enemies—who are beyond the pale of their goodwill and largesse.

By the early 1990s the young people entering the work force were the first generation in the history of the country never to know hunger or serious deprivation of any kind. They were also the first generation not to be compulsive workers content to labor for ten or more hours a day six and seven days a week. In a remarkable departure from the past, they had become the first Koreans to take for granted that they had a right to a life beyond work, including the pursuit of personal happiness.

129

논리

Nolli

(Nohl-lee)

"Beware of Being Logical"

Koreans were traditionally conditioned to depend on cultural intuition and customs rather than logic. They generally thought in subjective rather than objective terms and were content to conduct their lives on the basis of "approximations" rather than hard facts. Psychologist Jae Un Kim says that still today Koreans tend to dislike and shun people who are rational-minded and try to react and do things according to principles of *nolli* (nohl-lee), or "logic." He says that Koreans prefer a "round" or "smooth" approach to things—something that inspired Korean sociologist Chae Sok Choe to label this kind of Korean thinking "pumpkinism" (from the round shape of pumpkins).

Traditional Korean society was structured according to patterns that go back to the origin of family life, with father, mother, and children in that order of authority and privilege. But interpersonal relationships within families, among friends, in business, and in politics as well were based on a precisely ordered hierarchical protocol in which objective thought and individualistic behavior had no place. Sex, age, position within families, social class, and connections determined almost every aspect of life from birth to death. Whatever abilities or ambitions individuals possessed had to be exercised within the minutely defined limitations of these predetermined factors.

This cultural construct was diametrically opposed to *nolli*, which literally means "objective reasoning," as a result of which logic was an immoral concept in Korea until modern times. The word itself was virtually taboo. So powerful was this cultural conditioning that still today the typical Korean is turned off by the obvious, and especially the aggressive, use of logic. People who try to think and behave in a logical manner, with universal principles as their guidelines, are generally disliked and often shunned. They are considered cold and calculating and bereft of the personal, "human" qualities that are so important to the Korean psyche.

Sociologist Chae Sok Choe says that ordinary Koreans still believe that all things in life, including business matters, should be handled as if they were pumpkins—in other words, as smooth round things not requiring any close examination or special treatment. Many Westerners, with their built-in analytical and critical mind-set, invariably rub Koreans the wrong way, resulting in ill feelings and resistance.

It is therefore important for Westerners in Korea to keep in mind that *nollijogin*, or "logical-minded persons," are generally regarded as disruptive rather than constructive. People who are so logical minded that they are incapable of being flexible are viewed as social deviants. Choe blames this Korean characteristic on Confucianism, which emphasized the importance of "face" over virtually everything else, resulting in Koreans becoming formalistic, ritualistic, and nonrational in their behavior.

The only way around this cultural abhorrence for *nolli* is to take the time to introduce the subject, problem, or whatever in personal terms. The more emotion-charged these personal scenarios, the more likely the approach will work because that is the cultural medium in which Koreans have been conditioned to respond.

One of the traditional Korean (as well as Chinese and Japanese) complaints about Westerners, particularly Americans, is that they talk too much and say too little, and there is a special phrase used to described such people: *mal i manta* (mahl ee mahn-tah), which means "many words." It refers specifically to people who emphasize logic (words!) over feelings and "face."

Koreans for centuries have been conditioned to depend on a kind of visceral feeling known as *tongchal yok* (tohng-chahl yohk), which literally means "power of insight," rather than logic or so-called facts. Koreans have traditionally used *tongchal yok* as a kind of cultural telepathy. Older Koreans still today rely as much or more on *tongchal yok* as they do on other factors, a circumstance that can be especially upsetting to Westerners who have been weaned on facts and logical reasoning.

Koreans and Westerners also tend to clash over the concept and use of the term *kongpyonghan* (kohng-p'yohng-hahn), "fair" or "just." In its Korean context fairness is not an absolute principle. It is relative and changes with the circumstances. Korea, for example, is geographically minuscule compared to China, the United States, and other land-rich countries. Therefore, in the eyes of Koreans Korea should not be held to the same foreign trade standards of these larger nations.

The challenge facing Westerners in Korea is to adapt their own values, attitudes, and habits to the point that they can deal effectively with the emotional and personal characteristics of Koreans in work as well as in play. Americans in particular have difficulty dealing with nonlogical, nonpragmatic cultures, so it generally takes a great deal of effort for them to accept the idea that logic does not always prevail in Korea—that the personal element often takes precedence over what seems to them totally obvious and self-explanatory situations.

A key point in this understanding is that "face," expressed in terms of formalistic etiquette, generally means a lot more to Koreans than rational, practical solutions and behavior. But for all of their finicky attachment to precisely prescribed personalized etiquette, when Koreans are in a nonthreatening, informal setting they are among the world's most happy-go-lucky people, with an extraordinary penchant for singing, dancing, and making merry.

Of course, a growing number of Koreans have shed all or most of their traditional subjective skin and now conduct themselves and their businesses on the basis of objective reasoning. Lucky is the outsider who is able to team up with this impressive group of people.

130

뇌물

Noemul
(Noh-muhl)

"Bribery vs. Gift Giving"

In ancient Korea gift giving to tribal chiefs, headmen, shamans, and others who performed a variety of services began as payment for their services and was the original form of taxation. After the development of city-states, gifts were given regularly to local and regional officials and were regarded as part of their legitimate income—a custom that was sanctioned politically because it reduced the cost of government and was accepted socially because it was the only recourse common people had for getting help or cooperation from government officials.

Members of the elite ruling class routinely gave gifts to officials on all levels, including court ministers, to repay favors, to obligate people to them, and to achieve various other ends. For nearly two thousand years (from 108 B.C. until A.D. 1910) the various kingdoms on the Korean peninsula usually maintained their independence by paying annual tribute to China. This tribute included such things as gold, silver, celadon, ginseng, horses, eunuchs, and women.

In its traditional context, such tribute and gift giving itself was not seen as immoral as long as the custom was not abused. Officials and others were regarded as immoral, however, if they went beyond a certain norm in what they expected or demanded for their help.

Following the adoption of a very strict form of Confucianism by the new Choson dynasty in 1392, Korean society became increasingly hierarchical and authoritarian. Common people had few if any human or legal rights, making it even more essential for them to get on and stay on the good side of local officials by giving them bribes in the form of gifts. Thus *noemul* (noh-muhl), or "bribery," almost always disguised as gift giving—or, in the case of China, as tribute in return for protection from foreign invaders—became not only the oil that made the Korean political system work but also essential to the survival of the nation.

In the new administrative system that evolved during the early decades of the Choson dynasty (1392-1910), a hereditary class of officials called *hyangni* (h'yahng-nee) was assigned to carry out the orders of county magistrates in local areas. These petty officials received no government remuneration whatsoever for their services, resulting in their using their position to extort payment in kind in the form of "taxes" from farmers and craftsmen in their areas.

The prevalence of gift giving and bribery in Korea resulted in obscuring the nature of the two actions. Giving someone something, including cash, as a "gift," no matter what the motive might be, was traditionally not regarded as a bribe in the Korean sense, and no guilt, sin, or immorality was attached to the act.

But as Korea's population grew and government became much more complicated, bureaucratic, and controlled by an elite social class, officials began to take advantage of their power by extorting gifts from people beyond what they normally received for their services. Korean society remained in the hands of authoritarian regimes and military juntas until the 1980s, with gift giving and bribery as institutionalized as ever.

Korean society still suffers from the age-old syndrome of paying tribute to those in power, but it is no longer sanctified as moral behavior. The government has established strict guidelines in an effort to control *noemul* as well as gift giving that crosses the line, but it continues on a massive scale.

During the 1960s and 1970s, when Korea's economy was being transformed by the growing *chaebol* (chay-buhl) enterprise groups and the thousands of small manufacturers and traders vying with each for raw materials, government licenses, and contacts with foreign importers, bribery (and gift giving, its alter ego) flourished as never before. Few transactions were not engendered by or accompanied by some form of "favor" in return. The *chaebol* in particular attracted critical attention from the news media and the public for the way they obtained government contracts and other support from the various trade and finance agencies of the government.

The Korean concept of personal gifts varies in a fundamental way from the Western concept. When Koreans give a gift, it is not just a gesture of generosity or politeness. They expect something in return—a business or personal favor, not an exchange of gifts—and if not immediately, then sometime in the future. After Koreans have given a gift, especially a relatively expensive item, to someone and then approached them with a *putak* (puh-tahk), or "request" for a favor, it may be a serious breach of etiquette to refuse to grant the favor. In a Western context this smacks of blackmail, but in its Korean sense the gift was payment for the favor and they have a right to expect the favor.

The practice of giving gifts and being repaid by favors is a deeply entrenched and universal custom in Korea that is fully sanctioned by society. It has long been the custom in Korea for subordinates to give gifts several times a year to their superiors and for people in general to give periodic gifts to such people as teachers, doctors, and officials with whom they have any kind of relationship. This was one of the costs of maintaining harmonious relationships.

But some people abuse the gift-giving custom by taking it to extremes; some, in fact, use this approach as their primary business strategy. Westerners who are not familiar with this custom are frequently victimized by this category of unscrupulous people. Avoiding being burdened by this kind of social debt is touchy. There are occasions when gifts can be refused or returned to the sender, but this is practical only when the intended receiver is not in a vulnerable position and cannot be made to suffer by the would-be giver. Another way of "canceling" or countering the debt is to give some kind of gift in return.

In the early 1990s the government established precise guidelines for personal gift giving in an effort to make it clear when someone crossed the line. But the custom had been institutionalized so long that this measure simply resulted in a new label being applied to the practice. Nowadays it is more common to refer to gift giving as well as out-and-out bribes as *t'ukhye* (ttuk-hay), which means "special favors." Both business and political relationships in Korea are personal in nature, and both operate on the basis of "special favors."

The *t'ukhye* involved in daily life in Korea today range from nighttime entertainment, meals, and drinks to relatively expensive gifts, including sums of money on the occasion of weddings, funerals, and other special events. But Koreans still distinguish between such favors and bribes, pointing out that it is, in fact, the personal nature of public and business relations that has resulted in gift giving and favor exchanging playing a major role in Korean life and that what outsiders might view as bribery is no more than meeting traditional social obligations. The implication, of course, is that a *t'ukhye* is not a bribe unless it involves a substantial amount of money or benefit in kind and that Koreans are very sensitive to the difference between the two.

In November 1995 the new reform government of President Young Sam Kim arrested former president Tae Woo Roh on charges of accepting more than $600 million in bribes from thirty of the country's top business tycoons. Roh, an ex-general who had won fame during his presidency by calling for democratic elections that ended centuries of dictatorial rule, pleaded guilty to the charges and was sentenced to prison. Roh's predecessor, ex-general Doh Hwan Chun, was also arrested, convicted of complicity in the killing of several dozen students during antigovernment demonstrations in 1980, as well as for accepting bribes, and imprisoned.

Foreigners living and doing business in Korea are advised to exercise extra caution to avoid getting caught up in the quicksand of *noemul*. Once started it is difficult to stop. Besides, it is now illegal to give "gifts" of any significance to public officials, and government determination to eliminate the practice continues to grow. Foreigners in Korea who accept gifts should be aware that they have incurred a debt and that sometime in the future they may be asked to pay it.

131

농부
Nongbu
(Nohng-buu)
"The 'Good' People"

In 1948 an American army general stationed in Korea announced that Koreans would never be able to use technology to attain a high standard of living. He added that the economy of Korea would remain agricultural, primarily rice growing, presumably forever. Given the historical background of Koreans, and the state of Korea at that time, the American general may be at least partly forgiven for his myopic view of the future of Korea.

From the beginning of Korean history until the 1900s, some 80 percent of all Koreans were basically tenant farmers, bound to the plots of land they tilled by custom and by law, generally unable to change their occupations or ways of doing things. Farmers lived in villages clustered within or near the fields they tilled. Each of the villages was virtually self-sustaining, with each household producing its own food and clothing. Each village was also responsible for providing a specified quota of produce and other products (including mulberry leaves for silkworms, walnuts, and pine nuts) to landlords and to the government as taxes.

In the official hierarchical order of Korean society, farmers were often said to rank next to the ruling class and were referred to as *nongbu* (nohng-buu), or "good people." In reality, however, they were generally treated as people with few rights, only a step above slaves and outcasts. The term *nongbu* was used by the upper class as a ploy designed to placate farmers and encourage them to be proud of their role in society. It was generally recognized that Korea's peasants were, in fact, the ideal Confucian citizens—they were obedient, humble, polite, hardworking, and self-sacrificing—*nongbu* in every sense of the word.

Throughout Korea's pre-modern history scholars routinely wrote learned treatises on the obvious fact that farmers were the foundation of the state and that without them there would be no state—a truism that both rural landlords and the elite ruling class managed to play down, and often ignore entirely, in their compulsion to extract more and more taxes from the *nongbu* to maintain their relatively luxurious lifestyle and finance their factional struggles against each other.

Korea's peasants not only supported themselves and the rest of the country but were also the most disciplined and democratic in the way they managed community affairs. All decisions regarding farming villages were reached by discussion and consensus—something that the faction-prone scholar-official ruling class was often incapable of doing.

In times of war as well, it was invariably the peasant class that bore the brunt of the fighting and suffering. And despite the reputation that Koreans have traditionally had for being paragons of well-mannered behavior, and peaceful by nature, it was just as often peasant armies that came to the rescue of the country when it was threatened from the outside. (One indication of the martial spirit of Korean farmers was the custom for boys and young men from different villages to engage in orchestrated rock fights during festivals.)

It was also Korea's peasant class that was the most faithful in carrying on the ancient shamanistic rituals, from exorcisms to festivals, that helped to sustain the culture over the generations. Farmers had their own musical traditions, *nong ak* (nohng ahk), contributing significantly to the folk arts that are now regarded as cultural treasures.

Since the beginning of Korea's massive industrialization in the 1960s, the number of farmers has decreased dramatically and is still falling. By the late 1990s over half of the entire population of South Korea lived in just four cities—Seoul, Pusan, Taegu, and Inchon.

132

노래

Norae
(No-rye)

"Singing Your Way to Success"

Westerners visiting Korea for more than a few days, especially if they take up residence there, are inevitably presented with a challenge that few are capable of meeting with sufficient aplomb or skill to avoid being embarrassed, much less impress anyone. The challenge they are faced with is *norae* (no-rye), or "singing," more often than not in a solo act before an audience, something that the average Westerner has never done in his or her lifetime.

    Norae was traditionally an integral part of Korean culture, first as shamanistic rituals and celebrations that all people were required to participate in, then as personal and public entertainment in which everyone took part. Chinese travelers in Korea around 1000 B.C. reported that it was customary in some of the tribal nations they visited for the people to gather around open fires and hold impromptu songfests. One tribe was described as devoting the entire month of October to an ongoing celebration called *Muchon* (Muu-chohn), or "Dancing to Heaven."

    Korean records show that it was customary for the royal courts of the various kingdoms to maintain troupes of professional singers and dancers to entertain the royal family, ministers, and state guests. Singing was part of the training, and part of the normal activities, of the famed *hwarang* (whah-rahng) warrior corps that appeared during the midyears of the Shilla dynasty (57 B.C.–A.D. 669). A special kind of stylized theatrical entertainment that included dancing as well as singing, called *kamaugiak* (kah-mou-ghee-ahk), also dates from this period. (Japan's kabuki theater, which appeared some one thousand years later, was the Japanese equivalent of *kamaugiak*.)

    Probably the most famous—and most notorious—of the "singing groups" in early Korea were the *kisaeng* (kee-sang), young women trained in playing musical instruments, singing, dancing, and conversation to make them suitable companions and concubines for men of the upper class—an institution that originated some two thousand years ago and survived into modern times. Singing has also continued to be a mainstay of the shaman and other religious rituals that are common in Korea.

    As time passed, all Koreans began singing for the pleasure of it and over the millennia amassed a large number of folk tunes that became an integral part of the culture. All Korean children learned how to sing a number of these folk tunes as part of their upbringing. But unlike some societies, Koreans did not stop singing when they became adults. Everybody sang at festivals, parties, and other special occasions, in groups as well as solo. Until the post–World War II era the mainstay repertoire of professional entertainers as well as common people were folk songs. Professional singers also specialized in "epic story" songs that glorified the history of Korea.

    The traditional lifestyle that resulted in Koreans developing professional-like skill in singing persisted until well up into the twentieth century, and although the lifestyle has changed dramatically most Koreans can still sing well enough to be confident about performing individually. One of the reasons for this is another tradition that is known as *jang ki* (jahng kee), which literally means "favorite technique" and refers to the custom for Koreans to practice some kind of entertainment skill—generally singing—on their own and in private.

    While virtually all Koreans have traditionally gained some skill in singing as children, many people took it upon themselves to develop their singing ability well above the average to surprise and impress their friends and give themselves both a social and a professional advantage—goals that led them to spend a significant amount of time honing their *jang ki*.

    This tradition of singing is still alive and well in Korea—and not surprisingly was given an extraordinary boost by the great *karaoke* (kah-rah-oh-kay) boom that began in Japan in the 1970s and swept the world during the 1980s.* Koreans naturally expect non-Koreans to sing just like they do and are surprised and disappointed when they discover that most Westerners can't sing their way out of a paper bag and are so intimidated by the idea that they often refuse to try. This cultural difference is a considerable handicap for Westerners in Korea, including businesspeople who are there on short trips, because they are almost always put in a situation—in a bar or at a banquet party—where they are expected to sing.

Korean businessmen who take their customers and suppliers to bars and clubs that feature *karaoke* singing generally take turns at the microphone, belting out two or three of their favorite tunes in Korean, Japanese, or English. When the group is a large one, this can take a long time. At gatherings where singing is customary, the guest of honor or the senior person in the group is offered the honor of singing first. They may decline to go first, but they are expected to sing before the party breaks up. Foreigners who are guests of Koreans at *karaoke* places are expected to perform like everyone else. Not being able to fully participate in these *norae* exhibitions goes beyond personal embarrassment. It leaves one with a sense of being culturally disadvantaged. So the best recourse for people planning on going to Korea—or going to *karaoke* bars with Korean friends or associates in New York or elsewhere—is to be forewarned and to practice singing before going. "You definitely need a song that you can sing 'on demand.' If nothing else, 'You Are My Sunshine' works," adds Martin Sours, Professor of International Asian Studies at the American Graduate School of International Management.

Those who simply cannot carry a tune, and often don't know the words to any song, can sometimes save themselves by insisting that one or more Koreans in the party join them in a duo or trio (most singing bars have songbooks for those who need them). That way they can fake their way through the experience—something that I have done many times.

And for those who have never had the experience of *karaoke*-style singing in a bar or club, even when faking it in a group, it is a powerful male bonding experience that is part of establishing and nurturing the close relationships that are so important to doing business in Korea. Foreign businesspeople who can sing well and delight in (humbly) showing off their *jang ki* are especially well received by Koreans and often find that being able to bond with their Korean contacts through *norae* is one of their most valuable assets.

Karaoke is a term made up of the Japanese word *kara* (kah-rah), which means "empty," and the first two syllables from the Japanization of the English word *orchestra* (*okesutora*). The phrase *kara oke* literally means "empty orchestra," referring to the fact that singers perform to recorded orchestra music—not music provided by live musicians.

노래방
Norae Bang
(No-rye Bahng)
"The Singing Salons"

The importance of singing in Korean culture comes as a surprise to most Westerners, probably because of the image they have of Korea as a cold, rugged country and of Koreans as serious-minded, work-oriented people not given to levity or frivolous behavior. But behind their masks of formal decorum and obsessive ambition, Koreans are a fun-loving people given to puns, jokes, humorous stories, and singing.

Singing in Korea goes beyond being a well-entrenched cultural custom. By the early 1990s it had become virtually a national obsession that had been institutionalized and industrialized on a national scale. During the 1980s Korean entrepreneurs in Seoul began opening *norae bang* (no-rye bahng), or "singing salons," that quickly spread throughout the country.

Unlike the Japanese-invented *karaoke* (kah-rah-oh-kay) bars, which are bars first and singing venues second, Korea's ubiquitous *norae bang* do not stock, sell, or allow liquor on the premises. In fact they are famous for being used as "sobering up places" by men who have had too much to drink at other places and do not want to hire someone to take them home or go home drunk.

Korea's *norae bang* are designed specifically for people who want to express and enjoy themselves by singing in a semiformal situation where they will not disturb anyone, don't have to be concerned about shaming themselves, and are provided with professional-type loudspeaker and video equipment that enhances their performance while adding to the satisfaction and pleasure they get from the experience.

Norae bang feature private rooms of different sizes that are rented to patrons by the hour. The more individuals in a party, the larger the room. Snacks and soft drinks are served. Some larger "singing salons" offer a variety of special services, including parking attendants and transportation. Some also allow professional drummers to visit their rooms and offer to entertain patrons with exhibitions of traditional drumming.

Patrons of the singing salons usually go in groups and generally take turns staging solo performances, but before the evening is over most join together to perform in groups. Most patrons sing in at least Korean and English, and some also sing in Japanese. In addition to laser disc players that provide recorded music, the *norae bang* also feature videos that display on-screen lyrics for the convenience of those who need help.

The largest collection of singing salons in Seoul is located south of the Han River (which bisects the city). Reservations are needed to guarantee entry into some of the more popular places. Korean hosts often take foreign visitors to their favorite *norae bang* rather than the more expensive *kisaeng* houses or hostess-stocked cabarets.

Some Korean companies provide in-house *norae bang* for their employees, not only as a convenience but also as an officially approved means of reducing workplace stress. Foreign businesspeople stationed in or visiting Korea can gain important points by participating in *norae bang* song fests with their Korean contacts.

134

노 예

Noye
(Noh-yeh)

"The Pre-modern Slave Culture"

Noye (noh-yeh), or slaves, were an integral part of pre-modern Korean society. From the beginning of Korean history one of the primary aims of warfare was to obtain slaves. Generals and other ranking officers who were successful on the battlefields were awarded land grants and slaves. The ownership of both eventually became hereditary. It was also common for people who could not pay their taxes or their debts to be enslaved. When a man was convicted of a crime and executed, his family became slaves. The children of slaves became slaves, making the status hereditary and resulting in the number of slaves growing along with the rest of the population.

There were various terms for different categories of slaves, including *kano* (kah-noh), which referred to male slaves who worked in households; *kabi* (kah-bee), or domestic female slaves; and *kadong* (kah-dohng), young slave boys. In a draconian measure that was designed to perpetuate the social status of slaves and prevent them from gaining any kind of power, laws were passed disqualifying slaves and their descendants from holding civil service jobs.

In addition to privately owned slaves, the state itself owned slaves. Kyongju, capital of the Shilla kingdom from 57 B.C. until A.D. 935, became one of the largest and most attractive cities in the world primarily through the use of slave labor. Shilla kings also used slaves to build great tombs for themselves.

In addition to villages of free people, virtually every county in the country had "special communities" that were in fact labor camps specifically for slaves. Slaves lived in these settlements and went to and from the places where they worked. Large numbers of slave laborers and artisans were attached to the various palace and government agencies of Shilla. Some officials owned as many as three thousand slaves, indicating that the slave population of the capital was indeed large.

By the tenth century there were so many slaves in the country that a Slave Review Act was enacted by the Koryo court in a drastic measure to reduce the number of slaves—an action that was also taken to reduce the wealth and power of many officials, military officers, and clan lords.

Korean history is marked by slave uprisings. In most of these instances one of the primary purposes of these rebellions was to destroy the local and national governments' slave records so that the rebels and their descendants could no longer be officially identified as slaves. During some of these turbulent periods former slaves became affluent enough to buy their freedom; others became free by serving in the military. Some became high-ranking military officers and government officials.

In the mid-1400s there were 350,000 public slaves throughout Korea, meaning they were owned by different branches and agencies of the government. In 1462, during the first century of the Choson dynasty, there were more than 200,000 government-owned slaves on the rosters of Seoul agencies alone. Some top government officials personally owned as many as 3,000 slaves during this period. However, from this time on, the number of slaves and people held in bond decreased rapidly.

In 1592, when the Japanese invaded Korea and advanced on Seoul, causing the ruling king and his court to flee, slaves stormed the *noye* registration office and the Ministry of Punishments in Seoul and set fire to both of them, destroying all of their records. By the seventeenth century the number of public slaves had dropped to 200,000, but it was the middle of the eighteenth century before the number of privately held slaves began to decrease significantly. Finally, in 1801, the Choson court freed all the people in bond to government offices. One reason for this action was to eliminate the serious financial burden the large number of slaves had become on the court by returning them to tax-paying status.

The Choson court officially abolished private slavery in 1894, but it continued unofficially, particularly involving female slaves, for several more years, with some cases reported in the public press as late as the 1920s. By this time Korea had been annexed by Japan (in 1910), and the Japanese were to introduce new and heinous elements into the ancient practice of slavery.

Japanese occupation forces began by rounding up dozens of thousands of Korean men and women and shipping them to Manchuria and Japan to work as *noye* laborers in factories and mines. As the Japanese expansion onto the Asian mainland turned into full-scale war, the Japanese army commissioned civilian agents to round up thousands of young Korean girls and women to be used as slave prostitutes for Japan's armed forces.

In keeping with their custom of using flowery euphemisms to obscure reality, the Japanese high command listed these sex slaves as "comfort women." Forced to serve as many as fifty or more men a men a day, these young women had a very low survival rate. Some died of disease, others died of mistreatment, and some killed themselves. A number chose to become "suicide bombers," using concealed hand grenades to kill themselves and their Japanese "customers."

In the 1990s this inglorious behavior of the Japanese army came back to haunt Japan when several dozen former Korean "comfort women," then in their late sixties and seventies, came forward and demanded both an apology and some kind of redress from the Japanese government. These Korean women were joined quickly by women from the Philippines and other areas of Southeast Asia who had also been forced to serve as prostitutes for the Japanese military when Japan captured and occupied their homelands between 1940 and 1945.

At first the Japanese government denied that the Imperial Army had played any role in organizing and operating "sex rings." But voluminous records quickly surfaced proving that the Japanese army had done exactly that, not only in Korea but in all of the other countries that it occupied between 1941 and 1945.

In 1995 the Japanese government unofficially admitted that the charges of the Korean women (and the women from other Asian countries as well) were true but claimed that it was not obligated to make any kind of financial settlement because all such matters had been covered as part of the wartime reparations agreements signed at the end of World War II. Again in keeping with the Japanese (and Asian) custom of keeping such things off the record, the Japanese government in the spring of 1995 authorized the establishment of a private organization to raise "consolation" funds for the former sex slaves.

Pre-modern Korea, like other Buddhist countries of Asia, also had a class of "untouchables" who were known as *paekchong* (pake-chong), or "outcasts"—the old word for "butcher." These were people who worked with meats and hides and at other "unclean" occupations such as grave digging and lived in specially designated communities.

Part of the present-day mentality of Koreans is a legacy of this long history of institutionalized slavery enforced on them by their own governments as well as by foreign invaders. They are extremely sensitive to any hint of outsiders treating, or appearing to treat, them as if they were "slaves."

135

눈치

Nunchi
(Nuun-chee)

"Korea's Cultural Telepathy"

It is generally accepted that people who live together for many years, particularly husbands and wives, eventually arrive at the point that they understand each other so well they can "communicate" without words—that, in effect, they can virtually read each other's mind. To some degree this phenomenon also occurs on a larger scale, within groups of people who share the same set of knowledge, the same values, the same aspirations, the same fears, and so on.

Naturally, the older, the more structured, the more refined, and the more exclusive a society, the more its people can communicate nonverbally. Korea (like Japan) meets this description precisely. Koreans are very much aware and make a major to-do about a practice or a facility they call *nunchi* (nuun chee), which translates roughly as "reading feelings" or "reading minds"—and is something that I call "cultural telepathy."

Koreans are so culturally attuned to each other's thoughts and behavior, because they have been "living together" for several thousand years and until recent times were programmed deliberately and comprehensively to think alike and act alike, that they can, in fact, seemingly "read" each other's emotions and thoughts. Korean social scientist Chae Sok Choe says in his book *The Korean Social Character* that the role of *nunchi* in Korean life is so vital that he refers to Korean culture as "*nunchi* culture."

Foreigners in Korea are constantly encountering situations in which they misunderstand Koreans because Koreans customarily do not verbally explain their attitudes and actions, resulting in the foreigners being called down for their failure to have divined the feelings and intentions of their Korean co-workers, contacts, or friends through *nunchi*. Of course, there is nothing mysterious about *nunchi*. But foreigners who are not skilled in using it in their communication with Koreans can be at a serious disadvantage. The disadvantage can sometimes be especially devastating if they do not know, in the first place, that *nunchi* exists.

Becoming skilled at *nunchi* communication naturally goes well beyond non-verbal language. It requires an intimate familiarity with all of the nuances of the national character and personality of Koreans in general, as well as detailed knowledge about the educational background, social status, and work status of the individuals involved. Age and sex are also primary factors in *nunchi* communication, directly influencing the cultural content of the messages being sent and received. This makes it extremely important that people be able to access different "sex" and "age" channels and accurately "read" the messages that are being sent.

The higher the status of Korean individuals, the more likely they are to depend on *nunchi* for their own input and the more they expect their subordinates and others to be able to "read" their positions and wishes without words being spoken. Some Koreans in important positions routinely "test" the "Koreanness" and loyalty of their subordinates by putting them in positions where they have to divine their will through *nunchi*. Those who fail may thereafter be suspect.

Korean sociologist Se Chol O says in his book *The Social Psychology of the Korean People* that *nunchi* evolved out of the need for people to avoid offending others and maintain smooth human relations by communicating in vague, indirect terms rather than direct speech. To achieve this, O adds, it has traditionally been necessary for Koreans to conceal their true thoughts and intentions from others, especially people outside of their family and kinship circles. O goes on to say that this need for concealment is, in fact, one of the key reasons Koreans were traditionally selective in their friendships and generally limited their involvement to as few people as possible.

Foreigners in Korea can hardly avoid getting caught up in situations because they are unfamiliar with *nunchi* communication. Tales of such experiences range from hilarious to tragic. The only practical recourse that newcomers have is to develop a close relationship with trustworthy Korean contacts or colleagues who will willingly and discreetly act as their "*nunchi* guides" or "interpreters."

Having such a "cultural medium" is especially important for foreign businesspeople newly arrived in Korea, particularly those who are employed by Korean companies because a great deal of what they are expected to learn, know, and do is communicated through *nunchi* channels. Veteran expatriates in Korea say it generally takes from three to five years, and a great deal of effort, before foreigners develop the ability to "receive" in *nunchi* "code" and fully understand the messages they themselves are sending to their Korean counterparts.

"In any event," adds Martin Sours, Professor of International Asian studies at the American Graduate School of International Management, "the Korean mind-set is that foreigners *never* understand them."

136

외계인

Oegugin

(Oh-eh-guug-een)

"Encounters with Foreigners"

The first *oegugin* (oh-eh-guug-een), or "foreigners,"* of record to show up in Korea were Chinese who came as invaders some 4,000 years ago. This pattern was to be continued for some 3,500 years by more Chinese and by Mongols, Japanese, Manchus, and Jurchens. For much of this long period Korea was under the political and military domination of the Chinese, then the Mongols and the Manchus, and was required to pay annual tribute to these overlords to maintain a semblance of autonomy.

The first Western foreigners to set foot in Korea arrived in the sixteenth century, but they were so few in number that they were seen by only a few Koreans and were more curiosities than anything. Following a seven-year invasion by Japan between 1592 and 1598, and another invasion by the Manchus of Manchuria in the 1630s, Korea closed its doors to all outsiders except the Chinese and a limited number of Japanese traders.

Then, in the early 1600s, Korea had its own Will Adams, the real-life model for author James Clavell's Pilot Blackthorne in his famous novel (and later tele-

---

*Historically, geographical, social, and political divisions in Korea resulted in all nonlocal people being regarded as "foreigners" and treated differently. Local people referred to outsiders as *nam* (nahm), which literally means "other area people." Still today, regional feelings are strong and have a significant impact on society, influencing marriages, education, job placement, and politics.

vision show) about early Japan entitled *Shōgun*. The Korean version of the Englishman Will Adams was a Dutchman named Jan Janse Weltevree who, with two companions, was stranded on the coast of Korea in 1627. A tall, red-headed, blue-eyed man who was an expert at firearms, Weltevree and his skills so impressed the Choson court that he was made a member of the middle class (*chungin*), given a military post and a Korean name (Yon Pak), and allowed to marry a Korean girl. (His two companions died early.)

In 1653, when Weltevree was fifty-eight years old, he was sent to the Korean island of Cheju to interview the survivors of a shipwrecked Dutch ship that was under the command of a man named Hendrik Hamel. A year later the thirty-six survivors of that ship were taken to Seoul, where they were assigned to a military unit in the city. Several of the men died there. In 1663 the twenty-two who remained alive were sent to military units in Cholla Province. Ten years later eight of them escaped in a skiff and made their way to Japan. One of the escapees, the ship's former captain, Hendrik Hamel, later published a book about his adventures, bringing the first information about Korea to Europe and telling something about the story of Jan Weltevree. Weltevree lived out his life in Korea.

From 1832 on, an increasing number of English merchant ships and warships began appearing in Korean waters. Three French warships anchored off the coast in 1846, leaving a letter for the king requesting that formal relations be established. In 1854 two Russian naval vessels fired on Korean ships and coastal villages. In 1866 an American-owned ship, the *General Sherman*, sailed up the Taedong River to Pyongyang, reportedly intending to raid the royal tombs nearby. The prince regent, a man named Taewongun, known for his ruthlessness in defending Korea against foreign intrusions, ordered that the ship be forced to leave immediately or destroyed if it failed to do so. Soldiers and a mob of civilians attacked the ship, killing all of the crew and burning the vessel. In 1868 a Prussian who had been trying to convince the ruling prince regent to open trading relations created an uproar by violating the tomb of the regent's family.

Korea was finally forced by Japan to reopen its doors to the outside world in 1876 as a result of increasing pressure, including military action, by Japan, Russia, the United States, and the European colonial powers. Japanese nationalists had been publicly advocating an invasion of Korea since 1873.

With the opening of Korea in 1876 several hundred Westerners, mostly missionaries, educators, and professional people, some of whom were invited by the Choson court, flocked into Seoul and other Korean cities and began a concentrated effort to change Korea from a feudal Confucian society into a democratic Christian society. Most of these people were well received by Koreans on all levels and were treated with great respect as honored guests and friends of Korea.

In 1895 Japan usurped China's ancient position of suzerainty over Korea, installed its own puppet ruler on the Choson throne, and began turning the kingdom into a colony. Koreans objected to this new invasion by attacking the Japanese occupation forces. Japan retaliated by annexing the country, eliminating it as a national entity, then trying over the next thirty-five years to obliterate the national and cultural identity of Koreans as well. The Japanese also expelled virtually all Western residents from Korea during this period.

Thus except for a brief period between 1875 and 1910, and the few West-erners who lived and worked in Korea during that time, the Korean experience with foreigners throughout its history ranged from unpleasant and insulting to destructive on a massive scale. Even during this "honeymoon" period with for-eigners there were extreme nationalists who preached a violent form of *min-jokchuui* (meen-joak-chuu-we), or "racism," in their efforts to rid Korea of all foreigners.

But Koreans not only survived their encounters with foreigners; they were tempered by them and became stronger and more resilient. In Korea today *oegugin* are a common sight. The cities are teeming with foreign businesspeo-ple from many countries, and both cities and provincial areas are seasonally crowded with foreign tourists. But like all Asians in old societies with highly structured and exclusive cultures, Koreans remain extraordinarily sensitive to the sight and presence of foreigners. They automatically distinguish between outsiders and themselves by racial appearance, clothing, eating and drinking habits, and all the other tangible and intangible facets of culture.

Koreans automatically divide newly arrived foreigners into specific cate-gories, beginning with whether or not they have had any kind of prior connec-tion or relationship with Korea, Koreans, or Korean organizations. The more intimate or important such connections, whatever they might be, the faster and more completely Koreans accept the newcomers. Among the most meaningful prior relationships are having taught at Korean universities, studied at Korean universities, being related by blood or by marriage to Koreans, and having worked for well-known Korean companies. A foreign man with a Korean wife may be considered "half Korean" in a casual, social sort of way.

Koreans are delighted when foreigners show a genuine interest in their cul-ture and take great pride in showing them their arts and crafts and many of their customs. Foreigners who have social status, because of their professions or jobs (as professors, engineers, etc.), and marry Koreans are more or less looked on as "honorary Koreans," and may be welcomed at least into the outer circle of the families of their Korean relatives.

There is a variety of "tests" that Koreans have traditionally used to measure the commitment of foreigners to Korea—something that they may refer to in a humorous manner but that they take very seriously. The most unusual of these tests is to take the foreigner to a special restaurant, order *posintang* (poh-sint-ahng), or "dog-meat stew," and challenge the foreigner to eat it. Foreigners who eat the dish and say they like it are immediately declared to be "Korean" in spirit if not in body.

Posintang has long been a traditional dish in Korea, highly reputed for its health-giving properties and particularly efficacious during hot weather. In 1988, the year the Summer Olympics were held in Seoul, animal-rights advocates made such a fuss about the eating of dog meat and the prominent display of signs over Seoul restaurants that featured *posintang* that the government ordered the signs be taken down during the Olympics. This resulted in dog-meat aficionados charging international interference in Korea's internal affairs. (In Japan, a similar test involves *natto*/not-toe, or fermented soybean paste.)

Foreigners who are subjected to this test should, of course, be very diplo-matic if they choose to refrain from eating dog meat. The best way is to apologize good-naturedly and say it is against your religious beliefs and equate your position with the ancient Buddhist prohibition against eating meat of any kind—a custom that Koreans do not follow but understand.

On a more personal level, Koreans tend to look on foreigners with whom they become acquainted, particularly in the workplace, as sources of free instruction in English (or whatever their native language is), and it is common for people to go beyond the normal Western bounds of friendship in taking advantage of such relationships. In most instances this imposition is blatantly obvious, but in many cases the Westerners involved feel that they are also benefiting from the relationship to the point that they not only tolerate it but look forward to it.

Koreans are especially skilled at handling guests, making sure that they sit in the "right place" according to their social rank or status on that occasion. Where foreign visitors and guests are concerned, this custom often includes a hands-on approach when visitors hold back when told, or shown, where to sit, etc. It generally takes a while for newcomers to realize that this is a formal, ritualized process and that it applies to virtually all Korean behavior. The only appropriate and acceptable recourse is to relax and go with the flow.

The largest number of overseas Koreans reside in the United States. The Korean term for Korean-Americans is *Hangukkye Migugin* (Hahn-guuk-kay Me-guug-een). Many Korean immigrants to the United States established homes and businesses in minority neighborhoods, competing with Hispanic and African-Americans. One of the cultural code words that became vogue in the Korean community was *hindongi* (heen-dohn-ghee), or "whitey," a derogatory term for Anglo-Caucasian Americans.

137

외국인 선교사
Oegugin Songyosa
(Oh-eh-guug-een Sohn-gyoh-sah)

"Foreign Missionaries and Korea"

The first *oegugin songyosa* (oh-eh-guug-een sohn-gyoh-sah), or "foreign missionaries," to visit Korea were Chinese, following the invasion of Korea by the Chinese Han dynasty emperor Wu-Ti in 109 B.C. Wu-Ti defeated the Koreans, but rather than annexing the peninsula into the Han empire, he turned the small Korean tribal kingdoms in existence at that time into vassal states. During the following four centuries many Chinese Buddhist priests and Confucian scholars visited the Korean kingdoms, and Korean students in turn went to China to study these new philosophies.

The first Western missionary to set foot in Korea was a Spanish Jesuit priest named Gregorio de Cespedes who accompanied one of the Japanese armies that invaded Korea in 1597 (after an earlier invasion failed to conquer the peninsula in 1592). This curious event came about because the army leading the attack on Korea in this second invasion was composed of Japanese Christians, and the priest apparently went along to administer to the general and his troops. The Japanese overran the country, killed dozens of thousands of people, looted and then destroyed virtually everything in their path, then took other thousands of Korean artists and craftsmen back to Japan as captives before withdrawing from the peninsula in 1598 when Japan's de facto shogun, Hideyoshi Toyotomi, who had ordered the invasion, died. The second foreign missionary of record to enter Korea was a Jesuit priest named Peter Grammont, who crossed the border from China illegally in 1785 and began preaching and baptizing converts. Ten years later a Chinese Catholic priest named Mun-mo Chu openly entered Korea and began proselytizing even though teaching a foreign religion in Korea at that time was illegal.

By 1863 there were more than a dozen French priests and twelve Korean priests and some 23,000 Christian converts in the country. Like their brethren in other parts of the world, the foreign missionaries had immediately set about trying to establish a political as well as a religious power base. The new Korean prince regent, Taewongun, blamed the foreign missionaries and their teachings for many of the problems afflicting the kingdom and began systematically persecuting the priests and their church members. Finally, in 1866, a series of pogroms against the priests and converts began. Nine of the French missionaries were seized, taken to the banks of the Han River on the outskirts of Seoul, and beheaded. Over the next three years an estimated eight thousand Christian converts throughout Korea were killed.

In 1882 the United States signed a diplomatic protocol with Korea in which the Choson court agreed to allow American diplomatic personnel, traders, and missionaries into the country. Despite the dangers, dozens of American missionary families, particularly Methodists and Presbyterians, quickly flocked into Seoul and other major Korean cities. The first Protestant missionary in Korea was Dr. Horace N. Allen, an American, who arrived in 1884.

These American missionaries were greatly influenced by the experiences other Christian missionaries had continuously had in China over a period of more than three centuries—all of whom eventually were in for a rude awakening. These early missionaries, fanatic in their belief that Christianity was the one and only true religion, soon discovered that educated Chinese had absolutely no interest in Christian theology, that they had numerous gods in their own pantheon and were not about to give them up in exchange for a foreign god created by a small group of people they had never heard of. For the most part the only Chinese converts the missionaries made were oppressed women and poor people who were interested primarily in the material benefits gained from cooperating with the foreigners.

This repudiation of Christianity by the Chinese caused the foreign missionaries laboring there to suffer untold spiritual and intellectual agonies. But a few of these foreign missionaries, who were more scholarly and acquainted themselves with the tenets of Buddhism and other Oriental religions, came to realize that all of the world's major religions have basically the same origin and the same message and that none of them have an exclusive right to the souls of the world's inhabitants. But it was not until the 1880s that the entire Christian missionary community in China accepted the idea that they could not wean people away from the Buddhist and Confucianist beliefs and practices that had been an integral part of their social, political, and economic ideology for more than two thousand years.

Because of the failures and frustrations reported by Western missionaries in China, those who went to Korea from the 1880s on were not as obsessed with getting Koreans to repudiate their entire culture and history in favor of an alien theology. They went more as educators in Western knowledge than as theological zealots. They also learned early that there were many similarities in Christianity and the traditional beliefs of the people and did not attempt to force them to totally abandon their culture. The foreign missionaries in Korea were also wiser in that from the beginning they put Koreans in charge of their programs, making them by, as well as for, Koreans. Their efforts were therefore much more successful and soon became self-sustaining.

These American missionaries set about establishing Korea's first schools and colleges for women and the first Western-style clinics and hospitals, using these institutions to introduce Koreans to a wide range of Western ideas and technology. The first missionary school (Paichai Haktang) was established in 1884 by an American missionary group from the North Methodist Church led by the Rev. Henry G. Appenzeller. The following year a Presbyterian group opened a boys' high school (*Kyungshin*). The first girls' school in Korea, *Ewha Haktang*, was established in 1886 by a Methodist group. (It is now Ewha University, the most prestigious girls' school in the country.)

American missionaries also founded Choson Christian College (in 1905), which later became Seoul's famous Yonsei University. The following year missionaries founded Sungshil College in Pyongyang. Protestant missionaries from the United States were the first to introduce the concepts of human rights and democracy into Korea. (Later historians were to suggest that Protestant missionaries were also more successful in Korea than Catholic missionaries because the earlier Catholics spoke French and prayed in Latin, while the later Protestants spoke English and prayed in Korean.)

Not surprisingly, the missionary-run schools attracted large numbers of Korea's most ambitious and intelligent men and women, commoners as well as members of the ruling *yangban* class, with the result that a significant percentage of those who subsequently became leaders in the modern professions, including politics, were Christian converts.

Former students of these missionary schools established an organization called the Independence Club, whose members spearheaded Korea's independence movement following the takeover by Japan in 1910. Shortly after Japan annexed Korea, Japanese authorities arrested six hundred members of this group, tortured them to obtain information about other members, beat many of them to death, and imprisoned the rest.

One of the members of this club who was arrested when the Japanese cracked down on its activities, Syngman Rhee, authored a seminal book called *The Spirit of Independence* and half a century later became the first president of the Republic of Korea in 1948. (Rhee's original Korean name was Sung Man

Yi. He anglicized it to make it easier for Westerners to pronounce and remember. Rhee was a member of the famous Yi clan, one of whose members, Song Gye Yi, founded the famous Choson dynasty in 1392.)

Unlike most other foreigners taking up residence in Korea, missionaries were expected to learn the language as one of their first orders of business since there was no way they could carry out their mission without being able to communicate fluently in the language. The benefits provided by learning Korean gave the missionaries tremendous advantages since it made it possible for them to interact directly with the people socially as well as professionally.

One of the most extraordinary accomplishments of the Protestant Church during these early years was a "Million Souls for Christ" campaign staged in 1905. The campaign was built around large Bible-study conferences that were attended by several hundred thousand people anxious to learn about this new way of looking at people and society.

Among the cultural contributions foreign missionary-scholars made to Korea (in 1939) was a standardized system for romanizing the Korean alphabet, making it possible for foreigners to study and learn the language without having to learn either *Hangul*, the simplified Korean script devised by a team of scholars in the fifteenth century, or the far more complicated and difficult Chinese ideograms that were still in common use in the late 1800s.

As champions of the rights of the people, American missionaries in Korea favored a democratic form of government as opposed to the authoritarian system of the Choson dynasty. When Japan toppled the Choson government and annexed Korea in 1910, the American missionaries quietly supported the efforts of the Koreans to regain their independence from Japan. Finally, in 1940, Japan expelled all foreign missionaries from Korea.

Five years later, when World War II ended with Japan's defeat, many of the same missionaries returned to the southern portion of the country, but not to the North. The Russians who entered the war against Japan only weeks before it ended were in charge of disarming Japan's occupation forces in the northern half of the country and refused to let foreign missionaries back in.

Postwar South Korea was to prove an even more fertile ground for Christian missionary activity. Foreign missionaries are now well entrenched in Korea, with a nationwide infrastructure that supports them and their efforts. Close to 25 percent of the people of South Korea are registered as Christians (some 80 percent of this number are affiliated with the Methodist and Presbyterian Churches).

The Catholic Church had its fastest growth period after 1962, when the Vatican gave permission for Catholic missionaries to conduct mass in Korean and authorized the publication of a joint Catholic-Protestant translation of the Bible. In 1984, Pope John Paul II went to Korea to preside over the canonization of ninety-three Korean and ten French missionary martyrs. This was not only the first time that the Catholic Church had held a canonization ceremony outside of the Vatican, but gave Korea the fourth-largest number of saints in the world.

The anti-Christian pogroms of the 1860s, ordered by the notorious prince regent Taewongun, were the first and last major episodes of violence against foreign missionaries in Korea. From that time on, Koreans have probably been more hospitable and receptive to foreign missionaries than any other Asian country.

Because of the strict policy of segregating men and women that still existed in Korea during the 1880s, Mary Fitch Scrantan, the first American missionary sent to Korea by the Women's Foreign Missionary Society of the Methodist Church, introduced the subterfuge of having male preachers concealed behind a curtain so their audience could not see them. Another strategy for getting around sexual segregation was building churches in the shape of an angle, so that men could sit in one wing and women in the other wing, while the pastor was positioned at the corner where the wings joined.

Spencer J. Palmer, a specialist in East Asia and cultural history, notes in his book *Korea and Christianity* that the phenomenal success of Christian missionaries in Korea between 1895 and 1910 was due primarily to an incredible number of tragic events that struck the country during this period, including invasions by the Chinese and Japanese, the murder of the queen by Japanese troops, and occupation of the country by Japan, which resulted in feelings of loss and shame that pervaded the people. Palmer says the people were caught up in a degree of despondency and decline that Buddhists refer to as *kali yuga* (kah-lee yuu-gah), which means "the last days," and that Christianity offered the only hope.

Protestant pastors taught that men and women were equal and that men should respect the rights of women and be loyal to their wives. When female church members complained about their husbands, the pastors warned the men that if they did not change their ways they would be expelled from the church. The Protestant Church thereafter became the primary catalyst for bringing about change in the age-old custom of sexual segregation in Korea.

The Protestant Church was aided in its crusade by a triweekly journal called the *Tongnip Sinmun* (Tohng-neep Sheen-muun), or "Independence Newspaper," which continuously proclaimed in straightforward language that men who treated women as inferior were uncivilized and primitive and that it was the height of ignorance to abandon and waste half of the population.

In some respects Christian missionaries have been more successful in Korea than in any other Asian country, and the spread of Christianity among Koreans has now become self-sustaining. The growth of the various Christian denominations no longer depends on the activities of foreign missionaries. Notes Martin H. Sours, Professor of International Asian Studies at the American Graduate School of International Management, "The role of pastor has a great deal of prestige and is attractive to many Korean men. As a result, Christian churches are growing on their own."

138

오기
Ogi
(Oh-ghee)

"The Stubborn Streak"

There are many contradictions in the traditional attitudes and behavior of Koreans—some of them relatively benign and others explosively destructive. These contradictions became a deeply entrenched part of the character of Koreans because they were conditioned for centuries to repress many of their most natural inclinations and needs and to accept beliefs and follow customs that were in conflict with their most basic emotions and genetic programming.

On the one hand, common Koreans were conditioned to be humble, passive, and obedient no matter what the circumstances. This programming helped make Koreans incredibly resilient and malleable in the face of both natural and man-made disasters. It also made them equally stubborn. This obstinate factor in the Korean character is expressed in the term *ogi* (oh-ghee), which means "an unyielding spirit," and has both a positive and a negative side.

One of the negative facets of *ogi* makes it virtually impossible for Koreans to admit that they personally made a mistake or that they failed because of their own inability or weaknesses. At the same time, being caught up in situations where their competency is called into question creates a compulsive need for revenge. This aspect of the Korean character is especially difficult for Westerners to accept and deal with, because Westerners regard admitting mistakes and weaknesses as an admirable sign of moral courage and, conversely, the act of concealing mistakes and weaknesses as dishonest and destructive.

Cross-cultural business and political relationships in Korea therefore require an extraordinary sensitivity to this side of the *ogi* factor in the Korean character and skillful diplomacy in dealing with it effectively. Of course, the positive side of *ogi* allowed Koreans to survive long centuries of oppressive rule and one war after another and, since the 1960s, to prosper to an extraordinary degree. Expatriate businesspeople who have spent decades in Korea say that the economic successes of the Koreans as well as their own successes were due in great measure to the positive side of the *ogi* character of Koreans. Their Korean counterparts and employees simply refused to give up regardless of the hardships and odds they faced.

One Korean commentator described the character of Koreans as being like that of weeds. No matter how many times they are stepped on, cut down, or pulled up, they always come back. Few foreigners have ever spent any significant amount of time in Korea without encountering their stubbornness, and all are eventually impressed with it—for good and bad.

When businesspeople, foreign or Korean, are faced with an impasse caused by the negative side of Korean *ogi*, about the only recourse they have is to persist politely and then persist some more. Korean businesspeople themselves often joke that the primary qualifications needed to succeed in business in Korea are an iron stomach (the ability to drink a lot of alcohol and survive) and an iron butt (the ability to sit in meetings for hours without rigor mortis setting in) and simply to be more *ogi* than the other party.

Koreans have traditionally taken pride in their stubbornness because it was often the only asset they had in dealing with foreign invaders. One of the greatest demonstrations of *ogi* the world has ever seen is the one staged by North Korea at Panmunjom in the demilitarized zone established between North and South Korea at the end the Korean War in 1953. More than fifty years later, Communist-indoctrinated North Korean political and military leaders were still resisting the idea of reunifying the country.

On a personal basis, it should be kept in mind that the positive attributes of the *ogi* syndrome in Korean character generally apply only to in-group members and situations—to family members, employers, schools, etc., with whom they have ties that cannot be dismissed. Koreans feel no special obligation to persevere in unsatisfactory relationships with people outside this inner circle.

Another, more contemporary, term for the stubbornness that is especially associated with Koreans is *kojip* (koh-jeep).

139

어머니

Omoni
(Oh-moh-nee)

"Mothers as Saints"

Many Koreans regard *omoni* (oh-moh-nee), or "mother," as the second most important "cultural code word" in the Korean vocabulary, a ranking that is based on all of the obvious reasons as well as a number of reasons related specifically to the Confucian concept of a well-organized and well-ordered society. (Most Koreans put *aboji*/ah-boh-jee, or "father," first on the list of the most important culturally relevant words in the Korean language.)*

It is the Confucian factor in Korean society that is most important in the traditional image and role of Korean *omoni*. The Confucian ideology adopted by the

---

*Other key "cultural code words" almost always ranked in the top ten include *adul* (ah-duhl), which means "son"; *kongbu* (kohng-buu), meaning "study"; *uiri* (wee-ree), or "obligation"; and, in more recent times, *ton* (tohn), "money."

Choson dynasty during the last decade of the fourteenth century called for a total separation of the activities and obligations of males and females. Girls and women were strictly limited to household (and farming) chores (including weaving cloth and making wearing apparel), giving birth to children—preferably sons—and child raising. In urban areas this separation was so complete that females were confined to their homes and walled-in yards during the day, further limiting their participation in the social and public life of the country.

Until marriage and motherhood the 90 percent of young Korean girls who were not in the upper class were essentially servants and often slaves. Their situation typically became worse when they were married—by arrangement—and went to live with their in-laws. It was not until they had given birth to at least one son that they began to achieve any position of privilege or rights within their husbands' families, and the extent of these privileges was controlled tightly by their husbands and in-laws, particularly their *shiomoni* (she-oh-moh-nee), or "mothers-in-law." Korean mothers-in-law were traditionally strict taskmasters throughout their lives, and it was only with their death that their daughters-in-law were free for the first time from the supervision and demands of other women to whom they owed absolute subordination and obedience. Officially at least, females never escaped domination by males—first by their fathers, then by their husbands and fathers-in-law, and finally by their adult sons.

In actuality, however, Korean women often exercised considerable power behind the scenes. The discipline and frequent abuse they were subjected to generally made them mentally tough, and while they normally conformed to the sanctified rules of Confucian etiquette when in public and in the presence of males, when they were in their own *anbang* (ahn-bahng), or "inner room," domains, they could be and often were closet queens. This was particularly true because the traditional upbringing of boys did not teach them how to develop skills in interacting with females, often leaving men at a disadvantage when faced with the wiles of a determined wife and mother.

Despite their superior social position, Korean men were dependent on women not only for male children who were necessary for the continuation of the family line as well as conducting the rituals of ancestor worship, which was the responsibility of the oldest sons, but for running their households and keeping the family fed and clothed—a position that brought with it considerable power that women could use for positive or negative purposes, depending on their relationships with their husbands.

Because Korean men generally segregated themselves from their wives and children, the paramount influence on children naturally came from their *omoni*. This system resulted in Korean children being strongly attached to their mothers throughout their lives, with far fewer and weaker ties with their fathers. In fact, oldest sons often became estranged from their fathers because of the lasting control exercised over them.

The relationship between Korean mothers and fathers, and between fathers and their children, has changed dramatically since the mid-1900s, particularly among the generations born after 1960. The sexes are no longer segregated. Mothers are treated more as equal partners. Most fathers interact with their young children as often as possible. But there is still a father's world and a mother's world in present-day Korea, and sociologists say that Korea is slowly taking on the characteristics of a matriarchy, with mother and "mother's house" playing a central role in the thinking of both males and females.

The artificial ranking and roles forced onto the Korean people by Confucianism for more than half a millennium have left their mark, but it seems that the pendulum is now finally moving in the direction of mothers and women in general, gradually reversing a fundamental social ideology that has probably prevailed throughout most of Asia since the dawn of the human race.

140

엄살
Omsal
(Ohm-sahl)

"Gaining Sympathy"

The original Chinese name for Korea was *Choson* (Choh-suun), which is translated poetically as "Land of Morning Calm." Another old Chinese name for Korea might be translated as something like "Land of the People of the East Who Are Paragons of Politeness." Despite the calm demeanor and politeness that have long been associated with Koreans, however, they (along with their Asian cousins) are, in fact, an exceptionally emotional people who are prone to extremes of behavior when something happens to upset their harmonious equilibrium.

There is nothing mysterious about this contrast in Korean behavior. The politeness and harmony for which Koreans were traditionally famous were the result of strict behavioral conditioning that forced them to repress their natural impulses. This cultural conditioning did not totally eliminate their natural impulses, however, and on fairly regular and predictable occasions their control would snap and they would literally throw tantrums. When sorely provoked over a period of time, they would also resort to extreme violence.

The Korean propensity for emotional tantrums has diminished in recent decades because of fundamental lifestyle changes. The young are no longer conditioned to control their speech or their behavior to anywhere near the degree that was characteristic of Korean society until the 1970s. But the syndrome remains a constant factor in Korean life.

Koreans are still not free to give full rein to their natural impulses and must maintain a conspicuous degree of harmony in all of their interpersonal relationships—harmony that is based on a calculated level of polite speech and behavior designed to avoid hurting anyone's feelings. The existence of this syndrome in Korean culture contributed to the appearance of another common cultural habit, that of grossly exaggerating situations to gain sympathy. This institutionalized practice is called *omsal* (ohm-sahl), meaning "gaining sympathy."

Of course, it is normal for people to employ stronger-than-usual emotional appeals when they are trying to get sympathy. What makes the Korean way of going about *omsal* unusual is how far people go in their efforts. People engaging in *omsal* use many of the histrionics employed by actors in great dramatic roles, crying and carrying on with extraordinary intensity. Women in particular are noted for the vehemence of their *omsal*, especially when directed toward men whom they believe have wronged them. Foreign men who get emotionally involved with Korean women and are subjected to *omsal* performances often find that they cannot cope with them because they have had no experience in dealing with such raw and uninhibited emotions.

All Koreans are programmed to use *omsal* in manipulating their personal as well as their public or professional relationships. It is part of the skills all employees, executives, politicians, and professionals bring to any relationship.

Foreign businesspeople who are new to Korea or have had only limited experience in dealing with the emotional side of the Korean character are particularly susceptible to being manipulated by clever *omsal* tactics. This is often especially true for top foreign executives who come to Korea for brief high-level meetings and cannot see beyond the red carpet that their Korean hosts lay out for them. Just being familiar with the *omsal* syndrome is not always sufficient for Westerners to defend themselves because most have not had enough experience in dealing with fiercely expressed emotions. As a result, many are so intimidated by the threat of an emotional outburst that they lower their standards and expectations.

141

온돌

Ondol

(Ohn-dohl)

"Hot Times on the Floor"

Like most other Asians, Koreans traditionally lived on the floors of their homes—sitting on floor cushions to rest, eat, and do various kinds of work, and sleeping on floor mats. A long time ago, someone in the northern area of Korea, where it gets frigidly cold in winter, picked up on the old Chinese idea of using the heat from cooking fires to make life considerably more comfortable during the cold season.

This heating system, known as *ondol* (ohn-dohl) in Korean, consisted of funneling the heat from fireplaces into a series of flues or channels beneath the floor. Building on the Chinese concept, early Koreans first dug channels in the ground floor, covered them with thick slabs of granite, then spread a layer of clay over the stones. (In later centuries the clay was then covered by heavy sheets of oiled paper.) The hot smoke and heat from the fireplaces were funneled into the flues, heating the granite slabs and the clay covering. The stones and clay held the heat for several hours after the fires burned out.

The *ondol* was one of the world's first and most efficient central heating systems, not only because heat rises but also because Koreans literally lived on top of their built-in floor radiators. Both the original style of *ondol* and modernized systems are still in use in Korea today. (In earlier times, rice and barley straw as well as wood were burned in the fireplaces.) Korean sleeping mattresses are made thin so as not to block the heat rising from the floor, while quilts or comforters that go on top are generally quite thick to hold the heat in.

In modern homes, apartments, and office buildings in Korea, metal pipes installed under the floors carry heated water instead of the exhaust from fires. On the average, however, Korean homes and workplaces are not kept as warm in winter as Westerners generally like, not only as an economic measure but also because enduring cold weather without complaining has traditionally been a sign of strength of character. In addition to their custom of enduring cold temperatures, however, Koreans also traditionally wore padded clothing indoors as well as outdoors during the coldest months.

Modern technology has not yet improved on the ancient *ondol* concept of heating the floors in homes and buildings instead of heating the inside air, which is inefficient and wasteful. Foreigners who have occasion to visit some luxurious Korean homes and plush apartments in winter are often surprised—and delighted—to find the floors deliciously warm.

142

오렌지족

Orange Jok
(Orange Joak)

"Playboys and Playgirls"

The physical facade of Korea today is so different from Korea prior to the 1970s that it is like two different countries. The attitudes and behavior of the post-1970 generations of Koreans have also changed, in many instances to the point that they could be called a new kind of Korean. No longer programmed in Confucianism from childhood on, no longer separated by gender at an early age, no longer conditioned in rote behavior that homogenized them to a remarkable degree, and no longer punished for being different, these new-generation Koreans include many who behave very much like young people in other advanced countries around the world, wearing the same kinds of clothes and accessories, listening to the same kinds of music, eating the same kinds of food, and enjoying the same pastimes.

This internationalization of culture is, of course, nothing new, but some of its ramifications in Korea are so different from the still very near past that they attract extraordinary attention. As recent as the latter years of the 1950s most Koreans had to work incredibly hard, long hours to survive. Young, single men and women did not socialize with each other in public or date. Only a small percentage of the people of any age had sufficient income that some of it could be used for entertainment, impulse buying, or merely to show off. Among the most envied people in the country at that time were American military and civilian personnel stationed at the various camps. Their salaries and access to American-run post exchanges made them rich by Korean standards.

In the early 1970s the "good life" of plentiful food, stylish clothing, electronic gadgets, and the other appurtenances of affluence were still a dream for most Koreans. But by the end of the 1980s all of that had changed. For the first time in the history of the country, ordinary people were able to indulge themselves in a surfeit of material things. This affluence gave birth to a group of young people who came to be known as *orange jok* (orange joak), which translates as "orange group"—or "orange tribe" to give it more of the flavor it deserves.

The connotation of "orange" in this label depends to some extent on individual interpretations. The general consensus, however, is that the color orange is associated with both freshness and foreign things that are expensive, and the image therefore has an exotic appeal to those seeking to express themselves in nontraditional ways.

Members of the *orange jok* are young people from especially affluent families who are notorious for driving expensive foreign cars, wearing expensive imported fashions, and spending large amounts of money in restaurants and nightclubs and on travel and other things. Critics of the "orange tribe" say they are so spoiled that they do not take life seriously. They also say that many of them are from newly rich families and are poorly educated—comments intended to explain the un-Korean behavior of these maverick playboys and playgirls.

For Koreans whose memories go back beyond the 1970s the appearance of a distinctive group of people devoted to extravagance and life in the fast lane is both embarrassing and disturbing, a blot on their image of themselves as a serious-minded and diligent people who do not trivialize the challenges of life. Obviously a generational thing, the negative image of the *orange jok* will no doubt fade with the passing of time.

어리광 응석
Origwan-Unsok
(Oh-ree-gwahn-Uun-sohk)

"Selfless Love and Indulgence"

If Confucius can be forgiven for accepting and promoting the idea that sex, age, wisdom, and fortuitous birth—especially the latter—give some people the divine right to rule over others, his other contributions to the welfare and happiness of mankind would have been much more popular. His insight into the benefits of listening to good music, for example, should have been enough to earn him sainthood in any society. He preached not only that good music calms and civilizes the id but also that it contributes enormously to social harmony in general.

Confucius's primary goal was to achieve a total breakthrough in civilizing mankind. But before that challenge could even be addressed there had to be order and stability in society, and he chose to work through the existing political system because there was, in fact, no other practical choice.

The foundation for the kind of society that Confucius envisioned is summed up in the phrase *origwan-unsok* (oh-ree-gwahn-uun-soak), which can be translated as "selfless love and indulgence" (*amae* in Japanese). In simple terms, Confucius presumed that if all the attitudes and behavior of people were based on absolute selfless love and indulgence, there would be no disharmony among people and no need for strong, strict governments to enforce sanctions against evildoers.

The concept of *origwan-unsok* came to Korea with Confucianism, first from around the fourth century A.D. and then in an all-encompassing political, social, and cultural program launched by the new Choson dynasty in 1392, which adopted a new, strict form of Confucianism as the national ideology. But as in China, the concept of selfless love and indulgence took second place to a highly stratified social system and very strict protocols controlling all behavior and interpersonal relationships. In other words, Korean leaders, like their Chinese role models, gave eliminating disharmony through behavioral conditioning precedence over first trying to instruct the people in *origwan-unsok* and then depending on their own good nature to ensure order and stability.

As the generations passed, however, the philosophy of selfless love and indulgence gradually permeated Korean culture. The ruling class publicly paid homage to it, but in practice they regarded it as something that was appropriate only for common people and as a general rule continued loving and indulging only themselves. The first Westerners to spend time in Korea and talk or write about their experiences spoke glowingly of the unselfish nature and open-heartedness of ordinary Koreans. According to these foreign visitors, the poorer the people the more likely they were to be devout practitioners of *origwan-unsok*.

Origwan-unsok was traditionally the most conspicuous in Korea in child raising. Parents were almost endlessly tolerant of the behavior of young children until they reached the age of four or five, at which time they began to condition them in the highly stylized etiquette that was the hallmark of Korean behavior. Young boys were especially indulged, smothered with affection, and given priority over female children. This, according to contemporary sociologists, resulted in their growing up to be especially willful in their relationships with their families and sexist toward women.

In present-day Korea *origwan-unsok* is still held up as the ideal social ideology, and Koreans, especially affluent Koreans, often proudly bring it up as one of the superior facets of their culture. In fact it appears that the philosophy *is* gradually gaining credence among the very class that ignored it for so many centuries. And just as the first Western visitors in Korea were impressed with the innate selfless and indulgent nature of most Koreans, it is the same cultural character that subtly attracts contemporary foreigners to Korea and often results in their becoming longtime or permanent residents.

144

파

P'a
(Ppah)

"The Faction Syndrome"

One of the most conspicuous and influential characteristics of Koreans is a culturally imbued need to identify with and work within exclusive *p'a* (ppah), or "factions," to protect themselves, to contribute to a cause, and to achieve personal goals. This impulse is so strong and pervasive that it impacts on almost every aspect of life in the country and is especially significant in politics and commercial organizations.

The propensity for company employees, bureaucrats, and politicians to form *p'a* is a result of a number of primary social factors, some of which go back to ancient times. The most important of these elements was no doubt the clan system, which survived into modern times, and the Confucian emphasis on the people being divided into precise hierarchical units based on social class, family, sex, age, education, and occupation.

This social system did not permit personal independence or individual action. Everyone belonged to a finite number of groups of people and to specific categories within those groups, which together created and controlled their attitudes and behavior. No one who was a member of society in good standing could act on his or her own. Everything had to conform to the customs and laws detailing the rights and obligations of individuals in each group based on sex, age, seniority, and so on.

In virtually every group made up of more than five or six people, factions would coalesce around a strong or charismatic individual or on the basis of blood ties, class, age, birthplace, school ties, and common goals. During the long Choson dynasty (1392–1910) there were dozens of factions within the royal court. There were also numerous factions, large and small, within the elite circle of scholar-officials, and among the professional scholars who were outside government. In fact throughout Korean history, the successive governments have been dominated by factions made up of members from specific clans.

In present-day Korea there is substantially more leeway in personal attitudes and behavior than what was allowed in earlier years, but there are factions in every organization of any size in the country, commercial and political. In the political arena, especially, it is often necessary to be aware of and know how to deal effectively with these factions to get anything done. The influence of factions in commercial enterprises is generally subtler, but it is there, and knowing about the factions, especially their agendas and leaders, can be of vital importance.

Political factions and their leaders are well known to the public. Their strengths, successes, and failures are constantly being monitored by the press and by their opponents, so there is no problem in identifying them and determining the role they play in the day-to-day affairs of the government. However, *p'a* in business enterprises and in semi-independent government-sponsored organizations are usually invisible to outsiders and generally can be identified only by employees or people with inside knowledge.

Factions in larger Korean companies include blood relatives, alumni of the same schools, people who joined the company the same year, people who come from the same part of the country, and exceptionally talented, strong, ambitious individuals who attract groups of followers.

Naturally, foreign businesspeople approaching Korea for the first time should attempt to identify and qualify any factions that might concern them—something that should be done with as much finesse as possible. Bankers, consultants, customers, and suppliers are usually the best sources for information about *p'a* in Korean companies.

145

바둑

Paduk
(Pah-duke)

"A Learning Game"

Surviving and functioning effectively in Korean society has been a complicated and demanding process since the people first entered the pages of history. From the earliest times there was a precise etiquette for every facet of behavior and numerous lengthy rituals for the conduct of religious, social, and political affairs that required years to learn and constant reinforcing to master. This environment also gave rise to recreational and competitive activities that were equally demanding, including the game *paduk* (pah-duke), which originated in China.

Paduk, known as *wei-chi* (way-chee) in Chinese and as *go* (goh) in Japanese and English, is a game played with smooth black and white stones that are placed on intersecting lines inscribed on a square board. The rules of the game are simple—so simple, in fact, that at first the game appears to be similar to checkers. The game begins with the board clear. Players take turns placing one stone at a time on any of the dozens of intersections on the board. Once a stone has been placed it cannot be moved except when a opponent "captures" it and removes it from the board. When a group of stones becomes hemmed in by the stones of an opponent and does not have "two eyes"—separate enclosures of one or more intersections—it is considered "dead" within a territory. Whoever surrounds the most territory wins the game.

Paduk also reminds some people of chess, in which the pieces are arrayed in precise formation against the opponent and advance across the board to capture or trap the opponent's chess pieces. In *paduk*, however, there is no "front line." Players can set their stones down on any open intersection, giving them dozens of choices that eventually impact the outcome of the game. Another way that *paduk* differs from chess is that the stones are all of equal value. This eliminates the possibility of winning a game by blocking the movement of the opponent. There are always intersections on the board where stones can be placed.

The ultimate goal of *paduk* masters is not to quickly capture territory and end the game. It is to demonstrate superior strategic thinking and gradually crush the will of the opponent. The fewer stones used in the process of gaining control over territory all over the board, the more superiority is demonstrated. The dozens of choices in placing stones and how each stone relates to the stones of the opponent make the game far more complicated than it appears. Skilled players must be able to think the way a computer behaves, considering numerous possibilities well beyond each of their moves and the moves of their opponents.

Early Koreans attributed cosmic ramifications to *paduk*, believing that winning or losing would have a significant influence on their day-to-day activities and lives in general. It was considered a test of character and spirit as well as intellect and was ordinarily treated with the utmost seriousness. At the same time, skilled players were able to use their moves as a way of expressing humor. The game was often used by opponents in real-life situations as a way of expressing their opposition and, when possible, their intellectual superiority.

One of Korea's best-known amateur *paduk* players, businessman-diplomat-poet-philosopher Sung Pum Lee, has compared *paduk* to Zen, to higher mathematics, and to the creative process in which the inner mind is set free and the player is guided by cosmic intuition.

It is said that virtually anyone can learn how to play *paduk* at an enjoyable level after a short period of practice but that it takes years for a person who is not divinely gifted to become a true master of the game. The Korean equivalent of chess, *changgi* (chahng-ghee), is favored by "ordinary" people—meaning those not considered intellectuals.

Not surprisingly, Koreans see *paduk* as a Korean thing that is beyond the ken of foreigners. My editor, Martin H. Sours, recalls being told by a good Korean friend that there was no way he could learn *paduk* because he was not Korean. "My friend was not putting me down or anything like that," Sours said. "He was protecting my *kibun*—my feelings—he didn't want me to fail in my attempts to understand. But at the same time he was telling me that I should not expect him to explain *paduk* to me because I was a foreigner. Koreans, as well as Chinese and Japanese, typically have this elitist attitude toward the essence of their cultures."

146

백일

Paik Il
(Pake Eel)

"The Hundredth Day Party"

In pre-modern Korea infant mortality was high because of a variety of diseases and other health problems that did not respond to herbal medicines. Newborn babies were treated with extra care in an effort to preserve their lives. This generally included prohibiting visits by outsiders for the first twenty-one days of the baby's life and not formally recognizing the new family member until it was fairly certain that the child was going to survive.

A long time ago it also became customary for families to wait until the hundredth day to officially celebrate the birth of a new child with a *Paek Il* (Pake Eel), or "Hundredth Day Party"—making this one of the most auspicious social events in Korean life. Relatives and close friends were invited to participate in the happy event. *Paek Il* parties are still the custom in Korea and continue to be one of the more important social events that take place regularly throughout the year. Many families, in fact, stage three *Paek Il*—one for the father's family, one for the mother's family, and another one for the father's school friends and work colleagues. (*Paek* is also written and pronounced with a "b" sound—*baek*/bake.)

Paek Il are marked by feasts that include a variety of special foods. Guests are expected to bring gifts. Families generally take platters of rice cakes and other specialties to their closer neighbors, who respond by bringing gifts for the infants. Hundredth Day Parties are always occasions for taking numerous photographs that go into family albums. (In earlier times it was customary to take frontal pictures of baby boys in the nude as a public record of their maleness.)

The second milestone in the life of a new baby is its first birthday. The first-year birthday party, or *dol* (dohl), represents the official "coming out" of the newest addition to Korean families. Families go all out to provide popular festive foods and make sure guests enjoy themselves. Children are usually dressed in traditional Korean attire (called *Hanbok*, which means "Korean clothing") for this celebration. Their mothers, grandmothers, and sometimes other family members and relatives may also dress in *Hanbok*.

A special "floor table," piled high with traditional festive foods in colorful dishes, is set up for the child and the mother (who feeds the child and makes sure it doesn't knock things off the table). One of the key events of *dol* parties is to place money, a pen, a piece of thread, and a book on a table in front of the birthday child to see which one it will pick up first. According to old beliefs, what the child picks up first is an omen of its future. The money relates to wealth, the pen to writing, the book to scholarship, and the thread to a long life. Not surprisingly, most parents hope their child will go for the money.

Relatives and friends who are invited to *dol* parties are expected to bring gifts. Among the most prized and most common gifts are gold rings (which in the past were an important hedge against a variety of disasters), clothing, and toys.

On the hundredth day after a child's first birthday celebration it is customary for familes to make offerings of rice and seaweed soup to *Samshin Halmoni* (Sahm-sheen Hahl-mohn-ee), the "Grandmother Spirit," in recognition of the role that grandmothers have traditionally played in child raising in Korea. The family, relatives, and friends then celebrate by eating traditional good-luck foods such as red bean cakes and steamed rice cakes. On this occasion male children are dressed in modernized traditional clothing and headgear that indicates they are unmarried. Female children wear traditional clothing and cosmetics.

147

비평

Pipyong
(Peep-yohng)
"The Pitfalls of Criticism"

In pre-modern Korea, *pipyong* (peep-yohng, also pronounced beep-yohng), or "criticism," was a one-way affair. Superiors were privileged and obligated to criticize their immediate subordinates and inferiors in general, but it was strictly taboo for inferiors to criticize those who outranked them. This meant that the lower class was permanently enjoined from publicly criticizing the elite upper class. All females were regarded as inherently inferior to men. It was therefore considered a serious breach of Confucian morality for women to criticize men. Any woman who did so put herself in peril.

The higher the rank of superiors, the more immune they were to criticism— a principle that invariably resulted in superiors assuming an infallibility that made ineptitude, inefficiency, and corruption commonplace and was a major contributing factor in perpetuating the Confucian-oriented social system. Severe political and social injunctions against *pipyong*, combined with ancestor worship and its emphasis on looking back instead of forward, made social and economic progress in pre-modern Korea virtually impossible.

When people or organizations were criticized outside the approved cultural context, they were compelled to take some kind of action to eliminate the stain on their reputations. Interestingly, until recent times it was especially taboo to criticize famous artists and writers—the point being that if they were criticized they might become discouraged and stop trying to achieve perfection in their work.

Pipyong is no longer "officially" taboo in Korea, but it still contains a very real element of danger that entails personal as well as professional risk when those of lower rank criticize people above them. Public criticism of individuals, groups of people, or organizations still results in revenge seeking of one kind or another. Foreigners in Korea are repeatedly advised by professional consultants as well as close Korean friends to refrain from publicly criticizing anything or anybody and thereby avoid any possibility of damaging their relationships.

It is especially important for foreigners to keep in mind that Koreans, unlike Americans and other Western nationalities, do not like their *chalmot* (chahl-moat), or "faults, mistakes, and errors," to be pointed out to them. They also tend to take any kind of criticism about Korea, its people, or its institutions as a personal affront and thereafter to bear a grudge against those who voiced the criticism.

In contrast to the taboos against inferiors criticizing superiors—and outsiders criticizing Korea—the vehemence with which managers and executives in Korean corporations publicly criticize subordinates who make mistakes or fail to meet performance expectations can be shocking to outsiders who have never witnessed, and do not expect, such behavior from Koreans.

Some companies hold weekly meetings at which the sole purpose often seems to be for senior executives and managers present to harangue the group, and particular individuals, for perceived failings. The purpose of these sessions is to publicly humiliate and shame the employees as a way of motivating them to increase their efforts and diligence, which is standard Confucian psychology.* (See *Puseo Jang Hoe*.)

This approach is not recommended for foreign managers in Korea, however. In the Korean context of things, foreign managers are not entitled to treat employees the same way that Korean managers do. Not being Korean, foreigners do not have the pecking-order rights of Koreans, and any attempt to assume

---

*There is another facet to this technique and psychology that is characteristic of authoritarian societies and was epitomized during the so-called "Cultural Revolution" that devastated China from 1966 until 1976. Millions of people who were suspected of having been "tainted" by Western ideas were seized by Red Guard students, publicly humiliated, tortured until they confessed to having "anti-Mao thoughts," then deprived of their jobs and imprisoned or killed. Thousands were executed in public—often by being beaten to death—as a way of intimidating the population.

these rights is met with serious resistance. Foreigners are expected to do their criticizing of Korean employees in private. Part of this rationale derives from the fact that foreigners are viewed as outsiders in a racial, cultural, and social sense and therefore do not have the right to behave like Koreans. Another part of it comes from the fact that Koreans do not like to be shamed in public under any circumstances, and while they have to take it from their Korean superiors they refuse to take it from foreigners.

보호주의
Pohojuui
(Poh-hoh-juu-wee)
"Protectionism Korean Style"

Throughout most of Korea's early history it survived as a nation by playing the role of vassal to China, protecting itself primarily by paying tribute and allowing the Chinese to dictate most of its foreign policy, a system that forced Koreans to suppress their anger and remain polite to the Chinese. In 1945, as the victor in World War II, the United States became Korea's new suzerain.

Despite subsequent efforts by the United States to protect the sovereignty of Korea, and the contributions it made to the transformation of Korea into an advanced industrial nation, many younger Koreans, particularly university students, tend to view the United States as an economic tyrant that attempts to impose its will unfairly on the other countries of the world—a modern-day Western version of ancient China.

The position of these anti–United States dissidents brings to mind Rudyard Kipling's famous dictum "The East is East and the West is West, and never the twain shall meet." While Kipling's comment on the differences separating the East and the West is outdated in some respects, in others it is just as valid today as it was in the nineteenth century. The Korean concept of *pohojuui* (poh-hoh-juu-wee), or "protectionism," and its application to Korea's trade and other foreign relations, particularly those involving the United States, is one of the areas where the East and West are still divided.

Americans and other Westerners base their concept of trade relations on equal rights and reciprocity. Fairness, which includes some allowance for mitigating circumstances, is also a normal part of the Western mind-set. But generally speaking, the Western concept of fairness in trade relations is exclusive. It is not viewed as a golf game in which the inexperienced player gets a handicap to make the players more evenly matched. Koreans, on the other hand, take the position that it is only natural for them to protect their manufacturers and their market from foreign competition because Korea is a small country with few natural resources and should not be expected to compete on equal terms with anyone.

In its Korean context, *pohojuui* is more of a moral than an economic issue, with the morality concerned naturally being Korean morality. In the Korean mind-set, morality is multidimensional and holistic and is based on circumstances rather than absolute principles. Their reasoning is that it makes no sense at all for the Korean market to be compared with the American market. This position results in Westerners saying that Korea's trade policy is unfair and therefore immoral and Koreans saying that it is Western trade policies that are unfair and therefore immoral, creating a Kiplingish impasse.

Another facet of the moral judgment Koreans make in their foreign trade relations is that they have suffered so much, sacrificed so much, and worked so hard to achieve the success they now enjoy that the United States in particular should take this into consideration in its Korean trade policies.

The only solution to this impasse, with its nationalistic as well as moralistic elements, is for Korean companies to continue the process of integrating their operations with foreign companies—in technological transfers, manufacturing, and marketing—to the point that Koreans have full faith that they are equal partners in a vast array of international enterprises and can develop the confidence to open up their country economically as well as socially.

In the meantime, the United States government and American businesspeople need to be sensitive to the moral aspects of their trade relations with Korea and develop strategies for incorporating a moral dimension into their presentations and actions—an approach that would benefit both sides. Until these steps are taken, Korea's *pohojuui* will continue to be a major obstacle for all concerned.

149

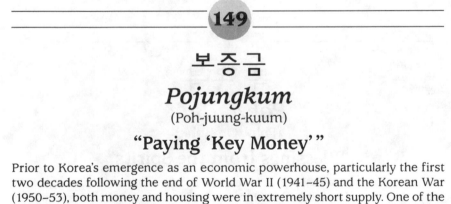

보증금
Pojungkum
(Poh-juung-kuum)
"Paying 'Key Money'"

Prior to Korea's emergence as an economic powerhouse, particularly the first two decades following the end of World War II (1941–45) and the Korean War (1950–53), both money and housing were in extremely short supply. One of the most important methods construction companies and would-be landlords used to raise money for building new homes and apartments was to require future tenants to make large *pojungkum* (poh-juung-kuum), or "key-money" deposits, before construction began. This method of "renting" homes and buildings is known as *chonse* (chohn-say).

Some builders and landlords, especially those catering to large companies and foreign residents (who were rich by Korean standards at that time), also required that rent be paid in advance, sometimes for as many as five years. The key money was fully refundable at the end of the lease contract, but in the meantime the builder could loan the money out for as much as 35 percent interest per year and have an immediate cash flow that sometimes exceeded what the annual rental or lease fees would amount to when the construction was completed.

Many of those whose needs were critical were willing to pay extra to speed up the process, giving rise to a nonrefundable type of key money that was called *kollykum* (kohl-lee-kuum).

The postwar conditions that led to up-front key money and the payment of rent a year or more in advance have long since disappeared, but the *pojungkum* system has not. Key money and the advance payment of rent are now the norm in Korea, making it difficult for the average family to build or rent new quarters.

There are now two rental systems in effect in Korea—one referred to as *junse* (june-say), or *chonse* (chohn-say), and the other called *wolse* (wohl-say). In the *junse* system the renter deposits approximately half of the value of the house or apartment, with the interest accruing on the deposit going to the landlord. Under the *wolse* system the renter makes a smaller, negotiable deposit, with the interest going to the owner, and pays a monthly rental fee. The larger the deposit, the lower the monthly payments. This system is the most common in the case of office rentals.

Housing and office space in Korea is measured in units called *pyong* (p'yohng), which is approximately six square feet or .54 square meter. In advertising the size of their rental offices, apartments, or homes some landlords include hallways, small outside balconies, and other nonlivable areas in their overall *pyong* numbers, so it is important to be aware of this and make detailed inquiries.

150

복 오복
Pok/O-Bok
(Pohk/Oh-Bohk)

"Blessings from the Spirits"

It seems to be a universal principle that the less freedom people have and the more they are subjected to the whims and idiosyncrasies of rulers who have absolute power, the more likely they are to depend on supernatural phenomena to provide them with solace and protection. Gods and spirits may not be the progeny of religious and political despots, but they thrive best in autocratic societies in which ordinary people have few if any rights and are obligated to serve the elite ruling class.

The kings and *yangban* (yahng-bahn) ruling class of pre-modern Korea were not especially harsh by world standards, but until the modern era—which in a real sense did not begin until the end of the Korean War in the 1950s—common people had few human rights and society in general was authoritarian, male dominated, and feudalistic to the core.

There had been benevolent rulers and *yangban* in earlier times in Korea, but their benevolence was the kind that one extends to a valued servant or slave—not the kind that includes freedom of thought or any semblance of independent behavior. In this environment the supernatural world played a key role in the lives of the common Koreans. They depended entirely on gods and spirits for *pok* (pohk), or "blessings," that would protect them from the ravages of nature as well as misuse and abuse by their overlords.

There was peace and stability in Korea except on rare occasions when these abuses became untenable and rebellions erupted. But this peace and stability was achieved only because the system required the people to subordinate themselves totally to their superiors and obey them without question or delay. Thus the only "good" that common Koreans could expect in their lives were *pok* from the spirits. They were therefore meticulous in praying and performing the rituals prescribed for the guardian spirits and gods that exercised domain over their homes, villages, larger communities, nearby mountains, and the afterlife.

Early Koreans were not bashful about what they wanted out of life. They created a list that came to be known as *O-Bok* (Oh-Bohk), or "The Five Blessings." These blessings were wealth, high status, a long healthy life, abundant offspring, and a painless and natural death. Needless to say, until recent times only a tiny percentage of the Korean population ever had any chance of achieving more than one or two of these goals because their social class and the quality of their lives were fixed at birth at little more than a survival level.

When it became apparent in the 1970s that many Koreans were going to be able to achieve most if not all of the traditional *O-Bok*, it resulted in a great deal of public dialogue and debate, with some people making the point that if everyone got what they wanted it might turn out to be a disaster rather than a blessing. The major point of the dialogue was that the desire of the poor to become wealthy, a prerequisite for most of the other blessings, could lead to a breakdown in morality that could result in the country becoming a quagmire of avarice, corruption, and depravity. Another point was that if families had as many children as they wanted and everyone lived to an advanced age the social and economic impact could be devastating.

A number of the more thoughtful commentators on *O-Bok* held that Korean mentality as a whole would have to be transformed before there could be positive progress toward a society in which the Five Blessings reigned. Among their observations was that Koreans would have to give up their traditional Confucian-driven compulsion to have many children, along with their obsession with male supremacy, male descent, and the second-class status of females.

What these people were saying in essence was that Koreans would have to give up the Confucian ideas on which their society and culture had been based for more than two thousand years and start over with a much more pragmatic approach to life. Despite the fact that Koreans have historically been known as the most Confucian of all the people in the Confucian sphere of Asia, that is exactly what the majority of them having been doing since the 1980s.

Most present-day Koreans no longer have to depend on spirits for all of their blessings. They now have enough freedom and affluence that they can help themselves to many of the intellectual, emotional, and material "blessings" of a prosperous industrialized society. But the superior-inferior nature of Korean society has basically remained the same. People are still ranked vertically according to their social class, sex, position, and age. The modern-day *pok* they receive varies with their relative positions within their families and within their work units.

The transformation of Korea from a totally Confucian society dependent on spiritual blessings to one based on practical efforts has been deeper and more dramatic than similar changes taking place in China and Japan. Individual Koreans have more self-confidence than the Japanese and they are more open and outgoing than the Chinese. They are also more at ease with the principles of individualism and democracy than the Japanese, and less given to intrigue than the Chinese.

One of the most dramatic and far-reaching examples of the willingness of Koreans to change began in the 1960s. Leading Korean companies began hiring people with foreign language ability and business experience or training abroad and putting them in responsible managerial positions. In contrast to this, with rare exceptions Japan's leading corporations refused to employ people with foreign experience. When their own employees came back from overseas assignments, their foreign experience was deliberately ignored. Many companies treated returned employees as outcasts. It was not until the early 1980s that senior Japanese executives of large firms began to overcome this insular, ethnocentric prejudice and both hire small numbers of foreigners and give their own veteran employees returning from overseas responsible positions.

Koreans, on the other hand, not having been handicapped by this extreme ethnocentric obsession, not only are well on their way toward achieving at least two and maybe more of their *O-Bok* but also believe they will eventually overtake Japan.

151

복수

Poksu
(Pohk-suu)

"The Need for Revenge"

Korean morality was based traditionally on a foundation of a carefully prescribed and almost inhumanly high standard of hierarchical social etiquette, which resulted in people becoming extraordinarily sensitivite to insults, real or imagined, and to any threat to their personal relationships, "face," or prerogatives. This sensitivity created a countervailing need for *poksu* (pohk-suu), or "revenge," which has long been a significant factor in the Korean character.

To make social relationships in Korea even more complicated, the family, kin, and group orientation of Korean society generally made it impossible to limit insults or threats and *poksu* to individuals. By the nature of the society, such incidents almost always became group affairs. Still today when untoward situations or conflicts occur, the characteristic reaction of individual Koreans is to seek allies in a *moryak* (moh-r'yahk), or "revenge plot," to inflict punishment of some kind on the other party. There is no sense of fair play in *moryak*. Plotters use whatever means they can to bring the other party down without endangering themselves.

Another historical reason for the *poksu* syndrome in Korean society was never-ending political, economic, and social competition between clans and other power groups, which made both survival and success a constant struggle that invariably had the characteristics of blood feuds.

Foreign businesspeople in Korea are frequently the victims of *moryak*—often without being aware of who their enemies are or why they are being victimized. In fact, some plots against foreign executives are so clever that they do not know they are being deliberately victimized and attribute their failure, transfer, or dismissal to other things.

Probably the two most common reasons for a *moryak* against an expatriate businessperson in Korea are that one or more members of the Korean staff regard him or her as arrogant, incompetent, undeserving (of the responsibility and high pay of an executive), or some combination of these qualities; or a member of the Korean staff believes that he or she should be the top person in the company and sets out to achieve that goal by undermining the foreign manager.

The potential success of this kind of revenge-taking in Korean companies and professional organizations is enhanced because stronger, more aggressive, and ambitious individuals invariably attract followers who cooperate with them in achieving such goals.

Koreans must spend a significant amount of time and energy avoiding *moryak* campaigns by following established protocol in all of their personal and professional relationships, by not antagonizing people, by protecting their "face," etc.—something that is always difficult and sometimes impossible to do, particularly with people who are especially sensitive for some reason or have a hidden agenda.

Foreigners living and working in Korea are especially vulnerable to *moryak* plots because they generally are not as aware of the danger as Koreans or as skilled as Koreans in avoiding adverse situations. The only practical recourse for foreigners in Korea is to attempt to develop the necessary awareness and skills as quickly as possible and to establish close relationships with Korean advisers or mentors to help them keep their relationships balanced.

폭력
Pongnyok
(Pohng-n'yohk)
"The Violent Side"

While Korea was long famous as "The Land of Morning Calm," there was a shocking dichotomy to this image that was much less well known. Particularly since the fifteenth century, ordinary Koreans have been prone to explode in outbursts of extreme *pongnyok* (pohng-n'yohk), or "violence," and violence was used customarily by the authorities at all levels of government. Not surprisingly, the reasons for the contradictions in the Korean character have their origin in religious and political ideologies.

When the Chinese first began to take notice of the tribes inhabiting the Korean peninsula, they found a wide variety of social customs and different levels of cultural sophistication. According to Chinese records, some of the tribes were peaceful and well behaved, while others were described as being hot-tempered, with robbing and killing commonplace.

Historical records show that Korea's early tribal states grew by conquest—by invading and capturing neighboring states and enslaving their populations. The three kingdoms of Koguryo, Paekche, and Shilla, particularly Koguryo, also warred against China. Koguryo built its own Great Wall to help deter invasions by China and northern tribesmen. The wall, stretched across the northwestern border with China, measured a thousand *li* in length (420 kilometers). Unification of the peninsula under the Shilla banner in 669 was accomplished by force of arms. Seizure of the government by military officers in 1170 inaugurated a period of violence that lasted for several decades. This included political assassinations and massacres among the ruling class and rebellions by peasants and slaves.

In the fifteenth century, when King Sejo (1455–68) seized power, he carried out a bloodbath, killing many of the leading scholars and statesmen of that era, including several members of the "Hall of Worthies," the royal research institute. A ruthless man, Sejo went on to enact a national code that totally bureaucratized the administrative system, putting government in the hands of scholar-officials and military officers—a system that was to prevail until 1910.

From 1392 on, the social and political systems imposed on Korea by successive generations of authoritarian kings brought long periods of peace among the general population, but there was frequent violence at the top, as elite factions squabbled and fought over power. By the late 1800s *pongnyok* had become endemic. Brought on by internal strife and by invasions and occupation, first by Chinese and then by Japanese military forces, it was to continue for several decades. The Korean War from 1950 to 1953 was an orgy of violence on a massive scale. After the end of the Korean War the government, students, and labor unions routinely used violence in battling each other in a phenomenon that did not begin to subside until the 1980s. The history of violence in Korea is the history of the two ideologies, Buddhism and Confucianism. After the tribal kingdoms of Korea under the influence of China in 108 B.C. subsequently adopted both Buddhism and Confucianism, the contradictions in these new philosophies imbued the people with split personalities. They were programmed to think and behave in ways that were diametrically opposed to each other and required the suppression of most natural feelings, resulting in intellectual and emotional conflicts that could not be reconciled without violence.

On the one hand Koreans were conditioned to treat family and friends with the greatest kindness and authorities with the greatest respect. Strangers, however, were outside the pale of courteous behavior. Koreans were also programmed to have the highest regard for learning, but with the exception of the *kisaeng*, or professional female entertainers, education was reserved almost exclusively for male members of the elite ruling class.

Korea's Confucian-oriented family and clan groupism was designed to ensure social stability and harmony, but all was not always harmonious among family members. At virtually all times in all families there was an undercurrent of anger and resentment that built up over the years because officially and formally all power was in the hands of fathers. All members of the family were subordinate to the will of the fathers, who could be arbitrary and unfair. Younger members of families were expected to be subservient to their older siblings, particularly males, who could and often did take advantage of their superior positions.

Arguments among family members were commonplace, and there were many occasions when their anger and resentment got out of control and resulted in physical violence between brothers and between sons and fathers. This enforced familism and groupism and also promoted extreme factionalism, resulting in both local and regional strife throughout the society, particularly among factions in the elite ruling class that were continuously vying for power.

These outbursts of violence, domestic as well as political, and by women as well as men, have been especially characteristic of Koreans since the ascendancy of Neo-Confucianism during the long Choson dynasty (1392–1910), a social and political ideology that was to force all Koreans to behave in a manner contrary to human emotions. All behavior, especially that of women, was so prescribed, so controlled, that they were forced to suppress virtually all of their emotions most of the time. Men could get drunk and engage in extramarital sex and relieve some of the stress that built up in their lives, but wives and nonprofessional women were not allowed any safety valve.

About the only emotional outlet ordinary women had was loving and taking care of their children after they were married. Their marriages were arranged, and there was little if any emotional bond between them and their husbands. Korean men (like their counterparts in most of the rest of the world) were not aware that their wives had sexual and emotional needs that were not fulfilled by pregnancies, child raising, and unending work.

Except for farm wives who had to work in the fields, women were required to stay in their homes or walled yards during the day. The only females allowed on the streets during the day were maids or other servants on emergency errands. Women could leave their homes only after dark when a great bell was sounded, and they had to be back in their homes by midnight.

Female illnesses resulting from frustrations and other stress were therefore commonplace. Relatively large numbers of women suffered mental break-downs, went into trances, and exhibited other symptoms of acute stress. When the symptoms exhibited by these women included trances, people presumed they had been possessed by spirits, resulting in many of them becoming *mudangs*, or "spiritual mediums," a profession that gave them some standing in the community.

Another aspect of the duality of the traditional character of Koreans was a significant disparity between what was officially presented as real and what was actual reality. This disparity, according to Kwang Kyu Yi, an authority on changes occurring in the traditional Korean family, resulted from the unattainably high standards and expectations set by Confucianism and the reality of daily life, especially in politics.

Yi said that such high expectations made an equally high level of discontent inevitable. Yi also pointed to the fact that the Confucian family system favored first-born sons over other children in families to the extent that younger off-spring were treated practically like outcasts, resulting in their suffering from intense feelings of injustice and frustration. The primary reason for the supremacy of the first-born son in the Korean family system was that he was responsible for maintaining the family line and performing the rituals of ances-tor worship, which was at the heart of filial piety.

Much of the long Choson era, particularly the first two centuries, was marked by periods of violence, including numerous *sahwa* (sah-wah), or "polit-ical purges," brought on by conflicts between the new Confucian-oriented scholar-officials and the traditional Buddhist factions.

A propensity for *pohngnyok* is still a very conspicuous facet of Koreans' character, not only as a reaction to the still heavy hand of Confucianism that con-ditions them to keep their emotions suppressed most of the time but also because they have not yet had enough experience with resolving personal or public conflicts through peaceful debate and reasoning.

Foreigners in Korea are less likely to be subjected to physical or verbal vio-lence than Koreans themselves because they are generally viewed as guests and therefore come under a different set of behavioral rules. Still, it is advisable for foreigners to avoid conduct that is known to upset Koreans, including such things as behaving in an obviously arrogant manner, using impolite or insulting speech, indulging in public criticism, and ignoring cultural taboos.

Unlike Chinese and Japanese, Koreans are characteristically confrontational in their approach to out-of-the-ordinary situations. However, their confronta-tional reactions are controlled carefully and generally do not result in a complete breakdown of communications or negotiations. In street demonstrations staged by students, workers, or others, the scene is often exceptionally violent and people often get hurt, but fatalities are extremely rare. From the 1960s until the early years of the 1990s, Korea was convulsed with labor strife that saw public violence reach new heights. The government and big business collaborated in an all-out war against labor unions, resulting in violent skirmishes becoming the norm. Newspapers of the day regularly carried accounts of union members going to extremes to attract public attention to their plight. Some of the more bizarre incidents included women demonstrating in the nude, a worker burning himself to death with gasoline, other workers committing suicide by leaping from buildings, union members capturing and holding hostages, and more.

The passing of a new labor law in 1996 resulted in a new outbreak of riots in December of that year and again in January 1997.

Despite these bloody incidents, Korean business writer Chan Sup Chang in his book *The Korean Management System—Cultural, Political, Economic Foundations* says that Koreans hate bloodshed "more than any other people in the world." Chang adds that Koreans can tell instinctively when to "confront a situation with violence" and when to approach it in a friendly manner. Unfortunately, throughout Korean history there has been no end of circumstances when the only recourse open to Koreans was violence.

It is obviously important that foreigners also learn how to "read" potentially dangerous situations in Korea to avoid taking inappropriate actions.

153

법

Pop
(Pope)

"The Less Law the Better"

Korean historians characterize *pop* (pope), or "laws," during the Three Kingdoms period (57 B.C.–A.D. 668) as being "simple and severe." Transgressions usually punished by execution included murder, bodily injury, theft, female adultery, and jealousy on the part of wives. Since polygamy was customary, the latter two "crimes" were especially designed by men to keep their wives quiet.

Confucianism, which became the primary political ideology of the Three Kingdoms during their final centuries, was both a bane and a blessing to Korea, but it got one thing right where laws were concerned. Confucius said that laws could not by themselves secure peace and tranquillity and that societies that depended on laws to enforce right thinking and right behavior were eventually torn apart by misconduct and violence. Confucius added that the more laws a country had, the more unlawful its citizens would be, and yet passing more and more *pop* was always the recourse of politicians in immoral, violent societies.

Koreans have actually had very little experience with the kind of laws familiar to Americans and other Westerners. Until the second half of the twentieth century, they were ruled by authoritarian governments that brooked no input from the people and no disobedience by ordinary citizens. In the Western sense Korea was a country not of laws but of government regulations and official administrators who enforced the regulations on behalf of the government, not the people. Naturally enough, this environment did not enthrall Koreans with the law. Generally speaking, they feared the law and often despised it, with good reason.

There were, in fact, few laws in pre-modern Korea because they were not needed. Korean behavior was actually prescribed by the law in only a few instances. Their daily conduct was controlled primarily by a religiouslike obedience to the principles and practices set down by Confucianism for individuals and families. Fathers were responsible for the behavior of their families; village and community leaders were responsible for the conduct of everyone within their jurisdiction.

Legal scholars in Korea, beginning in the 1960s, conducted a number of studies on Korean attitudes toward laws that revealed that people were basically indifferent to the values and "facts" represented by laws. Their concept of right and wrong, good behavior and bad behavior, was based on personal circumstances instead of abstract principles. They viewed behavior from a human rather than a legal aspect and simply ignored laws that conflicted with their view. The idea of laws upholding the virtue of people was a totally alien concept. The studies reemphasized that Koreans still overwhelmingly preferred a humanistic resolution to conflicts or problems instead of legal solutions arrived at in courts.

In 1965 Sung Jong Hyon noted in an article entitled "The Legal Consciousness of the Koreans," published in the May edition of *Sasang Gye* (*The World of Ideas*), that Koreans had not absorbed a sense of the law during the modernization of the country and that Koreans still did not believe in the principle of legalism.

The Korean attitude toward law has changed in the intervening decades, but not dramatically. Koreans are still wary of the government, of courts, and of the law. They still prefer to settle problems by arbitration. This attitude naturally impacts contracts and other areas of business in Korea and gives rise to a great deal of frustration among foreign businesspeople, many of whom stake their reputations and their companies on the written word.

For their part, Korean courts and government agencies routinely use the law to achieve personal and national goals, which frequently means that they rule against foreign interests regardless of what the national *pop* says or implies. In both a general and a specific sense, the Korean government takes the view that attorneys and courts are "agents" of the government and that their first responsibility is to the government—not to clients, petitioners, or anyone else.

In the traditional Confucian concept of society, the fundamental basis for the maintenance of order and harmony in society should not be laws but the elimination of all sources of discontent among the people and the guarantee of peace of mind. Studies of the character of present-day Koreans indicate this is still the fundamental belief of the people.

In Korean courts the reputation of judges depends more on how they handle cases from the viewpoint of family relations and humanism than how strictly they uphold the law. Judges who decide cases strictly on the basis of law are regarded as cruel and unfit for the bench.

Most young Koreans seem to have inherited the Confucian concept of the morally perfect character and the idea of giving spiritual well-being precedence over materialism. They tend to rate wisdom and virtue over technical skill and regard friendships and achievement in the arts as more desirable than wealth. These feelings result in young Koreans being highly critical of extravagant spending and wasteful customs, with elaborate birthday parties and wedding celebrations high on their list of such extravagances. And yet these practices remain common among all levels of society.

There has been one change in Korean attitudes toward the government that is of extraordinary significance. The ancient philosophical concept that the citizenry had a right to criticize an abusive and inefficient government is no longer just an abstract notion. They now demand the right to take part in national affairs regardless of how many laws they have to break in the process and the danger they may face because of such actions.

Visitors in Korea should especially keep one thing in mind. Suspects are considered guilty until their innocence is proven. The police and other investigative authorities assume it is their right to force suspects to confess. The concept of the suspect's innocence being proven in court by testimony is not well established. Suspects either confess or are released because they refuse to confess and there is no evidence to back up the police charges. Torture of suspects by police authorities has been traditional in Korea and according to the testimony of former prisoners and press reports is still common, although somewhat less horrendous than before.

The administration of Young Sam Kim, elected president in 1992, is credited with eliminating much of the reprehensible behavior of police authorities and is regarded by many as a bringing about a paradigm shift in the attitudes of both civilians and government employees. The public attitude is that the bad old days are gone and people no longer have to put up with such behavior.

In what seems to be a contradiction in the role of law and justice, it is against the law for a victim to injure a burglar, and if a victim should kill a burglar the victim is considered guilty of murder. The corollary to this behavior is that traditionally in Korea burglars were not violent and would immediately leave the premises if there was any indication that anyone was home. Automobile drivers involved in accidents resulting in injury to any other party can expect to be jailed, charged with committing an unlawful act, and required to pay a fine or spend time in prison.

154

복고춤
Pop Ko Chum
(Pope Koh Chuum)

"The Law Drum Dance"

Music and dancing have long played a vital role in Korean life, being considered a way of communicating with the spirits as well as essential for building character and keeping people in harmony with the cosmos. Traditionally many people in Korea's upper class, including kings and members of the royal court, spent a great portion of their lives pursuing these arts.

Music and dance have also long been one of the primary techniques used by Korean *musok* (muu-soak), or "shamans," to enter trances and act as psychic mediums. They use the same methods to put clients or patients into trancelike states and rid them of evil spirits and psychosomatic problems.

Drums are a key factor in the mind-altering effects of Korean music and dance, with one particular Buddhist dance, the *Pop Ko Chum* (Pope Koh Chuum), or "Law Drum Dance," being especially noted for the seductive effect it has on viewers. This dance, originally performed solo with a small drum and two drumsticks, builds up to a crescendo of drumming that arouses the passions to a remarkable degree.

There is a famous story about the power of the Law Drum Dance to incite the deepest passion. The incident took place in the sixteenth century and involved a *kisaeng* (kee-sang), or professional female entertainer who was renowned as a dancer, musician, poet, and lover, and a monk who was equally famous for his ability to withstand all fleshly temptations. Her professional instincts aroused, the *kisaeng* took it upon herself to seduce the monk. Donning a Buddhist robe and hat, the *kisaeng* went to the monk's temple and offered to perform a *Pop Ko Chum* on his behalf—a dance that was intended to demonstrate the power of Buddhist law over the eroticism of the flesh. The monk readily assented.

The *kisaeng* apparently put on a show for the ages. At the end of the performance she quickly disrobed and stood before the aroused monk stark naked. Needless to say, the monk's famed willpower went up in steam.

In recent times the *Pop Ko Chum* has been completely secularized and commercialized and is one of the most popular stage acts in Korea. In its contemporary reincarnation the dance is performed by five, nine, or twelve female dancers who are selected as much for their beauty as for their dancing and drumming skills. Glamorously costumed and made up, the dancers perform a thrilling repertoire of acrobatic actions in concert with drumming—a performance that is usually scheduled as the grand finale because it leaves audiences excited.

Foreigners who are invited by Korean hosts to attend *Pop Ko Chum* performances are generally not aware of their reputation for being an aphrodisiac in sound and do not consciously associate them with anything other than good entertainment. But few who have experienced one of these exhibitions can deny their libido-arousing effects.

Also in recent years, a number of *Pop Ko Chum* troupes have traveled abroad, putting on exhibitions that were officially designated as spreading Korean culture. Not surprisingly, the exhibitions drew much more enthusiastic responses than art and craft displays.

155

부정
Pujong
Puu-johng

"Keeping Women Down"

From the beginning of Korean history down to the twentieth century, women were officially regarded as *pujong* (puu-johng), "unclean" or "polluted," in both a physical and a spiritual sense, and were forbidden to participate in various rituals or set foot in certain male areas. This male attitude and behavior no doubt derived from the fact that men have always been frightened and repulsed by female menstruation, pregnancy, and childbirth and have used this biological function as an excuse to degrade women and to treat them as physically, intellectually, and spiritually inferior to men.

Ultimately, of course, as in other male-dominated societies, the Korean concept of *pujong* was a shameless ploy used by men to control the sexuality, work, and childbearing function of women for their own selfish interests. The concept of female *pujong* was not only sanctified and promoted by Korea's male religious leaders but institutionalized in the political system as well and thus permeated the culture. Korean women themselves came to believe that they were in fact inferior and to accept their lowly status. Absolute chastity was demanded of women before marriage and absolute faithfulness to husbands afterward. But premarital and extramarital sexual activity by men was not only permitted but also endorsed and promoted.

In the fourteenth century Korean men, inspired by the macho orientation of a new form of Confucianism, took this concept of women as inferior further than most of their counterparts around the world, ruling that women should be virtually segregated from the male world. Thereafter, males and females were separated at an early age, and while they lived side by side they were in different dimensions.

Western concepts of women and their place in society were introduced into Korea during the last decades of the nineteenth century, primarily by American missionaries. This Western influence very slowly began to erode the role of *pujong* in the lives of Korean women. However, it was not until the end of the Japanese colonial period in Korea in 1945 that the status of women in South Korea, which was then dominated by the United States, began to change dramatically. For the first time in the history of Korea, newly passed laws gave women most of the rights traditionally enjoyed by men.

But the attitudes and habits ingrained into people over many generations die hard. The new laws had practically no effect on the lives of most adult Koreans. It was the first postwar generation of Korean women who began to publicly ignore many of the ancient *pujong* customs, particularly those that kept them segregated from males from a young age.

These young women began flocking to schools, factories, and offices. Influenced by American music, movies, and television, they also began to date for the first time in the history of their country, and many began choosing their own marriage partners.

Korean society is still dominated by men, however. Women are still treated as second-class human beings, both politically and economically. But there are growing indications that Korean women will achieve equality, or at least near equality, faster than their sisters in other Confucian-influenced societies of Asia. Korean women tend to be more aggressive than their Asian counterparts, not only intellectually and emotionally but physically as well. When young Korean women want something (or somebody!), they are more likely to put everything they have into the struggle to get what they want.

Realizing full well that financial success and independence bring social as well as political empowerment, Korean women are becoming more and more active as business entrepreneurs. Some of the most successful and exciting start-up companies in Korea are the handiwork of these extremely ambitious and capable women.

Korean men can no longer justify trying to keep women "in their place" by using the old *pujong* ploy. It is now official government policy that Korea cannot achieve its full potential without the unfettered contribution of women.

156

불다

Pulda
(Puhl-dah)

"Eliminating Office Stress"

Conforming to Korean etiquette, particularly in offices of larger companies where the rules of behavior are especially strict, does not come easily or without cost. While growing up in the Korean environment obviously helps prepare Koreans for the experience, it nevertheless requires the expenditure of a great deal of psychic energy that results in building up *pulda* (puhl-dah), or what some Korean health authorities refer to as "office stress" (although *pulda* refers to stress in general). *Pulda* is recognized as a health factor in the lives of Korean office workers, and one of the aims of many of the company-organized after-hours activities, from bar hopping and bowling to mountain climbing, is to help relieve the pressures that cause it.

In Korean life in general it is only during certain organized after-hours activities that superiors and inferiors are free to dispense with the formalized etiquette that normally rules their relationships and to react to each other as equals. This relaxation of rules is not a subtle or casual thing. It is done openly and often vigorously, with both inferiors and superiors exaggerating their behavior to make the point that they are temporarily equal. In fact superiors will often announce that their roles have been switched, that juniors have become their "bosses" for the occasion (because the juniors are more experienced or skilled in whatever activity is going on).

This equalization of co-workers is the most conspicuous at parties where drinking alcoholic beverages is an institutionalized aspect of the gathering. On these occasions one of the primary "requirements" is that the participants dispense with the normal rigid etiquette that divides them and "let their hair down." Dancing together, singing, and performing humorous skits are routine at such parties. It is regarded as arrogant if not insulting behavior for anyone, including foreign employees or foreigners who happen to be there as guests, to refuse to participate in these activities.

Virtually everyone at such parties cooperates in the process of encouraging other participants to drink until they are drunk. Koreans, like the Japanese and Chinese, typically vie to see who can drink the most. They want and "need" to see other people drunk enough that their "true" character and personalities emerge—something that does not happen when they are sober and conforming to the role playing that is required by their social status and organizational rank.

However, in larger gatherings where senior executives are present, neither the structure nor the conduct is completely democratic. The seating arrangement invariably conforms to the traditional hierarchical relationships between inferiors and superiors, and inferiors, especially those who are young and lower ranked, are respectful of the seniors. Middle and senior executives, on the other hand, may be as informal and as forward as they wish in interacting with lower-ranking employees.

About the only way lower-ranking employees are permitted to criticize senior managers or the management practices of their companies is indirectly in humorous skits—a cultural tradition that is ancient in Korea. In fact, entertainment has traditionally been used as a psychological tool to influence people on all levels of Korean society, from the national government down to company managers.

Korean executives in larger firms are acutely aware of the dangers of *pulda* buildup and the importance of company-sponsored entertainment and cultural programs in controlling the attitudes and behavior of employees. Such things are a key part of the management policies in most companies. Foreign corporations operating in Korea should also be aware of the *pulda* factor in Korea's corporate culture, particularly the fact that it tends to be far more intense than in typical foreign companies, and develop ongoing programs to keep it under control.

157

불교

Pulgyo
(Puul-g'yoh)

"The Buddhist Wave"

In 109 B.C., armies of the newly founded Han dynasty in China invaded and captured the Korean peninsula, which at that time was the home of several small kingdoms. Over the next several decades the Chinese influence was instrumental in the coalescing of these small tribal states into three relatively large kingdoms: Shilla (57 B.C.–A.D. 935), Koguryo (37 B.C.–A.D. 668), and Paekche (18 B.C.–A.D. 660).

Existing more or less as tributary states under China, these new Korean kingdoms adopted the Chinese form of government but generally retained their traditional culture—something that was to change dramatically from the fourth century A.D. on, with the mass arrival of *Pulgyo* (Puul-g'yoh), or "Buddhism," in Korea. Korean historians give the precise date of the arrival of Buddhism in the Koguryo kingdom as A.D. 372, during the reign of King Sosurim, who became a devoted patron of the new religion. Buddhism became the national religion of Paekche in 384 and in Shilla, located far to the south of the peninsula, in 528.

Following the official adoption of Buddhism as the state religion by King Sosurim and his Paekche counterpart, large numbers of Chinese Buddhist priests took up residence in Korea, becoming teachers and advisers to Korea's ruling classes. With official patronage from the courts of the two kingdoms, the priests introduced the whole range of Chinese arts and crafts to their Korean sponsors, including the Chinese system of writing.

Over the next several centuries these Korean patrons of Buddhism and the arts and crafts of China sponsored their development on a national scale. Hundreds of *Chol* (Chohl), or Buddhist temples, some of them huge complexes, were built throughout the country. Many of the temples were located in remote mountainous areas that were selected especially for their scenic beauty and serenity. Religious historians also attribute the founding of several Buddhists schools of thought to newly converted Korean monks—schools that subsequently had profound influence not only in China but also in Southeast Asia, Tibet, and Japan. Leading Buddhist priests were honored with such titles as *Kuk Sa* (Kuuk Sah), or "National Master," and *Wang Sa* (Wahng Sah), or "Royal Master."

Buddhism taught that personal well-being as well as the state of the nation could be enhanced by pious acts, a belief that resulted in an extraordinary proliferation of Buddhist temples and monasteries throughout the country, and the daily observance of Buddhist rituals. Those in power believed that the more temples they built the more successful they would be. There were more than seventy temples in the Koryo capital of Kaesong. Other acts regarded as pious included copying the Buddhist scriptures, parading through the streets shouting Buddhist sutras or carrying banners inscribed with Buddhist sutras, and feeding mendicant monks. One of the biggest annual events in Koryo was a vegetarian banquet at which upwards of a hundred thousand monks feasted.

One of the most influential tenets of *Pulgyo* was the concept of reincarnation, something that had extraordinary appeal to Korea's lower classes because their lives were generally filled with uncertainty and hardship and were typically short, making them particularly susceptible to a belief that promised more than one lifetime. The upper class quickly became devout Buddhists not only because of the promise of life after death but also because Buddhism was seen as providing divine protection for the nation—a concept expressed in the term *Ho Guk* (Hoe Guuk), which might be translated as "Nation Protector."

Son, or Zen, Buddhism is said to have entered Korea in the seventh century, but it was the ninth century before it became a force to be reckoned with as a result of sponsorship by regional fief lords. By the end of the Shilla dynasty in 935, *Son* had become well established among the rural gentry and their private armies because it taught austerity, discipline, and an indomitable spirit in achieving goals, whether these goals were in art or war. Between the ninth and fourteenth centuries, *Pulgyo* was split between the original sect and *Son*, which emphasized meditation and perfection of the self through strenuous ascetic practices. All good was believed to come from pious acts.

But with Buddhism ensconced as the state religion throughout the Koryo dynasty (918–1392), Buddhist monks continued to play key roles as advisers to the kings, their ministers, and other key members of the elite ruling class. The common belief that the survival of the state was in the hands of the gods gave the Buddhists enormous power.

A key reason why the Pure Land Sect of Buddhism spread so rapidly in Korea was that according to its teachings the only thing people had to do to be reborn in the Buddhist paradise was to chant the sutra *Nammu Amita Pul* (Nahm-muu Ah-mee-tah Puhl). It was not necessary to study or to meditate on difficult metaphysical doctrines, which meant that even the illiterate common people could be good Buddhists and have guaranteed passage to the "Pure Land" upon their death.

Monks, temples, and monasteries received land grants in perpetuity from the state, and monks were exempt from providing conscription labor. Over the decades temples and monasteries became wealthy and powerful, making it possible for them to buy—or confiscate—more land and start a variety of commercial enterprises, resulting in their amassing even more wealth. To protect their wealth they began to train young monks as warriors. Eventually all monasteries had their own armed guards and garrisons, with the latter often fighting in large-scale battles. In the twelfth century one monk became so powerful that, failing to convince the king that he should move the capital to Pyongyang, where the geomancy powers were stronger, he fielded a large army and tried, unsuccessfully, to usurp the throne.

One of the more memorable events that occurred in the thirteenth century points up the role that Buddhism played in Korean society. In 1231 Genghis Khan, the scourge of Asia, attacked Korea, causing the entire Korean court to retreat to Kanghwa Island, just off the mainland coast in the Yellow Sea. There the reigning Koryo king ordered the engraving of the entire Chinese translation of the Buddhist scriptures on 81,258 wooden tablets, known as *Palman-Taejangkyong* or *Koryo Taejanggyong*. The feat required hundreds of craftsmen working for sixteen years. Each of the tablets was twenty-four centimeters wide, sixty centimeters long, and three centimeters thick and weighed 3.5 kilograms.

When the marathon undertaking was complete, the entire lot was destroyed—burned either by the king as an offering to win the favor of the gods in the court's battle against the Mongols or by the invading Mongols (historical accounts differ). The effort may not have been a total waste. The Mongols won the war but allowed Korea to survive as a vassal state within the Mongol empire. One of the ways the Mongols attempted to control the affairs of Korea was requiring that the crown princes be educated in Beijing, marry Mongol princesses, and remain in the Mongol capital until it became their time to assume the Koryo throne.

After this accommodation with the Mongols, the Koryo king had a second set of the Buddhist tablets carved. Now called *Tripitaka Koreana*, this set of tablets can be seen today in Haeinsa Temple near the city of Taegu, where they are stored in special bins that control the humidity and air flow. They are said to be in perfect condition and are ranked by the Ministry of Culture as "National Treasure No. 32." (*Tripitaka*, meaning "Three Baskets," is a Pali term referring to the Buddhist scriptures.)

Buddhism provided the impulse for the invention of movable metal type by a Korean in 1234, predating Johannes Gutenberg's accomplishment in Germany by some two hundred years. (The first metallic type to be made of copper was cast in Korea in 1403 on orders from the ruling Choson king.)

But by the beginning of the fourteenth century the Koryo dynasty had become corrupt and inefficient. Much of this was blamed on Buddhism, which had continued to absorb most of the attention of the court and the wealth of the country. Joining a Buddhist monastery became a way for young men to avoid regular work, taxes, and other day-to-day responsibilities while gaining many privileges. For most monks of this age, any religious piety they exhibited was a sham used to take advantage of their sacred calling and indulge themselves in pleasurable things, including the company of attractive women.

In the mid-1300s the Chinese rebelled against the Mongols and succeeded in expelling them from the country. The successful revolt of the Chinese against the Mongols also freed Korea from the Mongol yoke. But shortly after the victorious Chinese rebels established their own Ming dynasty, they marched on Korea in an attempt to reimpose hegemony over that hapless country. The king of Korea sent his most capable general, Song Gye Yi, to meet the invaders. When it became obvious to Yi that he could not defeat the Chinese, he turned back, deposed the Koryo king, and signed a peace treaty with the Chinese, saving the kingdom but once again making Korea a vassal state of China. A few years later (1392) General Yi invoked the mandate of heaven, declared himself king, and founded the Choson (or Yi) dynasty—which was to survive until 1910, when the country was annexed by Japan.

The new general-turned-king (King Taejo) struck down the laws and eliminated the practices that had made *Pulgyo* the national religion of Korea and began replacing it with so-called Neo-Confucianism, which established filial piety and ancestor worship as the new national religion. King Taejo confiscated most of the property of the temples and monasteries, banished most of the monks to the mountains, and limited the number of young boys who could join the order. No more than one son out of three in a family could become a monk.

In a further move in 1406, Taejo set the limit on Buddhist monasteries in the country at 242 and ordered all the others closed down. He also made it mandatory for all monks to register so the government could keep track of them. The fortunes of Buddhism waxed and waned over the next century, but by the end of the sixteenth century it was little more than a private faith practiced by women, its great temples little more than monuments to a glorious past. Some anthropologists and religious historians have referred to early Buddhism as a "cult of the dead" because of its emphasis on revering ancestors.

Contemporary Buddhist scholar Ki Yong Yi in an article in *Korean Studies* said that the positive influence of *Pulgyo* on Korean society included a sense of mercy and charity, the concept that good should be encouraged and evil punished, and that individuals should be willing to sacrifice for the benefit of their families, communities, and society in general. This may be history seen in idealized hindsight, but in any event the influence of Buddhism on Korea, combined with the other aspects of Chinese culture, was profound, and it is not over yet.

There are presently some twenty recognized sects of Buddhism in Korea and more than seven thousand temples and monasteries, some of which date from the Koryo period. Approximately 20 percent of the population list themselves as Buddhists. Buddhist holidays and festivals are celebrated throughout the country.

The two largest Buddhist sects are *Chogye* (Choh-geh) and *Taego* (Tie-goh), both of which are part of the Mahayana division of Buddhism. The *Chogye* sect is made up of two "schools," *Son* (Sohn) and *Kyo* (K'yoh). The *Son* school, known as Zen in English and Japanese, emphasizes meditating and attempting to solve intellectual riddles as a means of achieving enlightenment. *Kyo* emphasizes scriptural studies. Some 90 percent of all Korean Buddhists belong to the *Chogye* sect.

The *Taego* sect permits its monks to marry—a practice that some say was introduced by the Japanese when they occupied and annexed Korea (1910–45) because they figured that married monks would be a lot easier to control than monks who had to repress their sexual desires. (If this is true, the obvious question is why the Japanese didn't mandate that priests of the *Chogye* sect marry because they outnumbered *Taego* priests about nine to one.)

Korean sociologists relate the modern revival of Buddhism* to a growing need among Koreans for an identity that is not bound by the stifling philosophy of Neo-Confucianism, which marked the Choson dynasty, or "Westernism," which many see as destructive to the positive attributes of Korea's traditional culture.

---

*For those Westerners who may have been confused by what appears to be swastikas used to indicate the sites of Korea's Buddhist temples, the crossed mark, which is actually the reverse of the Nazi swastika, is an ancient Buddhist symbol that originated in India.

품질
Pumjil
(Puum-jeel)
"Quality as a Cultural Thing"

In the 1960s the Japanese became famous for the quality of their products. What most people don't know is that the Japanese got their first lessons in the importance of quality and quality control from Korean artists and handicraft masters more than a thousand years before made-in-Japan watches, motorcycles, and electronic products took the world by storm.

As early as the fourth century A.D. large numbers of Korean scholars and artisans settled in Japan under the patronage of the imperial court (which, according to some records, was itself founded by Koreans). Historical records indicate that from this period virtually all of the arts and crafts that appeared in Japan were introduced either by Korean masters or by Japanese who had apprenticed under Korean or Chinese masters.

Some historians also say that Japan's equally famous tea ceremony, which emerged as a major social and economic force in the sixteenth century and was to provide much of the philosophical and aesthetic foundation for Japan's traditions of quality, was based primarily on the work of Korean ceramists and potters.

In any event, as early as A.D. 100 Korea had already been introduced to the arts and crafts of China and in the following centuries absorbed not only the technology but also the aesthetic and utilitarian principles that Chinese masters built into their products. Records also show that Korean ceramists eventually surpassed their Chinese masters in the beauty and quality of celadon porcelain produced during the Koryo dynasty (918–1392), resulting in its becoming highly prized in China.

The blue-green shade of color achieved by the Korean ceramists of that era was so outstanding that a famous Chinese scholar of the Sung period wrote that the color was one of the ten most wonderful things in the world. (The other nine things, including silk and jade carvings, were all Chinese.)

Korea's traditions of *pumjil* (puum-jeel), which literally means "degree of excellence," like those that were to develop in Japan in later centuries, came about through the master-apprentice custom in the crafts and to the fact that the master craftsmen of the day were patronized by the royal court and the leading members of the society. This royal patronage provided extraordinary motivation for the craftsmen to attempt to achieve perfection in their work to maintain the royal favor, with the result that the standards of quality and aesthetics became higher with each generation.

In the 1590s the quality traditions of Korea were to suffer a setback that was so serious that they did not begin to recover their ancient standards until the 1960s—a setback for which Japan was held directly responsible. In 1592 the Japanese invaded Korea, beginning a seven-year war during which the arts and crafts industry in Korea was devastated. In addition to destroying the infrastructure of the handicraft industry (kilns, museums, manuals, etc.), Korean historians say the Japanese captured the most successful artists and craftsmen to take back to Japan as slaves, then killed most of the remaining craftsmen and their apprentices to prevent them from being able to revitalize the craft industry.

Soon after this tragic event Korea closed its doors and became known as the "hermit kingdom." Without masters the arts and crafts in Korea went into decline, and for a long period its traditions of quality were little more than a historical memory. Korea's "hermit" period did not end until 1873, when it was once again Japan that was to bring tragedy to the long-suffering peninsula. Japan forced Korea to reopen its doors to the outside world and in 1910, after yet another bloody struggle, annexed the country. It was not until the 1960s, after regaining their freedom from Japan and surviving a destructive civil war, that Koreans were finally free to begin rebuilding their country and returning to their historical traditions of *pumjil*.

Korea's *pumjil* standards, particularly in high-tech areas, have now caught up with those previously associated only with the West and Japan, but Koreans are not content just to match the Japanese. They believe they can and will surpass the Japanese, and in doing so right a wrong that they have lived with since the sixteenth century. A related word, *yangil* (yahn-geel), refers to a "good product."

159

풍요

Pungnyu
(Poong-n'yuu)

"Going with Nature's Flow"

Animism, the first religion of Korea, provided the intellectual, emotional, and spiritual foundation for the original Korean cosmos. It explained the "creation" of the Korean people and their relationship to the world around them. One of the most important lessons the Koreans learned from nature was that nature, in all of its forms, was the supreme power in the universe, and since they couldn't change it or defeat it the only logical recourse was to get along with it, to go with the *pungnyu* (poong-n'yuu), literally the "wind flow."

Korean scholars Jon Carter Covell and Alan Covell (a mother and son team), in their authoritative book *The World of Korean Ceramics*, note that *pungnyu* is an aesthetic principle, used in relation to the beauty of Korean ceramics, that suggests movement in a psychological sense. In this case the "wind flow" is what attracts and pulls the viewer into the material, the shape, and finally the essence of the ceramic piece. The Covells say that this "wind flow" does more than link man with a ceramic piece. They say that it links man with nature in the sense that both are a part of a continuum, constantly changing and yet at any one time frozen into a particular form.

Koreans learned the art of ceramic making from the Chinese, but they did not stop with just imitating the Chinese masters. They improved on them (and it was Korean potters and Korean pottery that gave impetus to the development of Japan's famed tea ceremony and its aesthetic principles in the sixteenth century*). *Pungnyu* was not limited to the creation of ceramics in Korean culture. It permeated all of their arts and crafts and might be called the essence of both their Koreanness and their beauty because it was an element that all artists and craftsmen tried unconsciously to infuse into their work. An additional secret of the power of *pungnyu* was that it was very subtle, so subtle, in fact, that people without considerable training or experience in aesthetics, or a great deal of natural sensitivity, could not see it or feel it.

The influence of *pungnyu* suffered a serious setback in 1592 when several Japanese armies, fielded by fief lords of southern and southwestern Japan on orders from Hideyoshi Toyotomi, the ruling warlord, invaded the country and made a special point of capturing large numbers of Korean potters and craftsmen and taking them back to Japan as spoils of war.

While the ceramic industry in Korea declined almost to the point of disappearing from this time on, it was to be reincarnated in Japan with astounding results. The Korean potters taken to Japan, working under the competitive patronage of the powerful provincial lords who had captured them, took the principle of *pungnyu* to new heights, first in the tea ceremony and then in all of the arts and crafts for which the Japanese were later to become famous.

The disruption of the arts and crafts in Korea by successive Japanese invasions in the 1590s and ongoing raids by the Manchus the following century was to have a long-term negative effect on role of *pungnyu* in Korean life. Then came the political turmoil of the 1800s, the annexation of Korea by Japan in 1910 and finally the Korean War in the 1950s, all of which continued to limit the role of the arts in Korea.

Despite these cataclysmic events, the concept of *pungnyu* did not disappear from Korean culture, and since the 1980s it has been experiencing a comeback. Now, rather than being used primarily in the production of traditional arts and crafts, the principle of "wind flow" is being used in the design and fabrication of a variety of modern products as well. The ancient forces of animism are still with the Koreans and will no doubt continue to give them a considerable advantage in competing with the rest of the world.

---

*Historical records indicate that Japan's greatest tea master and aesthete, Sen no Rikyu (1522–91), was himself the descendant of a Korean potter who took up residence in Japan some two generations earlier.

풍수
Pungsu
(Puung-su)

"Keeping in Cosmic Harmony"

More perceptive visitors to Korea may notice that the palaces, pagodas, temples, and other old structures have a specific geographic orientation as far as the compass and physical features of the site are concerned and conform to a design that is often simply described as "Oriental." This orientation and design derive from beliefs and concepts Koreans imported from China long ago, beliefs that hold that the health and welfare of the dead as well as the living are related directly to the natural forces that flow from the sun, from hills and mountains, from the wind, and from water.

This belief incorporates the idea that if a grave is not in harmony with its surroundings the spirit of the deceased person within cannot find peace and that if a building is facing in the "wrong" direction or its doors and windows are not in the "right" place, bad spirits will enter the building and bring misfortune to its inhabitants. In contrast, when graves are situated properly and buildings and their doors, windows, and surroundings are designed and positioned in accordance with the flow of good spirits, fortune will smile on the residents or employees, whichever the case may be.

Divining the proper design and orientation for graves, buildings, and doors is a folk "science" or art called *pungsu* (puung-su), which literally translates as "wind and water" and is known in the Western world as geomancy. It has been practiced by virtually all of the older, more advanced cultures of the past, in Africa and Europe as well as in Asia.

The *pungsu* theory regards the earth as the mother of all things and holds that the energy that imbues the earth varies with location and orientation, and this in turn has a fundamental effect on any person or any activity that takes place in or on that location. The same theory says that heaven is male, and that when the female (earth) and male (heaven) are in harmony energy will be released, producing wind and rain as well as invisible energy that penetrates and affects everything.

After a building design has been completed, the next challenge facing the geomancer is to locate "the breath of the cosmic dragon," to use Chinese terms, by means of a large, complicated magnetic compass (invented in China some two thousand years ago) made up of concentric lines and numbers related to the degree of deviance from the north and to the *yin-yang* forces in the cosmos. (Even numbers are *yin*; odd numbers are *yang*.)

At first in Korea geomancy was used only by members of the ruling class to choose sites for palaces and royal tombs. But as the noble families grew in numbers and rural clans became larger and more powerful, they too adopted the custom, and from there it spread among the general population. The Buddhist monk Toson (827–898) is credited with playing a leading role in popularizing *pungsu* by adding Buddhist concepts to its principles in his counseling and writing.

From Toson's time on, amost every new building, village, town, and city were laid out in accordance with the principles of *pungsu*, which included not only their physical orientation as a whole but also the size and design of individual buildings, trees, and other landscaping—even such things as flagpoles. The most propitious site for a building or burial site, etc., was known as *myong dang* (m'yohng dahng), or "bright place."

During the Koryo dynasty (936–1392) the influence of geomancy was such that in the early centuries the dynasty had three capitals at the same time, each located in a place that was believed to be especially favorable for the regime. The ruling kings divided their time among the capitals, spending various months in each of them during the year. Each time conditions in the country became unsettled there were demands that the central capital in Kaesang be abandoned completely in favor of a new site.

The growth of a well-to-do class of rural gentry contributed to the spread of geomancy, as these groups built family compounds, burial tombs, and temples and sought to keep the spirits on their side and enhance their power and standing in their districts. Among the more conspicuous of the buildings constructed by both rural gentry and urban nobility were so-called "prayer pagodas," designed to increase the efficacy of their prayers for good fortune.

King Taejo (formerly General Song Gye Yi), founder of the Choson dynasty in 1392, decided on Seoul as the location of his new capital after months of consideration by leading geomancers of the day. Among the features that were especially favorable for Seoul: the area was surrounded by mountains, and a large river (the Han) and a major stream (the Chong Gyechon) passed through the heart of the basin.

Rapid industrialization and building in Korea since the 1960s have made *pungsu* secondary to man-made forces, but building codes enacted by Seoul and other Korean cities in the 1980s were based in part on the principles of geomancy, particularly in the amount of open space that was mandated for buildings and how it was to be landscaped.

Most Koreans, regardless of where they live, still believe that ignoring the influence of *pungsu*, or having an incorrect *pungsu* reading, will have a negative effect on their health, their work, and their lives in general. Korean home builders who live in rural areas where there is space available, and city dwellers who are affluent enough to buy large lots, still consult geomancers in the design and placement of their homes. Graves are also automatically situated to comply with *pungsu* principles.

Foreigners involved in any renovation or building project in Korea can get a lot of positive mileage out of demonstrating an awareness and knowledge of *pungsu.** Recommended reading for that purpose: *Feng Shui for Business*, by Dr. Evelyn Lip, an architect and geomancer (Times Books International, Singapore and Kuala Lumpur, 1989).

Fortunately, most people have a built-in sense of what is right or wrong about a building design and its orientation without any professional training, and interestingly enough when they describe a building that they like and feel especially comfortable in, they sound very much like geomancers.

For those who question the validity of geomancy or are willing to accept the idea that there is something to it, consider this: experts in the art say that cosmic conditions change constantly and that to remain in harmony the orientation of some buildings, doors, etc., must be changed every twenty years. They add that other buildings can go for as long as thirty years without getting out of synch with the cosmos, depending on how the environment around them changes.

Some Western architects and industrial complex designers have taken up the study of *pungsu* and now routinely use its principles in their work.

161

풍수

Puseo Jang Hoe
(Puh-say-oh Jahng Hoh-eh)

"The Weekly Scoldings"

There is perhaps no better demonstration of the impact of the traditional Confucian-oriented family concept on personnel management in large-scale Korean companies than the institutionalized weekly managers' meetings. In these meetings, called *puseo jang hoe* (puh-say-oh jahng hoh-eh) in Korean, the senior manager running the meetings generally treats the lower-ranking members the way a very stern and demanding father would treat immature and irresponsible children.

Koreans who have attended *puseo jang hoe* say that the tone of the meetings varies somewhat with the character and personality of the presiding

---

*One of the most famous contemporary incidents involving *pungsu* occurred in Hong Kong, where the art is known as *feng shui*, or "wind and rain." When the original design of the Hong Kong and Shanghai Bank building was completed by the architectural firm assigned to the project, the Chinese investors in the building insisted that the design be shown to a geomancer. The geomancer gave the architects a detailed list of changes that would have to be made in the design before the building would be in harmony with its surroundings. The investors ordered that the changes be made, despite the delay and additional cost.

executives but that all of them are designed to chastise attendees for any inefficiencies in their work, to inspire them to be more diligent in their efforts and continue striving for perfection, and to reinforce both the concept and the reality of control that superiors exercise over their subordinates.

These commentators say that it is common for meeting leaders to use harsh language when criticizing the reports given by the individual members and sometimes to continue haranguing a particular individual for up to fifteen or twenty minutes. The vehemence of such scoldings can be startling to Westerners who have not been forewarned or developed some tolerance for the experience. Having witnessed such sessions dozens of times (in Korea as well as Japan), I can personally attest to how embarrassing and upsetting they can be to an outsider and how long it takes to understand and accept them in their cultural context.

Attendees at *puseo jang hoe* are expected to "sit and take it" without any attempt to defend themselves. Generally the only thing they are permitted to do besides answer specific, direct questions is to repeatedly apologize and promise to do better.

In their Korean context these "scold meetings" are regarded by top management as part of the ongoing training process that is designed to keep middle and lower managers sharp and doing their very best. Obviously individuals who are subject to regular scoldings can be sure that their chances for promotion are dramatically diminished, so the motivation to avoid being singled out and scolded is very strong. Middle and lower managers are expected to take the same approach in criticizing and controlling unranked staff members of their sections and departments. The more severe the scolding of any lower-level individual, the more likely the manager doing the haranguing will be to later invite the person out after hours for a round of drinks and eating to demonstrate that there was nothing personal in the "attack."

One of the more conspicuously negative aspects of this approach to management is that it makes middle- and lower-level managers reluctant to approve of anything on their own and has resulted in a bureaucratic system that requires anywhere from three or four to a dozen or more signatures (*tojang*/toh-jahng), or "name seals," of people on a gradually ascending level before a proposal or document is approved.

Another result of this system is that managers almost always find something to criticize in the work of their subordinates. Some managers I have dealt with who spoke little or no English made an unwavering practice of demanding some kind of change in copy I or some other native English speaker had written.

Not surprisingly, the seating arrangements at *puseo jang hoe* are a precise representation of the hierarchical ranking of all of the individuals at the meetings, with the senior man at the head of the table and the lowest-ranking people at the foot of the table.

룸살롱
Room Salon
(Room Sah-lohn)

"Sex in a Glass"

One of the most interesting and popular attractions of the nighttime entertainment trades in Korea are the so-called *room salons* (room sah-lohns), or night spots, that are similar to some of the more intimate cabarets and nightclubs in Japan, Hong Kong, Bangkok, Manila, and other Asian cities that feature beautiful female hostesses and cater exclusively to male clientele. But unlike their counterparts in most other Asian countries, Korea's *room salons* are usually more intimate in that they feature private rooms for each individual group of customers (and more closely resemble teahouses in Taiwan). The typical room is furnished "home" style with sofas arranged around one or more coffee tables, depending on its size. A small amount of floor space is left open for dancing.

Some of the larger *salons* have live music, with a band playing onstage in a central area and sometimes going from room to room. In the latter instance the musicians play for customers who want to sing to live music. Songbooks, usually with lyrics in Japanese and English as well as Korean, are invariably on hand for the use of patrons.

Each customer who enters a *room salon* is automatically assigned a hostess who acts as a dancing partner and a very convivial table companion, pouring drinks, engaging in word and hand games, and generally creating a stimulating atmosphere. There is an unwritten rule that a patron who is unhappy with a hostess assigned to him may ask for a different hostess at least once and sometimes twice. Most places frown on customers changing hostesses more than twice.

The most prestigious, and common, drink in the *salons* is Scotch whiskey. Some regular patrons have their own bottles kept for them at their favorite place. Thereafter they pay for the services of the hostesses and whatever they eat rather than their drinks. Snack items served at *room salons*, called *anju* (ahn-juu), include such things as nuts, dried peas, steamed beans in the pod, senbei crackers, fish, and fruit. Some regular patrons run tabs at their favorite places, which they, or their company, pay monthly. This makes it possible for them to entertain guests and then walk out without any reference to the bill, something that is quite impressive to first-time foreign visitors.

Some of the most beautiful, best-educated, and most talented women in Korea work in *salons* as full-time professional hostesses. Others are students or office workers during the day and hostesses at night. Some housewives also work as hostesses.

Korea's *salon* hostesses are a modern version of the traditional *kisaeng*, who ply their trade in *kisaeng* houses (in the manner of Japan's *geisha*) and are far too expensive for the average man-about-town. All *salons* are relatively expensive. High-class clubs, such as those in major international hotels, have high-class prices. The tip for a popular hostess in such places can run to a week's salary for an ordinary working man. Most of the patrons of Korean's provocative *salons* are therefore local businessmen who have generous allowances for entertaining clients and business prospects, and they make the most of them, especially where foreign visitors are concerned.

Because of the custom of entertaining business guests, *salons* generally offer foreign businessmen in Korea on short trips the only practical opportunity they have to meet and socialize in an intimate setting with young Korean women—a situation that Korean businessmen and politicians use to their fullest advantage. Korean businessmen (like their counterparts in Japan and other parts of Asia) learned a long time ago that nothing softens and disarms men more rapidly or completely than the company of women, and *salon* hostesses play a leading role in their business relationships. The services of some *salon* hostesses are used regularly by the same clients to impress and influence their own customers and when they are engaged in especially important negotiations and are seeking some additional favorable influence on the side.

Western businessmen who have traveled widely in Asia and experienced the charms of cabaret hostesses in Tokyo, Taipei, Hong Kong, Bangkok, Kuala Lumpur, Singapore, and Manila say that only the most outstanding hostesses in Manila compare with those in Korea in terms of both beauty and sensuality. While the "sex" they sell is mostly the intangible kind, it is nevertheless a potent combination of physical beauty and feminine charms made all the more powerful by the atmosphere.

Foreign businesspeople who are visiting in Korea or are still new on the local scene but want to use *room salons* for their own entertainment purposes are advised to get the help of an experienced Korean associate to brief them on how the system works so they will be able to control the cost of an evening's entertainment while making sure that the expectations of their guests are met and everyone has a good time.

Another popular choice for people who want to spend a less expensive evening on the town are so-called "Hofs," which are German-style beer halls featuring such typical German snack items as sausages and potatoes. Some people start out their evening at a Hofs, then go elsewhere for dinner. Others do just the opposite—have dinner and then go to a Hofs to talk, sing, drink, and have fun.

Western-style nightclubs (or cabarets) also abound in Korea, many of them on the premises of major international hotels. Like the *room salons*, their primary drawing cards are their elegantly dressed and perfectly coifed hostesses, many of whom literally radiate *maeryok* (mayer-yohk), or "sensual charm."

163

사과
Sagwa
(Sahg-wah)
"The Role of the Apology"

Chae Sok Choe, author of *The Korean Social Character*, says that Koreans are unable to function in an orderly manner in relationships between equals; that they are so conditioned to superior-inferior behavior in the use of language, demeanor, and other responses that encounters with "free" people who are their equals is upsetting. Choe adds that maintaining the proper form and order in superior-inferior relationships is very difficult and is a source of a great deal of tension and anxiety for Koreans because of the constant fear that they might make a mistake and damage the other party's "face."

This anxiety is one of the reasons the *sagwa* (sahg-wah), or "apology," has been symptomatic of Korean behavior for centuries. People are always apologizing for real as well as imagined mistakes, slights, or affronts. They learned over the centuries that apologizing to superiors, even when there was nothing to apologize for, was always the better part of valor.

Because apologies were so common, a casual or perfunctory *sagwa* could be as bad as not apologizing at all, resulting in people dramatizing their apologies to family members, friends, work associates, employers, and officials with deep bows and emotional declarations of regret. Choe goes on to say that Koreans were traditionally incapable of behaving in a humble manner toward strangers and apologizing to them with genuine regret. This factor is one of the reasons verbal battles and knock-down, drag-out fights were traditionally commonplace among Korean men. Men got into situations where conflicts, even minor ones, could not be resolved with conciliatory words, and they had no choice but to resort to fisticuffs to save face. (In more recent times, this propensity for Koreans to do battle has greatly diminished as society has become more open and people are freer to express themselves verbally.)

During the thirty-six-year period when the Japanese occupied Korea (1910–45), they kept sealed dossiers on all Koreans of any social, political, or business consequence. These dossiers, compiled and kept updated by the regular police as well as secret agents and local informers, covered every aspect of the lives of the Koreans concerned, from the personal, private comments they made, to who their friends were. Every time any of these people committed what the Japanese were able to construe as a minor offense, they were required to write a *simal so* (she-mahl soh), or "letter of apology," to the Japanese authorities, asking to be forgiven and promising never to repeat the offense.

If these people continued to commit minor offenses, they were arrested and the accumulation of apology letters was used as evidence to prove that they were habitual dissidents or criminals and to justify their being sentenced to prison. Japanese managers in charge of commercial enterprises in Korea also used the dossier system of keeping a record of the attitudes and behavior of their Korean employees to keep them under control and to use as evidence against them anytime it suited the Japanese goals.

The *simal so* custom institutionalized by the Japanese was continued by Korean authorities and company management after Korea regained its independence. While it is far less intrusive now than it was during the Japanese period in Korea, it is still an important part of Korean life.

Writing "apology letters" works just as well for foreigners as it does for Koreans, and foreigners who commit real or imagined transgressions are well advised to make use of this sanctified practice in their efforts to maintain harmonious relations with their Korean contacts and government entities.

Overall the role of the *sagwa* in Korean society has diminished considerably with the growing sense of individualism and self-confidence that began developing in conjunction with the introduction of democracy into the country. But an apologetic attitude and behavior is still characteristic of Koreans who are in an inferior position, and the apology continues to play a vital role in maintaining smooth interpersonal relationships.

All too often Westerners who are inexperienced in Korea take the typical apologetic behavior of lower-ranking Koreans as an indication that they are not as strong-willed, as capable, or as trustworthy as the Westerners would like. Most of the habitual apologies made by Koreans have nothing to do with any genuine transgression on their part. They are a form of traditional politeness that includes an element of humility practiced by people on all levels of society.

The humble element in Korean politeness is a double-edged product of Confucian influence. On the one hand Confucianism conditioned the people to be genuinely humble. On the other hand it also conditioned them to be outraged by any signs of arrogance on the part of superiors. Broadly speaking, Koreans were programmed to accept the social superiority of others because their superiority was "ordained by heaven" or by fate, but only as long as those in superior positions did not let their rank or power make them arrogant. The social factor that kept relations between the high and the low in harmony was ceremonial politeness and apparent humility expressed in the form of apologies.

Westerners who learn the role and power of the apology in Korea invariably get along much better in both their private and public relationships with Koreans.

사절그러 연즐
Sajokuro/Yonjul
(Sah-johk-ur-roh/Yohn-juul)

"Personalism and Connectionism"

For more than two millennia Korea's dynastic governments were authoritarian, and all human relationships were based on a hierarchical inferior-superior class system. There was no place for such concepts as equality and justice in the Western sense. Society was structured according to Confucian principles that were aimed at creating and maintaining political stability, peace, and harmony by eliminating individualism and making the collective family the primary social unit.

Eventually this system was to become the core of Korean culture, resulting in a society that was fragmented physically and emotionally into exclusive family groups and that generally forced family members to deal with the outside world as groups rather than as individuals. Relationships between families, between families and economic enterprises, and between families and officialdom were severely limited by this system because such relations were based more on emotional factors and arbitrary rules than on practical realities.

This resulted in the entire society being based on a foundation of *sajokuro* (sah-johk-ur-roh), or "personalism"—on bringing in a personal element, from sex, class, age, and position, into every attitude and action. And since personal attitudes and actions are emotional by definition, establishing and keeping effective, harmonious relationships with others, in private as well as public and business affairs, became an extremely difficult process of balancing feelings no matter what the conflicts or contradictions might be.

Because of this personal, emotion-based social, political, and economic system, all relationships in Korea, including business and professional, were expected to grow out of personal connections instead of common interests, common needs, or reciprocal advantages. *Yonjul* (yohn-juul), or "connectionism," thus became both the fuel and the lubricant that made Korea run. Family members wanting or needing something began with their own kinship group and then expanded outward, creating social networks with whatever individual, company, or government office whose cooperation or help they needed.

The most effective of these social networks, often referred to as *in maek* (inn make), were based on very precise commonalities beginning with blood kinship, then such things as being born in the same village or town, working in the same place, and, in modern times, attending the same schools and having the same teachers. *In maek* literally means something like "human pulse" and is indicative of the importance of these personal networks. Personalism and connections are still the preferred foundation for virtually all private and public interactions in Korea. When people are forced to interact with individuals with whom they do not have appropriate connections, they invariably go to great lengths to put the relationship on a personal basis as quickly as possible. This subconscious need is one of the factors that foreigners interacting with Korean businesspeople and government officials must deal with, quickly and effectively, to establish and sustain effective relationships with them.

My Korean business colleagues explain that when it is impossible for one reason or another for them to establish a truly personal relationship with a customer, supplier, or government official, they must pretend that the relationship is personal by their manner of speech and behavior in general. This does not mean that they treat the other parties in a casual manner. The appropriate social protocol must be followed even more carefully in such situations. What it does mean is that they must behave toward the other parties as if the interaction were very personal, very emotional, very important—not just a neutral business matter.

Another facet of the *sajokuro* syndrome in Korean culture that often impacts Westerners is that it did not allow for the development of the concept of *kukpiui* (kook-pee-wee), or "confidentiality." While Korea's traditional social system was based on personal relationships, it did not incorporate the idea of "personal matters" being confidential or private because virtually all matters concerned the family, clan, and community more than the individual. This historical conditioning is still a significant part of the character of Koreans. Most people do not consider personal affairs, financial matters, and the like as being confidential and talk about them far more openly than what is common in Western societies. The same situation also generally applies to business matters, making it necessary that new employees be briefed thoroughly on the importance of keeping certain things under wraps.

Old Korea hands point out that this weak concept of *kukpiui* is one of the reasons it is especially important for foreign managers in Korea to personally qualify and hire their *piso* (pee-soh), or "private secretaries," particularly when they are involved in joint venture partnerships. Old hands note that although Koreans are generally more loyal to individual *posu* (poh-sue), or "bosses," than they are to companies, this is often not the case where joint ventures are concerned. Personal secretaries who are hired by the Korean side of a joint venture for foreign managers tend to give their loyalty to the Korean side, a situation that can be both uncomfortable and dangerous for the foreign manager.

Personalism in Korea is often linked closely with nationalism, resulting in Koreans typically reacting as a cohesive group where popular causes are concerned. For one thing it is far easier to conduct a national *poikotu* (poy-kot-tuu), or "boycott," against foreign products in Korea than in most countries because Koreans take things more personally and are conditioned to act together.

One of the most important personalized "code" phrases in the Korean language is *Jal butak hamnida* (Jahl buu-tock hahm-nee-dah), which means something like, "Please do 'something' [whatever you can] for me." It is an institutionalized, ritualistic phrase that is commonly used by people to others when they want them to do something, to take care of something out of the ordinary.

It is used in both informal and formal situations, generally among people on the same social level, and by inferiors to superiors. It includes an element of humbling oneself and elevating the other party. The use of the term makes any request very personal, thereby appealing to the deepest cultural programming of the other party.

Foreign businesspeople and others in Korea can enhance the response they get from their Korean friends and contacts by the judicious use of *Jal butak hamnida*, keeping in mind that it should not be overdone—or used to lower-ranking employees except on special occasions when they are being asked to do something that is conspicuously over and above their normal duties.

Another key phrase that is closely related to *Jal butak hamnida* is *Oryo u shijiman* (Oh-ree-yo uu she-jee-mahn), which can be translated as "I know it is difficult, but please do your best anyway." This phrase also puts the order or request on a personal basis, thereby invoking the pride and "face" of the individual asked to take on the task.

165

산
San
(Sahn)

"Korea's Sacred Mountains"

In the traditional Korean cosmos every *san* (sahn), or "mountain," was a sacred place because it had its own *san shin* (sahn sheen), or "mountain god"—an idea that derived from the shamanistic belief that spirits dwell in all high places. Buddhism, introduced into Korea between the fourth and seventh centuries A.D., held mountains in high esteem for the same reason, and taught that the beauty and serenity of mountains was conducive to deep spiritual contemplation. As a result of these two concepts, mountains have traditionally played an especially important role in the history of Korea, and the higher and more spectacular the mountain, the more important this role.

Throughout Korean history shamans as well as ordinary people have made regular pilgrimages to mountains noted as the home of more powerful gods to commune with the spirits and seek their assistance. From the earliest times Buddhist priests have also sought out exceptionally scenic places on mountains to build temples and spend their lives in study and contemplation.

For shamans and their followers the most important mountain in Korea is *Paekdu San*, or Mt. Paekdu, located in North Korea. At 2,744 meters (9,000 feet), it is the highest mountain on the Korean peninsula. Mt. Paekdu, which is on the Korea-China border in Northern Korea, has been especially sacred to Koreans since ancient times because their creation myth tells them that is where the

Korean race began in the year 2333 B.C.* According to the myth, the lord of heaven (God) sent his son, Hwanung, down to earth where he met a bear and a tiger. The son offered the two a chance to become human by staying in a cave for a lengthy time, eating only garlic. The tiger failed the test, but the bear succeeded and became a beautiful woman. Hwanung and the woman mated and had a son, named Tangun, who became the Adam of the Korean race and the first king.

Like Mt. Fuji in Japan, *Paekdu San* is the cone of an extinct volcano that is visible for miles and is snow covered in winter. Close up it is made even more spectacular by a crater lake on its summit that is 14 kilometers (9 miles) in circumference and 380 meters (1,250 feet) deep.

The 1948 division of Korea into two political entities, separated by impassable military barriers at the thirty-eighth parallel, meant that South Koreans could no longer make pilgrimages to Mt. Paekdu. This eventually resulted in Mt. Taebaek in Kangwon province east of Seoul, facing the East Sea (Sea of Japan), being named as an alternate home of Tangun, the nation's founder. Mt. Mani on the offshore island of Kanghwa, west of Seoul, is a third "alternate" for shamanistic rites marking the birth of Tangun.

Other mountains that have traditionally been sacred to Korean shamanists include Mt. Kumgang and Mt. Myohyang in North Korea and Mt. Chiri, Mt. Moak, Mt. Mudung, Mt. Inwang (in west-central Seoul), and Mt. Pukan north of Seoul.

Mt. Halla, the volcanic mountain that makes up the bulk of Cheju Island (Korea's largest island and one of the nine provinces of South Korea), also has a small crater lake and is sometimes referred to as the Mt. Paekdu of the southern part of the country. Semitropical Cheju is some eighty-five kilometers (53 miles) off the southern tip of the Korean peninsula, and for many centuries was out of the mainstream of Korean life. Its relative isolation resulted in many of its shamanistic traditions surviving intact into modern times.**

(By the mid-1980s Cheju was anything but isolated. It had become a favorite vacation spot not only for Koreans but for Japanese as well, with world-class hotels and excellent restaurants with international menus. The island now boasts golf courses and many other amenities aimed at tourists. Some see it continuing to develop as a kind of Hong Kong and as an ideal jumping-off place for visiting mainland Korea as well as China, which is only a short jet hop away.)

---

*In a ploy to add to the prestige of Il Sung Kim, the first president of North Korea, the North Korean government had history books rewritten to show that Kim established a secret guerrilla headquarters on Mt. Paekdu during World War II and, operating from that camp, defeated the Japanese army that was occupying Korea. New history books also claim that Jong Il Kim, who succeeded his father, Il Sung Kim, as the president of North Korea in 1994, was born on Mt. Paeduk and that at his birth white horses were seen flying in the vicinity. Earlier sources list the Russian city of Khabarovsk as Jong Il Kim's birthplace.

**Native inhabitants of Cheju Island have their own creation myth, which is similar to that of the Hopi Indians in the American state of Arizona. Both the Hopi and the Chejuans say their ancestors came from the interior of the earth, entering this world through a hole in the ground.

Traditionally each village in Korea had its own special mountain, where there was a shrine to house the mountain spirit. Some villages in present-day Korea continue this traditional shamanistic practice, and each year hundreds of thousands of Koreans, from urban as well as rural areas, make pilgrimages to mountains to invoke the goodwill of the gods. For a growing number of young Koreans, however, the spectacular mountains on the peninsula are valued more as mountain-climbing and skiing destinations than as religious shrines.

166

산실
Sashil
(Sah-sheel)

"Forget the Facts!"

Encounters between Koreans and Westerners can sometimes leave the Westerners in a state of culture shock that ranges from mild to incapacitating. One of the reasons for this is that Koreans are conditioned to be human oriented, while Westerners are programmed to be fact oriented. Human values and facts often act very much like oil and water. They do not mix—especially when the human values were created in a society where such concepts as equality, fairness, directness, unvarnished truthfulness, and rational thinking in general were traditionally either immoral, unknown, or both—a description that fits traditional Korea precisely.

Present-day Koreans are certainly capable of rational thinking and very pragmatic behavior when it is advantageous for them to do so, but a great deal of their personal behavior in one-on-one relationships is still based on giving feelings precedence over *sashil* (sah-sheel), or "facts." Much of the time, *chong-shik* (chohng-sheek), "formality" or "formal process," is also more important than anything else.

Western businesspeople, particularly Americans, invariably emphasize two points when they engage Koreans in any kind of dialogue—facts and fairness. Koreans generally find this approach disturbing, and as often as not, depending on how aggressive the other parties are, it turns them off because they believe it is proper and best to deal with human factors first and work the "facts" in gradually, as circumstances warrant.

To further complicate matters, the traditional Korean idea of fairness often differs significantly from the Western concept. While fairness in its Western context is based on mutual equality, fairness where Koreans are concerned tends to be egocentric and interpreted from a hierarchical perspective.

In this context the inferior-superior relationship between people determines what is fair, and since some people are always "more equal" than others, fairness is an arbitrary thing based on social status. Where strangers—and foreigners—are concerned, the criterion for fairness becomes more personal and more subject to individual interpretation. Personal advantage becomes the overriding factor, not the obligation to be fair in an objective sense.

In business situations involving foreign companies there is generally an additional factor—a deep-seated belief that the business should favor Korea. The reason for this built-in attitude is the national concept that Korea is small, has limited natural resources, and has traditionally been preyed on by outsiders, so therefore Korean companies should not be expected to compete with foreign companies—or larger, richer foreign countries—on an equal footing.

Foreign businesspeople can generally work around the Korean custom of putting personal factors ahead of *sashil* by beginning with the personal, human facets of their proposal or project and thereafter working in the facts instead of the reverse. In addition to not triggering the Korean allergy to hard facts first, this approach is a clear signal that the foreign side is sensitive to Korean customs and has a corporate culture that is responsive to the Korean environment.

At the same time, it is essential that foreign companies not bend so far in the Korean wind that they are kept permanently off balance. Finding the right equilibrium between facts and harmonizing with the local scene requires a great deal of cultural insight that is generally best achieved on a short-term basis through the counsel of bilingual, bicultural Koreans who have had considerable experience in successfully bridging cultural gaps. Old-time expatriates say it takes three or four years of intensive cross-cultural exposure for a foreigner to absorb enough of the language and culture to personally read the signs and react effectively.

167

사양

Sayang

(Sah-yahng)

"Keeping a Low Profile"

In pre-modern Korea boasting in any form about anything, but especially about one's own intelligence and ability, was a serious transgression against the traditional morality. Bragging was equated with arrogance and was officially taboo in the Confucian concept of human relations. Koreans were conditioned from childhood to thoroughly despise people who boasted about their knowledge or accomplishments, and to exalt those who concealed their intelligence and ability out of consideration for the feelings of others. The lower the class of people, the stronger the taboos against displaying any kind of superiority.

This enforced *sayang* (sah-yahng), or "humility," went a long way toward preserving harmony in Korean society. But it also contributed to the preservation of ignorance and mediocrity among the vast majority of people and generally prevented those with natural or acquired intelligence and ability from demonstrating their learning and skills and thereby bringing about technical and social improvements. Among the educated ruling class as well, one of the most prized traits of the truly wise and talented person was a humble manner in all things.

At the same time, the pride and arrogance of people tended to increase in direct proportion to their political power, making humility a personal and arbitrary factor rather than a universal cultural trait. In this social and political environment inferiors tended to behave in a humble manner when interacting with superiors, and superiors tended to exercise their prerogatives of pride and privilege in their relations with inferiors. In other words, humility, like every other behavioral trait in the traditional Korean character, was circumstantial and was based primarily on the hierarchical relationship of the people involved.

Sayang continues to play an especially important role in Korean life. Modern etiquette requires that people downplay verbal references to their ability and accomplishments, but it does not preclude them from demonstrating what they know and can do. In fact the confidence that Koreans demonstrate in their ability is virtually unbounded. As long as this "can do" attitude is expressed in terms of a group, rather than as an individual, it is not only culturally acceptable but expected and admired.

Probably the most common manifestation of the *sayang* syndrome is when people are served tea or a meal. It is customary to wait until the invitation (or request) to drink or eat has been repeated at least three times before actually beginning. In this context the term refers to doing something that is against one's will (refusing to drink or eat when you are actually thirsty or hungry) but behavior that is an integral part of Korean etiquette.

The importance of maintaining a humble attitude in Korea contrasts sharply with the role of aggressive self-confidence, pride, and self-embellishment that is characteristic of Americans and other Westerners and is often the source of substantial misunderstanding and friction between Koreans and Westerners. Westerners who do not speak Korean and have had little or no exposure to Korean culture often misjudge the intelligence and competence of Koreans not only because Koreans downplay their abilities but also because the Westerners are not capable of judging them.

At the same time, Koreans are likely to view the aggressive, self-promoting behavior of many Westerners as arrogant and as a sign of callous disregard for the feelings of others, further compounding the problem of cross-cultural communication and cooperation. Koreans have special difficulty accepting and dealing with the type of curt, aggressive behavior that is often associated with some foreigners. When they encounter this kind of behavior, whether it is subtle or out in the open, their reaction is naturally negative, compounding the situation.

There are no fast, easy solutions to the problems caused by this particular cultural clash. Obviously, any effort to resolve the conflict must begin with both sides being aware of the underlying reasons for the friction, taking steps to alter their own behavior to achieve an acceptable compromise and develop tolerance for the things that cannot be changed quickly or easily.

Of course, for Westerners contemplating doing business in Korea, the ideal is to begin with a concentrated course in the Korean language and culture, then work out an approach that will allow them to behave in a straightforward and candid manner toward all Koreans, regardless of their status—something that will eventually gain them more respect and cooperation than trying to emulate Korean behavior.

168

세계화
Segyehwa
(Say-gay-hwah)
"Korean-Style Globalization"

Korean history has been linked intimately with that of Japan since ancient times. From around the fourth century A.D. until the first decades of the seventeenth century the relationship was one-sided, with cultural and technological influence flowing from Korea to Japan. In the 1630s both nations practically sealed themselves off from the world. The Japanese left only three tiny windows open for limited contact with the outside—one small group of Dutch traders who were kept isolated on a man-made islet in Nagasaki Bay and allowed one ship visit per year and periodic visits by Chinese and Korean trade ships that were controlled carefully by the shogunate.

Korea's only doors to the outside world were no more than tiny cracks, consisting of annual missions to Beijing, China, to deliver tribute, and limited contact with Japan, generally through the island of Tsushima, which lies midway between Pusan, Korea, and southwestern Japan. Both countries were to remain "hermit kingdoms" until the nineteenth century.

Japan's geographic position in the North Pacific, where it became known to early American whalers, Russian explorers, and European traders in the eighteenth century, resulted in it becoming the first to reopen its doors to the outside world. As more and more ships from Russia, the United States, and Europe's great colonial powers began entering Japanese waters, and now and then being wrecked offshore by typhoons, these countries began competing with each other to force Japan to end its isolation policy.

Using gunboat diplomacy, the United States won this competition and in the 1850s became the first foreign country to reestablish diplomatic and trade relations with Japan since it had closed its doors in 1637. Japan's shogunate system of government could not survive this encounter with the West and fell in 1867 to a group of young radicals determined to transform the country into a Western-style economic and military power.

Less than fifteen years later a rapidly industrializing Japan used military force to end Korea's isolation and ultimately to bring about the collapse of the Korean government. But rather than allow progressive elements in Korea to form a new government, the Japanese invaded, captured, and in 1910, annexed the country.

Although Japan took the lead in industrializing Korea between 1910 and 1945 (when Korea regained its sovereignty as a result of Japan's defeat in World War II), the industrialization was done as an appendage to Japan's own economy. Thus, in 1945, when Japan was defeated and Korea regained its independence, the Korean business community was some sixty-five years behind that of Japan in terms of management experience.

The situation in Korea was exacerbated by the division of the country in 1945 into North Korea and South Korea and then by the Korean War from 1950 until 1953, which further devastated the country's industrial infrastructure and killed hundreds of thousands of its best-educated and most experienced men.

It was not until the mid-1950s that Korea was able to turn its energy to rebuilding the country, and then it started out with an industrial base that was far smaller than that of Japan. Only a few hundred Korean managers had had limited experience in running large-scale operations, and practically none of them had had any international experience.

What Korea did have was a historical reverse in its traditional relationship with Japan. Japan had become an economic role model for Korea to follow, and it did so with such speed and efficiency that it astounded the world. Some maintain that the economic "miracle" accomplished by Korea was, in fact, more of a miracle than Japan's own rapid rise to economic prominence because Korea started with much less and had much further to go.

Korea has continued to emulate Japan in its economic policies and in some areas has virtually eliminated the managerial and technological gaps between the two countries. In fact many expatriate businesspeople in Korea say that Koreans are better managers than the Japanese because they are more candid, open-minded, and flexible, and that they take a much more pragmatic approach to research.

It may very well be that the last lesson Koreans take from the Japanese experience is both the process and the pace of the globalization of the Korean economy. In the 1980s some of Japan's more farsighted industrial and political leaders began talking about *kyosei* (k'yoh-say-ee), literally "symbiosis" or "living in harmony," in reference to integrating the Japanese economy into the global economy. But given the fact that the overwhelming majority of Japanese businessmen and bureaucrats were vehemently against the idea, believing it would destroy the country, those in favor of deregulating and globalizing the Japanese economy took the typical Japanese way of attempting to achieve *kyosei* in small increments over a period of several decades.

Beginning in the early 1990s, Korean business and political leaders began using the term *segyehwa* (say-gay-hwah) in their comments and speeches regarding their economic system and international trade relations. *Segyehwa* literally means "worldization," i.e., "globalization," and refers to a state of mind as well as to the structure of business. Like their Japanese counterparts, however, while these Korean leaders began publicly espousing *segyehwa*, they generally continued to do things the way they had always done them out of deep-seated fear of foreign competition in their home market.

Top executives of Korea's huge multinational firms were well aware that the globalization of the Korean economy would be inevitable in the future if they wanted to continue to have access to foreign markets. But the first aim of these newly converted globalists was to blunt growing criticism from foreign businesspeople and governments about the closed nature of the Korean market and the inroads Korean manufacturers were making abroad.

Segyehwa has since become something of a catchall slogan intended to impress foreign critics and to program both bureaucrats and businesspeople to accept the gradual globalization of the Korean economy. But given Korea's history as a victim of foreign powers, and a form of patriotic nationalism that is palpable, it is not likely that Koreans will voluntarily open their doors completely no matter how much pressure is brought against them. Those who oppose globalization point out that Korea is a tiny country with limited natural resources and could not possibly compete even in its own market with China, Europe, Japan, and the United States combined.

In the meantime, *segyehwa* will no doubt continue to be held up as Korea's official economic philosophy, as something that is very desirable but not possible for the time being.

Adds Martin H. Sours, a professor at the American Graduate School of International Management: "A few influential Korean elites are seeking globalization while preserving Korean roots. But the widespread mandatory study of English is irreversible. In the late 1990s one prestigious Korean university announced a plan to require all students, regardless of their major, to enroll in one class taught in English."

Some Korean company executives insist that the day-to-day business in their international departments be conducted in English.

169

선

Seon
(Say-own)

"Spouse Hunts"

Westerners customarily have regarded many of the traditional attitudes and much of the behavior of Asians as both impractical and irrational. The extreme formality, the presentation of "false fronts," and the custom of using vague, indirect speech that have long been characteristic of Asian cultures have frequently been used by Westerners to denigrate Asians and make themselves feel superior. The Asian tradition of "arranged marriages" rather than "love marriages" is another custom that Westerners tend to regard as dehumanizing.

But from the Asian viewpoint a dispassionate comparison of arranged marriages and love marriages clearly reveals that arranged marriages make more sense than "love knots." So-called love marriages are based primarily on emotional and sexual needs, which, as is well known, are "blind." Family background, education, physical and mental health, and genetic makeup are incidental things that play little or no role.

In arranged marriages, on the other hand, mature adults, who put the long-term interest of the households and their sons and daughters first, use a long list of objective criteria in bringing potential spouses together. In Korea the meeting of potential brides and grooms is a formal affair known as a *seon* (say-own). The "seconds" of the two young people—professional go-betweens, close relatives, employers, parents—escort the young people separately to a public meeting place, usually a restaurant, where they are introduced and allowed to look each other over. If both parties get past this first hurdle, a second meeting, usually just the two prospects, is arranged. A successful second meeting usually leads to an agreement to marry.

Despite the growing popularity of love marriages in Korea, the traditional *seon* remains an important social custom that is not likely to disappear in the foreseeable future. Korean traditionalists point out that it is far more rational and practical than the "hit-or-miss" method common in the West.

A new "courting code word" that became vogue among male and female college students during the 1980s is similar to *date* or *dating*. This term is the English word *meeting*, which has been incorporated into the Korean language to mean a rendezvous between young single men and women who are romantically interested in each other. It is also used in reference to small groups of male and female students who meet at special places to socialize with each other, with the idea being that couples who are attracted to each other will begin to date. Although the Koreanized version of *meeting* is still used most commonly by college students, it is gradually coming into use off campus as well.

170

시
Shi
(She)

"The Poetic Culture"

Like all cultures in the Buddhist sphere of Asia, the traditional Korean way of life incorporated a poetic dimension that exercised a fundamental influence on the intellectual, spiritual, and emotional life of the people. *Shi* (she), or "poetry," was important in Korea before the introduction of Buddhism, however. As in most ancient cultures, the first native Korean poetry was oral and consisted of chants and songs for ritual worship and ritualized work.

In 109 B.C., China invaded Korea and for the next four hundred years exercised considerable control over the various Korean kingdoms as provincial fiefdoms. During these centuries the Chinese system of writing as well as

Buddhism, Confucianism, and the Chinese system of education were introduced into Korea and became an integral part of Korean culture.

The study and writing of poetry had already been one of the primary facets of education in China for more than a thousand years. Among the educated class in China, knowledge of poetry and the ability to compose poetry, often on the spur of the moment, were regarded as the measure of a man's cultural achievements and his qualifications for responsibility and public office. This tradition was passed on to Korea.

Thus the first Korean poetry to be conceived as poetry (as opposed to oral songs and chants) was written in Chinese by Korean scholars and followed the Chinese model. Buddhist monks transformed shamanist chants and prayers into Korea's first written poetry, called *hyangga* (h'yahng-gah), or "native songs."

Korean literary historians say there were four primary characteristics, or requirements, for writing *Han shi* (Hahn she), or "Chinese-style poetry." First it had to be "I" centered; that is, it had to express the personal viewpoint or feelings of the composer. Second, it had to express the Buddhistic philosophy of transcendence through freedom and liberation as well as the Confucian concept of achieving ultimate wisdom through order and control.

The third criterion of poetry was that it should be spontaneous—not something that the writer would labor over for hours, days, or weeks—and that it should reflect a powerful universal emotion brought on by some sudden event or experience, such as seeing the moon rise, witnessing a bird in flight, or unexpectedly meeting an old friend. A fourth qualification was that poems be about the universal essence of things as opposed to their outward appearance. A flower covered with dew and struck by the morning sun, for example, would be seen as symbolic of the whole of nature.

During the unified Shilla period (669–935) Korean scholars developed a system of using Chinese ideograms phonetically to write the Korean language. This made it possible for Korean composers of *hyangga* to write their compositions and record many of those that had been passed down orally for generations.

During the Koryo dynasty (918–1392) a form of poetry called *changga* (chahng-gah), literally "long songs," replaced the earlier *hyangga*. There were two kinds of *changga*—a longer sophisticated type written in Chinese and a shorter version that was passed on orally and was called *sogyo* (soag-yoh), meaning "common" or "vulgar," but which, in fact, were very elegant and subtle (like Japanese haiku).

The traditions of *Han shi* continued during Korea's last dynasty (Choson, 1392–1910), evolving into two genres, *sijo* (she-joh) and *kasa* (kah-sah), which, together, were said to express the sensibilities that were the most characteristic of Koreans.

Kasa poetry, described as "prose poetry," celebrated the beauty of nature. *Sijo* poetry, which had originated during the Koryo dynasty (918–1392), was philosophical in nature.

Some examples of *Han shi*:

> Autumn winds are blowing;
> I chant a sad song.
> So few people in this world
> have ever understood me.
> It is the third watch;
> rain splatters the window.
> I sit in front of the lamp,
> my spirit 10,000 *li* away.
>
> —*Written in the eighth century by*
> *Chiwon Choe while serving as an*
> *official in China, far from his*
> *Korean home*

> Desolate the monk's room
> beside the ancient tree;
> one lamp burns in the shrine,
> one incense burner smokes.
> I ask the old monk
> how on earth he spends his days:
> A chat when a guest comes;
> when the guest goes, a nap.
>
> —*Kyu Bo Yi (1168–1241)*

> Rip your black robe asunder;
> fashion a pair of breeches.
> Take off your rosary;
> use it for a donkey's crupper.
> These ten years studying
> Buddha's Pure Land,
> invoking the Goddess of Mercy
> and Amithaba's saving hand,
> let them go where they will.
> Night on a nun's breast
> is no time for reciting sutras.
>
> —*Chol Chong (1536–1593)*

Contemporary Korean *shiin* (she-een), "poets," write in their own language, of course. Some write in the ancient Korean and Chinese traditions, others in the Western tradition. Some are creating traditions of their own. One example:

> So hushed the sky
> an orchid wondering why
> opened its petals wide.
>
> —*Author unknown*

시간

Shigan
(She-gahn)

"On Fast Time"

Expatriate businesspeople in Korea often have occasion to smile at first-time visitors from New York who are prone to brag—or complain—about the pace of business in that city. It usually doesn't take more than a week or ten days before these visitors change their tune and begin looking forward to getting back to their home bases so they can rest up.

The Korean view and use of time changed dramatically from 1961 on, when General Chung Hee Pak (Park) established a virtual military dictatorship and set out to turn South Korea into a Japan-style economic superpower. For the next eighteen years General Pak (who retired from the army in 1963 and won election to the presidency as a civilian) ran Korea with stern military efficiency. He was assassinated by the head of the Korean Central Intelligence Agency in 1979 as a result of growing discontent over his dictatorial policies and rigging of elections, but in the meantime he and his administration had successfully launched an economic miracle that was far more impressive than what the Japanese had succeeded in doing because they started with far less and got far less help from the United States and other Western nations.

Given the traditional Korean view and use of *shigan* (she-gahn), or "time," the dedication of the Koreans to General Pak's program was astounding. Factory hands and managers alike worked from sixty to eighty hours a week, with a diligence that was almost superhuman. Senior executives often lived in their offices for days and weeks at a time. Their wives brought them clean clothing and food. For more than thirty years the pace of work and business in Korea continued at a frenzy and still today is much faster and more intense than in most countries.

This extraordinary transformation in the character of Koreans obviously came about because for the first time in the history of the country the people were actually working for themselves and for the nation. The government, rather than blocking their efforts as it had traditionally done in the past, played a leading role in planning and promoting economic progress on a massive scale.

Having been subjected to the arbitrary rule of their own kings and ruling class from the beginning of their history until 1910, and then used as virtual slave laborers by the Japanese from 1910 until 1945, the Koreans literally exploded with energy and determination. Part of this transformation was complete repudiation of the harsh and unhappy past. The past was something to be forgotten.

Like modern-day computer software programs, the Koreans attempted to compress more and more activity into each hour of the day and night. Speed became one of the key values motivating the business world. Nothing was too big, too technical, or too complicated to attempt. During this period there was little distinction between private and public or work time. Generally speaking, income was not based on how many hours people worked but on how much they were able to produce. For some thirty years everything was secondary to work and productivity.

Business activity in Korea has since slowed down to something below the speed of light, but most Koreans, especially those in high-tech export industries and service industries catering to international clientele, still work with a dedication and energy that sets them apart from most other people.

Korean essayist Kyu Tae Yi says that *shigan* in Korea is intensely "tight and fast." He says that present-day Koreans regard rushing about, doing things as quickly as possible, and doing several things at the same time as a virtue. He adds that they like to be first and to "take the high ground" in everything. But despite this attitude and the kind of behavior it entails, on a personal basis typical Koreans are not nearly as time-bound as Americans and other Westerners. They regard time as more elastic or flexible. They do not see being "on time" as an inherently serious matter. Intentions take precedence over time.

As far as personal appointments are concerned, being thirty minutes "late" is culturally acceptable to Koreans. However, businesspeople, especially those who are used to dealing with foreigners, generally conform to the Western concept of time when making and keeping appointments.

Koreans still tend to blur private and public time. Their concept of time, Yi continues, is "human centered" and "work centered," so they do not automatically keep track of the hours they work as Westerners are wont to do. Employees do not dash for the door at the official quitting time. However, the attitude toward *shigan* among the younger generations is changing. They are becoming more and more interested in having a life away from their workplaces, and pressure for a more equitable division of their time is growing.

172

실패

Shilpae
(Sheel-pay)

"Avoiding Failure"

Koreans have a phobia about *shilpae* (sheel-pay), or "failure" in both an individual and personal sense. They were programmed for centuries to shun individualism and personal responsibility in favor of groupism and group responsibility, making them exceptionally wary of any kind of personal failure. The legacy of this conditioning remains a significant part of the national character of Koreans. This does not mean, however, that Koreans do not experience or recognize individual failure. It happens all the time, but there continues to be considerable effort to diffuse personal responsibility for failure by dealing with it in a group context. Being personally blamed for failure would result in shame, which is one of the worst things that can befall Koreans and is therefore avoided whenever possible.

Fear of personal *shilpae* is one of the factors that imbues Koreans with extraordinary energy and motivation to persevere, regardless of the odds, in anything they undertake in an effort to avoid failure—a cultural trait that is virtually the opposite of the attitude of Westerners, who rationalize failure as one of the best ways to learn, routinely take chances that are likely to end in failure, and preach the philosophy of getting up and trying again.

Generally speaking, Korea's early society was not tolerant of failure of any kind on any level. The Zen sect of Buddhism taught Koreans that the goal of all actions was perfection and that people should strive endlessly for that goal. At the same time, the social and economic ideology greatly limited all innovation and experimentation, correspondingly reducing the chances of failure because people were limited in what they could do.

In addition to the personal shame resulting from failure and taboos against trying to change things, there could also be punishment of some kind, ranging from loss of privileges to demotion in rank or social status. Because of these social sanctions against *shilpae*, Koreans generally did not undertake anything they felt might prove to be embarrassing or get them into trouble.

The end of the feudal social system in Korea in the mid-1900s freed Koreans for the first time to try new things and take chances, but it did not eliminate the centuries of conditioning to abhor failure. This led them to go to extremes to avoid failure by studying and working with almost superhuman energy and diligence. Between 1960 and 1990 Korea literally roared with a cacophony of noise rising from the incessant activity of people and machines.

Still today Koreans regularly note that Americans and people in other large industrialized countries can afford to make mistakes because they can start over again without any serious consequences, whereas they often have only one opportunity to succeed. Foreign businesspeople and diplomats involved with Korea invariably encounter this fear-of-*shilpae* syndrome and must devise ways of getting around it. This involves long-term indoctrination in the concept that failure is not the end of things if the effort was sincere and that more often than not failure is a valuable learning tool. To make this lesson stick, it is vital that Korean managers and employees have solid guarantees of job security.

The idea that it is better to try and fail than not to try at all was totally alien to Koreans until the aftermath of the Korean War (1950–53), when they literally had no choice if they wanted to survive.

173

신
Shin
(Sheen)

"Life Without God"

Koreans have never had a personalized concept of a "living God" in the form of a single spiritual being watching over them, passing judgment on their thoughts and actions, waiting to welcome them into heaven or to consign them to hell depending on their attitudes and behavior during life. The ancient Koreans did not create an all-powerful *Shin* (Sheen), or God, in their own idealized image. Neither did they create a heaven or hell in the popular Christian image.

The "heavenly beings" in the Korean cosmos might more appropriately be called *nature spirits*. There was a senior or supreme god in the shamanist pantheon of Korean thought, but it seems this was more of an honorary position than anything else because "he" was seldom if ever mentioned. People prayed to the individual gods and spirits who were directly responsible for the forces that affected their lives—those that controlled the rain, wind, the growth of crops, and other practical matters. Sociologist Tae Rim Yun notes in his book *Koreans: The Structure of Their Minds* that what Koreans want from "heaven" is a long life, wealth, comfort, social status, and to be remembered after death. They are "here and now" oriented.

There is no concept of original sin in the Korean cosmos, so Koreans do not start out having to seek "salvation" from a vengeful God. And praying to one or more gods and spirits does not ensure them of any kind of beyond-life salvation. When Koreans pray, it is for a concrete benefit in the real world, either right now or in the future. There is an old Korean proverb to the effect that "It is better to live in a field of dung in this world than hope for a better life in the afterworld."

Many Koreans therefore have difficulty understanding and accepting religions that have only one god and emphasize an uncertain and unknowable afterlife rather than the here and now. In the Korean context of things such religions are anti-life and do not really make sense. When Christian missionaries flocked into Korea in the 1870s and 1880s, they were overjoyed at the reception they received from many Koreans. But the attraction that Christianity had for Koreans was not theological. It was social and political. They were impressed by the Christian concept of spiritual, social, and political equality, human rights, and other concepts they had never before experienced.

These aspects of Christianity played a major role in the breakup of the Confucian-based Choson dynasty between 1880 and 1910 and in virtually all of the positive political, social, and economic changes that have occurred in Korea since that time. But Koreans do not attribute any of these changes to the Christian God. Instead they attribute them to the social and political philosophies that are an integral part of Christianity. "It's the Christian sense of values, love, charity, self, individualism, and living in a Christian community that makes Christianity attractive to many Koreans," says Martin H. Sours, Professor of International Asian Studies at the American Graduate School of International Management.

Generally speaking, Koreans believe that Buddhism and its various sects are superior in many ways to Christianity, Judaism, and Islam because these are intolerant "one God" religions that attempt to force people to behave in ways that are often both irrational and inhuman. In popular terms—if they give the matter any thought at all—most Koreans prefer to deal with several gods who are not as strict, not as vengeful, and more understanding of the nature of mankind.

Probably the most important thing that Christianized Westerners should keep in mind about Korean attitudes and behavior is that generally their morality—their sense of "sin"—is not based on any theologically oriented philosophy of right or wrong but on practical matters in the here and now. This means that their attitudes and behavior can vary in fundamental ways, depending on the circumstances.

174

신용
Shinyong
(Sheen-yohng)
"Operating on Trust"

Throughout the last five hundred years of Korea's pre-modern history its society functioned primarily on the basis of Confucian precepts that were an integral part of the culture. People absorbed these precepts naturally as they grew up. Their behavior was determined by this cultural and social programming rather than by written laws. In this environment all relationships were based on a combination of obligations and *shinyong* (sheen-yohng), or "trust." Each person was expected to conduct himself or herself according to a minutely prescribed etiquette based on the immutable factors of sex and age as well as social class and position.

The basis for social conduct, including the foundations of Korean morality, was the family unit. While the same etiquette and morality generally applied to all families, it was more of a personal thing than a universal thing, which had the effect of confining trust to family and to a limited number of others with whom one had some kind of personal relationship.

Shinyong based on family and personal ties remains a key factor in Korean life, particularly in the areas of personnel recruitment in business and government service, and in management in general. This has led Korean social scientists to list categories of people according to "trust scales" that went from 100 percent trust down to zero trust. Generally the only people who were rated at 100 percent on these scales were parents, spouses, children, and brothers and sisters. Next in line were nephews and nieces, who come in at 99 percent. Cousins were rated at 97 percent and other relatives at 96 percent. High school classmates came in at 97 percent, college classmates at 85 percent, and members of the same church at 95 percent. People with the same family name, as well as those whose ancestral homes were in the same part of the country, were ranked at 70 percent on the trust scale. Other Koreans who were strangers got a very low 5 percent. Lowest of all were foreigners with whom there was no relationship of any kind. They got a very conspicuous 1 percent.

Korean consultant and go-between H. J. Chang (Semco International) and others say these assessments are now much too narrow, but that "trust scales" continue to serve as the base from which Koreans contemplate, start, and manage any kind of venture involving employees or partners. In many common situations, these precise relationships take priority over all other considerations. They play some role in virtually every enterprise in Korea. In addition to a trust scale applied to individuals, high schools and colleges in Korea are rated according to a prestige scale. These two scales are generally combined when it comes to evaluating employee candidates. Until the early 1990s most larger Korean companies made a practice of hiring graduates from just one or two schools so as to take advantage of the relationship ties that exist among the alumni. Now hiring practices are more likely to be driven by individual qualifications as well.

Given this *shinyong* factor in Korea life, newly arrived foreign business-people who have no prior relationships with individual Koreans or with Korean schools are seriously handicapped. Old-timers say that it takes around three years for newcomers to be accepted and become productive, even when they are very much aware of the obstacles they face and work diligently to overcome them. This time frame may be shortened, however, by establishing a network of connections months in advance of actual entry into Korea. This can be done through Korean embassies, consulates, banks, universities, service organizations (Kiwanis and Rotarian contacts), professional associations, local groups of expatriate Koreans, the foreign subsidiaries of Korean companies, and the like.

Whatever the situation, foreigners should keep in mind that business and other relationships in Korea are invariably based more on personal trust and confidence than on contracts, laws, or such principles as equality, fairness, and justice.

십이지간
Shipijikan
(Sheep-ee-jee-kahn)

"Living by the Numbers"

During Korea's long pre-modern era, astrologers were a mainstay of society, consulted by virtually everyone. There were full-time astrologers attached to the king's court. Families in the elite *yangban* class also retained astrologers to guide them in making all kinds of decisions, from when to hold weddings to the most auspicious days for traveling or engaging in some enterprise. Astrologers, many of them part-time, also made their services available to common people, often by setting up temporary makeshift sidewalk "offices" in villages, towns, and cities in the evenings.

The key to Korean astrology, the *shipijikan* (sheep-ee-jee-kahn), or "zodiac," (literally "twelve earthly columns"), like so many other things, was imported from China some two thousand years ago. As in other areas of Asia, it is based on the lunar calendar rather than the solar calendar as in the West. Since the lunar calendar is shorter than the solar calendar, it is necessary to add a month every thirty months to keep the two calendars more or less synchronized. Because of this, astrological forecasts and the date of holidays based on the lunar calendar can vary by as much as thirty-eight days.

Korean astrology also differs from its Western counterpart in that a person's *tti* (tee) sign is based on the year of birth rather than the month. The role played by the exact time of birth is the same, however. Another difference in the Asian and Western *shipijikan* is that while the Western zodiac is based on the movement and relationships of the planets and stars, the Asian zodiac is symbolically based on twelve animals and various characteristics attributed to them.

There is a disarming story about how the names of animals came to be applied to lunar calendar. According to the story, Buddha commanded that all animals appear before him. The only ones who responded were the rat, ox (or cow), tiger, rabbit, dragon, snake, horse, goat, monkey, rooster, dog, and pig, in that order.

Since that time, these animals have been honored by being used to illustrate the attitudes and behavior demonstrated by people, with each characteristic related as closely as possible to the nature of the animal representing the year of birth—an approach that may better fit the traditional character and personality of Confucian and Buddhism-oriented Asians than people from other philosophical and religious traditions. (In my own case, I have some difficulty equating my personality and character with my "birth animal"— the dragon—even though it "sounds" a lot better than being compared to a rat, rabbit, goat, or pig.)

Astrology no longer plays the defining role in Korean life, but it is still an important cultural factor in the lives of many people, with the degree of its importance determined primarily by the individual's level of education and internationalization. Still, relatively sophisticated people pay careful attention to the *shipijikan* signs of prospective mates and to time cycles and dates in general.

176

실업가
Shiropka
(She-rope-kah)
"Businesspeople Redeemed"

Until modern times merchants, the businesspeople of preindustrial Korea, were officially one of the lowest of the social classes because of religious beliefs that making a profit from the labor of others was immoral. Skill in business as well as manual labor of any kind, no matter how expert a person might be or how much technology was involved, did not earn one special social status. The greatest carpenters, stonemasons, potters, or iron workers were not singled out for honor because that would usurp the vertical structure of the society.

Genuine social status was generally given only to scholars and government officials, especially the latter because only they had the power to make decisions and accumulate wealth. For this reason the dream of virtually every male Korean was to become a government official—something that was totally out of the question during most of Korea's history for all except the sons of the elite *yangban* class.

In the early decades of the Choson dynasty (1392–1910), the royal court issued licenses to a fairly large number of merchants authorizing them to act as purchasing agents for the government. The merchants receiving these licenses were known as *kong in* (kohng een), or "tribute men," in reference to the requirement that they remit a percentage of their income to the court.

These special licenses were hereditary and remained in effect for more than two hundred years. Because of their exclusive right to supply the needs of the court and all of its agencies, the income of these merchants was guaranteed, and eventually they became a well-to-do middle class—the first in the history of Korea. But because of the ongoing religious climate that regarded business as immoral and virtually no legal system for the protection of business activities, these merchants invested their surplus capital in land rather than new business, perpetuating the basic agricultural and cottage industry economy that had existed since ancient times.

It was not until 1791, in conjunction with the opening of three huge public markets in Seoul, that most of these royal licenses were withdrawn. One of these markets adjoined the East Gate just inside the great wall surrounding the city. Another was just outside the South Gate, and the third one was in the district that is now known as Chongno. The East and South Gate markets continue to flourish today and are among the most famous tourist attractions in the city.

From about 1880 until 1910 thousands of Koreans became entrepreneurs, starting all kinds of enterprises, from handicraft shops to major mining and manufacturing operations. Even during the "dark period" following annexation by Japan, many of these new businessmen were able to continue their companies even though they had to coordinate their operations with Japanese laws and demands. At the same time, several thousand Koreans gained experience in modern manufacturing and management techniques as employees of Japanese-owned companies, which proliferated on the peninsula after 1905. When Korea regained its sovereignty in 1945, the survivors of the Japanese occupation and World War II were able to put their experience to good use.

It was not until well after the end of the Korean War in 1953 that large numbers of ordinary individuals in South Korea were able to start their own businesses and begin to turn the image of the *shiropka* (she-rope-kah), or "businessperson," around. But during the first decades of South Korea's rise as an economic superpower, business was a free-for-all. The rules and regulations that existed were generally ignored. Tax evasion, bribery, collusion, fraud, and the theft of intellectual property were commonplace. Most company founders ran their firms like feudalistic family fiefs. But the anarchy worked. Freed for the first time in the history of the country to establish their own companies and do business with anyone, thousands of Koreans became manufacturers and exporters practically overnight.

With the few exceptions just mentioned, the Koreans who founded companies following the end of World War II in 1945 and the Korean War in 1953 had no experience or knowledge of modern business or personnel management techniques. They had only their cultural experience and accumulated folk wisdom. During this period Korean employees, including those in the largest enterprises, did not have the guaranteed lifetime job security that became famous in postwar Japan. They depended on Confucian philosophical and social sanctions to prevent employers from firing them to avoid shaming both themselves and their employees.

For many of Korea's post–Korean War companies the road to success was through a monthly English-language trade magazine (first called *Oriental America* and later renamed *The Importer*) founded in Tokyo in 1957 by American Ray A. Woodside, a graduate of the American Institute for Foreign Trade in Glendale, Arizona (now the American Graduate School of International Management, popularly known as Thunderbird).

The Importer, where I served as editor from 1958 through 1962, covered consumer products made in Japan, Korea, and Southeast Asia that were destined for the export market. The magazine was distributed by subscription to importers around the world, with the largest concentration of importer-subscribers in the United States. From 1959 on *The Importer* made it possible for Korean manufacturers and exporters, including one- and two-man operations, to reach importers on a monthly basis in the rich American and European markets. As a result of this access, many of *The Importer's* earliest Korean advertisers are now household names around the world.

Despite a natural tendency to depend on the government for support as well as protection from international competition, Korea's new breed of businesspeople proved to be more practical minded than their Japanese counterparts. Unlike top-ranked Japanese executives who regarded people with foreign educations and foreign work experience as somehow "tainted" and refused to employ them until well up into the 1980s, South Korea's company founders began sending their sons abroad as early as the 1960s to get MBAS from Harvard, Yale, Stanford, and other famous universities.

By the mid-1990s most of Korea's top corporations were being run by this foreign-educated second generation, and the ancient Confucian image of *shiropka* as people who lived off the labor of others like leeches had disappeared and been replaced by a new image of businesspeople as the primary pillars of the society. Nowadays, *chabonjuui* (chah-bohn-juu-we), or "capitalism," is in and business is the new religion of Korea. Successful businesspeople, rather than government officials, are the role models that most young Koreans would like to emulate. Another new key word in the Korean vocabulary is *saopkka* (sah-ohp-kah), or "entrepreneur," a concept that was totally alien to Korean culture until the final decades of the twentieth century.

Despite a number of fundamental differences in the way Koreans and their Japanese counterparts do business, there is one way in which Korean businesspeople closely resemble Japanese businessmen and that Westerners would be well advised to incorporate into their own philosophies. This similarity involves a cultural transformation that takes place as individuals become successful. The more successful Korean businessmen are, the more scholarly and moralistic they are apt to become. Generally speaking, once they have reached the top, they do not look like or act like the American image of a top executive—the hard-driving, dynamic individual who often behaves more like a buccaneer than a socially responsible businessperson. Like their Japanese counterparts, top Korean executives generally give up day-to-day management responsibilities and spend their time considering the philosophical and moral implications of their enterprises in an effort to make them more socially responsible and ensure that the principles they establish will become permanent.

There are other factors at play in Korea that have a profound influence on the economy and the country's international political and trade relations. One of these factors is the emergence of "economic nationalism." Broadly speaking, much of the motivation that drives Korean businesspeople is a strong desire to benefit the country, not just themselves and their families. They regard striving especially hard for success as their patriotic duty.

There is a special phrase in Korean that refers to the philosophy of being successful in business to contribute to the national welfare: *sanop bo guk* (sahn-ohp boh gook), which means something like "serving the country with business." Top business executives see themselves as a patriotic vanguard striving to build a powerful country in order to ensure Korea's survival.

Another important word in the business vocabulary of Korea is *kongchae* (kohng-chay), which refers to competitive entrance examinations given by companies to college students applying for jobs as managerial candidates. It is said that these open exams were originated specifically to eliminate the dependency of companies on hiring relatives of employees and on personal recommendations and allow them to hire new employees on the basis of character, education, and attitude.

Although *kongchae* examinations are common, some critics of the system say that its advantages (in hiring on the basis of test results rather than by kinship or personal recommendation) are often negated because such employees are often not as loyal as other people are to their companies. These critics say that managers hired through the *kongchae* process have a history of job hopping. (Despite the stigma that attaches to people who change jobs of their own accord, the number is growing. People who move from one company to another looking for more pay and better working conditions are frequently referred to as *chamsae jok*/chahm-sigh johk, or "a flock of sparrows.")

Despite movements toward democratizing hiring procedures in Korea, *yonjul* (yohn-juul), or "connectionism," continues to be a major factor in all areas of success in Korea, from business and politics to university professorships. The ideal connection is when a businessman has high school alumni brothers in high government offices and is their *sonbae* (sohn-bay), or "senior." Few factors are more important in the lives of businesspeople and politicians than *hak yun* (hahk yuun), or "school ties." Next in line after blood ties and school ties are *ji yun* (jee yuun), or "regional ties"—or the family's original home district.

Korean corporations subject new managerial candidates to several weeks of indoctrination that concentrate primarily on imbuing them with the philosophy and spirit of the company concerned and instructing them in how to behave and interact with other employees and outsiders. In all companies these training programs include learning the company motto and company song. Where white-collar female employees are concerned, company training programs consist primarily of instructing them in how to speak to superiors and outsiders (in person and on the phone), how to bow, how to serve refreshments, how to open doors for visitors and superiors, and where to stand or sit in a variety of common occasions.

Another key word in Korean business is *sungjin* (suung-jeen), or "promotion." In most Korean companies employees are promoted on the basis of longevity plus merit. And unlike in earlier times, when age came first, it is becoming more and more common for Korean companies to have managers who are younger than some members of their staff. Still, in many companies attitude and behavior are ranked right up with technical knowledge and skills, diligence, and loyalty as the attributes that lead to promotion.

In a growing number of larger Korean corporations the primary qualification for promotion to executive rank is *tongchal yok* (tong-chahl yahk), or "keen insight," a phrase that is of special importance because it incorporates both cultural sensitivity and cultural skills (in the use of language, in the ability to discern what other people are thinking, in inspiring loyalty and support) as well as the ability to understand intuitively the essentials of business situations and make the right decisions.

Social barriers between nonrelated individuals, families, clans, villages, and regions that were traditional in Korea for centuries have dissipated dramatically since the advent of democratic principles and mass industrialization between 1960 and 1980, but enough of them remain to have a discernible and often deleterious effect on communications within large companies and organizations.

People in sections and departments within larger organizations basically view themselves as members of an exclusive and inclusive group and regard people in other areas of the same organization as outsiders in competition with them. Communication among company units is generally controlled, and there is a precise protocol that must be followed to avoid friction and repercussions. This system obviously works well enough for Korean companies to function with varying degrees of efficiency, but it is often a major handicap where foreigners dealing with Korean companies are concerned because it slows down the communication process and often alters the content.

Another behavioral characteristic that often divides Korean and foreign businesspeople is the Korean custom of avoiding confrontations and resolutions that they do not agree with and do not want by telling people what they want to hear, doing the things they wanted to do in the first place, and later apologizing when confronted with their arbitrary actions.

Despite the dramatic changes that have taken place in Korean society in general from 1945 on, the overwhelming majority of businesspeople are still uniquely Korean in the traditional sense. S. H. Jang, one of Korea's post–World War II renaissance men who combined the careers of an international business executive, consultant, scholar, professor, columnist, and book author, describes the essence of the typical Korean businessman as friendly, with an extraordinary sense of humor, intensely energetic, easily embarrassed, with a volatile temper, outrageously self-confident, as patient as Job on one hand and intensely impatient in other circumstances, brimming over with powerful feelings, and subject to strong jealousy.

Jang adds that typical Korean businessmen are never satisfied and cannot rest until they are the top men in their companies—a deep-seated motivation that results in their being exceptionally hardworking and constantly striving to rise in the managerial hierarchy. Jang says that except when interacting with friends and guests, all Koreans are driven by a "me-first" syndrome that has few restraints—a holdover, no doubt, from centuries of cultural conditioning in being forced to play a secondary role.

Another of the most important ingredients in the character and qualifications of a successful Korean businessman is a strong sense of paternalism. He is expected to treat his employees with the careful respect due their station and to make most personnel management decisions on the basis of feelings rather than facts.

Company founders, or *shijo* (she-joh), played an especially significant role in the transformation of Korea into a major industrial power, giving rise to numerous articles and books on the "founders' spirit" that energized the economy from 1945 through the 1980s. The energy, vision, and convictions of *chaebol* (chay-buhl) founders like Byong Chol Yi (Lee) of Samsung, Chu Yong Chong of Hyundai, In Hoe Ku of the LG Group, Chung Hun Cho of Hanjin, and Chan U Ryu of Poongsan—the Fords, Rockefellers, Harrimans, and Carnegies of Korea—were duplicated on a smaller scale throughout the business world. Most Korean businessmen manage their companies like military units, with all the discipline, formalities, uniformity, seniority, ranks, and privileges that are the heart and soul of the best military organizations. And as in the military, rewards are generally slow in coming, but punishment for misbehavior is sure and swift. Employees are arranged in groups (squads, platoons), are treated as groups, and work as teams. Generally they are also rewarded and punished as groups—although individuals are routinely criticized, often at group meetings, by their superiors.

Also as in the military, Korean company protocol requires that subordinates address managers and executives by their titles or by their last names plus titles. Also as in the military, the way in which things are done is as important as what is done. Employees are generally required to "go by the book" at all times. This can be especially frustrating to Westerners, who tend to focus on facts and substance rather than form.

Despite the breakneck pace still maintained by most Korean businessmen, a growing number do not subscribe to lives of all work and no play. In addition to patronizing *kisaeng* houses, cabarets, *room salons*, and other venues where food, drink, and the companionship of especially seductive women are the main attractions, many Korean businessmen take advantage of the large number of sauna baths in the country.

The larger of these saunas are opulent havens that provide locker rooms, showers, steam rooms, dry saunas, herbal rooms, hot, medium, and cold baths, and "grooming rooms" where patrons may brush their teeth, shave, and have their hair cut and styled. Most patrons go to the saunas after work, spending from one to two hours there before going home or going out for the evening.

177

시샘

Shisaem
(She-same)

"The Jealousy Taboo"

Until the advent of a semidemocratic society in Korea following the end of World War II, there was a strong Confucian taboo against *shisaem* (she-same), or "jealousy," in Korean society. Historical records reveal that from the earliest times until the end of the last dynasty in 1910 there were laws prohibiting wives from exhibiting jealousy over the extramarital affairs of their husbands. In earlier days wives who crossed this line were subject to execution. In more recent centuries the punishment was divorce, dishonor, and usually a life of poverty.

Confucianism taught that being jealous of anyone over anything was immoral and would end up damaging not only the spirit of the jealous person but also having a negative impact on his or her family members and ultimately the country at large—and this latter threat made jealousy the business of the authorities.

From the early years of the fifteenth century until the twentieth century Korean society was divided into fixed classes. With rare exceptions those in the lower classes, which accounted for more than 80 percent of the population, could not move into a higher class. The *shisaem* that these people felt for those who were better off than they were had to be suppressed, and they had to continuously humble themselves before their betters.

In this environment it became particularly frustrating for common Koreans to see others placed above them in hereditary positions, with no possibility that they could ever change the situation. There was no rooting for the underdog or supporting people beyond what might simultaneously improve one's own circumstances. There were no celebrations if one's neighbors somehow improved their lot to even the slightest degree by working harder or being smarter. Any demonstration of superiority by one's peers, and especially by anyone below them, was regarded with hateful spite.

This extreme form of built-in prejudice has not yet disappeared from Korean culture. It is still characteristic of Koreans to be maliciously jealous of those around them who better themselves by legal or illegal means. Their traditional reaction is that their own average or inferior talents have been exposed and the only way they can expunge these bruised feelings is to bring the more successful people back down to their level.

Shisaem can be especially rampant in a Korean-foreign joint venture when the foreign side is responsible for the hiring and does not abide by the Korean custom of stratifying the staff by sex, social class, education, schools attended, school ties, even blood relationships among the employees. Jealousy also continues to play an important role in the lives of Korean women, especially among those who date and marry foreign men. Socially and legally free to exhibit jealousy since the mid-1950s, the degree of their jealousy and the violence with which they often react to being cheated on by boyfriends or spouses is one of the remarkable features of Korean society.

Korean wives of foreigners who do become jealous often suffer from the fact that the taboos against demonstrating jealousy are still deeply ingrained in their psyche, and although they are now socially free to exhibit jealous behavior, deep down they feel that such behavior is wrong, that they should not be jealous.

178

실학
Sil Hak
(Sheer Hahk)

"The Coming of Practical Learning"

From around the fifteenth century until the last decades of the nineteenth century the primary political and social focus in Korea was to conform to social and political forms detailed by the Chinese sage Confucius in the fifth century B.C. This focus included a hierarchical arrangement of people within society, an authoritarian government, male dominance, and ancestor worship—all factors that contributed to an intellectual emphasis on the past that virtually precluded social and economic progress.

Another element in the traditional mind-set of Koreans that contributed to universal stagnation was the Taoist philosophy that people should not attempt to change things, that they should be totally passive and spend their lives attempting to merge with the cosmos. Buddhism also encouraged a reflective and passive life that worked against innovation and evolution of any kind. The individuality, the spirit, the curiosity, and the ambitions inherent in the psyche of the people were stifled in the name of Confucian harmony.

As a result of these philosophical and religious influences, with only a few exceptions over the centuries, the only people in Korea who were permitted to become educated were caught up in a system that limited their education to philosophical, literary, and esoteric matters that could not be questioned or changed. From one century to the next the majority of the most learned men in the country spent their time contemplating, commenting on, and debating subjects that had no relevance at all to the problems of the state and society.

It was not until the seventeenth century and afterward that a few maverick Confucian scholars, most of whom were not government officials and had no political power, began to focus on *sil hak* (sheer hahk), or "practical learning," and to propose a variety of social, political, and economic reforms based on Western concepts seeping into Korea from China. Historians say that the greatest of the *sil hak* scholar-writers was Yag Yong Chong (1762–1836). Chong's critiques of Korean society and the political system of the day were greatly influenced by the Catholicism of Rome. Because of this relationship, Chong was exiled from Seoul for eighteen years and banned from holding public office for another seventeen years.

But the influence of these "practical learning" scholars was minimal at best and did not slow the downward spiral of the Choson dynasty. Said Yonsei University's Professor Chong Hong Pak: "All that the *sil hak* advocates could do was to remonstrate and rage ineffectually." Much of the impetus for these belated efforts resulted from the influence of Jesuit missionaries who had taken up residence in China in the sixteenth century, particularly the writings of the Catholic priest Matteo Ricci, which were brought back to Korea by the missions sent to Beijing each year to take tributary gifts to the Chinese emperor.

Commenting on this period in Korea's history, Professor Pak added that during the seventeenth and eighteenth centuries the Confucian factions in the elite ruling class spent their time "picking the dry bones of Confucian doctrine" and "sucking the thinning blood of the country."

By the mid-1800s the squabbling Confucian officials of the Choson court had exhausted themselves and the country, and the advocates of *sil hak* were gaining both strength and momentum. But events set in motion by foreign powers, notably Japan, were to prevent the "practical learning" scholars from being able to reverse the course of the country, and *sil hak* was not the vehicle of progress that was hoped for. Within twenty years of the opening of Korea to the West, Japan had virtually taken over the economy as well as the country's foreign relations and in 1910 formally annexed the country, making it an integral part of the Japanese empire.

It was not until after Korea regained its sovereignty in 1945, had been split in half, and then suffered a devastating civil war initiated by Communist-dominated North Korea and its Chinese allies that South Koreans were finally free to embark on a national program of *sil hak*. But again that was not to happen immediately. South Korea first had to overcome the destruction of the Korean War and the corruption of the first postwar governments. It was not until Chung Hee Park, an army general, took over the government in a bloodless coup in May 1961 that the people of South Korea were finally in a position to use their repressed ambitions in an all-out effort to industrialize and modernize the country.

Sil hak played a central role in this transformation. South Korea began importing technology on a massive scale. Thousands of young Koreans were sent abroad—or went on their own—to attend foreign universities and soak up the "practical learning" that had been denied to them throughout most of the country's history. The Korean thirst for *sil hak* was almost unbounded, and in one generation the country leaped into the age of technology, competing on many fronts with Japan, the United States, and the other advanced countries of the world. Today *sil hak* and its use are at the heart of the government's economic and political policies, often taking precedence over the interests of other countries. Today there are few people in the world who are more practical minded than Koreans or more interested in *so hak* (soh hahk), "Western learning," when it comes to their economic welfare.

179

소도

Sodo

(Soh-doh)

"Writing as a Cultural Discipline"

The system of writing that developed in China and subsequently spread to Korea and Japan has had more influence on more people than any of the world's other writing systems. The Chinese way of writing did not stop with simple pictographs or hieroglyphics, which were the basis for most writing systems. Over many centuries in the early history of China the basic symbols representing everyday life and the cosmos as the Chinese knew it were combined with other pictographs to form increasingly complex concepts that eventually numbered over a hundred thousand.

To be even moderately literate a person had to spend years memorizing several thousand of these "characters" and learning how to draw them properly—as opposed to having to memorize and draw only twenty-some letters that could be used to represent all of the sounds in a language, as the ABCs do in English. The ordeal involved in becoming literate in Chinese was a process that dramatically influenced the character and personality as well as the mental and manual abilities of those who were subjected to it.

Because of the extraordinary investment in time and energy that was required to become literate in Chinese, virtually all such learning in pre-modern China was limited to members of the elite ruling class and generally to male members of this class. Eventually education in writing was not only limited by economics but also circumscribed by law as a privilege of the upper class.

As the centuries passed, some writing teachers and scholars began to stylize the characters according to their own artistic inclinations, eventually creating a variety of "schools" that taught different writing styles. As more time passed, writing the characters became more and more of an art, with the masters of successive generations striving to emulate and surpass those of the past. Eventually these masters made writing the characters a fine art within itself, with the content of the chosen characters playing a secondary role. The Chinese word for the art was *shufa* (shuu-fah), or, in modern terms, "penmanship."

Chinese scholars began introducing their system of writing into Korea in 108 B.C., when the small kingdoms on the Korean peninsula came under the suzerainty of China. The art of *shufa* became *sodo* (soh-doh) in Korean. However, it was to be some five hundred years before Korean masters of *sodo* began appearing in relatively large numbers, and another millennium before it was to begin having a significant impact on people outside the elite class of male scholars who administered the national and local governments.

With the gradual spread of education following the establishment of the Choson (Yi) dynasty in 1392, the practice of *sodo* also became more common. Ultimately, skill in *sodo* came to be equated with not only one's educational achievements but one's morality as well. Developing skill in calligraphy was believed to elevate spirituality and refine behavior and therefore to provide a variety of social and cultural benefits.

The use of Chinese characters—and the practice of *sodo*—lost considerable favor in Korea between 1945 and 1985 because of the emergence of strong nationalist feelings against foreign things. But the characters were so deeply embedded in the literature as well as the culture in general that attempts to abolish their use were premature. By the end of the 1980s the growing self-confidence of Koreans and the country's growing involvement with China, Japan, and other countries in Southeast Asia with large populations of affluent overseas Chinese made it obvious that continuing to use the characters provided major economic and political benefits.

In modern-day Korea *sodo* art of the past is highly prized, and practicing the art is part of the education of virtually all Koreans. It is widely recognized in Korea that the discipline and process required to learn how to write Chinese characters, especially with any degree of stylized skill, contributes significantly to the aesthetic sensibilities, the manual skills, and the diligence of Koreans and is therefore a major factor in sustaining the attributes that help make Koreans a skilled, hardworking people.

While it does not have official recognition as such, *sodo* could certainly be described as one of Korea's cultural treasures.

180

소개

Sogae
(Soh-gay)

"Limiting Introductions"

In pre-modern Korea people did not meet and mix in a casual way. Korean society was segmented into strictly enforced social classes that were further divided into exclusive superior-inferior relationships within families and work groups. The exclusivity of the family and kinship groups was so encompassing that it virtually precluded people, particularly women, from forming casual friendships with outsiders. There were simply too many social barriers.

In this environment people did not have a wide circle of personal friends, even on their own social level. Nor did they want them, considering the various obligations that friendship involved and the dangers of exposing themselves to others. Because of the very real possibility that serious obligations might follow, *sogae* (soh-gay), or "introductions," were taken very seriously and involved a strict protocol.

This system, which existed for well over a thousand years, became so deeply embedded in the psyche of Koreans that today it still plays a significant role in their lives, in personal as well as professional relationships. Even though Korea's traditional social system with all its carefully defined ranks and taboos has changed dramatically since the last decades of the twentieth century, introductions are not taken lightly.

Most Koreans who are in public with friends do not automatically introduce them to other friends they meet. Generally they will not introduce them unless they specifically want the two parties to develop a formal relationship for business or political reasons. In such situations Koreans cannot ignore their respective social classes and take each other for granted. They must quickly determine their relative social status and then assume the accepted demeanor and level of respect language to use to each other.

When people make a point of performing introductions, they are careful to establish the relative social standing of each party as part of the introductions so that the two can respond to each other appropriately. In addition to the family and generational name, these introductions include such things as company or organization affiliation, rank or title, educational background, birthplace, and so on, because all of these things affect whom one can meet, the etiquette involved in the meeting, and the relationship that develops thereafter. Generally speaking, present-day Koreans still reserve their social time and resources for a small tightly knit circle of kin and friends made during their school years.

Introductions in Korea, particularly when they involve middle-aged and older adults, tend to be on the formal side. People stand and bow and give their names. Men, especially those involved with the international community, shake hands as well as bow. Ranking older men often just nod if they are being introduced to lower-ranking people. If they are meeting people in their age group of similar rank, they are more likely just to shake hands. It is a gesture of extra courtesy, respect, and enthusiasm to use both hands when shaking hands.

One of the reasons Koreans have traditionally been wary of meeting other people was that once a relationship had been established their new friends felt free to ask for favors—something they could hardly refuse because of their Confucian orientation. The more emotional an appeal for favors, the more pressure there was on people to grant them.

While the interpersonal behavior of Koreans is becoming more and more Westernized, the degree of the Westernization depends on many factors, from age and gender to education, place of residence, work experience, and interaction with Westerners, both in Korea and through travels abroad. And although the pace of these changes is speeding up as communication and cultural barriers continue to dissipate, it is generally not wise for outsiders to presume automatically that individuals they meet are Westernized in either attitudes or behavior. Until their degree of Westernization becomes obvious—which can happen in a matter of minutes— it is better to maintain a formal, polite manner in keeping with known Korean values.

181

소개장
Sogaejang
(Soh-gay-jahng)
"Letters of Introduction"

One of the reasons Koreans like living and working in the United States so much is that they can dispense with much of the age-old etiquette that controls—and fundamentally limits—their lives when they are in Korea. An example that is often mentioned is that in the United States they can telephone or walk up to and start talking to anyone without having to be concerned about sex, social class, rank, or any future complications. In Korea, on the other hand, it has traditionally been virtually unthinkable for people to make "cold calls" or introduce themselves to other businesspeople or government bureaucrats they need or want to meet. Such behavior was—and still is to a great degree—considered both rude (if not immoral) and unprofessional.

Where doing business in Korea is concerned, one must first have connections. Generally the next most important thing is *sogaejang* (soh-gay-jahng), or "letters of introduction." Koreans therefore spend a great deal of their time and energy arranging for *sogaejang* to people they want to do business with or get something from. Among the most valuable sources of introductions are relatives, university professors who taught the individuals they want to meet, classmates, alumni brothers and sisters, leading government bureaucrats, as well as bankers and businesspeople who have strong relationships with the people involved.

Ranking government bureaucrats and corporate executives who take up second careers as consultants and mediators after retirement are often valued as much for their introductions as for their advice. Those with high public profiles are especially effective as go-betweens.

Korean businesspeople and government bureaucrats tend to be tolerant of foreigners who approach them without introductions, particularly if the foreigners concerned are people they would like to know for their own benefit or if the reason the foreigners approach them is especially interesting to them. On almost all other occasions, however, the receptions foreigners get are usually very polite and hospitable but stop there.

The situation changes entirely if one goes in with a *sogaejang* from someone with whom the individual has a relationship. The stronger the connection, the more obligated the individual is to respond favorably. It therefore behooves foreign businesspeople in Korea to adopt the Korean custom of using introductions, making the practice a regular part of their overall approach to doing business. In this approach the personal factor in Korean society should not be ignored. Generally the more personal the relationship connecting two people, the stronger the social debt that binds them and the more concerned they are about fulfilling their obligations to each other.

There are, of course, exceptions to these general rules and customs, particularly among the growing number of Korean businesspeople who were educated abroad or spent years in overseas assignments, but it still pays to approach even these people with good, strong introductions because they dramatically speed up the process of establishing the desired relationship.

속담

Soktam

(Soak-tahm)

"Wisdom in Proverbs"

A great deal of the culture of Korea is reflected in its *soktam* (soak-tahm), or "proverbs," which incorporate not only the folk wisdom of the people but also their weaknesses, fears, and idiosyncrasies. In the 1970s Korean psychologist To Hwan Kim analyzed seventy-three hundred of the most common sayings and proverbs in the Korean language in an attempt to shed light on the Korean way of thinking and behaving and published the results in a book entitled *A Psychological Analysis of Korean Proverbs*.

Kim divided his findings into eleven categories having to do with poverty, economic pragmatism, hostility toward officials, hostility and envy toward the elite *yangban* ruling class, contempt for people who did menial labor, anxiety about social conditions, authoritarianism, optimism, fatalism, this-world orientation, and superstitious beliefs and prejudices.

References most often repeated in the *soktam* Kim studied grew out of the fact that it was the official policy of the last and longest Korean dynasty (1392–1910) to keep common people in a permanent state of poverty. When this was coupled with natural disasters and the vagaries of nature, the lives of ordinary Koreans were in constant danger.

Because of that state, Koreans became obsessed with the idea of achieving the wealth that would relieve them of the terrible burden of poverty, but because of social and political barriers all they could do was complain about their situation and dream about changing it.

Traditionally oppressed and exploited in every way imaginable by their own officials as well as invaders, common Koreans naturally developed an extreme hostility toward officialdom in whatever form and on all levels. Most of their ire was directed toward members of the *yangban* class because this elite group monopolized material wealth and political power in Korea and was symbolic of all that ordinary Koreans hated about government.

The strong sense of contempt for menial labor that was characteristic of Koreans during their long feudal period grew out of Buddhist taboos against such "unclean" occupations as butchering animals, working with hides, grave-digging, and collecting trash. People in these hereditary occupations were invariably at the bottom of the pecking order.

The strict etiquette demanded by Korea's male-dominated hierarchical society and the taboos against demonstrating emotions, particularly affection and love, made Korean life cold and frustrating. When this was coupled with the corruption that was rife among the ruling class, common people were in a constant state of anxiety. The whole Confucian system of order within the family, the government, and society in general was based on absolute authoritarianism and the constant threat of force, resulting in anxiety's becoming second nature to Koreans.

But Kim found that despite the hardships and dangers faced by Koreans there was an optimistic streak in their character and outlook that helped them endure their poverty and lack of freedom. He also found, however, that their optimism took second place to a profoundly fatalistic attitude that their primarily sorrowful lives were preordained and that there was nothing they could do to change them.

Kim also found many *soktam* that demonstrated the real-life orientation of Koreans as opposed to an afterlife. Their thoughts and efforts were directed toward meeting the day-to-day challenges of life and enjoying themselves as much as possible now. His eleventh point was that *soktam* show that Koreans were traditionally a superstitious people with many prejudices but were innately concerned about family members, kin, and close friends, as well as themselves. In this respect they were no different from most people everywhere, and hundreds of Korea's most repeated proverbs have their exact counterparts in other cultures.

Some examples: poverty is the mother of crime; don't try to teach your grandmother to suck eggs; fields have eyes and woods have ears; bad news travels fast; what's mine is mine and what's yours is mine.

183

선배 후배

Sonbae/Hubae
(Sohn-bay/Huuh-bay)

"Seniors and Juniors"

A careful study of Korea's business and professional worlds reveals that the whole economic and political spheres of activity in Korea revolve around personal rather than objective factors. The basis for employment in government and in private industry, relationships between government agencies and commercial companies, business ventures, and so on are more likely than not determined by where individuals were born, where they went to school (especially university), and other personal considerations.

Blood and childhood friendship ties are key elements in social and economic relationships in Korea. But school ties, particularly those created by attending the same high schools and universities, play an especially important role in public life. Graduates from the same schools feel an extraordinary obligation to cooperate with and help each other throughout life. The roles that older graduates play on behalf of younger graduates often take on the character of godparents.

Two key words express the special relationships that exist between students and graduates of the same school: *sonbae* (sohn-bay) and *hubae* (huuh-bay). *Sonbae* means "senior" or "superior," with a number of other connotations that include "master" and "patron." *Hubae* means "junior," "subordinate," or "follower." Once this relationship is fixed by attendance at the same school, it can never be changed or sundered. *Hubae* are obligated to show deference to their *sonbae* and to serve them in whatever way they can. *Sonbae* are similarly obligated to help their *hubae* in any way they can. This junior/senior relationship is fixed by who graduates first.

Probably the most common role played by *sonbae* who have gone into industry or the government and advanced to the managerial level is helping new graduates from their old schools get jobs in their own organizations or at places where they have strong contacts. This function of *sonbae* is so important that many high school graduates try to determine which university they attend by the number of its influential alumni. The more alumni a school has in powerful commercial and government positions, the higher its status among students.

Korea's university alumni associations, including those made up of graduates of foreign universities, are understandably strong, as are the alumni groups in individual government agencies and corporations. Generally each annual crop of graduates going into companies and government agencies from one university form their own individual alumni groups informally and become members of the organization's consolidated alumni group. *Tonggi* (tohng-ghee), referring to same-year students, and *tonggisaeng* (tohng-ghee-sang), meaning "classmates," are key words in these scenarios. Practices differ, but there are usually monthly or semimonthly and annual meetings, along with parties and other events.

Foreign businesspeople recruiting employees in Korea should be aware of the role and importance of the *sonbae/hubae* connections and take these connections into consideration. Generally speaking, employees from the same schools will be more cooperative with each other and therefore function more effectively as a group.

Another factor to be considered is that staff members and managers who are graduates of the most prestigious high schools and universities may resent being subordinates to managers who came out of lower-ranking schools. This social and class sensitivity can be a serious morale and efficiency problem, particularly if the "lower-class" managers are not diplomatic in their attitudes and behavior.

The easiest way for foreign companies to avoid this kind of problem is to relegate all hiring to their local staff. Koreans are old hands at dealing with age, sex, and social classes in the workplace. The obvious weakness of this approach, however, is that those given the authority to recruit new employees will generally favor those whom they can dominate. Veteran businesspeople in Korea say that the only way a foreign company can be assured of getting the best possible mix of employees is to have all of its recruiting handled by a well-established and reputable consulting firm.

184

선비
Sonbi
(Sohn-bee)
"The Ideal Human"

Christian countries have traditionally had their saints—selfless individuals of extraordinary virtue who were and still are held up as models for all mankind. Korea had its *sonbi* (sohn-bee). *Sonbi* is an old word that translates as "scholar" or "intellectual" in the sense of someone who exhibits all of the most admirable virtues attributed to Confucianism.

Korean legends and mythology presented the image and role of the *sonbi* as the ideal human being whose primary function was to guide the uneducated and act as their intermediary with the government and the gods. Korea's scholar-gentlemen were expected to embody the spirit of *sonbi*—which refers to selfless, disciplined men in control of their earthly desires who are dedicated to the welfare of the nation and the people. In reality, however, few people lived up to the ideals of *sonbi*.

Until modern times the only route to social mobility in Korea was generally through education, which was basically limited to the hereditary gentry—and they had to be affluent enough to afford the expense. Thus only families who could do without the labor of sons and afford to engage the best possible tutors for their sons had any chance of improving their social, political, and economic status. Success resulting from academic achievement was not itself hereditary. But once a son had achieved the exalted status of scholar-official, the political, economic, and social advantages generally made it possible for the family to continue the success from one generation to the next, thereby creating a permanent upper class that perpetuated itself—and limited its size.

The more entrenched the educated class became, the less opportunity there was for other families to improve their lot. Korean society thus became relatively static, made up of the elite ruling class at the top, and peasants, craftsmen, and merchants on the bottom. However, history notes that time and again it was the *sonbi* who stood up against government officials on behalf of the people even when it meant their complete ruin socially and politically and sometimes their death. It was this tradition of unselfishness and sacrifice that made the *sonbi* heroes of the people. But there were also *sonbi*, particularly in more recent times, who gave precedence to maintaining harmony through absolute obedience to superiors—an ideology that favored the elite over common people and did not sit well with the lower classes

In 1913 an educator-patriot named Chang Ho An founded an organization known as *Hung Sa Dan* (Huung Sah Dahn), or "Society for Raising Gentlemen," in an effort to educate young Koreans in *sonbi*like qualities to help combat the degeneration of Korea's famed manners caused by the colonization of the country by Japan. Some present-day social scientists, like Kyu Tae Yi, author of *The Structure of the Korean Mind* and several other books, often refer to *sonbi* as an ideology that has both a positive and a negative side and was therefore a mixed blessing to pre-modern Korea.

In Yi's view the central theme of *sonbi*-ism was filial piety, benevolence, righteousness, loyalty, and fidelity to one's principles, although *sonbi* scholars were also noted for their indifference to material possessions and their dedication to helping other people regardless of the sacrifices they had to make.

Few people in present-day Korea have the reputation of being *sonbi* in the traditional, positive sense, but their number appears to be growing and taking on new dimensions that incorporate success in business. Some of the founders of Korea's most successful corporate combines (Samsung, Hyundai, LG Group [formerly Lucky Gold-Star], Daewoo, Sunkyong, etc.) qualified as New Age *sonbi* because of their influence on Koreans at large.

Other modern-day critics give short shrift to the ideals expressed in *sonbi*-ism, accusing present-day scholars and intellectuals of being inconsistent in their publicly expressed beliefs and their private behavior. Critics say these modern-day *sonbi* still follow the formalistic morals of Confucianism and feudalistic authoritarianism and among other things resort to fortune-tellers and *yin-yang* practices in their private and professional affairs.

Some of the legacy of Korean scholars not soiling their hands with any kind of work has survived into modern times. Professors and other professional scholars usually have assistants do most or all of the mundane work involved with their projects. But generally speaking, throughout Korean society humanistic-oriented *sonbi* continue to be seen as ideal models for the people in their struggle to get an education and to succeed in business, the professions, or politics.

Generally speaking, however, Koreans do not view Western scholars or successful businesspeople as *sonbi*like individuals because of their endorsement and acceptance of individualism and materialism.

185

성
Song
(Sohng)

"Integrity vs. Law"

The Confucian ideology that became the foundation of Korean society in the early years of the Choson dynasty (1392–1910) was essentially an elitist philosophy that was used to justify a stern, authoritarian rule by a privileged few. Common people lived in a state of uncertainty and anxiety because there were no guarantees that their persons or their property were safe. In this environment laws that existed were designed primarily to preserve and protect the government, not the people.

This constant anxiety resulted in Koreans spending an inordinate amount of time and emotion in creating and nurturing connections with people who could help them in times of need and protect them when they were threatened. But there had to be more than just fear binding people together to make this system work. The Confucian answer to this challenge was an extraordinary emphasis on *song* (sohng), or "integrity," which was taught as one of the paramount virtues.

With both their livelihood and often their survival dependent on the goodwill and cooperation of other family members, their kin, neighbors, and local officials, *song* became a social, political, and economic imperative. However, the *song* that existed in this environment was not based on any universal principle of conduct. Generally speaking, it applied only to one's own family, relatives, circle of friends, and connections and was therefore circumstantial. Broadly speaking, there was no social mandate to demonstrate integrity to outsiders because there was very little, if any, interaction with outsiders.

A primary factor used by Koreans in judging the character of an individual is expressed in the phrase *chin shimuro* (cheen sheem-uu-roh), which is translated as "pure heart." To Koreans a person with a *chin shimuro* is one who has absolute integrity, is totally sincere, and can always be depended on to do the right thing (in terms of what Koreans consider right). When examining young candidates for employment, Korean personnel managers are generally more interested in applicants having "pure hearts" than good academic records.

Song has still not been universalized fully in Korea. Among Koreans it is still primarily a personal, circumstantial thing that applies only to people with whom one has a positive relationship. When foreigners are involved, however, other considerations often come into play.

Koreans tend to put all foreigners, particularly Westerners, in a "guest" category and to treat them differently because foreigners do not fit into any of the prescribed cultural categories that have traditionally made up Korean society.

Part of this special treatment is to apply more universal and higher moral standards, including *song*, in their interactions with foreigners. The rationale for treating guests exceptionally well is also an important element in Confucian philosophy. Confucianism teaches that being hospitable to guests is one of the primary virtues and one of the most important attributes of a civilized, cultivated person.

As a result of this conditioning, Koreans are noted for their generosity in spending money on guests and going out of their way to please them—something they regard as a national duty and essential for upholding both the reputation of all Koreans and the image of the country. This factor played an especially important role in the development of the Korean economy from 1960 on because many foreign importers were so impressed with the integrity, determination, and hard work of their Korean suppliers that they persevered despite many obstacles. Still today Western businesspeople and visitors in Korea typically become beneficiaries of both Korean integrity and hospitality.

186

성

Song
(Sohng)

"Sexual Mores"

One of the most conspicuous and powerful facets of Confucianism was its attempts to control human behavior by strictly limiting the role of love and by making *song* (sohng), or "sex," a restricted function that for women was basically reduced to producing offspring. Generally Confucianism did not recognize or condone sex as a pleasurable activity. Talking about sex, much less writing about it, was taboo, and those who broke this prohibition were often punished severely. As a result of this combined religious and political taboo against sex, ordinary Koreans became extraordinarily inhibited about sexual matters and conduct. Among other things, it was taught that indulgence in sex for pleasure had a negative effect on the life force, was therefore harmful to one's health, and reduced longevity.

But the sexual impulse was far too powerful to deny completely, and as in all societies that attempt to control sexual behavior, men, particularly those in the privileged upper class, exempted themselves from most sexual prohibitions. Upper-class Korean men of means maintained concubines and mistresses (*chop*/chope) and patronized a professional class of prostitute-entertainers called *kisaeng*. Cities, towns, and villages had their inns or houses of prostitution, where in many cases women were held against their will. (One of the reasons for the appeal of Taoism among upper-class men of early Korea was that it not only condoned sexual activity but prescribed it as one of the ways of achieving nirvana.)

The idea that women also needed sexual release to maintain mental and physical health appears to have been unknown in Korea (as it was virtually everywhere else until recent times). The sexual behavior of wives was generally limited to procreation, making a variety of psychological and physical maladies common among women and having a fundamental effect on the overall social and political system of pre-modern Korea.

In *The Koreans and Their Culture* (Ronald Press, New York), anthropologist Charles Osgood described pre-modern Korean men as the most aloof in the world when it came to women. He also said that Koreans were emotionally unstable because of their sexual inhibitions. He compared their typical reactions to that of a hibernating bear on one hand and the fury of a goaded tiger on the other—behavior that was no doubt linked to the suppression of the sexual impulse.

From the beginning of the Choson dynasty (1392), when a much stricter form of Confucianism was adopted as the state ideology, boys and girls were segregated at the age of seven (which is either six or five by the Western way of counting age because Korean infants were counted as one year old at birth and two years old on the first New Year after their birth). This official policy of segregating the sexes was known as *naeoebob* (niegh-oh-eh-bob), literally "inside-outside code." An expression commonly used to denote the social gap between the male and female sexes was *namjon-yobi* (nahm-joan-yoh-bee), or "honored men–lowly women."

In families young brothers and sisters could sit together for meals and play together but were segregated by sex when it came to interacting with other children. The lives of females in a household were centered around the *anbang* (ahn-bahng), or "inner rooms," while those of males were centered in *sarang-bang* (sah-rahng-bahng), or "outer rooms." Sons of the elite *yangban* class were educated in the Confucian classics and were eligible to take government-sponsored examinations for civil service positions. Girls were taught home-making skills and nothing else. When married, girls became virtual servants of their mothers-in-law. They gained a measure of personal freedom only after giving birth to sons and getting older.

The lives of Korean women were controlled strictly by a list of taboos known as the *chilgo chiak* (cheel-goh chee-ahk), or "seven evils," which were disobeying their in-laws, failing to have sons, committing adultery, exhibiting jealousy, having a hereditary disease, talking excessively, and committing larceny. If a woman committed any of these "evils," her husband or in-laws could sever the marriage ties, leaving her totally ostracized because her family would not take her back. There were no grounds for women divorcing their husbands.

During the more than five hundred years of the Choson dynasty (1392–1910) urban women were confined to their homes during the day to prevent them from being seen by or interacting with any males other than members of their own families. The only exception to this rule was that maids or other female servants could be sent out on special emergency errands, such as procuring medicines. Women were allowed to go out of their homes for a few hours at night after sundown but only after men had been warned to go indoors by the ringing of large bells. Even though it was dark during the time that women were outside their homes, they were required to wear shawls concealing their heads and partially concealing their faces in case they inadvertently encountered a male.

Although the virtual enslavement of women officially ended with the downfall of the Choson dynasty in 1910, it was to persist for several decades. As late as the 1950s many Korean women in larger cities had never been outside the walls of their home compounds during the day, and some had never been outside their yards in their lifetime.

Korean men were so obsessed with female chastity that women who were widowed or discarded by their husbands (for misbehavior or failure to have male children) were generally forbidden to remarry, resulting in large numbers of them resorting to a kind of common-law marriage known as "sack marriage"—referring to the practice of men wanting second wives or concubines to enter the homes of widows or divorcees at night, wrap them up in a sack, and carry them off—often with the connivance of the widows.

Legal prohibitions against women remarrying officially ended with the elimination of the feudal family system following the introduction of democratic principles into Korea from 1945. But social sanctions against women who married more than once continued to play a significant role in Korean life.

Sociologist Tong Se Han says in *The Korean Conception of Sex*, an article published in *Sedae* (*The Generation*), that the "procreation-centeredness" of sex was responsible for the family centrism, male supremacy, obsession with descent, and female submission and dependence that were characteristic of Korean society until modern times. In that environment, Han adds, it was the supreme duty of husbands and wives to have numerous offspring to ensure the continuation of the family line. One of the problems with this kind of thinking was that it gave the family line precedence over the welfare of women and all children except the first son.

Historically, Korean women were targeted by Chinese, Khitan, and Mongol invaders who sought them as both work and sex slaves, and women were included in the annual tribute that the early kingdoms of Korea paid to China. During the fifteenth and sixteenth centuries Japanese pirates regularly raided the Korean coast for women and other loot.

During the 1930s and early 1940s the Japanese conscripted large numbers of Korean women to serve as prostitutes for its military forces. In the mid-1990s survivors of this group, whom the Japanese military officially registered as "comfort women," were still trying to get the Japanese government to recognize their existence and make some kind of amends for the suffering they endured.

The Korean War (1950–53) was to be the watershed event in the lives of most Korean women. Once it was over and rebuilding began, large numbers of young women began to enter universities, go into industry, and take up professional careers. Another key factor in the social and sexual emancipation of Korean women was the stationing of large numbers of American and Allied troops and civil service personnel in Korea following the end of the Korean War.

With so many Korean men killed during the occupation of Korea by Japan, World War II, and the Korean War, and most Korean families reduced to absolute poverty by the wars, large numbers of young Korean women were drawn to the foreign troops stationed in the country. Fraternization between the Allied forces and Korean women gave new meaning to the term *foreign relations*.

The entertainment infrastructure that sprang up to serve the needs of the occupation forces included red light districts, independent brothels of every description, and nightclubs staffed by large contingents of hostesses. These nightclubs attracted some of the most beautiful, intelligent, and talented women in Korea—women whose physical attraction would hypnotize many of the male Western visitors. During the 1960s and 1970s thousands of young Korean women also worked as call girls in an industry that was as highly and efficiently organized as any other business. Male guests checking into Seoul hotels invariably got their first calls from these young women within a few minutes after they entered their rooms. Many of the young women who took up with foreigners during that period ended up marrying them. Others went into business on their own, and some built up small fortunes.

Korean women have come a long way since that heady postwar period, but today they are still treated as second-class citizens. Male children are still preferred, mothers have no legal rights over their children, and in divorce cases fathers generally get custody of any children. By the 1970s it was common for young single Korean men and women to court each other in the Western fashion and choose their spouses, but arranged marriages are still common, particularly in rural areas.

One interesting teenage response to the weakening of the traditional social barriers caused by separating the sexes might be described as a Korean version of "spin the bottle"—but without the element of chance. In this "game," a group of teenagers would meet at a prearranged place. Boys would place personal items together on a table or some other surface in front of the girls. It was then up to the girls to pick up one of the items. The owners of the items became their dates.

Recent surveys of university students indicate that their attitudes toward sex and sexual behavior are no longer Confucian, but they are not as liberal as come critics of contemporary behavior claim. Surveys show that about half of college-age Korean men and women believe that premarital sex is all right and that it should not necessarily presuppose marriage.

One of the legacies of Korea's lingering family clan system often has a negative impact on young couples wanting to get married. Korean law prohibits marriage between couples who have any paternal ancestors in common, no matter how far back the connection might be. The law allows maternal relatives to marry after the fourth generation. It was not until 1995 that a new law made it legal for members of the huge Kim clan to marry if there was no traceable relationship between the two parties.

성리학
Songnihak
(Sohng-nee-hahk)
"Cosmic Thinking"

There is an element in Korean thinking that is referred to as *songnihak* (sohng-nee-hahk), which can be translated loosely as "cosmic thinking"—a viewpoint that goes well beyond the visible and mundane world to incorporate ontology (being) as well as cosmology and the spiritual relationship between humanity and these concepts.

There is a native as well as a Chinese element in this concept of cosmic thinking. Korea's traditional animistic view of the world provided fertile ground for the Chinese schools of philosophy that began seeping into the country as early as 108 B.C., when China's so-called "military emperor" Wu-Ti established suzerainty over the Korean peninsula. From that point on Chinese scholars regularly visited Korea and young Koreans were sent to the capital of China to study. The adoption of China's ideographic writing system by Korea's elite class of rulers and administrators between 108 B.C. and the sixth century A.D. brought with it the whole Chinese package of philosophical ideas, including Buddhism, Confucianism, and Taoism—all of which were based on aspects of *songnihak*.

In broad terms cosmic thinking referred to taking into account all of the forces of nature and conducting oneself in harmony with the world at large. This is not to suggest, however, that traditional Korean culture was founded on cosmic principles or that all was harmonious. In fact virtually every facet of Korea's feudalistic social system contradicted *songnihak* as far as human relations were concerned.

Like their Chinese counterparts, Korean scholar-officials constantly preached the concept of cosmic thinking, but the concept was usurped by whatever group was in power to justify its rule, and like the modern-day use of the word *democratic* in Communist regimes, it was an Orwellian misuse of the phrase. The only thing cosmic or holistic about the old Korean social and political systems were their all-out attempts to control the attitudes and behavior of people on behalf of the ruling class.

Still, *songnihak* played and continues to play an important role in Korean society. In pre-modern Korea this role was limited primarily to the intellectual and spiritual spheres, where it provided some solace for the suffering caused by a complete lack of personal freedom and denial of the self. In present-day Korea the concept is gradually coming into its own in direct relation to the degree and quality of the freedom of thought and action allowed by the government.

Virtually every Korean is culturally imbued with the idea that humanity should be guided by cosmic thinking, that neither Korea nor the world at large will be right with the cosmos until this occurs, and that they must try to help make it happen. But they are restrained by memories of all that Koreans have suffered in the past from both domestic and foreign forces. These memories are the source of a Korean obsession with achieving the power necessary to eliminate evils that still exist in their own society, as well as to protect themselves from destructive forces from the outside.

Their obsession is reflected in an almost paranoid nationalism that continues to manifest itself in political authoritarianism, economic protectionism, and a "do whatever is necessary" attitude by the government and the business community.

Foreign response to Korean fears and ambitions and their ongoing mercantile behavior should be recognition of the sources of their obsession, guarantees of strong, cooperative action to help them achieve their goals, and equally strong pressure on them to make this cooperative relationship a mutual, reciprocal effort. If this is done, Koreans will have the opportunity to actually apply *songnihak* to their political, economic, and social systems for the first time in their history.

188

성실한
Songshilhan
(Sohng-sheel-hahn)

"The Importance of Loyalty"

In societies in which personal relationships define and control virtually all behavior, loyalty becomes one of the primary pillars of every aspect of life. But life in such societies is always uncertain and dangerous because it is ruled by the emotions of individuals, not universal principles.

Pre-modern Korea was an outstanding example of a personally oriented society in which *songshilhan* (sohng-sheel-hahn), or "loyalty," to one's family, clan, community, or faction usually took precedence over everything else, including the deepest emotions. Generally speaking, loyalty in its traditional Korean context was equated with suppressing one's own interests, inferiors obeying superiors without question, and acting only on behalf of the group.

Songshilhan in present-day Korea is still more personally oriented than principle oriented. In private affairs loyalty to families is still a given, but it no longer includes the concept of suppressing all personal feelings and desires or being absolutely obedient to fathers or other senior family members. Young Koreans now make many decisions on their own.

In companies and other places of employment, individual Koreans have traditionally attached themselves to seniors who had power and were on the advancement escalator. By demonstrating absolute loyalty to these seniors they made themselves indispensable and were pulled up by them. This kind of personal loyalty almost always took precedence over talent until the 1980s and 1990s. But as technical and managerial skills became more critical, more and more bosses found that both they and their companies were better served by giving precedence to ability rather than allegiance.

In general, however, personal loyalty remains an overriding trait that Korean managers demand of their subordinates. For talent to totally replace personal loyalty, the whole group relationship system of Korean culture will have to undergo fundamental changes as well.

Songshilhan between companies is just as important in Korea as it is between individuals. Once one company starts doing business with another company, it is very difficult to break off the relationship. Doing business with more than one company at the same time is also a sensitive matter. If a product or service is something that the most senior company can provide—or believes it can provide—going to another company may be regarded as a slight, as not showing respect to the first company.

Koreans are also upset by foreign companies coming in and publicly shopping around for agents or partners by approaching several companies at the same time. They regard this approach as unfair and opportunistic and have been known to blackball such companies. Veteran expatriate businesspeople in Korea say the best way to avoid ruffling corporate feelings is to discreetly research potential agents or partners and then approach the one that is best qualified.

Foreigners involved with Koreans, for whatever purpose, should keep in mind that the quality of the relationship will be determined to a considerable extent by Korean-style loyalty factors rather than principles or practical reasoning. In other words, the emotional content of the relationship generally takes precedence over the logical content.

189

선물

Sonmul

(Sohn-muul)

"Gift Giving as 'Social Oil'"

Establishing and nurturing personal relationships has traditionally been a key part of life in Korea. One of the ways that people developed and nurtured these relationships was through *sonmul* (sohn-muul), or "gifts." *Sonmul* were used to express friendship, respect, and loyalty and to build up social, economic, and moral obligations that could be drawn on at a later date.

Because gifts played such an important role in Korean life, their selection, presentation, and receipt involved a great deal of protocol and became one of the most distinctive features of Korean culture. The formalities that grew up around gift giving during the long feudal era in Korea have lessened considerably, but there is still substantial etiquette involved.

Gift-giving protocol includes the etiquette involved in handing other people objects of any kind. Which hand is used may signal very clearly which is the superior and which the inferior. The right hand is used when passing something to a person of superior status. In formal situations the amount of courtesy and respect demonstrated is increased greatly by supporting the right hand with the left hand (by placing the left hand under the right hand). Either hand may be used to pass things to people of lower status, but both hands are not used unless people are humbling themselves to a person as part of an apology for some serious mishap or transgression.

Among the gifts that are appropriate for home visits are fruit, fruit juices, pastries, wine, and other alcoholic drinks. Toys are always appropriate for families with small children. Koreans generally do not give household appliances or decorative items as gifts on the occasion of home visits. Packaging is also of special importance in Korea. With more than two thousand years of handicraft traditions, Koreans have high standards when it comes to wrapping and boxing gifts. But except for homemade gifts (cookies, for example), packaging is usually not a problem because department stores and other shops that specialize in selling gift items are also expert at packaging them appropriately.

Cash has long been a popular gift in Korea, but it took on new dimensions following Korea's emergence as a major industrial power and the spread of affluence among ordinary people. Now, giving cash gifts, particularly on the occasion of funerals, weddings, key birthdays, and other important celebrations, is a very important part of life in Korea.

Proper etiquette calls for gifts of money to be enclosed in an envelope or wrapped in a sheet of paper. Cash gifts given to hosts on ceremonial occasions are called *pujugum* (puu-juu-guhm), literally "help money"—that is, money to help pay the costs incurred by the hosts.

The importance of keeping track of gifts given and received is indicated by the fact that many people, families as well as individuals, have traditionally kept a *mulmokkye* (muhl-moak-keh), a kind of record book of gifts, particularly the names of people who bring gifts to special functions. One of the reasons for this is that it is also customary for hosts (at receptions, weddings, and so on) to give gifts to guests when they depart. These latter "guest gifts" are known as *dapryepoom* (dahp-reh-poom), which literally means "thank-you gifts." There is also a special word for people who attend such functions without bringing gifts: *pin son* (peen sohn), which means "empty hands."

When Koreans are traveling abroad, particularly when traveling on business or for professional reasons, they customarily carry a supply of small gifts known as *chonjimina* (choan-jee-mee-nah), which literally means "one centimeter of feelings," to give to people who help them out in any way during their trip. The *chonjimina* are meant to show appreciation and express thanks for small favors. It is a good idea for foreign businesspeople visiting Korea to emulate this custom and take along little "good feeling gifts." Care should be taken, however, to distinguish people who deserve—and may expect—a more substantial gift and not disappoint them with a *chonjimina*.

An equally important facet of gift giving in Korea is the country's own regional *myung mul* (me'yuung muul), or "famous products." Over the centuries all of the main regions in the country have developed *myung mul*, which are prized as gifts and souvenirs by people from other areas. People who go on pleasure as well as business trips (*chultchang*/chuhlt-chahng) within Korea are expected to bring back *myung mul*. Koreans who travel abroad are also expected to bring back gifts that are representative of the regions they visited.

190

손님

Sonnim
(Sohn-neem)

"Honorable Guests"

One of the dichotomies of Korean culture is the difference in the way Koreans treat known and unknown people and how their behavior changes toward previously unknown people once they are recognized as *sonnim* (sohn-neem), the common term for "guests." The honorific term for guest is *naebin* (nay-bean). Koreans, like Chinese and Japanese, were traditionally conditioned to avoid unnecessary contact with strangers to avoid complicating the loyalty they had to give to their families, work groups, and superiors—and, in earlier times, to avoid endangering their lives as well.

One of the key reasons for this avoidance syndrome was that all interpersonal relationships called for following a very precise etiquette, based on both language and physical behavior, that was determined by the social status of the people involved. Correctly determining this status was a touchy and often time-consuming process that simply wasn't worth the effort if an ongoing relationship was not going to be pursued.

Furthermore, it was socially unacceptable for a person of inferior social status to seek to establish a personal relationship with a person of superior rank for no specific reason. Vice versa, it was unheard of for ranking people to seek any kind of casual social relationship with people below them. Another factor in Korean behavior toward strangers that went beyond social stratification and snobbery was that the exclusivity of the family and close kinship system virtually eliminated establishing personal relationships with outsiders.

In sharp contrast to this restrained behavior toward outsiders, Koreans have traditionally treated *sonnim* with such effusive hospitality that it could be smothering. Going all out for guests was a matter of extraordinary personal pride and desire for "face." In earlier times it was one of the few occasions when ordinary Koreans could dispense with frugality, indulge themselves, and literally show off.

Koreans now have virtually unlimited opportunities to entertain themselves, their friends, and their business and professional contacts, but there are still significant cultural barriers to forming casual or close relationships indiscriminately, particularly with people who are outside their social class. These barriers can be breached, however, where guests are concerned, and still today being a guest of Koreans, whether in a business or personal relationship, is a special experience because their traditions of hospitality are not only alive and well but have grown in proportion to their affluence.

Present-day hospitality in Korea also continues to have a strong nationalistic as well as a personal element. Koreans have always been extraordinarily proud of their country, and this pride has become even stronger as a result of their economic accomplishments. Demonstrating profuse hospitality to *sonnim* remains one of the most important ways that Koreans gain face for themselves and their country. This cultural feature is especially conspicuous in the international hotel industry, where the level of service and hospitality far exceeds that found in most other countries and is a matter of national pride.

This pride in service to guests is one of the many cultural attributes of Koreans that has contributed to their success and competitiveness in international trade. In almost all cases foreigners *like* visiting Korea and doing business with Koreans because Koreans make the experience so pleasurable.

191

씨름

Ssirum
(Ssee-ruhm)
"Korean Wrestling"

Ssirum (see-ruhm), or Korean wrestling, is believed to have originated some time around A.D. 400 in the kingdom of Koguryo. The compound word itself means "competition of man." The first matches may have been associated with religious rituals. In any event they soon became a regular feature of festivals, particularly the *Tano* (Tahn-oh) holiday on the fifth day of the fifth lunar month, now usually celebrated in early May.

Tano, described as a "spring festival," was originally a shamanistic ceremony designed to bring about good harvests. It is now marked in villages, towns, and cities by a weeklong series of events that includes folk dancing, singing contests, wrestling, and various prayer rituals and is classified as "Intangible Cultural Asset No. 13" by the Ministry of Cultural Affairs and Sports.

Until recent times no consideration was given to size or weight in *ssirum* matches. Contestants met all comers, with the championship going to the one who eliminated all rivals or had the least amount of losses. Winners of these annual elimination contests were given the title "Super Strong Man" and awarded a bull as a prize. At first *ssirum* wrestlers were sponsored by well-to-do public officials and monasteries. Then the sport spread among the common people, becoming a favorite of farmers and fishermen because it was simple and required no special equipment. Nowadays one of the main *ssirum* tournaments of the year is held in September in conjunction with *Cursok* (Chuu-soak), the Korean Thanksgiving. Instead of a live bull, tournament winners are now given golden ox trophies, plus cash.

In the early 1980s *ssirum* was organized into a professional sport under the auspices of the Korean Ssirum Association (KSA), with weight divisions—those weighing over one hundred kilograms (220 pounds) and those weighing under one hundred kilograms. Wrestlers belong to teams of clubs consisting of a dozen or more members.

The KSA sponsors three "Top Super Strong Man Competition" tournaments and four "Super Strong Man Contests" annually, making it one of the most popular spectator sports in the country. Coaches scour the countryside for exceptionally strong teenage boys wanting to take up the profession. Those who are accepted become members of clubs or "stables," where they undergo rugged training. *Ssirum* wrestling is also part of the physical education program in all middle schools and high schools in Korea.

Ssirum might be called the Korean equivalent of sumo wrestling, but about the only real similarity is that like sumo it originally developed in ancient times as a semireligious ritual and over the centuries gradually became a spectator sport patronized by the court and well-to-do officials.

In *ssirum* the two opponents, dressed in trunks or a loincloth, face each other in a sandpit. They are tied together at their waists and their right legs by two bands of stout cloth called *satba* (saht-bah), one red and the other blue. The bands of cloth are about 1.5 meters (5 feet) long and prevent the wrestlers from moving away from each other. The referee wears a red band on one arm and a blue band on the other arm.

At the beginning of the match the wrestlers assume the starting position. Facing each other in a semisquatting position, each wrestler grasps the back of the other's neck with his right hand and the cloth around the other's right leg with his left hand. At a signal from the referee, who moves out of the way and strikes a massive gong, the wrestlers try to pull, push, or throw their opponents off balance, making them touch the sand with any part of their body other than their feet. The first wrestler to touch the ground loses the match. The referee signifies the winner by raising the arm bearing the band that corresponds to the color of the wrestler's *satba*. The best two out of three falls wins.

Some historical sources say that *ssirum* wrestling is Mongolian in origin, suggesting that its appearance in Korea was much more recent. The Mongols invaded Korea in A.D. 1231, gradually increased their control over the peninsula and from the 1260s exercised total hegemony over the country for the next one hundred years. During that relatively brief historical period the influence that the Mongols had on Korea was remarkable, given the country's long vassal relationship with China.

Korean food as well as Korea's traditional male and female costumes are much closer to Mongolian styles than to Chinese styles—which some historians suggest may be accounted for because there was already an ethnic and cultural affinity between the Mongols and the Koreans. But Korean historians date the origin of *ssirum* wrestling at least a thousand years before the arrival of the Mongols, and it is apparently a form of wrestling practiced nowhere else in the world.

Growing Westernization in Korea has done nothing to diminish the popularity of *ssirum*. On the contrary, as Koreans have become more affluent there has been a resurgence in their appreciation of such traditional practices as *ssirum*, and it is now more popular than ever and includes a growing number of female wrestlers.

192

수줍은

Sujupngun

(Suu-jupc-ngun)

"The Shyness Syndrome"

Korean social scientists, and Koreans in general, invariably include *sujupngun* (suu-jupe-ngun), or "shyness," as one of the most important facets of the traditional Korean character. The term is often used by Korean men when extolling the virtues of Korean women, as well as when they are explaining to Westerners the passive behavior of Korean employees in many work situations.

But as usual in the Confucian sphere of Asia, there are two sides and several facets to Korean shyness. In earlier times, when Korean society was totally dominated by men, females were conditioned to be shy, humble, and obedient at all times, particularly in expressing their sexuality. Males, on the other hand, were taught to be humble in the presence of superior males and to obey them without question, but to be aggressive toward females.

Much of the fabled charm of Korean women was due to this conditioning in shyness, passivity, and vulnerability, because all of these things traditionally were a sexual turn-on for most men. At the same time, the reputation that Korean men had of being peaceful by nature and paragons of Confucian etiquette was due in part to their conditioning in humility and passivity in the presence of superiors.

Culturally induced *pukkurowohaji*, a more colloquial term for shyness, is still a significant part of the Korean character, but it is now regularly mixed with a spirit of independence and aggressiveness by both males and females that can be startling to the outsider. Korean males still defer to their superiors, but they are no longer shy about voicing their opinions and speaking up for their rights, even though they may choose to do so only in group situations.

Korean women have changed the most, however. Even though their public demeanor is generally very shy by Western standards, they can be as positive and as forward as men, if not more so, in business and in private, intimate situations. They are generally even more forthright where Western men are concerned because they are not inhibited by cultural taboos that still influence their reaction to Korean and other Asian men.

All things considered, there is still enough of the pure *pukkurowohaji* of traditional Korea to provide an appealing factor to life in modern Korea, especially for Westerners whose own cultures no longer value shyness as an attractive asset for men or women.

193

슬픔
Sulpum
(Suhl-puum)
"Sadness in Korean Culture"

Westerners who are newly arrived in Korea are frequently taken aback by a traditional style of folksinging called *chang* (chahng), which, according to newcomers, sounds like the singers are crying in agony. *Chang* singing is, in fact, one of the traditional ways Koreans have of expressing the soul-deep *sulpum* (suhl-puum), or "sadness," that is so much a part of their psyche. Songs sung in this manner are charged with expressions of sadness about the problems of life.

Aigo chukketta (aye-go chuke-ket-tah), which literally means "I could just die," is another reference to the sadness that has been so much a part of Korean life since ancient times and is common in everyday speech.

Sulpum has been a major element in Korean culture for well over a thousand years—more precisely, since the adoption of Buddhism as the national religion and Confucianism as the national political and social ideology. Buddhist philosophy emphasizes the fragility and briefness of human life and predisposes people to a fatalistic and essentially sad attitude about life. Buddhist inspired poetry typically compares human existence with that of flowers—short and bittersweet.

Son (Sohn), the Zen sect of Buddhism, which was intimately associated with Japan's samurai warriors and less so with the *hwarang*, or "warriors of the flower circle," of Korea, teaches that one should disdain the soft, the easy, and the fear of death and embrace the hardships and sadness of life.

Confucianism imbued Korean culture with an element of sadness through its prohibition of the verbal and physical expression of emotions that forced people to behave unnaturally and to suffer their frustrations in silence. The lives of women in particular were so limited by law and custom that they had no concept of deliberately pursuing happiness for themselves alone. Sadness was built into their lifestyle.

With rare exceptions, such as festivals and other celebrations, the women of pre-modern Korean could not socially interact with non–family members for purposes of recreation and self-fulfillment. Meeting, talking to, even making eye contact with males other than family members was taboo for women. People in general were not free to make even minor decisions about their lives. Behaving as an individual was immoral and resulted in serious consequences. The family and the group came first.

In this environment sadness was a more natural state than happiness because it is unnatural and damaging not to express emotion, associate freely, hug, or embrace each other, or have skin contact.

One of the ways Koreans traditionally expressed feelings of unhappiness with the social obligations and other restraints on their lives was by yearning for the simple, uncomplicated, and safer life of the *sonin* (soan-een), or "hermit"— a theme that appears over and over in the literature of old Korea.

Modern-day Koreans are now free of most of the programming that traditionally distorted their lives and created a culture of sadness. But a cultural legacy that was nearly two thousand years in the making cannot be exorcised in one generation. An element of sadness is still discernible in the attitudes and behavior of most older Koreans when they are in repose—sadness that wells up from the inherited pain of the past and from all the joys and opportunities that their forbears missed. This sadness adds a special kind of poignancy to Korean life that makes it especially appealing to some people who are sensitive to the human condition.

Another key term in the understanding of Korean culture that is related to *sulpum* is *omsuk* (ohm-suuk), which means "gravity, solemnity, sternness"—the mood and attitude promoted by shamanism, Buddhism, and particularly Confucianism as the only appropriate and acceptable manner for the conduct of private as well as public affairs. Most Koreans still conduct themselves with a stern dignity that generally sets them apart from Americans and others.

194

수영

Suyong
(Suu-yohng)

"Cleansing Body and Spirit"

Koreans learned a long time ago that as people grow up they generally accumulate a lot of emotional baggage that gets heavier and heavier and unless this weight is somehow relieved it causes all kinds of mental and physical ailments. In later centuries, especially after the founding of the Choson dynasty in 1392, most Koreans, women in particular, came under some of the most devastating kinds of emotional stress imaginable.

Virtually every aspect of the behavior of both men and women was so carefully prescribed by a strict form of state-sponsored Confucian ethics, morality, and etiquette that there was almost nothing natural or spontaneous in their lives. Males and females were separated at an early age. The sexuality of women was almost totally denied. Parents, especially fathers, had to be obeyed regardless of how irrational or damaging their behavior.

The ultimate goal of the social ideology that prevailed during the long Choson dynasty (1391–1910) was to destroy the concept of individuality and self and replace it with a group consciousness that was programmed to obey and support the government.

People who lived in that era and earlier may not have realized the source of the stress that built up in their lives—and again especially in the lives of women—but they did come up with a variety of ways to relieve the stress and restore people to emotional and spiritual health. Korean men commonly resorted to drinking, fighting among themselves, and extramarital relations as a means of relieving stress—things that were totally denied to women.

But there was one recourse that was available to women—a kind of spiritual-emotional cleansing called *suyong* (suu-yohng). This cleansing process, conducted by shamans, is the same one that has been used by people throughout the world, apparently since humans beings became self-aware. It consisted of incantations, singing, dancing, and the use of a variety of objects ranging from herbs and hallucinogens to religious talismans to increase the power of the shamans' spells.

Illnesses, especially mental ailments that did not respond to the traditional herbal medicines, and deaths that were traumatic were among the most common occasions for making use of *suyong*. In the case of mental and other unexplained illnesses it was assumed that the body had become inhabited by evil spirits and that they could be expelled from the body by a *suyong*. In the case of death, the purpose of the cleansing process was to rid the survivors of their grief by allowing them to make their final farewells to the dead and sever the emotional ties that had held them together in life.

Suyong are still a vital part of the lives of many Koreans, especially those who live in rural areas and follow most or all of the old ways that appear to have a considerable advantage over the psychoanalytical methods used in the Western world. The Korean patient of a shaman generally needs only one treatment instead of a series of talk-sessions that may not work.

195

다방

Tabang
(Tah-bahng)

"Coffee Shops and Cafés"

The abundance of bars, cabarets, coffee shops, restaurants, and teahouses in modern-day urban Korea belies the traditional Confucian-oriented family and social system, which did not lend itself to such extravagances. The public entertainment facilities that did exist in pre-modern Korea were for men only and were designed primarily for men to indulge themselves in drinking and carrying on with prostitutes. Villages had their community halls, but there was no historical precedent for mixed-sex entertaining and socializing with groups of casual friends, acquaintances, or business contacts in the home.

But like both their contemporary Chinese and Japanese neighbors, Koreans, women as well as men, now eat out and "drink out" to a degree that is overwhelming to more home-oriented Westerners. Because of this custom, the number of restaurants, *shiktang* (sheek-tahng); cafés, *kyongyang shick* (kyohng-yahng sheek); coffee shops, *tabang* (tah-bahng); tearooms, *tagwahoe* (tah-gwah-hoh-eh); and beer houses, *saeng maekchu chip* (sang make-chuu cheep), in Korea is astounding.

All of these places are well patronized, but the ones that play the most important role in social life in Korea may very well be the ubiquitous *tabang*, or "coffee shops." *Tabang* are where Koreans meet to get acquainted, talk, conduct business, read, listen to music, escape the cold in winter and the heat and humidity in summer, or just rest. They are a favorite place for beginning and ending evenings on the town.

Prices in *tabang* are relatively high for coffee, tea, fruit juice, and various other soft drinks, but patrons are free to stay as long as they wish and the extra-high prices are payment for this privilege. Also as in Japan, the role of *tabang* in Korean life has resulted in the creation of what can be called a "coffee shop culture," in reference to the decor of the shops, the kind of music they feature, their overall ambiance, and the behavior they encourage.

Newly arrived foreign bachelors in Seoul and other larger cities soon learn that *tabang* are one of the best places in the country for girl watching (another popular place for this venerable custom is the lobby and coffee shops of major international hotels). People in Korea as tourists are also well advised to visit at least two or three *tabang* during the course of their stay to rub elbows with students, office workers, housewives, and others. It is in such places that one begins to feel the pulse of Korea.

Kyongyang shick, or "cafés," in Korea are similar to coffee shops as popular meeting places, but unlike coffee shops they are licensed to serve food and alcoholic drinks and are generally more upscale in their construction and furnishings. They also tend to cater to specific age groups, with some of them oriented toward men and women in their twenties and others favoring an older crowd. There are also "rock cafés," a hybrid of rock-and-roll clubs and cafés, where patrons can dance and drink.

대도

Taedo
(Tay-doh)

"Manners as Morality"

Koreans have always associated morality with *taedo* (tay-doh), or "manners." Speaking in broad terms, the traditional morality of Koreans was based on absolute conformity to a precise set of rules governing relationships between parents and children and between inferiors and superiors. This Confucian-based etiquette system was not founded on abstract principles that guided Koreans in the decisions they made or in their day-to-day behavior. They had no decisions to ponder, no choices to make.

Virtually everything Koreans were expected and allowed to do was carefully ritualized down to the last small detail. This included all of the mundane actions of life, from sitting, eating, dressing, talking, and working to walking. Any deviation from the established way was glaringly conspicuous and taboo. This social system, which was made the law of the land during the early decades of the Choson dynasty (1392–1910), was superimposed over a tradition of refined manners that had made Koreans famous for well over two thousand years.

Korea's original *taedo* apparently grew out of animistic rituals that were an integral part of daily life—rituals that were designed to please the spirits and keep everyone and everything in harmony with the cosmos. As time passed and the population grew, the elite ruling class added new rules to these ancient rituals in an effort to ensure an obedient citizenry and a harmonious society. Etiquette gradually became equated with ethics, making morality a physical thing that was visible for all to see.

Koreans are no longer bound by the all-encompassing etiquette of the feudal era. But among family members, friends, and acquaintances, their behavior is still distinguished by a level of *taedo* that is rare outside the Confucian sphere of Asia and adds a special quality and ambience to life in the country. In fact, Korean *taedo* has a noticeably positive influence on most Westerners who spend more than a few weeks in the country, subtly resulting in their becoming more sensitive about their own behavior and adopting Korean manners to varying degrees. Foreigners who spend several years in Korea, especially if they learn the language and are able to get inside the culture, usually find themselves bowing and behaving very much like Koreans in their more casual personal relationships.

This tendency for foreigners in Korea to take on some of the coloration of the culture has both good and bad aspects. On the positive side, it helps reduce the cultural stress that affects both foreigners and Koreans when they associate with each other. This is often more of a benefit to the Korean side than to the foreign side because associating with foreigners puts un-Westernized Koreans under an exceptionally severe strain, particularly if the burden of communicating in English or some other foreign language is put on them.

The negative aspects of foreigners "going native" range from being very subtle to blatant, but all result from the same thing—the propensity for Koreans to treat foreigners more as they treat other Koreans when the foreigners in question act like Koreans. Some experienced Westerners say this reaction by Koreans can be so detrimental that they deliberately continue "acting like foreigners" no matter how long they have been in Korea, how well they speak the language, or how familiar they are with all of the nuances of Korean behavior. Their rationale is simply that Koreans generally treat foreigners as guests, going out of their way to accommodate them, and are far more tolerant of any transgressions they may commit—something that translates into a major advantage for foreign visitors and residents alike if they do not abuse it.

Another facet of this syndrome is that most Koreans personally do not appreciate the idea of foreigners acting too much like Koreans. To them it is both irrational and impractical because they are acutely aware that traditional Korean etiquette, with all of its obligations, is often so restrictive and burdensome that it no longer makes any sense.

Old-timers say the most practical solution to this challenge is to follow the niceties of Korean *taedo* in casual personal relationships but to follow Western patterns of behavior in all matters of substance, thereby keeping both the respect and cooperation of Koreans.

197

대접

Taejop
(Tay-jope)

"Let the Good Times Roll"

The positive effects of enthusiastically entertaining guests with food, drinks, and warm, friendly conversation is well known, but some people do it more energetically and are better at it than others. Koreans entertain each other, friends, and guests with a gusto that is unsurpassed in any country. In fact Korean *taejop* (tay-jope), or "entertainment," could be listed as one of the country's most effective defensive and offensive weapons.

Korean social authorities explain their national penchant for vigorous entertainment as part of their traditional philosophical emphasis on the here and now—not waiting for the promise of good times in some afterlife. Another obvious factor in the traditional popularity of *taejop* in Korea is that life for most Koreans was extremely hard most of the time, and when they had an opportunity to enjoy themselves they were not restrained by the idea of saving anything or themselves for some other time. Equally important was the fact that the only time people could dispense with the highly stylized and restrictive etiquette that made up the heart of the social system was when they were engaged in a party that included drinking.

The most common form of *taejop* in Korea is food and drink—copious amounts of mostly spicy food that is always accompanied by equally large amounts of beer, wine, or whiskey—whether the location is a private home, a restaurant, or an inn.* Drinking alcoholic beverages has long been an especially important ingredient in Korean entertainment because strict etiquette prevented Koreans from revealing their true character and personality except when drinking.

Koreans still believe they cannot really get to know people until they have gotten drunk with them and seen behind their masks of manners and moral pretensions. Consequently, a great deal of business and other important matters in Korea is conducted in restaurants, inns, and other public places that specialize in providing good food, drinks, and a high level of service.

Another aspect of hospitality that is of extraordinary importance in Korean *taejop* are young, beautiful women who exude an aura of sexual promise. Koreans, like other Asians in particular, learned long ago that the company of beautiful women—combined with liquor—has a remarkably mellowing effect on men and will do more than virtually any other experience to bond males and encourage business relationships in a matter of hours.

The most intriguing—and, to some people, infamous—of the places that Koreans have traditionally used for sex-enhanced business purposes are the *kisaeng* houses, which feature women trained as perfect party companions. Korea's most commonly used sex-as-entertainment places, however, are the hundreds of cabarets and nightclubs throughout the country that provide beautiful young hostesses as dancing and drinking companions for their guests. Generally speaking, however, it is the allure of sex, not its reality, that male guests pay for in these popular night spots—although some of the young women are available for private arrangements after an evening of drinking, singing, and dancing.

Such entertainment does not come cheaply, and it goes without saying that businessmen who are hosted at such parties are expected to reciprocate at the first opportunity—something that has made the nighttime entertainment trades one of the biggest industries in Korea. And while the role of *kisaeng* houses, cabarets, and nightclubs in doing business in Korea has been diminishing steadily since the 1980s, there is little likelihood that it will disappear altogether because it is too deeply rooted in the culture and its attractions are too deeply ensconced in the male psyche.

---

*Until the 1980s most Korean restaurants and clubs that serve food automatically served *boli cha* (boh-lee chah), or "barley tea," instead of water. People who preferred water generally had to order it. Now it is more common to serve bottled mineral water. I recommend that newcomers make a point of trying *boli cha*, however. Its musky taste grows on one quickly, and it is especially delicious when chilled as a summer drink.

Foreign businesspeople are not exempted from the demands of business *taejop* in Korea. They too are aggressively and often expensively entertained, and failure to follow this deeply entrenched Korean custom can have decidedly negative effects on a budding relationship.

Chopttae (chope-tay), commonly used to mean "reception" and "party," is also used in the sense of "entertain."

택시
Taekshi
(Tack-she)
"Riding Korean Taxis"

Catching and riding regular run-of-the-street *taekshi* (tack-she), or "taxis," in Korea has long been an adventure that many foreign visitors would just as soon do without. There are elite taxis called *mobom* (moh-bohm) that are especially licensed to cater to foreign visitors to avoid language and other problems, but they are expensive and limited in number. International hotels also have a covey of "standard" cabs that serve their guests almost exclusively. These cabs, operated by independent companies and private owners, do not offer the standard of service featured by the *mobom* class of cabs.

Deluxe cabs are painted black and have a wide gold-colored stripe on their sides and a yellow sign on top. Their drivers, who have been licensed especially to serve foreign visitors, have undergone both courtesy and language training and have passed examinations on the location of the more important destinations in their respective cities. They wear uniforms and go about their business in a very professional manner. Ordinary taxi drivers who serve primarily international hotel guests are also usually very knowledgeable about popular destinations, but their foreign language ability is usually limited or nil. They get around this by having the hotel doormen tell them where their passengers want to go.

In addition to the taxi lines at major hotels, there are city-maintained taxi stands along major streets and in the front of some major office buildings. These public taxi stands usually have paid "enforcers" on hand to make sure that both cabs and would-be passengers line up and take their turn.

For foreigners the adventuresome part of catching and riding taxis in Korea (especially in Seoul) begins when they flag them down—or try to flag them down—in the streets or in front of a building where there is no taxi stand. Drivers who are new in the business and do not speak English (which they assume all foreigners speak) will often ignore foreigners frantically waving at them because they assume—usually correctly—that they would not understand where it is the passenger wants to go. Even the Korean names of first-class hotels and other major buildings, restaurants, and the like sound different when pronounced by Koreans in "proper" Korean.

Another factor in catching cruising cabs on the street is that there is generally no such thing as first-come, first-served or "ladies first." It is whoever can get into the cab first regardless of who flagged it down, who has been waiting the longest, or who is closest to the cab when it stops. When a taxi stops at any place other than a taxi stand or in front of a hotel with a doorman, there are no rules. People in general have no qualms about pushing in front of, or sprinting in front of, someone else and commandeering "their" cab. This is one of the most conspicuous situations when the famed politeness and courtesy of Koreans does not apply, and the term *shillye* (sheel-yeh), "rudeness" or "discourtesy," is most often heard. It is also is one of the sorest points of many foreign visitors in Korea as well as growing numbers of Koreans.

Another upsetting factor for uninitiated foreign visitors is a custom called *hapsung* (hop-suung), or "ride sharing." Cab drivers routinely solicit two, three, or more passengers at the same taxi stand or pick up additional fares as they are driving along if there is still room in their cabs. The only criterion for the driver is that the additional passengers say they are going in the same general direction. Drivers who are already carrying one or more passengers and spot other would-be passengers waving at them from the sidewalks pull up and slow down or stop altogether. Those wanting cabs shout out their destinations. If any of them are in the general direction of the fares already aboard, the cabby loads up. Fares picked up along the way pay a basic fare plus what is added to the meter after they board.

Communication problems can be even more serious if the driver speaks very little or no English, the passenger speaks little or no Korean, and the destination is not a well-known landmark. Part of this problem can be solved easily with a little forethought and planning. Prior to embarking on a trip, anyone who doesn't speak survival Korean should have a Korean friend, hotel clerk, etc., write out the destination in *Hangul* (Hahn-guhl), the native Korean writing system, on a card or slip of paper to show to taxi drivers.

Even this approach works well only when the address is a common destination. If it is a private home or some other out-of-the way place and the passenger has not been provided with a detailed map, finding it can be a hit-or-miss experience because few streets are named and the address system has nothing to do with the streets that buildings or houses are on. (See *Chuso*.)

Of course, getting back to their starting point can also be a serious problem for visitors, and the same technique can be used. Wisely, most hotels and some other places of business in Korea provide preprinted address cards in Korean for their guests and customers to show to taxi drivers.* Since there is a constant turnover among taxi drivers, and new ones are invariably newcomers to that particular city, there are no guaranteed or permanent solutions to the problem. Some taxi drivers cruising the streets while empty or looking for additional *hapsung* fares ignore foreigners, especially if they look like tourists, assuming that they will not be able to communicate with them and preferring to avoid problems.

There are a number of other unusual factors involving taxis in Korea. Tunnels, of which there are several in hilly Seoul and in other cities, often charge tolls. Taxi drivers usually pay the toll fee, then add the charge to the fare at the end of the trip. Taxi drivers work in shifts, from early morning until mid-afternoon, and from that time until midnight or later. At the end of their shift, drivers head for their respective headquarters. Some will pick up fares who are going in that direction. Others whiz on by. Some longtime foreign residents in Korea say that by the mid-1990s rising crime rates had made it unsafe for women to ride taxis alone late at night.

199

태권도

Tae Kwon Do
(Tie Kwahn Doh)
"Hand-and-Foot Combat"

Korea, like other Asian countries, has a long history of martial arts, particularly those that were developed for use in self-defense and hand-to-hand combat without weapons. The reason for this traditional emphasis on weaponless self-defense was simply that ordinary Koreans of old, like other Asians, were generally not allowed to own or carry weapons and needed an effective way of protecting themselves because they were regularly subject to attack by brigands and other lawless individuals.

Another reason for developing skill in fighting without weapons was that warriors and others who *were* allowed to carry arms were often attacked when they were unarmed or were caught off guard and had no time to use their weapons. In addition, weaponless martial arts were used for physical exercise and in competition for positions in the royal court.

Korea's most popular martial art is *tae kwon do* (tie kwahn doh), usually written in roman letters as one word, *taekwondo*, which literally means "the way of the hands and feet"—the "weapons" that are used the most in the art. "Some weapons, notably short sticks, long poles, knives and swords, were traditionally used by *taekwondo* practitioners, but the focus was on weaponless defense," notes American *taekwondo* master Ernest G. Beck.

Taekwondo is somewhat similar to China's *kung fu*, which was created and made famous by priests of the Shaolin Temple, and Okinawa's *kara te do* (kahrah tay doh), or "the way of the empty hand," but the Korean art developed independently of these well-known fighting methods. *Taekwondo* has been practiced in Korea for around two thousand years and is therefore much older than *kara te*.

Like *kung fu*, *taekwondo* was based more on the use of mental energy than raw physical power and on knowing exactly where to strike opponents to stun or kill them with a single blow. The "secret" to the power of *taekwondo* is said to be *ki* (kee), which, according to Oriental philosophy, is the cosmic energy that animates all life. Practitioners of the art of *taekwondo* mentally concentrate this energy in their hands or feet so that each blow is more like an explosion. Adds *taekwondo* master Ernest Beck: "Considerable effort is put into training the hands and feet to move with incredible speed, which dramatically multiplies the energy that is released when they strike an object." This burst of energy penetrates deep into the target area in a shock wave that can cause considerable damage.

Of course the primary goal of present-day *taekwondo* masters is not to teach their students how to kill or maim opponents. It is to teach them physical and mental coordination, discipline, self-respect, and respect for others.

The world certifying body for *taekwondo* is the Korea Taekwondo Association (KTA), which was founded in 1961 and is headquartered in Seoul, Korea. In 1973 the KTA established the World Taekwondo Federation to train and certify foreign students in traditional *taekwondo*. However, over the years the World Taekwondo Federation moved strongly toward teaching the martial art as a sport and succeeded in getting the art admitted to the Olympic Games as a demonstration sport in 1988 and 1992. In 1996 the art was officially accepted by the Olympic Committee as a medaled sport beginning with the year 2000 games.

In the meantime, the Korea Taekwondo Association, the parent entity, has remained a traditional martial arts organization. To maintain the teaching of *taekwondo* as a traditional martial art, the Korea Taekwondo Association has designated a number of American Taekwondo Master Instructors as representatives who are authorized to certify black belts in traditional *taekwondo*. This program has met with considerable success in the United States, resulting in other traditional Korean martial arts schools instituting similar certification programs.

Such recognized Korean organizations as the Korean Hapkido Federation and the Republic of Korea Yudo Association work closely with American masters to maintain the teaching of the traditional ways. Considerable support for these programs has also come from the Korean Martial Arts Instructors Association in Korea, which provides coordination and training in the United States by Senior Master Instructors from the respective school systems in Korea.

Foreign *taekwondo* practitioners may become members of such Korean organizations as the Korea Tang Soo Do Moo Duk Kwan Society and the Korea Ancient Martial Arts Society.

A *Hanmadang* (Hahn-mah-dahng), or "Martial Arts Festival," has been staged each year in Korea since 1962 and in the United States since 1995. Practitioners from all of the martial arts are invited to participate in the annual festivals, competing in their respective forms—poomse, hung, kata, sets, etc.—for trophies. There is no "free-fighting" (sport fighting) in the *Hanmadang*. The primary aim of the festivals is to promote the study and practice of the traditional martial ways.

Taekwondo, also an official event in the Asian Games, is taught as a sport in more than one hundred countries around the world. Although there is body contact in the sports version of the art, it is limited to prevent injury. Master Beck says that another long-term goal among American devotees of *taekwondo* is to get the teaching of the traditional art established in primary schools and high schools as a standard curriculum. He adds: "More and more people are recognizing that the discipline students learn in traditional *taekwondo* programs carries over into their school work—their grades go up!—and into their homes—they are more respectful toward their parents and others!"

Visitors in Seoul can see exhibitions of *taekwondo* at the World Tae Kwon Do Federation headquarters.

The second most popular martial art in Korea is *yudo* (*judo* in Japanese), which means "the way of gentleness," in reference to its emphasis on giving way, being passive, and letting opponents defeat themselves by taking advantage of their moves and turning their strength against them. *Yudo* was developed in China in ancient times and introduced into Korea in the twelfth century, where it enjoyed a minor boom and then faded away.

However, Koreans did take the art to Japan, where it became a major part of the training of Japan's famous samurai warrior class which ruled Japan from the latter part of the twelfth century until 1868. When Japan occupied Korea in 1905 and finally annexed the country in 1910, the Japanese occupation forces reintroduced *yudo* to Koreans by making it a part of the physical and mental education of Korean youths (as part of their overall campaign to Japanize all Koreans).

Yudo is still taught in Korean schools as a sport and is a part of the training of all Korean military and police. A number of Korean judoists have won gold medals in the Olympic Games.

200

단골

Tangol

(Tahn-gohl)

"Creating Special Customers"

Some shopkeepers, wholesalers, and other businesses in Korea have relationships with customers that go back for several generations. Virtually all shopkeepers and other businesses in Korea have traditionally made it a practice to develop what is known as a *tangol* (tahn-gohl) or *tankol* (tahn-kohl) relationship

---

*Japan has the same address system as Korea. In the 1950s Japanese restaurants solved part of the problem of making themselves known to customers by printing their addresses on tiny matchboxes and passing them out for free. In 1959 I introduced the idea of printing addresses as well as locator maps on small "flash" cards, in both English and Japanese, for several hundred key destinations in Tokyo (*De Mente's Self-Guide to Tokyo*). The practice quickly spread throughout the country.

with customers. *Tangol* literally means "frequent customer" and refers to a "good customer" or "loyal customer"—one who always comes back and is therefore especially valued by the seller.

Shopkeepers and other businesses in Korea often begin the process of creating *tangol* relationships by voluntarily extending *oesang* (oh-eh-sahng), or "credit," to customers of choice. This action obligates the buyer to continue patronizing the same seller. Some *tangol* relationships are forged rather quickly, particularly when they are on a small scale and involve neighborhood merchants. Others may require months to years of careful cultivation. The *tangol/oesang* system adds considerably to the recordkeeping of merchants, but it also guarantees them a steady clientele.

In villages and other long-established neighborhoods *tangol* relationships that have existed for one or more generations generally take on an institutionalized character sanctified by time and custom. Tradespeople and their *tangol* customers become bound to each other in a kinship fashion that is virtually unbreakable. In colloquial terms, customers "belong" to the merchants they have traditionally patronized.

Foreign companies seeking to gain market share in Korea will find their approach much easier if they are able to introduce the *tangol* element into their programs—which means, however, that they must be aware of and develop strategies for working around, through, or over already existing *tangol* relationships. Generally speaking, Korean consumers in rural areas, and retailers and wholesalers anywhere in the country, will not automatically change their suppliers because of price or other factors that keep markets in the United States and elsewhere in a state of flux. Loyalty to their traditional suppliers normally takes precedence over such matters.

(The Japanese equivalent of *tangol* is *tokui*/toh-kuu-ee, usually with the honorific *san*/sahn attached—e.g., *tokui san*, or "honorable valued customer.")

201

도덕

Todok
(Toh-dohk)

"Circumstantial Morality"

In the traditional Korean social environment, *todok* (toh-dohk), or "ethics," was more a matter of etiquette than adhering to absolute principles of right or wrong. This resulted in what sociologist Kyong Dong Kim refers to as "moralistic ritualism." In other words, moral behavior consisted of abiding by the inferior-superior rituals prescribed by Confucius, rather than basing morality on the common good. Kim went on to say that the gentry of Korea used the concept and practice of moralistic ritualism to justify their right to rule and to use force and authoritarianism in administering the country.

In other words, Korean morality was not based on absolute universal concepts of right or wrong encoded in religion or any other philosophy. It was more of a personalized set of circumstantial guidelines that applied to the individual in relation to his or her family, kin, professional connections, friends, and the government. A key word in all behavior and relationships was *sagong* (sah-gohng), or "circumstances."

Korea's traditional *todok* evolved from the Confucian concept that the proper—and therefore ethical—order in society was an inferior-superior relationship between people based on their sex, age, social class, and position. Whatever sustained and enhanced these vertical relationships was ethical; whatever threatened or damaged them was unethical. This meant that traditional Korean ethics were not universal principles that applied to everyone on all occasions in the same way. They were "situational" or "circumstantial" in that they were determined by personal as well as emotional factors at a particular time and place.

The circumstantial nature of morality in Korea has long been recognized in attitudes toward the poor. The poor, it is said, cannot afford the luxury of *todok*. It is also said that if people lose their *hyongpyon* (h'yohng-p'yohn), or "position," and the survival of their family is in jeopardy, they may be justified in ignoring morality and taking extreme measures.

In practice Korean ethics were behavioral guidelines based on a variety of obligations inferiors had to superiors and, in theory at least, that superiors had to inferiors. They were not designed to measure or ensure high standards of equality, fairness, and justice as these terms are understood in principle in the West. Generally speaking, their aim was exactly the opposite of these "Western" principles. Their goal was to maintain the status quo in a society based on inequalities.

The personal orientation of traditional Korean ethics was a powerful detriment to innovative thinking and action by individuals. Although ethics were based on personal interpretations, they could be expressed only in terms of *chang* (chahng), a word that implies a strong emotional sense of belonging—body and soul—to a specific social group. It implies the ultimate in group consciousness and group morality, not in public consciousness or universal morality.

Todok based on Western principles was introduced into Korea in the latter decades of the nineteenth century by American missionary-scholars who established schools and became tutors and advisers to many individuals who were to play leading roles in the subsequent modernization of the country. Present-day Korea continues to have two standards of morality—the traditional one, which is based primarily on circumstances, and Western morality, which is more or less based on absolute principles of right and wrong. Not surprisingly, Koreans mix the two and switch from one to the other according to the circumstances.

It is generally easy for outsiders to recognize which *todok* Koreans are using because the difference is so obvious that there is no question. Koreans themselves distinguished between the two moralities by regarding one as "the

Korean way" and the other as "the foreign way" or "the Western way." There are many instances when Westerners dealing with Koreans must also mix the two moralities and on some occasions go "the Korean way" to make progress. In either of these two situations, the challenge facing Westerners is to see beyond their own cultural view to make the most effective decision.

Although the Western concept of ethics was brought to Korea in the late 1800s, it was only a cursory introduction to a tiny group of people. It would be well after the mid-1900s before the bulk of the population was introduced to the concept. Generally speaking, however, "Korean ethics" are still the rule in Korea, despite the growing influence of Western thinking and behavior. Attitudes and habits that were built up over several millennia cannot be exorcised from the cultural that easily—even when there is considerable pressure, both internally and externally, to do so.

A significant part of the reason for the survival of Korean ethics into modern times goes beyond their built-in cultural tenacity. Many older Koreans sincerely believe that Korean ethics are superior to Western ethics, and they are doing everything they can to preserve them. The more economically successful Korea becomes, the more convinced these people are that this success is a result of their traditional morality.

Naturally, Korean ethics are the strongest in group situations rather than on an individual basis, particularly in government ministries, corporations, and other public and private institutions. Westerners who encounter Korea's group-based situational ethics for the first time are generally taken aback. From their viewpoint the behavior of government officials and company executives is often devious, dishonest, and unfair. However, the more international Korean corporations are, the more likely they are to adhere to strict Western ethics as far as their foreign activities is concerned. In fact some Korean behavior might be described as textbook American. Following the Korean War in 1951–53, Koreans were under so much pressure to perform and achieve results that "resultism" became an obsession, spawning a plethora of evils that continue to plague the country—from bribery and collusion to a raft of one-sided trade policies.

Still today it is common for many Korean businesspeople to be more interested in the end result than the manner in which something is achieved. In other words, the end justifies the means—a philosophy that has long been well known and appreciated in the West but is apt to be castigated by Westerners when it is used by Koreans to gain an advantage over foreigners.

Among the interesting aspects of Korean ethics mentioned by Se Chol O in a study called *Culture and the Theory of Social Psychology* was his assertion that Korean women are more ethical and dependable than Korean men (which, it could be argued, is usually the case with women in all cultures). O adds that Koreans typically attribute any success they have to the assistance they received from others. But when they fail, they blame others for not having given them enough aid rather than accept any of the blame themselves. Sociologist Yong Bok Koh adds that the "moral dualism" of Korea continues to be the root cause of the social and political problems afflicting the country by preventing what he calls "moral integration."

An odd facet of Korean behavior emphasized by O was that the more public onlookers there are, the less likely any Korean will come to the aid of a stranger in trouble—a phenomenon that is becoming increasingly common in the United States and other Western countries. Along these lines, it seems that Western ethics are becoming more and more like Korean *todok*—situational rather than absolute—or rather a combination of the two that varies with the circumstances. While the two sides continue to differ in principle, they are not that far apart in practice, and once Westerners get over the initial emotional shock they are usually able to do business.

202

도장

Tojang
(Toh-jahng)

"Sealed with a Chop"

In 109 B.C. a Chinese army under the command of the reigning emperor, Wu-Ti, invaded the several small kingdoms on the Korean peninsula, occupied them, and turned them into vassal states that were required to pay annual tribute to China. Over the next several centuries the ruling classes of these kingdoms adopted and assimilated Buddhism, Confucianism, and numerous arts and crafts, including the Chinese writing system, from their huge, highly advanced neighbor.

Another Chinese custom adopted by Koreans during this period was the use of the *tojang* (toh-jahng), "name-seal" or "chop," for affixing their names on letters, documents, paintings, and drawings. *Tojang*, consisting of family names rendered in Chinese ideograms and carved onto the ends of small cylinders of wood, ivory, or other materials, apparently originated in India, where they were known in the Hindi language as *chhap*, pronounced "chop," meaning "seal." Korea's early kingdoms also adopted the Chinese military and civil administration systems, creating a professional class of bureaucrats whose power eventually came to be represented in their *tojang*. Government edicts and other documents had to bear the seals of all the appropriate ministry officials or bureaucrats to be official.

As time went by, the use of *tojang* spread among all members of the gentry, commercial class, and eventually common people, as their official "signature," resulting in the appearance of large numbers of professional *tojang* carvers. This custom caused a great deal of confusion in Korea because so many of the people had the same family name—with Kim, Lee, Choi, and Pak accounting for over half of the entire population. About the only way one Kim could have his seal different from the seals of other Kims was to have the carving of the

Chinese ideographic writing of his name stylized in a way that made it different from all others—more or less as fingerprints differ.

Despite these built-in differences, *tojang* presented a serious problem. Since they were the official signature of the individual, anyone who found, stole, or otherwise got hold of someone's seal could legally obligate that person, it being the same thing as having their power of attorney. Finally this danger led to government officials and merchants having one version of their *tojang* registered at their local city, town, or ward office to authenticate it as their official signature. This registered seal was then locked away when not being used. Generally, people who had registered *tojang* for official purposes also had unregistered seals that they used for ordinary letters, drawings, and so on.

With the spread of literacy in Korea from the end of the nineteenth century on, and especially with the dramatic increase in international business and other affairs from the 1950s on, the use of *tojang* gradually diminished in favor of the written signature. Shortly after Korea regained its sovereignty (from Japan) in 1945, a law was passed recognizing the written signature as the only legally valid signature. This action could have consigned *tojang* to Korea's colorful past, but it did not for several reasons: the carving of the seals was an important handicraft industry; many Koreans liked the traditional flavor of the seals on their private papers and other things; and visiting tourists began buying generic seals as souvenirs as well as having their own *tojang* made, with their names rendered in phonetic Chinese or in *Hangul* (Hahn-guhl), the purely Korean system of writing.

Modern-day *tojang* carvers use a variety of materials that include less expensive wood, plastic, marble, and metal, as well as expensive jade. Despite the international ban on ivory trade, seals made of ivory are still found in Korea.

203

도망가다
Tomanghada
(Toh-mahng-hah-dah)
"Escaping from Obligations"

One of the hallmarks of Korean culture is the number of social obligations involved in maintaining good relations with family members, friends, co-workers, and company superiors—obligations that are usually time-consuming and often expensive. These obligations include attending funerals, weddings, and special birthday celebrations, all of which require substantial outlays of cash. In the past fulfilling such personal obligations was mandatory for anyone who did not want to be ostracized and end up as an outcast on the fringe of society.

As Korea's economy grew from the mid-1950s on, Korean companies began adding to these private social obligations by requiring employees to participate in such company-sponsored events as athletic competitions, mountain hiking, and picnics. Employees were expected to go on these *sawon yohaeng* (sah-wohn yoh-hang), or "employee excursions," to reinforce and demonstrate their loyalty to their group and the company as well as to reconfirm and reinforce the personal bonds tying them together.

For the first several decades these company outings, which included trips to famous recreational areas, food, and drinks, were very popular among employees. But as the standard of living rose and the younger generations became more individualistic and independent minded, many of them began to resent this enforced togetherness. A growing number of them began engaging in *tomanghada* (toh-mahng-hah-dah), or "escaping" from these obligations by making up excuses.

Another break with tradition that is becoming more common involves after-hours drinking sessions sponsored by individual managers of sections and departments as part of developing interpersonal relations, relieving stress, and dealing with complaints. Younger Korean men often prefer to go out drinking with their friends, meet their girlfriends, or go home rather than spend their evenings with bosses and co-workers.

Some middle-aged and older Korean businessmen now also balk at corporate demands on their personal time, especially some of the old practices that involved excessive drinking. Like their Japanese counterparts, when Korean businessmen take guests out for dinner and drinks, they usually don't stop with just a meal and a few drinks at a restaurant. They feel compelled to go on to a karaoke bar or to a cabaret where there are hostesses and dancing. There is often a third stop and sometimes a fourth stop, depending on how much the hosts want to impress their guests with their own capacity for drinking as well as to measure the "sincerity" and stamina of their guests.

Anthropologist Roger L. Janelli notes in *Making Capitalism—The Social and Cultural Construction of a South Korean Conglomerate* that there are sometimes humorous references to the fourth stop as being a "killer"—implying that by that time everyone usually ends up dead drunk—because *sa* (sah), the word for "four," is a homonym for "death."

Skipping these togetherness rituals is a major challenge to tradition and is indicative of the fundamental changes taking place in Korean society. But despite these changes, foreign businesspeople in Korea must be especially cautious about turning down invitations to go out on the town at night. Obviously ducking such social rituals can damage relationships or prevent them from being established in the first place if the *tomanghada* is not legitimate or not handled diplomatically. Whether or not one can safely decline a particular invitation or keep the outing short is a judgment call based on the circumstances at hand.

Some companies and managers continue to emphasize the importance of *sawon yohaeng*, and there are occasions when they invite their foreign partners to join them on such outings. It is both good politics and fun to do so.

동창회
Tongchang Hoe
(Tohng-chahng Hoh-eh)
"Alumni Groupism"

American companies that set up operations in Korea and do their own staffing have a history of personnel problems that are so far outside the realm of their experience that they often don't recognize the factors causing them. The reason for this is that American managers are often blinded and therefore handicapped by their lack of class consciousness—one of the things that makes American society the most comfortable society in the world.

In contrast to this, Koreans are class-conscious to the point that when their relative social status is ignored they are uncomfortable and have difficulty relating to and cooperating with each other. In some cases, such as when younger, "lower-class" people are put in charge of people who are older and are higher in the social hierarchy that exists in Korea, the emotional consequences are so extreme that both morale and efficiency are seriously damaged.

There have been examples of expatriate American managers in Korea who were made aware of the "class" friction among their Korean employees and tried to solve the problem by calling everyone in and lecturing them on democracy, equality, and management by merit rather than social status. In most cases this only made the problems worse because it encouraged the lower-class employees in managerial positions to be more aggressive and demanding. Old Korean hands, along with Korean business consultants, say that despite the American abhorrence for class distinctions, there are occasions when doing as the Koreans do is the only practical solution.

Another cultural factor in relationships in Korea that foreign executives should be aware of is the importance of *tongchang hoe* (tohng-chahng hoe-eh), or "alumni groups." School ties, particularly among individuals who attended the same schools from primary grades through university, are especially strong in Korea. In larger companies and government agencies there are almost always *tongchang hoe* that impact on management and the success potential of the companies.

In the context of traditional Korean culture, common school experiences establish ties that last for life. Graduates of the same school feel a moral obligation to help each other. The higher an individual rises in the political or business world, the more likely he is to surround himself with employees who attended his old schools—a system that then perpetuates itself as each new generation of alumni follows the same practice.

Alumni groups within companies form generational layers of employees who are especially cooperative and loyal, enhancing the effectiveness of teamwork. Ties between *tongchang hoe* from the same schools who are in different companies and government ministries serve as connections that play vital roles in their relationships.

There are numerous success stories in Korea that illustrate the importance of *tongchang hoe*. Foreign companies going into Korea should be aware of this factor and take advantage of it by hiring graduates from schools with especially well-placed alumni as well as tapping into existing alumni groups when looking for new employees.

Among the most valuable connections businessperson can have in Korea are junior alumni brothers in high government offices. Alumni who are senior to the president of Korea and cabinet ministers are in an especially enviable position.

205

동학
Tong Hak
(Tohng Hahk)
"The Eastern Learning War"

Korean intellectuals of the sixteenth, seventeenth, and eighteenth centuries, through links with China, were generally aware that great scientific and technological changes were taking place in the outside world. By the closing decades of the sixteenth century the Korean army and navy had rifles and cannon and used the latter (in conjunction with ironclad ships) to defeat Japanese invasion fleets on two occasions—in 1592 and 1597.

But as far as most Korean scholar-officials were concerned, the industrial revolution in Europe might as well have been on the moon. Imbued in the Confucian philosophy of conservatism and emphasis on the past, they were content to let the outside world go its own way. By the first decades of the nineteenth century the impact of these changes could no longer be ignored. But the greater the pressure and the more ominous the threat from China, Japan, and the Western colonial powers, the more xenophobic and conservative the great majority of Koreans became. By the 1850s these feelings had begun to manifest themselves in a grassroots socioreligious movement to combat foreign influence and keep foreigners out of Korea. Che U Choe, a lower-class aristocrat who lived in the countryside, is credited with founding this movement, which came to be known as *Tong Hak* (Tohng Hahk), or "Eastern Learning," in reference to Confucian teachings. Some Korean historians say that the *Tong Hak* movement was in part a reaction against the growing influence of Catholicism in Korea, which was known as "Western Learning."

Choe began preaching that the only salvation for Korea lay in resisting "Western learning" by using the Confucian wisdom that had been the basis of their society for more than five hundred years. *Tong Hak* groups were formed throughout the country and became more and more militant as foreign powers continued their colonization efforts and Japan in particular increased its presence in Korea. Finally, in 1894, these *Tong Hak* groups staged a series of uprisings in an attempt to overthrow the weak Choson court and bring about the formation of a stronger government that would be more capable of defending the country. When one of these *Tong Hak*–inspired rebel groups won a number of decisive victories over government forces, the Choson king petitioned China for help. Beijing immediately sent a contingent of troops across the Yalu River into Korea.

Japan reacted to this move by dispatching a larger and much better-equipped army into Korea to repel the Chinese, resulting in the Sino-Japanese War, which ended with China suffering an ignoble defeat and Korea at the mercy of Japan. Choe was captured, tried on a charge of heresy, and executed.

Later Korean critics were to note that the Confucian learning that had molded the culture of Korea and sustained Korean society for many centuries had betrayed them and had ignited a series of events that was very quickly to result in the total demise of the Korean state and eventually lead to war between Japan and the United States.

Although Koreans were and still are the most Confucian in their beliefs and behavior among all of the people in the Confucian sphere of Asia, including China itself, the lesson they learned as a result of the failure of *Tong Hak* was not lost on them. Following the end of World War II and the regaining of their sovereignty, Koreans took to Western technology with a special vengeance, quickly creating a powerful industrialized economy. They also began laying the foundation for a society that combines Eastern learning and the rationalism and humanism of the West.

Koreans have made extraordinary progress in their goal of creating a new culture based on the best of the East and West, but it is far from uniform. They are, however, far ahead of China and Japan in pursuit of this goal because they are more realistic and pragmatic—a heritage that probably derives from the fact that historically they were victims rather than aggressors.

While modern-day Koreans are imbued with extraordinary confidence in their abilities, they are not burdened by the kind of superiority complex that afflicts the Chinese and Japanese and are therefore much more practical in their outlook on life and their relations with other people.

206

동일
Tong Il
(Tohng Eel)

"The Great Reunification Dream"

The Korean peninsula first appears in history as the home of several small clan tribes that eventually fused into a number of kingdoms—notably Koguryo, Paekche, Shilla, and Kaya. In the late 600s the Shilla kingdom, located on the southern portion of the peninsula, succeeding in unifying the kingdoms under a single national banner. The peninsula was to remain unified until 1948, when it was divided into North and South Korea as part of the post–World War II conflict between the Soviet Union and the United States.

In 1950 Communist-dominated North Korea invaded South Korea in an attempt to reunite the two halves of the peninsula by force. The United States and other members of the United Nations joined the war on behalf of South Korea. The Soviet Union and China backed North Korea with troops and equipment. The fighting lasted for three years, ending in July 1953.

Both North and South Korea were devastated by the war. More than a million people were killed, and other millions were left homeless and separated from their families. The truce left the two halves of the peninsula in a wary standoff, with each side rearmed by its patrons and the degree of acrimony so virulent, particularly on the part of the North Korean leadership, that it verged on insanity. For the next several decades the passionate desire of most ordinary Koreans for *tong il* (tohng eel), or "reunification," remained a frustrating holy grail.

The term *tong il* took on a life of its own, generating an ongoing debate and endless meetings between North and South Korean representatives, along with their American advisers, that had the aura of a macabre drama constantly on the verge of total violence. These meetings, in the village of Panmunjom less than an hour north of Seoul, with their staged theatrics, became a tourist attraction.

It was not until the early 1990s, when the Soviet Union broke up and East and West Germany were reunited, that North Korean leaders began to show signs of flexibility in their stance on *tong il*. But by that time it was suspected that North Korea had, or was on the verge of producing, nuclear weapons. This became a new bone of contention that kept the two sides in a bitter stalemate. In the following years there were other calculated signs of progress in the pursuit of *tong il*, but in each case they turned out to be delaying tactics designed by the Communist leaders of North Korea.

By 1995 the economy of North Korea appeared on the verge of collapse. With aid from Russia, China, and other Eastern Bloc nations greatly reduced, and in some cases stopped altogether, combined with a number of natural disasters, shortages of food and fuel forced the Communist authorities in Pyongang to appeal to the international community for help. This resulted in renewed hope that the leaders of North Korea would be more amenable to *tong il*. But once again these hopes were in vain.

By 1997 the consensus outside of North Korea appeared to be that barring a revolution by the people of North Korea—a revolution that all or most of the North Korean army would have to support for it to be successful—any *tong il* would have to take place very gradually over a period of decades. Given the historical acrimony between the northern and southern portions of Korea, even this prediction may be overly optimistic.

In the meantime, *tong il* remains one of the most politically, economically, and socially sensitive and provocative terms in the Korean language, stirring longings, fears, and anger over this new suffering imposed on Korea by outsiders.

207

독립
Tongnip
(Tohng-neep)

"Independence vs. Tradition"

Many "old Korea hands" say that Koreans are not as ethnocentric as their Chinese and Japanese neighbors and are more at ease with Westerners and other foreigners. But they add that because of the lingering influence of generations of conditioning in Confucianism, Koreans tend to be ambivalent in their attitudes toward the individualistic philosophy and behavior of Westerners.

Americans in particular generally elicit both the most admiration and the most criticism from Koreans, not only because there are more contrasts between American and Korean behavior but also because they have had far more exposure to American ways. Most Koreans, particularly younger generations, are envious of the *tongnip* (tohng-neep), or "independence," of Americans (in the sense of being able to make personal choices and please oneself) and yearn for more of it in their own lives. But many of them are quick to criticize Americans as being selfish and uncaring— which, of course, is diametrically opposed to the view that Americans have of themselves.

In the Korean mind-set all the good that Americans have done, individually, in organized groups, and as a nation, is often overshadowed by the negative reaction of Koreans to American attitudes and behavior that were traditionally taboo in Korean culture. Because of so many centuries of conditioning in selflessness and groupism, Koreans tend to regard the American way of interacting with other people, the competitive nature of capitalism, and American-style business management as symptomatic of a selfish and uncaring nature.

Despite their admiration and imitation of many facets of American culture, the average Korean is generally unable to distinguish between the American way of being individualistic and selfish on one hand and kind and caring on the other simply because these seemingly contradictory concepts were never a part of their historical experience.

When questioned closely about *tongnip*, Koreans generally say that American-style independence is not suitable for Koreans and that they must create their own style within the context of their ongoing culture. They point to the violence that is endemic in American society as one of the results of "selfish and excessive" independence. But personal *tongnip* is increasing in Korea because of affluence and human nature, not because Koreans are consciously imitating the American lifestyle. More and more younger people with successful business careers have gotten used to privacy and independence and prefer to live in their own homes or apartments rather than with their parents. For the very same reasons older, retired parents who have become well-to-do are choosing to live by themselves rather than move in with one of their sons or daughters.

One of the many challenges facing Korea is to merge the human desire for self-identity and independence with Confucian-style family and social responsibilities and come up with a happy medium. And little by little Koreans are redefining the meaning of *tongnip* to suit their own cultural viewpoint.

208

의무

Uimu
(We-muu)

"Duty and Morality"

Although Korea has a history that is well over four thousand years old, the traditional character and morality associated with Koreans were forged primarily during the last and longest of the country's royal dynasties—the Choson or Yi dynasty, which began in 1392 and ended in 1910. The founder of this dynasty was a professional soldier, General Song Gye Yi, who staged a successful coup against the ruling Koryo court, made peace with an invading Chinese army, and adopted China's Neo-Confucianism as the political and social ideology of his new regime.

Neo-Confucianism was a form of the great sage's teachings that made filial piety and ancestor worship the building blocks of a hierarchical society divided by sex and class, with morality based on a precisely defined duty following gender and social distinctions. Thereafter, *uimu* (we-muu), or "duty," became a key part of the emotional, spiritual, and intellectual force that held Korean society together. There was the *uimu* of children to parents, of individuals to their families, of inferiors to superiors, of people to governmental authorities, and of the living to the dead.

These duties took precedence over virtually all other considerations, particularly over personal feelings, including love, and personal goals. The system required inferiors to obey superiors on all levels of society and called for group or collective responsibility, beginning with the family. In broad terms *uimu* refers to social obligations that people are born with, along with those that are a natural outgrowth of the care and training that one receives in the process of growing up.

In this Orwellian-type environment, the family, beginning with the senior male member, was responsible for the behavior of every member of the family, and all were subject to punishment for the transgressions of any member. This collective responsibility was applied to whole communities and villages, forcing people to police the behavior of everyone in their group. In some cases the insidious nature of collective responsibility and collective punishment resulted in the neighbors of people who broke some law or social taboo taking matters into their own hands, vigilante fashion, and meting out punishment.

While collective responsibility is no longer the official ideology in Korea, the lives of most Koreans are still influenced significantly by *uimu* to their families, teachers, classmates, close friends, and bosses. Koreans continue to be family oriented to an extraordinary degree and to take their families and close personal relationships into consideration in all of the more important decisions they make. Acting as individuals, on their own, is still relatively rare.

Foreigners who are not familiar with the duty obligations that Koreans are under and become involved with them for business and other purposes often find many of their attitudes and much of their behavior confusing and frustrating. There is no quick and often no easy solution to this problem. In the case of foreign businesspeople dealing with employees as well as clients and outside contacts, there is often no choice but to make some kind of accommodation to avoid creating more serious obstacles.

This cross-cultural problem is often exacerbated by Koreans who have become bilingual and bicultural. They generally think and act "Western" when dealing with Westerners but must conform to Korean attitudes and behavior when interacting with other Koreans—a situation that frequently results in misunderstandings and friction in foreign-managed companies (and in diplomatic circles) in Korea.

The only practical response to this common problem is for both sides to be culturally sensitive enough to be aware that the problem exists and diplomatic enough to discuss it calmly and rationally as each occasion arises so as to reach a mutually acceptable accommodation.

209

의리
Uiri
(Wee-ree)

"The Burden of Obligations"

In traditional Korean society (much of which has survived into modern times), family life revolved around fathers. Fathers had the exclusive right to make all decisions of any consequence in all families and were responsible for the behavior of each family member. In every sense of the phrase fathers were the lords and masters of their homes and often used the threat of force and punishment in controlling family members. But there had to be something other than force and punishment to make this system work smoothly and contribute to the *hwa* (whah), or "harmony," that was so important in Korean society. This something was *uiri* (wee-ree), which in its simplest context means "obligations" but when fully extrapolated includes the concepts of absolute integrity, loyalty, and the highest standards of Confucian morality.

Uiri was the cultural glue that bound the people to one another in their respective hierarchical places—the loyalty that parents and children owed to each other and to their kin and friends, to their teachers, employers, and government officials. *Uiri* was not something that people were free to accept or ignore. As with "original sin" in Christianity, all Koreans were born with a certain number of preordained obligations and incurred new ones as time passed. The "original obligation" of all Koreans was the one they owed to their parents for giving them life and raising them, often at considerable sacrifice. This obligation included doing everything they could to make their parents happy and contented during their lifetime and then honoring them after their death.

Another of the more powerful obligations in Korean society was paying respect to all elders, not just to parents and grandparents. This resulted in younger and older people being labeled with specific terms that identified their category: *noin* (noh-een), "elders" or "older people," and *cholmun saram* (chohl-muun sah-rahm), or "young people." *Noin* was by far the most important of these words because Koreans were conditioned from infancy to respect those who were older, and the older the individual the more respect that was due.

Failure to properly discharge all obligations when they were due was one of the most shameful—and sometimes dangerous—things that could befall Koreans. And such failures brought shame not only to the individual who failed but to their families and friends as well.

There were many things that Koreans were required to do to fulfill the demands of *uiri*. These included obeying all of the dictates of Confucian-style filial piety, from interpersonal relationships within families and ancestor worship to abiding by a highly stylized etiquette that required the careful use of respect words and language in general. There were precise obligations having to do with weddings, births, birthday celebrations, funerals, festivals, and other events that were both time-consuming and expensive; things that people dared not ignore or downplay for fear of losing "face" and damaging their own status as well as that of their families.

The primary sanction used to enforce the fulfillment of *uiri* was the very real threat of social ostracization—and worse. People who deliberately and repeatedly failed to conform to the precise rules of behavior literally lost their place in society and became outcasts. If their failure to abide by established protocol involved a high-ranking official, the repercussions could be even more serious.

The power of *uiri* in Korean life has diminished considerably since democracy began gradually replacing Confucianism as the official social ideology in the 1960s. But it remains the overriding factor in the lives of most people. All Koreans today are bound to their families, relatives, friends, co-workers, employers, etc., by obligations that are an integral part of their identity as Koreans in good standing.

Foreigners wanting to deal effectively and pleasantly with Koreans must establish a *uiri*-bound relationship with them—one in which both parties have the necessary trust and confidence in each other to be frank, cooperative, and supportive and to be able to impose on each other in times of need.

210

의식

Uishik

(We-sheek)

"Contents of the Korean Mind"

Koreans, like the Japanese, are fascinated by their own psychic makeup. Social scientists as well as professional laypeople are constantly trying to analyze and explain Korean attitudes and behavior. In their efforts to understand themselves, Korean intellectuals have come up with a number of theories and terms based on exhaustive studies of the country's intellectual heritage as reflected in poetry, literature, and books in virtually every field of knowledge—even commentaries written by foreign residents and visitors.

One of the terms that is used regularly in this effort is *uishik* (we-sheek), which is usually translated as "consciousness" but actually goes well beyond the idea of being awake and aware. It incorporates the entire "contents" of the Korean mind—beliefs, attitudes, values, everything that makes up the traditional Korean philosophy and psychology.

Researchers into the *uishik* of Koreans readily admit that their approach is not "scientific" and that their conclusions are "approximations" rather than "scientific fact," but they add that most of their judgments are still self-evident in the attitudes and behavior of present-day Koreans. One of the aspects of the Korean mind that the researchers emphasized was its "this-worldness," meaning that Koreans traditionally have tended to ignore both abstract thinking and behavior based on abstract concepts in favor of the here and now, the tangible—things they could see, feel, and make use of in their daily lives. The researchers suggest that this typical Korean characteristic derived from the fact that until recent times common Koreans did not have the luxury of contemplating abstract notions; that all of their energy and efforts were needed to survive from one day and one season to the next.

A key factor in the creation of this kind of national character of Koreans, the researchers add, was the fact that political rule in Korea had traditionally been authoritarian and that ordinary people had been conditioned for century after century to passively accept that their destiny, like that of grass and trees, was predetermined. Other "contents" of the traditional Korean mind listed by both professional and amateur researchers included an obsession to achieve wealth and power, a compulsion to learn and constantly improve themselves, tremendous pride, extraordinary sensitivity about their reputations, and overriding confidence in their ability to accomplish whatever they set out to do.

Korean society, from the family unit to the government, is no longer totally authoritarian, and obviously the *uishik* of Koreans has changed dramatically and is changing still. But enough of the traditional character still exists to be readily identifiable in all Koreans, including those who have been educated abroad or worked abroad and become conspicuously Westernized. Furthermore, there is a point beyond which the *uishik* of Koreans is not likely to change, no matter how much or how long they are exposed to other mind-sets. Koreans regard only part of their traditional *uishik* as negative and as something they are determined to eliminate. They are not only satisfied with most of the "contents" of their "national mind." They regard them as superior, are proud of them, and are deeply committed to perpetuating them.

211

위정

Ujong
(Uh-johng)

"Friendships in Korean Life"

The Confucian-oriented political and social system in Korea's last and longest royal dynasty (1392–1910) defined and limited personal relationships by relegating people to precise classes and occupations, then establishing a wide range of requirements and taboos to control behavior within and between the different groups. This system precluded people from establishing personal relationships outside their immediate groups, which generally meant their families and relatives, their workplaces, and, in the case of boys in the upper class, their schools. One of the most far-reaching effects of this social system was that it conditioned people to think only in terms of their own groups and to view all others as outsiders to whom they owed no sympathy, no trust, and no support.

Because people were prevented from establishing close ties with outsiders, the ties they were able to establish within their own groups were especially important. In this environment *ujong* (uh-johng), or "friendship," had special meaning for Koreans. The friendships that people formed with a few relatives, neighbors, and classmates of the same sex and age when they were children and teenagers were generally the only friends they were to have during their lifetimes. Another key reason these early same-sex *ujong* were so important in Korean life was the fact that as much as was physically possible boys and girls were separated at the age of seven, and thereafter the two sexes basically lived apart.

Korean sociologists describe traditional friendships as intimate and lifelong. But the Western terms *blood brothers* and *blood sisters* probably give a better idea of the depth and importance of traditional *ujong* ties in Korean society.

The Confucian conditioning that was responsible for limiting Korean friendships and intensifying those that did exist prior to the 1960s has diminished dramatically in present-day Korea, but its influence lingers on. Still today Koreans do not make friends anywhere near as casually as most Westerners, and their social as well as their work and business activities are often based on and guided by ties that go back to their childhood and teenage years.

Strangely enough, Korean sociologists say that given the nature of the relationships between family members and their kin, the concept of Korean fathers and sons being friends, or uncles and nephews being friends, was traditionally inconceivable. Sociologist Kyung Soo Chun relates in a study published as *Reciprocity and Korean Society: An Ethnograpy of Hasami* that as late as the 1970s in rural areas it was common for sons literally to hate their fathers and to avoid meeting them except in formal situations required by their mutual obligations.

No doubt the traditional restrictions on friendships within Korean society is one of the reasons Koreans are so amenable to making friends with foreigners. Not being Korean, foreigners are basically "culture free," and there are few if any barriers to establishing friendships with them. This friendship factor has played a leading role in relations between Korea and the West since the opening of Korea to the Western world in the 1880s. The first Westerners in Korea—diplomats, missionaries, teachers, and businessmen—were able to quickly establish relationships that were to transcend all cultural differences and last not only for their lifetimes but be passed on to the next generation as well.

Since business as well as virtually all professional matters in Korea are keyed to personal relationships, Westerners proposing to spend time in Korea today for whatever purpose will find that the greatest asset they can have are friendships with as many Koreans as possible. Establishing *ujong* relationships should be high on their list of priorities.

212

음주
Umju
(Uhm-juu)

"The Great Equalizer"

Group-oriented societies in which people are divided hierarchically into inferiors and superiors on the basis of class, sex, age, and occupation require an extraordinarily detailed and strictly enforced etiquette to make the system work. Such systems invariably limit communication between people in the same group and make it extremely difficult, and often impossible, for people in different groups to communicate effectively.

This social system is, in fact, so impractical that it is absolutely essential that such societies come up with ways of bypassing all of the etiquette and taboos that normally prevent full, candid communication. Asia's group-oriented societies generally resolved this problem by allowing their members to ignore traditional etiquette, to talk openly and honestly with each other, across class as well as culturally imposed lines, when they were drinking alcoholic beverages in a specific kind of setting.

Korean society has traditionally been an outstanding example of this rule—but in Korea as elsewhere in Asia, it had its downside as well. One of the more deleterious aspects of ritualized *umju* (uhm-juu), or "drinking," in Korea was the concept that people were not responsible for their behavior when they were intoxicated, leading to acts of violence often going unpunished. Eventually the custom of excusing disruptive and destructive behavior of people who were inebriated became institutionalized into law that was not eliminated until modern times.

Still today, despite significant changes in attitudes and behavior, virtually every social, economic, and political action that takes place in the country is lubricated with alcohol. One foreign resident described drinking as "the national sport." Korean men have traditionally drunk for the purpose of becoming *chwihada* (chwee-hah-dah), or "inebriated"—not just to get a little high and have an excuse for breaking the rules. But there have also traditionally been behavioral boundaries beyond which they could not go with impunity. Making a *silsu* (sheel-suu), or "mistake in etiquette," toward a superior during a drinking spree is still taboo.

Because of the cultural taboos that traditionally limited the amount of communication between Koreans and generally prevented them from speaking openly and honestly except when they were drinking, it naturally came about that people could not believe or trust one another—could not really get to know each other—until they had engaged in a number of *umju* bouts that allowed them to remove their masks and reveal their true selves to each other.

While the absolute necessity for people to get drunk together before they can establish trusting relationships has diminished greatly in recent decades, drinking continues to be an essential part of virtually all male relationships in Korea, and *Hanchan hapshita* (Hahn-chahn hahp-sshtah), or "Let's have a drink," is one of the most often heard expressions in Korea. When Koreans want to discuss something personal or about business, it often begins with *Hanchan hapshita*. A related phrase often used in conjunction with "Let's have a drink" is *han jan man* (hahn jahn mahn), meaning "just one glass." It should not be taken literally.

It is tradition for Korean hosts to repeatedly press their guests to drink, often exchanging glasses or cups as a mark of friendship and respect. Failing to follow this long-established etiquette can be considered rude. In this environment, men who refuse to drink are invariably suspect unless they have a solid medical reason, and not being willing or able to drink puts both them and their associates or counterparts in an awkward position. Particularly when nondrinking foreigners are involved, Koreans feel especially constrained.

Foreigners in Korea who are light drinkers or nondrinkers must be very diplomatic in handling this situation. One gambit that can be, and often is, used successfully by light drinkers—Koreans as well as foreigners—is to simulate drunkenness after only one or two drinks and only sip at drinks for the rest of the party. A ploy increasingly used by Koreans themselves is to say they are taking some kind of antibiotic that precludes them from drinking—which is good enough in social situations but is weak, to say the least, when one is out with business contacts and trying to make the best impression possible.

The pressure to drink is real and is strong enough that many Koreans who have a low tolerance for alcohol, and in many cases are actually allergic to it, will drink anyway, knowing that it is going to make them ill. Another cultural factor that can be upsetting to foreigners is that when Korean men drink—more so in bars than at banquet dinners—they typically become loud, boisterous, and physical as part of "forgetting etiquette" and letting off emotional steam. Koreans are naturally tolerant of this kind of behavior, since it has been socially permissible for centuries. But it can be awkward and embarrassing to people who are used to more sedate manners, especially when they are in a public place.

As is also common in societies where drinking is a major cultural expression, Koreans follow a precise etiquette that is a key part of the ritual. At the onset it is customary for the host of the event to pour drinks for the key guest or guests. If the party is small and made up mostly of equals, the host may get up from his seat and pour drinks for everyone. After the initial round, members of the party vie for the honor of pouring drinks for the host. Throughout the party, inferiors make a big show of pouring drinks for superiors, sometimes circumnavigating the table. When someone pours a drink for you, etiquette calls for you to return the favor. Hard-core tradition calls for you to down your drink, hand the empty glass to whoever poured the drink, and pour that person one.

If your glass is not empty when someone offers to pour for you, strict etiquette calls for you to quickly finish it off. In most cases you can get by with taking just a modest-sized swallow, but some especially aggressive participants will pressure you until you empty your glass. Proper etiquette calls for lower-ranking people to hold their glasses with both hands or with their left hands supporting their right hands when someone is serving them. Servers are expected to hold bottles in the same way.

In a direct contradiction of their normally reserved behavior when sober, Korean men typically become very physical and affectionate with other men as soon as they have had a few drinks and gotten a little tipsy—linking arms, squeezing hands and legs, holding on to each other, etc. They commonly apologize for this kind of behavior, especially when they are out with Westerners who do not behave in the same way and often cringe noticeably when their legs or hands are fondled.

In earlier times Korean women generally did not drink alcoholic beverages. Some, however, took up drinking after they passed the age of sixty and were no longer responsible for taking care of their families. The most conspicuous exception to this rule were the *kisaeng*—professional women who catered exclusively to affluent men as drinking companions and entertainers (Korea's equivalent of Japan's better-known *geisha*). Today most Korean women drink modestly as part of their social activities.

Another term intimately associated with drinking customs in Korea is *ich'a hoe* (eech-ah hoh-eh), which can be translated as "second party." When Korean businesspeople and others take guests out drinking at night, they almost always go to at least two places, an *ich'a hoe* and sometimes a third or even a fourth as well. Foreign guests accepting invitations for a night out should keep this in mind and not go overboard at the first stop.

The drinking facilities patronized by Koreans are generically referred to as *muljangsa* (muhl-jahng-sah), which includes bars, *room salons* (with hostesses), and nightclubs.

Most Korean businessmen have one or more *seiryuk kwon* (say-ruuk kwahn), or "power places," meaning favorite bars and cabarets that they frequent often and are well known by the staff and managers. They know they will get special service at these places and habitually take guests, clients, and prospective clients there to impress them. Another commonly used word for drinking places where patrons have developed a close relationship with the owner or manager and the hostesses is *tan gol* (tahn gohl), literally "sweet place."

Another insightful term used in reference to wining and dining people to maintain good relations with them or to soften them up for some purpose is *bang suk ul galda* (bahng suuk uhl gahl-dah), which means to "put a cushion under" them—in other words, to make them comfortable, put them in a good mood, and greatly enhance the possibility that you will get what you want.

Koreans use the word *daepochip* (die-poh-cheep) in reference to traditional drinking places (that also serve a variety of food). *Daipochip* is the Korean equivalent of the Japanese word *akachin* (ah-kah-cheen), which means "red lantern" and is used as a symbol for drinking establishments. But *daipochip* has an entirely different meaning and is not hung up in front of drinking places as *akachin* are in Japan. *Daipochip* means "house of artillery," or a place where big guns are kept. The implication is that when people drink they shoot off their mouths, and the more they drink the bigger the "shots" they fire.

There is another world of drinking in Korea that revolves around *cha* (chah), or "tea." Tea drinking was apparently introduced into Korea by Buddhist monks from China some time after the Chinese invaded the Korean peninsula in 109 B.C.

and made the small kingdoms existing at that time into vassal states. Prior to this, Koreans had been drinking a variety of herbal potions for health purposes for centuries if not millennia. But the Chinese custom of tea drinking that was introduced at that time had long since been formalized into a recreational and social ritual by the Chinese and quickly became a favorite of Korean nobles and the ruling class.

Korea boasts several kinds of tea made from a variety of grains, dried fruit, and leaves. Among the most common of these are *boli cha* (boh-lee chah), or barley tea, *mogwa cha* (mohg-wah chah), or quince tea (quince is a tree, native to Asia, that produces an applelike fruit), *hodo cha* (hoh-doh chah), or walnut tea, *insam cha* (een-sahm chah), or ginseng tea, and *hong cha* (hohng chah), or black tea. (Barley tea is also written as *bari cha* /bah-ree chah in roman letters.)

Barley tea (the barley is roasted) is the most commonly served tea in Korea. In virtually all homes and restaurants it is served instead of water. In winter it is usually served heated. And since the advent of refrigeration in the 1960s it is generally served chilled in the summer.

Koreans drink a lot of *cha*, summer and winter, and offering tea to guests is a sanctified ritual. The various kinds of tea served in Korea are not seen just as refreshments; they are regarded as health drinks.

Martin H. Sours, Professor of International Asian Studies at the American Graduate School of International Management, adds that the Korean concept of drinking is directly the opposite of the anti-alcohol stance built into American culture. When young men and women who don't drink, for whatever reason, go to Korea they are often taken aback by the contrast and the pressure on everyone to drink on regular occasions. It should be noted, however, that the legal sanctions against driving while under the influence of alcohol are very severe in Korea, and professional drivers do not drink when they are on duty.

213

음양

Um-Yang
(Umm-Yahng)

"Duality of the Korean Mind"

Traditional Korean beliefs having to do with the cosmos as well as the day-to-day attitudes and behavior of the people were influenced fundamentally by the *yin-yang* (yeen-yahng) or duality concept proposed and taught by early Chinese philosophers. In Korean the ideogram for *yin* is pronounced "umm." The *um-yang* principle is generally defined as referring to the passive, "female," dark, cool, cosmic element in contrast to the aggressive, "masculine," bright, hot elements in nature.

According to this belief, all things in nature are either *um* or *yang* or a combination of the two, and when they are combined in living organisms they must complement each other in the proper balance for the organisms to function properly. Some Korean scholars regard the *um-yang* concept as the principle on which Korea's traditional culture was founded, from the segregation of the sexes, male superiority, and the way children were supposed to behave toward their parents to the obligation that people had to obey their seniors, particularly government officials, without question.

While these cultural factors are normally explained in terms of Confucianism, Korean scholar Shin Pyo Kang says in his book *The Korean Outlook on Life* that Confucianism itself is based on the *um-yang* principle and that it is the *um-yang* principle that brings order and harmony to society as well as nature. Kang explains that this concept presupposes that a person is foreordained to be an inferior or a superior in relation to other people and that one's social status varies from one encounter to the next, alternating between superior and subordinate. Therefore, he adds, stability and harmony in Korean society are based on people knowing the role they were supposed to play in each encounter with others and playing it properly.

In Kang's view understanding Korean mentality and behavior must begin with an understanding of the *um-yang* principle. Other Koreans, including business scholar Chan Sup Chang, say that the *um-yang* concept of the cosmos is actually value-free, that all the opposites are needed to balance each other, and that the ultimate message is the coexistence of all things.

But it appears to be human nature to emphasize some *um* elements while downplaying the *yang* and vice versa, with the result that there are invariably contradictions and inconsistencies in the character as well as the treatment of people in any society based on the *um-yang* principle.

Korean psychologist Pu Yong Yi undertook the challenge of systematically and objectively analyzing contradictions in Korean character from the viewpoint of medical and analytical psychology and reported his findings in several treatises, including *The National Character of Modern Koreans: A Psychological Study of the Korean Personality*, and *The Ethical Conceptions of the Korean People*, published by the Academy of Korean Studies.

Yi summarized his findings by saying that Koreans are humane, peace-loving, patient, pliable, polite, simple, submissive, unsophisticated, family oriented, open, creative, and progressive and that they are also extremely emotional, cruel, masochistic, sadistic, crude, hot-tempered, dependent, deceitful, and jealous. They also do not distinguish between private and public things, are lazy, lack an aesthetic sense, are narrow-minded, and factional, put great stock in protecting their feelings and "face," and do not like others to enter their private space.

This indicates that Korean culture is characterized by an overload of *yang*, no doubt because it was the male side of the ruling class that decided on the relative strength of the *um* and *yang* in the cultural brew, and they chose to emphasize their own element over that of women and common people.

Analyzing Korean attitudes and behavior from the *um-yang* viewpoint is fascinating as an intellectual exercise, and it does, in fact, explain the dichotomies in Korean character, but it doesn't take the frustration or the pain out of dealing with their dual personalities. Koreans have, of course, been conditioned for centuries to deal with these dualities but only by suppressing most of their natural inclinations and needs. The frustrations and pain can be especially excruciating for Westerners who have not been programmed to accept the inferior-superior concept and other imbalances in Korean behavior. Still, there is some solace in being able to intellectually understand the dual forces at work in typical Korean behavior. Just as it helps to know when someone has a headache, you can adjust your own behavior accordingly.

The duality of the Korean character is reflected directly in their reaction to *sasaengwal* (sah-sang-wahl), or "privacy." Koreans appear to be obsessed with finding out intimate details about others, but in direct contradiction to this they resent it when people pry into their private lives. This, according to psychologist Jae Un Kim, is a reaction to the self-centered orientation of the Korean mind-set, which prevents them from being able to view others objectively or put themselves in the place of others.

Um-yang dualism is conspicuous not only in interpersonal relationships in Korea but in aesthetic and graphic forms as well. The *kukki* (kuuk-kee) or national flag of the Republic of Korea includes the time-honored *um-yang* symbol. (The four trigrams on the flag also have specific readings: *kun*/kuun, *kon*/kone, *gan*/gahn and *i*/ee, and meanings. *Kun* represents heaven, spring, the east, and benevolence; *kon* represents earth, summer, the west, and righteousness; *gan* refers to the sun, autumn, south, and courtesy; *i* represents the moon, winter, north, and knowledge.)

214

은 혜

Unhye
(Uhn-heh)

"Social Indebtedness"

Every Korean is burdened with a variety of social and moral debts he or she owes from birth, and new ones are added as each person grows older and becomes active outside the family. The most important of these debts are to one's parents. Other debts include those that are owed to teachers, to schoolmates, to employers, and so on—all the people who contribute directly to one's livelihood and life goals.

All of this social indebtedness is subsumed in the Confucian-laden word *unhye* (uhn-heh), which means "benefits" and is one of the most important terms in the Korean lexicon. The more benefits people receive from others, the more obligated they are to repay them somehow. Parents in particular can make heavy demands on their children. Teachers are also morally empowered to expect payment of some kind for the benefits they bestowed on students.

As a result of the moral force of *unhye*, the influence that university professors have over their students may last for a lifetime, particularly when the professors use their outside connections to help students obtain jobs in prestigious companies and government agencies. Students who later rise to prominent positions in government or industry may be visited by their former teachers seeking some kind of favor. Generally speaking, the higher the educational level of Koreans, the more beholden they feel toward their teachers and the more willing they are to help them in later years.

The lifelong relationships growing out of the *unhye* factor in Korean society are still another of the many webs or ties that Koreans have traditionally depended on to function in a social and political system that was essentially anti-human and antagonistic, despite its philosophy and facade of harmony and virtue. Because people were virtually confined within the circle of specific groups (families, kin, classmates, benefactors) and were not free to establish and use other relationships based on such practical issues as goodwill and mutual need, the social indebtedness resulting from *unhye* played a primary role in their lives.

The *unhye* factor is still alive and well in present-day Korean society. It no longer has the almost sacred status that it enjoyed when there were no other options available to most people, but it continues to survive and play a significant role because acknowledging social indebtedness is still regarded as one of the highest virtues. Anyone who fails to aid a former benefactor is regarded as having no honor, no shame.

One of the few ways that foreigners can gain entrance into the inner circle of Korean families is to become benefactors to a family member. This especially applies to foreigners who are in teaching positions, because Koreans value education and hold scholars in high esteem. Foreign families who have acted as hosts for Korean students studying abroad also become heirs to an ongoing social debt that Koreans take seriously.

Foreigners who help individual Koreans get into business or succeed in business also earn *unhye* points that build up interest as time goes by.

215

운명

Unmyong
(Uhn-m'yohng)

"The Demise of Fate"

Early Western residents of Korea were struck by a character trait of Koreans that seemed entirely out of place in a Confucian-oriented society that was controlled so rigidly that people often seemed incapable of independent thought. These Westerners noted that during celebrations and other informal occasions Koreans exhibited a lighthearted, carefree, quixotic, and often volatile character that the Westerners equated with the Irish, and more than one chronicler of this period described Koreans as "the Irish of the Orient."

This was quite a remarkable thing to be able to say about a people who were steeped in animism, Buddhism, Taoism, and Confucianism—a process that conditioned them to behave more like drones than free-spirited individuals and to believe that their lives were in the hands of *unmyong* (uhn-m'yohng), or "fate."

Until modern times Koreans had no choice but to believe in fate. On the secular side, their lives were programmed for them by authoritarian governments and an even more autocratic family system in which they virtually had no free-will options. On the spiritual side they were conditioned to believe that their lives were in the hands of gods and spirits and that mundane things such as their choice of names and the direction their homes and doors faced controlled their fortunes.

In a commentary on the fatalism of Koreans, writer Sang Bok Han noted in an article entitled "The Korean Patterns of Life and Ways of Thinking" that until recent times Koreans were virtually prisoners of their social class and local environment. There was practically nothing in their lives that they could change without resorting to extreme violence, and there were powerful sanctions to prevent such changes. Han added that the lives of common Koreans consisted of "chronic poverty" and "dreadful anxiety," and since they were politically powerless, their only recourse was to put their lives in the hands of household spirits and village gods.

Philosopher Il Chol Shin elaborated on this theme in his book *Explore Korea*, saying that Koreans were traditionally forced to live in a state of passive and resigned endurance, unable to protest and without pathos for others. This social system was justified as totally moral and correct by the ideology of Confucianism, which from 1392 until 1910 was the official doctrine undergirding the reigning dynasty.

Belief in the supernatural and in communicating with spirits continues to play a significant role in the lives of many Koreans, particularly those who live in rural areas. Many people in urban as well as rural areas still consult astrologers and other kinds of fortune-tellers. Large numbers call in *mudang* (muu-dahng), "shaman spiritual mediums," to help them deal with deaths in the family and various psychological problems. Well-educated and sophisticated people still consult geomancers when they construct new homes or office buildings.

However, *unmyong* is no longer an overriding force in the lives of Koreans. For the first time in the history of their country they have achieved enough freedom and power to influence their fate in the personal as well as the public sphere, and they are doing so with increasing enthusiasm and imagination. Now, rather than seeing their fate as dark and dreadful, Koreans are predicting that their future will be bright and that they will finally achieve "The Five Blessings." (See *Pok/O-Bok*.)

It may very well be that freeing the "Irish factor" in the character of Koreans will be the thing that makes it possible for them to become the first Asians to join the international community, intellectually as well as spiritually and emotionally, as full-fledged members.

216

우리나라사람
Uri Nara Saram
(Uh-ree Nah-rah Sah-rahm)

"Our Country's People"

The exclusivity of Korean culture manifests itself in ways that are strange and often shocking to outsiders—and no people are more shocked at this cultural exclusivity than those of Korean ancestry who were born and raised outside Korea. When Korean-Americans, Korean-Canadians, and so forth go to their homeland to work or just to visit, it is a pilgrimage that affects them deeply. They are going back to their roots and arrive in an emotional high that makes them extraordinarily sensitive to every sight, every sound.

But much to the shock and chagrin of most "overseas Koreans," especially those who have gone to Korea on job assignments, they quickly discover that they are not always welcomed back as long-lost sons by Koreans in general. Some Koreans, in fact, treat them with the kind of disdain usually reserved for traitors. Few if any of the returnees speak Korean fluently, and what they do speak is old-fashioned. They also do not know, or are awkward in using, Korean etiquette in their personal and business relationships. As a result they are often looked on by strangers and newly met acquaintances as curiosities at best and as cultural dummies at worst.

When native-born Koreans encounter people who look exactly like they do but who talk like and act like foreigners, they are first of all surprised and then disbelieving. Among some Koreans—taxi drivers are good examples—this disbelief can readily turn to anger because their spontaneous reaction is that the individual is putting on airs, pretending not to be Korean. Korea's efforts to globalize its economy and internationalize its people are thus at odds with the emotional reaction of those who have not yet accepted these principles.

Because of this ongoing cultural exclusivity, foreign-born and -raised Koreans do not automatically benefit from the special guest category that Koreans almost always extend to non-Korean foreigners, especially Caucasian Westerners. Instead they are seen as Koreans who willingly gave up their motherland and their culture and in doing so have diminished themselves.

However, if overseas Koreans are aware of the cultural barriers they face in trying to "fit" into present-day Korea, have pleasant personalities, and are deliberately humble and polite, they can eventually earn a status that is known as *uri nara saram* (uh-ree nah-rah sah-rahm), which means "our country's people." This label is something like being given the status of "honorary Korean." But it is generally effective only among an individual's circle of friends and associates on whom one has already worked his or her charms. The individual has to go through the same complex routine of developing an *uri nara saram* relationship with each new person met.

As is generally the case when cultures collide, the higher the social and economic level of the Koreans that overseas Koreans meet, the less prejudice they are likely to encounter. There are exceptions, especially in the case of "foreign Koreans" who have become diplomats in the service of their adopted countries and have achieved fluency in the Korean language as part of their professional training. They are likely to be resented by their counterparts as "selling out" their homeland.

Foreign-born Koreans and Koreans who have become naturalized citizens of other countries, achieved prominence as engineers, scientists, scholars, and so on, and are invited back to Korea by corporations or universities are also put in a special category by those who invited them. Once outside these specific circles, however, they face the same problem in being accepted as *uri nara saram*.

Overseas Koreans planning a trip to their ancestral homeland for any purpose would be well advised to obtain a number of personal introductions to people who are able and willing to help ease their entry into Korean society—travel agents, hotel managers, business executives, teachers, government officials, et al. One of the best of all contacts for getting inside Korean society is a former Korean student who was befriended by the family of the overseas Korean. Church connections are also especially helpful.

217

위엄

Wiom
(We-ohm)

"Dignity Comes First"

Early Western visitors to Korea invariably commented, usually in glowing terms, on the extraordinary dignity with which Koreans of all classes behaved at virtually all times. These visitors found that ordinary day laborers who were illiterate behaved with the studied dignity that foreigners associated with members of the upper class who had had special training in manners. Older Koreans in particular presented a classic picture of *wiom* (we-ohm), or "dignity."

There was a reason for this. Historically Koreans had to repress their personal judgments, preferences, and hopes in favor of their family, workplace, and other membership groups. This cultural imperative resulted in outward appearances, expressed in the term *wiom*, often being more important than personal opinions and convictions. *Wiom* often took precedence over candor and truth and any other personal factor that might force Koreans to reveal their innermost thoughts. Maintaining a high standard of dignity made it possible for them to reveal nothing about their innermost thoughts, thereby protecting their face and often their lives as well.

In addition to the appearance of dignity reflected in the traditional Korean etiquette—formalized bowing, refined body movements, great attention to wearing apparel, etc.—Koreans were imbued, over many centuries, with the Confucian concept that dignified behavior was in itself a great virtue. Conforming to the same standards of dignified behavior that was characteristic of the elite *yangban* (yahng-bahn) was one of the few things that lower-class people had in common with the upper class.

Present-day Koreans, particularly the younger generations, are much more unrestrained in their behavior and freer in exchanging personal information about themselves, complaining about the government, and otherwise voicing their opinions. But *wiom* in its traditional sense is still very much a part of the Korean mind-set and sets Koreans apart from their contemporaries in the United States and elsewhere.

One of the ways present-day Koreans preserve their dignity is to be as passive and as accommodating as possible when in the presence of elders, seniors, and particularly higher-ranking executives and government officials. Another way that Koreans preserve their dignity is by ignoring strangers who cross or enter their space and do not approach them directly or speak to them. This behavior takes place in office situations as well as in public. Visitors to offices, stores, and similar private places often find themselves totally ignored until they take the initiative and address someone. People in public tend to "look through" those who are in their vicinity.

Since *wiom* and "face" are closely connected in the Korean psyche, Koreans are conditioned to be very sensitive to any kind of verbal or physical slight. Any slight not only wounds their dignity but requires some kind of redress. Common slights include failing to use or misusing a person's title, asking a person to do something that he or she feels is not his or her responsibility or is belittling, publicly criticizing anyone without being that person's direct superior, and speaking ill of or making fun of someone.

Foreign managers in Korea must walk a fairly fine line to avoid damaging the dignity of their employees. One way of broadening this line is to make a point of expressing ignorance of proper Korean etiquette and apologizing in advance for any transgressions. Interestingly, Koreans have a great affinity for people who have a good sense of humor, and this can be one of the most important qualifications for a foreign manager.

Traditionally, the only time Korean men deliberately "let go" of their dignity was when they were inebriated in private, with friends and family, which is still generally true today. Koreans who are hosting foreigners at drinking parties expect the foreigners as well to let their dignity go and have fun.

원망
Wonmang
(Wun-mahng)

"The Grudge Syndrome"

In Korea's traditional culture maintaining an unsullied "face," which meant one's own self-image, was a key part of the social morality. Virtually all relationships and interactions were personalized and depended on maintaining "face," so people became extraordinarily sensitive about any kind of behavior that caused them to lose face in the eyes of others or to lose respect for themselves.

Because people were basically regarded as extensions of their families, rather than as individuals, when a member of a family lost face, whatever the cause, the reputation of the whole family suffered. The higher the social level of the family, the more seriously these things were taken and the more extensive their repercussions could be. A slight or insult to one member of a clan, for example, especially if the member was high ranking, was regarded as a blemish on the whole clan.

Relatively minor slights could be wiped out by formal apologies, particularly if the transgressions were inadvertent. But if they were deliberate and especially if they involved people of rank, apologies were usually not enough to wipe the slate clean. Some kind of action on the part of the insulted party was necessary.

In this environment it became symptomatic for people to harbor *wonmang* (wun-mahng), or "grudges," sometimes for generations, and to seek opportunities to get revenge. Much of the internal violence that occurred historically in Korea was the result of *wonmang* feuds carried on between clans contending for scholarly prestige and political power. Most grudges, however, grew out of competition and discrimination within families and neighborhoods.

The cultlike practice of respecting and revering the male sex at the expense of females and the law designating the first son as the primary heir at the expense of other siblings were just two of the cultural factors that made competition and clashes between people inevitable. Sons being subjected to the wills of their fathers until the fathers died created a volatile situation that often strained emotions beyond their limits.

Most of the more feudalistic practices that were the foundation of premodern Korean society have gone by the wayside, but contemporary Korean etiquette and ethics continue to be demanding enough that they create significant emotional tension among people in general, keep them on the lookout for unfavorable comments or actions, and result in *wonmang* being common.

Foreign businesspeople in Korea are especially liable to unknowingly cause their Korean employees and others to hold grudges against them personally or against their company as a whole because they are not aware of all the things that can trigger *wonmang*. Obviously these things can include simple cultural blunders, especially when they are repeated over and over, overbearing behavior by the foreigners, insensitivity to the social relationships among their employees, and hidden personal agendas being pursued by staff members.

Only knowledge of Korean ways, the help of friendly and supportive employees or adviser-mentors, steadfast resolve to bridge cultural gaps, and luck can prevent foreigners in Korea from becoming the object of *wonmang*. But there is something that newcomers can do to reduce the possibility of creating enemies before they learn better, and that is to regularly apologize, sincerely, for inadvertent mistakes and ask for continuing forbearance and support. Koreans appreciate and react positively to genuine expressions of humility.

219

양반
Yangban
(Yahng-bahn)
"The Mandarins of Korea"

Westerners who began visiting Korea after the country opened its doors to the outside world in the 1880s were both mystified and fascinated by a class of men, usually middle-aged or elderly, who were treated with extraordinary respect and were referred to as *yangban* (yahng-bahn). Missionaries, businesspeople, and tourists alike all commented at length on the *yangban*, a term that was sometimes translated as "gentlemen scholars."

James S. Gale, in a book entitled *Korea Sketches*, wrote that the *yangban* did no productive work although they were well educated; that they were clean and soft, wore their fingernails long, spent most of their lives sitting on the floor leaning over low tables, and thus became permanently bent over by the time they reached middle age. Gale, a Christian missionary, added that the *yangban* were not good at business, were passive and fatalistic, despised women, and were parsimonious but extraordinarily self-disciplined, composed, dignified, easygoing, and kind.

Gale, who lived in Korea from 1889 to 1892, admitted that he could not understand the role that the *yangban* played in Korean life or how they could be so respected by the lower class. He made many comparisons between the *yangban* and the working class, noting that the "miserable poverty" in which ordinary Koreans lived was no doubt a result of Confucianism, which extolled poverty as a virtue. The *yangban* encountered by Gale and other Western visitors were members of an elite class that had ruled Korea since ancient times. Below them, supposedly in the order of their social status, were farmers, artisans, and merchants. Merchants were at the bottom of the social ranking because it was believed that profit making through trade was immoral.

Yangban was not a legal term, but over the centuries, and particularly during the early decades of the Choson dynasty, which began in 1392, it came to be synonymous with "ruling class," "gentry," "upper class," and so on. *So-ol* (soh-ohl) were the children of *yangban* by concubines or "second wives" and were treated as illegitimate. *Soja* were the descendants of the second wives of *yangban* men.

By the end of the nineteenth century Korea's *yangban* had had a long but generally inglorious history. Between 57 B.C. and the seventh century A.D. the various kingdoms on the Korean peninsula adopted the Chinese system of government, which was based on Confucian principles and administered by a class of scholar-officials and military officers. Eventually these scholar-officials and military men came to be known collectively as *yang ban* (yahng bahn), which literally means "double order" in reference to the fact that the ruling class was made up of two "orders" or "branches."

Korean society at that time was made up of a relatively small number of clans whose histories went back to the founding of the first dynasty in 2333 B.C. Two of the most powerful clans were the Kim and Yi. Other well-known clans were Ko, Sok, Yun, and Choe. Their families dominated the new *yangban* class, whose primary duty was to devote itself to the study of the Confucian doctrines and other Chinese classics, administer the government, and serve as military officers. From the seventh century until modern times the *yangban* were to have a virtual monopoly on education and both political and economic power in Korea.

The honor and status of the earliest *yangban* families depended on the academic accomplishment of their sons and how many of them succeeded in becoming government officials and high-ranking officers. Education was therefore a serious family affair. During some periods any aristocrat family that did not produce a scholar able to pass the civil service exams over a three-generation period had to give up its privileged class and become commoners.

Yangban officials themselves did no manual work of any kind. They were strictly administrators whose scholarly achievements were supposed to create the moral climate that would result in a perfectly harmonious society. With the passing generations it became customary for the *yangban* to marry only among their own class and to live in special locations in the dynastic capitals or in walled compounds in the countryside.

Over the generations these scholar-officials formed a new, elite class that eventually became hereditary and no longer dependent on its male members passing the national civil service exams. As the number of people in the *yangban* class increased during the Koryo dynasty (918–1392), they outgrew the number of government positions available. This resulted in large numbers of gentry outside the government, the more successful of whom became powerful provincial landlords.

In the century following the establishment of the Choson dynasty in 1392, most of the nobles (relatives of the kings) holding government positions were gradually replaced by non-noble Confucian scholars who had passed the civil service exams, thus putting the government bureaucracy entirely in the hands of the *yangban*.

Also as time passed, many grades or ranks developed among the *yangban*, some based on regional factors and others on lineage. Those born to concubines or second wives instead of primary wives were lower in status. Those who lived in the northern provinces were lower ranked than those in the central and southern regions. As the power of the government *yangban* grew, they exempted themselves from taxes and began to reward themselves with land grants that included all of the farmers working the land. Revenues from these grants made the scholar-officials wealthy and concentrated more power in their hands. In 1556 the Choson court made an effort to reduce the power of *yangban* officials by decreeing that they would be paid salaries rather than receive taxes from lands assigned to them. However, the court began issuing land grants to high-ranking military officers and to local officials who were also members of the *yangban* class, greatly diluting this reform measure.

In 1585 dissension among the *yangban* resulted in the class splitting into two factions—the Eastern Faction and the Western Faction. The Eastern Faction later split into a north group and south group, all of them contesting for influence and power and sometimes engaging in assassinations and open warfare.

In the 1630s the Manchus invaded Korea in a prelude to invading and capturing China. The Choson court was compelled to swear allegiance to the Manchus, further dividing the ruling *yangban* factions. (Throughout virtually all of the pre-modern history of Korea its various dynasties ruled only with the advice and consent of the successive imperial courts of China.)

Following the death of King Hyojong in 1659, the *yangban* were exempted from paying the universal military service tax and, for the most part, from military service as well. Continuing efforts to preserve the ancient *yangban* system only made the economic situation worse and increased the ferment among the oppressed peasant class and the gentry who were out of power. Factional struggles among the *yangban* became fiercer with each passing generation.

Every generation or so, crises that were especially severe resulted in reforms that contributed to brief periods of economic growth, but the inherent weaknesses of the system invariably reappeared and became more serious. By the late 1600s there were four hereditary groups in the *yangban* family clans, each with their own provincial estates or fiefs. Many of the leaders of these clans lived in special areas of Seoul and spent most of their time scheming to win power at court.

Since government office was the only route to wealth, power, and security, competition for positions as government officials became extreme. Rivalries became increasingly fierce. Pogroms and assassinations became commonplace. *Yangban* landlords added to their properties by buying and renting other lands. Poor peasants flocked to the cities to look for jobs in new industries. In some areas the nonworking elite class outnumbered all the other classes. At the same time, some *yangban* became destitute, gave up their exalted status, and married into more affluent families of farmers and merchants in the commoner class.

Aristocrats who did not have official positions in the government lived as artists, scholars, teachers, and landlords. When not engaged in factional intrigue, a great deal of their time was spent in performing the various rituals that had to do with interpersonal relationships and ancestor worship.

Those *yangban* who did not go into government service, either by choice, because of the intrigues of opposing factions, or because there were no positions available for them, and lived in rural areas for several generations were eventually classified as *hyangban* (he-yahng-bahn), or "former *yangban*," and were free to engage in commercial activity. As more generations passed, the number of so-called gentry who were uneducated and poor became substantial. However, because of the prestige adhering to the class, some of these poor gentry were able to dominate society and politics in their rural areas.

During the latter part of the seventeenth century clashes between the different *yangban* factions became even fiercer. A younger group of aristocrats who were not in power began to advance the idea that a nation can survive without a ruler but cannot survive without peasants and that reform was therefore essential. These doctrinal differences resulted in more factions splitting off. The old guard became known as the *Noron* (Noh-rohn), or "Elder Group," and the new reform-minded liberals were known as *Soron* (Soh-rohn), or "Younger Group." Many of the younger group of *yangban* were those who were out of power and had to engage in farming or some kind of business to survive and identified with the peasants rather than the elite.

Members of the *yangban* class who were reduced to earning a livelihood as small farmers were known derisively as *chanban* (chahn-bahn), or "ruined *yangban*." They were families who had been living in rural areas for generations, had not been able to produce sons who could pass the civil service examinations, and therefore were not eligible for appointments to government posts. To meet the demands of the times, the government issued more and more licenses for supplier guilds (wholesalers) to increase its own income. These licenses became the seeds for the development of a well-to-do merchant class. Some farmers also became wealthy and bought *yangban* status for themselves and their families.

In the late 1600s discontent with the *yangban* system and with Confucianism as the state ideology led a number of the out-of-power aristocrats to begin a *Sil Hak* (Sheer Hahk), or "Practical Learning" movement. Their position was that the Confucian classics that candidates for public office were required to master had absolutely no relevance to the political and economic problems besetting the country and that the education system should be replaced with one based on practical knowledge.

But overall the influence of this new breed of "Practical Learning" scholars continued to be blunted for the next two hundred years by factionalism in the government. The traditionally dogmatic Confucian scholars continued theorizing, debating, and stalemating all efforts to bring about fundamental changes in the political system.

In 1714 a maverick member of the ruling Yi family named Chung Hwan Yi published a treatise on the Korean character in which he blamed virtually all of the negative attributes of the people on the *yangban*—his own class. Yi wrote that by allying themselves in factions, plundering the poor peasantry, continuously vying for power, and accusing other factions of perfidy and base actions, the gentry set the worst possible example for common people and spread immorality wherever they took up residence. Yi accused the gentry factions of being caught up in trivial disputes that were continued from one generation to the next, poisoning the atmosphere for everyone.

During the last centuries of the Choson dynasty there were three classes of *yangban* families—the "true" *yangban* made up of families with members that had ranking government officials within the past four generations; the *hyang-*

ban or "fallen *yangban*" that had not had any ranking offices in more than four generations, and the *toban* (toh-bahn), or families that had not had any members in high government positions for many generations.

Below these three classes were four other categories of people: *jung-in* (juung-een), *so-ol* (soh-ohl), *sangmin* (sahng-meen), and *chommin* (chohm-meen). The *jung-in* were the technocrats—the doctors, interpreters, and historians. The *so-ol* were the offspring of *yangban* and their concubines. The *sangmin* were the commoners—farmers, fishermen, and craftsmen. *Chommin* were people who worked with meats and hides, dancers, fortune-tellers, and shamans.

In Korea's Confucian-oriented social system there were two sets of virtues—one that applied to common people and another that applied to the ruling *yangban* class. Confucianism was used by the *yangban* class to justify their political and economic monopoly and their use of armed power, incarceration, and execution to impose absolute obedience on the common people. This system naturally alienated common people from the government. Farmers in particular distrusted officials, and peasant rebellions became more and more common.

Jae Un Kim, author of *The Koreans: Their Mind and Behavior*, says that during the last generations of the Choson dynasty most of the *yangban* spent their time and energy seeking wisdom, polishing their virtue, nurturing friendships, dabbling in art, and seeking physical gratification in food and sex.

Confucian ideology, the foundation of Choson society, taught that the basis for human relations was respect for others and justice for all. But the *yangban*, says Pae Ho Han in *The Nature and Function of Korean Politics*, applied this ideology only within their own class. They believed that the basis for behavior among common people was absolute obedience to any superior.

Common Koreans were traditionally conditioned to believe that people of superior status were in positions of power because of superior character and to accept the disparity between their social levels as the natural order of things. But Han adds that the *yangban* system survived for as long as it did because in the early centuries the Choson government, Korea's last and longest dynasty (1392–1910), had the power and the will to force this ideology intellectually and physically on the common people.

But by the end of the nineteenth century the *yangban* class had become so impotent and divided that it was unable to create any kind of effective policy to defend the country from increasing encroachments by foreign powers, particularly Japan, resulting in Korea's being absorbed into the growing Japanese empire.

The official rank of *yangban* was abolished by the Choson court in 1894, but it was so much a part of Korean society that as late as the 1970s and 1980s many ex-*yangban*, particularly those in rural areas of the country, still considered themselves gentry, behaved like aristocrats, and were generally accorded the status of a superior class by the common people in their regions.

Following the annexation of Korea by Japan in 1910, the Japanese used many of the former gentry as surrogates in their administration of the country. A number of *yangban* landlords willingly collaborated with the Japanese colonizers, earning them even more hatred from their tenant farmers.

When the Japanese were defeated and expelled from Korea in 1945, the descendants of the *yangban* were there to resume the role they had played for more than a thousand years, and although they no longer had a legal monopoly on political power and the means of accumulating wealth, as a group they were nevertheless still the best educated and most experienced in both business and government and still had the social prestige of their traditionally elite status.

Most senior bureaucrats in Korea's government as well as the senior members of the country's military establishment are direct descendants of the *yangban* families of the past. And some Korean critics equate their mentality and behavior with that of the *yangban* of old. But there have been fundamental changes in class attitudes and behavior that used to keep *yangban* and commoners apart. Marriages between the descendants of *yangban* and "commoners"—especially commoners who have become affluent—have been generally accepted since the emergence of Korea as a major economic power in the 1970s.

220

얕보다
Yatpoda
(Yaht-poh-dah)

"Underestimating Koreans"

Strictly speaking, *yatpoda* (yaht-poh-dah), which means "underestimating," is not a cultural code word as far as Koreans themselves are concerned. But it refers to a syndrome that historically has influenced the attitudes and behavior of a great many Westerners toward Korea.

When Western businesspeople first began visiting Korea in the late 1800s, many of them assumed a superior attitude toward Koreans in general because of the country's technological backwardness and archaic social institutions. The naive and passive attitude of the majority of Koreans at that time added to this common reaction, reinforcing the superiority complex of the Westerners.

Westerners who had not had substantial cross-cultural experience in other personalized cultures found it difficult, and sometimes impossible, to accept the idea that what they regarded as irrational and impractical thinking and behavior by Koreans could lead to success in any endeavor. To them such thinking and behavior "didn't make sense," was inefficient, time-consuming, and ultimately self-defeating—a mind-set that invariably led to frustration and friction.

This misreading of the intellectual capacity as well as the character and personality of Koreans was caused by Westerners' inability to understand, appreciate, or judge the mentality or cultural programming of Koreans and tendency to assume the worst—a cross-cultural failing common to all people.

Still today foreigners who are involved with Korea all too often become victims of *yatpoda*—underestimating un-Westernized Korean businesspeople and government officials simply because the Koreans do not speak English and typically do not act in the forthright, aggressive, individualistic manner that is characteristic of Western behavior. Of course these Westerners are making the mistake of judging Koreans by their own values and standards, which they firmly believe are the best. Obviously the Korean way of doing things works too, and the challenge facing foreigners is to discover how it works and coordinate their own attitudes and behavior to get the best out of a combination of their way and the Korean way.

Koreans, like other Buddhist- and Confucian-oriented Asians, learned a long time ago how to use surface passivity, politeness, subtlety, and stubbornness, along with groupism, to achieve their goals, usually in slow increments. Learning to recognize and cope with this kind of thinking and behavior is a major obstacle for Western businesspeople and diplomats dealing with Korea. It requires absorbing a new mind-set and developing cross-cultural skills in using the new knowledge—which is best achieved by a period of professional training followed by on-the-job training.

The language barrier remains one of the biggest contributors to *yatpoda*. Westerners who are involved with Korea but do not speak Korean—the vast majority—must depend on Koreans who speak enough English (or some other language) to communicate with them. Since the number of Koreans who speak English fluently is limited, the level and quality of communication between Koreans and Westerners is dangerously low. When this mutual barrier to understanding is combined with fundamental differences in values and behavior, the possibility of misunderstandings and mistakes is virtually assured.

But just speaking Korean does not mean that a person can communicate with Koreans in the fullest sense of the word. That is only a small part of the challenge. The major part of the challenge is having and being able to use the historical knowledge that gives cultural meaning to the language, the cultural nuances that make Koreans and their language unique. Once past this barrier there is still another obstacle—being able to deal effectively with the cultural differences.

A significant part of the *yatpoda* that separates foreigners and Koreans is a combination of cultural *and* racial prejudices. Chinese and Japanese feel culturally superior to Koreans. Anglo-Americans, Canadians, and other Caucasians feel both culturally *and* racially superior to Koreans. This complicates all but the most casual relationships between foreigners and Koreans, often in ways that are so subtle they pass unnoticed and become significant only after they accumulate over a period of time.

It would seem that Korea's economic success would have gone a long way toward eliminating the *yatpoda* syndrome of Westerners, including those who have had little or no personal experience in Korea, but that has not always been the case. Rather than give Koreans any personal credit, these people attribute the rise of Korea to fortuitous circumstances and their having taken unfair advantage, rather than to the intelligence and talents of the people. In reality, of course, it was a combination of all of these factors.

연 연줄
Yeon/Yonjul
(Yohn/Yohn-juhl)
"Relationships and Connections"

It is, of course, a universal truism that having friends in high places—as well as in other "right" places—can make all the difference in the world in the quality, and sometimes the length, of people's lives. Nowhere is this more so than in Korea. The legacy of a Confucian-oriented social system that was based on a hierarchical arrangement of people within strictly divided classes continues to control the attitudes and behavior of most Koreans.

One of the most important facets of this conditioning in precisely defined and segregated classes and ranks was that it generally prevented casual contact and communication between people who were not related by blood and limited informal communication between family members, particularly sons and fathers. This vertically oriented social segregation, combined with both class and occupations generally being hereditary, greatly restricted business as well as social relationships.

A key part of this system was that it was all based on personal factors that were fixed by birth—sex, order within the family, class, the father's occupation, ancestry, even birthplace. Because of this system, *yeon* (yohn), or "personal relationships," became the foundation for all interactions, including business. The most important reason for basing business relationships on personal connections was that there was no historical precedent or legal foundation for doing business at arm's length. People simply did not associate with or do business with strangers.

Developing the necessary *yeon* with people was complicated, usually time-consuming, and often expensive in pre-modern Korea because the protocol controlling relations between people was based on the fixed factors mentioned above and was very precise and demanding. Strictly objective factors took second place to abiding by the prescribed etiquette.

Creating appropriate *yeon* in present-day Korea is not nearly as demanding as it was in the past, but it is no less important in establishing and maintaining business ties. There is nothing mysterious or unusual about creating such personal relationships. Initiating a relationship with self-introductions is no longer taboo, but it is far better to begin the process through introductions from individuals or companies well known and respected by the parties concerned. The next phase is the old universal practice of meeting face to face, eating and drinking together a number of times, getting to know each other's social, educational, and business background, and so on.

As common as all of this sounds, the importance of *yeon* in doing business in Korea should not be ignored or underestimated. Business relationships seldom begin, and never run smoothly, until the parties concerned have established a significant degree of trust and confidence in each other.

The Korean code word that refers to personal connections is *yonjul* (yohn-juhl) or *yeon jul*. People who have a wide circle of acquaintances and friends in the government, in private industry, and in the professions and have the reputation of being able to get virtually anything done through these *yonjul*, or "connections," are often described as *bal i nulba* (bahl ee nuhl-bah), or "having a wide foot." (The equivalent in Japan is *kao ga hiroi*/kah-oh gah he-roe-e, or "having a wide face.")

Bal i nulba had its origin in the exclusive and inclusive nature of traditional Korean society, which was divided into specific groups of people, beginning with families, kin, and local communities. The exclusivity of these groups, and their need to be as self-sufficient as possible, made it almost unthinkable for them to associate with and do business with outside groups on a casual, arm's-length basis. These social, economic, and political requirements greatly limited the number of outside relationships people developed, and all that they did develop first had to be personalized.

When the political basis for this social system was discarded at the end of the nineteenth century and Korea began industrializing, it became absolutely necessary for people to develop numerous relationships with many people. But Koreans did not give up all of the traditional cultural strings that controlled their relationships in both personal and business affairs. They continued to personalize them to whatever extent was possible or necessary.

Present-day Korea still operates on *yonjul*. People who do not have and cannot make connections with the "right people" are greatly limited in what they can do. In business there is almost no way they can succeed on any significant scale without both commercial and political connections. Koreans therefore spend a great deal of time, energy, and money creating and nurturing personal networks that are designed specifically to contribute to their goals.

Foreigners who want to succeed in Korea would be well advised to do the same. The most practical approach for newcomers is to go through their embassies, chambers of commerce, university affiliations, and members of the expatriate community in general. Membership in the Rotary and Kiwanis Clubs also provides access to inner circles in Korea.

예의범절
Yeui Pomjol
(Yeh-we Pohm-johl)

"Etiquette as Morality"

The traditional ethics and etiquette of Korea, as in the other Confucian-oriented countries of Asia, were based more on the outward behavior of people than on inner convictions having to do with universal right and wrong or absolutes based on human and antihuman principles. Generally speaking, Korean *yeui pomjol* (yeh-we pohm-johl), or "etiquette," was more a matter of programmed role playing based on gender, age, social status, and other arbitrary factors that changed with the circumstances.

Of equal importance in the shaping of the Korean character and mind-set was the fact that etiquette in pre-modern Korea was officially prescribed—down to the smallest detail—and enforced by an authoritarian government that exercised absolute religious as well as political and economic power and was therefore able to bend people to its will.

This environment made the behavior of people almost perfectly predictable, which, of course, was the aim of the government, but it was at the expense of individuality, diversity, spontaneity, creativity, and invention. Because etiquette was equated with morality, the ethics of people were visible for all to see. A highly stylized form of behavior, from bowing to observing other physical and verbal forms of protocol in all interpersonal relationships, took the place of a higher form of principles.

Knowing and observing the prescribed *yeui pomjol* became the fundamental guidelines for Korean life. The system required that one's feelings be suppressed in favor of playing the role assigned to one's gender, social status, and occupation. It was a Pavlovian concept that gave precedence to form and formality over the uniqueness, the individuality, and the spirit of human beings.

Very early in their history, in fact, before the introduction of Confucianism, Koreans were noted for their adherence to a highly refined and stylized etiquette, so much so that early Chinese visitors referred to the country as "The Land of Etiquette" or some similar sobriquet. Confucianism, which began to gain mass influence from the seventh century and became the paramount political ideology and the primary basis for society altogether in the last decade of the fifteenth century, resulted in *yeui pumjol* being officially institutionalized as a key part of the Korean culture.

While the rules of interpersonal behavior dictated by Confucianism for nearly five centuries are no longer as rigid and stifling as they once were, they nevertheless continue to be a significant factor in contemporary Korean culture. Manners are still equated with both education and morality. Standards of polite and proper behavior are still high enough that they generally take precedence over other matters, including the content of relationships.

Westerners who are conditioned to a much freer form of behavior and more concern with hard facts and practicalities sometimes find the Korean way mystifying and frustrating. To most Westerners there is no acceptable rationale behind such things as ignoring serious mistakes and allowing situations to deteriorate to protect one's own "face" or the feelings of someone else. But those who attempt to do business in Korea quickly discover that they must learn how to deal with *yeui pumjol*, no matter how irrational it might seem to be.

Korean etiquette has many ramifications that go beyond respect language, bowing, and other behavior. For one, it impacts on the "territoriality" of Koreans. Conditioned for centuries to live and work in close quarters, with little concept of personal privacy, the "territorial boundaries" of Koreans are much smaller than those of most Westerners. Physical contact, whether in a crowded cabaret or in the streets, is accepted as normal. Being jostled in boarding buses, subways, and trains, for example, is also typically taken in stride.

223

여보 여보세요

Yobo/Yoboseyo
(Yoh-boh/Yoh-boh-say-yoh)

"Hey There, Darling, Hello!"

Affection between Korean husbands and wives was regarded as socially undesirable until well beyond the midway mark of the twentieth century because it introduced an emotional element into a relationship that was prescribed in detail by laws and customs designed to maintain a system of gender segregation and discrimination against the female sex and to ensure absolute harmony in a vertically structured society in which order took precedence over virtually everything else.

This system, which prevailed in Korea from the end of the fourteenth century until modern times as the foundation of the culture, from ethics and etiquette to the state-sponsored religion, relegated women to the position of bonded servants, first to their parents and older male siblings and then to husbands, mothers-in-law, and others senior to them.

Husbands did not call their wives by their first names or by the nicknames almost all females were given as infants. Generally speaking, the relationship between husbands and wives was such that they did not socialize with each other in a casual way during leisure time. Their lives were divided into strictly maintained male and female spheres. When husbands wanted to call their wives—attract their attention—they used the term *yobo* (yoh-boh), which historically was more or less the equivalent of "hey," or "hey, you."

With the abolition of the traditional—and legalized—separation of the sexes and the gradual diminishing of the taboos against demonstrating emotion, particularly affection and love, the word *yobo* gradually absorbed affectionate nuances that made it somewhat like the English term "dear," or "darling," and in the last decades of the twentieth century these were the terms used in officially sanctioned Korean-English dictionaries as definitions of *yobo*. However, according to social surveys, some older women whose husbands have not significantly changed their traditional attitudes and behavior dispute this official definition and report that there is no element of affection in the way their husbands use the term. Younger Koreans are gradually giving up the use of these terms altogether.

An elaboration of *yobo, yoboseyo* (yoh-boh-say-yoh) has two other distinct uses. It is used as "hello" when answering the telephone and is also used in the sense of "excuse me" when calling out to someone, such as one's wife, a restaurant waitress or waiter, or a store clerk.

224

여자

Yoja
(Yoh-jah)

"Korean Women"

Chinese officials visiting the Korean peninsula during the age of tribal states recorded that women who became jealous of the extramarital sexual behavior of their husbands were subject to execution by decapitation. One tribe that imposed this penalty on women would then expose the body of the woman in public, requiring her family to pay a substantial ransom if they wanted to bury the corpse. The treatment of *yoja* (yoh-jah), or "women," improved dramatically following the introduction of Buddhism into Korea in the fourth century A.D., but with few exceptions Korean women have traditionally been treated as fundamentally inferior to men.

During the Three Kingdoms period (57 B.C.–A.D. 668) and early years of the unified Shilla dynasty (669–935), several queen mothers became regents for their underage sons. Shortly after the founding of the Shilla dynasty three women served as queens in their own right because they were the ranking members of the royal families at that time. The first of these queens, Sondok, reigned from 632 until 647 and was followed by a female cousin, Chindok, who ruled from 647 to 654.

Two classes of women resided in the Shilla court as *kungnyo* (kuung-n'yoh), or "palace women." Those from noble families and the families of provincial lords served as court ladies-in-waiting; those chosen from commoner families became servants and entertainer-prostitutes.

The invasion of Korea by Mongols in 1231, along with almost continuous warfare for the next forty years and then domination by the Mongol Yuan dynasty in China until the 1380s was an especially cruel time for Korean women. In addition to being subject to rape by Mongol soldiers, many were rounded up and shipped to the Yuan court in China as slaves and prostitutes. With Korean princes forced to marry Mongol princesses, the latter often made the life of Korean court ladies both difficult and dangerous. The Mongols also ordered the Korean court to round up hundreds of young women each year to be given to soldiers in distant outposts as wives. At first the Korean court filled the quota by choosing widows of criminals and the mistresses of Buddhist monks, but the Mongols objected to this practice and ordered that only the most attractive daughters of upper-class Koreans be selected. This resulted in families doing everything possible to hide their daughters, with many parents being punished severely for disobeying the Mongol order.

During the last century of the Koryo dynasty (918–1392) public morals reached a new low. There were numerous reports of men and women bathing together in the nude in rivers and women flocking to temples to stay overnight with monks. This resulted in new laws severely limiting the rights of women to appear in public. These restrictions were gradually increased over the next century. The fall of Korean women from grace to virtual slavery began to occur around 1200 in conjunction with the rise of Confucianism.

In 1392 the fate of Korean women was sealed for the next five hundred or so years when the new Choson dynasty made Neo-Confucianism, a very strict form of the sage's teachings, the political and social ideology of the country. As the years of the Choson dynasty passed, women were gradually segregated from the male world in a system known as *naeoebop* (nigh-oh-eh-bohp), which means something like "inside (women) outside (men) code/regulation." Homes of the upper-class families consisted of walled compounds containing several structures, including separate quarters for men and boys over the age of seven, for females and children under the age of seven, and for servants.

Still, well up into the first century of the Choson dynasty, the status of daughters remained fairly high. Their names were registered in the father's *chok po* (chohk poh), or "clan record," along with those of sons. Wives had rights that were similar to male rights in matters of property and succession. It was not until well into the sixteenth century that daughters came to be treated more like nonpersons and wives as chattel.

By the late 1400s upper-class women in urban areas were not permitted out of their walled-in yards during the day. They were allowed to go out only at night during a *sodung* (soh-duung), or "curfew," when men were restricted to their homes. This system was designed to prevent women from being seen by and having any kind of contact with males other than their own family members. At social events, including the very important sixtieth birthday celebrations, weddings, and funerals, husbands and wives did not sit together, segregating themselves into same-sex groups. Farmers' wives working in the fields were normally segregated from male workers. After the age of ten girls were not permitted outside the home to play, visit friends, or go to school. They could no longer associate with their own brothers.

Boys, on the other hand, were moved from the female quarters to the *sarang* (sah-rahng), or "men's quarters," at the age of ten and thereafter were enjoined never to enter the female quarters. Urban females caught outside their homes during the day without special permission were subjected to being lashed one hundred times with bamboo staffs. Generally the only time husbands went into the female quarters was to have sex with their wives or concubines.

The custom of isolating females behind doors and walls during the daytime resulted in one of the traditional children's games assuming special importance in the lives of young girls. This game was the Korean version of "seesawing" on a *nul* (nuhl). A *nul* consists of a thick board about seven feet long and two feet wide balanced seesaw fashion on a large bag of rice straw (or in contemporary times some other kind of centerpiece).

Instead of sitting on each end and just going up and down, however, Korean players stand on the ends of the board. One jumps into the air and comes back down on the board, sending the player on the other end flying into the air. The player who is to fly up into the air contributes to the height he or she is able to reach by leaping upward at the precise time his or her partner comes down on the other end of the board, dramatically increasing the upward thrust.

Young girls used their *nul* to "fly" up into the air and catch glimpses of the outside world over their yard walls. Eventually the practice became so common that it was institutionalized and was regarded as an interesting and colorful facet of Korean culture. Nowadays one generally sees the *nul-ddwee-gee* (nuhl-ddway-ghee) only on special holidays, at festival celebrations, and in commercially operated "folk villages."

One of the earliest marriage customs in Korea was described by the term *minmyonuri* (meen-m'yoh-nuu-ree), which referred to marrying a girl off when she was anywhere from six to eleven years old and sending her to live with her husband's family—where in most cases she worked as a maid to her mother-in-law. The marriage was generally not consummated until the girl reached puberty. Records left by some of these child brides reveal that the experience for many if not most of them was a terrible, sad ordeal. In some cases the husband was as much as thirty years older than his *minmyonuri* bride. (The practice of *minmyonuri* marriages in Korea continued until well up into the 1900s.)

Legal and social sanctions against widows remarrying were severe during the Choson (Yi) dynasty. In 1406 the Choson court ordered the establishment of *Chanyoan* (Chahn-yoh-ahn), or "Registries of Licentious Women," throughout the country and instructed local officials to keep detailed records of women who married more than two times. In one case recounted in *Women of the Yi Dynasty* (Research Center for Asian Women, Sookmyung Women's University, Seoul), the neighbors of a woman who remarried chased her down, tied a heavy rock to her neck, and threw her in a river. In another case a son killed his own widowed mother because she began an affair with another man. In another bizarre case, when the government learned that the inhabitants of a small island just off the coast allowed widows and widowers to marry, it had all of the houses on the island destroyed and evacuated all of the women, leaving only men on the island. Female chastity was so sanctified that during war women were expected to kill themselves rather than submit to rape by enemy soldiers.

One of the results of this inhuman social system was the development of a custom among the common people that was known as "sack marriages" or "carrying away widows." Friends of a widower, or a married man who wanted a second wife, would locate a widow in a nearby village or town, sneak into her home at night, cover her mouth, tie her up, put her in a sack, and carry her to the widower's home. In some cases willing widows were informed in advance of the plan and cooperated in the conspiracy. In other cases they were not informed and did not always go willingly. In these latter cases it was customary for the friends of the man to tie her on the back of the man carrying her in such a way that she could not bite or scratch him.

There were rules applying to stealing women for "sack marriages." If the men doing the stealing were discovered inside a widow's home, her family could fight against the intruders. But if the men managed to get just one of her feet outside the gate, all efforts to free her had to cease. Records of this period show that when the families of sacked widows complained to the authorities, they almost never required that the widows be returned, on the basis that it was a well-established custom. There were also frequent instances when families cooperated in "sack marriages" to avoid the expense of wedding ceremonies.

The lot of Korean women during the Choson dynasty was influenced profoundly by the queen mother of King Songjong, who was known as the "Tyrannical Queen." In 1475 she compiled and published a book called *Naehun* (Nie-huun), which can be translated as "Woman's Guide." Utilizing more than forty other books and treatises on Confucian-oriented morality and manners as her sources, the queen came up with a set of rules for the education and behavior of women that virtually became the law of the land. Among the guidelines set down for the parents of girls and for women: girls should be married at an early age; husbands should be provided with mistresses so their wives would not be distracted by sex; wives should not leave their homes during the day; wives should never make decisions on their own; wives should never speak about anything that they have not personally experienced.

Probably the worst period in history for Korean women was the Japanese invasion of the peninsula from 1592 to 1598. The small, inexperienced Korean army was no match for the ferocious Japanese warriors who had been hardened in battle. The Japanese overran the entire peninsula within months, combining their killing and destroying with rape on a massive scale. The Japanese troops captured large numbers of Korean women and confined them in camps as workers and sex slaves. Thousands of these women killed themselves rather than submit to the Japanese. The low status of women in Korean society was made even more shocking by the widespread practice for Korean men to disguise themselves as Japanese soldiers and group-rape girls and women.

Following the end of the war, so many Korean women, including the wives and daughters of gentry and nobles, had been dishonored by Japanese soldiers that the refusal of Korean men to marry them or keep them as wives became a national crisis, making it necessary for the government to issue an edict forcing men to marry the single women and stay married to wives who had been assaulted.

When the Manchu invaded Korea in 1627 and again in 1636, their soldiers also treated Korean women as slaves for the taking. Dozens of thousands of them were abducted to Manchuria, where many died in the first few months. The survivors were held until 1637, when they were permitted to return home after paying a ransom. During this period a few of Korea's more enlightened and outspoken scholars severely criticized the Korean government and Korean men in general for their inhuman attitudes and behavior toward women, but to no avail.

According to some Korean interpretations, women were forbidden to associate with males outside their families and were confined to their homes (except when required to do farm work) not because they were inherently inferior in any way but because the social system defined the role of women as "within" (the home) while the domain of the male was "outside" (the home).

This explanation goes on to say that it was the duty of women to take care of the home, care for the children, prepare the meals, make clothes for the family, and help their husbands with the farm work, as well as maintain an atmosphere of peace so their husbands would be free to handle the public responsibilities of the families. Within this context women were subject to the "law of three obediences": obeying the father before marriage, obeying the husband following marriage, and obeying the oldest son after the husband's death. Affection and love, including between husbands and wives, were not to be expressed openly or allowed to influence behavior.

When wives failed to produce sons, husbands either divorced them or took concubines. The higher the social status of wives, the more pressure there was on husbands to take concubines rather than divorce their wives because divorce not only shamed the wives and their families but at different times in history meant they could not remarry. However, the custom for Korean men to take concubines was to have a deleterious effect on society until modern times because sons born to "secondary wives" were not accorded total legitimacy as sons or heirs. The male children of concubines usually ended up forming "branch" families that often suffered the stigma of illegitimacy for several generations.

In Korea's upper class there were exceptions to the rules pertaining to women. In some scholarly families, girls were educated both overtly and covertly, and some went on to become artists, calligraphers, poets, and writers. But the best known of these rare exceptions was a category of professional female entertainers known as *kisaeng* (kee-sang), who were exempt from practically all of the rules applying to other women.

In addition to the "three laws of obedience," married women were required by both custom and law to eschew seven "evils," some of which overlapped the "three laws." These seven evils, known as *chilgo chiak* (cheel-goh chee-ahck), were disobeying in-laws, failing to give birth to a son, committing adultery, displaying jealousy, having a hereditary disease, talking excessively, and stealing. Succumbing to or being guilty of any one of these seven sins was enough to destroy the lives of women.

Upon marriage, arranged by parents or go-betweens, brides went to live in the homes of their husbands (in ancient times husbands lived in their wives' homes until the birth of their first child). Both husbands and their mothers and fathers had the right to evict wives who were guilty of any of the seven sins, something that was often more tragic than it sounds because the women could not return to their own families. For many, the only recourse was prostitution, isolated from the mainstream of society.

The higher the social class of women, the more they were required to segregate themselves from males. Foreign residents of Seoul in the early 1900s (just before the short-lived annexation of Korea by Japan) reported that wives and female relatives of officials still could leave their family compounds only at night after the sounding of a great bell that was the signal for all men to get off the streets. On these outings higher-class women were carried in closed palanquins, with most of them going to the female quarters of other family compounds to visit close relatives.

Upper-class women who walked in the nighttime streets were required to cover their heads and wear a veil that prevented anyone from seeing their faces. The type of veil was designated by law to distinguish upper-class women from lower-class women. Only female slaves, female entertainers, prostitutes, and the like appeared in public without veils. Early Western visitors in Korea reported that the costumes of slave women were designed to leave their breasts exposed.

The status of women from the early decades of the Choson era until the middle of the twentieth century was also influenced dramatically by laws under which only paternal-line relatives were considered family members, social class and rights were transmitted only from fathers to sons, the father was the sole authority in a family, marriages were allowed only outside the blood clan, and first-born males held the right to lineal succession.

Until the early 1900s young girls and women in the commoner class were also sold regularly into servitude and prostitution by their parents. But the lot of all daughters in Korean families was not all bad. As in most families everywhere, the youngest daughter was often singled out for special treatment, especially by grandparents, and traditionally was referred to as *usum kkot* (uh-suum kkhot), which may be translated as "smiling flower" and was a term of endearment.

Traditionally Korean women achieved some measure of freedom in their behavior only after they reached the age of sixty, especially if they had many children and grandchildren, since this was regarded as the completion of a life cycle. Generally it was only at this stage in their lives that commoner women were permitted to indulge themselves by drinking alcoholic beverages, smoking, and using rough and often ribald language. In fact older Korean women in general were far from being the passive creatures so often depicted. Westerners in Korea at the beginning of the twentieth century recorded that they had often seen commoner wives grabbing the topknots (hairdos) of drunken husbands, berating them loudly, and sometimes dragging them home by their hair. There were no such freedoms for upper-class women.

These historical experiences were to have an impact on the psyche of Korean women that persisted down to modern times. Anthropologist Roger L. Janelli reports that in the 1970s, when the village of Kagong-ni Hubuk staged a kind of public event and memorial photographs were taken, the men and women involved posed in separate groups. Janelli also says that even after village wives had given birth to sons they might not be considered members of their husbands' families and that membership was not guaranteed until they died and their death dates were officially recorded in their husbands' family registers.

The fact that a number of the first Western physicians, missionaries, and teachers to arrive in Korea in the late 1800s were women had a tremendous impact on the growing concept that the Confucian degradation of women and the legal restrictions placed on women were both immoral and seriously damaging to both society and the economy. Many of the young Korean girls taught by these foreign women went on to play leading roles in furthering the movement to free Korean women from the shackles of the past.

The first Korean woman to break with tradition and wear Western attire was a lady named Ko Ra Yun, who created a stir when she appeared on the streets of Seoul in 1899. The second woman to break this age-old tradition was Emily Hwang, formerly a teacher at Chinmyong Girls' School. It was to be twenty more years, however, before women in Western dress became common in Korean cities. The first women's organization in Korea was formed in 1896. Called the *Sun Song* (Suun Song), or "Adoration Society," the society established and operated the Sun Song Girls' School, whose goal was to emancipate women by educating them and encouraging them to become involved in the movement to keep Korea free from domination by foreign powers. In 1907 a group of women organized the Women's Society for the Payment of National Debts and initiated a nationwide campaign to raise funds for the national government.

The first nationwide women's organization in Korea was formed in 1927 as part of the women's liberalization and independence movement that had started in the 1890s. The platform of this organization was ambitious: eliminate social, economic, and legal discrimination against women; abolish early marriages; and guarantee freedom of choice in marriage. It was not successful because this was the period when Korea was occupied by Japan, and things only got worse until Japan's defeat and expulsion from the country in 1945. Between 1910 and 1920 a number of women's rights advocates were arrested and executed by Japanese authorities.

Leaders in the women's liberation movement in Korea say that of all the various women's organizations founded in the country during the first quarter of the twentieth century, the most outstanding and the one that was to have the most lasting effect was the Young Women's Christian Association (YWCA), established in 1922 by Helen Kim, a 1917 graduate of Ehwa Women's University and a major figure in bringing education to Korean women, and Pil Ye Kim, also an educator.

With so many Korean men killed during World War II and the following Korean War, the surviving male establishment was forced to allow women to work outside the home in far greater numbers than ever before. Increased automation in industry, particularly in the burgeoning electronics industry, increased the demand for female employees. In fact a great deal of the economic miracle accomplished by Korea was the result of labor by Korean women. Hundreds of thousands of girls and young women worked just as hard as men during the amazing growth period that began in the early 1960s and lasted until the 1990s.

But despite laws mandating equality in the workplace, female workers in Korea are paid less than men and have few if any opportunities to become managers or executives. There are other areas of discrimination as well. Not only are women expected to be efficient and productive in their work, but it is also generally company policy that they be conspicuously feminine in their behavior and attire. Some companies have been known to fire young female employees who did not meet their femininity standards. Male business consultants add, however, that as women rise in rank in companies their femininity becomes less important in their evaluation.

Female employees are also expected to conduct themselves according to the traditional Confucian standards of *in* (inn) or *induck* (inn-dook), which refers to virtuous living, long associated with the idealized Korean concept of a lady— or gentleman. It was not until 1991 that a revised Family Law guaranteeing women equal property rights with men and the opportunity to seek custody of any children in divorce proceedings went into effect.

Today there are more than two thousand women's organizations in Korea that engage in the same kinds of domestic and international activities as their counterparts in the United States and elsewhere. And although Korean women were leaders in breaking the Confucian chains that bound and gagged them from the fourteenth century until the mid-1900s, they do not think of freedom and equality with men in Western feminist terms. Korean women do not want to think like men or act like men. They want the right to be women in the fullest sense of the word. They also want to be equal partners with men in all things, but within the context of their feminine nature. They prefer a clearly defined "women's world" that is on an equal footing with the "men's world."

Despite all the advances that Korean women have made since the end of the nineteenth century, health authorities report that today a disproportionate number of Korean women still suffer from a form of hysteria because of emotional frustration resulting from suppressed and unfulfilled sexual yearnings.

Korean girls and young women seem to be especially concerned about their appearance and spend a considerable amount of time on grooming themselves, but it also appears that they dress and make up to impress other women as much as men. No doubt the primary reason for this is also historical. In the past women did not have to depend on their looks to attract mates. Marriages were arranged. Men did not compliment women on their appearance, in part because women were required by law and custom to dress in the costumes designated for their class, wear their hair in the same fashion, and look and act as much alike as possible. In fact, generally speaking, men did not compliment women on anything. Of course, all this is now changing among the younger generations, but it will no doubt continue to be a part of life in Korea for the foreseeable future.

열심히 합시다
Yolshimhi Hapsida
(Yohl-sheem-he Hahp-she-dah)

"Let's Do Our Best!"

Life in Korea has never been easy for the majority of the population. In addition to having to put up with a relatively harsh climate, a limited amount of arable land, repeated invasions by outsiders, and internal strife brought on by factions competing for power, Koreans were traditionally oppressed by their own authoritarian governments and a social system that forced them to suppress their emotions, their individuality, their ambitions—even their very natures.

From around 1870 until the 1970s, the conditions under which Koreans were forced to live were even worse. Riots, rebellions, the invasion and annexation of the country by Japan, followed by thirty-six years of brutal treatment by Japanese administrators, soldiers, and police, a devastating civil war that left the country divided, and the continuation of cruel authoritarian rule until the 1980s left the surviving Koreans tough and cynical but determined to create a better world for themselves.

In fact the determination of Koreans to build a better world became an obsession, an obsession that grew out of more than a thousand years of suffering and frustration that, rather than destroying the spirit of the people, strengthened their resolve in proportion to the suffering they had endured. One of the facets of this obsession with achievement and success is summed up in the phrase *Yolshimhi hapsida!* (yohl-sheem-he hahp-she-dah), which literally means "Let's do our best!"

Again as is so often the case in English translations of Korean words and phrases, "Let's do our best!" does not do justice to *Yolshimhi hapsida!* The Korean version of this phrase is more like a blood oath than a mere declaration. It overflows with emotion, with yearnings that have been stifled for generations and only now can be expressed in both word and deed. It is a phrase by which Koreans set and measure standards of effort. Anything less than one's best is not only unacceptable but un-Korean.

This expression, and the feelings that are part of it, is one of the secrets of the incredible transformation of Korea from a wasteland of rubble, disruption, and death in the early 1950s to a shining example of high-tech industry and affluence only three decades later. It is not limited, however, to industry. It also applies to virtually everything Koreans do, from studying to sports and other recreational activities. *Yolsshim* (yohl-ssheem) by itself means "enthusiasm, eagerness."

Foreigners setting up operations in Korea are well advised to get the professional cultural and business consultation that is necessary to harness the ambition and energy that comes with the commitment of Koreans to do their best.

Other key words and phrases having to do with the character and personality of Koreans include *Amukuto anida* (Ah-muu-kuu-toh ah-nee-dah)—"It's nothing. I can do it easily," a common response from Koreans, regardless of the nature of the task they are confronted with. The man who has little or no capital but still succeeds in building up a business by working especially hard is said to have done it *bural an chok* (buu-rahl ahn choak), or "only with balls." Part of these aspects of the Korean character is included in the often used-word *chisongnyok* (chee-song-n'yoke), which refers to the capacity that Koreans have for enduring incredible physical and mental hardships and succeeding despite all odds.

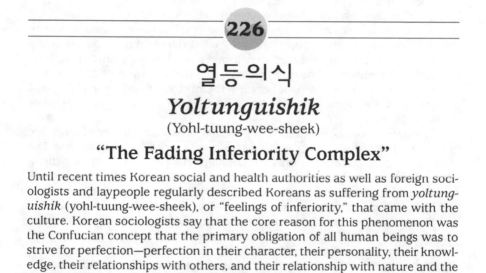

226

열등의식
Yoltunguishik
(Yohl-tuung-wee-sheek)

"The Fading Inferiority Complex"

Until recent times Korean social and health authorities as well as foreign sociologists and laypeople regularly described Koreans as suffering from *yoltunguishik* (yohl-tuung-wee-sheek), or "feelings of inferiority," that came with the culture. Korean sociologists say that the core reason for this phenomenon was the Confucian concept that the primary obligation of all human beings was to strive for perfection—perfection in their character, their personality, their knowledge, their relationships with others, and their relationship with nature and the spirit world.

Since it is virtually impossible to achieve perfection in any of these areas, the scientists add, Koreans were afflicted by an obsession that could never be realized. This obsession was internalized and manifested itself in a number of ways, from an exaggerated sense of "face" and dignity to feelings of inferiority. Confucianism, they add, also prevented the development of strong feelings of independence and competence among the people, further adding to the general feelings of inferiority.

Another primary factor that contributed to strong feelings of inferiority becoming a national trait among Koreans was the authoritarian nature of the government, which forced the people to be humble, passive, and obedient. Still another source of inferior feelings was the contradictions between the tight exclusivity of the family and the demands of society in general. Because of their responsibilities to their families, Koreans simply could not interact freely with

others on an individual basis. This meant that each person was more or less segregated from the rest of society and, except for close kinship groups, was virtually alone.

Then there was the awesome power and influence of China that must have
made the Koreans feel totally inconsequential by comparison. Until 1910 Korea
survived only by playing the humble vassal to the Chinese court. Another factor
contributing to the inferiority feelings of Koreans were frequent raids and invasions by the Japanese, a warlike people whose society was dominated by the
martial spirit and professional warriors—while Korea, in contrast, was dominated by scholars and artists from the sixteenth century until modern times.

Japan finally ended up capturing and colonizing Korea, then implementing
a program to convert the Koreans into Japanese while simultaneously attempting to destroy the last vestige of their culture. This campaign against Korean culture was terminated by Japan's defeat in World War II.

Yang Un Chong, a Korean social scientist who conducted a special study of
the inferiority complex of Koreans (*On the Korean Inferiority*, Sasanggye, The
World of Ideas), says that people habitually used the old term *yop chon* (yohp
chohn), or "old coin," to refer to their self-perceived inferior status or the inferior ability of themselves and others. Chong said this *yop chon* attitude derived
from comparisons Koreans made between themselves and advanced industrial
nations from the nineteenth century on and from the harsh colonization of
Korea by Japan between 1910 and 1945.

The division of Korea into Communist and American spheres of influence
at the end of World War II was another cataclysmic setback for all Koreans. The
Communist rulers of North Korea did not allow the people to think for themselves. They were indoctrinated with the concept that communism was the savior of mankind. Their supreme leader, Il Sung Kim, was deified. Their historical
feelings of inferiority were replaced with a robotlike sense of superiority.

South Koreans fared better under the authority of the United States and
Korean leaders, but the first postwar governments were in the hands of prewar
nationalists and others who were little more than latterday mandarins whose
ideology was primarily authoritarian and Confucian and whose administrations
were totally corrupt, brutal, and inefficient. The invasion of South Korea by
North Korea in the spring of 1950 added the devastation of war to the cultural
chaos and feelings of inferiority that Koreans had been experiencing since the
opening of the country to the outside world in 1876.

The end of the Korean War in 1953 did not remedy matters. The Communists stayed in power in North Korea and South Korea continued to be dominated by old-line authoritarian leaders and dependent on the United States. All
the foreign aid and foreign culture that poured into South Korea from 1945
until well up into the 1960s did nothing to boost the self-esteem of South Koreans, but it presaged a superhuman effort that was virtually to end their inferiority complex in one short generation.

Korea's amazing economic success between 1960 and 1990 went a long
way toward wiping out the inferiority complex with which Koreans had lived for
centuries. In addition to the obvious results of the incredible effort it took to

transform South Korea from a devastated wasteland into a world-class industrial power, government and industry used the latest advertising and public relations techniques to foster the idea that Koreans could do anything. One of the largest and most effective of these campaigns was built around the slogan "Can Do!" The pace of progress was, in fact, so fast that it was easy for the Koreans to believe that they were capable of almost anything.

Individually, *yoltunguishik* is no longer a factor in Korean thinking and behavior, but collectively Koreans still feel extremely vulnerable to being over-powered militarily as well as economically by foreign powers, and this fear is a major source of their nationalism and their mercantilist approach to the rest of the world.

227

연 애

Yonae
(Yohn-aye)

"Courting and Mating"

Yonae (yohn-aye), "courting" or "dating," in the Western sense did not exist in Korea until the latter part of the 1950s, and this is a new connotation for an old word. Prior to the abolition of feudal family laws in the late 1940s and the introduction of some democratic principles in the following years, Korean boys and girls were basically separated at the age of seven (six, according to the Western way of counting). Male and female siblings were allowed to play together until around the age of ten, but they ate and slept separately. From the age of ten the two sexes, including husbands and wives, lived in virtually separate worlds during their waking and working hours. Young boys and girls simply did not socialize with each other.

With rare exceptions that occurred mostly in the distant past, marriages in Korea were traditionally arranged by parents, close relatives, or professional go-betweens. In earlier times brides and grooms often met for the first time on their wedding day. Love or affection played absolutely no role in selecting spouses. Such feelings were seen as an obstacle to a successful marriage because they could lead to attitudes and behavior that were incompatible with the main purposes of marriage—to have children, perform the proper rituals, and ensure the continuation of the family.

When the last of Korea's royal dynasties began breaking up in the late 1800s, a few young Korean men and women who came under the influence of foreign missionaries and other foreigners formed emotional attachments, and some of them married. But such incidents were very rare. The annexation of Korea by Japan in 1910 and the following thirty-six years of harsh colonial rule by Confucian-oriented Japanese administrators meant a continuation of the same attitude toward male-female relationships that had traditionally existed in Korea.

All this was to change dramatically in the late 1950s and early 1960s, however. With a new constitution based on democratic rather than Confucian principles, the growing presence of Westerners in the country, and the influence of American movies, young Koreans began to break gender and social taboos that had been in place for millennia. Not surprisingly, young Korean girls were the first to publicly break these ancient taboos, mostly dating foreign men.

Since courting and love marriages had previously been unknown in Korea, there were no Korean (or adopted Chinese) words for courting or dating, resulting in the English words *date* and *dating* being Koreanized. Date became *teitu* (tay-e-tu), and dating became *teitingu* (tay-e-teen-guu), with the initial *t* sounding somewhat like a *d*.

With young girls streaming into colleges and universities by the hundreds of thousands from 1953 on, there was no way the sexes could be kept apart. But dating in the Western fashion was not common until well into the 1960s, by which time hundreds of thousands of young men and women were also working in close proximity to each other in factories and offices.

In addition to the deep-seated cultural barriers to dating that young Koreans had to overcome, there was an economic element. It was not until well into the 1960s that young Korean men could afford to spend money on anything other than the basics they and their families needed to survive. Furthermore, spending money on a date was a totally alien concept.

During the 1970s teahouses, coffee shops (including those in international hotels), and restaurants overflowed with young people almost every evening except Sundays and Mondays, but the majority of them were in separate groups of two, three, or four. It was not until well up into the 1970s that it became common to see dating couples in public places in the evenings. The most popular place for courting couples to meet were the coffee shops of top Western-style hotels because they felt less conspicuous there and were more at ease in a "foreign" setting.

Still, male-female relations in Korea remain far more formal and restrained than they are in the United States and other Western countries. Foreign men who date Korean women or have Korean wives are frequently cautioned by Korean friends or other foreigners who have been in the country for some time to avoid making a spectacle of themselves and shaming their female companions by holding their hands, walking with their arms around them, or kissing them in public—taboos that young American GIs stationed in Korea over the years routinely ignored.

Among the most ostentatious public displays of interest in the opposite sex in Korea are the customs surrounding Valentine's Day in February and a so-called "White Day" the following month. In the 1970s Japanese merchandisers of chocolate candies came up with the idea of encouraging women to give chocolates to their husbands, boyfriends, male associates, and any male they had a romantic interest in on Valentine's Day. This was soon followed by the custom for men to give women peppermint candies on "White Day" in March.

Korean merchants were quick to introduce both customs to Korea, where they now thrive.

Another key word that is used in courting and marriage in Korea is *kuhon* (kuu-hohn), which means "marriage proposal," a term that originally had no romantic connotations but is now an integral part of the new custom of love marriages.

Public displays of affection are no longer rare in Korea, and it is common to see mixed-race couples in public places.

228

용무

Yongmu
(Yohng-muu)

"Business as Religion"

For well over a thousand years Koreans were indoctrinated with the idea that engaging in commercial business for profit was a dishonorable and immoral occupation, and businesspeople were near the bottom of the country's social hierarchy. This moral attitude toward commercial activities was one of the primary reasons the Korean economy remained virtually stagnant from ancient times until the end of the nineteenth century.

However, this is one traditional religious concept that Koreans put behind them as soon as they were politically free to do so, and a reevaluation of Confucianism now holds that the great master was not against making profits as long as *yongmu* (yohng-muu), or "business," was conducted in a moral manner.

With or without the blessings of Confucius, Koreans have since proven that they are masters at making profits and in the process transformed Korea into one of the world's leading economies in less than three decades. (In addition to their competitive prices and proven skills, Koreans had a work ethic during the period of high economic growth that would put most Westerners to shame. Anthropologist Choong Soon Kim said Koreans worked as if they were soldiers in a combat zone fighting for their lives.)

Although Korean executives have adopted many Western management techniques, they are still primarily motivated and guided by traditional Confucian mores. As a result the social content of business in Korea continues to be one of the most significant—and, to Westerners, often troublesome—characteristics of the business world. Generally speaking, Korean companies and other professional organizations are operated more like social groups than purely economic units. Their management is personalized to a degree that Westerners find extraordinary, a factor that is often a major barrier to getting things done quickly—or, in many cases, at all.

In a broad sense, doing business in Korea is engaging in social relationships, and until Americans and other Westerners understand this approach and learn how to deal with it they will continue to make things difficult for themselves and their Korean counterparts.

Another key factor in business in Korea is the role played by the government. In the United States businessmen took the lead in building the American economy and came up with the concept that government and business are separate entities in an effort to preclude government restraints on their behavior. In Korea, on the other hand, the government made itself the "senior partner" in virtually all economic effort in the country.

Yongmu in Korea is still primarily a joint effort between the government and private enterprise, and Korean management retains many practices that are right out of the Confucian manual. But business per se is no longer morally suspect and, in fact, is rapidly replacing Confucianism as the prevailing religion.

By the mid-1990s the biggest challenge facing Korean business was to eliminate or get around government regulations that were enacted in the 1950s and 1960s to control and guide them, as well as to protect them from foreign competition. These regulations were obviously very successful in helping transform Korea into a major industrial power. But the more successful Korean businesses became, the more the regulations interfered with the development of a free-market economy, resulting in growing demands from the United States and others that Korea deregulate its economy and open its markets to exports from foreign countries.

Having played the leading role in transforming *yongmu* from a despised occupation to the lifeblood of Korea and then guiding the country to unprecedented prosperity, it is not likely that the government will rush to relinquish its control anytime soon.

Among the interesting code words that are of particular relevance in business: *daedulpo* (die-duhl-poh), literally "stone and pillar," refers to an individual in a company, agency, or organization who is primarily responsible for its success—the "backbone" of the group. *Stone* refers to the foundation stones on which buildings traditionally rested, and *pillars* are what hold buildings up.

Dong changsaeng (dohng chahng-sang) refers to the "network" of classmates, alumni brothers, relatives, friends made in the military, and other contacts that make up the most important assets one can have in business and politics.

All larger Korean manufacturing companies have groups of *hachong* (hah-chohng), or "subsidiaries," beneath them that act as parts suppliers and also, inadvertently, as buffers when slowdowns occur. Parent companies use the *hachong* to shield themselves against negative demand, price, and currency fluctuations.

The *hoegyesa* (hoag-yah-sah), or "accountant," is a far more important individual in the executive lineup of Korean companies than in most Western companies and is therefore someone that foreign businesspeople should make a point of meeting and developing a good relationship with.

Korean employees, particularly those in the large internationally known companies, typically work at a pace that is surprising and often disconcerting to foreign visitors. The Koreans themselves have a word for this: *ilbulrae* (eelbuhl-rie), which means "working like an insect"—a reference to the way bees and ants work.

The Korean equivalent of Japan's *kanban* (kahn-bahn), in reference to the "just-in-time" parts delivery system made famous by Japanese manufacturers, is *kanpan* (kahn-pahn). Koreans were among the first to adapt the system to their own manufacturing processes.

When Western importers began visiting Seoul and other Korean cities from the mid-1950s on, their increasing presence in the major international hotels created a phenomenon unlike anything that had ever happened in Korea—the buyers attracted large numbers of Korean traders and manufacturers seeking *korae* (koe-ray), or "business deals." The lobbies of the hotels were beehives of activity, excitement, and drama from the breakfast hour until late in the evening, as the Koreans, desperate for any kind of export order, vied with each other for the time and attention of foreign buyers.

Seeking *korae* with foreign visitors is still a major activity in Korea and continues to attract people who will promise almost anything to get a deal. First-time visitors to Korea who take the easy way out and attempt to conduct all of their business in their hotels may be setting themselves up for future problems. Holding initial meetings in hotels is fine, but unless the Korean company concerned is a well-known enterprise, visitors are strongly advised to inspect the facilities of the firm.

Another old culture-laden term that is of special interest is *maeddugi hanchul* (may-duu-ghee hahn-chuul), which literally means "grasshopper season." During Korea's short harvest season in the fall, grasshoppers eat with an intense fury in preparation for the coming cold winter, when there will be nothing to eat. Businesspeople picked up on the phrase to describe the seasons when retail outlets are the busiest and make the most profits—the major gift-giving periods in midyear and just before the end of the year.

Chonmae (choan-my) is another economic term of special importance in Korea. It means "monopoly." For a long time two of the most profitable monopolies operated by the Korean government were the sale of ginseng and tobacco. Tobacco has since been "liberalized" but continues to be a major source of revenue for the government. A term similar to this in appearance, *chonmae tukho* (choan-my tuuk-hoh), means "patent." Foreign patent applications in Korea must be in two languages—Korean and the language of the originating country.

As in Japan, economic success in Korea in the 1970s and 1980s attracted the attention of the underworld and more unsavory types of individuals not associated with organized gangs. These individuals, called *sokaiya* (soh-kie-yah) in Japan and *chonghoeggun* (chohng-hoh-eh-gguun) in Korea, are people who specialize in extorting money from major corporations by buying a few shares of their stock and then threatening to disrupt stockholder meetings if they are not paid off.

Korean companies, like their Japanese counterparts, have been susceptible to this kind of criminal extortion because they traditionally kept their more intimate records confidential not only from the public but generally from their stockholders as well and did not want to endanger their control by having to answer stockholder questions or respond to any possible demands for changes in management and operational policies. Typically, stockholder meetings in Korea last for less than an hour, most of which is taken up by top executives telling the audience how well the company is doing.

229

영어

Yongo
(Yohn-goh)

"The Language Burden"

Well over half of all young Koreans have studied *Yongo* (Yohn-goh), or "English," for one or more years by the time they finish high school. They study English because it is impressed upon them by their parents and their teachers that most of the world's foreign trade, on which Korea is so dependent, is carried on in the English language and that English is the primary language in international communications in most other fields as well.

But this universalization of the English language constitutes a major burden for large numbers of Koreans (and other nationalities as well) because it links their economic viability, their standard of living, and most of the things they would like to achieve for themselves and their country to their ability to understand and use English. Many Koreans do not accept this burden willingly or in good spirit. They look on it as being part of the cultural imperialism that is being inflicted on them, with the United States being the major offender. The fact that most American businesspeople with whom they must deal do not make any serious effort to learn Korean to the point that they can conduct business in it serves to convince their Korean counterparts that this linguistic imperialism is deliberate.

Most American businesspeople who go to Korea automatically presume that whoever they meet will either speak English or have interpreters on hand. To Koreans this is at best a sign of cultural arrogance and at worst a signal that the foreign side is forcing them to communicate in a foreign language to gain an advantage over them.

For most Koreans gaining fluency and ease in speaking *Yongo* requires several years of study and regular sustained use. Without this, trying to communicate on a sophisticated level for even short periods of time is a frustrating and exhausting experience. The more important the subject, the more onerous the ordeal. Koreans who are subjected regularly to this trial in their business with English speakers frequently complain about it among themselves. They say that they dread it and that it is hard for them not to feel anger toward the people who put them through the ordeal.

Interestingly, there are racial and cultural overtones to this Korean reaction to being forced to speak a foreign language in their business affairs. According to my Korean friends, the dread that they feel and the exhaustion they experience are much more pronounced when the foreign language they must speak is English, as opposed to Chinese or Japanese, at which they are often equally poor.

However, in my experience at formal meetings the higher the level of the Korean managers, the less likely they are to try to speak any foreign language in which they are not fairly fluent because they recognize the advantage that the foreign side has and refuse to handicap themselves. At after-hours meetings, these people will enthusiastically practice their English on their foreign guests or hosts. Foreign businesspeople in Korea who do not speak Korean should make a practice of apologizing for their lack of ability in the language. This is not the final solution, but it will help to mitigate the Korean feeling that the burden of understanding is being placed unfairly on them.

Of course, it goes without saying that when non-Korean-speaking foreigners are involved in meetings they should also take steps to make sure that their Korean counterparts do fully understand their side of the story by providing interpreters as well as having their main points translated into Korean, printed, and given to the Korean participants.

Another factor in the use of English by Koreans is that speaking English, which they described as a "horizontal language," for sustained periods of time is extremely tiring to them and they are often put into situations by foreigners where they have become exhausted. The reason for this problem, according to both Koreans and Japanese (who suffer from the same syndrome), is that remembering and speaking English uses a different part of the brain than Korean and is therefore a strain. Obviously foreigners involved in long negotiations or other sessions in which Koreans are required to speak English should take this factor into consideration and arrange for rest periods.

230

연세

Yonse

(Yohn-seh)

"Venerating Age"

Extraordinary respect for the elderly has traditionally been one of the defining features of Korean culture. Not only have Koreans themselves pointed to this custom with pride, but foreign observers as well have traditionally paid homage to this very conspicuous practice. Over the centuries the custom of venerating *yonse* (yohn-seh), or "age," became so deeply entrenched and so comprehensive in social relationships and interaction in Korea that it had an equally deep and comprehensive impact on both the politics and economy of the country.

In fact, if one extrapolates on the variety of influences this custom had on

Korea it would probably rank as among the top four or five factors that were responsible for the nature and tone of the overall culture and economy from ancient times until the last quarter of the twentieth century.

It was not until contemporary times that some Korean social scientists and intellectuals began to take a new, closer look at the old custom of exalting and catering to the aged, with some surprising conclusions. In their view the custom of respecting and catering to the elderly was generally misplaced and did more harm than good. They point out that the custom was based on age itself, not on the character, wisdom, intelligence, or accomplishments of the individuals concerned.

When this blind catering to the aged was combined with ongoing superstitions, the scientists add, it enhanced and perpetuated ignorance, prejudice, selfishness, and vanity and stifled the ambitions and energy of each new generation. These same critics acknowledge, however, that there was also a positive side to the custom of respecting and caring for the aged. First of all, not all aged people were callous about the feelings and challenges facing their offspring and the young in general, and these people were seldom if ever overly demanding. Second, the custom added a very humane facet to life in Korea since it virtually guaranteed that elderly people would not be abandoned or made to suffer from want or isolation.

Of course, the greatest motivation for respecting the elderly was the Confucian concept of ancestor worship. Confucianism taught that the spirits of people who died survived on another plane of existence and had the power to continue influencing the lives of their families. Confucianism required that people follow a number of rituals designed to placate and please the spirits of dead ancestors going back four generations.

Most Koreans still venerate their parents and grandparents and still follow the ancient custom of honoring them at the annual *Chusok* (Chuu-soak), or "Harvest Moon Festival," traditionally held on the fifteenth day of the eighth month on the lunar calendar, now on different dates in September or October. (This is the Korean version of Thanksgiving Day.) People enjoy sumptuous feasts, and memorial services are held at family grave sites.

Many Koreans also continue to honor their deceased ancestors at other times during the year, although the practice is far less formal and hidebound than it was before the coming of democracy and economic affluence. For the most part, remembering and honoring ancestors today is limited to praying before ancestral "name tablets" and photographs kept on small "shrine shelves" in homes.

In earlier times Korean men formally became *noin* (no-een), or "elders," at around the age of fifty-five.* The classification of *cholmun saram* (chohl-muun

---

*Traditionally, Koreans counted babies one year old at birth and two years old the first January after their birth. This meant that a child born close to the end of the year was considered two years old on January 1 when in actuality they might be only one month old. In later times it became common for newborns to be described as one year old at birth and two years old on their first birthday. Some Koreans still follow this system, so it often happens that someone who gives his or her age as fifty-five, for example, may actually be only fifty-four.

sah-rahm), or "young people," was considerably more arbitrary. Generally men were considered "young" until they reached the age of forty. In some cases, however, fifty-year olds and even fifty-five-year olds were still classified as *chol-mun saram*.

One of the more delightful legacies of this respect for the aged that still persists in Korea is the custom of calling all elderly men *halabuji* (hah-lah-buu-jee), or "grandfather," and all elderly women *halmoni* (hahl-moh-nee), or "grandmother," and treating them with extra courtesy.

The use of honorifics in speech and bowing to elders and superiors has changed to accommodate the times. Nowadays, among acquaintances people are expected to use honorifics to those who are ten years or more older than themselves. If the age range is less than ten years, they generally address each other as equals.

By the 1990s the age-old custom for elder, retired parents to live with their children (usually eldest sons) had begun to undergo a dramatic change. Part of the reason for this change was that children had begun to chafe at the custom. Equally important was the fact that many affluent parents had gotten used to the advantages of living alone and did not want to give up their freedom. This change was accompanied by increasing demands for national welfare programs for the less-than-affluent elderly.

Probably the most fundamental factor in the breakup of extended families was that so many of Korea's young couples moved into houses or apartments that were simply too small to accommodate their parents and grandparents, and they could not afford larger quarters.

231

엽전 사상
Yopjon Sasang
(Yohp-joan Sah-sahng)
"Looking Down on History"

Yopjon sasang (yohp-joan sah-sahng), an old term seldom if ever used by lay-people, literally refers to the coins that were used as legal tender in pre-modern Korea, but the words have long been used by scholars in reference to what some Korean critics describe as the self-degrading, self-destructive attitude that many Koreans had toward their history, culture, and traditional character from the latter decades of the nineteenth century until recent times. These critics say this *yopjon-sasang* feeling was a result of the political and military oppression inflicted on Koreans over the centuries by their own rulers, by the Chinese, the Mongols, the Manchus, and in more recent times by the Japanese who annexed the country in 1910 and, before being defeated and expelled from Korea in 1945, attempted to totally eradicate Korean culture and turn the Koreans into Japanese.

Some of these critics, particularly Tong Shik Yi,* also blame these neurotic feelings on the aid given to Korea by the United States following its liberation from Japan at the end of World War II and the aid it received from the U.S. during the Korean War. But recent psychological surveys of adult Koreans reveal that the *yopjon-sasang* attitude is gradually diminishing, particularly among those who were born after 1960. Unlike older Koreans, the post-1960 generations were not plagued with the anxieties, fears, and frustrations that had previously been the cultural and historical diet fed to every Korean from infancy on. Their image of themselves was more independent and more positive than that of older generations. And since the post-1960 generations have no memories—and often very little knowledge—of the role the United States and the other Allied powers played in keeping South Korea free of communism and its subsequent economic growth, they do not feel that they owe anything to anybody.

Responses by older generations as well indicate that the economic and social changes that have occurred in Korea since the end of the Korean War in 1953 have resulted in their distancing themselves from both their ancient and more recent history and improving their image of themselves and of Korea.

The *yopjon-sasang* syndrome is not likely to totally disappear from the psyche of Koreans, however, because the conditions that brought it about, along with the political and social ideology of Confucianism and the fact that they survived as a nation, will remain one of the most important aspects of their history. What is already happening, in fact, is that the ancient feelings of *yopjon sasang* are acting as a powerful catalyst in the development of aggressive tendencies that were historically absent from the Korean character. Koreans are no longer submissive when they feel their rights are being denied. They are not reticent about speaking up for those rights and readily using force to get them.

This means that foreigners dealing with Koreans can no longer force their will on them. They must deal with them as equals and be especially cautious about giving any impression of the kind of aggressive arrogance that Koreans have historically associated with foreign powers.

---

*Yi, Tong Shik, *The Self-Identity of the Koreans and Tao* (Seoul, Ilchisa: 1974).

Selected Bibliography

Chang, Chan Sup. *The Korean Management System—Cultural, Political, Economic Foundations*. Westport, CT: Quorum Books, 1994.

Choe, Chae Sok. *The Korean Social Character*. Seoul: Kaemunsa, 1976.

Choe, Sang Su. *Annual Customs of Korea*. Seoul: Seomun-dong Publishers, 1986.

Choi, Min Hong. *A Modern History of Korean Philosophy*. Seoul: Sung Mun Sam, 1980.

Chong, Yang Un. "On the Korean Inferiority," *The World of Ideas* (April 1961). Seoul: Sasanggye.

Chun, Kyung Ja. *Peace Under Heaven*. New York: M. E. Sharpe, 1993.

Chun, Kyung So. *Reciprocity and Korean Society—An Ethnograpy of Hasami*. Seoul: Seoul National University Press, 1984.

Chun, Shin Yong. *Korean Society*. Seoul: Sisayongosa Publishers, 1982.

Covell, Alan Carter. *Ecstasy—Shamanism in Korea*. Elizabeth, NJ, and Seoul: Hollym, 1983.

Covell, Dr. Jon Carter. *Korea's Cultural Roots*. Seoul: Hollym, 1981.

Covell, Dr. Jon Carter, and Covell, Alan. *The World of Korean Ceramics*. Seoul: Sisayongosa, Inc., 1986.

——. *Korean Impact on Japanese Culture*. Elizabeth, NJ: Hollym International Corp., 1984/1986.

Crane, Paul S. *Korean Patterns*. Seoul: Royal Asiatic Society, 1967/1978.

De Bary, William, and Kim, Jai-hyun, editors. *The Rise of Confucianism in Korea*. New York: Columbia University Press, 1985.

De Mente, Boyé Lafayette. *Korean Etiquette & Ethics in Business*. Lincolnwood, IL: NTC Publishing Group, 1994.

Deuchler, Martina. *The Confucian Transformation of Korea: A Study of Society and Ideology*. Cambridge, MA: Harvard University Press, 1992.

——. *Confucian Gentlemen and Barbarian Envoys*. Seoul: Royal Asiatic Society, 1983.

Eckert, Carter J., Lee, et al. *Korea: Old and New—A History*. Seoul: Ilchokak Publishers, for the Korea Institute and Harvard University, 1990.

Gale, James S. *Korea Sketches*. New York: Fleming H. Revell Publishing Co., 1898.

Grayson, James H. *Korea: A Religious History*. Oxford: Clarendon Press, 1989.

Ha, Tae Hung. *Guide to Korean Culture*. Seoul: Yonsei University Press, 1978.

——. *Maxims and Proverbs of Old Korea*. Seoul: Yonsei University Press, 1970.

Hahm, Pyong Choon. *Korean Political Tradition and Law*. Seoul: Royal Asiatic Society, 1982.

Han, Pae Ho. *The Nature and Function of Korean Politics*. Seoul: Academy of Korean Studies, 1979.

Han, Sang Bok. *The Korean Patterns of Life and Way of Thinking*. Seoul: The Academy of Korean Studies, 1987.

Han, Tong Se. "The Korean Conception of Sex," *The Generations* (May 1970). Seoul: Sedae.

Hong, Won Tack. *Relationship Between Korea and Japan in Early Period: Paekche and Yamato Wa*. Seoul: Ilsimsa: 1988.

Hong, Yi Sup. *Korea's Self-Identity*. Seoul: Yonsei University Press, 1973.

Hur, Ben Seunghwa, and Vegdahl, Sonja. *Culture Shock: Korea*. Singapore: Times Editions Pte Ltd., 1993.

Hyun, Peter. *Koreana*. Seoul: Korea Britannica, 1984.

Janelli, Roger L., with Yim, Dawn Hee. *Making Capitalism—The Social and Cultural Construction of a South Korean Conglomerate*. Stanford: Stanford University Press, 1993.

———. *Ancestor Worship and Korean Society*. Stanford: Stanford University Press, 1982.

Jang, Song Hyon. *The Key to Successful Business in Korea*. Seoul: Yong Ahn Publishing Co., 1988.

Kang, Shin Pyo. "The Korean Outlook on Life," *The Plaza* (January 1983). Seoul: Kwang Jang.

Kendall, Laurel. *The Life and Hard Times of a Korean Shaman*. Honolulu: University of Hawaii Press, 1988.

Kendall, Laurel, and Peterson, Mark, editors. *Korean Women—View from the Inner Room*. New Haven, CT: East Rock Press, Inc., 1983.

Kim, Choong Soon. *The Culture of Korean Industry: An Ethnography of Poongsan Corporation*. Tucson: University of Arizona Press, 1992.

Kim, Dong Ki, and Kim, Lin Su. *Management Behind Industrialization: Readings in Korean Business*. Seoul: Korea University Press, 1989.

Kim, Jae Un. *The Koreans: Their Mind and Behavior*. Seoul: Kyobo Book Centre Co., Ltd., 1991.

Kim, To Hwan. *A Psychological Analysis of Korean Proverbs*. Pusan: Haeyang Publishers, 1976.

Kim, Yong Un. *The Japanese and the Koreans*. Seoul: Purigipum Namu, 1981.

Kim, Yung Chung. *Women of Korea*. Seoul: Ewha Women's University, 1983.

Kim, Yung, and Key, Renaud, editors. *King Sejong the Great: The Light of Fifteenth Century Korea*. Washington, DC: George Washington University Press, 1992.

Koo, Bon Ho. *Socio-Cultural Factors in the Industrialization of Korea*. San Francisco: ICS Press, 1992.

Korean National Commission for UNESCO. *Korean Thought*. Seoul: Sisayongosa Publishers, 1983.

Korean Press Center. *Facts About Korea*. Seoul: Korean Overseas Information Service, 1993.

Lancaster, Lewis R., and Yu, Chai-shin, editors. *Assimilation of Buddhism in Korea*. Berkeley: Asian Humanities Press, 1991.

Lee, Chang So, editor. *Modernization of Korea and the Impact of the West*. Los Angeles: East Asian Studies Center, USC, 1981.

Lee, Dal Soon. *Rediscovery of the Political History of Korea*. University of Suwon Press, 1993.

Lee, Hye Ku. *Essays on Korean Traditional Music.* Seoul: Royal Asiatic Society, 1981.

Lee, Ki Baik. *A New History of Korea.* Cambridge, MA: Harvard-Yenching Institute/Harvard Press, 1984.

Lee, Man Gap. *Sociology and Social Change in Korea.* Seoul: Seoul National University Press, 1986.

Lee, Peter H. *Sourcebook of Korean Civilization: From Earliest Times to the Sixteenth Century.* New York: Columbia University Press, 1993.

——. *Modern Korean Literature.* Honolulu: University of Hawaii Press, 1990.

Lew, Young Ick, et al. *Korean Culture and Fine Art: A Historical View.* Seoul: The Korean Foundation, 1993.

Lip, Dr. Evelyn. *Feng Shui for Business.* Singapore and Kuala Lumpur: Times Books International, 1989.

Macdonald, Donald Stone. *The Koreans—Contemporary Politics and Society.* Boulder: Westview Press, 1996.

McKenzie, Frederick Arthur. *The Tragedy of Korea.* Seoul: Yonsei University Press, 1908/1975.

Min, Kyung Hyun; translated by Kim, Halla. *Korean Gardens.* Seoul: Borim Editions, 1992.

Nahm, Andrew C. *Introduction to Korean History and Culture.* Elizabeth, NJ, and Seoul: Hollym International Corp., 1993.

O, Se Chol. *Culture and the Theory of Social Psychology.* Seoul: Pakyongsa, 1979.

——. *The Social Psychology of the Korean People.* Seoul: Pakyongsa, 1982.

Osgood, Charles. *The Koreans and Their Culture.* New York: Ronald Press, 1951.

Paik, Wan Ki. *Korean Administrative Culture.* Seoul: Korea University Press, 1990.

Palmer, Spencer J. *Confucian Rituals in Korea.* Berkeley: Asian Humanities Press; Seoul: Po Chin Chai Ltd., 1989.

——. *Korea and Christianity.* Seoul: Royal Asiatic Society, 1986.

Pares, Susan. *Crosscurrents—Korean and Western Culture in Contrast.* Seoul: Seoul International Publishing House, 1985.

Popham, Peter. *The Insider's Guide to Korea.* Edison, NJ: Hunter Publishing, Inc., 1988.

Research Center for Asian Women. *Women of the Yi Dynasty.* Seoul: Sookmyung Women's University, 1986.

Rutt, Richard. *Korean Works and Days.* Seoul: Pakmun Publishing Company, 1965.

Rutt, Richard, and Kim, Chong-un. *Virtuous Women.* Seoul: Royal Asiatic Society, 1982.

Saccone, Richard. *The Business of Korean Culture.* Seoul: Hollym, 1994.

Scalapino, R. A., and Lee, Chong-sik. *Communism in Korea.* Seoul: Ilchogak, 1992.

Shin, Il Chol. *Explore Korea.* Seoul: Tamgudang, 1965.

Soh, Chung Hee. *The Chosen Women in Korean Politics: An Anthropological Study.* New York: Praeger Publishers, 1991.

Steinberg, David I. *The Republic of Korea.* Boulder: Westview Press, 1993.

Story, Robert, and Crowther, Geoff. *Korea*. Hawthorn, Australia: Lonely Planet Publications, 1995.

———. *Women of the Yi Dynasty*. Seoul: Research Center for Asian Women, Sookmyung Women's University, 1986.

———. *The Ethical Conceptions of the Korean People*. Seoul: Academy of Korean Studies, 1983.

Underwood, L. H. *Fifteen Years Among the Top-Knots*. American Tract Society, 1904.

Yi, Ki Yong, "Religions in Korea," *Korean Studies*. Seoul: Hyonamsa, 1983.

Yi, Kyu Tae. *Rediscovery of the Koreans*. Seoul: Mullisa, 1977.

———. *The Shape of Korean Life*. Seoul: Choson-Ilbo Sa, 1984.

———. *The Structure of the Korean Mind, Vol 2*. Seoul: Shin-won Munwhasa, 1983.

Yi, Pu Yong. *The National Character of Modern Koreans: A Psychological Study of the Korean Personality*. Seoul: Academy of Korean Studies, 1983.

———. *The Self-Identity of the Koreans and Tao*. Seoul: Ichisa, 1974.

Yu, Eui Young, and Kandall, Terry R., editors. *The Korean Peninsula in the Changing World Order*. Los Angeles: Center for Korean-American and Korean Studies, California State University, 1992.

Yu, Tong Shik. *Korean Religions and Christianity*. Seoul: Kiddokyo Sohoe, 1965.

Yu-Tull, Ducksoon Diana. *Winds of Change*. Silver Spring, MD: The Women's Institute Press, 1991/1995.

Yun, Tae Rim. *Koreans: The Structure of Their Minds*. Seoul: Hyonamsa, 1971.

Yun, Yi Hum, et al. *Religions in Korea*. Seoul: Korean Overseas Information Service, 1986.